The Theory of Trade Policy Reform

The International Library of Critical Writings in Economics

Series Editor: Mark Blaug

Professor Emeritus, University of London, UK
Professor Emeritus, University of Buckingham, UK
Visiting Professor, University of Amsterdam, The Netherlands

This series is an essential reference source for students, researchers and lecturers in economics. It presents by theme a selection of the most important articles across the entire spectrum of economics. Each volume has been prepared by a leading specialist who has written an authoritative introduction to the literature included.

A full list of published and future titles in this series is printed at the end of this volume.

Wherever possible, the articles in these volumes have been reproduced as originally published using facsimile reproduction, inclusive of footnotes and pagination to facilitate ease of reference.

For a list of all Edward Elgar published titles visit our site on the World Wide Web at
http://www.e-elgar.co.uk

The Theory of Trade Policy Reform

Edited by

Carsten Kowalczyk

Associate Professor of International Economics,
Tufts University and
Visiting Professor of Economics,
Harvard University, USA

THE INTERNATIONAL LIBRARY OF CRITICAL WRITINGS IN ECONOMICS

An Elgar Reference Collection
Cheltenham, UK • Northampton, MA, USA

Published by
Edward Elgar Publishing Limited
Glensanda House
Montpellier Parade
Cheltenham
Glos GL50 1UA
UK

Edward Elgar Publishing, Inc.
136 West Street
Suite 202
Northampton
Massachusetts 01060
USA

A catalogue record for this book is available from the British Library.

Library of Congress Cataloguing in Publication Data

The theory of trade policy reform / edited by Carsten Kowalczyk.
p. cm. — (The international library of critical writings in economics ; 127) (An Elgar reference collection)
Includes bibliographical references and index.
1. Commercial policy. 2. International economic relations. 3. International trade. 4. Free trade. 5. Welfare economics. 6. Second best, Theory of. 7. Tariff. 8. Taxation. 9. Subsidies. I. Kowalczyk, Carsten, 1956- II. Series. III. Series: An Elgar reference collection.

HF1411 .T429 2001
382'.3—dc21 00-065422

ISBN 1 84064 403 6

Printed and bound in Great Britain by MPG Books Ltd, Bodmin, Cornwall

Contents

Acknowledgements

The editor and publishers wish to thank the authors and the following publishers who have kindly given permission for the use of copyright material.

American Economic Association for articles: Trent J. Bertrand and Jaroslav Vanek (1971), 'The Theory of Tariffs, Taxes, and Subsidies: Some Aspects of the Second Best', *American Economic Review*, **LXI** (5), December, 925–31; Carsten Kowalczyk (1989), 'Trade Negotiations and World Welfare', *American Economic Review*, **79** (3), June, 552–9; Ramón López and Arvind Panagariya (1992), 'On the Theory of Piecemeal Tariff Reform: The Case of Pure Imported Intermediate Inputs', *American Economic Review*, **82** (3), June, 615–25.

Blackwell Publishers, Inc. for articles: Takashi Fukushima (1979), 'Tariff Structure, Nontraded Goods and Theory of Piecemeal Policy Recommendations', *International Economic Review*, **20** (2), June, 427–35; Kenzo Abe (1992), 'Tariff Reform in a Small Open Economy with Public Production', *International Economic Review*, **33** (1), February, 209–22; Carsten Kowalczyk (2000), 'Welfare and Integration', *International Economic Review*, **41** (2), May, 483–94.

Blackwell Publishers Ltd for article: Michael Keen (1989), 'Multilateral Tax and Tariff Reform', *Economic Studies Quarterly*, **40** (3), September, 195–202.

Econometric Society for articles: Edward Foster and Hugo Sonnenschein (1970), 'Price Distortion and Economic Welfare', *Econometrica*, **38** (2), March, 281–97; Tatsuo Hatta (1977), 'A Recommendation for a Better Tariff Structure', *Econometrica*, **45** (8), November, 1859–69; Arja H. Turunen-Red and Alan D. Woodland (1991), 'Strict Pareto-Improving Multilateral Reforms of Tariffs', *Econometrica*, **59** (4), July, 1127–52; James E. Anderson and J. Peter Neary (1992), 'Trade Reform with Quotas, Partial Rent Retention, and Tariffs', *Econometrica*, **60** (1), January, 57–76.

Elsevier Science Ltd for articles: P.J. Lloyd (1974), 'A More General Theory of Price Distortions in Open Economies', *Journal of International Economics*, **4** (4), November, 365–86; Avinash Dixit (1975), 'Welfare Effects of Tax and Price Changes', *Journal of Public Economics*, **4** (2), February, 103–23; Roger Guesnerie (1977), 'On the Direction of Tax Reform', *Journal of Public Economics*, **7** (2), April, 179–202; W.E. Diewert (1978), 'Optimal Tax Perturbations', *Journal of Public Economics*, **10** (2), October, 139–77; John A. Weymark (1979), 'A Reconciliation of Recent Results in Optimal Taxation Theory', *Journal of Public Economics*, **12** (2), October, 171–89; Tatsuo Hatta and Takashi Fukushima (1979), 'The Welfare Effect of Tariff Rate Reductions in a Many Country World', *Journal of International Economics*, **9** (4), November, 503–11; Takashi Fukushima (1981), 'A Dynamic Quantity Adjustment Process in a Small Open Economy, and Welfare Effects of Tariff Changes', *Journal of International Economics*, **11** (4), November, 513–29; W. Max Corden and Rodney E. Falvey (1985), 'Quotas and the Second Best', *Economics Letters*, **18** (1), 67–70; Rodney E. Falvey (1988), 'Tariffs, Quotas and Piecemeal Policy Reform', *Journal of International Economics*, **25**, 177–83; Takashi Fukushima and Namdoo Kim (1989), 'Welfare Improving Tariff Changes', *Journal of International Economics*, **26**, 383–8; John C. Beghin and Larry S. Karp (1992), 'Piecemeal Trade Reform in Presence of Producer-Specific Domestic Subsidies, *Economics Letters*, **39**, 65–71.

Harvard University Press for excerpt: Jaroslav Vanek (1965), 'Global Gains from Restricted Trade in a Two-Country World', in *General Equilibrium of International Discrimination: The Case of Customs Unions*, Chapter IV, 53–87.

Kiel Institute of World Economics for article: Rod Falvey (1994), 'Revenue Enhancing Tariff Reform', *Weltwirtschaftliches Archiv*, **130** (1), 175–90.

MIT Press Journals for article: Jaroslav Vanek (1964), 'Unilateral Trade Liberalization and Global World Income', *Quarterly Journal of Economics*, **LXXVIII** (1), February, 139–47.

Oxford University Press for excerpts: J.E. Meade (1955), 'The Second-Best Argument for Trade Control: (2) The Partial Freeing of Trade', in *Trade and Welfare*, Chapter XIII, 200–225; J.E. Meade (1955), 'The Partial Freeing of Trade: (1) Unilateral Tariff Reductions', in *Trade and Welfare*, Chapter XXXI, 513–20; J.E. Meade (1955), 'The Partial Freeing of Trade: (2) Discriminatory and Preferential Tariff Reductions', in *Trade and Welfare*, Chapter XXXII, 521–38.

Review of Economic Studies Ltd for articles: W.J. Corlett and D.C. Hague (1953–54), 'Complementarity and the Excess Burden of Taxation', *Review of Economic Studies*, **XXI** (1), 21–30; Michael Bruno (1972), 'Market Distortions and Gradual Reform', *Review of Economic Studies*, **XXXIX** (3), July, 373–83; W.E. Diewert, A.H. Turunen-Red and A.D. Woodland (1989), 'Productivity- and Pareto-Improving Changes in Taxes and Tariffs', *Review of Economic Studies*, **56**, 199–215.

University of Chicago Press for article: S.A. Ozga (1955), 'An Essay in the Theory of Tariffs', *Journal of Political Economy*, **LXIII**, February–December, 489–99.

Every effort has been made to trace all the copyright holders but if any have been inadvertently overlooked the publishers will be pleased to make the necessary arrangement at the first opportunity.

In addition the publishers wish to thank the Library of the London School of Economics and Political Science, the Marshall Library of Economics, Cambridge University, and B & N Microfilm, London, for their assistance in obtaining these articles.

Introduction

Carsten Kowalczyk

It has long been recognized that free trade maximizes the gains from international exchange. Yet getting there is a slow process, as trade liberalization remains incomplete both in depth and in breadth: Industrial tariffs have not been eliminated in spite of more than 50 years of arduous efforts; other sectors of important traded goods, such as agriculture and textiles, have only recently been subjected to discipline or slated for liberalization; and the recent proliferation of various preferential trading arrangements indicates a desire by nations to liberalize at different speeds with different trading partners.

Whatever are the reasons why trade liberalization is gradual – be it a fear of change, a lack of ability or willingness to compensate import competing interests, or a limited ability to cooperate fully between sovereign nations – the time dimension of liberalization is an important issue as negotiators address the lengths of tariff adjustment periods and tariff reduction formulae.[1] Both the length of period and the exact reform path matter greatly for economic welfare: The extension in time of protection means foregone income, and a concern for economic welfare would tend, therefore, to call for rapid tariff reduction, if not instantaneous elimination. Furthermore, while free trade has desirable economic welfare properties, Viner's (1950) demonstration that a customs union can be harmful implies that the same is not necessarily true for a partial reduction of trade barriers and, as a corollary, that even if the final destination is beneficial – as is the case for global free trade – it matters which route is traveled to get there. Thus, whether the purpose is to reduce political resistance to reform, or to avoid transitory economic losses, it is important to identify which types of trade policy change are welfare improving.

Defining trade policy reform broadly as a change in trade policy, or in other policy instruments with consequences for trade and prices, the theory of trade policy reform is the body of knowledge of how these changes in policy affect key economic variables, including economic welfare. The present volume surveys this theory and presents the most significant contributions to the literature. Albeit theoretical, it is a literature which is motivated by concrete policy challenges – and it is a literature which has informed policy. For example, the research on equi-proportionate tariff reductions is motivated in part by the Kennedy and Tokyo Round negotiations, and the research on extreme rates has informed the recommendation that tariff peaks be eliminated, now a common element in World Bank conditionality programs.

This Introduction presents the main policy and analytic questions of trade policy reform, and it discusses how the individual papers in this collection have contributed to their understanding. After the key issues within the context of a simple equilibrium model, some early findings on the significance of substitutability for welfare from reform are presented. This is followed by a discussion of how distortions affect welfare, and a review of the results on the welfare effects of reforms of tariffs, subsidies, and quotas in various economic environments. The question of when Pareto-improving reforms exist is then considered. The Introduction closes with suggestions for further research.[2]

Theoretical Structure and Issues

Consider a small open economy where price taking consumers and producers trade many goods, and let an increase in national welfare (which will at times be referred to as national income) be defined by an increase in the utility of a representative household.[3]

The economy has in place trade distorting policies. These could take many forms, including tariffs, quotas, subsidies, VER's or VIE's, or they could be the consequences of domestic policies such as, for example, production subsidies or consumption taxes. For the illustrative purpose of this section, suppose the policy in place is an array of import tariffs. How does a change in tariffs affect the nation's income? To answer this, we identify the channels through which a change in trade policy affects income.

Assuming that any tariff revenue or subsidy expenditure is returned to, or raised from, households in a lump-sum manner, the nation's budget constraint can be expressed either as the requirement that the value of exports equals the value of imports, or that expenditure equals the value of production plus tariff revenue. As originally considered by Meade (1955), and as further developed by Jones (1969) for small changes, and by Ohyama (1972) for large changes, it is possible to derive from the budget constraint – or, for large changes, from revealed preference – that a change in the welfare of a trading nation can be expressed as the sum of a *terms-of-trade effect* and a *volume-of-trade effect*. The former is defined as the weighted sum of the country's external export and import prices, where each price change is multiplied by the corresponding initial trade volume, and the latter is defined as the change in the trade volume of each good multiplied by the absolute difference between domestic valuation and world market price. A nation benefits from paying lower world market prices on its imports and from receiving higher world market prices on its exports. A nation benefits also from increased imports of a good that has a higher domestic valuation than world market price, and from increased exports of a good that has a higher world market price than domestic valuation, i.e., from increased trade in goods that are taxed.[4]

Suppose the country under consideration undertakes a liberalization of its trade, and that its terms of trade do not change. Consider now whether the reduction of the tariff on an imported good *i* raises or lowers national welfare. If all goods are normal in consumption, then imports of good *i,* and of any complement good, will increase, and welfare will improve. Imports of substitutes will fall, however, causing lower welfare. If the net effect on welfare of these opposing effects is positive, the tariff reduction is welfare improving.

Which effect is larger could be explored *ex ante* if sufficient data for calibration and estimation exist. Theorists have pursued an alternative approach, however, seeking to identify reforms that are welfare improving even in the presence of extensive substitutability. This search has led to the identification of two reforms which, if all goods are substitutes and normal in consumption, will raise welfare at every step of the path of adjustment: the reduction of extreme distortions, which is known as *concertina* reform, and the reduction of all distortions in the same proportion, referred to as *radial* reform.

Under substitutability, a lower tariff on good *i* raises exports of substitute goods and thus, due to balanced trade, the value of imports. This will tend to raise welfare if high tariff imports expand and low tariff imports contract – in which case *concertina* reform of distortions is beneficial. *Radial* reform of distortions raises welfare because, while leaving relative prices among distorted goods unaffected, it reduces their prices relative to the undistorted goods thereby raising the value of imports of the taxed goods with no first-order welfare effect from the reduced imports of the non-distorted goods.

Jones (1969), Bruno (1972, Chapter 7 in this volume), and Hatta (1977) show that it is possible to express the change in trade volume in terms of changes in underlying prices and income or, after some manipulation, as the combined effect from compensated substitutability and changed income. If a gift of income raises utility, the partial welfare contribution from reducing the price distortion between any pair of substitute goods is, *ceteris paribus*, positive, while the partial welfare contribution from reducing the price distortion between any pair of complement goods is, *ceteris paribus*, to reduce welfare.[5]

Much of the literature considers the reform of *distortions* rather than the reform of policy *rates*. The distinction is important since, as shown by Kowalczyk (1989, Chapter 18 in this volume), whether or not a *rate* reduction implies a *distortion* reduction may depend on how rates are quoted. The literature is also characterized by some maintained, and sometimes implicit, assumptions. For example, initial policies are usually assumed to be arbitrary and are not explained. As in conventional comparative statics analysis, the underlying shock to policy, i.e., the sudden interest in welfare improving changes, is also exogenous. And, finally, there is usually no reason offered why a reform, if undertaken, would be gradual rather than discrete.[6]

Early Analysis of Complements versus Substitutes

After Viner's demonstration that a partial trade liberalization may be harmful, effort is put into uncovering the conditions under which intuitively appealing tax reductions might be harmful. Research on taxation in public finance, and the work leading to the formulation of the general theory of second-best and reform, as expounded by Lipsey and Lancaster (1956), make it clear that a key issue is the substitutability and complementarity relations between commodities.

Corlett and Hague (1953–54, Chapter 1 in this volume) present an early formal equilibrium analysis of how substitutability versus complementarity affects the response of welfare to changes in tax rates. They show, for an individual consuming two goods and leisure, that a lower tax on a consumption good (while raising the labor tax to keep the tax revenue constant) raises utility if the good is a substitute to leisure, but reduces utility if the good is a complement to leisure, and they discuss the implications of this finding for optimal tax theory.

Meade, in his celebrated volume *Trade and Welfare*, applies his criterion for welfare-improving policy change – that goods be reallocated to where their valuation is higher – to a discussion of tariff changes. In Meade (1955, Chapter 2 in this volume) he discusses, in a two-country world, how a trading country's policy change affects its trade volume through what he defines as primary (change in own good), secondary (changes in close substitutes or complements), and tertiary effects (changes in other goods, and feedback effects as prices adjust to equilibrium). Meade (1955, Chapter 3 in this volume) furthers the analysis by considering non-discriminatory unilateral liberalization in a three-country setting, stressing how the reduction of an arbitrary tariff, even if done in a non-discriminatory fashion, may lead to a misallocation of goods. He presents also, in this chapter, a discussion of when initial tariffs and trade volumes are more likely to be such that a unilateral liberalization will raise global welfare.

Ozga (1955, Chapter 4 in this volume) makes the similar point, that a unilateral non-discriminating tariff liberalization may lower rather than raise world welfare, by calculating prices, production, trade volumes, and income for before- and after-reform tariff equilibria, in a numerical three-country equilibrium model.

Rather than assume, as Meade does, that utility is additive across nations, Vanek (1965, Chapter 5 in this volume) assumes the existence of international lump-sum income transfers and applies the Pareto criterion to the analysis of world welfare. He shows, in a two-country, two-good model, that if one of the goods is inferior in consumption, then there is an equilibrium from which a tariff reduction lowers world welfare; however, in this case, there is always another equilibrium with higher world welfare.[7] He shows, finally, that if no good is inferior, then any liberalization of trade raises world welfare in this two-good model where substitutability necessarily holds.

Income Effects, Distortions, and Radial Reform

Following the early contributions to the general theory of second best and the theory of reform, researchers bring formal general equilibrium techniques to the problem in search of robust structural relations. This permits the analysis of multiple distortions, and it makes clear, among other things, the role of income effects for the outcome of reform.

Foster and Sonnenschein (1970, Chapter 6 in this volume) provide a general analysis of distortions for a closed economy, and derive conditions under which a *radial* reform of uniform reductions of all distortions raises welfare.

Bruno (1972, Chapter 7 in this volume) extends their analysis to a small open economy with positive tariffs on imports, and he shows that convex technology and aggregate normality in consumption (a gift of income raises utility) together imply that a *radial* reduction of all tariffs raises welfare.

Lloyd (1974, Chapter 8 in this volume) considers consumer and producer taxes together with tariffs for a small open economy. He shows that if the aggregate marginal propensity to consume is positive, and if all pairs of goods are compensated substitutes in consumption, reducing the largest distortion in consumer prices raises welfare. He shows a similar result for producer prices, and emphasizes that both findings hold for negative as well as positive distortions. He demonstrates also that reducing the highest tariff raises welfare if that good also has the largest price distortion, and he stresses that if the economy has in place production or consumption taxes or subsidies, the highest tariff good may no longer be the good which is most distorted in price. He shows, finally, that a *radial* reduction in all distortions, whether caused by production, consumption, or trade taxes or subsidies – or any combination of them – raises welfare, and that a *radial* reduction of distortions of a subset of goods raises welfare if these goods are, on average, substitutes for the goods whose prices are not distorted.

Rather than assume that distortions are the control variables of the government, Dixit (1975, Chapter 9 in this volume) analyzes the welfare effects from changing *specific* rate commodity and trade taxes. Assuming convex technology and offsetting changes in lump-sum taxes to leave the government budget unaffected, he shows that a *radial* reduction of *specific* taxes raises national welfare, and, with additional assumptions, that a *radial* reduction in *ad valorem* taxes does so as well.[8]

Hatta (1977) presents an extensive analysis of the interaction between substitution and aggregate income effects. He shows that a *radial* reform of reducing all price distortions in the same proportion, and the *concertina* reform of reducing the highest distortion, improve welfare if the good with the highest distortion is a substitute for all other goods and if aggregate non-inferiority holds. He shows also that Marshallian stability implies aggregate non-inferiority.

Finally, Fukushima (1981, Chapter 10 in this volume) provides an extensive discussion of Marshallian stability for a small open economy, and he shows that Hatta's results on reform hold for an open economy as well, and that stability rules out Vanek's and Bhagwati's paradox.

Further Results on Unilateral Tariff Liberalization

With the improved understanding of the underlying structure of distortions, including the role of income effects, it has become possible to extend the scope of analysis to include non-traded goods and to consider additional distortionary policies such as consumption and production taxes and subsidies.

Bertrand and Vanek (1971, Chapter 11 in this volume) consider a small country which trades many goods, and they show that, if all goods are substitutes, eliminating extreme distortions raises national welfare through a positive volume of trade effect. Hatta (1977, Chapter 12 in this volume) applies instead the compensated approach, and he shows that if there are no inferior goods, if the good with the highest tariff is a net substitute to other traded goods, and if non-traded goods are net substitutes with all traded goods, then the *concertina* reform of reducing the highest tariff to the level of the next highest rate raises welfare of a small open economy. For the same model and conditions, Fukushima (1979, Chapter 13 in this volume) shows that a uniform tariff change, which has the *radial* reform of reducing all tariffs towards zero as a special case, raises utility.

Beghin and Karp (1992, Chapter 14 in this volume) demonstrate, for a small country with producer subsidies, no inferior goods, and non-tradeables being substitutable for all other goods, that a *radial* reform of equi-proportionate reduction of all tariffs and producer subsidies raises welfare. They show also that the *concertina* reform of reducing the highest tariff may not raise welfare when there are fixed producer subsidies in place, since the highest tariff may not imply the largest distortion. However, reducing the highest tariff can raise welfare if the corresponding producer subsidy is adjusted to leave price constant.

The assumption of extensive net substitutability, while made widely, is more than sufficient for welfare improvement. Furthermore, and as demonstrated by Lopez and Panagariya (1992, Chapter 15 in this volume), there are important economic situations where the assumption fails to hold. Thus, if a country imports a good which is not produced domestically, and if that good is used as an input in production, then complementarity necessarily arises in some standard production models. In these cases, reducing the highest tariff may lower rather than raise the small country's welfare whether that tariff is on the intermediate or on a final good.

Multilateral and Preferential Liberalization

Due to the activities of GATT/WTO, and the proliferation of preferential trading arrangements, there is considerable policy interest in results on reform involving many countries. Applying the compensated approach to multilateral reform, the literature has developed positive results for the reform of tariffs, and a caution for the joint liberalization of tariffs and subsidies. Modern approaches to tariffs and reform are also useful for the analysis of preferential trading arrangements, which have, until recently, been discussed in terms of the trade diversion and trade creation taxonomy introduced by Viner (1950).

Vanek (1964, Chapter 16 in this volume) demonstrates that a unilateral tariff reduction by the country which has the highest domestic relative price of a good improves the utility possibility of the world, while unilateral reform of a country with a non-extreme rate, as argued earlier by Meade (1955, Chapter 3 in this volume) and by Ozga (1955, Chapter 4 in this volume), may lower world welfare.

Hatta and Fukushima (1979, Chapter 17 in this volume) apply the compensated approach to world welfare and show that the *concertina* reform of lowering the world's highest tariff raises world welfare in a many-country, two-good world economy with no inferior goods and where all countries levy non-negative *ad valorem* tariffs. They show also that a *radial* reform, where all countries reduce simultaneously their tariffs by the same proportion, has a desirable effect on world welfare.

Kowalczyk (1989, Chapter 18 in this volume) shows that both the *concertina* and *radial* rules of reform may lower world welfare if the initial situation is one of both tariffs and subsidies. For the *concertina* result, the tariff may offset the distortionary effect from a given subsidy, and the tariff reduction may thus create or expand a distortion and hence reduce world welfare. For a *radial* reform, the uniform rate reduction of *ad valorem* tariffs and subsidies may expand rather than reduce price distortions along the reform path.[9] Fukushima and Kim (1989, Chapter 19 in this volume) show that the *radial* reform paradox does not occur when tariffs and subsidies are *specific*. Keen (1989, Chapter 20 in this volume) demonstrates that an equi-proportionate reduction of *specific* rate trade and consumption taxes raises world welfare.

In a consideration of discriminatory trade liberalization, Meade (1955, Chapter 21 in this volume) applies his framework of primary, secondary, and tertiary effects to explore how trade flows are affected by unilateral and reciprocal agreements such as a free trade area. He presents conditions under which a preferential agreement is likely to be welfare improving, and he argues that, in general, the optimal intra-club tariff is not zero.[10]

Kowalczyk (2000, Chapter 22 in this volume) presents a critique of Viner's trade diversion and trade creation approach, and argues that the analysis of customs unions and other preferential arrangements does not require a unique language but should be considered, instead, as a type of multi-country tariff reform and be analyzed by use of corresponding techniques. Assuming aggregate normality in consumption, and that all goods are net substitutes, the paper establishes that the welfare of a small country, and of the world, increase if the small country joins all the world's free trade areas, acceding to each through bilateral equi-proportionate tariff rate reductions.

Reforming Quotas and Tariffs

Quotas remain an important policy of protection for developing countries, and their relative impact on world trade has been increasing with the worldwide reduction of tariffs. It has been a stated policy goal of GATT and the World Bank to seek the elimination of quotas by recommending their conversion to tariff equivalents followed by rate reductions.

For a small open economy, Corden and Falvey (1985, Chapter 23 in this volume) argue that it is not possible to offset quota distortions with other trade restrictions since taxing substitutes only reduces welfare through reducing imports of the taxed goods. They conclude that the second-best implications from quota distortions are different from the implications from tariff distortions.

Falvey (1988, Chapter 24 in this volume) shows that if there are no tariffs then any quota relaxation raises welfare. If tariffs exist, and if all commodities are net substitutes, a loosening of any quota whose implicit tariff is higher than the highest explicit tariff will increase welfare, as will a tightening of the quota with a lower implicit tariff than the lowest explicit tariff. Falvey shows also that if the quota-restricted goods are net substitutes for all other goods, *concertina* and *radial* reforms of tariffs continue to be welfare improving. He concludes that, while there are many reasons to prefer tariffs to quotas, quotas do have the advantage that their reform is less prone to be welfare reducing.

From a general equilibrium perspective, this asymmetry between tariffs and quotas is surprising, because tariff changes could affect the intensity with which import quotas bind. By assuming that foreign exporters capture some of the quota rent, Anderson and Neary (1992, Chapter 25 in this volume) are able to explore the welfare consequences of the fact that, if volumes are not permitted to adjust, (shadow) prices will. *Ceteris paribus*, an increase in the marginal valuation of an already binding quota good will thus reduce welfare, as more rent is lost to foreigners. Anderson and Neary derive the quota-rent-sharing version of the condition that a gift of real income be welfare improving, and they show, among other results, that when no tariffs exist, and goods are net substitutes, all quota relaxations raise welfare, and that the *concertina* and *radial* reforms of tariff rates continue to be beneficial under less than full rent retention.

Government Activities – Additional Distortions and Revenue

The previous chapters have considered reform in standard competitive economies where production and consumption are undertaken by private producers and consumers, and where any tax or subsidy revenue is returned to, or raised from, households in lump-sum fashion. If the public sector provides goods and services at prices that differ from what competitive suppliers would charge, or if tariff revenue is an important source of government financing, new issues arise.

Abe (1992, Chapter 26 in this volume) presents sufficient conditions for when *concertina* and *radial* reforms are welfare improving for a small open economy where the government provides a consumption good free of charge. Among these is that the publicly provided good be over supplied, i.e., that the marginal benefit of it, financed by a lump-sum tax, exceeds its marginal cost of provision.

Falvey (1994, Chapter 27 in this volume), also for a small open economy, identifies tariff reforms which are both welfare and revenue enhancing. Among his findings are that the raising of the lowest tax and the increase of the highest subsidy are the only reforms of single rates that clearly meet both criteria. For the reduction of other rates, including the highest tariff, the effect on welfare depends on whether the rate exceeds or falls short of its revenue maximizing value. Similarly, a *radial* reduction of all tariff rates, while reducing distortions, will raise or reduce revenue depending on whether the initial overall structure is above or below that which maximizes revenue.

On the Existence of Welfare Improving Reforms

Most of the papers in this volume explore the conditions for, or the consequences from, some particular reforms, notably the *concertina* and *radial* rules of reduction of either distortions or of rates. However, some researchers have considered the question of when welfare improving rate reductions exist at all.

Guesnerie (1977, Chapter 28 in this volume) demonstrates, for a competitive closed economy with many consumers, the existence of Pareto-improving changes in consumer and producer taxes, and argues that such reform paths may involve temporary production inefficiencies. Diewert (1978, Chapter 29 in this volume) uses duality theory to demonstrate the existence of Pareto-improving reform paths, and he characterizes the direction of change that maximizes the increase in national welfare for a small change. Weymark (1979, Chapter 30 in this volume) reconciles these contributions, and he shows that critical assumptions for the existence of Pareto-improving reforms are that there is some good for which all households are either net sellers or net buyers, and that production responds to a small change in producer taxes.

Diewert, Turunen-Red, and Woodland (1989, Chapter 31 in this volume) show, for a small open economy with multiple households, that if there exists a tariff reform, such that the value of traded goods at world prices is increased while maintaining the initial net output vector for non-traded goods (they define such a reform to be productivity-improving), and if Weymark's condition that all consumers are on the same side of the market is satisfied, then there exists a differential change in tariffs and commodity taxes that yields a strict Pareto improvement in welfare. As special cases, they show that a *radial* tariff reduction is strictly Pareto improving, and that the *concertina* reform raises welfare if all goods are net substitutes in production.

Finally, Turunen-Red and Woodland (1991, Chapter 32 in this volume) extend the analysis of strictly Pareto-improving reform to many countries. They show, among other results, that a multilateral *radial* tariff reduction is strictly Pareto improving. Defining the concept of a shadow tariff, they show also that, if all goods are net substitutes, a unilateral reduction of any country's highest shadow *ad valorem* tariff implies a strict Pareto improvement.[11]

Further Work

As is evident from the contributions in this volume, and from the survey in this Introduction, the theory of trade policy reform has provided extensive analysis of *concertina* and *radial* reforms of tariffs. Both reforms have the appeal that higher rates are cut by more and, therefore, that industries and countries that deviate by more from free trade are requested to make larger adjustments. The *concertina* and *radial* reforms are also appealing in that they require only information about the signs of elasticities of substitution rather than estimates of their values. Both types of reform continue to be welfare improving when quotas co-exist with tariffs and in the presence of non-traded goods. However, trade subsidies or complementarities may cause either of these reforms to be welfare reducing, at least along segments of the reform paths.

It is a maintained assumption through the contributions presented in this volume that trade policy reform is undertaken by governments seeking to raise national income. Some recent work, not discussed in this volume, stresses that international agreements must specify such policies which national governments find it in their interest to uphold.[12] Other work emphasizes that government policies are set by political parties influenced through voting, lobbying, or contributions.[13] Finally, since the focus of this volume is on the theory of trade policy reform, it does not discuss work in the tradition of computable general equilibrium modeling, a branch of economic analysis of considerable practical use for policy makers.[14]

There are outstanding theoretical and empirical research challenges, in part to complete, extend, and document the theoretical landscape described in this volume, in part to provide insight into some policy issues of immediate concern.

Often trade reform does not include all goods or all countries, and further analysis that involves only a subset of goods or countries would be useful. It would be valuable also to extend the analysis of reform from tariffs, subsidies and quotas to include other policies, and to develop results on gradual trade liberalization in economies with extensive domestic distortions. Finally, there is only little work, theoretical or empirical, on the important questions of what determines the pace and formulae for rate reductions in trade policy reform.

Notes

1. Early GATT rounds were primarily over bindings, often at levels higher than the applied rates, and usually went into effect immediately upon a country's signing. Explicit phase-out periods were introduced with the Kennedy Round Agreement to reduce tariffs by 35 percent over a five year period. Later, the Tokyo Round Agreement specified eight years, and the Uruguay Round Agreement five years, to implement 33 percent and 40 percent tariff reductions, respectively. The Uruguay Round also tightened the permitted length of tariff phase-outs in Article XXIV interim agreements from "a reasonable length of time" to "exceed 10 years only in exceptional cases." See Kowalczyk and Davis (1998) for further discussion.
2. Dixit (1985), Vousden (1990), and Anderson (1994) provide surveys of the theory of protection including discussions of reform.
3. See Wong (1995) for a discussion of different approaches to welfare analysis in international trade.
4. The terms-of-trade and volume-of-trade effects are important also in the welfare analysis of groups of countries, and the volume-of-trade effects in the analysis of world welfare. See Ohyama (1972), Kowalczyk (2000, Chapter 22 in this volume), and Kowalczyk and Wonnacott (1992).
5. If a gift of income lowers utility, reducing a distortion between substitutes or raising a distortion between complements will, on the other hand, lower welfare. However, and as discussed in the literature surveyed in this volume, the case of a gift of income being immiserizing is associated with an unstable equilibrium and it is possible, then, to identify a welfare-superior equilibrium at which a gift of income will be welfare-improving.
6. Feldstein (1976) provides a discussion of why reform is often gradual. Leamer (1980) demonstrates formally that adjustment costs do not necessarily make a gradual phasing-out of tariffs preferable to their immediate elimination. Bagwell and Staiger (1997a, b) and Chisik (1999) show that evolving cooperation among non-cooperative governments can generate gradual tariff adjustment paths.
7. See also Bhagwati (1968) for a discussion of this paradox for the single-country case. Kowalczyk (1992) presents a unified analysis of the findings of Viner, Meade, Ozga, and Vanek.
8. Dixit and Munk (1977) discuss the role of numeraire for this analysis.

9. Kowalczyk (2000) shows that the same concerns apply to unilateral reform.
10. McMillan and McCann (1981) present a formal proof of this proposition.
11. Turunen-Red and Woodland (1993) consider the existence of multilateral welfare improving tariff reforms when international income transfers are not feasible.
12. Bagwell and Staiger (1997a, b). Kowalczyk and Sjöström (1994) analyze how international sidepayments can affect policy outcomes and derive an explicit financial mechanism.
13. Grossman and Helpman (1994, 1995).
14. Whalley (1985) provides an analysis of multilateral reform.

References

J.E. Anderson (1994), 'The Theory of Protection', in D. Greenaway and L.A. Winters (eds), *Surveys in International Trade,* Oxford, UK: Blackwell.

K. Bagwell and R.W. Staiger (1997a), 'Multilateral Tariff Cooperation During the Formation of Free Trade Areas', *International Economic Review*, **38**, 291–319.

K. Bagwell and R.W. Staiger (1997b), 'Multilateral Tariff Cooperation During the Formation of Customs Unions', *Journal of International Economics*, **42**, 91–123.

J.N. Bhagwati (1968), 'The Gains from Trade Once Again', *Oxford Economic Papers*, **20**, 137–48.

R.A. Chisik (1999), 'Gradualism and Free Trade Agreements: A Theoretical Justification', Department of Economics, University of Connecticut, December, mimeo.

A.K. Dixit (1985), 'Tax Policy in Open Economies', in A. Auerbach and M. Feldstein (eds), *Handbook of Public Economics, Vol. I*, Amsterdam: North-Holland.

A.K. Dixit and K.J. Munk (1977), 'Welfare Effects of Tax and Price Changes: A Correction', *Journal of Public Economics*, **8**, 103–7.

M.S. Feldstein (1976), 'On the Theory of Tax Reform', *Journal of Public Economics*, **6**, 77–104.

G.M. Grossman and E. Helpman (1994), 'Protection for Sale', *American Economic Review*, **84**, 833–50.

G.M. Grossman and E. Helpman (1995), 'The Politics of Free Trade Agreements', *American Economic Review*, **85**, 667–90.

T. Hatta (1977), 'A Theory of Piecemeal Policy Recommendations', *Review of Economic Studies*, **44**, 1–21. Reprinted as Chapter 10 in C. Kowalczyk (ed.) (1999), *Economic Integration and International Trade*, Cheltenham, UK and Northampton, MA: Edward Elgar.

R.W. Jones (1969), 'Tariffs and Trade in General Equilibrium: Comment', *American Economic Review*, **59**, 418–24. Reprinted as Chapter 4 in C. Kowalczyk (ed.) (1999), *Economic Integration and International Trade*, Cheltenham, UK and Northampton, MA: Edward Elgar.

C. Kowalczyk (1992), 'Paradoxes in Integration Theory', *Open Economies Review*, **3**, 51–9. Reprinted as Chapter 18 in C. Kowalczyk (ed.) (1999), *Economic Integration and International Trade*, Cheltenham, UK and Northampton, MA: Edward Elgar.

C. Kowalczyk (2000), 'Reforming Tariffs and Subsidies in International Trade', The Fletcher School of Law and Diplomacy, Tufts University, February, mimeo. (Revision of paper presented at the University of Washington Conference 'WTO and World Trade', Seattle, December 4, 1999.)

C. Kowalczyk and D. Davis (1998), 'Tariff Phase-Outs: Theory and Evidence from GATT and NAFTA', in J.A. Frankel (ed.), *The Regionalization of the World Economy*, Chicago: The University of Chicago Press.

C. Kowalczyk and T. Sjöström (1994), 'Bringing GATT into the Core', *Economica*, **61**, 301–17. Reprinted as Chapter 26 in C. Kowalczyk (ed.) (1999), *Economic Integration and International Trade*, Cheltenham, UK and Northampton, MA: Edward Elgar.

C. Kowalczyk and R.J. Wonnacott (1992), 'Hubs and Spokes, and Free Trade in the Americas', National Bureau of Economic Research Working Paper No. 4198, October.

E. Leamer (1980), 'Welfare Computations and the Optimal Staging of Tariff Reductions in Models with Adjustment Costs', *Journal of International Economics*, **10**, 21–36.

R.G. Lipsey and K. Lancaster (1956), 'The General Theory of Second Best', *Review of Economic Studies*, **24**, 11–32. Reprinted as Chapter 2 in C. Kowalczyk (ed.) (1999), *Economic Integration and International Trade*, Cheltenham, UK and Northampton, MA: Edward Elgar.

J. McMillan and E. McCann (1981), 'Welfare Effects in Customs Unions', *Economic Journal*, **91**, 697–703. Reprinted as Chapter 15 in C. Kowalczyk (ed.) (1999), *Economic Integration and International Trade*, Cheltenham, UK and Northampton, MA: Edward Elgar.
J.E. Meade (1955), *Trade and Welfare*, London: Oxford University Press.
M. Ohyama (1972), 'Trade and Welfare in General Equilibrium', *Keio Economic Studies*, **9**, 37–73. Reprinted as Chapter 5 in C. Kowalczyk (ed.) (1999), *Economic Integration and International Trade*, Cheltenham, UK and Northampton, MA: Edward Elgar.
A.H. Turunen-Red and A.D. Woodland (1993), 'Multilateral Reforms of Tariffs without Transfer Compensation', in H. Herberg and N. van Long (eds), *Trade, Welfare, and Economic Policies*, Ann Arbor: The University of Michigan Press.
J. Viner (1950), 'The Economics of Customs Unions', in *The Customs Union Issue*, Chapter IV, New York: Carnegie Endowment for International Peace, 41–81. Reprinted as Chapter 1 in C. Kowalczyk (ed.) (1999), *Economic Integration and International Trade*, Cheltenham, UK and Northampton, MA: Edward Elgar.
N. Vousden (1990), *The Economics of Trade Protection*, Cambridge, UK: Cambridge University Press.
J. Whalley (1985), *Trade Liberalization Among Major World Trading Areas*, Cambridge, MA: The MIT Press.
K. Wong (1995), *International Trade in Goods and Factor Mobility*, Cambridge, MA: The MIT Press.

Part I
Early Contributions to the Theory of Reform

[1]

Complementarity and the Excess Burden of Taxation

I

Recent discussion on the respective merits of direct and indirect taxes has reached the point where Mr. Little has shown that, if the supply of labour is allowed to vary, the argument against indirect taxation is not perfectly general.[1] This article states the conditions where a change from an income tax to a system of indirect taxes, raising the same revenue from an individual, can increase the supply of effort and raise real income.

Our main, and simplest, model considers a consumer who is able to decide how much leisure he will take and how much he will work. All marginal costs are constant and competition is perfect. The consumer is initially in equilibrium buying three goods X, Y and L (leisure), and paying a flat rate income tax. We assume that all the consumer's income is spent and none saved. The rate of income tax is now slightly reduced and a small *ad valorem* indirect tax is introduced on one of the two goods, X or Y, so that the same tax revenue is raised from the consumer. We shall show that whenever this tax change makes the consumer work harder, he will reach a higher indifference surface ; whenever it means that he takes more leisure, his real income will fall. In general the consumer will work harder when the higher rate of tax is levied on that good (X or Y) which is " more complementary " with leisure, and *vice versa*. These conditions hold whatever the size and direction of income effects. The only exceptions can occur in a " crazy " case where tax rates are so high that an increase in the rate of tax on *one* good lowers the total yield of the tax system.

When we say that X is " more complementary " with leisure than Y we do not necessarily mean that X and leisure are complementary in the sense used by Professor Hicks.[2] Both could be competitive with leisure but, in some sense, X is " less competitive " (more complementary) than Y. Degrees of competitiveness are measured along a continuous scale from very competitive goods at one end to very complementary goods at the other. The exact way in which this is done will be explained later.

The main analysis considers small changes in tax rates and does not indicate the size of the movements away from the initial equilibrium position needed to obtain an " optimum " system of taxation. This problem will be discussed briefly, together with the effects of the relaxation of some of our assumptions, towards the end of the article.

II

Let us consider an individual consumer who is in equilibrium, paying a flat-rate income tax at the rate $\frac{r}{1+r}$. He has acquired those amounts of three goods, X, Y and L which give maximum satisfactions from his post-tax income. Leisure is considered as a good providing satisfactions just like X and Y. Because of the difficulty of measur-

[1] Haskell P. Wald, " The Classical Indictment of Indirect Taxation," *Quarterly Journal of Economics*, 1944–45, p. 577.
A. Henderson, " The Case for Indirect Taxation," *Economic Journal*, 1948, p. 538.
I. M. D. Little, " Direct versus Indirect Taxes," *Economic Journal*, 1951, p. 577.

[2] J. R. Hicks, " A Reconsideration of the Theory of Value," *Economica*, 1934, pp. 69–71.

ing leisure, our algebraic analysis is formulated in terms of X, Y and W (work). In other words, we consider hours of work as numbers of hours not taken as leisure and *vice versa.*

The formula for the rate of income tax may look cumbersome. It is given this particular value because we follow the usual procedure of regarding an income tax as the equivalent of a purchase tax levied at the same *ad valorem* rate on all goods, except leisure. Purchase taxes are usually calculated as a proportion of price *excluding* tax. A direct tax on a commodity at the rate $r = \frac{1}{3}$, would thus be called, in the real world, a $33\frac{1}{3}$ per cent purchase tax. Income taxes, however, are usually expressed as a percentage of pre-tax income. Therefore, an *ad valorem* tax of $33\frac{1}{3}$ per cent levied on all goods (except leisure) is the equivalent, for the tax payer, of an income tax. But the rate of this equivalent income tax is called 25 per cent and not $33\frac{1}{3}$ per cent. The initial income tax can therefore be considered as an *ad valorem* tax on all goods and since the rate of *ad valorem* tax is r, the corresponding income tax rate is $\frac{r}{1+r}$.

This *ad valorem* tax, levied at the equal rate of r on both X and Y, is now replaced by *ad valorem* taxes on X and Y levied at the *unequal* rates of r_1 and r_2 respectively. These rates are fixed so that the total tax paid remains the same (in money terms), after the change takes place. It follows that the *ad valorem* rate of tax on one of the two goods, X or Y, will normally be lower than in the original situation where the income tax was simulated by the tax at the rate r on both X and Y. Similarly, the *ad valorem* rate of tax on the other good will be greater than initially. Symbolically, either $r_1 > r > r_2$; or $r_1 < r < r_2$.[1]

When the tax change occurs there will be an income effect and a substitution effect. The income effect will cause the consumer's real income to rise or fall—he will reach a higher or a lower indifference surface. The income and substitution effects combined will determine whether the consumer will hold more or less of the goods, X, Y and L with the indirect tax than with the income tax.

The term " income effect " is not used here in quite its normal sense. An income effect shows the influence on a consumer's satisfactions and on his purchases of goods of an increase in his money income—all prices being constant. It does not normally take a change in the amount of his leisure into account. But the income effects in this article show the change in the consumer's holdings of X, Y and L, when he is given an increment of income which does not depend on the amount of work he does. They show the effects of a " poll subsidy," increased family allowances or increased investment income, for example. It is clearly realistic to look on income effects in this way. A consumer's satisfactions can be altered just as much by a change in the amount of his leisure as by a change in his purchases of consumer goods. We shall use the term " income effect " in this special sense to include any effect on the amount of leisure which a consumer takes.

We can now tackle our first main problem. Under what conditions will the introduction of unequal tax rates (the tax paid remaining constant) alter the amount of work done by a consumer ?

Suppose that when the *ad valorem* rates on X and Y are equal the prices of X and Y (before tax) are p_1 and p_2, and after tax are P_1 and P_2. The tax revenue is then $X(P_1 - p_1) + Y(P_2 - p_2)$. When the tax change takes place, these prices become $P_1 + dP_1$ and $P_2 + dP_2$. Since we assume constant marginal costs and perfect com-

[1] These conditions will not always hold. In the " crazy " case mentioned in Section I, r might not lie between r_1 and r_2.

petition, p_1 and p_2 do not alter. So, the change in revenue, caused by the tax change is :

$$\left[(P_1 - p_1)\frac{\partial X}{\partial P_1} + (P_2 - p_2)\frac{\partial Y}{\partial P_1} + X\right] dP_1$$
$$+ \left[(P_1 - p_1)\frac{\partial X}{\partial P_2} + (P_2 - p_2)\frac{\partial Y}{\partial P_2} + Y\right] dP_2 \quad \ldots\ldots\ldots\ldots (1)$$

Since in the initial " quasi income tax " position the rate of tax on X and Y is the same, this reduces to :

$$\left[p_1 r\frac{\partial X}{\partial P_1} + p_2 r\frac{\partial Y}{\partial P_1} + X\right] dP_1$$
$$+ \left[p_1 r\frac{\partial X}{\partial P_2} + p_2 r\frac{\partial Y}{\partial P_2} + Y\right] dP_2 \quad \ldots\ldots\ldots\ldots (2)$$

and, as we assume that tax revenue remains constant when the tax system changes, this must equal zero.

Let $U(X, Y, W)$ be a utility function. In any equilibrium, where a tax is being levied, the consumer maximises this function, subject to the constraint :

$$M + W = XP_1 + YP_2$$

where W is work done, measured in pounds earned, and M is " unearned " income. If M is positive it represents the " poll subsidy " mentioned above ; if M is negative, it represents a poll tax. In the usual way, the conditions for maximising satisfaction are :

$$\begin{aligned} XP_1 + YP_2 - W - M &= 0 \\ U_x - \lambda P_1 &= 0 \\ U_y - \lambda P_2 &= 0 \\ U_w + \lambda &= 0 \quad \ldots\ldots\ldots\ldots (3) \end{aligned}$$

where λ, the Lagrange multiplier, is the marginal utility of money.

The price changes in which we are interested are a change of P_1 to $P_1 + dP_1$ and of P_2 to $P_2 + dP_2$. The resulting change in the amount of work done, dW, is given by :

$$dW = \frac{\partial W}{\partial P_1} dP_1 + \frac{\partial W}{\partial P_2} dP_2 \quad \ldots\ldots\ldots\ldots (4)$$

From the first relation in (3), it follows that :

$$P_1 \frac{\partial X}{\partial P_1} + P_2 \frac{\partial Y}{\partial P_1} - \frac{\partial W}{\partial P_1} + X = 0$$
$$\text{and } P_1 \frac{\partial X}{\partial P_2} + P_2 \frac{\partial Y}{\partial P_2} - \frac{\partial W}{\partial P_2} + Y = 0 \quad \ldots\ldots\ldots\ldots (5)$$

Since $P_1 = p_1(1 + r)$ and $P_2 = p_2(1 + r)$ we can use (5) to eliminate $\frac{\partial X}{\partial P_1}$, $\frac{\partial X}{\partial P_2}$, $\frac{\partial Y}{\partial P_1}$, and $\frac{\partial Y}{\partial P_2}$ from (2). We then have as the change in tax revenue :

$$\left[\frac{r}{1 + r}\frac{\partial W}{\partial P_1} + \frac{1}{1 + r}X\right] dP_1 + \left[\frac{r}{1 + r}\frac{\partial W}{\partial P_2} + \frac{1}{1 + r}Y\right] dP_2 \quad \ldots\ldots\ldots (6)$$

In order that the total tax revenue should be unchanged we thus require the changes in the two prices to satisfy :

$$\left[r\frac{\partial W}{\partial P_1} + X\right] dP_1 + \left[r\frac{\partial W}{\partial P_2} + Y\right] dP_2 = 0 \quad \ldots\ldots\ldots\ldots (7)$$

Substituting in (4) we have :

$$dW = \left[\frac{\partial W}{\partial P_1} - \frac{r\frac{\partial W}{\partial P_1} + X}{r\frac{\partial W}{\partial P_2} + Y} \frac{\partial W}{\partial P_2} \right] dP_1 = \left[\frac{Y\frac{\partial W}{\partial P_1} - X\frac{\partial W}{dP_2}}{r\frac{\partial W}{\partial P_2} + Y} \right] dP_1$$

Therefore :

$$dW = \left[\frac{YV_{wx} - XV_{wy}}{r\frac{\partial W}{\partial P_2} + Y} \right] dP_1 \quad \ldots\ldots (8)$$

Similarly, expressing dW in terms of the change in the price of Y :

$$dW = \left[\frac{XV_{wy} - YV_{wx}}{r\frac{\partial W}{\partial P_1} + X} \right] dP_2$$

In these equations V_{wx} and V_{wy} are the substitution terms in the Slutsky equation which shows the change in the amount of work done by the consumer resulting from changes in the prices of X and Y respectively. This change in the amount of work done (dW) will be positive whenever the expression on the right hand side of equation (8) is positive.

The denominator in this expression can only be negative in our " crazy " case. For the denominator is equal to $(1 + r)$ times the rate of change of tax receipts resulting from an increase in the tax on Y (with no change in the tax on X). It will only be negative if this change in the tax receipts is negative, and our crazy case occurs where an increase in the tax on one good, with no change in the tax on the other, *will* reduce tax receipts. We shall, therefore, ignore for the present the possibility that the denominator might be negative.

The expression $YV_{wx} - XV_{wy}$ in equation (8) will be positive if, in some sense, Y is more complementary with work than X is (or if X is more complementary with leisure). dW will then have the same sign as dP_1. If there are three goods, X, Y and L, a consumer will always work harder as the result of the introduction of the indirect tax (total tax paid remaining constant) if it is levied on *that good* (X *or* Y) *which is more complementary with leisure.* For example, suppose that the indirect tax is levied on X so that $r_1 > r_2$. If X is more complementary with L than Y is, the consumer will take less leisure in the indirect tax equilibrium. He will work harder.

Let us now say precisely what we mean when we say that X is more complementary with leisure than Y is. A greater or smaller degree of complementarity could easily be defined if it were possible to measure the quantity of leisure, as could be done if there were a maximum to the income which could be earned however hard an individual were to work. The quantity of leisure could then be measured by the difference between this maximum income and his actual earnings. In that case, our condition would be that the elasticity of complementarity[1] between X and leisure should be higher than the elasticity of complementarity between Y and leisure.

We can now proceed to show in what conditions the tax change will raise the consumer's real income by putting him on a higher indifference surface.

[1] Cf. R. G. D. Allen, " A Reconsideration of the Theory of Value," *Economica*, 1934, pp. 205–6.

The change in the utility function (dU) is given by :

$$dU = \left[U_x\frac{\partial X}{\partial P_1} + U_y\frac{\partial Y}{\partial P_1} + U_w\frac{\partial W}{\partial P_1}\right] dP_1 + \left[U_x\frac{\partial X}{\partial P_2} + U_y\frac{\partial Y}{\partial P_2} + U_w\frac{\partial W}{\partial P_2}\right] dP_2$$

$$= \lambda\left[P_1\frac{\partial X}{\partial P_1} + P_2\frac{\partial Y}{\partial P_1} - \frac{\partial W}{\partial P_1}\right]dP_1 + \lambda\left[P_1\frac{\partial X}{\partial P_2} + P_2\frac{\partial Y}{\partial P_2} - \frac{\partial W}{\partial P_2}\right] dP_2$$

(from equation (3))

Therefore $dU = -\lambda\,(XdP_1 + YdP_2)$ (from equation (5))

$$= +\lambda\left(r\frac{\partial W}{\partial P_1}dP_1 + r\frac{\partial W}{\partial P_2}dP_2\right) \text{ (from equation (7))}$$

$$= r\lambda dW \text{ (from equation (4))}$$

where dU is the increment of the utility index (the increase in satisfaction) ; r is the *ad valorem* rate of purchase tax in the initial " quasi income tax " equilibrium ; λ is the Langrange multiplier (the " marginal utility of money ") ; and dW is the increment of work done by the consumer, measured in money earned.

The consumer will only reach a higher real income as a result of the tax change—the increment in the utility function will only be positive—if $r\lambda dW$ is positive. Now r is the rate of tax and must be positive ; so must λ, the marginal utility of money. The consumer will, therefore, have a higher real income whenever dW is positive—whenever he works harder as a result of the tax change.

The above equation also shows that the rise in real income is equal to the marginal utility of the increase in money income, multipied by the *ad valorem* tax rate in the initial equilibrium. Thus for any given increase of work, the resulting rise in the consumer's real income will be larger the greater the marginal utility of money and the higher the *ad valorem* rate of tax.

Although this formula is simple, its meaning is not immediately obvious. One way of looking at it is this. If there had been no change in leisure, the consumer's money income would have been constant and the change in the tax system would have reduced his real income. This is shown by the traditional indifference curve diagram,[1] where a change from direct to indirect taxes (with money income and the tax yield constant) always leaves the consumer worse off. But if the consumer works harder after the tax change, his money income rises. In our model his increased income is dW and its utility λdW. Not all the satisfactions from spending this extra income represent a net gain to the consumer. Some of the utility derived from the extra income is cancelled out by the reduction in the amount of leisure now that the consumer works harder.

Again, some utility derived from the extra income has to make good the loss of satisfaction which would have occurred if the tax change had led to no increase in work. This latter loss of satisfaction is the one usually studied in this kind of analysis, but it is only a second order change (i.e. $dU = 0$, $d^2U < 0$) for an infinitesimal change like that we are studying, and we can ignore it.

The reason why the gain in satisfaction is only $r\lambda dW$ is, therefore, as follows. If the consumer is in the income tax equilibrium, a move away from that equilibrium position along the budget plane (including work) would cause a loss of satisfaction, but only of the second order. In order to buy the extra amounts of X and Y taken in the indirect tax equilibrium, the consumer would have to supply extra work equal to $(1 + r)\,dW$. With the indirect tax, however, the necessary extra work is only dW.

[1] Cf. for example, Henderson, op. cit., p. 540, and Little, op. cit., p. 577.

(Since no extra tax revenue is needed, expenditure and income increase by equal amounts.) There is thus a net gain of $r\lambda dW$, over a movement along the old budget plane. Our results for infinitesimal changes show the direction in which the tax system should change if real income is to rise. With finite changes, the loss of satisfaction caused by movements along the old budget plane would no longer be negligible. To find the " optimum " indirect tax system, we should have to take account of these second order changes along the old budget plane.

We cannot say with certainty what the effect of the tax change on the purchases of X and Y will be. This will depend both on the actual magnitudes of the substitution terms and on the income effects.

An illustration may make the position clearer. Let us suppose that the three goods, X, Y and L are cricket matches, food and leisure respectively. We assume that cricket matches[1] are more complementary with leisure than food is. We further assume that when the change takes place, the *ad valorem* rate of tax on cricket matches is higher than in the " quasi income tax " equilibrium and the rate of tax on food is lower. The tax change will thus make the consumer work harder. He will do more work and his real and money incomes will rise. Normally he will buy more food and watch less cricket, but neither result is certain.

The *rationale* of such a change from direct to indirect taxation is quite simple. The " ideal " tax would be one which was levied at the same *ad valorem* rate on all goods, including leisure.[2] By taxing those goods which are more complementary with leisure, one is to some extent taxing leisure itself. One is, therefore, moving in the direction of the " ideal " tax which is levied at equal *ad valorem* rates on all goods. This explains why the consumer reaches a higher indifference surface. We may also note that, since the total tax payment is constant, a smaller proportion of the consumer's money income is paid in taxes when he works harder. This provides part of the reason why more work raises the consumer's real income. The relative simplicity of the conditions under which real income rises or falls is the result of the constraint introduced by the central assumption of constant tax payments.

It is also possible to use our results to show whether one tax system can raise more revenue than another, from a given consumer on a given indifference surface. It can be shown that an indirect tax can raise more revenue, at a given level of real income, than an income tax, if the *ad valorem* rate of tax is higher on that good which is more complementary with leisure.

In discussing this subject, one finds that confusion sometimes arises because of attempts to divide leisure into two parts, that used in conjunction with other goods, for example, in listening to symphony concerts, and that used as " pure leisure "— when one does nothing at all. This distinction is a dangerous one. But even if the distinction is valid, the conclusions of the foregoing analysis are unaffected. An increase in, say, theatre prices, may induce a consumer to spend time which he previously spent at the theatre in " doing nothing." But since prices of goods like food are now lower, extra work must become a less unpleasant alternative to leisure. In this simple model, the consumer may spend more time " just sitting " in the garden as a result of the tax change. But, at least, he will spend some time he previously used in watching plays in doing a little extra work.

We can now show what change in the relative prices of X and Y is needed to

[1] Cf. Henderson, op. cit., p. 546.
[2] This is essentially equivalent to a poll tax.

keep the tax paid constant. We have seen from (7) that the ratio between the two price changes :

$$\frac{dP_2}{dP_1} = -\frac{r\frac{\partial W}{\partial P_1} + X}{r\frac{\partial W}{\partial P_2} + Y} \quad \ldots\ldots (9)$$

$$\text{therefore : } \frac{dP_2}{dP_1} = -\frac{-rX\frac{\partial W}{\partial M} + X + rV_{wx}}{-rY\frac{\partial W}{\partial M} + Y + rV_{wy}}$$

$$= -\frac{X}{Y} - \frac{r}{Y}\frac{YV_{wx} - XV_{wy}}{Y\left(1 - r\frac{\partial W}{\partial M}\right) + rV_{wy}} \quad \ldots\ldots (10)$$

The change in the price of Y is greater relatively to the change in the price of X the greater is :

$$\frac{r}{Y} \cdot \frac{YV_{wx} - XV_{yw}}{Y\left(1 - r\frac{\partial W}{\partial M}\right) + rV_{wy}}$$

That is to say, the price of Y will change more, relatively to the price of X, if X is more complementary with leisure, than Y is. The greater the difference between the complementarity of the two goods with leisure, the greater this relative price change.

Let us now consider the " crazy " case mentioned earlier. Here either the numerator or the denominator, or both, in the right hand side of equation (9) are negative. The numerator will be negative if an increase in the rate of tax on X (with the tax on Y constant) lowers the total tax yield. Similarly, the denominator will be negative if an increase in the rate of tax on Y has this result. These results can only occur if (*i*) the tax rates are high, and *either* (*ii*) leisure is an inferior good, *or* (*iii*) the good in question is so strongly competitive with leisure (in Hicks' sense) that the substitution effect outweighs the (positive) income effect. It would obviously be ridiculous to allow such a situation to persist, since a tax reduction would raise the revenue received by the Exchequer. Nevertheless, such a situation might conceivably occur and is worth analysing.

Let us first see what happens where the " crazy " case is reached for Y but not for X. This can only happen, whether leisure is an inferior good or not, if X is more complementary with leisure than Y is. To obtain the same tax revenue when a change from direct to indirect taxation occurs, both prices have to change in the same direction. An *increase* in tax rates would inevitably mean less work done and lower real incomes. A *reduction* in tax rates would increase both the supply of effort and real income. Similarly when the " crazy " case has been reached for X but not for Y.

When the " crazy " situation exists for both goods, the normal rules are reversed whether or not leisure is an inferior good. If tax revenue is to be constant, the tax rates will have to change in opposite directions. But the consumer will only work harder if the higher *ad valorem* tax rate is levied on the good which is *less complementary* with leisure. The consumer will then become " better off " in the usual way.

An illustration of a position where both X and Y are " crazy " may be useful. The notion that leisure might be an inferior good is improbable so we ignore it. If the " crazy " situation has nevertheless been reached for both X and Y, it follows that an increase in the tax rate on either good alone will reduce both the total tax yield and the supply of effort. If there is a rise in the rate of tax on the good which is more complementary with leisure, however, a greater part of the loss of tax revenue resulting from the reduction in work will be offset by the increased yield on the good in question.

The problem we are considering occurs where the two tax rates change in opposite directions and give the same yield. Here, a small increase in the tax on the good which is less complementary with leisure means the loss of much tax revenue and to offset this there must be a relatively large reduction in the tax on the other good. It is the relative largeness of this second change which causes the net effect to be favourable.

These exceptions to our main conclusions should be noted. The main argument relates to a model where tax rates are moderate. It should also be remembered that a change to indirect taxation *cannot* raise the consumer's real income if his supply of effort has zero elasticity, or if there is no additional work available. This should be borne in mind in any attempt to relate our conclusions to present day conditions.

Some of the restrictions in the analysis can now be relaxed. First, what happens where there are more than two consumer goods as well as leisure? We can again consider the initial income tax position by assuming that an *ad valorem* tax at the rate r is levied on all goods except leisure. The tax change can now be looked upon as a change in the rate of tax on any two of these goods, say, X_1 and X_2, the money tax yield being unaltered.

Equation (2), showing the necessary relative price-changes, is modified simply by including similar terms for the other goods in each of the brackets. The same modification has to be made in equation (5), but the result is that the relationship shown in equation (7) remains :

$$\left[r\frac{\partial W}{\partial P_1} + X\right] dP_1 + \left[r\frac{\partial W}{\partial P_2} + Y\right] dP_2 = 0.$$

The remainder of the argument applies as before. Where the tax rate is changed on more than two out of any collection of goods, our conclusions still hold, provided that the "average" (in some sense) rate of tax is raised on those goods which are most complementary with leisure.

The same type of analysis can be applied for a tax change from any initial tax system, starting from a modified form of equation (2) with differing values for r for the various terms. Putting $dU = 0$, or $XdP_1 + YdP_2 = 0$, and similar relations for changes affecting other pairs of goods, we can obtain the formal conditions for the "optimum" system of indirect taxes. The solution gives a system of equations in the n tax rates with coefficients involving the elasticities of complementarity between all pairs of goods. It does not follow, however, that goods most complementary with leisure would then bear the highest rate of tax. For example, if one of the goods had both zero income and substitution elasticities, the "optimum" position would be where the whole tax was raised from that good.

By assuming constant marginal costs our analysis has ignored the effects of changing marginal rates of transformation. We have assumed away the difficulties which arise because the Treasury does not want to acquire money from tax payers, but real resources. Since, in practice, marginal rates of transformation are bound to change, this problem is important if we are to make the transition from one to many consumers. We make this transition now.

Let us follow Mr. Little[1] in constructing a transformation surface showing those combinations of the various goods and leisure (or work) which remain to consumers

[1] Op. cit., pp. 581–3.

after the Government has taken all the goods it requires. We can express the nature of this transformation surface by the function :

$$\phi\ (X_1, X_2 \ldots X_n, W) = 0.$$

Let us now consider a change from an income tax situation. The condition that in any equilibrium position the Government has a given collection of goods, takes the place of our assumption that the total tax paid is constant.

It follows that the changes in the quantities of goods, and in work done must satisfy the relation :

$$\frac{\partial\phi}{\partial X_1}dX_1 + \frac{\partial\phi}{\partial X_2}dX_2 \ldots \frac{\partial\phi}{\partial X_n}dX_n + \frac{\partial\phi}{\partial W}dW = 0.$$

Consider again the case where the tax rate changes on the goods X_1 and X_2 only. We then have :

$$dP_1\left[\frac{\partial\phi}{\partial X_1}\frac{\partial X_1}{\partial P_1} + \frac{\partial\phi}{\partial X_2}\frac{\partial X_2}{\partial P_1} + \ldots \frac{\partial\phi}{\partial X_n}\frac{\partial X_n}{\partial P_1} + \frac{\partial\phi}{\partial W}\frac{\partial W}{\partial P_1}\right] +$$
$$dP_2\left[\frac{\partial\phi}{\partial X_1}\frac{\partial X_1}{\partial P_2} + \frac{\partial\phi}{\partial X_2}\frac{\partial X_2}{\partial P_2} + \ldots \frac{\partial\phi}{\partial X_n}\frac{\partial X_n}{\partial P_2} + \frac{\partial\phi}{\partial W}\frac{\partial W}{\partial P_2}\right] = 0 \quad \ldots\ldots\ldots\ldots (11)$$

In the initial equilibrium position with the income tax, the ratios of the partial derivatives of ϕ give the marginal rates of transformation between the different goods. Since we are assuming perfect competition, these marginal rates of transformation will be equal to relative prices before tax. That is to say :

$$\frac{\partial\phi}{\partial X_1} : \frac{\partial\phi}{\partial X_2} : \ldots \frac{\partial\phi}{\partial X_n} : \frac{\partial\phi}{\partial W} = p_1 : p_2 : \ldots p_n : -1 = P_1 : P_2 : \ldots P_n : -(1 + r)$$

Substituting this into equation (11) we have :

$$dP_1\left[P_1\frac{\partial X_1}{\partial P_1} + P_2\frac{\partial X_2}{\partial P_1} + \ldots P_n\frac{\partial X_n}{\partial P_1} - (1 + r)\frac{\partial W}{\partial P_1}\right] +$$
$$dP_2\left[P_1\frac{\partial X_1}{\partial P_2} + P_2\frac{\partial X_2}{\partial P_2} + \ldots P_n\frac{\partial X_n}{\partial P_2} - (1 + r)\frac{\partial W}{\partial P_2}\right] = 0.$$

It follows from an equation similar to that given in (5) that :

$$dP_1\left[-r\frac{\partial W}{\partial P_1} - X\right] + dP_2\left[-r\frac{\partial W}{\partial P_2} - Y\right] = 0.$$

This, once again, is the condition we had in (7).

It follows that changing marginal costs do not invalidate the conditions which we have outlined. The community will work more, and will have a higher real income, under exactly the same conditions as for the individual consumer. But the *final equilibrium position* is likely to differ.

What has been said above relates, strictly, only to the respective effects of indirect taxes and of proportional, " flat rate," income taxes. In the real world, however, a " progressive " income tax system usually includes a fixed allowance, granted by exempting a certain initial income from tax. Once the exemption limit is passed the marginal rate of tax usually changes only discontinuously so that over considerable ranges of income the " progressive " income tax really represents a flat rate tax plus a " poll subsidy." For small changes from this position towards indirect taxation, the foregoing analysis appears to be valid.[1]

[1] It might be worth mentioning that the case cited by Mr. Wald (op. cit., pp. 588–9), where a shift from a proportional to a progressive income tax makes the consumer better off, is the equivalent of our " crazy " case. As shown in his diagram, a lower marginal rate of tax, together with tax free allowances is raising as much revenue as a higher flat rate tax.

An interesting point emerges if one considers a true progressive tax. Mr. Henderson suggested that one way to compare direct and indirect taxes was to discover that system of indirect taxes which yielded, at each level of income, the same amount of revenue as a progressive income tax.[1] He then showed that, *if money income is held constant* (if leisure is held constant) the direct tax proves " superior " in the conventional sense of this term. But if leisure is *not* held constant, we know that the indirect tax can be the " superior " tax. The comparison of direct and indirect taxes with the same " tax formula " then becomes difficult. For, one reason why a change from direct to indirect taxation can increase a man's real income, is that it reduces the proportion of his income paid in tax. In other words, it reduces the progressiveness of the tax system. Mr. Henderson is, therefore, right, in a sense, when he claims that " it is not the change of method which is causing the change in output but the change in the tax formula from the point of view of the tax payer."[2] Once one moves away from a two-dimensional world, however, it is no longer true that there will be a direct tax system which has the same formula from the point of view of the Exchequer and is always " less onerous to the payer."[3]

Mr. Henderson is perfectly correct in claiming that a direct tax system can always raise a *given* amount of revenue from a *given* money income more painlessly than an indirect tax. But once the amount of leisure is allowed to vary, money income will vary too. The best way in which the problem can then be approached is by discovering which tax system raises a given revenue most efficaceously from a given " potential income " or a given " income earning capacity." It will then be found that a direct tax system will nearly always impose an " excess burden " as compared with some system of indirect taxes.

Let us now sum up the argument and consider some implications of our results. We have seen that some form of indirect taxation will be superior to direct taxation *if individuals are able to decide how much they work*. The discovery of the goods on which indirect taxes are required remains unsolved until we have more adequate statistical information about demand equations. Only in particular cases—such as the practically unimportant one of *completely* inelastic demand—can one make dogmatic statements about the " optimum " system of indirect taxation.

It should, however, be made quite clear that nothing in our analysis conflicts with the acknowledged superiority of the poll tax over all other forms of tax. Nor, of course, does anything in this article deny that a change from direct to indirect taxation might well reduce the progressiveness of the tax system, without enabling anyone to prove that it was less progressive. Such a proof is obviously impossible because no one knows the shape of all indifference maps.

London.

W. J. Corlett.
D. C. Hague.

[1] Op. cit., pp. 541–3.
[2] Op. cit., p. 545.
[3] Op. cit., p. 544.

[2]

THE SECOND-BEST ARGUMENT FOR TRADE CONTROL: (2) THE PARTIAL FREEING OF TRADE

LET us now leave on one side the problems raised by the existence of divergences between marginal values and costs due to the necessity for taxation for the purpose of raising revenue. We will assume, that is to say, that sufficient is received from State-owned income-bearing property or can be raised by other means—such as progressive lump-sum taxes—which do not cause any divergence between marginal values and costs. It is no longer required that taxes on international trade should raise any given revenue.

The problem which we intend to discuss in this chapter is whether it is always desirable on grounds of economic efficiency to eliminate a particular divergence between marginal values and costs in international trade by removing a tax or subsidy or other control of the international trade in the commodity concerned, when there are other divergences between marginal values and costs in the case of other commodities entering into international trade.

We wish to confine ourselves in this chapter to problems of economic efficiency. We shall, therefore, continue to assume that the same distributional weights are allotted by the policy-makers to all citizens in all the trading countries. That is to say, we should consider it an improvement if, at current prices, we could give an additional $1 of income to any one individual provided that that involved taking less than $1 of income away from any other individual.

We wish to confine ourselves in this chapter also to marginal changes. We shall, therefore, continue to assume that the structure of industry remains unchanged in each trading country and that we are concerned solely with such changes in trade taxes or other controls as will cause only marginal changes in the amounts produced, consumed, and traded of the products concerned.

But we are concerned in this chapter with another problem of second-best, as opposed to utopian, policy. We wish to consider in what conditions a reduction in one particular rate of import tax or other trade control will increase economic welfare not on the assumption that no other trade taxes exist, but on the assumption that for one reason or another a given structure of trade controls on the rest of international trade exists and will continue to exist.[1] But, in order to isolate certain

[1] In this chapter we shall argue as if these existing divergences between marginal values and costs in international trade were all due to trade controls—import and export duties, subsidies, quotas, State-trading controls, etc. There

basic considerations, we shall assume in this chapter that these unalterable divergences between marginal values and costs exist only in international trade and not in domestic production, consumption, or trade. In other words, we assume that within each of the trading countries a policy of modified laissez-faire is successfully adopted so that there are no domestic divergences between marginal values and costs.

We are left then with the following type of problem. Suppose that there is a duty in A on the import of blankets from B, and that the government in A reduces this duty. Suppose at the same time that there are duties or subsidies in A or in B on the movement of other goods from B into A or on some or all of A's exports to B. In these conditions does the reduction of the particular barrier on the sale of blankets by B to A necessarily lead to an increase in economic efficiency?

In accordance with the analysis of Chapter VII, in order to answer this question, we need to know what will be the effect of the reduction in A's duty levied on imports of blankets from B upon the amount of blankets which will be exported from B to A and, indirectly, upon the amounts of all the other products which will be exported from B to A and from A to B. We need to value the change in the volume of trade in each particular product by the supply prices of each product in the exporting country, since with modified laissez-faire policies within each country these supply prices will be equal to the marginal social net costs of production. We must then weight each of these changes in trade by the *ad valorem* rate of incidence of the trade barrier to which that particular line of trade is subject, since the trade barrier is the only cause of an excess of marginal value over marginal social cost. If the sum of all such changes so valued and weighted is greater than zero, then there is an increase in economic efficiency as a result of the partial move to free trade which the reduction of A's duty on imports of blankets represents. If, however, this sum is less than zero, the partial move towards free trade will have reduced and not increased world economic efficiency.

In making these calculations it is interesting to note the following points.

First, we can leave out of our calculation all changes in domestic trade within each country because we are assuming that there are modified laissez-faire policies within each country, which have the result that there is no divergence between marginal values and costs in any line of domestic transaction.

---

might, however, be divergences between marginal values and costs in international markets due to elements of monopoly or monopsony or, less probably, to external economies or diseconomies. The analysis is, of course, exactly similar in these cases, and the reader is left to apply the conclusions of this chapter to these other kinds of divergence for himself.

Second, we can leave out of our calculations all changes in international trade in commodities in which there is free trade, because in these cases too there are no existing divergences between marginal values and costs so that marginal changes in these transactions also have no effect upon economic welfare.

Third, we can leave out of our calculations all those products in international trade which are controlled not by taxes and subsidies but by quota arrangements which fix a rigid quantitative limit to the volume of trade. The reason for this is obvious. There will normally be no change in the volume of such trade, so that it can make no marginal contribution to an increase or decrease in economic welfare.[1]

Fourth, if subsidies to certain lines of international trade exist, then in those cases marginal costs will exceed marginal values and we shall be dealing with negative rates of divergence. An increase in the volume of such trade reduces economic efficiency since the marginal value of the increase in trade is less than its marginal cost. In such a case, therefore, any reduction of trade which would result as an indirect effect of the reduction of A's duty on the import of blankets from B will raise economic efficiency.

Our essential task is, therefore, to inquire what will be the effects upon the various flows of trade between A and B of a reduction in A's duty on the import of blankets from B. A complete answer to this question would involve a complete analysis of every change in both economies, since the supply and demand of each product entering into trade depends to a smaller or greater degree upon what has happened to the income of every factor of production in every country and to the price of every other product being produced or consumed in either country. Such a total analysis is completely impracticable except in a very elaborate mathematical form, and even this would provide results only of such generality that very few useful conclusions could be drawn from it. We must be content with a less rigorous analysis which will neglect a number of possible indirect repercussions but which may enable us to understand some of the most important tendencies at work.

Accordingly, in considering the effect of the reduction of A's duty on

[1] The one case in which imports which are restricted by a quantitative quota might be changed is where the repercussions of the reduction in A's duty on imports of blankets are such as to reduce the demand for or supply of this other product below the permitted quota. In such a case there would be a reduction in the volume of trade in this commodity. But we could still neglect the change in our calculations. The volume would not fall below the permitted quantity until the quota arrangement had lost all its protective effect, i.e. until all divergence between supply and demand price had disappeared as a result of the reduction in demand or the reduction in supply. Either the volume of trade is not changed or else there is no remaining divergence between marginal values and costs in the case of this commodity. In either case it makes no marginal contribution to increased or decreased economic welfare.

imports of blankets from B upon the flows of trade between A and B, we shall treat these effects under three separate headings, although in a full analysis these three types of effect could not be assumed to be independent of each other. We shall call these three types of effect the primary, secondary, and tertiary effects.

The direct effect of a reduction in the duty on imports of blankets from B into A will be to lower the price at which A's consumers can purchase B's blankets and/or to raise the price at which B's producers can sell blankets to A's consumers. By the *primary effect* of a reduction in A's duty on imports of B's blankets we mean the change in the amount of blankets which would be imported from B into A if there were no change of incomes in A or B and no change in the price of any product in A or B except the changes in the prices of blankets in A and B which were directly caused by the change in the duty on blankets.

But blankets may be a close substitute for or complement with some other particular product in A and/or in B. Because of this the change in the prices of blankets in A and B which are directly caused by the change in duty may cause shifts of supply and demand for these other products for which blankets are close substitutes or with which blankets are very complementary. This may, therefore, lead to shifts in the trade between A and B in these other products. By the *primary plus secondary effects* of the reduction in A's duty on imports of B's blankets we mean the changes which would take place in the amount of trade between A and B in blankets and in these other products which are close substitutes for or complements with blankets, if incomes remained constant in A and B and if the prices of all products remained constant in A and B except the prices of blankets and of these other products which were close substitutes for or complements with blankets in A or B.[1]

But when we have allowed for all the primary and secondary effects so defined, we may still not have reached a final equilibrium. We can illustrate this best in our present problem by saying that there might still remain a disequilibrium in the general balance of payments between A and B. The reduction in the import duty on blankets from B is likely to have caused A's consumers to purchase more imports from B and thus to have imposed some strain upon A's balance of payments with B. There is no reason to believe that the secondary changes, if any, as we have defined them will have removed this deficit on A's balance of payments. Its removal may, therefore, involve a fall in the general level of the incomes of the factors of production and of costs of products in A relatively to those in B, brought about either by the gold standard mechanism of general deflation in A and inflation in B or by

[1] Some important examples of primary and secondary effects are analysed in Sections VII–X of the mathematical supplement to this volume.

a depreciation of A's currency in terms of B's currency.[1] Such a development will encourage exports from A to B and discourage imports from B into A. These changes in trade flows due to the general adjustments required to restore equilibrium to the balance of payments between A and B we shall call the *tertiary effects* of the change in duty.

We do not need a very lengthy discussion of the primary effect of the reduction in A's duty on imported blankets. The effect will be partly to reduce the price of the imported blankets in A and partly to raise the price of the exported blankets in B. The reduction in the price charged to consumers in A for imported blankets will encourage them to purchase more of them,[2] and the better price which B's exporters can obtain for blankets sold to B will encourage them to export more of them. There will therefore be an increase in the volume of sales of blankets from A to B; and since there is a positive excess of marginal value over marginal cost in this trade due to the existing duty the primary effect of the reduction in the duty will always be to improve economic efficiency.

How great the increase in economic efficiency due to this factor will be depends upon two factors, the initial height of the duty and the size of the increase in the volume of trade caused by the reduction in the duty. With any given increase in the volume of trade the gain will be the greater, the greater is the initial level of the duty, since a high rate of duty will mean that there is a large excess of marginal value over marginal cost on the increment of trade. With any given duty the gain will be the greater, the greater is the increase in the volume of trade on which this excess of marginal value over marginal cost is enjoyed.

Now the increase in the volume of trade will be greater, the greater is the increase in the volume which A's consumers will want to import when the price they must pay for imported blankets falls by any small amount and the greater is the increase in the volume which B's exporters will want to sell abroad when the price they can obtain for exported blankets rises by any small amount. In other words, the primary increase in the trade in blankets will be large if the elasticity of demand for imports of blankets in A is large and if the elasticity of supply of exports of blankets in B is large.

Now the demand for imports of blankets in A will be the greater, the greater is the elasticity of demand in A for blankets in general—i.e. whether home-produced or imported. This is obvious. A fall in the price of imported blankets will cheapen the price of blankets in A, and the more this leads to an expansion in the consumption of blankets the more it will raise imports of blankets. But imported blankets may

[1] See Part IV of Volume I of this work.

[2] We rule out of consideration the remote possibility that the imported blankets may be so inferior a good in A's consumption that A's consumers purchase less of them when they become cheaper.

compete with home-produced blankets in A. The fall in the price of blankets in A due to the reduction in the duty on imported blankets will then reduce the price which home producers in A can obtain for their blankets. If as a result of this fall in price producers of blankets in A greatly cut down their supply, a large void will exist in the market for blankets in A to be filled by increased imports. In other words, the elasticity of demand for imported blankets in A will be the greater, the greater is the elasticity of supply of home-produced blankets in A. And, finally, the elasticity of demand for imported blankets in A will also be the greater, the smaller is the proportion of the total consumption of blankets in A which is supplied by imports. If imported blankets in A make up only a very small part of the total consumption of blankets in A, then only a very small proportionate increase in the total demand for blankets in A and only a very small proportionate decrease in the home supply of blankets in A is required to lead to an enormous proportionate increase in the amount of imported blankets which are required to fill the gap in A's market.[1]

Similarly, it can be shown that the elasticity of supply of exports of blankets from B will be the greater, (i) the greater is the elasticity of supply of the production of blankets in B whether for home consumption or for export, (ii) the greater is the elasticity of demand for blankets for home consumption in B, and (iii) the smaller is the proportion of the output of blankets in B which is exported. The reduction in A's duty on imports of blankets will raise the price offered for blankets in B. If this rise in price causes a large increase in B's production and a large decrease in B's consumption of blankets, this will release a large quantity for export. And if existing exports are small relatively to the total production of blankets in B, this increase in the supplies available for export will represent an enormous proportionate increase in the volume of exports.[2]

We may, therefore conclude that the primary effect of a reduction in A's duty on imported blankets will be to increase economic efficiency, and that the increase in economic efficiency will be the greater, (i) the higher is the initial rate of duty, (ii) the greater is the elasticity of demand for blankets in A, (iii) the greater is the elasticity of supply of blankets in A, (iv) the smaller is the proportion of A's consumption of blankets which comes from imports, (v) the greater is the elasticity of supply of blankets in B, (vi) the greater is the elasticity of demand for blankets in B, and (vii) the smaller is the proportion of B's output of blankets which is sold for export.[3]

[1] See Table XVIII (p. 198). [2] See Table XVII (p. 196).

[3] The above propositions can readily be proved algebraically. Let x be the volume of trade in blankets; $D_a(p_a)$ the volume of blankets consumed in A where p_a is the price of blankets in A and D_a is the demand function in A; $S_a(p_a)$ the supply of blankets produced in A; $D_b(p_b)$ the amount of blankets

We can turn next to the *secondary effects* of the reduction of B's duty on imported blankets upon the flows of trade. The reduction in the duty will, as we have seen, have the effect of lowering the price of blankets in A and increasing the amount of blankets flowing into the market in A and the opposite effect of raising the price of blankets in B and increasing the amount of blankets flowing out of the market in B. We will first consider the possible secondary effects of this which may take place in A's market, and we will then turn to the corresponding effects which may take place in B's market.

The extra blankets imported into A may be close substitutes for or close complements either with other goods which A imports or with goods which A exports. This gives us four possible types of secondary effect upon A's trade, namely: (1) where the extra blankets imported

---

consumed in B; $S_b(p_b)$ the amount of blankets produced in B; and t the *ad valorem* rate of import duty in A. We have the following three equations:

$$x = D_a(p_a) - S_a(p_a) = S_b(p_b) - D_b(p_b), \text{ and } p_a = p_b(1 + t)$$

since the volume of trade equals the excess of demand over supply in the importing country and the excess of supply over demand in the exporting country and since the price in A equals the price in B raised by the *ad valorem* rate of duty. Differentiating these equations we have:

$$dx = -(\varepsilon_a D_a + \eta_a S_a)\frac{dp_a}{p_a} = (\varepsilon_b D_b + \eta_b S_b)\frac{dp_b}{p_b}, \text{ and } \frac{dp_a}{p_a} = \frac{dp_b}{p_b} + \frac{dt}{1 + t}$$

where ε_a and ε_b are the numerical values of the elasticities of demand for blankets in A and B and η_a and η_b are the corresponding elasticities of supply. If we eliminate $\frac{dp_a}{p_a}$ and $\frac{dp_b}{p_b}$ from the last three equations and remember that $D_a = S_a + x$ and $S_b = D_b + x$ we have:

$$dx = \frac{-dt}{1 + t} \cdot \frac{\left\{\varepsilon_a + (\varepsilon_a + \eta_a)\frac{S_a}{x}\right\}\left\{(\varepsilon_b + \eta_b)\frac{D_b}{x} + \eta_b\right\}}{\varepsilon_a + (\varepsilon_a + \eta_a)\frac{S_a}{x} + (\varepsilon_b + \eta_b)\frac{D_b}{x} + \eta_b}$$

The gain in economic welfare is measured by the change in the volume of trade valued at the supply price and weighted by the *ad valorem* tax, i.e. by $dx \cdot p_b \cdot t$. The gain due to a given fall in duty $(-\,dt)$ is therefore measured by the expression:

$$p_b \frac{t}{1 + t} \cdot \frac{\left\{\varepsilon_a + (\varepsilon_a + \eta_a)\frac{S_a}{x}\right\}\left\{(\varepsilon_b + \eta_b)\frac{D_b}{x} + \eta_b\right\}}{\varepsilon_a + (\varepsilon_a + \eta_a)\frac{S_a}{x} + (\varepsilon_b + \eta_b)\frac{D_b}{x} + \eta_b}$$

It is clear that an increase in t will increase this expression.

The right-hand fraction of the expression is of the form $\frac{(a + b)(c + d)}{a + b + c + d}$.

Let this equal e. Now $\frac{de}{da} = \left(\frac{c + d}{a + b + c + d}\right)^2$ and is therefore positive, and similarly $\frac{de}{db}$, $\frac{de}{dc}$, and $\frac{de}{dd}$ are positive.

It follows that the expression for the increase in economic welfare consequent upon a given decrease in duty $(-\,dt)$ will be greater, the greater are t, ε_a, η_a, $\frac{S_a}{x}$, ε_b, η_b, and $\frac{D_b}{x}$.

are substitutes for other goods imported by A, (2) where they are complementary with other goods imported by A, (3) where they are substitutes for goods exported by A, and (4) where they are complementary with goods exported from A.

(1) Where the extra blankets imported into A—which we will call the primary goods—are close substitutes for other imports in A, we shall have a case of what may be called ***secondary import trade destruction in A***. Thus suppose that A imports two types of blanket from B—wool blankets and cotton blankets—and suppose that these two products are close substitutes for each other in A's consumption. Suppose then that there were a reduction in A's duty on imports of wool blankets without any reduction in her duty on imports of cotton blankets. Then the lower price and increased supplies of wool blankets in A would cause A's consumers to purchase less cotton blankets. Thus there would be a secondary destruction of the import trade in cotton blankets due to the primary increase in imports of wool blankets.

In the above example we have given a case in which there is direct competition in the demand of A's final consumers between the primary import (wool blankets) and the secondary import (cotton blankets). But there are at least two other forms of substitutability between the two imported products on A's market which may have exactly similar effects.

Suppose that A imports from B not only wool blankets but also raw wool which is used in A's industry to work up into home-produced blankets. Suppose then that in A an import duty on blankets is reduced without any accompanying reduction in duty on imports of raw wool. There will now be especially strong pressure on A's blanket industry to contract, since the price of the imported finished product will have been reduced without any corresponding reduction in the price of the imported raw material. As a result of this contraction in A's blanket industry, A's imports of raw wool will be reduced. In A's import demand finished blankets and raw wool are to a considerable extent substitutes for each other; according to the relative prices of imported raw wool and imported finished blankets, A's traders can choose between importing raw wool to be made up into blankets at home or importing the finished product itself.

There is yet another way in which substitutability may show itself between A's primary and secondary imports. Suppose that A imports from B both blankets and underwear and suppose that these are not close substitutes for each other in A's consumption. But suppose that blankets and underwear are close substitutes for each other in A's production in the sense that the factors of production which are used in A to produce blankets are extremely well suited to produce underwear—the same skill of labour and the same machines being required in both lines of production. Then a reduction in the price of blankets will cause a contraction in the blanket industry in A; this will release resources which will move into the production of underwear, which in turn will compete with imported supplies of underwear. As a final result the increased imports of blankets will have led to some reduction in the imports of underwear because of the competition of the two industries in A for the same factors of production.

Where there are secondary imports into A which in any one of these three ways are close substitutes for A's primary imports of blankets, the reduction in the import duty on blankets will cause a reduction in the imports of these secondary products. If there is any duty in A on the import of the secondary products, the reduction in the imports of the secondary product will in itself tend to reduce economic welfare, since there will be a smaller import of something whose marginal value in A exceeds its marginal cost in B. Now whether there is a net increase in economic welfare or not as a result of these combined primary and secondary changes will depend upon two things: first, upon the relationship between the rate of *ad valorem* import duty on the primary imports and the rate of duty on the secondary imports; and, secondly, upon the relationship which the reduction of the secondary imports bears to the increase of the primary imports.[1]

It is obvious that there is more likely to be a gain in economic welfare if the rate of duty is high on the primary imports which will come in in increased volume and is low on the secondary imports which will come in in reduced volume. We can be more confident about the good effects of a reduction of duty if it is high relatively to the rates of duty on the goods which may be the subject of secondary trade destruction.

It is equally obvious that the partial tariff reduction will do more

[1] By the primary imports we mean, of course, the imports of the product on which the duty is reduced, and by the secondary imports the imports of the product which is a close substitute for or complement with the primary import. But the increase in the primary imports is not, strictly speaking, the same as the primary increase in imports. Suppose that there is a reduction in a duty levied on the import of woollen blankets into A. We defined the primary increase in imports as the increase in the imports of woollen blankets which would then take place if money incomes and the price of everything other than woollen blankets remained unchanged. But suppose that this leads to a decreased import of some close substitute—cotton blankets. The decreased demand for cotton blankets may cause the supply price of cotton blankets to fall, and this may to some extent divert demand back again away from woollen blankets. This consequential reduction in the import of woollen blankets is part of the secondary change in imports. Thus the change in the amount of primary imports is equal to the primary increase in imports plus any parts of the secondary and tertiary changes in trade which may happen to take the form of changes in the amount of trade in the primary import. The reader should bear this distinction in mind in what follows where, solely for simplicity of exposition, we shall talk of changes in the amounts of primary and secondary commodities which are traded rather than of the primary and secondary changes in the volume of trade.

good if the volume of secondary trade destruction is low, relatively to the volume of primary trade creation.[1] The factors which will cause the ratio of secondary trade destruction to be low relatively to the primary trade creation are fairly clear. The first point is almost too obvious to need mention. The greater is the degree of substitutability in A's demand between the primary imports and the secondary imports in any of the three ways described above, the greater will be the shift of demand away from the secondary on to the primary goods and the greater, in consequence, the fall in the volume of the secondary imports relatively to the rise in the volume of the primary imports.

But this leads to a second consideration. A given shift of demand away from the secondary imports, however large, will have little effect upon the volume of those imports if the elasticity of supply of their export in B is sufficiently low. If when consumers in A shift from purchases of imported cotton blankets to imported wool blankets the exporters of cotton blankets in B—having no alternative uses for their factors of production—merely lower the price of cotton blankets and continue to export as many as before, there will be no decline in the volume of trade in cotton blankets. The reduction in the volume of the secondary imports will be large relatively to the increase in the volume of the primary imports only if the elasticity of supply of the exports of the secondary goods from B is large.

The primary increase in imports of blankets into A as a result of the reduced price of blankets in A is due to the substitutability between imported blankets on the one hand and home-produced goods and other imports on the other hand. The secondary reduction in imports will be the smaller relatively to the primary increase in imports, not only the smaller is the substitutability between the primary imports and other secondary imports (as we have already observed) but also the greater is the substitutability between the primary imports and other goods which are produced domestically in A. Thus if A also produces blankets or other goods which are close substitutes for blankets, the increase in the primary import of blankets can be large without relying upon an equivalent reduction in the import of other things.

Finally, the degree to which the volume of secondary imports will fall off will also depend upon the degree to which these secondary imports are good substitutes for other things produced in A. Thus when the demand for the secondary imports declines their price will be reduced unless the elasticity of supply of their export from B is infinitely high. As their price falls demand will shift back on to them away from

[1] On the assumption, of course, that the secondary product is subject to a trade duty and not to a trade subsidy. If trade in the secondary product were subsidized, reduction in it would increase economic welfare. In this case both the primary trade creation and the secondary trade destruction would raise economic welfare.

other goods produced in A if these secondary imports are good substitutes in A for other goods produced in A. We can, therefore, say that the reduction in the volume of secondary imports will be smaller relatively to the increase in the volume of primary imports, the greater is the substitutability between the secondary imports and the whole range of other products produced in A.

To summarize, where the blankets on which A's duty is reduced are close substitutes in A (in any of the three ways which we have described) for some other imports from B into A, there will be a secondary reduction in A's imports of these substitutes associated with the primary increase in A's imports of blankets. If there is a positive divergence between marginal values and costs (due, for example, to an import duty) in the case of the import of these substitutes, this secondary effect will tend to reduce economic welfare. The increase in economic welfare due to the primary increase in the import of blankets is, however, the more likely to outweigh this secondary loss, (i) the higher is the rate of duty on the primary trade relatively to the rate of duty on the secondary trade, (ii) the less the degree of substitutability between the primary import and the secondary import, (iii) the greater the degree of substitutability between the primary import and the general range of goods produced in A, (iv) the smaller the elasticity of supply of export from B of the secondary imports, and (v) the greater the degree of substitutability between the secondary imports and the general range of goods produced in A.

We have dwelt at very considerable length with this case of substitutability in A between the blankets on which A's import duty is reduced and other imports into A from B. We shall now deal much more shortly with the remaining three cases of substitutability or complementarity in A between the blankets imported from B and other of A's traded products, and with the corresponding four cases in B's market. The reader must for himself apply to these remaining seven cases the detailed analysis which corresponds to the points which we have discussed in detail in this first case.[1]

(2) We turn then to the case in which the blankets imported into A from B are complementary with some other good—let us say beds—which are also imported into A from B. The more blankets are available in A the more beds are required. A reduction in the duty on imported blankets in A is therefore likely to increase the demand in A for imported beds, so that we now have a case of ***secondary import trade creation in A.***

This complementarity is perhaps more likely to show itself in the import of two materials which are jointly used in A to produce some

[1] The mathematical reader may be helped in this task by consulting Sections VII–X of the mathematical supplement to this volume.

finished product. For example, A may import coal and iron ore to produce steel. A reduction in a duty on imported coal may reduce the cost of producing steel and thus, by increasing the demand for home-produced steel in A, raise the demand for imported iron ore. Or the complementarity between A's two imports may not be in A's consumption at all but in her production. Suppose that blankets in A can, for technical reasons, be produced only in the winter and that some other product—wireless sets—which are also imported into A can also be made in A in the summer by the same labour which produces blankets during the winter. Then a reduction in the duty on imported blankets will contract the blanket industry in A; this will reduce the labour available in the summer to produce wireless sets; and this will raise A's demand for imported wireless sets.

In any of these three cases a reduction in the import duty on blankets in A will lead to a secondary increase in the demand in A for some other import. If this import is also subject to an import duty so that there is a positive excess of marginal value over marginal cost in this case, then the increase in these secondary imports will also raise economic welfare so that the secondary change will in this case reinforce the primary change.

How much it will reinforce the primary change will depend upon two factors: the rate of tax on the secondary imports as compared with the rate of tax on the primary imports, and the increase in the volume of the primary imports as compared with the increase in the volume of the secondary imports. The greater are both these ratios, the greater the secondary reinforcement to the increase in economic welfare.

The secondary increase in imports will be the greater: (i) the greater the degree of complementarity between the primary and secondary imports, which is obvious; (ii) the more elastic is the supply of exports of the secondary product from B, so that their export is much increased when the demand for them in A is raised; (iii) the less good substitutes are the secondary imports for other products in A, so that when the increase in their importation raises their supply price this will not choke off A's demand for them; and (iv) the less good substitutes the primary import is in A with the other products of A, so that the reduction of duty on the primary import can lead to a fall in the price of the import in A and so to a large increase in demand for the complementary secondary import.

In this complementary case the increase in economic welfare due to the primary increase in imports when the duty on imports of blankets into A is reduced, will be reinforced by the increase in imports of the complementary secondary product, beds. It follows that the duty on blankets should not merely be reduced to zero, but should be still further lowered, or, in other words, the import of blankets should be subsidized. Suppose blankets are imported freely. The payment of a small subsidy on imported blankets will also increase the import of beds, upon which an appreciable rate of import duty is levied. The increased import of blankets will now do harm, since the subsidy lowers the marginal value in A below the marginal cost in B. But the increased import of beds will still do good since the marginal value in A exceeds the marginal cost in B by the amount of the duty. But the secondary good exceeds the primary damage when the rate of duty on beds is high relatively to the rate of subsidy on blankets. The raising of the subsidy on imports of blankets should obviously go further the greater is the increase in the volume of the secondary import (beds) in relation to any given increase in the volume of the primary import (blankets). The four considerations enumerated in the previous paragraph show, therefore, the conditions in which the rate of subsidy on the primary import should be raised to a high level relatively to the rate of duty on the secondary import.

(3) We pass now to the case of ***secondary export trade creation in A***. This is the case in which the primary imports into A on which the duty is lowered are close substitutes in A for some products which are exported from A. Thus if the duty on imports of wines into country A is reduced, this may cause people in A to drink more wine at the expense of drinking less home-produced whisky, and this may release more whisky for export from A. Or the substitutability may be between a raw material and the finished product. Thus a reduction in a duty on the import of raw cotton into A may lead to an increase in the output of finished cotton textiles in A and so to an increase in the export of cotton textiles from A. Or the substitutability may be on the side of production. A reduction in the duty on the import of machine tools in A may lead to a contraction of the machine tool industry in A. This in turn may release factors of production—skilled engineering labour—which are most readily re-employed in the industry producing motor cars; and this may lead to an increase in the export of motor cars from A.

If there is a duty and so a divergence between marginal social values and costs on the export of the secondary products from A to B, then any reduction in the duty on the primary import into A will be bound to increase economic welfare. It will cause an increase in the primary import (on which there is a divergence between value and cost) as well as in the secondary export (in which there is also such a divergence). Indeed, if the rate of duty on the export of the secondary product from A to B cannot be reduced—and such is our present assumption—economic welfare demands that there should be some subsidy paid on the import of the primary product into A. If the primary import is subsidized, this means that there will be some direct loss incurred by a further stimulation of this import, since its marginal cost will now exceed its marginal value; but if the rate of subsidy on the primary import is not too high relatively to the rate of duty on the secondary export, some increase in the rate of subsidy and in the volume of the primary import will still raise economic welfare, because the direct loss due to the greater import of the primary product (on which marginal cost slightly exceeds marginal value) will be more than outweighed by the indirect gain from the stimulation of exports of the secondary product (on which marginal value greatly exceeds marginal cost).

The increase in the secondary exports will be large relatively to the increase in the primary imports (and thus the rate of subsidy on the primary imports should be high relatively to the rate of duty on the secondary exports) (i) if the degree of substitutability in A between the primary import and the secondary export is high; (ii) if the elasticity of demand for the secondary export in B is high, so that there can be a large increase in the secondary export without much fall in its price and so without much discouragement to its supply in A; (iii) if the secondary export is not a very good substitute in production in A with all other products in A, so that any given fall in the price offered for it in B does not much reduce its supply in A; and (iv) if the primary import in A is not a very good substitute with all the other products in A (apart from the secondary export) so that its price will fall considerably in A when the duty on it is reduced (or the subsidy on it is raised) with the consequence that there will be a large stimulation of the secondary export which is a close substitute for it.

(4) The last type of repercussion in A is that of *secondary export trade destruction in A*. This occurs when, in one of the three ways already mentioned, the primary imports in A are complementary in A's consumption or production with some export from A. In this case the increased import into A of the primary import will increase the home demand (or reduce the home supply) of the secondary commodity and the volume of its exports will in consequence be reduced. In this case some rate of duty should be maintained upon the primary import if the secondary export is also subject to a duty. A rise in the duty on the primary imports will reduce the primary imports and thus increase the secondary exports; and while there will be some direct loss of welfare on the decrease in the trade in the taxed primary imports, there will be a more than counterbalancing gain of economic welfare in the increased trade on the taxed secondary exports provided that the tax on the latter is high enough relatively to that on the former.

The tax on the primary imports should be high relatively to that on the secondary exports if the increased volume of secondary exports which will be associated with any decreased volume of primary imports is large. This will be so, if (i) there is a high degree of complementarity in A between the primary imports and the secondary exports; (ii) if the elasticity of demand in B for the secondary export is high; (iii) if the secondary export is not a very good substitute in A with all the rest of A's products, so that its supply to B is not much discouraged by any fall in its price in B; and (iv) if the primary import in A is not a very good substitute with all the other products of A so that its price will rise considerably in A when the duty on it is raised with the consequence that there will be a large stimulation of the secondary export which is a close substitute for it.

So far we have considered the repercussions of a reduction of a duty on imports into A only upon the demand or supply in A of exports or imports. But the reduction in the duty and the consequential increase in the flow of the primary commodity from B to A may also have similar repercussions in B, if the primary export from B is a particularly close substitute for or complement with other imports or exports of B. These possible repercussions may also take any one of four forms. Here we shall merely enumerate the four possibilities. The reader is left to apply to them the same detailed analysis which we have already applied to the similar repercussions in A.

(1) *Secondary export trade destruction in B.* The primary export from B may, in B's production or consumption, be a close substitute for some other secondary commodity which is also exported from B. In this case a reduction in the duty on the import of the primary product into A will reduce the consumption or increase the production of that primary product in B which will lead to a reduction in the export of the secondary substitute commodity from B.

(2) *Secondary export trade creation in B.* The primary export from B may be complementary in B's consumption or production with some other product which is exported from B. In this case an increase in the export of the primary product from B to A will release larger supplies of the secondary product also for export from B to A.

(3) *Secondary import trade creation in B.* The primary export from B to A might be a close substitute in B's consumption or production for some commodity imported into B. In this case an increased export of the primary commodity would lead to increased imports of the secondary product.

(4) *Secondary import trade destruction in B.* The primary export from B to A might be complementary in B's production or consumption with some commodity which is imported into B. In this case the increased export of the primary commodity would lead to a reduced import of the secondary complementary commodity.

These primary and secondary repercussions of a reduction in an import duty in A upon the volume of trade between A and B are summarized in columns *a* and *b* of Table XIX.[1] Thus the primary effect

[1] Columns *c* and *d* will be used at a later stage in this chapter to illustrate different points.

of a reduction in A's duty is to increase the flow of the product directly affected from B into A, and this represents a primary creation of import trade in A and of export trade in B (column *b*, rows 1 and 2). Rows 3–6 of the table deal with the four possible secondary repercussions on A's trade with B which may result from repercussion in A's markets (see pp. 206–14 above). To take row 3 as an example, if the primary imports into A are close substitutes with other imports into A (SI in column *a*), then there will be a secondary reduction of these other imports which have now to face fiercer competition from the primary imports into A on which the import duty has been reduced (ID in column *b*). And similarly for all the other rows of columns *a* and *b* in the table.

Now if one takes into account the possible secondary repercussions in B (rows 7–10 of Table XIX), as well as the possible secondary repercussions in A (rows 3–6 of the table), it becomes clear that quite large indirect gains or losses might be associated with any given reduction in duty on a primary import from B into A. Let us consider an example of great secondary gain. Suppose that A reduces a duty on the import of raw wool from B. Suppose that A also exports woollen textiles manufactured out of imported raw wool, and suppose that the raw wool in B is jointly produced with mutton, which is also exported from B to A. Then the reduction in A's import duty on raw wool will increase A's imports of raw wool from B. But this will cause both a secondary export trade creation in A (which will now have more woollen textiles to offer for export) and secondary export trade creation in B (which will now be producing more mutton for export as a result of its increased production of raw wool). It is quite possible that the value of the increased trade in mutton and in woollen textiles might be greater than the value of the increased trade in raw wool. In this case the maximization of economic welfare might require a rate of subsidy to be paid on the import of raw wool into A which was higher than the rate of duty levied either on the export of woollen textiles from A to B or of mutton from B to A.

Other combinations of repercussion in A and B might mean that very large secondary losses were associated with any primary increase of imports into A. Suppose that A reduces a duty on the import of butter from B. Suppose that in A's consumption imports of butter are closely substitutable for imports of margarine, and suppose that in B's production the preparation of butter for export competes very closely with the same factors of production which are needed to produce cheese for export. Then the reduction in the duty in A on imports of butter and the consequential primary increase in butter imports will be associated with a secondary import-trade destruction in A (since a smaller amount of margarine imports will now be wanted in A) as well

TABLE XIX

The Primary and Secondary Effects of a Partial Reduction in A's Import Duties on the Volume, Balance, and Terms of Trade

(a)		Import (I) or export (E) trade is created (C) or destroyed (D) (b)	Movement of balance of trade in favour of A or of B (c)	Movement of terms of trade in favour of A or of B (d)
Primary effect in A	(1)	IC	} B	B
,, ,, ,, B	(2)	EC		
Secondary effects: In A the primary import is a substitute (S) or complement (C) for A's other imports (I) or exports (E)				
(i) SI	(3)	ID	A	A
(ii) CI	(4)	IC	B	B
(iii) SE	(5)	EC	A*	B
(iv) CE	(6)	ED	B*	A
In B the primary export is a substitute (S) or complement (C) for B's other exports (E) or imports (I)				
(i) SE	(7)	ED	A†	B
(ii) CE	(8)	EC	B†	A
(iii) SI	(9)	IC	A	A
(iv) CI	(10)	ID	B	B

* These two letters would be reversed if the elasticity of demand in B for the relevant imports was less than unity.

† These two letters would be reversed if the elasticity of demand in A for the relevant imports was less than unity.

as a secondary export-trade destruction in B (since less cheese will now be produced for export by B). It is now possible that the rate of duty on butter imports into A should be kept at a higher level than that on either margarine or cheese imports, since any loss in the trade in butter may be offset by a still greater increase in the value of the trade in margarine and cheese combined.

It may be worth while noting before we leave these secondary repercussions that they may take rather more complicated forms than those which we have already discussed. For example, the relationship of substitutability or complementarity may be indirect through some third commodity. Thus coal and fertilizers may be close substitutes in one country's imports, not because coal can be used as a fertilizer or the fertilizer used as a fuel, but because there is some third commodity produced at home—such as cow-dung—which can be used as a fuel or as a fertilizer. Then increased imports of coal will mean that less home-produced cow-dung will be used as a fuel, more will be used as a fertilizer, and less imported fertilizer will be needed. Or, to take another example, imports of thick underwear may not be directly complementary with imports of iron ore. But increased imports of warm underwear may reduce the demand for coal for domestic heating; increased supplies of coal for industrial purposes may stimulate the steel industry and so the import of a complementary material, iron ore.

In the examples which we have so far discussed we have not allowed any of the secondary changes in trade themselves to have secondary repercussions. But it may not always be possible to neglect such changes. For example, a reduced duty on the import of wheat into A by causing an increase in the supply of wheat in A may lead to a secondary reduction in the demand for imported barley into A. But the reduced demand for exports of barley from B may itself have a marked secondary repercussion—the land and labour previously used for the production of barley exports in B being almost wholly shifted to the production of, say, cheese exports from B. There would then be an increase of cheese exports from B to A as a secondary secondary repercussion of the primary increase of wheat imports into A.

How far it is useful to carry an analysis of this kind will always depend upon the particular problem which is under discussion. When the effects of any particular duty reduction are under consideration, we must always consider the principal secondary changes which will take place in other lines of trade which are subject to a duty or subsidy or to any other form of divergence between marginal values and costs. Only the particular circumstances of each case can finally decide how far it is worth while carrying through each series of repercussions. Normally direct primary repercussions will be greater than indirect secondary repercussions, and secondary will be greater than secondary secondary repercussions. At each link in the chain of repercussions the amount of change which is passed on to another single specific commodity is likely to become smaller and smaller. The changes are soon likely to be diffused in the form of very small changes affecting a very large number of commodities.

This consideration leads to an examination of the *tertiary* repercussions of any primary change. When we have made allowance for all the primary and noticeable secondary changes, we shall have allowed for all the significant changes which are concentrated upon trade in the one or two commodities most markedly affected by the change. But we shall not necessarily have considered all the relevant changes. The attainment of full equilibrium may still require many very small further changes spread over the trade in a very large number of other commodities, and if these other commodities are all subject to taxes or subsidies, the aggregate effect of a very large number of changes, even though each change is very small in itself, may not be negligible *in toto*. In our present problem these further, or what we shall call tertiary, changes will show themselves most clearly in what we may call balance-of-payments adjustments.

The primary and secondary changes are those changes in the trade in the commodities most directly affected which would take place if money incomes in A and in B remain unchanged and if all prices other than those of the primary and secondary commodities remained unchanged. But there is no reason to believe that general equilibrium can be restored after the primary reduction of duty without some change in the general level of money incomes and prices in A relatively to the general level of money incomes and prices in B. Such a general adjustment of money incomes and prices will be necessary if the primary and secondary changes alone so affect the trade between A and B that a general balance-of-payments problem remains which requires a solution by means of a domestic deflation of money prices and incomes in the deficit country combined with a domestic inflation of money prices and incomes in the surplus country (the gold-standard mechanism), or by means of a depreciation of the domestic currency of the deficit country in terms of the domestic currency of the surplus country (the method of variable exchange rates).[1]

The primary change itself will certainly put A's balance of payments into deficit, assuming that previously A was in balance. When the duty on A's imports of, say, blankets from B is reduced, there will be an increase in the amount of blankets bought by A from B, and in consequence A will spend a greater amount of money than before on her imports of blankets from B.

This effect of the primary change upon A's balance of payments with B may be aggravated or may be in whole or in part offset by the secondary changes. Let us first give an example where it will be much aggravated by the secondary changes. Suppose A reduces a duty on imports

[1] Cf. Part IV of Volume I of this work.

of raw wool from B. If the raw wool in A is jointly demanded with imported spinning and weaving machinery to make woollen textiles, A's demand for imports will be further stimulated by the secondary repercussions in A. If the raw wool is jointly produced with exported mutton in B, more mutton will be offered for export by B to A; and if A's demand for imported mutton has an elasticity greater than unity, then A's expenditure on imports will increase still further because of this secondary repercussion upon the supply of mutton in B. In this case the reduction in A's duty on imported raw wool will have caused a threefold strain on A's balance of payments—because of the primary effect upon imports of raw wool and because of the secondary effects upon the imports of textile machinery and of mutton.

But the secondary effects may be to mitigate and even—though this is less likely—more than to offset the primary strain on A's balance of payments. Thus suppose, to repeat an example which we have already used, that A reduces a duty on imports of butter from B, that the butter imports into A are close substitutes in A's consumption for imports of margarine, and that the butter exports from B are close substitutes in B's production for exports of cheese. Then if, broadly speaking, more than one-half of A's increased expenditure on butter imports were met by an economy of A's expenditure on margarine imports, and if, at the same time, more than one-half of the value of the factors newly used in butter exports in B were drained away from the provision of cheese exports by B to A,[1] and thus represented a reduction in the value of A's cheese imports from B, then the secondary changes might more than outweigh the primary deterioration in A's balance of payments, so that there was a net surplus on A's balance of payments to be cared for by the remaining tertiary changes.

The possible effects of the primary and secondary changes in trade upon the balance of trade between A and B are summarized in column *c* of Table XIX. The primary effect (rows 1 and 2) will necessarily be favourable to B's balance of trade, since it represents an increase in A's demand for B's exports. Whether the secondary repercussions will be favourable to A's or to B's balance of trade will depend upon the character of the secondary repercussion itself. Thus (row 3) if the primary import into A competes closely with other imports into A, there will be a secondary decline in A's other imports and so some secondary improvement in A's balance of trade. But (row 4) if the primary imports into A had been complementary with some other imports, there would have been an additional secondary increase in A's demand for imports and so a secondary intensification of the improvement in B's balance of trade. If the primary imports into A were substitutes in A (row 5)

[1] Assuming that A's demand for imports of cheese were very elastic so that she did not pay a much higher price for the cheese which B continued to export to her.

with exports from A to B, then they would increase the supply of products available for export from A to B, and thus—provided that the elasticity of demand for imports of these products into B was greater than unity—would improve A's balance of trade. And the opposite would be the case if the primary imports into A were complementary in A with other products exported from A to B.

Similar repercussions on the balance of trade may arise from repercussions in B's markets. If the primary exports from B are substitutes in B for other exports from B (row 7), then the supply of these other exports from B to A will be reduced, which will improve A's balance of trade, provided that the elasticity of demand for imports of these products into A is greater than unity. The opposite would be the case if the primary exports from B were complementary in B with other exports from B to A and so increased the supply by B of these other exports to A (row 8). If the primary exports from B are substitutes in B with imports of B from A (row 9), then B's demand for these other imports will be raised, and this will aid A's balance of trade. And, finally (row 10), the opposite will be the case if the primary exports of B are complementary in B with imports into B, so that B's demand for these imports is reduced.

Now any element of substitutability between the primary product and tradeable products (whether imports or exports) in either country (whether A or B) will give rise to secondary repercussions which will help to offset the primary strain on A's balance of trade. In Table XIX this is shown by the fact that whenever an S (i.e. substitutability) appears in column *a*, an A (i.e. an improvement in A's balance of trade) appears in column *c*. But it is to be noted that there is no direct corelation between secondary trade creation or trade destruction on the one hand and a secondary alleviation to A's balance of trade on the other. In Table XIX, in rows 3–10, D and C in column *b* are associated an equal number of times each with A and B in column *c*. A frequent secondary connexion may be where most of A's imports are fairly good substitutes for each other (A importing products of the same type which can serve similar purposes in consumption and/or need similar factors for their production), and where most of B's exports are fairly good substitutes for each other (B exporting products of the same type which can serve similar purposes in consumption and/or which need similar resources for their production). In this case we should have secondary adjustments of the kinds shown in rows 3 and 7 of Table XIX. There would be secondary trade destruction and so a secondary loss of economic welfare to set against the primary gain. But at the same time and for similar reasons there would be a secondary improvement in A's balance of trade to set against the primary strain on A's balance of trade.

But this is by no means the only possible case. In the real world the actual secondary repercussions will depend upon the particular country which reduces the duty and the particular product on which the duty is reduced. As we have seen (p. 219), if all the secondary repercussions were favourable, it is possible that the secondary relief to A's balance of trade might outweigh the primary strain on A's balance of trade. But if all secondary repercussions were unfavourable, there might be a very heavy combined primary and secondary strain on A's balance of trade.[1]

But whatever is the outcome, it would be a mere coincidence if the secondary repercussions exactly offset the primary strain on A's balance of payments and left the payments between A and B in full equilibrium. There is likely to be some balance-of-payments problem in one direction or the other. In what follows we shall suppose that the primary and secondary changes leave A with some deficit on her balance of payments, and shall consider the effect upon economic welfare of the further or tertiary adjustments which are necessary to remove this deficit. We have chosen to consider the case of a deficit on A's balance of payments because this would seem to be on balance the more probable case. But the reader can readily apply for himself the following type of analysis to the case in which there is a surplus, and not a deficit, on A's balance of payments which needs to be corrected.

If the primary and secondary changes leave a deficit on A's balance of payments, we assume that this will be closed by means of the price mechanism—i.e. either by a domestic deflation of money prices and incomes in A and a domestic inflation of money prices and incomes in

[1] For our present purpose, since we are not concerned with the distribution of income between A and B, we are not interested in the effect of the primary and secondary trade changes upon the real terms of trade between A and B. But in Table XIX, column *d*, these effects are also summarized. It is clear that the primary effect of the increased demand for imports in A will be to raise the price which must be paid to producers of the primary export in B and so to turn the terms of trade against A. This primary movement of the terms of trade against A may be mitigated or intensified by the secondary repercussions. Anything which reduces A's demand for imports (and thus reduces the price which B's exporters can profitably charge), or which reduces A's supply of exports (and thus encourages B's importers to offer a better price for the reduced supplies), will tend to move the terms of trade back in A's favour. Thus (rows 3 and 6 of Table XIX) anything which causes a secondary destruction of trade in A will help A's terms of trade, whereas (rows 4 and 5) anything which causes a secondary creation of trade in A will worsen A's terms of trade—either by increasing A's demand for imports or by increasing the supply of exports which she puts on B's market. In B, on the other hand, anything which creates trade will help A's terms of trade either by increasing B's demand for imports from A (row 8) or else by increasing the supply of exports which B puts on A's markets (row 9). Conversely, anything which destroys trade in B (rows 7 and 10) will worsen the terms of trade for A. It can be seen from Table XIX that there is no correlation between the three effects—on volume, balance, and terms of trade in columns *b*, *c*, and *d*—of the various interrelationships of substitutability and complementarity between traded goods in column *a*.

B, or else by a depreciation of A's currency in terms of B's currency. As we have already argued (see Chapter XV of Volume I of this work), the ultimate real effects of both methods will in all relevant aspects be the same. The fall in A's prices and incomes relatively to B's prices and incomes will lead to a general contraction in the volume of A's imports from B and a general expansion in the volume of A's exports to B; and if these changes in the volumes of trade are sufficiently large relatively to the price changes which cause them, the result will be to remove the deficit on A's balance of trade.

Now these tertiary changes in the volume of trade—the general contraction of A's imports and expansion of her exports—will be spread over the whole range of A's imports and exports. It will affect the primary and the secondary commodities as well as all the other items in A's import and export list. Thus the reduction in A's incomes and prices may cause A's consumers to reduce their consumption slightly of the primary product, the initial increase in the import of which has been the cause of the whole disequilibrium. It may also cause them to reduce slightly their consumption of some other imports, the volume of which has already been powerfully affected by some secondary repercussion from the change in A's primary import. But the tertiary or balance-of-payments adjustments will be spread over all A's imports and exports and, unless the primary and secondary products make up an important section of A's total international trade, their effect on the balance of payments is likely to operate mainly through all the other items of A's imports and exports. We will call these the tertiary products and will examine the effect of changes in them upon economic welfare, although the careful reader will realize that the tertiary effects influence all commodities—primary, secondary, and tertiary—and not only these other imports and exports which we are calling the tertiary products.

As we have seen, the restoration of balance to A's international payments comes about through an expansion of A's tertiary exports and a contraction of her tertiary imports. Now if there are taxes levied on most of A's imports and exports, so that there is an excess of marginal value over marginal cost in the case of most of her trade, then there will be a loss of economic welfare due to the tertiary contraction of A's imports and a gain of economic welfare due to the tertiary expansion of her exports. In what circumstances will the tertiary gain exceed the tertiary loss, and vice versa?

Now if A is a heavily protectionist country and B has only a moderately protectionist policy, then the *ad valorem* incidence of the general level of duties on A's imports is likely to be much higher than the *ad valorem* incidence of the general level of duties on A's exports.[1] In this

[1] It is assumed that both countries carry out their protectionist policies by taxing imports and not exports.

case the loss of economic welfare due to a tertiary reduction in the volume of A's imports will be greater than the gain of economic welfare due to an equal tertiary expansion of A's exports. A high level of import duties in A relatively to the level in B will be a factor tending to cause a net tertiary loss of economic welfare.

But suppose that the general level of duties on the tertiary trade was the same in both countries. It would still be possible for there to be a net tertiary gain or loss to economic welfare. For example, there would still be a net tertiary loss if the tertiary adjustment to A's balance of payments was brought about mainly by a contraction in the volume of her imports and very little by an expansion in the volume of her exports. Now this would be the case if the elasticities of demand for imports in A and of the supply of exports in B were very high (so that a small rise in the price charged for B's products by B's exporters in terms of A's currency caused A to import very much less of them, and a small fall in the price offered for B's products by A's consumers in terms of B's currency caused B to export very much less of them), and if, at the same time, the elasticities of demand for imports in B and of the supply of exports in A were very small (so that a large fall in the price charged to B's consumers for A's products in terms of B's currency did not cause B to buy very much more of them and a large rise in the price offered to A's producers for A's products in terms of A's currency did not cause A to export very much more of them). In this case the adjustment of A's deficit would be mainly by tertiary trade destruction (contraction of her imports) rather than by tertiary trade creation (expansion of her exports). But unless there is reason in any particular case to believe either that A's tertiary imports will be subject to a markedly different rate of tax than B's tertiary imports, or else that the elasticity of demand and supply for A's tertiary imports is much bigger or smaller than that for B's tertiary imports, there is no reason to believe that the tertiary adjustments will cause any significant net addition to or subtraction from economic welfare.

It may be useful at this stage to summarize this chapter by enumerating briefly the conditions which will make it probable that a reduction in the rate of import duty on one particular import will lead to a rise rather than a fall in economic welfare.

(1) First, the reduction in duty is likely to cause an increase of imports of the commodity concerned. This will certainly increase economic welfare. This primary increase in economic welfare will be the greater, (*a*) the greater the consequential increase in the volume imported, i.e. the more elastic is the demand for the import in A and the supply of the export in B, and (*b*) the higher is the initial rate of duty on the commodity concerned. This last point means that if a particular duty is reduced in successive stages—e.g. from 60 per cent to 50 per cent,

from 50 per cent to 40 per cent, and so on—the earlier stages of reduction are more likely to cause a net increase in economic welfare than the later ones.

(2) Second, if we assume that all other elements of trade between A and B are subject to some degree of tax and that none are subject to subsidization, there may be further increases of economic welfare if the commodity primarily concerned has the appropriate close relationships of substitutability or complementarity in consumption or production in A or B with other goods which may enter into trade between A and B. The relationships which will cause a secondary expansion of trade and so a still further increase of economic welfare are (i) substitutability in A between the primary product and other goods which are exportable from A and in B between the primary product and other goods which are imported into B, and (ii) complementarity of the primary product in A with other imports into A and in B with other goods which are exported from B. The opposite relationships will lead to a secondary destruction of trade and so to a loss of economic welfare which might outweigh the gain of welfare through increased trade in the primary good. The secondary gains are, of course, more likely to outweigh any secondary losses if the rates of duty which are currently levied on any secondarily created trade are high relatively to those currently levied on any secondarily destroyed trade.

Since we want to avoid substitutability between the primary import into A and A's other imports and substitutability between the export from B and B's other exports, there will be a greater chance of gain from the primary reduction of an import duty in A if the duty is cut on a whole class of goods than if it is cut on only one particular good in a whole class of goods. For in the latter case the particular commodity in question is very likely to be a close substitute in A's consumption for some other imported products in the same class and also a close substitute in B's production for some other exported products in the same class of goods.

(3) Third, if we assume that the primary and secondary changes just described will leave A with some deficit on its balance of trade, there may be some further tertiary gain of economic welfare if the general level of duties on A's imports (which must be contracted on balance-of-payments grounds) is low and the general level of duties on A's exports (which will be generally expanded) is high. Also the tertiary gain is likely to outweigh the tertiary loss if the elasticities of supply and demand for A's imports are less than the elasticities of supply and demand for A's exports, so that the balance-of-payments adjustment comes about more by a tertiary expansion of A's export trade than by a tertiary contraction of her import trade.

It is very difficult to reach any really general conclusions on this subject. There would seem to be some presumption in favour of a reduction in a particular duty, since the primary effect is always beneficial and the secondary and tertiary effects may be unimportant and may work one way or the other. There is a still stronger presumption in making cuts in those particular duties which have a specially high *ad valorem* incidence, because in this case the certain primary expansion of trade will receive a very high welfare weight (being the subject of a high rate of divergence between marginal values and costs) relatively to the welfare weights to be applied to any possible secondary or tertiary trade destruction. Finally, the presumption in favour of the cut is increased if it applies to a whole class of similar goods rather than to a particular good in a general class.

[3]

THE PARTIAL FREEING OF TRADE : (1) UNILATERAL TARIFF REDUCTIONS

In this chapter we intend to discuss certain problems connected with the unilateral reduction of barriers to trade by the authorities in one country in a world in which there are a number of other countries whose authorities maintain an existing structure of trade barriers unchanged. For the sake of simplicity we will suppose that there are only three countries in the world, A (the country whose authorities make a unilateral reduction in its trade barriers) and B and C (the other countries of the world whose authorities maintain unchanged an existing structure of barriers to their trade with A and with each other).

For many purposes a unilateral reduction by A's authorities of barriers to trade with B and C can be treated by the methods which were developed in Part II in the consideration of a two-country world. A can be regarded as one of the two countries and B-C, i.e. the rest of the world, as the other of the two countries. Thus if we are concerned with the effect of the reduction of a duty on imports into A from B and C upon the distribution of income between A on the one hand and B-C on the other or upon the distribution of income within A or B and C, we can use with little or no modification the analysis developed in Chapters XVII and XVIII in Part I.

Thus a reduction of A's barriers to trade with B and C is likely to increase the demand in A for the products of B and C and/or to increase in B and C the supply of the products of A. The price at which traders in B and C will be willing to supply exports to A is likely to be somewhat raised and the price at which they will be willing to take imports from A is likely to be somewhat lowered. The terms of trade will turn against A. There will be some redistribution of real income from the citizens of A to the citizens of B and C.

The reduction by A's authorities of a barrier to trade with B and C is likely to cause some change in the relative prices which producers in A can obtain for the products which compete with imports in A and for the products which are exported from A. The more normal case is perhaps where a larger flow of imports on to A's domestic market and a larger flow of exports out of A's domestic market will cause the price offered to A's producers for products which compete with imports to fall relatively to the price offered for exportable products. In this case there will within A be some redistribution of income away from the factors which are specially adapted to produce import-competing products and in favour of the factors which are specially adapted to produce exportable products.[1]

If the effects of a unilateral reduction of trade barriers by A upon economic welfare are to be finally assessed, these effects upon the international and domestic redistributions of income must be taken into account. But as they do not differ essentially from those discussed in our previous discussion of the two-country world, we shall neglect them in this chapter. It is our present intention to consider certain special features of the efficiency, as opposed to the equity, aspects of a unilateral reduction of trade barriers—features which are essentially due to the fact that there are more than two countries each of which has its own apparatus of trade controls.

Accordingly we will assume that the same distributional weights are allotted to marginal changes of income for all recipients of income in all countries. Welfare is unaffected by any small redistribution of a given world income. We are concerned only with the effect of the unilateral reduction of A's trade barriers upon the size of world income. We shall also assume that within each country there are no divergences between marginal social values and costs. On the other hand each country maintains non-discriminatory import duties on its imports from the other two countries. Thus while there are no divergences between marginal values and costs in production in any one country for consumption in that same country, marginal value does exceed marginal cost when production is undertaken in one country for consumption in another.[2] We can therefore proceed upon the basis that anything which leads to a shift from domestic trade to international trade will help to increase economic welfare, because (i) marginal values are no higher than marginal costs in respect of the domestic trade which is lost, (ii) marginal values are higher than marginal costs in respect of the

[1] From Chapter XVIII (pp. 291–295) it can be seen that if the elasticity of demand for imports from A in the rest of the world (i.e. B-C) were sufficiently low, the terms of trade might move so much against A that even in A's own domestic market the price offered for A's exportable products fell relatively to the price offered for A's import-competing products. In this case the effect upon the distribution of income within A would be the opposite to that mentioned in the text.

[2] This unreal assumption greatly simplifies our argument. But the basic form of the argument would remain even if this assumption were removed. We shall be arguing that anything which helps to increase trade between B and C at the expense of trade within B or within C will help to raise economic welfare because marginal values are no greater than marginal costs in the case of domestic trade whereas they are greater than marginal costs by the amount of the import duty in the case of international trade. But even if marginal values do exceed marginal costs in the case of domestic trade, the basic argument remains unchanged so long as the import duties are the cause of additional divergences between marginal values and costs which affect international but not domestic trade. So long as the rate of divergence between marginal values and marginal costs is likely for this reason to be higher in international than in domestic trade, the basic arguments of this chapter remain valid.

international trade which is encouraged, and (iii) distributional weights are the same for all recipients of income, so that any redistribution of income which incidentally takes place has no effect upon economic welfare.

Let us suppose that in these conditions the authorities in A reduce their non-discriminatory duties on imports from B and C, the authorities in B and C keeping their non-discriminatory duties on imports unchanged. The immediate effect of this will be to lead to a larger quantity of imports into A from B and C. The preservation of equilibrium in A's balance of payments will mean that some further readjustments must take place in A's trade. The strain on A's balance of payments due to the freer inflow of imports into A will cause the prices of A's products to fall relatively to the prices of the products of B and C either through a depreciation of the foreign-exchange value of A's currency or through a flow of gold from A to B and to C with consequential deflation of prices in A and inflation of prices in B and C. These changes will somewhat restrain the increase of imports into A and will stimulate A's exports to B and C. In the normal case the ultimate effect of the reduction of A's tariff will be an increase in the volume of A's imports from B and C, and an increase in the volume of A's exports to B and C in payment for the larger volume of imports purchased at rather worse terms of trade.[1]

Now there will be a gain in economic welfare on what—modifying somewhat the terminology employed in Chapter XIII—may be called the 'primary' increase in trade, namely, the increased imports and exports of A caused by the reduction of A's trade barriers. This gain will be large if:

(i) the elasticities of demand in A for imports from B and C and in B and C for imports from A are large, so that there is a large increase in these two volumes of international trade;

(ii) the rate of duty in A on the imports which are now more freely admitted into A was itself at a high initial level so that there was a large divergence between marginal value and marginal cost in the case of this expanded import trade; and

(iii) the rates of duty in B and C on the type of A's exports which are expanded to keep A's balance of payments in balance are also high, so that there is a large divergence between marginal value and marginal cost in the case of A's increased exports.

[1] For the reasons discussed in Chapter XVIII (pp. 291–295) it is possible that if the elasticity of demand for A's exports in B and C is sufficiently low the final result of the reduction in A's tariff will be an increase in the volume of A's exports to B and C in payment for a *decreased* volume of A's imports from B and C, acquired at very much worse terms of trade. In this case all that is said in the rest of this chapter about the indirect effects upon welfare of the *increase* in A's imports would have to be reversed and related to the indirect effects upon welfare of the *decrease* in A's imports. The reader is left to do this for himself.

But this primary gain in economic welfare may be reinforced by a secondary gain in economic welfare due to an indirect encouragement to the trade between B and C on which also there is a divergence between marginal values and costs due to import duties imposed on each other's product by the authorities in B and C. Alternatively, the gain in economic welfare due to the primary increase in A's trade with B and C might in part or in whole be offset by a secondary loss in economic welfare due to the indirect effects of the primary change in discouraging trade between B and C on which there is a divergence between marginal values and costs. What we must next consider is the way in which the change in A's import duty may affect trade between B and C.

If the authorities in A make a general non-discriminatory reduction in A's duties on all imports from all countries, the strong presumption is that A's imports will be increased both from B and from C. There is also a strong probability that the increase in A's exports which will have to take place to keep A's balance of payments in equilibrium will take the form partly of an increase in exports to B and partly of an increase in exports to C. Accordingly, we shall proceed as follows. We shall consider in some detail the possible 'secondary' effects[1] upon the desire of B's citizens to trade with C of an increase in A's imports from B and of an increase in A's exports to B. We can then allow for the fact that there are corresponding possible secondary effects of A's increased trade with C upon the desire of C's citizens to trade with B. The secondary changes in trade between B and C, whose effect upon economic welfare we must take into account in making a final assessment of the desirability of A's unilateral tariff reduction, will be the result of these two sets of forces in B and in C.

Let us then first consider the effect upon the incentives of B's citizens to trade with C of A's increased demand for imports from B. We will enumerate the conditions in which there is most likely to be a reduction in B's trade with C. Suppose that the products which A imports in greater quantity from B and of which there is now a greater scarcity in B are close substitutes in B for products which B exports to C. There will then be some reduction in the volume of B's exports to C.

This is most obviously the case when the products which B now sells in greater quantity to A are identically the same as products which B sells also to C; then the increased demand in A for these products (due to the reduction in A's tariff on them) will divert B's supplies from C's market to A's market. But the same is true if the products which B sells to A are only close substitutes either in B's consumption or in B's production with the products which B sells to C. When A's demand for certain of B's products is increased because of the reduction in A's duty

[1] For the meaning of the term 'secondary' in this context the reader is referred to Chapter XIII, p. 203.

on them, the price of these products in B's market will be driven up. This will divert the demand of consumers in B away from these products on to any close substitutes for these products; and if B's exports to C are among the close substitutes for these products, there will be an increased consumption in B itself of products which were previously exported to C and thus there will be a reduction in B's exports to C. The rise in the price in B of the products which are now in greater demand in A will at the same time encourage the production in B of these products at the expense of other products which employ the sort of factors of production which are needed to produce the additional exports for A's market (i.e. at the expense of products which are good substitutes in production in B for the products exported to A). Now if B's exports to C are among those products which require for their manufacture the same factors as are required for the manufacture of B's exports to A, then there will once again be a reduction in the supply of B's exports to C when A's demand for B's exports is raised.

Another case in which an increased import into A from B might reduce B's trade with C would be where the products imported into A were in B's consumption or production complementary with products imported into B from C. A imports more cups from B; there is a shortage of cups in B so that B's citizens require less saucers, which happen to be imported from C. Then an increase in A's demand for B's cups causes a reduction in B's demand for C's saucers. Or A imports more mutton from B; there is in consequence an increased production in B of sheep and so of wool, which B imports from C. Once again an increase in A's demand for B's mutton causes a reduction in B's demand for C's wool.

Similar considerations will determine the effect of A's increased exports to B upon the desire of B's citizens to trade with C. If A's exports to B are good substitutes in B's consumption or production for things which B imports from C, then there is likely to be a secondary reduction in B's imports from C. A exports more apples to B; and as a result the price of apples falls in B. B's consumers shift to the consumption of apples away from the consumption of pears which are a close substitute for apples in their consumption and which happen to be imported from C. Or else B's producers shift from the production of apples in B to the production of cherries in B (which can be produced easily on the land previously used to produce apples), thus reducing the demand for imported cherries from C.

A secondary reduction in B's trade with C would also take place if A's exports to B were complementary in B's consumption or production with products which B exports to C. Thus A exports more ink to B, which encourages writing in B, so that B's citizens consume more pens which were previously being exported from B to C. Or A exports more coke to B, so that less coke is produced in B. In consequence less gas is produced in B for export to C.

Such are the relationships in B between the products which A trades with B and the products which B trades with C which are most likely to cause an increase in B's trade with A to lead to a decrease in B's trade with C. But the relationships might just as well be reversed, in which case an increase in A's trade with B would lead to an increase in B's trade with C. If A's imports from B are good substitutes in B for the things which B imports from C or are complementary in B with the products which B exports to C, then an increase in A's imports from B would stimulate B's trade with C. Similarly, if A's exports to B are good substitutes in B for the things which B exports to C or are complementary in B with the products which B imports from C, then an increase in A's exports to B will stimulate B's trade with C.

If we remember that similar relationships are possible between A's increased trade with C and the willingness of C's citizens to trade with B, that B's imports from C are the same as C's exports to B, and that B's exports to C are C's imports from B, we can generalize the relationship in the following way. A primary increase in A's imports from B and C and her exports to B and C is the more likely to cause a secondary decrease in the trade between B and C:

(i) if A's imports are good substitutes in B or are complementary in C with the products which are exported from B to C;
(ii) if A's imports are complementary in B or are good substitutes in C with the products which are exported from C to B;
(iii) if A's exports are good substitutes in B or complementary in C with the products which are exported from C to B; and
(iv) if A's exports are complementary in B or good substitutes in C with the products which are exported from B to C.

In so far as the relationships are of this kind a primary increase in the foreign trade of A will lead to a secondary contraction in the trade between B and C, and in so far as they are the opposite to this a primary increase in A's foreign trade will lead to a secondary expansion in the trade between B and C.[1]

Let us first of all consider the case where the four relationships just mentioned are of a kind to cause negligible net secondary effects in the trade between B and C. In such a case a unilateral reduction of A's

[1] In the rest of this chapter we shall neglect the possible need for tertiary adjustments in trade due to the fact that even though A's balance of payments is in equilibrium, the result of the changes may be to leave B in deficit and C in surplus in its balance of payments. There may then have to follow some fall of B's prices relatively to C's which will reduce C's export trade and B's import trade and increase C's import trade and B's export trade. The welfare effects of these adjustments ought to be taken into account in the final sum. But they are perhaps unlikely to affect the issue very much one way or the other. See the argument developed in Chapter XIII (pp. 217–223).

duties is bound to be favourable to economic welfare. It will cause a primary increase in trade on which there is an excess of marginal values over marginal costs (because of the trade taxes) without any adverse secondary repercussions. Indeed, in the interests of world economic welfare A's authorities would have not merely to remove their barriers on imports but even to subsidize A's imports from B and C. The reason for this is the existence of import duties in B and C on their imports from A. If A increases a subsidy on imports from B and C, this is to encourage further a trade on which there is already some loss of economic welfare, because the existing rate of subsidy on A's imports from B and C means that the marginal value of the imports in A's market is already lower than their marginal cost in B's and C's markets. But the increase in imports into A must be paid for by increased exports from A to B and C; in so far as these products are subject to import duties in B and C there will be a gain of economic welfare in this expansion of A's export trade. If the terms of trade remained unchanged, so that to preserve equilibrium in the balance of payments the increase in the volume of A's exports to B and C had to be equal at current prices to the increase in the volume of A's imports from B and C, then the loss of welfare on an increase in subsidized imports into A would only be as great as the gain of welfare on the corresponding increase in taxed exports from A if the rate of excess of marginal cost over marginal value in the case of the imports were as great as the rate of excess of marginal value over marginal cost in the case of the exports. In other words, the rate of subsidy on imports would have to be raised as high as the rate of tax on exports in order to maximize welfare. The real rate of tax on trade between A and the rest of the world is a compound of A's tax on the trade and the tax imposed by the rest of the world on the trade. The nearest approach to free trade, in the absence of action by the authorities in the rest of the world, is that A's authorities should pay a subsidy which just offsets the tax imposed by the other authorities.

Now suppose that the four relationships discussed on p. 518 are such that the secondary repercussion of an increase in A's foreign trade is to stimulate the taxed trade between B and C. *A fortiori* it can now be argued that a unilateral reduction of A's duties is desirable in the interests of world economic welfare. Indeed, A's imports ought now to be subsidized at a rate which not merely offsets the duty raised in B and C on imports from A but which was even higher than this, because of the indirect secondary advantages to be gained in the expansion of trade between B and C resulting from a further expansion of A's trade with B and C.

It follows from all this that rather special conditions must be fulfilled for it to be true that a unilateral reduction of A's import duties is not desirable on grounds of world economic efficiency. For this to be so the four relationships discussed on p. 518 must clearly be of a kind which cause there to be a secondary contraction of the trade between B and C; and the loss from this secondary contraction of trade between B and C must be sufficiently great to outweigh the gain in economic welfare to be derived not only from the increased imports of A from B and C but also from the increased exports of A to B and C. This is the more likely to be the case:

(i) the more nearly the four conditions discussed on p. 518 conform to those required to cause a secondary contraction of trade between B and C;

(ii) the higher is the *ad valorem* rate of duty levied in B and C on the sort of products which they import from each other (i.e. the larger the loss in economic welfare on each unit of secondary trade which is lost);

(iii) the lower the rate of the import duty in A which is in the process of reduction (i.e. the smaller the gain in economic welfare on each unit of primary import trade which is gained); and

(iv) finally—what is not always remembered—the lower the rates of the import duties levied in B and C on the sort of goods which they import from A (i.e. the smaller the gain in economic welfare on each unit of primary export trade which is gained).[1]

[1] Dr. S. A. Ozga of the London School of Economics has by means of a rather different technique of analysis also reached the conclusion that even a non-discriminating reduction of duties by one country in a many-country world may represent a movement away from, rather than towards, the free-trade position.

[4]

AN ESSAY IN THE THEORY OF TARIFFS[1]

S. A. OZGA
London School of Economics and Political Science

I

MANY arguments for lower tariffs derive from intuitive generalizations of such simple theoretical constructions as, for instance, Ricardo's example of England and Portugal exchanging wine for cloth. Professor Viner, in his path-breaking study of customs unions,[2] has raised doubts about the validity of such generalizations for preferential reductions of tariffs; they may lead not toward but away from the free-trade position. The present paper goes further than that. It questions the validity of such generalizations for nonpreferential reductions of tariffs as well; if there are more than two countries, each with its own tariff system, nonpreferential reductions of tariffs may also lead not toward but away from the free-trade position.

The main line of attack, however, is not on the generalizations; the objective is the basic construction. The purpose of this paper is to investigate the effects of tariffs on the allocation of productive resources in more than two countries by using models of such a high degree of simplification and such techniques of representation as to make it possible to illustrate the conclusions by means of numerical examples.

[1] I am deeply indebted to Professor J. E. Meade and Dr. H. Makower for valuable advice and stimulating criticism. I wish also to express my thanks to Professor E. H. Phelps Brown for helpful comment.

[2] Jacob Viner, *The Customs Union Issue* (New York: Carnegie Endowment for International Peace, 1950).

II

1. Let us take first the techniques of representation. The basic assumption of this paper is that of constant opportunity costs. The production opportunities of each country are given in the form of the function

$$\alpha x + y + \beta z \ldots = C ,$$

where x, y, z, . . . , are the variable quantities of the commodities X, Y, Z, . . . , which can be produced; the commodity Y is the numeraire; α, β, . . . , are the constant opportunity costs of the commodities X, Z, . . . , in terms of the numeraire Y; and C is the amount of the numeraire Y which the country could produce if it specialized completely in the production of this single commodity. If there are only three commodities, X, Y, and Z, the production opportunity function may be represented by a plane on a three-dimensional diagram. In Figure 1 the quantities of the three commodities are measured along the three axes. The opportunity costs of X in terms of Y are represented by the slope of the line CA,

$$\alpha = \frac{CO}{OA} ;$$

the opportunity costs of Z are represented by the slope of the line CB,

$$\beta = \frac{CO}{OB} ;$$

the constant coefficient C is equal to CO; and the production opportunity function is represented by the plane ABC.

The analysis does not require any assumptions about the nature of real costs, although, of course, it begs the question of how constant opportunity costs can be reconciled with the existence of several factors of production. No attempt is made in this article to give a satisfactory answer to this question. The assumption of constant opportunity costs is not an ideal method of simplifying exposition, but in the present case it is a very effective one.

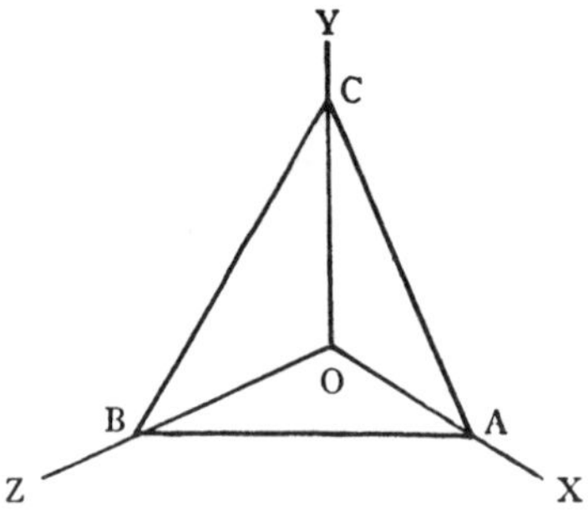

FIG. 1

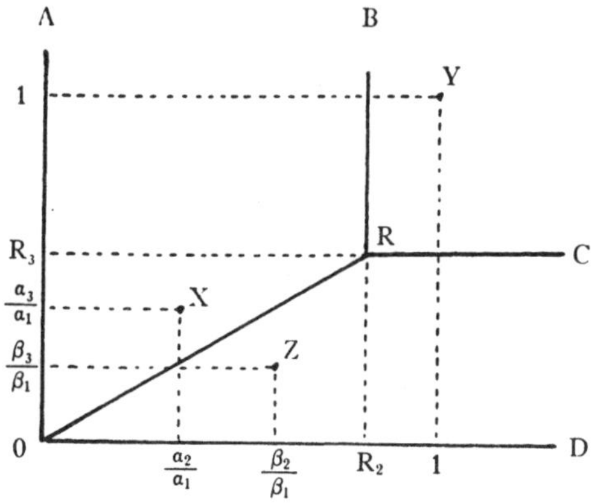

FIG. 2

2. The following technique is used to represent geometrically the differences in the opportunity costs among three countries. In Figure 2 the ratios of the opportunity costs in Countries II and I, α_2/α_1, β_2/β_1, . . . , are measured along the horizontal axis, and the ratios of the opportunity costs in Countries III and I, α_3/α_1, β_3/β_1, . . . , along the vertical axis. They determine the positions of the respective commodities on the diagram. The coordinates of the commodity X are thus α_3/α_1 on the vertical axis and α_2/α_1 on the horizontal axis; the position of the commodity Z is determined by the ratios β_3/β_1 and β_2/β_1; the numeraire Y is obviously at unity. The diagram represents the comparative cost differences and may be called the "field of comparative advantage."

The relative positions of the commodities on the diagram are independent of the choice of the numeraire. If the numeraire were not Y but X, the opportunity costs of Y in terms of X would be $1/\alpha$; those of Z would be β/α; and so on. The opportunity costs of X would, of course, be unity. This means that all ratios along the horizontal axis would have to be multiplied by a constant α_1/α_2, and the points representing all commodities would move to the right, all of them in the same proportion. The ratios along the vertical axis would have to be multiplied by α_1/α_3, and again all points would move in the same proportion in the upward direction.

An alternative procedure is to adjust the scales along the two axes so as to have unity where α_2/α_1, is now on the horizontal axis and where α_3/α_1 is now on the vertical axis; in this case the points representing the commodities would not move at all. The absolute positions of all commodities on the diagram can always be made independent of the choice of the numeraire by a suitable adjustment of the scales along both axes. The essential condition is only that the same commodity be the numeraire in all the three countries.

3. In the analysis given below there is no place for money or monetary institutions. But for the purpose of exposition the following rules are accepted for expressing prices. It is assumed that each country has its own unit of accounting—the dollar in Country I, the pound in Country II, and the franc in Country III—and that the value of these units is so adjusted as to make the supply price of the commodity *Y* (the numeraire in Fig. 2) equal to one dollar in Country I, one pound in Country II, and one franc in Country III. This means that in each country the supply prices of different commodities in terms of that country's unit of accounting are always equal to their opportunity costs in terms of *Y*; thus the supply price of *X* in Country I is α_1 dollars, that of *Y* in Country II is one pound, and that of *Z* in Country III is β_3 francs. As the opportunity costs are constant, the supply prices must also be constant.

With constant supply prices in terms of home currencies, the process of adjustment of relative prices reduces to adjustments of the rates of exchange among the currencies. Such adjustments are equivalent to changes in the terms of trade.

4. Suppose now that the rate of exchange of pounds into dollars (r_2) is OR_2 in Figure 2; $r_2 = OR_2$ pounds exchange for one dollar. It follows that, as the commodity *X* is to the left of R_2,

$$\frac{\alpha_2}{\alpha_1} < r_2 ;$$

$$\therefore \alpha_2 < \alpha_1 r_2 .$$

In other words, with the rate of exchange $r_2 = OR_2$ the supply price of the commodity *X* in Country II is lower than the supply price in Country I, both prices expressed in the same currency. The same is true, of course, of any other commodity to the left of the point R_2. The supply prices of the commodities to the right of R_2 are lower in Country I than in Country II.

Similarly, if the rate of exchange of francs into dollars is $r_3 = OR_3$ francs for one dollar, the supply prices of the commodities below the point R_3 are lower in Country III than in Country I, and those of the commodities above R_3 are lower in Country I than in Country III. It follows that Country I can supply the commodity *Y* and all other commodities within the area *BRC* at lower prices than either Country II or Country III. These are therefore the commodities which Country I would produce and export in the conditions of free trade; *BRC* is Country I's area of specialization. Other commodities can be supplied at lower prices by other countries.

If the rate of exchange of pounds for dollars is $r_2 = OR_2$ and that of francs for dollars is $r_3 = OR_3$, the rate of exchange of francs into pounds must be

$$\frac{r_3}{r_2} = \frac{OR_3}{OR_2}$$

francs for one pound. In other words, the rate of exchange of francs into pounds is measured by the slope of the line *OR*.

It follows that for the commodity Z, as well as for any other commodity below the line OR,

$$\frac{\beta_3}{\beta_1} \div \frac{\beta_2}{\beta_1} = \frac{\beta_3}{\beta_2} < \frac{r_3}{r_2},$$

$$\therefore \beta_3 < \beta_2 \frac{r_3}{r_2};$$

that is, Country III is able to supply them at lower prices than Country II. The opposite is obviously true for the commodities above the line OR; Country II is able to supply them at lower prices than Country III. The area of specialization of Country II is thus $AORB$, and that of Country III is $DORC$.

The boundaries of the three areas of specialization depend on the position of the point R. Free-trade equilibrium prevails when it is so adjusted to the conditions of demand that each country is able to satisfy the demand of all three countries for those commodities which are within its area of specialization. If, for instance, the situation is as in Figure 2 but Country I is not able to satisfy the whole demand for all the commodities which are within the area BRC, the relative prices of these commodities must rise and the terms of trade and the rates of exchange must become more favorable for Country I. Point R moves upward and to the right, the area BRC contracts, and the range of the commodities in the production of which Country I specializes is reduced. Equilibrium is established when the point R has moved so high up and so far to the right that the reduced area BRC contains only those commodities which Country I is able to produce in sufficient quantities to satisfy the demand.

5. As far as free trade is concerned, the technique of the field of comparative advantage serves the same purpose as Edgeworth's and Viner's logarithmic scales of comparative costs;[3] the movements of the point R are equivalent to the shifts of their scales up and down. The advantage of the new technique, however, is that it is also applicable to the analysis of the effects of tariffs.

Suppose that Country I has a uniform ad valorem tariff imposed on all commodities at the rate $t_1 = (T_1R_2/OT_1) = (T'R_3/OT')$ in Figure 3. This means that commodity X can be imported from Country II by Country I only if at the current rate of exchange the import price of X including the tariff is lower than the supply price of X in Country I; that is, if

$$\alpha_2\left(1+\frac{T_1R_2}{OT_1}\right) < \alpha_1 OR_2;$$

$$\therefore \frac{\alpha_2}{\alpha_1} < OT_1.$$

In other words, it is possible to import from Country II only those commodities which are above the line OR and to the left of T_1E. Similarly, only those commodities can be imported from Country III which are below the lines OR and $T'F$. The area $EHFCRB$ may therefore be called Country I's "area of protection"; it contains the commodities which are produced in Country I under protection of the tariff.

If Country III has its uniform tariff too, and if the rate of the tariff is $t_3 = T_3R_3/R_3O$, Country III will not import commodity Z from Country I if

$$\beta_3 < \beta_1\left(1+\frac{T_3R_2}{OR_3}\right) OR_3;$$

$$\therefore \frac{\beta_3}{\beta_1} < OT_3;$$

[3] F. Y. Edgeworth, *Papers Relating to Political Economy* (London: Macmillan & Co., 1925), II, 53; Jacob Viner, *Studies in International Trade* (New York: Harper & Bros., 1937), p. 465.

that is, if the commodity is below the line *MN*. It will not import commodity *X* from Country II because

$$a_3 < a_2\left(1+\frac{T_3R_3}{OR_3}\right)\frac{RR_2}{OR_2};$$

$$\therefore \frac{a_3}{a_2}=\frac{a_3}{a_1}\div\frac{a_2}{a_1}<\frac{MR_2}{OR_2};$$

that is, because the commodity is below the line *OM*. Country III's area of protection is thus *NMORC*. Similarly, if the rate of the tariff in Country II is $t_2 = R_2T_2/OR_2$, its area of protection is *PLORB*.

From the location of particular commodities in different areas of Figure 3 it is now possible to say in which country they are produced, from which country they are exported, and by which countries they are imported. The commodities located in the area *AOSE*, for instance, are produced only in Country II and exported to both Country I and Country III. Those in *ESMB* are produced in Countries II and I; they are exported from Country II to Country III; in Country I they are produced under the protection of the tariff. The commodities in the area *BMKP* are produced in the same countries, but now Country II produces them under protection of the tariff, and Country I exports them to Country III. The area *KLWHSM* contains the commodities which, owing to tariffs, are produced in all three countries simultaneously; there is no trade in them.

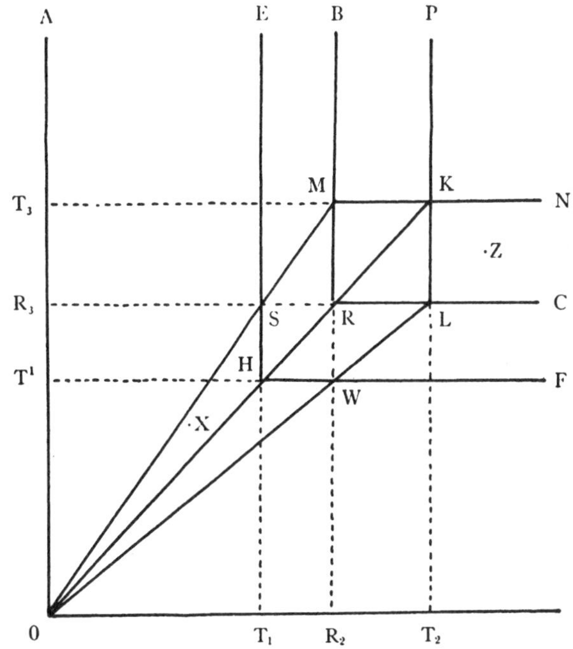

FIG. 3

The equilibrium position of the point *R* may not be the same with tariffs as without them. Tariffs may lead to a change in terms of trade, and the rates of exchange must be adjusted accordingly. But the essential condition of equilibrium remains the same: the quantities of the commodities supplied must be equal to the quantities demanded.

III

As the second step let us apply the technique described above to a particular numerical example. Suppose that our three countries are producing three commodities only. The general form of the three production opportunity functions is thus

$$\alpha x + y + \beta z = C \, .$$

1. Suppose that the numerical values chosen for their constant coefficients are

$$3\tfrac{1}{2}x_1 + y_1 + 2\tfrac{1}{2}z_1 = 1{,}300 \text{ in Country I},$$

$$4x_2 + y_2 + 2\tfrac{1}{2}z_2 = 2{,}600 \text{ in Country II},$$

$$6x_3 + y_3 + 2z_3 = 1{,}050 \text{ in Country III}.$$

The positions of the three commodities in the field of comparative advantage are then as shown in Figure 4; the numerical values along the axes represent the opportunity-cost ratios which determine the positions of the commodities.

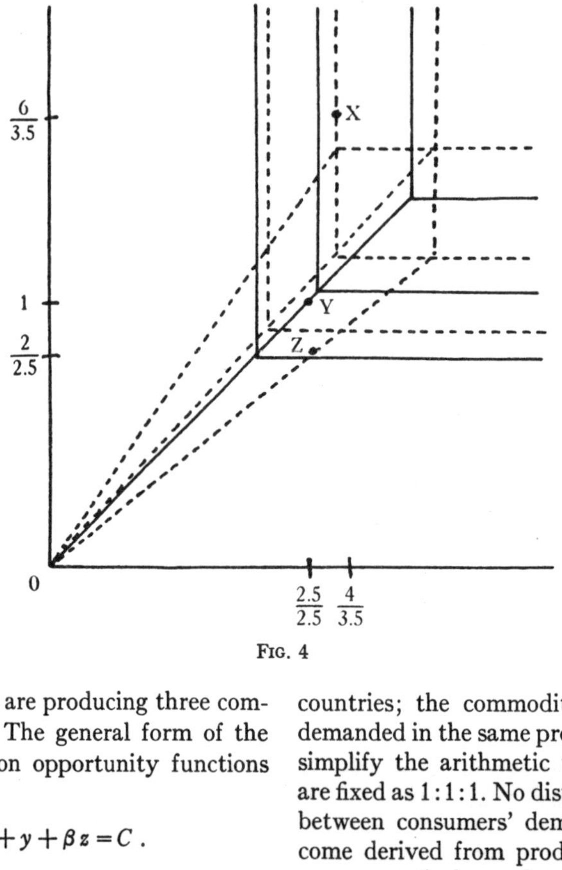

FIG. 4

On the side of demand the basic assumption is that of a constant pattern of consumption, the same in all the three countries; the commodities are always demanded in the same proportion, and to simplify the arithmetic the proportions are fixed as 1 : 1 : 1. No distinction is made between consumers' demand out of income derived from production and the government's demand out of the revenue from tariffs; the assumption of the constant pattern applies to both of them. The quantity of any of the three commodities consumed by both the government and private individuals may therefore be regarded as a measure of the community's real income.

The rules for expressing prices, devised solely for the purpose of exposition, are the same as in the general analysis: each country has its own currency (unit of accounting) the value of which is always so adjusted that the supply prices of all commodities in terms of the currencies of the countries in which they are produced are always equal to their opportunity costs in terms of the numeraire Y.

2. Suppose further that in all the three countries there are tariffs at the ad valorem rate of $t = \frac{1}{3}$ and that the position of the point R is as shown in Figure 4; the dotted lines then represent the boundaries of the three areas of protection. There is no trade in commodity Y. Commodity X is exported from Countries I and II to Country III; its world market price in terms of Country II's currency is thus equal to

$$p_X = \alpha_2 = 4 \ ,$$

that is, to its opportunity costs (in terms of commodity Y) in Country II; in terms of Country I's currency it is equal to $\alpha_1 = 3\frac{1}{2}$. Commodity Z is exported from Country III to Countries I and II. However, since it is at the margin of Country II's area of protection, it may be produced also in Country II; its supply price in Country II is equal to the world market price plus tariff. This means that, if both prices are expressed in Country II's currency

$$p_Z(1+t) = \beta_2 \ ,$$

and

$$p_Z = \frac{\beta_2}{1+t} = 2\tfrac{1}{2} \div (1+\tfrac{1}{3}) = \tfrac{15}{8} .$$

In international trade one unit of X exchanges, therefore, for $p_X/p_Z = 32/15$ units of Z.

If this is to be the position of equilibrium, the quantities of the commodities produced in each country must be consistent with the pattern of production corresponding to the dotted lines in Figure 4, and they must satisfy the conditions of the given production opportunity functions, of the constant pattern of consumption, and of balanced trade at the exchange ratio of one unit of X for 32/15 units of Z. The pattern of production in Country III is that Y is produced for home consumption only, X is not produced at all, and Z is produced for home consumption as well as for export. If the quantity of each of the three commodities consumed (the same owing to the constant pattern of consumption 1:1:1) is denoted by I_3, and the quantity of exports of Z is denoted by ${}_ZE_3$, the condition of balanced trade is that for ${}_ZE_3$ units of Z Country III must obtain I_3 units of X. As the exchange ratio is 32/15 units of Z for one unit of X, the condition is

$${}_ZE_3 = \tfrac{32}{15}\, I_3 .$$

The quantities produced by Country III are thus I_3 of Y and $I_3 + 32/15 I_3$ of Z; and the condition of the production opportunity function is satisfied if

$$I_3 + 2\,(I_3 + \tfrac{32}{15}\, I_3) = 1{,}050 .$$

The solution is

$$I_3 = 145 \ ,$$

and

$${}_ZE_3 = 308 \ .$$

The quantities produced in Country III are thus 145 units (I_3) of Y and 453 units ($I_3 + {}_ZE_3$) of Z. They satisfy all the conditions of equilibrium; minor inconsistencies are due to the solution being given in round figures.

The same procedure may be applied to Country I, which is in a very similar position to that of Country III. The only difference is that it is exporting not Z

but X and that it is importing not X but Z. The solution for Country I is

$$I_1 = 212$$

$$_XE_1 = 99\ ,$$

and the quantities produced are 212 units of Y and 311 units of X.

The solution for Country II is as follows. As Country I is exporting 99 units of X and Country III is importing 145 units of X, Country II must be exporting 46 units of X; and as Country III is exporting 308 units of Z and Country I is importing 212 units of Z, Country II must be importing 96 units of Z. There is no trade in Y. The conditions of Country II's production opportunity function are thus satisfied if

$$4(I_2+46)+I_2+2\tfrac{1}{2}(I_2-96)=2{,}600\ .$$

The solution is $I_2 = 354$, and the quantities produced are 400 units of X, 354 of Y, and 258 of Z.

The quantities of each commodity produced in each country which satisfy all the conditions of equilibrium are thus shown by the following production matrix:

		Countries		
		I	II	III
Commodities	X	311	400	0
	Y	212	354	145
	Z	0	258	453

and the quantities of each commodity traded by each country are shown by the following trade matrix:

		Countries		
		I	II	III
Commodities	X	− 99	− 46	+145
	Y	0	0	0
	Z	+212	+ 96	−308

where minus means exports and plus means imports. The quantities consumed can be obtained by subtracting exports from the production figures and adding imports. They are the same for all commodities:

212 in Country I
354 in Country II
145 in Country III

The total, 711, is the measure of the world's real income.

3. Now, starting from the above position, let us examine the effects of certain reductions of tariffs. Suppose first that Countries II and III form a customs union. The immediate result is that the areas of protection between these two countries disappear, and Country I must lose its export market for X in Country III; it cannot compete with Country II, which does not pay the tariff. The terms of trade therefore move against Country I, and the point R moves toward the origin at 0. This, however, means that it becomes unprofitable for Country I to import Z, and Country I becomes eliminated from trade.

The solid lines in Figure 4 represent the new position of equilibrium. There is no need to go again into the details of how the solution is obtained. Its main characteristics are as follows. Countries II and III form a free-trade area completely separated from the rest of the world. Neither of them is small enough to specialize in the production of one commodity only; both therefore produce Y, and the prices of X and Z in terms of Y (or in terms of Country II's and Country III's currency) are

$$p_X = \alpha_2 = 4\ ,$$

$$p_Z = \beta_3 = 2\ .$$

The production matrix which satisfies all the conditions of equilibrium is:

		Countries		
		I	II	III
Commodities	X	186	522	0
	Y	186	516	6
	Z	186	0	522

the trade matrix is:

		Countries I	II	III
Commodities	X	0	−150	+150
	Y	0	−144	+144
	Z	0	+372	−372

and the quantities consumed are:

186 in Country I
372 in Country II
150 in Country III

The world's real income (708) is thus smaller than in the initial position. The customs union leads to a less efficient allocation of the world's productive resources.

4. In the example above the decline of the world's real income is not due to any special arrangement of the comparative cost differences. It is possible to construct an example with the same comparative cost differences, the same level of tariffs, and the same pattern of consumption, in which, however, the effect of the preferential removal of tariffs is favorable. A change in the productive capacity of Country I, that is, in the coefficient C_1, is sufficient to bring about this result.

Suppose that $C_1 = 130$; that the productive capacity of Country I is one-tenth of what it was before. The geometrical solution is then exactly the same as before, and Figure 4 remains valid. In the initial position one unit of *X* exchanges for 32/15 units of *Z;* the production matrix is:

		Countries I	II	III
Commodities	X	31	505	0
	Y	21	370	145
	Z	0	83	453

the trade matrix is:

		Countries I	II	III
Commodities	X	−10	−135	+145
	Y	0	0	0
	Z	+21	+287	−308

and the quantities consumed are:

21 in Country I
370 in Country II
145 in Country III
—
536

An interesting feature of this solution is that, as a result of the over-all reduction of the productive capacity in Country I, real income in Country II has increased (from 354 to 370).

In the final position, after the establishment of the customs union, Country I is completely eliminated from trade. The only effect of the reduction of its productive capacity is thus that it now produces and consumes only one-tenth of what it produced and consumed with the larger productive capacity. Its real income is thus 19, and the quantities consumed in the other two countries remain the same as they were in the previous example. The world's real income consists of

19 in Country I
372 in Country II
150 in Country III
—
541

It is higher than in the initial position. Now, therefore, in spite of the fact that comparative cost differences, the level of tariffs, and the pattern of consumption are the same, the customs union is favorable from the point of view of the world's real income; it leads to a more efficient allocation of the world's productive resources.

5. The possibility of an unfavorable effect on the world's real income is not restricted to preferential reductions of tariffs. Suppose that, starting from the same initial position as before (with $C_1 =$ 1,300), instead of Countries II and III forming a customs union, Country I re-

moves its tariffs on all imports irrespective of the country of origin. The result is that, as long as the exchange rates remain unchanged, it is more profitable for Country I to import *Y* from Country III than to produce it at home. Since, however, Country III cannot satisfy the whole demand for *Y* and *Z*, and Country I can produce more of *X* than is demanded, the terms of trade and the rates

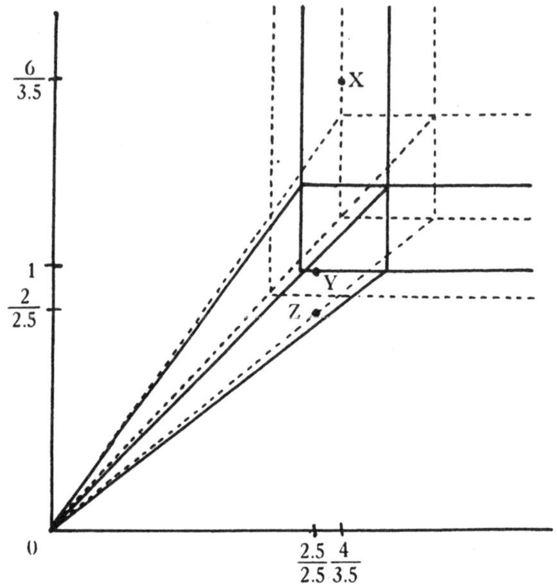

FIG. 5

of exchange must move against Country I and in favor of Country III. The point *R* moves downward. This, however, means that it is no longer profitable for Country II to import *Z* from country III, and Country II becomes eliminated from trade.

The new position which satisfies all the conditions of equilibrium is represented by the solid lines in Figure 5; the dotted lines represent the initial position as in Figure 4. The world market prices of *X* and *Z* in terms of *Y* (and in terms of Country I's or III's currency) are

$$p_X = \alpha_1 = 3\tfrac{1}{2} \,,$$
$$p_Z = \beta_3 = 2 \,,$$

the production matrix is:

		Countries		
		I	II	III
	X	361	347	0
Commodities	*Y*	35	347	326
	Z	0	347	361

the trade matrix is:

		Countries		
		I	II	III
	X	−161	0	+161
Commodities	*Y*	+165	0	−165
	Z	+200	0	−200

and the quantities consumed are:

200 in Country I
347 in Country II
161 in Country III
———
708

The removal of tariffs in Country I is thus unfavorable from the point of view of the allocation of the world's productive resources; the world's real income has declined from 711 to 708.

IV

The interpretation of the results of these examples is as follows. Viner's case is that, if two countries form a customs union, the effect may be more trade between the two countries concerned and less trade between either of them and the rest of the world. The former effect is what Viner calls "trade creation"; the latter is trade diversion.[4] The result is that the world's income may either increase or decrease.

The same conclusion, however, applies to nonpreferential reductions of tariffs, provided only that the rest of the world consists of more than one country. Nonpreferential reductions of tariffs in one country may lead not only to more trade between the country reducing its tariffs and the rest of the world but also to less trade among particular countries of the rest of the world. Suppose, for instance, that an agricultural country removes its tariffs on its imports consisting of industrial products. Its imports increase. This, however, may mean that at the same time imports of the same products by some other country may have to decline. In the example given in the last paragraph of the preceding section, Country I removed its tariffs on imports of the commodity Z, and the result was that, owing to a shift in the terms of trade in favor of Z, the tariff of some other country importing Z (Country II) became more effective, and this latter country was eliminated from trade altogether; the world's real income declined.

The conclusion is thus that, in a world consisting of several countries, each with its own system of tariffs, the removal of some tariffs, no matter whether they are preferential or not, may lead either toward or away from the optimum allocation of the world's productive resources. And this means that it is impossible to say on a priori grounds whether in the world of today the establishment of a free-trade area in a part of it, for instance, in western Europe, or a general reduction of tariffs by one country, for instance, the United States, not followed by the complete removal of all tariffs and universal free trade, would lead to a greater or smaller income for the world as a whole.

[4] Incidentally, it may be worth mentioning that the technique of the field of comparative advantage can be used to represent Viner's case geometrically (as well as that of nonpreferential reductions of tariffs) with an unlimited number of commodities. The commodities subject to trade creation, to trade diversion, and to various secondary effects due to a shift in the terms of trade can be represented by areas delimited by the solid and the dotted lines in Figs. 4 and 5.

[5]

CHAPTER IV · GLOBAL GAINS FROM RESTRICTED TRADE IN A TWO-COUNTRY WORLD

IV-1. INTRODUCTION

Thus far we have dealt primarily with the quantitative production, consumption, and trade effects of customs unions, and have presented some examples of the effects of unions on the welfare of individual countries. Because we have assumed a single preference map for each union member and for the rest of the world, the problem of aggregating levels of social satisfaction of different consuming units (countries) was absent. In this and the following chapters we will study the effects of customs unions and other world-market imperfections on total world income and on income of different parts of the world other than individual countries. Indeed, it is on such considerations that any objective evaluation of customs unions must be based.

The method of producing a single index of social welfare for a number of independent consuming units (countries or individuals) is neither unique nor unambiguous. The problem can be approached in a number of different ways. The first and perhaps most significant distinction to be made is that between the "cardinalist" and "ordinalist" approaches. We are using these terms for the sake of brief identification, while realizing that they are not fully descriptive. Broadly speaking, the cardinalist approach is based on the assumption that human satisfaction, or utility, is as quantifiable as, say, industrial output, and, moreover, that utilities and/or changes in utilities of different individuals, positive or negative, can be added to form a single index of social satisfaction. The ordinalist approach, on the other hand, requires neither the assumption of cardinal measurability nor that of interpersonal comparability or additivity. While a good deal more realistic, the ordinalist approach makes it very difficult, at least at first, to speak about aggregate welfare effects.

Now it ought to be pointed out at this stage of our argument that most of the important literature on the subject of customs unions is based on the cardinalist method. Both Professors Meade[1] and Viner,[2] though in somewhat different ways and with different degress of methodological refinement, add losses of income by some countries to gains of others in appraising the aggregate effects of customs unions. For purposes of the present monograph, at least, I reject that approach. Not only do I have philosophical objections to it, but I believe, and hope to show in most of what follows, that the ordinalist method, even in the context of imperfect market situations, can take us far beyond that of cardinal utility and interpersonal comparability.

If we want to compare two different economic situations involving more than one individual and do not believe that utilities of different individuals can be measured cardinally and compared with each other, we cannot do otherwise than to reformulate the problem. Instead of asking whether one situation is preferable to the other, we have to ask whether one situation could be made preferable to all individuals if resources were transferred among individuals in an appropriate way. Different forms of such a "compensation criterion" have been suggested by different writers,[3] each depending on different circumstances,

[1] Meade, *The Theory of Customs Unions.*

[2] J. Viner, *The Customs Union Issue* (New York, 1950).

[3] The most important contributions are those of N. Kaldor, "Welfare Propositions of Economics and Interpersonal Comparisons of Utility," *Economic Journal* 49:549–552 (September 1939); J. R. Hicks, "The

or different environments, wherein the transfer is to be performed. Kaldor's original test is based on the assumption that the two situations being compared are characterized by given and invariant bundles of products (or products and factor supplies) available to the society. In the process of transfer from the gainers to the losers, the conditions of production are not permitted to adjust to changing market conditions. Now, as pointed out by Scitovsky, such a criterion can render the Kaldor criterion nontransitive and may lead to contradictory results. Specifically, one situation can, on the basis of Kaldor's test, be preferred to the other, and vice-versa.

Professor Samuelson's method of compensating transfers, associated with his well-known concept of utility-possibility function, permits all markets to adjust to changing distribution of resources. To any prescribed set of parameters defining an economic situation and a prescribed distribution of income there will generally correspond a unique optimal set of utilities of different individuals. To all possible distributions of income will then correspond a unique collection of points in the utility space. Such a collection is the utility-possibility locus corresponding to the economic parameters defining the situation.

Using the Samuelson utility-possibility function, one situation can then be considered definitely preferable to another, if the utility possibility of the latter lies entirely within the utility possibility of the former. If the two loci intersect, either a Bergsonian social welfare function is needed in order to rank different situations, or it has to be stipulated that one situation is preferable to another for certain specific ranges of distribution of income. While intersection of utility possibilities makes it impos-

---

Foundations of Welfare Economics," *Economic Journal* 49:696–711 (December 1939); T. Scitovsky, "A Note on Welfare Propositions in Economics," *Review of Economic Studies*, 9:77–88 (November 1941); P. A. Samuelson, "Evaluation of Real National Income," *Oxford Economic Papers* (n.s.) 2:1–29 (January 1950).

sible to rank unambiguously alternative situations, as much as the Kaldor criterion does in some cases, the definite advantage of Samuelson's method is that transfers envisaged by him are a good deal more efficient as well as more feasible. Indeed, it is difficult to visualize how a government (on Kaldor's assumptions) could ever "freeze" any bundle of products while redistributing resources among individuals. But we can quite well imagine a situation where (lump-sum) transfers are effected between different individuals while the general-equilibrium solution of the system is adjusting to such transfers. The compensating transfers can be deemed efficient (that is, not distorting the general-equilibrium solution) and feasible, especially in the context of our present analysis, where the different economic units among whom transfers are to be performed are countries rather than individuals.

Moreover, in many situations the utility-possibility criterion will yield unambiguous results while the Kaldor criterion will not. We will encounter some of these situations later in our analysis. For the moment let us at least give an intuitive argument in support of this assertion. The Samuelson utility-possibility curve being an envelope of an infinite number of the Kaldor redistribution loci (which, necessarily, will intersect), a utility-possibility function that is preferable at all its points to another such locus will correspond to a family of the Kaldor loci that are very likely to intersect the Kaldor loci underlying the inferior utility-possibility locus.

It is Professor Samuelson's concept of the utility-possibility frontier, as discussed above, that we will be using in this and subsequent chapters in analyzing the welfare effects of customs unions. In summary, it is defined as the locus of optimal levels of individual satisfactions attainable by a society through optimal compensating transfers, given a set of prescribed parameters such as technologies, factor supplies, demand conditions, and institutional distortions of price relationships. The latter set of parameters (such as tariffs) takes the welfare analysis from its usual setting of Pareto optimality into that of market imperfections of all kinds. However, it does not affect its validity. On the contrary, the cardinalist second-best approach becomes largely obsolete through the extension of the utility-possibility method to imperfect market situations. Not only does the ordinalist approach permit of comparisons of situations resulting from finite changes of the prescribed parameters; not only is it based on assumptions that are a good deal more realistic; but results obtained through it can easily be reworked into, and have a definite bearing on, Professor Meade's second-best index. The latter index, on the other hand, has very little bearing, if any, on the comparative positions of the utility-possibility loci corresponding to other than infinitesimal changes of policy parameters.

But perhaps the most significant advantage of the method employed here is its general applicability. Using the utility-possibility approach, situations where both output and institutional parameters — or either one — are changing, can be compared. The Meade index, on the other hand, is valid only for a given economic structure, and permits changes only in price-cost-distorting institutional parameters (such as tariffs). For example, under Pareto-optimal conditions an increase in the supply of a nonlabor factor will unambiguously result in a uniform outward shift of the utility-possibility function, while the Meade index cannot tell us anything about the merits of the situations compared.

The use of the utility-possibility analysis in the context of imperfect market situations is not entirely new. Nevertheless, it seems to be desirable to expound the fundamentals of that analysis before we approach more complicated situations arising from the formation of discriminatory customs unions. This we will do in the present chapter while deriving some other interesting results.

IV-2. THE UTILITY FRONTIER AND TRADING UNDER IMPERFECT MARKET CONDITIONS

The principal purpose of this section is to derive and make operational a utility-possibility curve, and show its consistency with trading situations, in the case where the marginal rates of substitution are permitted to be different for different individuals or countries. This market imperfection actually is, as we have observed in earlier chapters, the key factor in the analysis of discriminatory trading practices.

To start with a simple case, we assume here that outputs are invariant, and that there are only two products and two countries involved in world trading, consumption, and output. While it is obvious that the last assumption is too restrictive to deal with a situation of a customs union, we make it here at first in order to develop our analytical technique and illustrate its logic.

One other assumption is made in this section, namely, that preferences of each country are such that Giffen's paradox could never arise, *whatever* the endowments — or availability — of each country prior to trading. As this assumption will play an important role in a good deal of our subsequent analysis, and as it simplifies matters substantially, we may elaborate on it somewhat. First we ought to emphasize the "whatever" in the statement of the assumption. It implies, among other things, endowments that can for some products be negative in quantity — that is, amounts of products used as inputs in other commodities. Stated in this way, our assumption is actually equivalent to the assumption of "no inferior goods" — and some readers might prefer this interpretation. The important reason why we prefer our formulation is that the "absence of Giffen's paradox" is a good deal more illuminating than the "absence of inferior goods" in the presentation of a number of subsequent proofs. Specifically, it is required in those proofs that nowhere (in a usual indifference map drawn in the first quadrant) would a marginal rate of substitution greater (smaller) in algebraic value than another marginal rate at point *A* fall within the second (fourth) quadrant in relation to point *A*. Clearly, this — with indifference curves convex everywhere — is the same thing as excluding the existence of inferior goods. However, the proofs made later in this study are based on the absence of the above-stated different marginal rates in the different quadrants rather than on the absence of negatively sloped income consumption lines.

Suppose, as in our discussion in Chapter II, that outputs of two countries, *a* and *b*, are added to form the usual box dia-

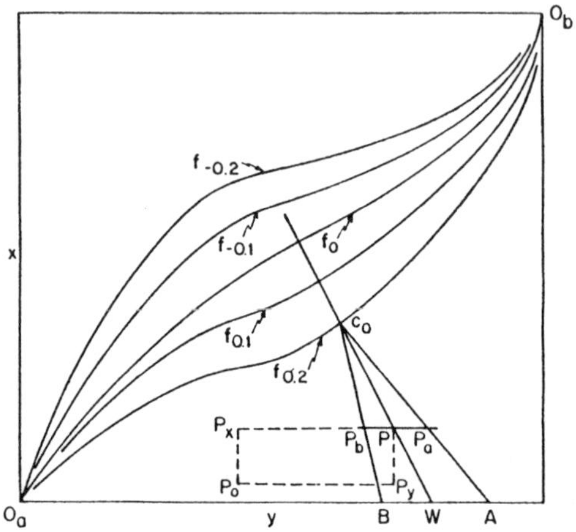

FIGURE 4.2.1

gram, whose dimensions reflect the invariant world output of two products. Such a box is shown in Figure 4.2.1. Within it we find the usual Pareto-optimal contract curve f_o, characterized by the equality of marginal rates of substitution of *a* and *b* (one indifference map being measured from O_a, the other from O_b). We know that under perfectly competitive market conditions, the consumption point of the two countries must be somewhere on f_o, its exact position depending on the outputs, or resource availability of the two countries.

Now consider a situation where the marginal rates of substitution M_a and M_b no longer are equal, but are in a given prescribed proportion:

$$M_a/M_b = 1 + r, \tag{4.1}$$

where r is a positive or a negative constant. Relation (4.1) then defines another locus in the box, also going from O_a to O_b. At any point of that locus the indifference curves of countries a and b will be intersecting, the difference in their respective slopes being given by r. Provided that the indifference curves are convex at all points, this locus f_r will consist of a single infinity of points (that is, will be a line). Two such loci, defined by r_1 and r_2, cannot intersect, as follows from our definition. On the assumption of "no Giffen's paradox" made above, f_{r_1} will be nearer at all its points to f_o than will f_{r_2}, for

$$0 < r_1 < r_2, \tag{4.2}$$

or

$$0 > r_1 > r_2. \tag{4.3}$$

Four such loci corresponding to values of r of -0.1, -0.2, $+0.1$, and $+0.2$, are illustrated in Figure 4.2.1 as $f_{-0.2}$, $f_{-0.1}$, and so on. It is now apparent that the Pareto-optimal locus f_o is only a special case belonging to the family of loci f_r defined by $r = 0$.

Now suppose that the world prices of products x and y are given as p_x and p_y respectively, and that country a levies an *ad valorem* tariff of the rate t_a on its imports of x, and country b levies an *ad valorem* tariff of t_b on its imports of y. There are no other countries engaging in international trading. Under these conditions the equilibrium marginal rate of substitution in country a will be given by

$$M_a = \frac{p_x(1 + t_a)}{p_y}, \tag{4.4}$$

and in country b by

$$M_b = \frac{p_x}{p_y(1 + t_b)}. \quad (4.5)$$

From relation (4.1) it then follows that r, expressing the divergence between the marginal rates of substitution in the two countries, is given as

$$r = t_a + t_b + t_a t_b. \quad (4.6)$$

Let us refer henceforth to the value of r given by relation (4.6), that is, defined by prescribed levels of t_a and t_b, as r'. The locus $f_{r'}$ now gives us all the points attainable by trading, countries a and b imposing tariffs t_a and t_b on their respective imports, corresponding to all possible allocations of outputs.

This is now to be shown in greater detail. Suppose that t_a and t_b both are about 10 per cent, so that the locus $f_{0.2}$ pertains as reproduced in Figure 4.2.1. Now consider a point on that locus, such as c_o. Through that point pass two indifference curves (not in the diagram) one for each country, whose slopes (marginal rates of substitution) are different by r', that is 20 per cent. The two slopes and point c_o define two lines, c_oA and c_oB. Finally, a third line passes through c_o, namely, c_oW, whose slope is given by the ratio of world prices, p_x/p_y, that is, prices not including the tariffs levied by the two countries.

Now any point on c_oW represents an allocation of outputs consistent with consumption of the two countries at point c_o and with the prescribed *ad valorem* tariffs t_a and t_b. Of course, as in our earlier chapters, it is assumed that the tariff revenue is redistributed to the private sector of the respective economies. To show the trading situation that must lead to the solution-point c_o, consider point P on c_oW, representing the outputs of x and y produced by countries a and b, measured from the two countries' respective origins O_a and O_b.

As in Chapter II, we can draw a horizontal line through P, and obtain points P_a and P_b at the intersections of that line with c_0A and c_0B. Point P_a represents the products x and y available to the private sector of country a, that is, output plus transfer of tariff revenue, and point P_b represents similar magnitudes for country b. P_ac_0 is the trading vector of the private sector in country a, and P_bc_0 the trading vector of the private sector of country b. The segments P_aP and P_bP represent the tariff revenue of the two countries respectively. It is this revenue that is redistributed to the private sectors. We have stated here only the essentials of the trading solution as it has been discussed with greater thoroughness in Chapter II.

Now it will be observed that any point on c_0W would have led to the same consumption point c_0 as the situation just described, the level of satisfactions remaining unchanged in the two countries; only the volume of trade would have been different. On the limit, if point P were exactly at c_0, there would have been no international exchange; yet the equilibrium relationships between domestic and world prices and marginal rates of substitution would have been preserved.

On the other hand, if the production point were placed on the line defined by c_0 and W, but between f_0 and c_0, with the prescribed levels of tariff t_a and t_b (that is, with the prescribed divergence between the marginal rates of substitution in the two countries r') no international trade could have materialized, and the divergence between the marginal rates of substitution in a and b would have been indeterminate; we can be sure only that it could not have been larger than r'. On the limit, if the hypothetical production point P were on the intersection of c_0W with f_0, the marginal rates of substitution and relative product prices in the two countries would have been equal to each other. It is also evident that whenever there would be no trade in the situations just described, point P would coincide with the consumption-allocation point c_0.

Now let us alter somewhat the definition of point P, and say that instead of being a production point, it is a resource (endowment) allocation point of the two countries before trading, attainable through a transfer of real resources from a true production point such as P_o in Figure 4.2.1. In the situation illustrated in the diagram it would have required a transfer of P_oP_x of x and P_oP_y of y from country b to country a to attain the availability point P.

From this it is clear that any point such as P can be attained through transfers of real resources between the two countries, and consequently any point such as c_o on $f_{0.2}$ can be attained through trading (as studied above) and tariff imposition of the prescribed magnitude of about 10 per cent by both countries. Of course, it has to be stressed that any availability point P fulfilling these conditions would have to be on or to the south of $f_{0.2}$. If transfer of real resources were to lead to a point P within the area enclosed by $f_{0.2}$ and $f_{-0.2}$ — on the assumption that the countries impose a 10 per cent *ad valorem* tariff on any imports — there would have been no trade, and the marginal relationships postulated for $f_{0.2}$ could no longer hold. However — and this is fairly important for our present analysis — in such a case both countries would be better off without trade than in a situation consistent with trade. Indeed, if tariffs imposed by countries a and b make trade impossible, then we can be sure that, given world resources, the two countries taken together are better off than if the availabilities were such as to generate trade, *ceteris paribus*. But we will return to this point in greater detail below, once we have introduced the concept of utility possibility.

All that has been shown in Figure 4.2.1 can be summarized using the concept of utility-possibility functions. Consider the ordinal utility plane (that is, the plane where points can only be compared according to whether their coordinates are "greater than," "smaller than," or "equal") shown in Figure 4.2.2. On the vertical axis we measure an (ordinal) utility index of country a, and on the horizontal axis a utility index of country b. The locus f_o from Figure 4.2.1 yields in Figure 4.2.2 the Pareto-optimal utility-possibility curve for countries a and b. All its points are attainable by the community under conditions of free trade, through appropriate transfers of real resources from a to b or from b to a, given total world resources. Because, for

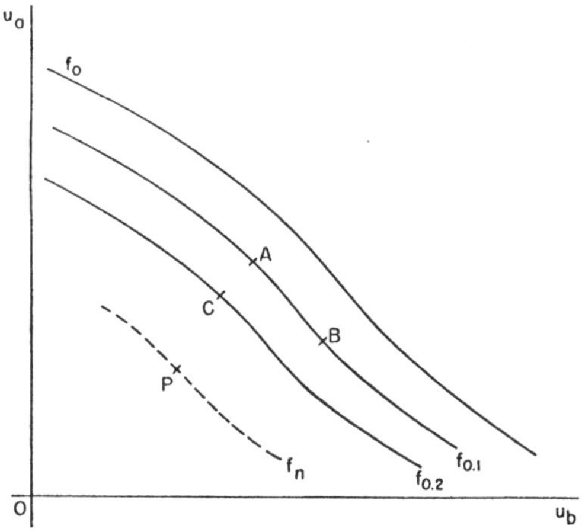

FIGURE 4.2.2

increasing values of r from its initial zero level (corresponding to the Pareto-optimum), the f_r loci are farther and farther away from f_o in the box diagram of Figure 4.2.1, the utility-possibility functions corresponding to increasing values of r will at all points be closer and closer to the origin of the u_a–u_o plane. The same holds for decreasing values of r, starting from $r = 0$.

Not to clutter the diagram, we have illustrated in Figure 4.2.2 only the two utility-possibility curves corresponding to the values of $r = 0.1$ and $r = 0.2$, together with the Pareto-optimal utility possibility curve. The interpretation of the comparative positions of these three curves is that

$$f_0 > f_{0.1} > f_{0.2}, \tag{4.7}$$

where the inequality signs are used to indicate "uniform superiority" in the sense discussed in the preceding section. Specifically, it has been shown that whatever the trading equilibria, both countries can be made better off through redistribution of resources, at lower positive values (higher negative values) of r, than they were at relatively higher positive (lower negative) values of r.

Recalling here that the world is assumed to consist of only two countries, our analysis leads immediately to interesting although not new results pertaining to that case. Since the situations with positive r are symmetrical in all respects to the situation with negative r, let us restrict ourselves to the former of those two cases, and consider relation (4.6). As shown by that relation, r is a uniformly increasing function of t_a and t_b. From this it follows that any trade liberalization, whether by country a or country b, or by both, will reduce r. But a lower r necessarily implies a higher utility-possibility function. Hence, it can be concluded that in a two-country world free of Giffen's paradox, any trade liberalization will lead to an increase in world potential income. For example, suppose that the trading equilibrium with 10 per cent tariffs imposed by both countries leads to the allocation point C on $f_{0.2}$ in Figure 4.2.2. If country a now frees its trade entirely, and no redistribution of resources in the world is effected, a point such as B may result, showing a decline in satisfaction of country a and an increase in country b. However, if with the newly prevailing trading conditions, resources are redistributed (in the way shown above) from b to a, a point such as C on $f_{0.1}$ can be attained, where both countries are better off than they were at point A.

Assuming a production point such as P in Figure 4.2.1, there will be some unique level of r, corresponding to combinations of tariffs of the two countries given by relation (4.6), that will just eliminate all international exchange. That level of r will be given by the (unique) f_r contour passing through P. Corresponding to that contour we have the utility-possibility curve f_n in Figure 4.2.2 passing through point *P*, showing the distribution of utilities if both countries *a* and *b* are in autarky.

If situations of both trade and no trade are considered, the utility possibility curves in Figure 4.2.2 can be interpreted as "minimal" curves, in the sense that they indicate the minimum utility possibility of the world (endowed with given amounts of resources), corresponding to prescribed levels of tariffs by the two countries. If the tariffs are prohibitive, the (autarky) allocation point cannot be inferior to combinations of utilities indicated by the utility-possibility curve corresponding to those tariffs (as given by relation 4.6).

One important point remains to be discussed. So far, we have dealt with the simple case where total world output is invariant. It is this simplifying assumption that rendered the utility-possibility locus identical with the Kaldor redistribution locus. Suppose now that this assumption is relaxed, and that the two countries forming the world economy are permitted to transform *x* into *y* and *y* into *x*, according to a prescribed production-possibility curve. It is intuitively plausible, and it can be proved, that none of the conclusions of the analysis presented so far will be altered. Specifically, the utility-possibility curves in Figure 4.2.2 will be in the same relation to each other irrespective of whether outputs are fixed or substitutable.

As we will be dealing with this case later in the context of a three-country world [4] we restrict ourselves here to a verbal outline of the proof. Suppose that in the box diagram in Figure 4.2.1, *P* and point c_0 illustrate the state of affairs with *r* equal to 0.2 in the more general case where outputs are substitutable. Point *P* now represents a point on both countries' production possibilities, and the marginal rates of transformation at that point must be equal to the corresponding internal marginal rates

[4] See Chapter VI, section 4, below.

of substitution M_a and M_b. Point O_b now lies on a world-production possibility curve $K_{0.2}$ defined by the requirement that the marginal rates of transformation in the two countries must be in the same relation (defined by $r = 0.2$) as the marginal rates of substitution. In the product plane there will be another world production possibility curve, $K_{0.1}$, corresponding to $r = 0.1$. It is easy to show that $K_{0.1}$ will be at all its points superior to $K_{0.2}$; the method of proving this is quite analogous to that used in showing the superiority of $f_{0.1}$ over $f_{0.2}$.

Now consider point O_b on $K_{0.2}$. To it corresponds, with $r = 0.2$, a unique utility possibility curve $f_{0.2}$ in the ordinal utility plane. To any point on $K_{0.2}$, such as O_b, will correspond another utility possibility curve $f_{0.2}$. The envelope of such $f_{0.2}$ curves is the utility possibility locus of the world defined by the production possibilities of a and b, and by the requirement that $r = 0.2$. Only some of the $f_{0.2}$ loci will have a point of contact with the envelope, that we may call $F_{0.2}$. Now let us consider any single $f_{0.2}$. It corresponds to some definite point such as O_b on $K_{0.2}$. Now consider any point on $K_{0.1}$, to the right and above that point, and call it O'_b. To it will correspond a utility possibility curve $f'_{0.2}$ that can be shown entirely superior to the underlying locus $f_{0.2}$ (based on O_b to the left and below O'_b). To O'_b also must correspond a utility possibility $f'_{0.1}$, entirely superior to $f'_{0.2}$; this we have proven in the main portion of this section. Now repeating for all optimal points such as O_b on $K_{0.2}$ the same argument, we come out with a family of production possibilities such as $f'_{0.1}$, each superior to the underlying $f'_{0.2}$ and $f_{0.2}$. The envelope of that family of loci is the utility possibility curve of a and b, defined by the production possibilities of the two countries and the requirement $r = 0.1$. We may call it $F_{0.1}$. From what has been said about the relation between the loci f and f', it follows that $F_{0.1}$ must be to the right of and above (that is, superior to) $F_{0.2}$.

IV-3. THE ASSUMPTION OF "NO GIFFEN'S PARADOX" RELAXED

In the preceding section we have made, and explained, the assumption of "no Giffen's paradox." Although we have not shown it, the principal results of that section depend on that assumption. In this section, we first want to show that this is actually so: specifically, that on the assumption made, any liberalization of trade in a two-country, two-commodity world will be beneficial to potential world welfare.

While proving that Giffen's paradox cannot be present if the argument of the preceding section is to hold, we will also be able to show simultaneously what will or can happen if it is present. The existence of the paradox can have an important bearing on both the utility-possibility curves corresponding to imperfect international markets and the trading equilibria determining those curves. Finally, the analysis in the present section will permit us to generalize in some important respects the results of the foregoing section.

Perhaps the most convenient procedure to adopt is to reiterate the analysis of the preceding section, relaxing the crucial assumption made so far. The first thing to be observed is that whether Giffen's paradox is present or not in the preference maps of the two countries a and b, the principal characteristic of the Pareto-optimal contract curve will not be altered: this characteristic is that the contract curve can cross each attainable indifference curve of each individual only once. This characteristic is translated in terms of the utility-possibility curve by the postulate that the latter is a uniformly declining locus.

Now the same will hold for what we may call the *subcontract curves* — that is, the efficient loci of resource allocation corresponding to different prescribed divergences of the marginal rates of substitution r — if the possibility of Giffen's paradox is entirely absent. In other words, and more precisely, the absence of Giffen's paradox is a sufficient (but not necessary) condition for the subcontract curves to pass through each level of satisfaction only once, and hence for the utility-possibility loci f_r (defined in the preceding section) to be uniformly declining functions. We have encountered such loci in the preceding section.

If the possibility of Giffen's paradox cannot be ruled out for some endowments of either country, the situation can become

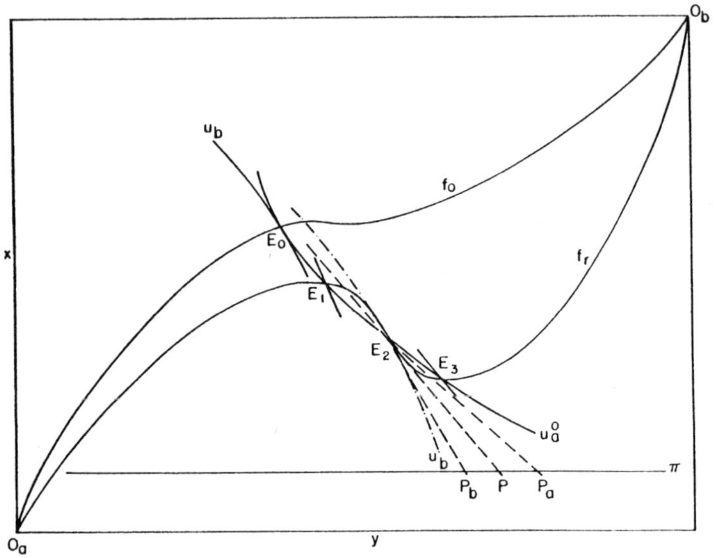

FIGURE 4.3.1

different. This we can see from Figure 4.3.1. In this diagram we find the usual consumption-box for two countries, a and b, and two commodities x and y. Consider within that box the indifference curve $u_a{}^0$ of country a and point E_3 on that curve. The slope of the indifference curve of country b (the marginal rate of substitution of b) at that point is indicated by a segment of a straight line passing through E_3. The divergence r of that slope and the slope of $u_a{}^0$ defines the subcontract curve f_r. Now from the convexity of u_a^o it follows that f_r can encounter again u_a^o at a point other than E_3 only if the Giffen paradox is present for a certain range of initial endowments in country b. Such is effectively the situation described in the diagram: the marginal rate of substitution of b at point E_2 is indicated by the slope of E_2P_b, which is steeper than the line indicating the marginal rate of b at E_3. By definition, the divergence of the rates at E_2 and E_3 is the same, indicated by r.

Observing that u_a^o must reach the contract curve f_o somewhere to the left of and above E_2, namely, at E_o, it follows that

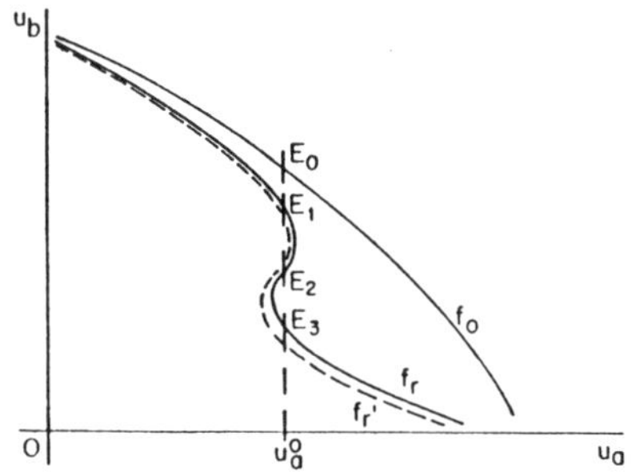

FIGURE 4.3.2

there must be at least one other point, such as E_1, between E_2 and E_o, also consistent with the divergence r. The locus f_r will also pass through that point.

The contract curve f_o in Figure 4.3.1 gives rise to the Pareto-optimal utility-possibility frontier for the world f_o in Figure 4.3.2. It must be uniformly declining, as drawn. As in the preceding section, the utility-possibility curve f_r, stemming from the subcontract curve defined by r, must be enclosed entirely by f_o. However — in opposition to the case discussed in the preceding section — the utility-possibility curve f_r in Figure 4.3.2 no longer has to have everywhere a negative slope. Actually, f_r now will have a shape typified in Figure 4.3.2, that is, for some levels of u_a it will permit more than one equilibrium value of u_b. Such is the case — reflecting our construction in Figure 4.3.1 — for u_a^o: E_1, E_2, and E_3 all correspond to u_a^o, but to different levels of u_b.

Now suppose that $r(>0)$, defining f_r in our two diagrams, is increased a little in absolute value to r'. There will be a new utility-possibility curve (in Figure 4.3.2), $f_{r'}$ corresponding to that level of the divergence between marginal rates of substitution in the two countries, caused, in turn, by a new, higher degree of commercial protection. By definition, $f_{r'}$ cannot intersect f_r. However, it no longer holds that $f_{r'}$ should everywhere lie below f_r. We can say only that it must be located in the area enclosed by the two axes and by f_r.

The important consequence of this new situation is that a reduction of r in absolute value no longer has necessarily to lead to an improved welfare of the world. For certain regions of income distribution between countries a and b, reduction in the absolute value of r — that is, trade liberalization between a and b — can lead to lower satisfaction for one country given a constant satisfaction of the other, and vice-versa.

Specifically, if the initial equilibrium is at E_2 in Figure 4.3.2 and r is increased (assuming r positive), while redistributing resources through efficient transfers in such a way as to keep the satisfaction of country a unchanged, and preserving trading between the two countries, the new equilibrium point will fall above E_2, on the broken line $f_{r'}$. But this indicates an increased satisfaction of country b. On the other hand, if the initial equilibrium were at E_1 or E_3, the "normally expected" result would have been obtained; the satisfaction of b would have declined as a result of intensified trade protection, as indicated by the position of $f_{r'}$ in the vicinity of these two equilibria.

The practical question now arises, whether these results upset seriously the usual expectation that liberalization of trade will lead to increased potential world welfare. It may appear intuitively plausible, but indeed, it is not immediately evident, that equilibria such as E_2 in Figure 4.3.2 could arise only from unstable trading situations. If this were so, we would not have to be unduly worried about our results because, even if Giffen's paradox is present, it would be possible to argue that perverse situations are excluded on grounds of instability. Indeed, if, starting from E_2, tariff in one country were raised, the normal result would be obtained because the disturbance caused by such a policy would make the new equilibrium settle on $f_{r'}$ in the vicinity of E_3 rather than of E_2.

But it remains to be shown whether trading situations leading to equilibria such as E_2 actually are unstable or not. The answer is that they may be either, and consequently it is not possible to play down the importance of the "pathology of liberalization" just outlined. We are now going to show the possibility of E_2 stemming from a stable trading equilibrium. Indeed this is the more important result because it upsets — at least to a degree — the traditionally accepted expectation with respect to liberalization and world potential welfare. Afterward we will only indicate the possibility of instability at E_2.

Let us return to Figure 4.3.1 and consider the equilibrium E_2. The two marginal rates of substitution at E_2 are indicated by the slopes of E_2P_b and E_2P_a — the first corresponds to country b, the second to country a. As in our previous discussion P_a and P_b are the availability points of the private sectors of the two countries obtained by adding to the production point (not yet determined) the subsidies deriving from tariff revenue. The actual point P reflecting outputs of the two countries within the box diagram will be determined by the two tariff levels in the two countries, adding up to the total divergence of marginal rates of substitution r. For example, with a production point P we would have tariffs in the two countries of approximately equal magnitude.

Now for the purpose of our proof let us make the simple assumption that country b is a free-trade country while the tariff of country a explains the entire divergence of marginal rates. This places the production point P at P_b: there is no tariff and no transfer in country b.

Let us now consider all possible redistributions of product y between countries a and b — indicated by π. Point P_b, identical with P (on our assumptions) is one of the distribution points. To each point on π such as P will correspond one or more points on f_r such as E_2. The latter are the points of consumption of the two countries corresponding to a given divergence of marginal rates of substitution r. If there is only one point on f_r for every point on π, and only one point on π for every point on f_r (that is, if there is a one-one onto correspondence between f_r and π), all equilibria under trading and protection corresponding to π and f_r must be stable. This follows from the easily verifiable fact that if there is only one equilibrium in a general-equilibrium barter situation, that equilibrium must be stable. Indeed, if offer curves intersect in such a way as to yield an unstable situation, there must necessarily be other equilibria present.

Now to show that E_2 (as in the diagram) can be stable, all we have to show is that the desired one-one onto relationship between f_r and π can exist in the particular situation studied. Suppose that the segments O_aE_1 and E_3O_b of f_r are not only the most efficient allocation of consumption between a and b, given trading and a specified divergence r, but also represent the income consumption lines of a and b, defined by the marginal rates of substitution found at E_1 and E_3, respectively. Moreover, f_r in the vicinity of E_2 also coincides with the income consumption lines of a and b, defined by the marginal rates of substitution at E_2 (that is, by the slopes of E_2P_b and E_2P_a). In the remaining segments of the portion of f_r defined by E_1 and E_2, the marginal rate of substitution in the two countries, and hence the slope of E_2P_b, changes gradually and uniformly from its value consistent with E_2 to its value (steeper slope) consistent with E_1. Similarly for the transitions between E_2 and E_3: the slope of the trading vector gradually and uniformly becomes flatter. Nothing in the nature of the particular problem can prevent this situation from arising.

Under these conditions, to every initial endowment point on π such as P_b (identical in our particular situation to P) will correspond only one efficient consumption point on f_r and hence only one trading vector. Consequently, all trading equilibria thus generated must be stable, including the equilibrium at E_2.

The discussion just presented can be further clarified by a mechanical representation. Suppose that we have a moving point F_r sliding along f_r from east to west. As it moves, the trading vector corresponding to it (such as E_2P_b) will generally also move, and in particular its origin (such as P_b) will travel along the endowment locus π. It is evident from what precedes that if the itinerary of the point such as P_b is uniformly from east to west as F_r moves from east to west, then all equilibria are stable. If, however, the point such as P_b for certain ranges of the east-west movement of F_r returns to positions it has assumed already — that is, moves from west to east — there will be multiple equilibria corresponding to such positions of the point such as P_b. Moreover, we know that equilibria corresponding to the west-east movement of the endowment point will be unstable; those corresponding to the east-west movement of the point such as P_b (as F_r moves from east to west) will be stable.

This is illustrated graphically in Figure 4.3.3 where the movement of a point such as P_b along π is indicated by an arrow. It corresponds to a uniform east-west movement of F_r along f_r. The region above the line π represents stable situations, that below, unstable situations. For example, we observe that at the position indicated by P on π there will be three equilibria because the traveling point such as P_b will reach that position three times. Two will be stable and one unstable, as the traveling endowment point reaches twice the point P while moving east-west, and once while moving west-east. It will reach position P in the order stable-unstable-stable; in other words, if we were to draw the offer curves corresponding to position P, they

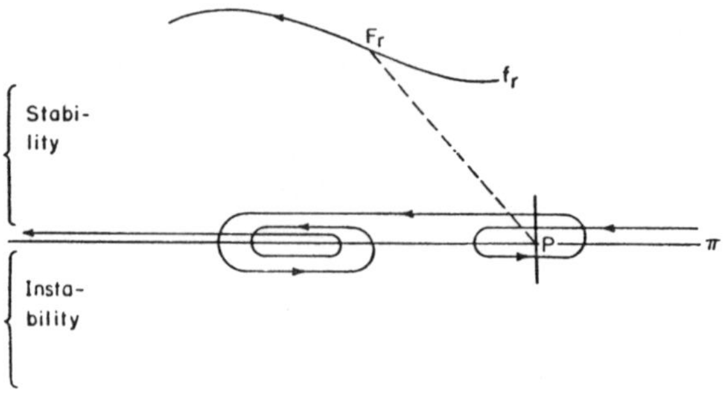

FIGURE 4.3.3

would intersect three times, and the unstable equilibrium would be bordered by two stable equilibria.

As we travel further in the general east-west direction, we reach a region where five equilibria will correspond to each point on π, two unstable and three stable. At the intersections of the itinerary-arrow with π we find endowment-points characterized by one stable equilibrium and one stable-unstable equilibrium. Also the traveling point such as P_b can rest at certain positions, while F_r keeps moving. Such is the situation with offer curves coinciding with each other and with f_r within a certain region. In this case the equilibrium price ratio is indeterminate.

But let us return to the main thread of our argument and consider the world utility-possibility function. The case studied so far is one where the utility-possibility function f_r in Fgure 4.3.2 in its "abnormal" range has a portion that is upward sloping, that is, for which redistribution of available world output makes both countries gain or lose depending on the direction of redistribution. This follows from the fact that f_r in the vicinity of

E_2 in Figure 4.3.1 passes through a region enclosed by $u_a{}^o$ and u_b.

But it is perfectly possible — still on the assumption of Giffen's paradox — to have a situation even more abnormal than that illustrated in Figure 4.3.2, where in the "abnormal" region we would find not only the possibility of both countries' welfare moving in the same direction with redistribution of resources, but a new "normal" region of declining welfare of one with increasing welfare of the other. In Figure 4.3.4, f_r illustrates this situation.

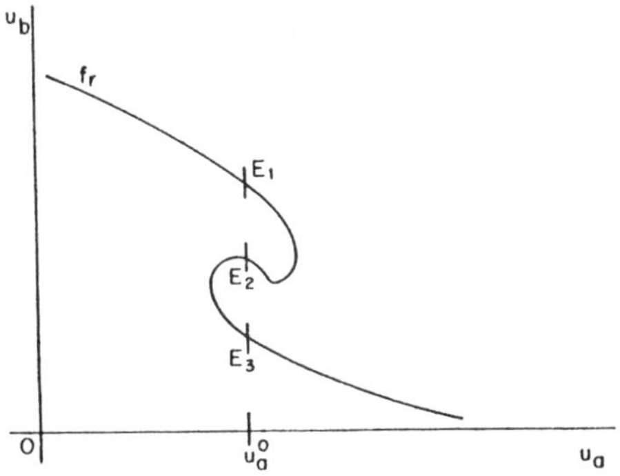

FIGURE 4.3.4

Equilibria at points such as E_2 in that diagram are most likely to be unstable (we will elaborate on this point presently), while those in the vicinity of E_2 in Figure 4.3.2 are most likely to be stable. We have shown only the possibility of stability at E_2 in the latter case, but the reader can verify, using the tools presented here, that this is also the most likely outcome, precisely because of the fact that welfare of both countries is moving in the same direction with redistribution. Similarly, it may be interesting to study more closely the equilibria leading to points such as E_2 in Figure 4.3.4. We will not do so here. Let us only point out that, as before, for a given level of satisfaction $u_a{}^o$, in country *a*, trade liberalization can lead to reduced welfare for country *b*. But, as we have pointed out previously, the market instability most likely at E_2 reduces even further the likelihood of this situation being relevant for any real trading situations.

A typical configuration of offer curves of the two countries leading to an unstable equilibrium such as E_2 in Figure 4.3.4 is represented by *OA* and *OB* in Figure 4.3.5. In that diagram, e_2 is the unstable equilibrium corresponding to E_2 on the utility-possibility function of the preceding figure. The important fact will be observed here, contrary to the free-trade situation, that

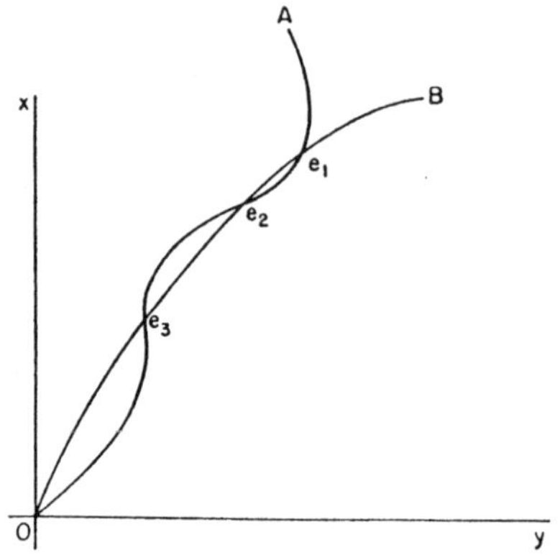

FIGURE 4.3.5

the offer curves (here *OA*) no longer have to be single-valued with respect to a ray (terms of trade line) through the origin.

To substantiate this proposition and to illustrate the case of a utility-possibility function with three declining regions (such as that of Figure 4.3.4) let us consider a special case where three trading equilibria, two stable and one unstable, are obtained for one and the same terms-of-trade ratio. This case, obviously, is impossible in the free-trade situation.

To take the simplest situation first, let us assume that country *a* is facing an infinitely elastic offer curve, such as *Ot* in

Figure 4.3.6. With a tariff imposed by that country reflected by the divergence of the international price ratio and the internal price ratio Op'_1, point c_2 in the second quadrant (using Professor Meade's representation) is a possible consumption point, consistent with the consumption indifference curve u_a. Op_2, in this case, is the external trading vector of country *a*, and Op'_2

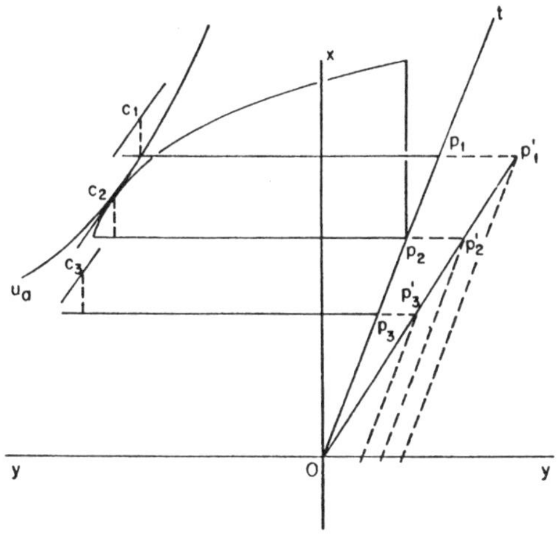

FIGURE 4.3.6

is the trading vector of the private sector of the economy. A total tariff of $p_2p'_2$ in terms of product *y* is levied on that trade and redistributed to the private sector of the economy. (This augments the production block by $P_2P'_2$ of product *y*.)

But, as we see from the diagram, points c_1 and c_3 in the second quadrant are equally conceivable consumption points of country *a* and points p_1 and p_3 — on the same international trading line — equally conceivable trading points. Observe that the marginal rates of substitution at c_1 and c_3 are the same as at c_2, and equal to the internal trading ratio of country *a*, given by the slope of Op'_1. The only requirement for this to be possible is that the income consumption line of country *a* corresponding to that marginal rate of substitution pass through c_1, c_2, and c_3. It is immediately apparent that such a line must necessarily imply the existence of inferior goods (here product y, or a-exportable), or, what is the same thing, the existence of Giffen's paradox for some (positive or negative) initial endowments.

While the trading ratio is the same for all three equilibria, the amount of trade will be different for the three; the subsidy received and total tariff paid will be different, and — what is essential for our present argument — the levels of satisfaction of country a will differ according to the equilibrium actually prevailing.

Instead of assuming a perfectly elastic offer curve of country a, it is possible to visualize a symmetrical situation for country b, yielding the same three equilibria of international barter exchange as those just shown. Again, the condition of an inferior good in country b is necessary. The awkwardness of this particular situation, and hence its limited relevance for any real situations, is apparent from the fact that in country b the inferior good would have to be product x, while — as pointed out already — in country a it would have to be product y.

From our previous discussion it follows that p_1 and p_3 are stable equilibria while p_2 is an unstable one. Translated into the context of the utility-possibility function in Figure 4.3.4, the situation just studied would yield three points on f_r, that corresponding to p_1 to the northeast of that corresponding to p_2, and the latter to the northeast of that corresponding to p_3. Clearly, if such a situation ever were to arise in the real world, the government (or governments) of the country (or countries) involved could devise such policies as to generate the situation most desirable for everybody. But this ought not to distract us from the fact that the ideal policy for the two countries would be to liberalize trade entirely, possibly redistributing income in such a way as to improve the lot of everyone.

The two important conclusions of this section are: 1) that if Giffen's paradox and inferior goods are present the utility-possibility functions corresponding to imperfect international markets may not be single-valued with respect to all axes; and 2) that trading equilibria corresponding to the "pathological regions" of the utility-possibility loci can be stable. Consequently, liberalization of world trade can reduce welfare of one country while welfare of the other (or others) remains unchanged. It is of paramount importance to point out at this stage of the argument that this does not imply that higher protection in some cases must be potentially preferable, from the world point of view, to lower protection. The important fact still remains that the utility-possibility function corresponding to a greater distortion of marginal rates must necessarily be enclosed by the utility-possibility function corresponding to a lesser distortion of those rates. And consequently, a world authority using any Bergson-type social welfare function — showing higher levels of social satisfaction for higher satisfactions of all individuals — could always attain an allocation-point that would be socially preferable in a world of lesser protection. Indeed, given such a social welfare function and optimal income redistribution between countries, what we have termed the "pathological region" of the utility-possibility loci would become quite irrelevant as equilibria within it could never arise.

The analysis presented here has a good deal of relevance for the discussion of more complicated trading situations where more than two countries and more than two products enter the general-equilibrium solution of the world economy. In such situations, as much as in the simple case considered here, inferior goods and Giffen's paradox can lead to analogous complications. In most of our later analysis the assumption of no inferior goods and no Giffen's paradox is usually made in order to keep the arguments sufficiently simple, and especially not to indulge in matters that have virtually no application to the real world.

However, even if there were some residual relevance left, the argument of the preceding paragraph pertains: if unorthodox results can arise *locally* from tariff alterations, such results are impossible once the entire utility possibilities are considered in conjunction with a social welfare function.

IV-4. WORLD UTILITY POSSIBILITY WITH RESPECT TO INDIVIDUAL WELFARE

One important point remains to be made that is applicable both to our present analysis and to that of subsequent chapters. Thus far we have represented the preferences of each country by a single indifference map comparable to that of a single individual. Accordingly, all the utility-possibility functions studied expressed the maximum attainable levels of "aggregate" satisfaction of the different countries composing the world economy.

It is a fact well known to economists that except under rather unrealistic conditions, use of single social indifference maps is not justifiable in dealing with actual trading situations. As trade takes place, or changes in trade arise, income of individuals will generally be redistributed, and this will generally lead to a different social indifference map for each different trading situation.

Now it is interesting to note — and it is the principal point of this section — that a similar difficulty can be avoided when we examine the impact of changing economic conditions on the utility-possibility function.

It can be shown that all the conclusions with respect to the utility-possibility function obtained so far, for the case where the consuming units are countries, are equally valid for the case where the consuming units are individuals in those countries. Specifically, if we have established that the utility-possibility function

$$f_r(u_a, u_b) = 0 \qquad (4.8)$$

is entirely contained within the area enclosed by the two (utility) axes and another utility-possibility function

$$f_{r'}(u_a,u_b) = 0 \qquad (4.9)$$

for

$$r > r' > 0 \qquad (4.10)$$

or

$$r < r' < 0, \qquad (4.11)$$

then, we also know that the "individuals'" utility-possibility function,

$$F_r(u_a^1, \ldots, u_a^n; u_b^1, \ldots, u_b^m) = 0, \qquad (4.12)$$

is entirely within

$$F_{r'}(u_a^1, \ldots, u_a^n; u_b^1, \ldots, u_b^m) = 0, \qquad (4.13)$$

provided that there is free trade within each of the countries; the superscripts are used here to distinguish individuals. This holds whether the outputs of the different countries are fixed or whether they are variable according to some preassigned production possibility function. The conclusion also is valid for any number of commodities actually produced and exchanged.

It will also be noted that the only restrictions placed on the preferences of individuals are the same as those placed on the preferences of *a* and *b*, originally used; that is, the ordinal indifference maps have to be convex and nonintersecting, but they can be different for different individuals.

The theorem just stated in relation to the problem discussed in this chapter is only a minor application of a much more general theorem extending over the entire field of utility-possibility analysis. The latter is stated and proved in the appendix to this chapter; consequently we omit the proof of the theorem stated here.

APPENDIX TO CHAPTER IV · A REHABILITATION OF "WELL-BEHAVED" SOCIAL INDIFFERENCE CURVES [1]

The discussion concerning the permissibility and adequacy of social indifference curves that has been conducted now for almost three decades is well known to all students of welfare economics and international trade theory. Without reiterating, it may be useful to note that the most recent significant step in that discussion was made — quite independently of each other, it seems — by Paul A. Samuelson[2] and J. de V. Graaf,[3] who have shown that if there is a Bergson-type social welfare function, and income is optimally redistributed at all times according to such a function, then nonintersecting social indifference curves exist. They can be used both for derivation of market equilibria (not necessarily unique) and evaluation of social welfare effects of different economic situations.

The purpose of these pages is to establish a theorem making it possible to use single, convex, and nonintersecting social indifference curves (fields) in handling a very significant class of problems in welfare economics, in situations where no Bergson-

[1] I express thanks to my students, Mssrs. R. Miller, L. Officer, D. Schydlowsky, and R. Webb of Harvard University, whose discussion was instrumental in deriving this theorem.

[2] "Social Indifference Curves," *Quarterly Journal of Economics*, February 1956.

[3] *Theoretical Welfare Economics* (Cambridge, 1957), p. 49.

function is given and where individuals belonging to different societies (countries) have different preferences.

THEOREM:

Suppose that $U^a, U^b, \ldots, U^k$ are ordinal utility indexes corresponding to the entire class of convex and non-intersecting indifference fields of individuals $a, b, \ldots, k$ (pertaining to any number of products consumed). Satisfaction of an individual depends only on amounts consumed by that individual. $f(U^a, U^b, \ldots, U^k) = 0$ is the utility-possibility function corresponding to given economic conditions (such as supplies of fixed factors, state of technology, characteristics of markets such as free trade or tariffs, and so forth). On the other hand, $F(u^a{}_1, \ldots, u^a{}_m; \ldots; u^k{}_1, \ldots, u^k{}_n) = 0$ is a utility-possibility function corresponding to *the same* conditions, of groups $a, b, \ldots, k$ of individuals $1, \ldots, m$; $1, \ldots, n$, and so on, perfect competition prevailing *within* each group $a, b, \ldots k$. All u's also correspond to nonintersecting and convex preference fields. Then if it can be shown for two prescribed sets of conditions A and B that

$$f_A \text{ is uniformly superior to } f_B \qquad (1)$$

for *all U's* convex and nonintersecting, it must follow that

$$F_A \text{ is uniformly superior to}^{4}\ F_B \qquad (2)$$

for all u's convex and nonintersecting. Similarly, we can substitute for "uniformly superior to" (i) "uniformly inferior to," (ii) "either superior or inferior or intersecting," (iii) "not inferior to," or (iv) "not superior to" (the last two qualifications permitting of points of tangency between utility-possibility loci) in both relations.

[4] By a uniformly superior utility-possibility function we understand a function entirely enclosing, together with the coordinate axes, another utility-possibility function.

Proof:

Proposition (1) implies that any arbitrarily chosen individual (among the k individuals) can be made better off in situation A than he was in situation B, all other $(k-1)$ individuals' satisfaction being held unchanged (through appropriate lump-sum transfers), whatever the distribution of income in situation B. Analytically we are using given indifference surfaces $\bar{U}$ for all but one of the $a,b,\ldots,k$ individuals and the entire (convex and nonintersecting) preference field of one individual, U'. The proof of the theorem is immediately established if we redefine the $\bar{U}$'s as the Scitovsky social indifference loci of all the $a,b,\ldots,k$ countries but one (arbitrarily chosen) corresponding to any equilibrium income distribution in situation B, and U' as the Scitovsky (convex and nonintersecting) preference *field* corresponding to all but one (arbitrarily chosen) individual's (in the remaining one of the $a,b,\ldots,k$ countries) utility at the level of situation B and to the entire preference *field* of the remaining individual (in the remaining country). Indeed, with these redefinitions, proposition (2) is implied by proposition (1), because proposition (1) implies that any one of the many individuals in countries $a,b,\ldots,k$ can be made better off in situation A while keeping all other individuals $[(m+n+\ldots)-1]$ as well off as in situation B for any distribution of individual utilities in situation B.

The practical significance of the theorem is that it rehabilitates — for the purposes of ordinal welfare analysis — the use of single convex and nonintersecting indifference fields for entire countries; of course, on the assumption that *within* (not outside) each country prevail competitive conditions. Whatever we prove concerning a world composed of countries of Robinson Crusoes we have also (and already) proved for a world composed of countries with arbitrary numbers of inhabitants, each having any convex and nonintersecting indifference field.

Let us point out a few applications. From the simple case where there is only one Robinson Crusoe we immediately know, for any number of individuals and for any foreign reciprocal demand, that any trade is "uniformly superior" to no trade, and that for any number of individuals an optimum tariff is "uniformly superior" to free trade whenever the foreign offer curve is less than infinitely elastic. For example, to establish the first proposition, all we have to do is to realize that an individual, whatever his convex and nonintersecting preferences, must be made better off while trading than he was without trade.

As an application of a situation with two Robinson Crusoes, let us recall the conclusion (derivable for two individuals and two products through a box diagram of exchange) that a greater tariff by one Robinson and free trade on the part of the other is uniformly inferior (for the world) to a smaller tariff, as long as neither tariff is prohibitive. Our theorem extends the conclusion to two countries with any number of different individuals.

For convenience we have assumed thus far that only products consumed enter the *U*'s and the *u*'s. However, it is possible to envisage consumption of leisure entering the utility functions as one of the products. In that case the characteristics of situations A and B would have to include as one of the specifications the transformation function between leisure and attainable outputs (given technology and supplies of nonlabor factors). The one somewhat anomalous consideration in this case is that we have to think of each Robinson Crusoe as having as much maximum available leisure as the nation to come in his place in relation (2). But this does not in any way impair the validity of the theorem.

A little reflection will make it clear to the reader that in Pareto-optimal situations defined by production possibility loci and no intergroup (international) trade, uniform shifts of utility-possibility functions must correspond to uniform shifts in production possibilities. In such cases the application of the theorem is the most straightforward and, perhaps, most trivial. Our second example above, concerning optimum tariff situations, illustrates indirectly such an instance. Indeed, the Baldwin curve (envelope) is formally nothing else but a production possibility function, from the point of view of a country, entirely superior to the "true" physical production possibility of that country, except for one point of contact corresponding to no trade.

The theorem becomes a good deal more useful where trading under perfect or imperfect market conditions among social groups (countries) is considered. In this sphere there are innumerable applications, of which our first and third illustrations above are only the most simple and straightforward examples.

Part II
Distortions: Income Effects and Substitutability

[6]

Econometrica, Vol. 38, No. 2 (March, 1970)

PRICE DISTORTION AND ECONOMIC WELFARE[1]

BY EDWARD FOSTER AND HUGO SONNENSCHEIN[2]

We study a standard n-commodity model in which equilibrium positions are characterized by specified inequalities between society's marginal rates of transformation in production and a single consumer's marginal rates of substitution in consumption; these inequalities are exemplified by, but not limited to, excise taxes and subsidies. We explore circumstances under which certain increases in these "taxes" and "subsidies" can be said to decrease welfare. In order to do so, we look for conditions under which the equilibrium consumption vector is well defined by a specification of the taxes and subsidies, and find that the conditions required are stringent. Among our conclusions is the proposition that the validity of consumers' surplus measures for analyzing such problems may depend on assumptions that are more strict than their users have realized.

INTRODUCTION

IN THIS PAPER we study a simple n-commodity model in which equilibrium positions are characterized by specified inequalities between society's marginal rates of transformation in production and consumers' marginal rates of substitution in consumption. Our purpose is to introduce a very natural analytic device to investigate the effect on welfare of changes in these inequalities. The device takes the form of certain mappings defined on the set of efficient production. It enables us, for example, to guess immediately the negative result that the loss in welfare associated with a given set of distortions is *not* generally well defined. We proceed to explore the mathematical restrictions that these mappings must satisfy in order to yield positive results, and to specify conditions on the economy sufficient to guarantee that these restrictions will be satisfied.[3]

THE MODEL

There are n final goods, whose quantities are indicated by the coordinates of an n-vector, $x = (x_1, \ldots, x_n)$. The efficient frontier of the set of production possibilities is denoted by Π; Π is thus the n-dimensional generalization of society's transformation curve. We assume that Π can be represented by the solutions to an equation $\pi(x) = 0$ where, for any $x > 0$ and for all i, $0 \leqslant i \leqslant n$, $\pi_i(x) > 0$ ($\pi_i(x) = \partial\pi/\partial x_i$). The preferences of the single consumer in the model are represented by a nonnegative utility function u (defined on the collection of vectors having all of

[1] This paper is dedicated to the memory of our dear friend and colleague Professor Jacob Schmookler (1919–1967).

[2] We should like to thank the referee for his valuable comments.

[3] The question posed in this paper concerns movement from an initial nonoptimal situation. It thus falls within the class of problems that have come to be known as "second-best" problems. It also falls within the compass of a class of problems that has been treated by consumers' surplus analysis. The model we employ is at least as specialized as those most often used in second-best and consumers' surplus analysis, so our results should be special cases of the ones obtained there. On the contrary we find that positive results, when they can be obtained, are the consequence of assumptions not generally considered in those theories.

their coordinates nonnegative) and we will assume that both u and π have continuous first partial derivatives.[4] In addition we shall require that Π be concave to the origin, that $u_i = \partial u/\partial x_i > 0$ for all $x > 0$ and for all i, $0 \leqslant i \leqslant n$, and that the indifference contours of u be strictly convex to the origin.[5] For simplicity of exposition we shall further restrict our attention to a consumer whose utility is zero for all bundles containing zero amounts of one or more commodities. This assumption will rule out corner equilibria.

Denote the set of elements of Π with all coordinates strictly positive by Π^0 ($\Pi^0 = \{x \in \Pi : x > 0\}$). Define $P : \Pi^0 \to E^{n-1}$ by

$$P(x) = \left(\frac{u_1(x)}{u_n(x)}, \frac{u_2(x)}{u_n(x)}, \ldots, \frac{u_{n-1}(x)}{u_n(x)}\right) = (p_1(x), \ldots, p_{n-1}(x)).$$

The expression $P(x)$ represents the marginal rates of substitution in consumption at x. Define $R : \Pi^0 \to E^{n-1}$ by

$$R(x) = \left(\frac{\pi_1(x)}{\pi_n(x)}, \frac{\pi_2(x)}{\pi_n(x)}, \ldots, \frac{\pi_{n-1}(x)}{\pi_n(x)}\right) = (r_1(x), \ldots, r_{n-1}(x)).$$

The expression $R(x)$ represents the marginal rates of transformation at x. Further define two continuous functions $\phi_s : \Pi^0 \to E^{n-1}$ by $\phi_s = P - R$, and $\phi_a : \Pi^0 \to E^{n-1}$ by

$$\phi_a(x) = \left(\frac{p_1(x) - r_1(x)}{r_1(x)}, \frac{p_2(x) - r_2(x)}{r_2(x)}, \ldots, \frac{p_{n-1}(x) - r_{n-1}(x)}{r_{n-1}(x)}\right).$$

The expression $\phi_s(x)$ is the vector of differences between the consumer's marginal rates of substitution and the producers' marginal rates of transformation at x (called the *specific distortion* at x), and $\phi_a(x)$ is the vector of the corresponding percentage differences (called the *ad valorem* distortion at x). We will say that x is an *s-equilibrium* for the distortion $S = (s_1, s_2, \ldots, s_{n-1})$ if $\phi_s(x) = S$, and that x is an *a-equilibrium* for the distortion $A = (a_1, a_2, \ldots, a_{n-1})$ if $\phi_a(x) = A$. That is, x is an s-equilibrium for the set of distortions S if the vector of specific distortions between marginal rates of transformation and substitution calculated at the point x is equal to S. Similarly, x is an a-equilibrium for the distortion vector A if the vector of ad valorem distortions calculated at the point x is equal to A. We shall use the function ϕ, the distortion vector D, and use the term *d-equilibrium* when

[4] In order to avoid the need to weigh one man's gain against another's loss, we must do one of the following: either avoid the issue in a forthright way, by specifying that there be just one consumer; or specify a mechanism whereby in moving from one equilibrium to another every man's utility will rise or fall together. For most of the paper we hold to the first alternative so that welfare becomes synonymous with the individual consumer's utility. But this choice is inessential to the argument. For example, the second alternative could be used if one were prepared to accept the fiction of an omniscient government knowing everyone's utility function, and making ideal lump-sum transfers in the background so as to maximize a quasi-concave social welfare function. In this case the social welfare function will specify a set of social indifference surfaces with all the properties of an individual's indifference surface [6, p. 16] and this is sufficient for the theory.

[5] Note that this restriction applies only to u, not to Π; Π may be flat, or contain flat segments, so long as it is smooth.

a statement can be interpreted as referring to either ad valorem or specific distortions. When the distortion is not specified to be one or the other, the statement should be interpreted as applying to either.

Here is a familiar proposition presented in the above terminology. It states that the distortion-free equilibrium coincides with the point of maximum utility in Π. The proof is well known (see, e.g., [**4**]).

PROPOSITION 1: *If x^0 is a d-equilibrium for the distortion $D = 0$, and x is a d-equilibrium for the distortion $D' \neq 0$, then $u(x^0) > u(x)$.*

We draw special attention to the fact that the distortion vector $D = 0$ is associated with a unique d-equilibrium. The association of d-equilibria with distortions will be unique for all distortion vectors only if ϕ has a special property: x, y in Π^0 and $x \neq y$ must imply $\phi(x) \neq \phi(y)$.[6] If ϕ does not have this property there will exist a distortion D and distinct commodity bundles x and y such that both x and y are d-equilibria for D. In this situation the utility associated with D is well defined only in a degenerate case ($u(x) = u(y)$). We note further that when multiple equilibria are associated with a given distortion vector, it will always be possible (except in two degenerate cases) to find a pair of equilibria x^1 and x^2 such that x^1 is associated with more distortion than x^2 (in a very strong sense) and greater utility.[7]

The preceding observations indicate that a great deal rests on the uniqueness of the d-equilibrium associated with any given distortion vector. This condition implicitly has been assumed in most treatments of the welfare economics of price distortion.[8] As a case in point, consider the analysis of consumers' surplus presented in [3]. The starting point is a model similar to the one presented here, and yet the measure of loss that is derived assigns a single loss to each distortion vector. This assignment must then bear the burden of approximating several possible losses, and moreover gives the misleading impression that the sign of the change in loss is a well defined function of the change in the distortion vector—a proposition that is not generally true.

The following examples demonstrate that even in exceptionally simple models there may be multiple equilibria associated with some distortion vectors.

Example 1: In Figure 1, both L and N are d-equilibria associated with the same distortion; M is a d-equilibrium associated with a larger distortion. Note that a movement from L to M and a movement from N to M represent increases in

[6] A mapping with this property is said to be one-to-one.

[7] Formally, if there exist x, y in $\phi^{-1}(D)$ such that $u(x) > u(y)$, then (i) there will exist a pair of d-equilibria x^1 and x^2 having the property that $u(x^1) > u(x^2)$ and $\phi(x^1) = k\phi(x^2)$, $k > 1$, or (ii) every indifference surface representing utility between $u(x)$ and $u(y)$ will have a point in $\phi^{-1}(D)$.

PROOF: The continuity of ϕ implies that, for all $0 < t < 1$, there exists $k > 0$ such that the indifference surface corresponding to a utility level of $tu(x) + (1 - t)u(y)$ contains a point in $\phi^{-1}(kD)$ (see Section 1, below, for discussion). If (ii) is not satisfied then one of these points (call it z) is not in $\phi^{-1}(D)$. Thus $\phi(z) = kD$ for some $0 < k \neq 1$. If $k > 1$ then (i) is satisfied by $u(z) > u(y)$ and $\phi(z) = k\phi(y)$. If $k < 1$ then (i) is satisfied by $u(x) > u(z)$ and $\phi(x) = (1/k)\phi(z)$. This establishes the proposition.

[8] For an exception, see [**1**, p. 13].

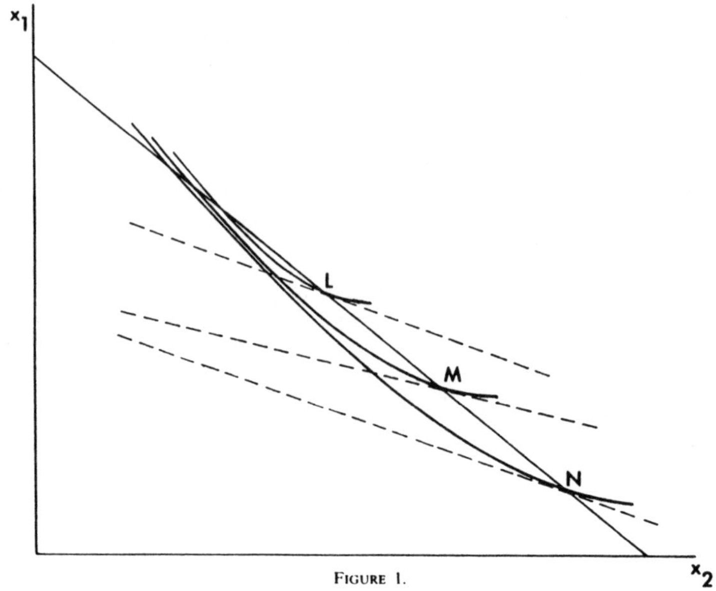

FIGURE 1.

distortion; but the movement from L to M is associated with a fall in utility, and the movement from N to M is associated with a rise in utility.[9]

Example 2: Let

$$x^1 = (5, 5, 5), \qquad x^2 = (7, 4, 4),$$
$$R(x^1) = (0.5, 0.1), \qquad R(x^2) = (5, 5),$$
$$P(x^1) = (1, 0.5), \qquad P(x^2) = (10, 25).$$

Then $\phi_a(x^1) = \phi_a(x^2) = (1, 4)$. It is clearly possible to fit a Π concave to the origin and an indifference surface convex to the origin, each containing x^1 and x^2, and satisfying the above slope requirements.[10] The remaining indifference surfaces

[9] The indifference curves in Example 1 stand in a rather special relationship; x_2 is inferior for at least some levels of income. If there are only two commodities, an unambiguous connection between an increase in distortion and the direction of change of utility is rescued by the following proposition.

PROPOSITION 2: *If there are only two commodities, and if neither is inferior, then a rise in distortion implies a fall in utility*. (The proof follows easily from revealed preference techniques used below.)

[10] To show that a concave Π may be fitted to the two points, observe that if we treat the third good as the numeraire setting its price at 1.0 for both producers and consumers, producers' prices consistent with a given vector R of marginal rates of transformation are $R^* = (R, 1)$ and consumers' prices consistent with a given vector P of marginal rates of substitution are $P^* = (P, 1)$. Then note that $R^*(x^1) \cdot x^1 = 8.0 > R^*(x^1) \cdot x^2 = 7.9$, and $R^*(x^2) \cdot x^2 = 59 > R^*(x^2) \cdot x^1 = 55$. To show that a convex indifference surface could be fitted to the same points, observe that $P^*(x^1) \cdot x^1 = 12.5 < P^*(x^1) \cdot x^2 = 13.0$, and $P^*(x^2) \cdot x^2 = 174 < P^*(x^2) \cdot x^1 = 180$.

for a well behaved preference ordering can be obtained by the condition that along any ray from the origin they all share the same slope as the reference indifference surface. The example therefore demonstrates a case of multiple a-equilibria for a single producer and a single consumer whose tastes can be represented by a homogeneous utility function. In addition it illustrates that two points with the same ad valorem distortion can lie on the same indifference surface. We prove later that this cannot happen for specific distortions.

Example 3: Let

$$x^1 = (20, 200, 20), \qquad x^2 = (15, 188, 36),$$
$$R(x^1) = (1, 1), \qquad R(x^2) = (1.75, .25),$$
$$P(x^1) = (3.75, 1), \qquad P(x^2) = (4.5, .25).$$

Then $S = \phi_s(x^1) = \phi_s(x^2) = (2.75, 0)$ and x^1 and x^2 are two equilibria for the same specific distortion. It is clearly possible to fit a Π concave to the origin through x^1 and x^2 with the slopes dictated by $R(x^1)$ and $R(x^2)$.[11] We now must specify a well behaved indifference map consistent with the example. Notice that x^1 is revealed preferred to x^2.[12] Suppose that at prices $P^*(x^1) = (P(x^1), 1)$ and income $P^*(x^1) \cdot (x^2)$, the consumer chooses $y = (19, 190, 19)$. Note that the line through y and x^1 passes through the origin. Now construct a *reference indifference surface* through x^2 having the usual convexity and satisfying two restrictions: at x^2 it must have slopes consistent with $P(x^2)$, and where it cuts the ray from the origin through y and x^1 it must be below y, and have slopes consistent with prices $P(x^1)$. This is clearly possible, because $P^*(x^2) \cdot y > P^*(x^2) \cdot x^2$. All other indifference surfaces are constructed from this one by giving the utility function constant marginal rates of substitution along any ray from the origin; thus all indifference surfaces will be convex, and the indifference surfaces passing through y and x^1 will have the slopes already specified at those points. The example therefore demonstrates a case of multiple s-equilibria for a single producer and a single consumer whose tastes can be represented by a homogeneous utility function. In addition it illustrates that multiple equilibria can exist with just one price distorted.

In order to obtain positive results we shall adopt two natural methods of attack. The completely "static" approach is to investigate conditions under which there is a single equilibrium for a given distortion. This alone is not sufficient to guarantee that utility must diminish as distortion increases, but it is sufficient when coupled with the assumption that Π is flat. The other approach requires dynamics. If we assume that more than one equilibrium might be consistent with a given distortion vector, we can in some cases say which equilibrium, and therefore which level of utility, will obtain under a specified adjustment mechanism. The dynamic analysis is given in Section 2. In Section 1 we introduce notation and then investigate the "single equilibrium" theory.

[11] $R^*(x^1) \cdot x^1 = 240 > R^*(x^1) \cdot x^2 = 239$. $R^*(x^2) \cdot x^2 = 109.25 > R^*(x^2) \cdot x^1 = 105$.

[12] $P^*(x^1) \cdot x^1 = 295 > P^*(x^1) \cdot x^2 = 280.25$. $P^*(x^2) \cdot x^1 = 160 > P^*(x^2) \cdot x^2 = 150.5$.

1. THE SINGLE EQUILIBRIUM THEORY

We begin by making precise the notion of an increase in distortion. Let x be a d-equilibrium for the distortion D. If x' is a d-equilibrium for the distortion $kD(k > 1)$, then we will say that x' is associated with a *radial increase in distortion* relative to x.[13] One reason for studying radial increases in distortion is that, in a loose sense, they preserve the balance of distortion, and so may be thought to be the increases for which we are most likely to find decreases in utility.[14]

In what follows it will be convenient to have a geometric realization. For this purpose, we restrict attention to a world with three commodities; hence Π, the set of efficient production possibilities, will be a two-dimensional surface in the three-dimensional commodity space, and the distortion vector will be defined by a point in a plane (this plane is called the *distortion space*). Note that a radial increase in distortion means a movement out along a ray from the origin in distortion space. Denote by x^0 the welfare optimum in Π, i.e., the distortion-free equilibrium, and let I_i denote the locus of points in Π for which utility is $u(x^i)$. I_i is the intersection of an indifference surface with the production surface; it forms a loop[15] on Π around the point x^0 (an indifference loop). Furthermore, no two such loops intersect, and if I_i lies closer to x^0 than does I_j, then $u(x^i) > u(x^j)$ (see Figure 2).

The function ϕ maps points on Π^0 in commodity space into points in distortion space. We know (Proposition 1) that ϕ maps x^0 into the origin. One might expect that ϕ maps the indifference loops on Π into loops around the origin in distortion space. This is in fact the case, *if* there is only one equilibrium associated with each distortion vector.[16] When the images under ϕ of indifference loops form loops in distortion space, then we will call these loops indifference loops as well.

We now wish to find conditions under which a radial increase in distortion necessarily implies a decrease in utility; more precisely, we seek conditions under

[13] Clearly, if x' is associated with a radial increase in specific distortion relative to x, then it will usually *not* be associated with a radial increase in ad valorem distortion relative to x.

[14] We say "in a loose sense" because the choice of numeraire affects what is to be called a "balanced" increase (we owe this comment to the referee and to Lionel McKenzie). But once a numeraire has been chosen, we have the following relationship between a radial increase in distortion and increases in distortion in individual markets: Define $D = (d_1, d_2, \ldots, d_{n-1})$ to represent a *single-coordinate increase in distortion* over $D' = (d'_1, d'_2, \ldots, d'_{n-1})$ if $d_i = kd'_i$, $k > 1$, for some index i, and $d_j = d'_j$ for all $j \neq i$. If ϕ is one-to-one and there exist radial increases in distortion that are associated with increases in u, then there will exist single-coordinate increases in distortion that are associated with increases in u (because a radial increase may be decomposed into a succession of single-coordinate increases). In other words, conditions sufficient to ensure that a single-coordinate increase in distortion will decrease utility must be stronger than conditions necessary to ensure that a radial increase in distortion will decrease utility.

[15] A loop, L, or simple closed curve, is a closed curve that does not intersect itself; formally, L is a loop if there exists a continuous $f:[0, 1] \to \Pi$ with L as its image, such that $f(0) = f(1)$ and $f(t) \neq f(t')$ for all distinct t and t' in the interval $(0, 1)$.

[16] Let $B[I_i]$ represent the closed and bounded region of Π that is enclosed by I_i; if there is only one equilibrium associated with each distortion vector, then ϕ is one-to-one and continuous on $B[I_i]$ (and is therefore a homeomorphism). Thus ϕ preserves topological equivalence, so that it maps loops into loops, and if a point (x^0) lies in the interior of a loop I_j in $B[I_i]$, its image (the origin) lies in the interior of $\phi[I_j]$. (The details of this argument are dealt with later.)

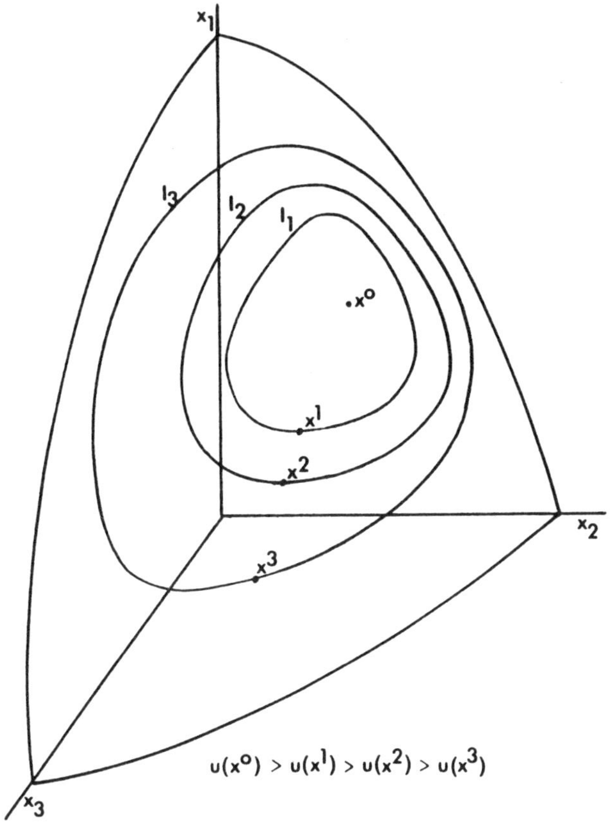

FIGURE 2.

which the following will hold:

(A) *Given any pair of distortion vectors D and kD(k > 1) in* $\phi(\Pi^0)$, *and given the associated d-equilibria* x^1, x^k, *then* $u(x^1) > u(x^k)$.

That is, we seek conditions under which, in moving out along any ray from the origin in distortion space, we cut indifference loops with successively lower utility indices. From a geometric point of view, it might seem that (A) cannot be negated

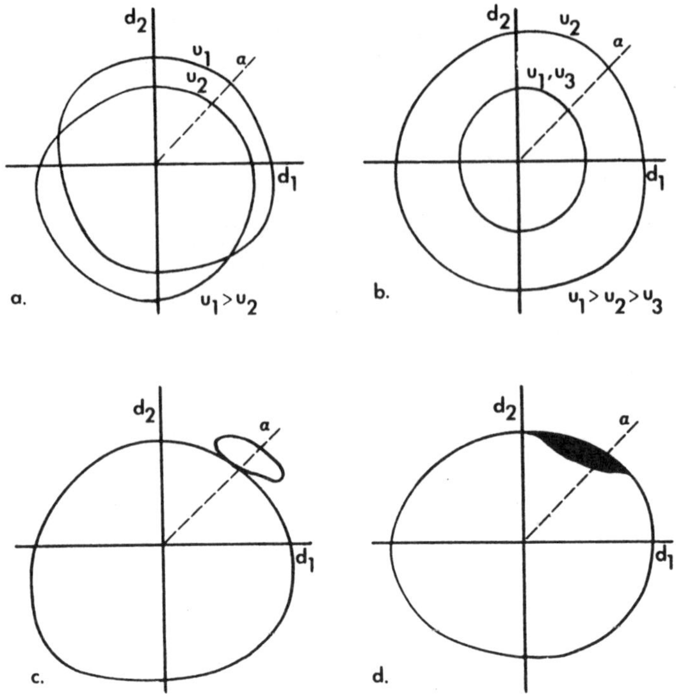

FIGURE 3.

when we restrict attention to the single equilibrium theory;[17] however this is not the case, as is illustrated in Figure 4. The indifference loops of Figure 4 are sufficiently deformed by the mapping ϕ so that a rise in distortion from a to b represents a rise in utility. (Examples in which the loops *are* deformed in this way remain to be provided, but we have no a priori reason to rule out the possibility.[18]) Can we be sure that the situation of Figure 4 is the only situation in which, with unique equilibria, more distortion may mean more utility? The following theorem,

[17] Figures 3a–3d all show situations in which the conclusion of (A) would not hold for movements along ray α, but for each of these our assumptions are violated (in Figures 3a–3c, there are multiple equilibria associated with a given distortion, and in Figure 3d there is more than one distortion associated with a given equilibrium, hence either the production surface or the indifference surface has a corner).

[18] We have not been able to construct such an example. The difficulty that we have encountered has been to find satisfactory conditions on Π and u sufficient to guarantee that ϕ is one-to-one everywhere.

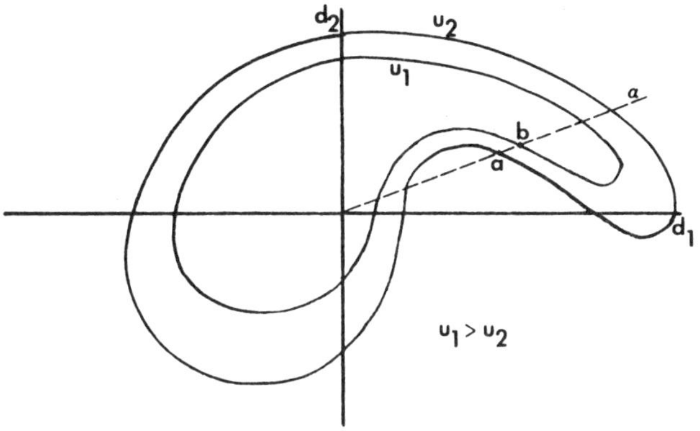

FIGURE 4.

fundamental for the single equilibrium theory, shows this to be the case. The language of the theorem is that of our three commodity example; but the proof is completely general.[19]

THEOREM 1: *If ϕ is one-to-one, then a necessary and sufficient condition for all radial increases in distortion to be associated with reductions in utility is the following:*

(B) *There exist no two points x^1 and x^k in Π^0 having the same utility, and such that x^k is associated with a radial increase in distortion relative to x^1.*

PROOF: The necessity of (B) is clear. We proceed to prove the sufficiency of (B). Assume $\phi(x^1) = D$ and $\phi(x^k) = kD$ $(k > 1)$. Consider the indifference loops $I_i = \{x \in \Pi : u(x) = u(x_i)\}$ $(i = 1, k)$. We shall now prove that if (B) holds, the loop I_1 lies closer to the distortion-free equilibrium than the loop I_k, or in other words that $u(x^1) > u(x^k)$. This of course will establish the result.

We will assume that I_1 is farther out than I_k and establish a contradiction. Consider $B[I_1]$, the closed and bounded region of Π that is enclosed by I_1. Its image under the transformation ϕ is a closed and bounded region in $\phi(\Pi)$ containing the origin. Furthermore, since ϕ is one-to-one and continuous on $B[I_1]$, Γ is a boundary point of $\phi(B[I_1])$ if and only if $\phi^{-1}(\Gamma)$ is in I_1.[20] It follows that $\phi(B[I_1])$ contains $\phi(I_k)$ in its interior. Hence there exists an $m > k$ such that mD is on the

[19] "Loop" in the three commodity case takes the ungainly form "topologically equivalent to an $(n - 1)$-dimensional sphere" in the n-commodity case; otherwise the proof is identical.

[20] Since ϕ is one-to-one and continuous on a compact set, it is a homeomorphism. Hence it maps interior points into interior points and boundary points into boundary points. This is the consequence of a highly nontrivial and important theorem on the topology of Euclidean n-space, *Brouwer's theorem on invariance of domain*. See, e.g., [2, p. 359].

boundary of $\phi(B[I_1])$; thus $mD \in \phi(I_1)$. Examine $x^m = \phi^{-1}(mD)$ and x^1. They have the same utility, yet x_m is associated with a radial increase in distortion relative to x^1. This contradicts (B), so the theorem is proved.

We now proceed to state and prove the main positive result in the single equilibrium theory.

THEOREM 2: *If Π is flat (aggregate production takes place at constant marginal cost) and if no commodity is inferior in the utility function, then a radial increase in distortion is associated with a reduction in utility.*

Before proceeding to the proof of Theorem 2, we establish a Lemma.

LEMMA 1:[21] *For specific distortions we have the following:*

(C) *There exists no two points x^1 and x^k in Π^0 having the same utility, with* (a) *x^k associated with the same specific distortion as x^1 or* (b) *x^k associated with a radial increase in specific distortion relative to x^1.*

Of course (C) implies (B), hence Lemma 1 asserts that the situation of Figure 4 cannot occur for specific distortions.

PROOF OF LEMMA 1: If (C) were not satisfied, there would exist two points x^1 and x^k such that

(1a) $(x^k - x^1)\cdot(P(x^1), 1) > 0,$

(1b) $(x^k - x^1)\cdot(P(x^k), 1) < 0,$

where

(2a) $P(x^1) = R(x^1) + S,$

(2b) $P(x^k) = R(x^k) + kS (k > 0).$

Since Π is concave to the origin,

(3a) $(x^k - x^1)\cdot(R(x^1), 1) \leqslant 0,$

(3b) $(x^k - x^1)\cdot(R(x^k), 1) \geqslant 0.$

Subtracting (3a) from (1a) and (3b) from (1b), using (2), yields $(x^k - x^1)\cdot(S, 0) > 0$; $(x^k - x^1)\cdot(kS, 0) < 0$. Because $k > 0$ this is a contradiction and the lemma is proved.

PROOF OF THEOREM 2: Since Π is flat, $R(x)$ is a constant (vector-valued) function of x. In this case x^k is associated with a radial increase in specific distortion relative to x^1 if and only if x^k is associated with a radial increase in ad valorem distortion

[21] Note that Lemma 1 is not restricted to the case where Π is flat.

relative to x^1. As a result of Theorem 1, Lemma 1, and the preceding remark, Theorem 2 will be established when we show that, under the conditions of the Theorem, ϕ_s is one-to-one.

Suppose that ϕ_s is not one-to-one. Then there exist $x^1 = (x_1^1, \ldots, x_n^1)$, $x^2 = (x_1^2, \ldots, x_n^2)$, and S such that $x^1 \neq x^2$ and $S = \phi_s(x^1) = \phi_s(x^2)$. From the definition of S, $P(x^1) = R(x) + S = P(x^2)$. Therefore, from the point of view of our single consumer, the movement from x^1 to x^2 (or x^2 to x^1) is purely the result of an increase in income. Without loss of generality, assume $(P(x^1), 1) \cdot x^1 > (P(x^2), 1) \cdot x^2$. Now, $x^1 \neq x^2$ and $(R(x^1), 1) \cdot x^1 = (R(x^2), 1) \cdot x^2$ imply that, for some i, $x_i^1 - x_i^2 < 0$. But this means that the ith commodity is inferior. This contradiction establishes the theorem.

2. THE MULTIPLE EQUILIBRIUM THEORY

In Section 1 we provided conditions under which a unique equilibrium consumption vector is associated with a given distortion vector, and in that framework investigated the welfare implications of radial changes in distortions. When there are multiple equilibria one cannot in general determine the relation between welfare and distortion without reference to an adjustment mechanism that will single out just one of the alternative equilibria. In this section we examine the relation between welfare and distortion for three adjustment mechanisms. For the first two of these we assume that Π is flat.[22] The third adjustment mechanism operates when Π is strictly concave to the origin.

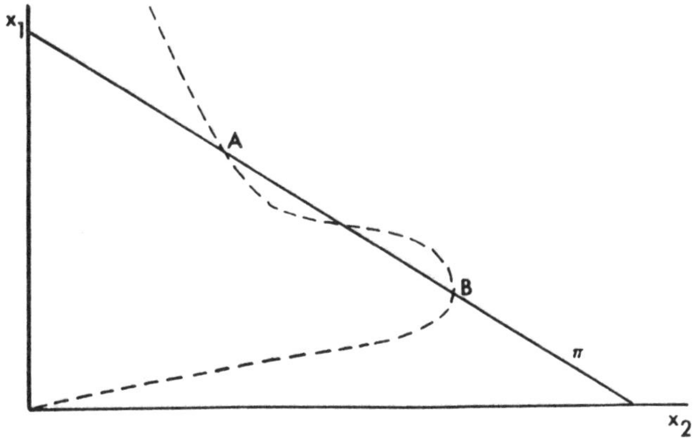

FIGURE 5.

[22] Hence multiple equilibria can exist only if the utility function has inferior goods. The essential property for the following argument is that Π be flat, however, not that some goods be inferior in consumption.

If Π is flat then $R(x) = R$ is constant, and any vector S of specific distortions will define a constant vector P of marginal rates of substitution satisfying $P = R + S$. Interpret the vector P as a vector of $n - 1$ prices confronting the consumer (with the price of the nth commodity set equal to 1), and consider the consumer's equilibrium commodity bundles for prices P and alternative budget levels. The locus of such points is an income expansion path, and excluding degenerate cases this path must cross Π an odd number of times (see Figure 5). Each point at which the income expansion path cuts Π is an s-equilibrium for the distortion vector S. No two of these s-equilibria have the same utility (by Lemma 1), hence there will always be an s-equilibrium with highest utility, such as A in Figure 5, and one with lowest utility, such as B in Figure 5. (If there is only one s-equilibrium, these two will coincide.) Refer again to Figure 5. If when the distortion vector S is introduced, the adjustment mechanism starts the consumer with a budget greater than that needed to attain A, and moves the budget plane smoothly inward until his equilibrium is on Π, the equilibrium attained will of course have higher utility than any other equilibrium associated with the same distortion vector on S. If, on the other hand, the adjustment mechanism starts the consumer with a budget smaller than that needed to attain B, and moves the budget plane smoothly outward until his equilibrium is on Π, the equilibrium attained will have lower utility than any other equilibrium associated with S.

We now will exhibit two adjustment mechanisms that achieve those contrasting results. Both are interpreted as applying to distortions in the form of taxes (and subsidies) on consumption goods.

Process 1: *An Overcompensating Transfer by Government*

For any tax vector, the government starts by giving the consumer a lump-sum transfer that would just permit him to buy his no-tax consumption bundle (if the tax vector includes some subsidies, the transfer required might be negative); this will create excess demand at the relative prices that include taxes. To remove the excess demand, the government reduces the lump-sum transfer until the consumer's desired consumption bundle is on the boundary of his no-tax consumption set (assume that this income adjustment takes place by a recontracting process, with consumption taking place only after the equilibrium is attained). This process clearly guides the consumer to the s-equilibrium yielding highest utility for the given tax vector.

Process 2: *A Flexible Wage Adjustment Process*

We now assume that there is more than one consumer, and that labor, the single unproduced factor of production, is supplied inelastically by each individual. We further assume that the technology is that of the open Leontief model and competition keeps profits at zero. Thus Π, the transformation surface, is flat, and income distribution is determined solely by the distribution of employment.

For Process 1, we assumed that as excise taxes were imposed, lump-sum taxes were correspondingly diminished (or transfers increased) so as to maintain equilibrium consumption on Π. Here we assume that when the government imposes excise taxes at nonnegative rates, it makes no compensating lump-sum transfers. We further assume that immediately after the tax is imposed, consumers obey the same budget constraint as they did without the tax; that is, where x^0 is the no-tax equilibrium,

$$R^* = (r_1^*, \ldots, r_n^*) = (r_1, \ldots, r_{n-1}, 1),$$

$$S^* = (s_1^*, \ldots, s_n^*) = (s_1, \ldots, s_{n-1}, 0),$$

$$P^* = R^* + S^*.$$

We assume that immediately after the tax is imposed, consumers face the aggregate budget constraint:

$$(4) \qquad P^* \cdot x = R^* \cdot x^0.$$

The budget plane defined by (4) lies strictly inside Π except at points on the boundary representing zero consumption of all taxed commodities. The equilibrium attained with this budget plane is thus an unemployment equilibrium; we assume that each individual's employment is a monotone function of total employment, so everyone's budget, and everyone's utility, is lower with the unemployment equilibrium than at the lowest s-equilibrium for the distortion vector S. We now assume that full employment is attained by a flexible wage–flexible price process: unemployment causes wages to fall, this causes prices to fall, which stimulates demand, and each consumer's budget plane moves outward until equilibrium is on Π.[23] This chain of events will bring the economy back to full employment, and each consumer will be brought to the s-equilibrium with lowest utility for the distortion vector S. In aggregative terms, community indifference surfaces can be defined for each level of employment by taking the Scitovsky contour of the relevant individual indifference surfaces; the economy's income expansion path for prices P^* may be traced out by reference to these nonintersecting community indifference surfaces, and the equilibrium attained on Π will have the lowest utility of all s-equilibria defined for the distortion vector S.

It is interesting to note that, with either of the above two widely divergent adjustment processes, we still have the result that a radial increase in distortion means a decrease in utility. This is demonstrated by another theorem.

THEOREM 3: *Assume that Π is defined by $R^* \cdot x = 1$, $x \geqslant 0$, and the consumer's prices are given by $R^* + S^*$; assume further that a single consumer maximizes utility subject to a budget constraint which he regards as fixed, and that he treats prices as parameters. Then if the equilibrium attained is* (i) *always the equilibrium*

[23] A formal specification of the process is given in the appendix.

with highest utility of all equilibria associated with S^*, or (ii) *always the equilibrium with lowest utility of all equilibria associated with S^*, a radial increase in distortion means a decrease in utility.*

PROOF: We shall give a proof for (i); the proof for (ii) is similar. Let x^i represent the equilibrium attained with distortion vector iS^*, $i = 0, 1, k > 1$, and consider the income expansion path associated with prices $R^* + S^*$. Let y be the point on this income expansion path for income $(R^* + S^*) \cdot x^k$, and let z be the point on the path for income $(R^* + S^*) \cdot x^0$. We shall show that z lies outside Π, y lies inside Π, and conclude that $u(x^1) > u(x^k)$.

First, $R^* \cdot z > R^* \cdot x^0$ because z is chosen when both are available yet x^0 is chosen at prices R^*. Next we have, by revealed preference,

$$(5) \qquad (R^* + S^*) \cdot y = (R^* + S^*) \cdot x^k,$$

$$(6) \qquad (R^* + kS^*) \cdot y > (R^* + kS^*) \cdot x^k.$$

Since $k > 1$, subtracting (5) from (6) gives

$$(7) \qquad S^* \cdot y > S^* \cdot x^k$$

and hence, from (5) and (7), $R^* \cdot y < R^* \cdot x^k$. Thus y is inside Π and z is outside Π. By the continuity of the income expansion path, there must be at least one point x^* on Π, for a budget intermediate between those at which y and z are bought. Clearly the budget at which y is bought is lower than the budget at which z is bought, since z is preferred to x^0 and x^0 is preferred to y. Hence x^* is purchased with a higher budget than is y, so x^* is revealed preferred to y, and to x^k. But $u(x^1) \geqslant u(x^*)$ and therefore $u(x^1) > u(x^k)$, which completes the proof.

These two examples suggest that the adjustment mechanism does make a difference. When there are multiple equilibria, a small distortion may keep the economy in the neighborhood of the distortion-free equilibrium or it may drive it far away, even when alternative equilibria that yield higher utility exist.

We now assume that Π is strictly concave, and suggest a result that complements the results attained for the two previous adjustment mechanisms.

Process 3: A Flexible-Price Adjustment Process

For any $S = (s_1, s_2, \ldots, s_{n-1})$ consider the points on Π that are compatible with the distortion kS, for some $k \geqslant 0$. Call this set H_s. By Lemma 1 no two points of H_s have the same level of utility, and therefore H_s may be parameterized by $f: [0, 1) \rightarrow H_s$, where $f(0)$ is the distortion free equilibrium, and $v > v'$ implies $f(v)$ is further along H_s from the distortion free equilibrium than $f(v')$.

Assume that the consumer purchases the first $(n - 1)$ commodities at prices $(R + S)$, that producers sell these commodities at prices R, that the price of the nth commodity is fixed at unity and that the prices, net of distortions, of the remaining commodities are adjusted according to $\dot{r}_i = \alpha_i E_i(R, S)$ $(i = 1, 2, \ldots, n - 1)$.

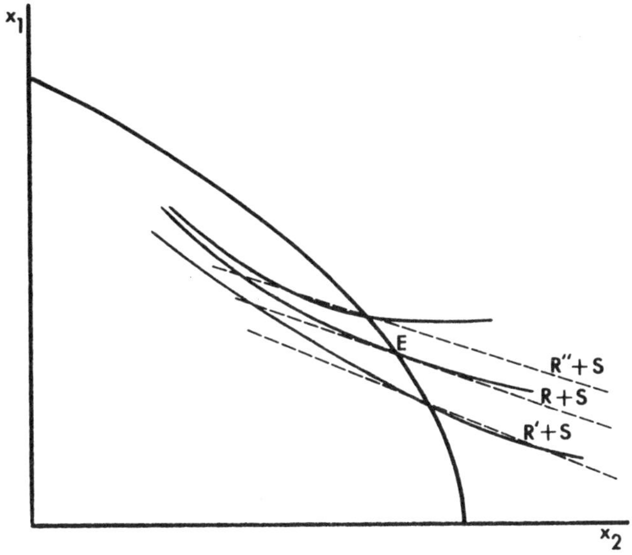

FIGURE 6.

(The α_i are positive constants, and $E_i(R, S)$ denotes the excess demand by consumers for the ith commodity when producers are maximizing profits at prices R and the distortion is S.)

Consider now the case of exactly two commodities and a region in which an increase in distortion can be associated with an increase in utility. Such a region is displayed in Figure 6. Suppose that we are in equilibrium at point $E = f(v_0)$, with the distortion at S. Formally, we assume that in some neighborhood of E, increases in distortion correspond to decreases in v, and decreases in distortion correspond to increases in v. If the distortion remains S, and if producers' prices are displaced to R', then the profit maximizing action of producers and the utility maximizing action of consumers will imply a negative excess demand for commodity 1 and a movement still further away from E. (Similarly, if producers' prices are displaced to R'', the economy moves away from E.) Thus E is not a stable equilibrium for this adjustment mechanism.

If we now return to the case of more than two commodities, the instability of equilibrium, in regions where increases in the distortion rate may be associated with increases in utility, is no longer clear. The above argument suggests, however, that in these regions the initial movement (after displacement) will be away from equilibrium for this adjustment process.

3. CONCLUSION

Economists generally accept the proposition that in an economy rich in distortions the abolition or reduction of a single distortion may lead to a reduction in welfare. We have examined conditions under which a radial decrease in distortion will unambiguously improve welfare. If production takes place at constant cost and no commodities are inferior, then there will be a single equilibrium associated with each vector of distortions and a radial decrease in distortion will improve welfare. The analysis becomes more complex, however, if production does not take place at constant cost. When an economy is characterized by a strictly concave production frontier, it is possible for there to be more than one equilibrium compatible with a given vector of distortions, and under these conditions, there will exist (except for degenerate cases) equilibria x and y, with x having a lower utility than y and the distortion associated with x representing a radial decrease from the distortion associated with y. Not even the strong assumption that the economy contains a single individual, whose tastes are represented by a homogeneous utility function, is sufficient to eliminate this possibility. In order to obtain definite results for the multiple equilibria case, it is necessary to specify mechanisms for adjustment to equilibria characterized by distortions. Our analysis of three such mechanisms leads to the presumption that a radial decrease in specific distortion will improve welfare.

University of Minnesota
and
The Pennsylvania State University

Manuscript received November, 1967; revision received December, 1968.

APPENDIX

A FLEXIBLE WAGE ADJUSTMENT PROCESS FOR A LEONTIEF ECONOMY

Production and employment for the economy are specified by

(8) $$v = (I - A)^{-1}x,$$

(9) $$e = a_0'v,$$

where v is an n-vector showing production levels for each good, x is an n-vector showing levels of final demand for each good, and A is the usual input-output matrix. The expression e is employment, and $a_0 = (a_{0i})$ shows labor requirements per unit of output in each industry; the prime symbol denotes the matrix transpose.

Prices for sale of intermediate goods are assumed equal to production costs, measured by a vector R^*; R^* is determined by equations dual to (8),

(10) $$R^* = (I - A')^{-1}a_0 w,$$

where w is the wage rate. If consumers' prices P^* are also equal to unit costs, the value of final demand equals labor income; $P^{*\prime}x = we$.

THE WAGE-PRICE ADJUSTMENT PROCESS

Let L represent the full employment labor force, and assume that

(11) $$\dot{w} = k(e - L), \qquad k > 0;$$

the dot indicates the derivative with respect to time. Suppose that $x = x(P^*)$, and write $H = [h_{ij}] = [\partial x_i/\partial p_j^*]$. We shall assume that H is bounded for all relevant P^*, and has a negative dominant diagonal in the sense of McKenzie [5] realized with the unit costs r_i^* as weights; that is, $h_{jj} < 0$ for all j, and

$$r_j^*|h_{jj}| > \sum_{i \neq j} r_i^*|h_{ij}| \qquad (j = 1, \ldots, n).$$

This strong restriction says roughly that demand for each good responds more to changes in its own price than does the demand for all other goods taken together; the restriction is used to help guarantee convergence to full employment equilibrium.

When there are no excise taxes, suppose that $P^* = R^*$, and initially $e < L$. Using equations (9) to (11) we may write

$$\dot{e} = (k/w^2)R^{*\prime}HR^*(e - L). \tag{12}$$

The restriction on H guarantees [5, Theorem 2] that $R^{*\prime}HR^*$ is negative, hence $\dot{e} > 0$ when $e < L$, and $\dot{e} = 0$ when $e = L$. So $\lim_{t\to\infty} e = L$.

THE PROCESS OF ADJUSTMENT TO AN EXCISE TAX

Starting from a full employment equilibrium, the government imposes excise taxes at nonnegative rates on final sales, but not on sales of intermediate goods; thus receipts from the excise tax are simply removed from the private economy, causing a deficiency of demand and unemployment. Write R^* as prices before taxes, and $P^* = R^* + S^* = (I + E)R^*$ as prices after taxes (whether the economy is at full employment or not). The matrix E is a diagonal matrix of excise tax rates (e_i) with $e_n = 0$. We assume that the initial impact of the tax is to preserve the money value of final demand, but reduce the real demand below the full employment level; i.e.,

$$R^* \cdot x(R^*) = P^* \cdot x(P^*), \qquad R^* \cdot x(P^*) < R^* \cdot x(R^*).$$

The employment adjustment process, from that point on, can be described exactly as before, except that equation (12) is modified slightly to $\dot{e} = (k/w^2)R^{*\prime}H(I + E)R^*(e - L)$. Given our assumptions, this again yields $\dot{e} > 0$ when $e < L$.[24] ($H(I + E)$ has a negative dominant diagonal if H does.) So again $\lim_{t\to\infty} e = L$.

REFERENCES

[1] Davis, O. A., and A. B. Whinston: "Welfare Economics and the Theory of Second Best," *Review of Economic Studies*, January, 1965.

[2] Dugundji, James: *Topology*. Boston: Allyn and Bacon, 1965.

[3] Harberger, Arnold C.: "Taxation, Resource Allocation, and Welfare," in National Bureau of Economic Research and the Brookings Institution, *The Role of Direct and Indirect Taxes in the Federal Revenue System*. Princeton, N.J.: Princeton University Press, 1964.

[4] Hotelling, Harold: "The General Welfare in Relation to Problems of Taxation and of Railway and Utility Rates," *Econometrica*, July, 1938.

[5] McKenzie, Lionel: "Matrices with Dominant Diagonals and Economic Theory," Chapter 4 of Arrow, Karlin, and Suppes (eds.), *Mathematical Methods in the Social Sciences, 1959*. Stanford University Press, 1960.

[6] Samuelson, Paul A.: "Social Indifference Curves," *The Quarterly Journal of Economics*, February, 1956.

[24] The assumption of diagonal dominance of H is stronger, now, than before; the price weights used are not market prices, but producers' prices; diagonal dominance with these weights is a somewhat unnatural restriction to place on a demand function.

[7]

Market Distortions and Gradual Reform[1, 2]

MICHAEL BRUNO

The Hebrew University, Jerusalem

I. INTRODUCTION

Consider a mixed private-public, partially controlled economy for which two different price vectors are determined. One is a shadow price vector $\bar{p}$ given exogenously or by some social optimization procedure. This motivates government policy and is the price vector used in public investment decisions. The other " distorted " price vector is the actual equilibrium price p, which is determined in the market, affecting both private producers' and consumers' decisions. Suppose the government can use the tax system, or a process of institutional change, to bring the market price system " closer " to the true social optimum price, but it is unable to do so all at once, either because of very high adjustment costs, or because of political and institutional constraints, etc. Can one say anything about the welfare implications of a *gradual* reform of the price system, as the economy moves from one sub-optimum to another?

As is well known, no general theories exist for the case of second best adjustments, except the relatively trivial ones which suggest that the true optimum will be preferred to any suboptimum. It is in general, except for very special circumstances, not the case that partial equilibrium component by component adjustment of prices would improve things. Quite the opposite can often be shown to be the case. Yet it would be wrong to conclude that choice between two suboptima is *never* possible. There are situations in which this *can* be done and where a class of aggregate adjustment processes, involving uniform across-the-board [3] reductions in the distance $\bar{p}-p$, can be shown to enable a general aggregate welfare improvement at *each* stage, even when no predictions about specific sector or resource allocations can be made.[4]

The present study is an attempt to analyse the implications of this type of adjustment rule in the context outlined above, when the technology is of a general convex kind but the shadow price for " most " goods is given independently of market prices. One situation where this would apply is an open economy that faces given international prices for its tradable goods, and attempts to reform a distorted domestic tariff structure. The theory would also apply to the case of constant cost home goods or factors which are traded in institutionally constrained monopolistic markets and where the government can affect market prices by gradual trading of its inventories (or output) of such goods (e.g. natural resources, buffer stocks, labour in a " dual " economy).

1 *First version received July* 1971; *final version received October* 1971 (*Eds*.).

2 I would like to acknowledge helpful discussions with Jagdish Bhagwati, Peter Diamond, Frank Hahn, and Robert Solow. I am also indebted to G. M. Heal and to a referee for very helpful comments on a draft.

This paper was partly written during tenure of a 1971 Ford Faculty Fellowship at M.I.T. and partly supported by an NSF grant to the Project for Quantitative Research in Economic Development at Harvard University.

3 Call this AB for short.

4 A major reference that has, at least, in part inspired the present study is Foster and Sonnenschein [2]. They apply such a rule in the context of a closed economy with a constant cost technology, to adjust the tax wedge between production and consumption.

Section II discusses and proves the basic proposition that the application of the AB rule increases total net output evaluated at *shadow* prices. A geometric interpretation is given in the Appendix. The next section analyses the aggregate welfare implications in terms of revealed consumers' preferences. Section IV proves modified theorems for a more general economy in which some prices and commodities are not controlled by government at all (e.g. non-tradables). We end with some concluding remarks about the limitations of the model and a possible " dual " interpretation.

II. PRICE ADJUSTMENT AND NET OUTPUT RESPONSE

Consider an economy producing a net output (input) [1] vector y with a (strictly) convex technology. Its producers, who are profit maximizers, as well as its consumers, face a vector of (relative) market prices p. This " private " price vector may be different from the " social " or shadow (relative) price vector $\bar{p}$ which is the one that motivates government decisions. For the time being we shall assume that $\bar{p}$ is fixed for *all* goods and given independently of p and that the government alone can in fact meet excess demand (supply) at the price $\bar{p}$. It can affect the " private " price vector p by changing it gradually but is assumed to be unable to affect this transition at once.

Let us use a subscript to denote the stage of adjustment, i.e. p_1 is the price at the first stage, p_2 at the second, etc. and assume the following AB *adjustment rule*:

$$p_2 - p_1 = -\beta(p_1 - \bar{p}) \quad \text{where } 0<\beta<1 \qquad \text{...(1)}$$

or

$$p_2 - p_1 = -\frac{\beta}{1-\beta}(p_2 - \bar{p}) \qquad \text{...(2)}$$

i.e. always cut the *distance* between p and $\bar{p}$ by a proportionate (not necessarily constant) amount. This can also be written in a form that shows p_2 as a convex combination of p_1 and $\bar{p}$: $p_2 = (1-\beta)p_1 + \beta\bar{p}$. Note that in general $p_2 - p_1$, like $p_1 - \bar{p}$, will consist of both positive and negative elements.[2]

Obviously the two extreme limits $\beta = 0, 1$ stand for the respective cases where prices are not changed at all or changed the whole way, both of which are of no particular interest to us. It is, however, important to note that the above rule allows one to reach the full optimum eventually, in all prices.[3] Our first proposition concerns potential welfare in the sense of net output response.

Theorem 1. *If the technology is (strictly) convex and producers maximize their profits at given market prices, any AB cut in the distance between the market prices (p) and the independently given shadow prices ($\bar{p}$) of all goods constitutes a potential improvement in welfare in the sense that net output, evaluated at shadow prices, must (strictly) increase.*

Proof.[4] Profit maximization under strict convexity entails the following two inequalities (dot means scalar product):

$$p_2 \cdot y_2 > p_2 \cdot y_1 \qquad \text{...(3)}$$

$$p_1 \cdot y_1 > p_1 \cdot y_2 \qquad \text{...(4)}$$

1 We follow the convention of having outputs represented by positive entries, net inputs by negative ones.

2 Note also that the distance $p - \bar{p}$ and the *relative* prices in p_2 are not independent of the normalization rules chosen for p_1 and $\bar{p}$. What is really involved is a gradual reduction in the *angle* between p and $\bar{p}$ (see the Appendix).

3 This could not be said for a composite good rule that would, say, change all *prices* proportionately. Here relative prices *do* change.

4 The Appendix and Figures 1 and 2 give a geometric interpretation of the theorem and the proof.

from which it follows that $(p_2-p_1).(y_2-y_1)>0$. From (1) and (2) we thus get:

$$(p_j-\bar{p}).(y_2-y_1)<0 \quad (j = 1, 2). \qquad ...(5)$$

By (3) and (5) it follows that

$$\bar{p}.(y_2-y_1) = p_2.(y_2-y_1)-(p_2-\bar{p}).(y_2-y_1)>0.$$

If we have convexity, rather than *strict* convexity, the strict inequality sign in (3), (4) and (5) must be replaced by weak inequality, and in that case we can only state

$$\bar{p}.(y_2-y_1) \geqq 0. \quad \text{Q.E.D.}$$

Before proceeding with further analysis let us briefly mention relevant situations for the application of this type of model. The most obvious case is that of a small open economy, without externalities, in which relative international prices ($\bar{p}$) are given (subject to normalization by choice of the exchange rate) and $p-\bar{p}$ is a vector of domestic tariffs.[1]

Note that Theorem 1 constitutes an *extension of the classical gains-from-trade theory*. We have shown that, in the AB tariff change sense, less restricted trade is potentially superior to more restricted trade, not only in the vicinity of the polar autarchy [2] or free trade positions, but for any two " convex " intermediate positions.[3]

The analysis likewise holds for the case in which a domestic good gets transacted in an institutionally monopolized market which keeps the price p constrained away from the true opportunity cost price $\bar{p}$, but the government can gradually change p. The assumption that the government uses $\bar{p}$ rather than p for its own accounts would in such a case imply that it can either produce (buy) the good (or factor) at that price or else that it holds inventories of these commodities which it can accumulate or run down. Examples of the latter might be: natural resources like land, stocks of minerals, water, unskilled labour in a less developed " dual " economy, or agricultural surpluses, etc. Note, however, that the assumption of *fixed* $\bar{p}$ is quite restrictive and would imply that social marginal rates of substitution (or transformation) must be fixed for these goods.

III. DECENTRALIZED EXPENDITURE PATTERNS AND REVEALED PREFERENCE

So far we have analysed the implication of the AB adjustment rule only on the production side. To make more specific welfare statements we must now go one step further and discuss consumer behaviour and the effect on expenditure patterns.

Let the difference $x = y-c$ between net output (y) and (domestic) expenditure (c) stand for net trade (in the case of international trade) or for net public inventory accumulation (in the " natural resource " illustration). Obviously there is nothing that will guarantee that $p \cdot x = 0$. However, we shall show that under a very simple version of Walras' Law we must have $\bar{p} \cdot x = 0$.

1 Let t be the vector of *ad valorem* tariff (or subsidy) rates and T the diagonal matrix having the elements of t spread along the diagonal. Then $p = (I+T)\bar{p}$ and the adjustment rule becomes an AB tariff cut: $t_2-t_1 = -\beta t_1$ or $t_2-t_1 = -\dfrac{\beta}{1-\beta}t_2$.

Note that as long as *all* goods are tradable (for non-tradables see Section IV) *any* across-the-board adjustment to an *arbitrary* uniform rate would constitute a potential improvement. This follows from the free choice of an exchange rate as numeraire; e.g., suppose we have three goods with domestic prices (in pesos) of 200, 50, 300 and foreign ($) prices of 10, 20, 50. For an exchange rate base of 5 pesos/$ the implied tariff rates are, respectively 3, $-1/2$, 0·2. If, however, we choose to unify to an " effective " exchange rate that is 10 peso/$ (or, alternatively, an exchange rate of 5+uniform 100 per cent tariff) the implied initial tariff rates are 1, $-3/4$, $-0{\cdot}4$ (negative tariffs always entail subsidies). Theorem 1 says that AB unification to either one or the other will qualitatively improve things. Obviously the actual resource allocation at any intermediate stage will depend on the choice of strategy.

2 Autarchy can here be represented by the vector p which makes zero trade in all goods *just* profitable. A similar device can be used for quantitative restrictions.

3 Cf. Samuelson ([6], [7]), Kemp ([3], [4]), Bhagwati [1]. See also in this connection, Krueger and Sonnenschein [5].

Lemma. *If the government transfers all its surplus (or deficit) to (from) the private sector in a lump sum fashion and private income equals private expenditure,* $\bar{p}\cdot x = 0$.

Proof. Net government transfers to the private sector are given by

$$(\bar{p}-p)\cdot x = (p-\bar{p})\cdot(c-y).$$

Private earned income is $p\cdot y$ Private sector's expenditure is $p\cdot c$. Thus we get:

$$p\cdot y+(p-\bar{p})\cdot(c-y) = p\cdot c. \qquad \ldots(7)$$

From which it follows that $\bar{p}\cdot x = 0$, Q.E.D.[1]

Theorem 1 plus the Lemma now imply that we also have:

$$\bar{p}\cdot c_2-\bar{p}\cdot c_1>0 \text{ (or } \geqq 0 \text{ if convexity is not strict).} \qquad \ldots(8)$$

Given the AB adjustment rule and the assumption that the government can make lump sum payments or transfers, can one show that aggregate consumption will not only potentially improve but will, in fact, be *revealed* to have been increased? In other words, can we show, using *market* prices, that $p_2\cdot(c_2-c_1)>0$ (or $p_1\cdot(c_2-c_1)>0$)?

Consider an individual spending C_1 at prices p_1 (and income $p_1\cdot C_1$) and C_2 at prices p_2 (income $p_2\cdot C_2$). Suppose he would spend $\tilde{C}_2$ at prices p_2 and income $p_2\cdot C_1$, i.e. if real income remained unchanged. We have $p_2\cdot\tilde{C}_2 = p_2\cdot C_1$ and by revealed preference considerations $p_1\cdot\tilde{C}_2 \geqq p_1\cdot C_1$. Summing over all individuals we thus have ($\tilde{c}_2 = \Sigma\tilde{C}_2$ and $c_i = \Sigma C_i$, $i = 1, 2$):

$$p_2.\tilde{c}_2 = p_2.c_1 \qquad \ldots(9)$$

$$p_1.\tilde{c}_2 \geqq p_1.c_1. \qquad \ldots(10)$$

Next consider the identity

$$\bar{p}.(c_2-\tilde{c}_2) = \bar{p}.(c_2-c_1)+(p_2-\bar{p}).(\tilde{c}_2-c_1)+p_2.(c_1-\tilde{c}_2).$$

We have:

$$\bar{p}.(c_2-c_1)>0, \text{ by (8).}$$

$$(p_2-\bar{p}).(\tilde{c}_2-c_1) = -\frac{1-\beta}{\beta}(p_2-p_1).(\tilde{c}_2-c_1) = \frac{1-\beta}{\beta}p_1.(\tilde{c}_2-c_1) \geqq 0,$$

by (2), (9) and (10) and

$$p_2.(c_1-\tilde{c}_2) = 0, \text{ by (9).}$$

Therefore we have

$$\bar{p}.(c_2-\tilde{c}_2)>0 \text{ (or } \geqq 0 \text{ if production is not strictly convex).} \qquad \ldots(11)$$

(11) means that the partial aggregate consumption increment due to a change in income $p_2.(c_2-c_1)$ and evaluated at shadow prices ($\bar{p}$), must be positive. From this it follows that unless $p_2.(c_2-c_1)$ happens by fluke to be zero,[2] we must have

$$p_2.(c_2-c_1)>0 \text{ if and only if}$$

$$\bar{p}.m_2>0 \qquad \ldots(12)$$

where $m_2 = \dfrac{1}{p_2.(c_2-c_1)}(c_2-\tilde{c}_2) =$ " marginal " propensity to consume[3] (a vector).

1 If all goods are internationally traded, the lemma would imply that the net trade balance (in foreign currency) is zero. Since c stands for any purchases of goods, not necessarily consumption goods, any case of a non-balanced current trade balance can always be accommodated in the present framework by suitable purchases or sales of claims on real assets. In the more general case, if some of the goods are " natural resources ", what this means is that the net total social asset change (of trade plus public inventory accumulation) must be zero.

2 Since eventually in a continued adjustment process p gets close to $\bar{p}$, (9) and (11) rule out a *permanent* $p_2.(c_2-c_1) = 0$. If our economy were to consist of one aggregate consumer with strictly quasi-concave utility function and strictly convex production set this could *never* happen, since $p_2.(c_2-c_1) = 0$ would imply $c_2 = \tilde{c}_2$, which violates (11).

3 Had we chosen to measure aggregate expenditure at first period's prices we would get an exactly analogous result:

$$p_1.(c_2-c_1)>0 \text{ if } \bar{p}.m_1>0, \text{ where } m_1 = \frac{1}{p_1.(c_2-c_1)}(c_1-\tilde{c}_1)$$

and $\tilde{c}_1$ is the consumption vector chosen at prices p_1 and income $p_1.c_2$. m_2 and m_1 are not point mpc's in the strict sense of the word (hence the inverted commas) since there is nothing in our analysis that requires the adjustment process to be infinitesimal.

If all goods are normal, in an *aggregate* sense,[1] $m_2>0$ and (12) will always hold. In fact, (12) may not hold only if some goods are inferior. However, such (aggregate) inferiority would have to be pretty strong to make $\bar{p}\cdot m_2$ come out negative.[2] Moreover, even if we had inferiority, since $p_2.m_2 = 1$, continuity considerations (p_2 getting "close" to $\bar{p}$) would eventually make (12) hold.

Let us summarize these results in a Theorem:

Theorem 2. *If individual consumption behaviour satisfies the (weak) axiom of revealed preference and if the aggregate marginal propensity to consume (spend), evaluated at shadow prices. is positive, then the AB adjustment rule increases aggregate consumption (expenditure) at market prices.*

Theorem 2 clearly constitutes a stronger statement about welfare implications than did Theorem 1. It shows that under certain assumptions about decentralized behaviour society will behave so as to be revealed better off in an aggregate consumption sense. Note, however, that even that is quite restrictive. We have ignored income distribution considerations here. *Everybody* can be made better (or no worse) off only if compensatory transfers between consumers are possible.[3] A government cannot confine itself to price adjustment alone.

IV. PARTIAL CONTROL AND TARIFF UNIFICATION

So far we have assumed all goods to be fully controllable (i.e. "tradable", in the open economy case). We now extend the analysis to the case in which there is an output (y) of controllable goods and in addition an output vector (y') of different goods which are not controlled at all. A price vector (p') clears the latter markets ($c' = y'$)[4] without government intervention or taxation for these goods.[5] The government is now assumed to apply the AB adjustment rule only to the first set, thus determining p_2. The remaining prices p_2' will adjust endogenously as a result of producer and consumer optimizing behaviour.

To avoid having to repeat all of the previous analysis for this case one can employ a simple device. Define a fictitious shadow price vector $\bar{p}' = (p_2'-(1-\beta)p_1')/\beta$. This corresponds to the imaginary experiment of applying the AB adjustment rule to *all* goods with extended shadow price vector ($\bar{p}$, $\bar{p}'$) and resulting in the actually observed new market price (p_2, p_2'). Obviously $\bar{p}'$ has no inherent economic meaning as a "price". It is an endogenous variable in the system and may take negative values. However, it now allows us to use the same argument leading to Theorem 1 this time for both controllable and non-controllable goods combined. We obtain an analogous result:

$$\bar{p}.(y_2-y_1)+\bar{p}'.(y_2'-y_1')>0 \quad (\text{or } \geqq 0)$$

[1] Unless one assumes that $\bar{p}.M_2$ (M_2 = "mpc" for a representative individual) is the *same* for all individuals, normality for the micro-units ($M_2>0$) is neither a necessary nor a sufficient condition for "normality" in the aggregate ($m_2>0$), since changes in income distribution might upset things in aggregation. We ignore these questions here.

[2] Condition (12) and the "perverse" case of inferiority generalize the 2-sector trade model discussion of Bhagwati [1] and Kemp [4]. We also note that (12) is at the same time a stability-of-equilibrium condition. If it is violated one could, as in the two-sector model, show that there always exists a preferred equilibrium that would be stable (a point attributed to Samuelson—see Bhagwati [1]). In an n-good real world (as distinct from 2-sector illustrations) it is hard to envisage inferiority to be sufficiently strong to upset (12).

Note also that in the Foster-Sonnenschein analysis [2] non-inferiority had to be assumed.

[3] If this is impossible it is quite clear that consumers who had previously enjoyed a relatively subsidized bill of goods may now actually lose (i.e. $p_2.(C_2-C_1)$ may be negative for some individuals).

[4] Strictly speaking we have $y' \geqq c'$ and $p' \geqq 0$ with complementary slackness.

[5] In the open economy case "non-controlled" goods will be non-tradables.

which can be written out in the form

$$\bar{p}.(y_2-y_1)+p_2'.(y_2'-y_1')+\frac{1-\beta}{\beta}(p_2'-p_1').(y_2'-y_1')>0 \qquad ...(13)$$

or

$$\bar{p}.(y_2-y_1)+p_1'.(y_2'-y_1')+\frac{1}{\beta}(p_2'-p_1').(y_2'-y_1')>0.$$

A modified statement, instead of Theorem 1, that now suggests itself from (13) is in terms of the change in output where controlled goods are evaluated at shadow prices whereas the uncontrolled goods are evaluated at either present or past market prices. Such a hybrid net output measure will show an increase in any of the following cases:

1. Uncontrolled commodity quantities stay constant ($y_2' = y_1'$). This would, for example, cover the case of fixed non-tradable factors of production.[1]
2. Uncontrolled goods prices stay constant ($p_2' = p_1'$). This could correspond to the case in which marginal rates of substitution or marginal rates of transformation for these goods are fixed,[2] or where the economy can effectively be decomposed into the two groups of goods with no interdependence.
3. The case $\frac{1}{\beta}(p_2'-p_1').(y_2'-y_1')<0$ or where it is >0 but "small" in relation to the value of output.

Next we note that the Lemma remains correct in the modified case (since $p'.c' = p'.y'$) and all of the argument leading to Theorem 2 can likewise be repeated step by step to find that

$$p_2.(c_2-c_1)+p_2'.(c_2'-c_1')>0 \quad \text{(unless it is } = 0)$$

if and only if $\bar{p}.m_2+\bar{p}'.m_2'>0$ or, written out:

$$\bar{p}.m_2+\frac{1}{\beta}(p_2'-(1-\beta)p_1').m_2'>0 \qquad ...(14)$$

where we now redefine $m_2=(c_2-\tilde{c}_2)/(p_2.(c_2-c_1)+p_2'.(c_2'-c_1'))$, and similarly for m_2'.

This shows the exact modification that has to be introduced in Theorem 2 if the same welfare statement is to hold in the more general case. It is now not enough to have m_2 and m_2' non-negative. However, one can see from (14) that if $p_2' \geqq p_1'$ or if β is "sufficiently" large or if the term relating to the uncontrolled (non-traded) goods is small in relation to $\bar{p}.m_2$, the same result will still hold. A more precise statement cannot be made unless we have more information about the nature of the supply and/or demand interdependences between the two types of goods. However, there is one clear case that might merit special mention. Suppose we are dealing with an open economy in which there are many tariff-ridden tradable goods and one composite non-tradable good (other than fixed factors).[3]

If one applies an AB tariff (subsidy) reduction towards a uniform effective exchange (or tariff) rate, there is good reason to expect the price of non-tradables p' to go up in relative terms (i.e., $p_2' \geqq p_1'$). The argument would run as follows: as tariff distortions

[1] In that case one can see from (13) that any price tag put on y' will in fact do because it does not affect the value of the change in net output.

[2] Cf. Foster and Sonnenschein [2] *op. cit.*

[3] Fixed factors do not affect (14), since the appropriate elements in (c_2-c_1) are zero by definition.

are reduced the production of tradables (i.e. foreign exchange) becomes relatively more efficient, like technical progress that is trade-good biased. If the non-tradable good is not an inferior good, the new equilibrium must take place at a point in which the price of non-tradables relative to the tradable goods (i.e. foreign exchange) must have increased. In other words, with $\bar{p}$ kept constant by some normalization, we have $p_2' \geqq p_1'$ so that (14) will hold.

The implication of this finding for trade policy is of considerable practical importance since it implies that even without precise prior knowledge of the future equilibrium real exchange rate between tradables and non-tradables, a unilateral AB cut in distortionary tariffs (subsidies) increases aggregate welfare in the sense discussed above.[1] We summarize this discussion in a Theorem.

Theorem 3. *In a small open economy without externalities an AB reduction in tariff distortions will increase aggregate income (expenditure) if condition (14) holds. If there is only one (composite) non-tradable good, in addition to fixed factors, and if all goods are normal in the aggregate sense, condition (14) can be expected to hold.*

We should warn the reader on two issues: one is the obvious point already made about the restrictiveness of the notion of " aggregate " welfare. The other relates to the qualitative nature of this as well as the previous theorems. There are many ways of normalizing $\bar{p}$ and choosing β's and some of them may be better than others, in the sense that they may make welfare rise at a more rapid rate from one suboptimum to the next.[2] Obviously the Theorem is not an optimality statement. In real life, however, such qualitative rules may sometimes be of greater practical importance.[3]

V. CONCLUDING REMARKS

There are a number of minor ways in which this simple model could be generalized to cover various cases. Examples are: the treatment of domestic intermediate goods, existence of quantitative restrictions and other corner solutions, exogenous technical progress. Likewise, as Foster and Sonnenschein [2] have shown, similar results apply to AB cuts in *ad valorem* excise taxes that form a wedge between production and consumption, providing marginal rates of substitution in production remain constant.[4] In our model this could apply to the case of tradables (given international prices) or where the non-tradable goods are produced at constant marginal costs. The question of extension to the more general convex technology case remains open. As FS have shown for their model this may often lead to multiple equilibria. This also brings us to the most restrictive aspect of our own analysis.

[1] Uniform unilateral tariff-reduction plans have been applied in practice. For example, a currently running Israeli import-liberalization programme has as its declared objective an annual AB tariff reduction towards a uniform effective exchange rate of 5.50 IL/\$ to be reached by 1975. The official rate today is 4.20. Effective tariff rates vary from this to 3 times that level. The higher uniform rate can be reached either by devaluation or by having a 1.30 IL/\$ uniform tariff cum subsidy. (The shadow exchange rate presently in use for project evaluation is 5.00-5.50).

[2] Since we ignore monetary phenomena here and deal with a model in which only *relative* prices matter, price normalization and the choice of β's can only affect the sequence of intermediate stages but not the " final " optimum (relative) price vector (p, p'; where $p = \bar{p}$), it if is unique. It would, however, make practical sense, for example, to apply from the start a reference " effective " exchange rate that approximates a future equilibrium exchange rate and couple the AB cuts with suitable devaluations, so as to minimize extreme back and forth changes in *absolute* prices.

[3] Witness the enormous resource expense involved in measuring detailed effective tariff rates whose practical use for policy purposes such as the above is rather dubious.

[4] Cf. FS's Theorem 2 for a closed economy. The latter could actually be proved more directly by applying the method leading to our inequality (11). Suppose $\bar{p}$ = constant production prices, p = consumption prices. Here $y = c$ (closed economy) and $\bar{p}.(c_2-c_1) = \bar{p}.(y_2-y_1) = 0$. Applying the AB rule to $(p-\bar{p})$ we find that $p_2.(c_2-c_1)>0$ if and only if (11) holds, which is also weaker than FS's condition of no inferiority.

Of all the assumptions made so far, the most restrictive may be the one that assumes the shadow prices $\bar{p}$ to be given independently of the rest of the system. There are two immediate examples for which this assumption would be violated. One is the case of monopoly in trade. Here $\bar{p}$ will no longer be independent of p. The other example that comes to mind is the Ramsey-Diamond-Mirrlees case in which indirect taxes are the only way in which revenue can be raised, and no lump sum transfers are allowed. At first sight it would look as if our propositions would break down for this case, and it may be worth exploring further.

Obviously other instances could be cited where the simple price independence assumption might break down or where it would at least have to be modified, as would be the case whenever shadow prices depend in an important way on the adjustment process chosen.[1]

Finally, there is a " dual " to the present analysis that might merit further exploration. Consider an idealized command economy in which the government plans by fixing the target bundle of outputs (inputs) $\bar{y}$ and allocates resources and production orders in such a way as to minimize costs of production. Suppose for some historical reason the actual bundle being produced y is not " optimal ". The government plans to adjust the economy towards production of the optimal bundle but can do so only by small steps (because of high adjustment costs, institutional inertia, etc.) A dual proposition to Theorem 1 could be conjectured, this time with respect to a gradual AB reduction of the difference $y-\bar{y}$.[2] The basic proposition should now read that a uniform adjustment of the " target " bundle towards $\bar{y}$, would involve the ability to produce the optimal bundle at gradually decreasing real costs of production. As with other applications of duality theory, it would seem that mixed primal-dual theorems could also be conjectured, involving a partition into quantity or price determination, depending on the nature of the institutional mechanism involved.

REFERENCES

[1] Bhagwati, J. "The Gains from Trade Once Again ", *Oxford Economic Papers* (July 1968).

[2] Foster, E. and Sonnenschein, H. " Price Distortion and Economic Welfare ", *Econometrica* (March 1970).

[3] Kemp, M. C. " The Gain from International Trade ", *Economic Journal* (December 1962).

[4] Kemp, M. C. " Some Issues in the Analysis of Trade Gains ", *Oxford Economic Papers* (July 1968).

[5] Krueger, A. O. and Sonnenschein, H. " The Terms of Trade, the Gains from Trade and Price Divergence ", *International Economic Review* (February 1967).

[6] Samuelson, P. A. " The Gains from International Trade ", *Canadian Journal of Economics and Political Science* (May 1939).

[7] Samuelson, P. A. " The Gains from International Trade Once Again ", *Economic Journal* (December 1962).

1 Any adjustment theory for these more general cases would probably have to centre around convergence of the (normalized) distance $p-\bar{p}$ (or the angle between p and $\bar{p}$).

2 The tool to be used for the proof of such a proposition would be the dual minimum cost frontier, i.e., the concave envelope in the price space which is the locus of minimum production costs for all goods. The tangent plane to this surface at any point would be given in terms of the quantities produced.

APPENDIX

A Geometric Interpretation of Theorem 1

Consider a geometric illustration of what is involved in our model and in Theorem 1.

Figure 1 gives a 2-dimensional illustration of the production possibility surface in the strictly convex case. The " true " optimum takes place at point *R*, the normal to the surface at that point being the shadow price vector $\bar{p}$. The tangent hyperplane at *R* gives the government's trading possibilities. The economy is actually producing at the point *A*, with price vector p_1 (again normal to the surface at that point). The vector *OA* is the output (input) vector y_1. Similarly for the point $B(y_2, p_2)$.

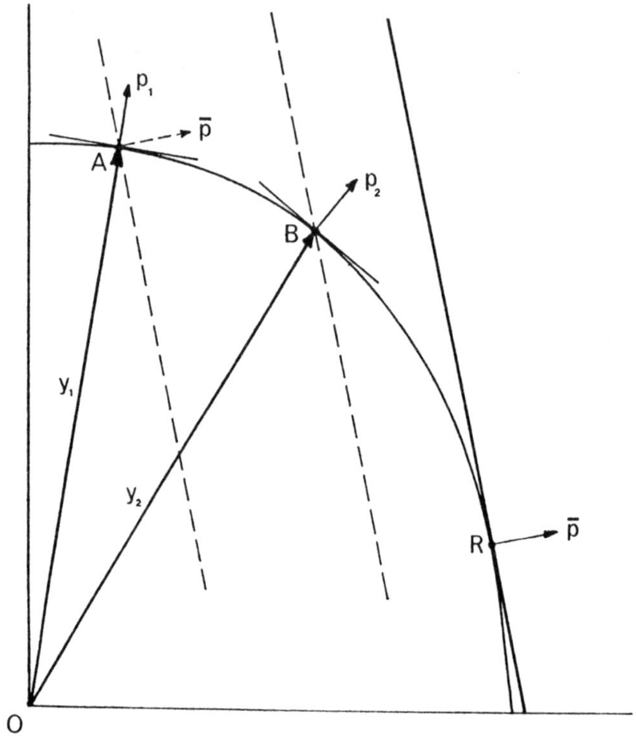

FIGURE 1

Figure 2 is a schematic vector diagram from which the meaning of the adjustment rule and Theorem 1 can be more clearly read. We start from vectors $y_1(OA)$, $p_1(AC)$ and $\bar{p}$ (*AD*) in general *n*-dimensional space. The output increment vector (y_2-y_1) is given by *AB*. For any two price vectors p_1 and p_2 and the corresponding vector (y_2-y_1), the orthogonal hyperplane (*AF*) through the point *A* must leave p_2 in the same halfspace as y_2-y_1 while p_1 must be in the other half space. This is the meaning of inequalities (3) and (4) respectively, when interpreted in terms of the angles between the respective vectors.[1]

[1] The angle between two vectors *a* and *b* being θ, we have $\cos\theta = \frac{a.b}{|a|.|b|}$. Alternatively we can say that the projection of p_2 on (y_2-y_1) is positive ($\theta<90°$, $\cos\theta>0$) that of p_1 is negative ($\theta>90°$, $\cos\theta<0$).

Next, the vectors p_1 and $\bar{p}$ generate a convex cone (vertex A, the two extreme half lines along the directions of p_1 and $\bar{p}$). Our adjustment rule (1) or (2) for choice of p_2 means: " Choose *any* price vector p_2 inside that convex cone." What Theorem 1 says is: " Such a choice of p_2 will generate an output increment vector $AB(y_2-y_1)$ on which the projection of $AD(\bar{p})$ must be positive $(\bar{p}.(y_2-y_1)>0)$, i.e. the angle between the latter two vectors must be less than 90°."

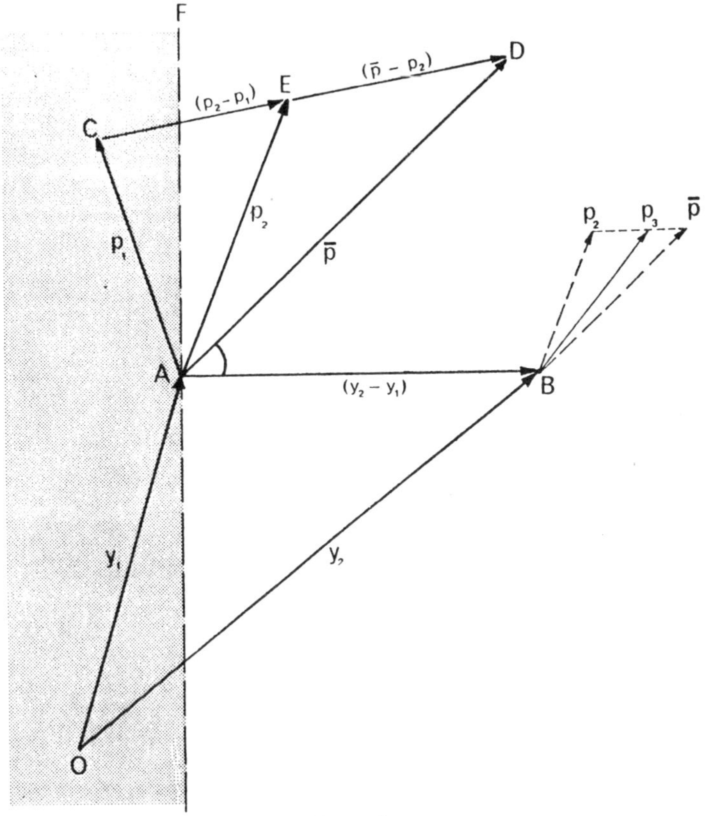

FIGURE 2

Note that the way the adjustment rule works p_2 must lie in the same hyperplane as p_1 and $\bar{p}$ (but not necessarily with (y_2-y_1)) and is a convex combination thereof. However, since we only care about *relative* prices any constant (or normalization) multiple of p_1 or $\bar{p}$ will do and therefore any point E that cuts the distance (CD) between such direction vectors will do too. This latter geometric construction plus the previously stated rule about the location of AC and AE with respect to the hyperplane AF suffice to ensure the required result.[1] The next adjustment stage can now be started from point B, by drawing the vectors p_2 and $\bar{p}$ from that point and choosing a new price vector p_3 as before.

[1] Note that the proof in the text involves showing that the projections of both $AE(p_2)$ and $ED(p-\bar{p}_2)$ on AB are positive. In terms of Figure 1 what is involved is showing that as we move from A to B the trading hyperplane gets closer to R.

This geometric illustration should also help to convince one that although the adjustment rule chosen is a sufficient condition to ensure the required result, it is by no means necessary. There may be many other constellations that will satisfy (3) and (4) and give an "acceptable" angle between *AD* and *AB* without the specific convex construction of *AE*.

[8]

A MORE GENERAL THEORY OF PRICE DISTORTIONS IN OPEN ECONOMIES*

P. J. LLOYD

Research School of Pacific Studies, Australian National University, Canberra, A.C.T., Australia

1. Introduction

A standard welfare problem that has been considered is to maximise a social utility function $U = U(C_0, \ldots, C_n)$ with the aggregate consumption of the final consumable commodities as its arguments, subject to a transformation surface or production set and, in an open economy, the balance of payments requirement that total import payments not exceed total export receipts. The first-order conditions of this constrained maximisation are familiar. For tradable final consumable commodities, the marginal rates of substitution in consumption, transformation in domestic production and transformation through international trade must be equal to each other, for all pairs of commodities. Welfare losses are incurred whenever market prices diverge from the shadow price duals of this Pareto-optimal situation which they may do for several reasons.

The problems of piecemeal policy-making considered here are a particular kind of second-best optimisation and policy determination in which the sub-Pareto-optimal situations come about from additional constraints on relative prices. It is assumed there are unremovable taxes–subsidies[1] or monopolies which distort the relative prices of a subset of commodities while the relative prices of at least some of the remaining commodities are adjustable. In particular, there is a set of commodities, A_1, whose prices to consumers (p_i) are distorted away from the relative prices in world markets ($\bar{p}_i^*$),

$$p_i = \bar{p}_i^*(1+r_i), \qquad r_i = \bar{r}_i \neq 0 \text{ for } i \in A_1. \tag{1}$$

*I am indebted to Jeff Fishburn, Murray Kemp, Ted Sieper, Sundrum, Stephen Turnovsky and an unknown referee for valuable comments on an earlier draft.

[1]Domestic political and international commitments commonly rule out changes to some taxes–subsidies. Some tax–subsidy instruments are not adjustable simultaneously because different Government authorities are responsible by law for different instruments and they act independently of each other; for example, a Treasury may adjust commodity taxes while an independent tariff fixing authority adjusts tariffs periodically.

Instruments may also be alterable within limits but not removable. This kind of alteration is the basis of the conditions that are sufficient for a welfare increase.

There is a set of commodities, A_2, whose prices to producers (q_i) are distorted away from the relative prices on world markets,

$$q_i = \bar{p}_i^*(1+s_i), \qquad s_i = \bar{s}_i \neq 0 \text{ for } i \in A_2. \tag{2}$$

Bars denote distortions which are not alterable. We shall, following convention, assume that the degree of distortion for each commodity whose relative price is distorted is constant in ad valorem terms, except when considering reductions in all or some of the distortions themselves. These distortions may be due simply to taxes–subsidies on consumption or production or imports or exports, or to net combinations of these. In international trade models in which the domestically-produced and imported commodities are assumed to be perfect substitutes for each other and there are no quantitative constraints, there can be no domestic monopolies. However, the problems of unremovable monopolies and/or commodity taxes in a closed economy will emerge as a special case.

The term 'price distortions' has been adopted as a short hand to distinguish this area of policy-making and propositions from closely related areas of 'non-price distortions' which arise because of different additional constraints on variables other than the prices. One such area is the problem in public finance which arises because of the necessity to raise a total revenue through some levels of distortionary commodity taxes (to be decided) in order to pay for the provision of goods by the public sector [see Little (1951), Meade (1955, pp. 112–118), Diamond and Mirrlees (1971a, b), Dixit (1970), Lerner (1970) and Stiglitz and Dasgupta (1971)]. A second related area of discussion is the long search for optimal taxes to pay for losses of producers in industries subject to increasing returns to scale who sell their commodities at marginal cost [see Baumol and Bradford (1970) and references therein]. A third related divergence from Pareto-optimality arises when there are assumed to be non-economic objectives in the form of direct constraints on the *quantities* of goods produced, consumed or traded [see Bhagwati (1971) and references therein].[2] Finally, externalities in production or consumption and the terms-of-trade effects of trade restrictions may also provide market failures. All of the policy-making questions discussed here could be paralleled in each of the areas of 'non-price distortions'.

Three aspects of policy-making in the presence of unremovable price distortions are considered. (a) The sets of adjustable taxes–subsidies which are

[2]Relating this area to the theory of price distortions, Bhagwati (1971) noted the symmetry of the ranking of instruments between the situations with price distortions and the situations with additional constraints on corresponding production, consumption or trade. Ohyama (1972, pp. 56–58) and Lloyd (1973) proved the optimality of policies subject to constraints on the volume or value of production, consumption or trade of certain commodities carries over to a model with price distortions elsewhere in the economy.

implied by the first-order conditions of the constrained maximum are derived and some propositions concerning them are developed (section 2). An alternative interpretation of these results is given in terms of the Hicks–Allen (1934) concept of complementarity or substitutability, from the sign of the first partial derivatives of the inverse price functions. (b) The effects on welfare of preselected changes in the adjustable taxes–subsidies such as a uniform reduction in all distortions or a reduction of extreme distortions (section 3). (c) The ranking of alternative instruments for commodities whose relative prices are adjustable (section 4). We shall see that propositions for each of these three aspects of social welfare are related.[3]

2. Second-best rules

Formally the basic welfare problem is to maximise the social utility function

$$U = U(C_0, \ldots, C_n) \tag{3}$$

subject to

$$F(X_0, \ldots, X_n) = 0, \tag{4}$$

$$C_i = X_i + Z_i, \qquad i = 0, \ldots, n \tag{5}$$

$$\sum_i \bar{p}_i^* Z_i = 0, \tag{6}$$

[3]Elements of a general theory of price distortions have been emerging for several years. The first substantial attack on the theory of these problems was made by Meade (1955, ch. VII and Mathematical Supplement). Meade assumed the existence of a number of tariffs, domestic taxes–subsidies, monopolies and externalities and then enquired whether changing any one of them would increase or decrease welfare. The later more pragmatic approaches by Foster and Sonnenschein (1970), Bruno (1972) and Bertrand and Vanek (1971), the first two of whom examined the effect on national welfare of an across-the-board or radial reduction in all distortions and the last of whom examined the effects of reducing extreme distortions, are an extension of this method but they were all developed from the assumption of a social utility function rather than by following Meade's cumbersome method of retaining the utilities of individuals in a Bergson-type utility function. Similarly, the problem of whether the formation of a customs union increases the welfare of member countries is an application of this basic method. The literature on this subject is not considered.

Meade (1955, Mathematical Supplement) also made comparisons of pairs of instruments in different situations. Bhagwati and Ramaswami (1963), Bhagwati, Ramaswami and Srinivasan (1969), and Bhagwati (1971) developed independently and extended this approach by obtaining the best instrument and ranking other inferior instruments for several situations, given the social utility function.

The first attempts to devise second-best rules in the theory of price distortions were in the early general equilibrium discussions of monopoly. For the three-commodity model Lipsey and Lancaster (1956) and McManus (1959) derived the rules which Green (1961) extended to the multi-commodity case.

Bhagwati (1971) drew together some propositions concerning the welfare effects of single tax–subsidy changes and the ranking of instruments but he did not discuss any conditions which are sufficient for an increase in welfare and his analysis is severely restricted to only two commodities. The latter restriction does not permit any relations of net complementarity between two commodities.

and such domestic distortions as are given by eqs. (1) and (2). The social utility function is assumed to be continuous and twice differentiable and strictly quasi-concave. The transformation surface in eq. (4) is assumed to be continuous, twice differentiable and strictly concave from below. The assumption of a fixed transformation surface prevents us from examining distortions in relative input prices. Eqs. (5) and (6), respectively, define domestic aggregate consumption (C_i) equal to domestic production (X_i) plus net imports (Z_i) or less net exports, and the budget condition that import payments equal export receipts, both measured in foreign prices ($\bar{p}_i^*$). To isolate the problems due to price distortions we adopt the small country assumption that all prices are fixed on the world market independently of the demands and supplies of the country concerned. Commodity zero is taken as the numeraire commodity and we set $p_0^* = 1$.

Most authors assumed that the social utility function is derived from an individualistic Bergson-type social welfare function which weights the utilities of individual consumers and that an omniscient government makes ideal lump-sum transfers among consumers so as to maximise the social utility of any available set of commodities. With the added assumption of no externalities of consumption, the marginal rates of substitution between any two commodities must be equal among all consumers and equal to the social rate of substitution [see v.d. Graaff (1967, p. 54)]. Since we shall be concerned solely with cases in which the same distortion is assumed to apply to all consumers and lump-sum transfers are feasible, nothing is gained by retaining individual utilities as Meade (1955) originally did. Under analogous assumptions on the supply side we shall consider the aggregate supplies of each commodity rather than the supplies from each producer.[4]

We may consider all three welfare questions by deriving an expression for the change in utility in terms of total differentials which incorporates all of the constraints including the price distortions. This method of total differentials reduces the constrained maximisation to an unconstrained maximisation by successive substitution in the maximand. Differentiating totally eqs. (3)–(6):

$$\mathrm{d}U/U_0 = \mathrm{d}C_0 + \sum_i (U_i/U_0)\,\mathrm{d}C_i, \tag{7}$$

$$\mathrm{d}X_0 = -\sum_i (F_i/F_0)\,\mathrm{d}X_i, \tag{8}$$

$$\mathrm{d}C_i = \mathrm{d}X_i + \mathrm{d}Z_i, \qquad i = 0, \ldots, n \tag{9}$$

$$\mathrm{d}Z_0 = -\sum_i \bar{p}_i^* \mathrm{d}Z_i. \tag{10}$$

U_i and F_i are the first partial derivatives of U and F with respect to C_i and X_i. Unless otherwise indicated the summations are over $i = 1, \ldots, n$. Using

[4]The use of aggregated relations means that we can only consider one of the three sets of first-order conditions that are conventionally considered in welfare economics [see for example, Bator (1957)]; namely, the so-called production-cum-distribution conditions. We cannot in this model consider taxes on commodities which differentiate among individual consumers or producers, though the methods may be extended to these distortions.

eq. (9) for $i = 0$ and substituting eqs. (8) and (10) in (7) yields

$$\mathrm{d}U/U_0 = \sum_i (\bar{p}_i^* - F_i/F_0)\,\mathrm{d}X_i + (U_i/U_0 - \bar{p}_i^*)\,\mathrm{d}C_i. \qquad (11)$$

This form incorporates the constraint of the transformation surface and trading possibilities but no distortions. The control variables here are the amounts of all commodities produced and consumed. We assume that a unique interior solution exists in all distortion and distortion-free situations.[5]

The necessary (and sufficient) first-order conditions for Pareto-optimality are obtained by setting the coefficients of the total differentials equal to zero,

$$U_i/U_0 = F_i/F_0 = \bar{p}_i^*, \qquad i = 1, \ldots, n. \qquad (12)$$

Eq. (12) states the familiar conditions that the marginal rates of substitution in consumption, transformation in domestic production and transformation through international trade be equal to each other, for all pairs of commodities.

Under the assumptions that consumers maximise utility and producers maximise profits and zero externalities, we have, respectively,

$$p_i = U_i/U_0, \qquad i = 1, \ldots, n, \qquad (13)$$

and

$$q_i = F_i/F_0, \qquad i = 1, \ldots, n. \qquad (14)$$

It is assumed that $p_0 = q_0 = 1$. With no price distortion or other additional constraints perfectly competitive behaviour realises Pareto-optimality.

The price distortions of eqs. (1) and (2) violate the two sets of conditions for Pareto-optimality in eq. (12) given competitive behaviour. It should be noted that the price distortions in eqs. (1) and (2) are derived from two assumptions; the assumption that there is some unremovable distortion in the price of commodity i and the assumption, implied by setting the price of the numeraire commodity equal to unity, that no offsetting tax–subsidy can be imposed on commodity zero. The second assumption and the choice of numeraire affect the solution of each problem.[6] This gives the following not-quite-trivial proposition.

Proposition 1. If there are unalterable taxes–subsidies of a particular kind or monopolies on a set of commodities, but the relative prices of these commodities may be varied by imposing other taxes–subsidies on the same commodities, the distortions of the prices of these commodities may be eliminated.

[5] Vanek (1965), Bhagwati (1968), and Foster and Sonnenschein (1970) established that multiple equilibria may arise with a given set of distortions if there are inferior goods. Foster and Sonnenschein (1970) derive some propositions concerning welfare changes in the presence of alternative equilibria by introducing different adjustment mechanisms. Sontheimer (1971) derives a very general set of conditions, including convexity of consumer preferences and the production possibility set, which are sufficient to prove the existence of a competitive equilibrium in the presence of tax–subsidy distortions.

[6] McManus (1959, pp. 210–211) criticised the original treatment of monopoly and related problems by Lipsey and Lancaster (1956) for their erroneous interpretation of the numeraire.

This has been well-known since the early controversy concerning proportionality of marginal cost and price when there are unremovable monopolies but commodity taxes may be levied [see, for example, v.d. Graaff (1967, ch. X)]. In this case Pareto-optimality may be restored by granting subsidies at the rate $e_i/1+e_i$ on the consumption of the commodities whose production is monopolised, where e_i are the Lerner degrees of monopoly. Another illustration is the use of uniform import tariffs and export duties to offset a fixed overvalued exchange rate. In fact, positive non-distortionary taxes–subsidies are required for the implied lump-sum transfers of the second-best.

With price distortions, substituting from eqs. (1)–(2) and (13)–(14) into (11) yields

$$\mathrm{d}U/U_0 = \sum_i \bar{p}_i^* s_i \,\mathrm{d}X_i + \sum_i \bar{p}_i^* r_i \,\mathrm{d}C_i. \tag{15}$$

In the presence of constraints on relative prices the solution is obtained most directly by setting up the relative prices as the control variables. Commodity demand functions with relative price arguments are obtained by maximising social utility for a given expenditure. Since these functions are homogeneous of degree zero we have, choosing commodity zero as the numeraire,

$$C_i = \psi_i(p_1, \ldots, p_n; y), \qquad i = 0, \ldots, n, \tag{16}$$

where $y = C_0 + \sum_i p_i C_i$ is real income in terms of the numeraire commodity.

From eqs. (14) and (4) we obtain the general equilibrium supply functions

$$X_i = X_i(q_1, \ldots, q_n), \qquad i = 0, \ldots, n. \tag{17}$$

Differentiating (16) and (17) and substituting in (15) yields

$$1/U_0 \,\mathrm{d}U = \sum_j \bar{p}_i^* r_i \Big(\sum_j \partial\psi_i/\partial p_j \,\mathrm{d}p_j + \partial C_i/\partial y \,\mathrm{d}y\Big)$$

$$- \sum_i \bar{p}_i^* s_i \sum_i \partial X_i/\partial q_j \,\mathrm{d}q_j.$$

Since

$$\mathrm{d}y = \Big(\mathrm{d}C_0 + \sum_i p_i \,\mathrm{d}C_i\Big) + \sum C_i \,\mathrm{d}p_i,$$

and in view of eq. (7), we have

$$m \,\mathrm{d}U = \sum_i \bar{p}_i^* r_i \sum_j \partial C_i/\partial p_j \,\mathrm{d}p_j - \sum_i \bar{p}_i^* s_i \sum_j \partial X_i/\partial q_j \,\mathrm{d}q_j, \tag{18}$$

where

$$\partial C_i/\partial p_j = \partial\psi_i/\partial p_j + C_j \partial C_i/\partial Y$$

is the income-compensated price change, and

$$m = 1/U_0\Big(1 - \sum_i \bar{p}_i^* r_i \partial C_i/\partial y\Big)$$

is the marginal propensity to consume all commodities evaluated at world prices. The latter follows because

$$1/U_0 = p_0/U_0 = \lambda = \partial Y/\partial U,$$

where λ is the Lagrange multiplier in the consumers' problem of minimising expenditure (Y) for $U = \bar{U}$. Hence,

$$\begin{aligned} m &= \partial Y/\partial U - \sum_i \bar{p}_i^* r_i \partial C_i/\partial U \\ &= \sum_i \bar{p}_i^*(1+r_i)\partial C_i/\partial U + \partial C_0/\partial U - \sum_i \bar{p}_i^* r_i \partial C_i/\partial U \\ &= \sum_i \bar{p}_i^* \partial C_i/\partial U + \partial C_0/\partial U. \end{aligned} \tag{19}$$

Eq. (18) is the basic equation that may be used to examine different welfare questions by choosing the appropriate relative prices to adjust.

The question we consider in this section is the second-best level of all adjustable taxes–subsidies, given that there is a subset of some non-zero unalterable distortions. With fixed international prices, variations in domestic prices to consumers or producers now reflect solely variations in taxes–subsidies on domestic consumption and/or production. In eq. (18) setting the coefficients of the total differentials for those prices which are variable equal to zero yields the two systems of equations

$$\begin{aligned} &\sum_i \bar{p}_i^* r_i \partial C_i/\partial p_j = 0, \qquad j \notin (A_1 \cup B_1), \\ &\sum_i \bar{p}_i^* s_i \partial X_i/\partial q_j = 0, \qquad j \notin (A_2 \cup B_2). \end{aligned} \tag{20}$$

B_1 and B_2 are, respectively, the sets of commodities whose consumer and producer prices are not distorted but because of domestic or international commitments cannot be varied by imposing consumer or producer taxes–subsidies. Transferring the terms involving fixed distortions to the right-hand side of each equation and applying Cramer's Rule, the system of equations yields the desired solution values for the taxes–subsidies on consumption and production, respectively,[7]

$$r_v = -\sum_j \Big(\sum_{i \in A_1} \bar{p}_i^* \bar{r}_i \partial C_i/\partial p_j \Big) D_{jv}/D, \qquad j \notin (A_1 \cup B_1), \tag{21}$$

where D is the determinant of the square matrix $[p_i^* \partial C_i/\partial p_j]$ and D_{jv} is the cofactor of the element $(p_v^* \partial C_v/\partial p_j)$, and

$$s_w = -\sum_j \Big(\sum_{i \in A_2} \bar{p}_i^* \bar{s}_i \partial X_i/\partial q_j \Big) E_{jw}/E, \qquad j \notin (A_2 \cup B_2), \tag{22}$$

where E is the determinant of the square matrix $[p_i^* \partial X_i/\partial q_j]$ and E_{jw} is the

[7]I am indebted to a referee for pointing out that Kolm (1971) has obtained a more general set of first-order conditions for constrained maximisation which includes this set in the presence of price distortions as a special case.

cofactor of the element $(p_w^* \partial X_w / \partial q_j)$.

This general formulation covers both the case in which all relative prices, other than those which are subject to non-zero unalterable distortions, are variable and the case in which the instrument set is further restricted because some of the tax–subsidy instruments on commodities not subject to non-zero distortions are assumed to be not variable, that is, committed at zero level. In the former case the sets B_1 and B_2 in eqs. (21) and (22) are empty. In the latter case the fixing of some taxes–subsidies at zero does impose a cost as the economy forgoes the opportunity of varying them to offset the harm of the distortions. Cases in which taxes–subsidies on production (consumption) of a set of commodities are constrained to be equal or otherwise fixed in relation to each other, may be handled by treating these commodities as a composite commodity in production (consumption) because of fixed world prices. Finally if tariffs–import subsidies are the only available instrument to compensate for distortions we set $\mathrm{d}p_i = \mathrm{d}q_i$ for these commodities.

While this rule and later rules are stated in terms of the determination of the levels of explicit taxes–subsidies they also provide shadow prices that a Government should use for commodity prices in cost–benefit analyses which evaluate Government projects and direct Government purchases in a distortion-ridden economy.

It is customary to define a pair of commodities as being substitutes or complements for each other in consumption according as the partial derivatives of the income-compensated commodity demand functions in eq. (16),

$$\partial C_i / \partial p_j \gtrless 0.$$

This is the Hicksian definition of net substitutes and complements. In an analogous way we define a pair of commodities as substitutes or complements for each other in production according as the partial derivatives of the general equilibrium supply function in eq. (17),

$$\partial X_i / \partial q_j \lesseqgtr 0.$$

Using this terminology the second-best tax–subsidy set given by eqs. (21) and (22) will in general depend on the relations of substitutability and complementarity between all commodities and those whose prices are adjustable, taken in pairs, and on the unalterable distortions. In fact, each adjustable consumption or production tax–subsidy may be written as a weighted average of the unalterable consumption or production distortions,

$$r_v = \sum_{i \in A_1} \bar{r}_i w_i, \qquad s_w = \sum_{i \in A_2} \bar{s}_i z_i, \tag{23}$$

where the weights are

$$w_i = -\sum_j (\bar{p}_i^* \partial C_i / \partial p_j) D_{jv} / D, \qquad z_i = -\sum_j (\bar{p}_i^* \partial X_i / \partial q_j) E_{jw} / E.$$

One feature of the second-best tax–subsidy set emerges immediately from eqs. (21) and (22).

Proposition 2. If commodities are traded internationally at fixed prices, there is a second-best set of taxes–subsidies on consumption which depend only on the distortions of prices to consumers and the relations of Hicksian complementarity and substitutability in consumption between all pairs of commodities, and a second-best set of taxes–subsidies on production which depend only on the distortions of prices to producers and the relations of complementarity and substitutability in production between all pairs of commodities.

Thus the corrective taxes–subsidies on production and consumption are entirely separated. Utility maximisation is a two-layer optimisation because of the assumptions that inputs do not enter the utility function and final commodities do not enter production functions. The first layer is the maximisation of the value of national output which puts the economy somewhere on the highest budget surface. The second layer is the maximisation of utility given the value of national output.

One result of the separation of stages is that this consumption tax–subsidy problem with international trade at fixed prices is identical to the general equilibrium problem of monopoly which was considered by Lipsey and Lancaster (1956), McManus (1959) and Green (1961). They assumed there is no international trade and a linear transformation surface. With constant Lerner degrees of monopoly, creating the divergence between the marginal cost ratios and relative prices, this implies that the relative producer prices of all commodities cannot vary. The resulting second-best tax–subsidy set, obtained by Green (1961, p. 73) in a slightly different way, is then given by the eq. (21) alone. Thus the special feature of this sub-model is that the optimal tax–subsidy set depends only on the relations of complementarity and substitutability in consumption.[8]

Although the general expressions giving the optimal levels of taxes–subsidies in eqs. (21) and (22) are rather complex, useful propositions emerge when we consider restrictions on the form of the utility or transformation functions.

Proposition 3. If all pairs of commodities are Hicksian substitutes in consumption (or production) for each other, the taxes or subsidies on consumption (or production) on all commodities which are adjustable must lie between the largest and the smallest of the values of the unalterable distortions of consumer (or producer) prices.

[8]An alternative second-best set of taxes–subsidies on production in this case is given by eq. (22). The assumption of a fixed distortion is less satisfactory for the analysis of monopolies than it is for unremovable taxes–subsidies. Profit-maximising behaviour by a monopolist in a general equilibrium model implies a variable degree of monopoly; see Negishi (1961–62).

This theorem was proven by Green (1961, pp. 73–74) for consumption taxes–subsidies in the monopoly case, by proving the weights w_i in eq. (23) are positive and sum to unity, but it applies equally to production taxes–subsidies in this model.

Other propositions that follow from the restrictions on the utility or transformation function are derived later in this section.

The rules for the second-best sets of instrument values can be stated more simply through the use of the inverse price functions. Consider first the consumption taxes–subsidies. The partial derivatives in eq. (21), $\partial C_i/\partial p_j$, are the derivatives of the income-compensated commodity demand functions,

$$C_i = C_i(p_1, \ldots, p_n; U), \qquad i = 0, \ldots n. \tag{24}$$

Inverting the last n equations of these equations we obtain n price functions,

$$p_i = p_i(C_1, \ldots, C_n; U), \qquad i = 1, \ldots, n. \tag{25}$$

A sufficient condition for the inversion of the commodity demand functions is that the Jacobian does not vanish. Later we wish to invert the functions while holding some subset of prices constant. A sufficient condition for these inversions is that the principal minors of the Jacobian not vanish. This condition is satisfied under the assumed 'stability conditions' of consumer equilibrium, that is, by the strict quasi-concavity of U. Since C_i and p_i are inverse functions, their respective Jacobians are inverse matrices

$$[\partial C_i/\partial p_j] = [\partial p_j/\partial C_i]^{-1}, \qquad i, j = 1, \ldots, n. \tag{26}$$

Eq. (21) can be rewritten, by reversing the order of summation, as

$$\begin{aligned} r_v &= -\sum_{i \in A_1} \bar{p}_i^* \bar{r}_i (\sum_j \partial C_i/\partial p_j D_{jv}/D), \qquad j \notin (A_1 \cup B_1), \\ &= -\sum_{i \in A_1} \bar{p}_i^* \bar{r}_i (\sum_j \partial C_i/\partial p_j K_{jv}/K p_v^*), \end{aligned}$$

where K is the determinant of the $k \times k$ sub-matrix of Slutsky terms $(\partial C_i/\partial p_j)$ and K_{jv} is the cofactor of the element $\partial C_v/\partial p_j$ of this matrix. Using eq. (26),

$$r_v = -\sum_{i \in A_1} \bar{p}_i^* \bar{r}_i (\sum_j \partial C_i/\partial p_j \cdot \partial p_j/\partial C_v)/p_v^*, \quad j \notin (A_1 \cup B_1).$$

Noting that from eq. (26),

$$\sum_j \partial C_i/\partial p_j \partial p_j/\partial C_v = 0, \qquad i \neq v, \tag{27}$$

and that $\bar{p}_i^* r_i = 0$ for $i \in B_1$ and rewriting the summations we now have

$$\begin{aligned} r_v &= [\sum_{i \in A_1} (\sum_{j \in A_1} \bar{p}_j^* \bar{r}_j \partial C_j/\partial p_i) \partial p_i/\partial C_v]/p_v^* \\ &= [\sum_{i \in A_1} \delta_i \partial p_i/\partial C_v]/p_v^*. \end{aligned} \tag{28}$$

The analogous expression for the second-best set of production taxes–subsidies is

$$s_w = [\sum_{i \in A_2} \phi_i \partial q_i / \partial X_w] / p_w^*. \tag{29}$$

It can be seen from eq. (18) that $\delta_i = m\partial U/\partial p_i$ and $\phi_i = m\partial U/\partial q_i$. These are the Lagrange multipliers associated with the constraints on the relative consumer and producer prices, respectively, of commodity i in the direct constrained maximisation of U.[9] Thus each expression for the second-best consumption or production tax–subsidy is a simple sum of terms involving the derivatives of the inverse price functions.

The interpretation of eqs. (28) and (29) requires the Hicks–Allen (1934) definition of substitutes and complements.[10] They defined a pair of commodities, i and j, to be substitutes or complements for each other in consumption according as the derivative of the utility surface,

$$\partial(U_j/U_0)/\partial C_i = \partial p_j/\partial C_i \lesseqgtr 0. \tag{30}$$

Analogously, a pair of commodities i and j may be said to be substitutes or complements for each other in production according as the derivative of the transformation surface,

$$\partial(F_j/F_0)/\partial X_i = \partial q_j/\partial X_i \gtreqless 0. \tag{31}$$

The relationship between the Hicksian definition and the Hicks–Allen definition of substitutes and complements in consumption (or production) for a pair of commodities can be obtained by identifying elements on the right-hand and left-hand side of eq. (26) (or the analogous expression in terms of q_i). The relationship is in general complex. As with the Hicksian definition, the definition in terms of elements of inverse price functions is symmetric, but with

[9]These expressions for the second-best tax–subsidy set can be obtained directly by using the Lagrangian function with an indirect utility and an indirect transformation function [Lloyd (1973)]. However, the total differential method has the advantage that it can also be used to evaluate pre-determined or alternative instrument changes.

In their original formulation of the second-best theory, Lipsey and Lancaster (1956, pp. 28–31) did explore the relationships between the signs of the terms $\partial(U_i/U_0)/\partial C_j$ and the Edgeworth–Pareto definition of substitutes and complements in terms of the signs of the second derivatives of the utility function (U_{ij}) and the nature of the sub-optimal tax–subsidy set. The interpretation in the text follows from setting $U_i/U_0 = p_i$ and identifying these terms as the partial derivatives of the inverse price functions.

[10]The concept has been the subject of considerable confusion. Hicks and Allen (1934) and Hicks in the text of 'Value and Capital' (1939, p. 44) actually defined substitutes and complements in the theory on consumption in terms of $\partial(U_j/U_0)/\partial C_i$ for the case of three commodities with Hicks' money as the numeraire commodity. However, in his Appendix, Hicks (1939, p. 311) gives the 'Hicksian' definition in terms of the signs of the elements of the Slutsky matrix. These two definitions are now known not to be equivalent when $n > 3$ [for example, Samuelson (1950, p. 379, n.)].

The definition used in the text in terms of $\partial p_j/\partial C_i$ is equivalent to the Hicks–Allen definition [see Morishima (1955–56) for a formal proof].

$n > 3$ it is possible for two commodities to be substitutes in the Hicksian sense and complements in the Hicks–Allen sense. One convenient relationship can be readily established. If all pairs of commodities are net substitutes in the Hicksian sense then all pairs of commodities are net substitutes in the Hicks–Allen sense. These properties follow from the theorem of Mosak (1944) that if we have a Hicks matrix whose principal minors alternate in sign and if the off-diagonal elements are all positive, the inverse matrix is composed solely of negative elements.

The economic interpretation of the second-best rules in terms of the Hicks–Allen concept of substitutes and complements helps to explain the meaning of the more complex determinantal expressions. It is remarkable that almost all of the authors who have obtained determinantal expressions for optimal tax–subsidies whose elements are the partial derivatives of the income-compensated demand functions, have not attempted to explain the economic meaning of their results.[11] The reason may be found by considering an example such as the case of a good the consumption of which is reduced below the Pareto-optimal level because it is subject to an unalterable consumption tax. Welfare may be increased if we partially offset this distortion by taxing the substitutes of this commodity and subsidising its complements in the Hicksian sense. But this is not sufficient. Welfare may be further increased by taxing the complements of substitutes and subsidising the complements of complements and so on, taking account of the effects of each alterable instrument on the commodities whose prices are distorted. It is all these Hicksian relationships among commodities which are contained neatly in the Hicks–Allen concepts of substitutes and complements. Algebraically in this case the term of the constraint $(1+\bar{r}_i) > 1$ and $\delta_i < 0$; that is, social utility would be increased by a decrease in the relative price of the commodity. Failing a change in the distortion, utility will be increased by taxes on this commodity's Hicks–Allen substitutes and subsidies on its complements. If the price of a commodity is constrained below the free trade relative price, viz., $(1+\bar{r}_i) < 1$, the rule is reversed; the complements should be taxed and the substitutes subsidised.

In eq. (28) the summation terms average the relations of substitutability and complementarity between each commodity whose relative price is alterable and those whose relative prices are unalterable. The values of the Lagrange multiplier weights used in the averaging, δ_i, will depend on the extent of the distortion and the utility function. The production taxes–subsidies which are called for because of unalterable taxes–subsidies on the production of other commodities can be interpreted in the same way, after noting that lowering the relative price of a commodity to producers reduces domestic production.

With the Hicks–Allen definitions we can give an alternative economic interpretation of Proposition 2.

[11] A few have given explanations for the simpler cases of models with two or three commodities; for example, Green (1961, pp. 71–73) and Dornsbusch (1971).

Proposition 4. If commodities are traded internationally at fixed prices the second-best calls for (a) taxes on the consumption of those commodities which are Hicks–Allen complements (substitutes) for those commodities whose relative prices to consumers are constrained below (above) the free trade relative prices in the sense that $\sum \delta_i \partial p_i / \partial C_v > 0$, *and (b) taxes on the production of those commodities which are Hicks–Allen substitutes (complements) for those commodities whose relative prices are constrained below (above) the free trade relative prices to producers in the sense that* $\sum \phi_i \partial q_i / \partial X_w > 0$.

The use of inverse price functions in eqs. (28) and (29) leads to another proposition.

Proposition 5. (a) If the utility surface is separable into two or more subsets of variables, one of which contains all commodities whose prices to consumers are unalterably distorted, the optimal tax–subsidy on the consumption of any commodity which is not in this set and whose price is variable, is zero. (b) If the transformation surface is separable into two or more subsets of variables, one of which contains all commodities whose prices to producers are unalterably distorted, the optimal tax–subsidy on the production of any commodity which is not in this set and whose price is variable, is zero.

This proposition was stated by Lloyd (1973).[12] A function $f(x_i, \ldots, x_s)$ is said here to be separable with respect to two sets of variables, $(x_1, \ldots, x_h)$ and $(x_{h+1}, \ldots, x_s)$, if

$$\partial\left(\frac{\partial f / \partial x_i}{\partial f / \partial x_j}\right) / \partial x_k = 0, \tag{32}$$

where i and j, but not k, belong to the same set and movement is constrained to a level surface of the function. Alternatively, the function is separable if the partial derivatives of the inverse compensated price functions of the commodities subject to unalterable distortions with respect to commodities in the other group are zero. Hence, the second-best does not call for corrective taxes–subsidies on commodities whose prices are variable but which are separable in production or consumption from the commodities whose prices are unalterably distorted.

3. Welfare effects of pre-selected changes

Propositions concerning the effects on welfare of arbitrary changes in the values of unconstrained instruments can easily be obtained.

[12]The importance of separability in second-best theory was first noted by Davis and Whinston (1965). However, they assumed the strongest form of separability, namely, additivity, and did not constrain movements to the level surface of a function. The definition in the text may not be invariant with respect to the choice of numeraire. It is an application of Leontief's concept at 'functional' (or weak) separability [Leontief (1947)] to a case where $f(x)$ is a surface.

Consider that changes can be made only to taxes–subsidies on consumption; that is, under the assumption that all international prices are fixed, the relative prices of all commodities to producers are fixed. If variation in only one consumption tax–subsidy is considered, the effect on welfare is, from eq. (18),

$$m\,\mathrm{d}U = [\sum_i \bar{p}_i^* r_i \partial C_i/\partial p_v]\,\mathrm{d}p_v.$$

By analogy, a change in only one tax–subsidy on production has the following effect on welfare,

$$m\,\mathrm{d}U = [\sum_i \bar{p}_i^* s_i \partial X_i/\partial q_v]\,\mathrm{d}q_v.$$

Differentiating eqs. (1) and (2) and substituting

$$m\,\mathrm{d}U = [\sum_i (\bar{p}_i^* r_i)\partial C_i/\partial p_v]\bar{p}_v^*\,\mathrm{d}r_v,$$

and (33)

$$m\,\mathrm{d}U = [\sum_i (\bar{p}_i^* s_i)\partial X_i/\partial q_v]\bar{p}_v^*\,\mathrm{d}s_v.$$

The necessary and sufficient condition for a welfare improvement by a single tax–subsidy change is that the relevant square bracketed terms be positive (negative) for a tax increase (decrease). These terms represent weighted average relationships of substitutability or complementarity with the weights being the specific values of the taxes–subsidies. Thus welfare is increased if a (small) consumption tax is imposed on a commodity which is on average in this sense a Hicksian substitute in consumption for all commodities whose consumer prices are distorted upwards ($\bar{r}_i > 0$). The sign of the tax change is reversed if the prices are distorted downwards by means of subsidies ($\bar{r}_i < 0$), or the commodity is a complement for the commodities whose prices are distorted.

It is convenient now to write eq. (33) in another form[13]

$$m\,\mathrm{d}U = [\bar{p}_v^* r_v \partial C_v/\partial p_v + \sum_{i \neq v} \bar{p}_i^* \bar{r}_i \partial C_i/\partial p_v]\bar{p}_v^*\,\mathrm{d}r_v$$

$$= [\sum_{i \neq v} \bar{p}_i^*(\bar{r}_i - r_v)\partial C_i/\partial p_v]p_v^*\,\mathrm{d}r_v/(1+r_v),$$

and (34)

$$m\,\mathrm{d}U = -[\sum_{i \neq v} \bar{p}_i^*(\bar{s}_i - s_v)\partial X_i/\partial q_v]\bar{p}_v^*\,\mathrm{d}s_v/(1+s_v).$$

The most important application of these equations is the following proposition concerning extreme distortions. A distortion of consumer prices, for example, is the extreme if $|r_v| > |r_i|$ for all i other than v. A reduction in this distortion requires $\mathrm{d}r_v \lesseqgtr 0$ as $r_v \gtreqless 0$.

[13]This utilises the well-known relation among Slutsky terms

$$\sum_i p_i \partial C_i/\partial p_v + \partial C_0/\partial p_v = 0.$$

Note that $r_0 = 0$.

Proposition 6. If all pairs of commodities are Hicksian substitutes in consumption (or production) and the aggregate marginal propensity to consume evaluated at world prices is positive, a sufficient condition for an increase in welfare is that the single most extreme distortion of consumer (or producer) prices be reduced.

Proposition 6 was hinted at by Meade (1955, pp. 103–104) and proven by Lipsey and Lancaster (1956, p. 25) for the case of a change in relative consumer prices due to taxes–subsidies with a Cobb–Douglas utility function which has the sufficient properties that all commodities are net substitutes and all goods are superior. Vanek (1964) proved a related proposition for trade liberalisation in a multi-country world. All of these authors considered only positive distortions due to monopoly or tariffs but one can see by inspection of eq. (34) that the proposition can be generalised to include negative distortions. However, as noted by Meade (1955, p. 103, n. 1), welfare is not necessarily increased under the same circumstances if the distortion is reduced to zero. This result is implied by Proposition 3.

Alternatively, Proposition 6 provides a generalisation of the proposition, noted by Bhagwati (1971, p. 84) and Foster and Sonnenschein (1970, p. 284) for a model with only two commodities, that if there is only one distortion in an economy a reduction in this distortion by any amount necessarily increases welfare.[14] Both Proposition 6 above and Bhagwati's proposition include as a special case the propositions of Kemp (1962) that restricted trade is superior to no trade and that a lower tariff is superior to a higher tariff, provided as Bhagwati (1968) noted and is evident from Proposition 6 there are no other distortions due to consumption or production taxes–subsidies, and no commodity is inferior (and hence there is no possibility of multiple equilibria).[15] An interesting case arises with international trade when we consider the effect of changing a tariff which distorts prices to both consumers and producers. From eq. (18), in this case

$$m\,\mathrm{d}U = [\sum_{i \neq v} \bar{p}_i^*(\bar{r}_v - r_v)\partial C_i/\partial p_v - \sum_{i \neq v} \bar{p}_i^*(\bar{s}_i - s_v)\partial X_i/\partial q_v]\bar{p}_i^*\mathrm{d}\tau_v/(1+\tau_v). \tag{35}$$

If the prices to both consumers and producers of the commodity subject to the most extreme of all tariffs are the most distorted of all relative prices then a reduction in this tariff must increase welfare (by Proposition 6 a fortiori, provided all commodities are net substitutes in consumption *and* production).

[14]It is apparent, as Bhagwati (1971, p. 86) noted in another proposition, that if one among multiple distortions is reduced, welfare is not necessarily increased. This is a straightforward application of Lipsey and Lancaster's basic theorem of the second-best. However, other propositions developed above indicate that we can make useful generalisations when Pareto-optimality is not attainable.

[15]The assumption of no inferiority plays a dual role. It ensures that the aggregate marginal propensity to consume is positive and it eliminates the possibility of multiple equilibria.

Bertrand and Vanek (1971) proved this result for a version of this model which incorporated tariffs but no other distortions. But if there are taxes–subsidies on production or consumption in addition to the tariffs on the trade of commodities, it is no longer true that a reduction in the most extreme *tariff* will necessarily increase welfare because the prices of some other commodities may be more distorted.

The effect of a simultaneous change in more than one pre-selected instrument is the sum of the effects of each instrument taken singly, some of which are likely to be positive and some negative. Differentiating eqs. (1) and (2) and subsitituting in eq. (18),

$$m\,\mathrm{d}U = \sum_i \bar{p}_i^* r_i [\sum_v \partial C_i/\partial p_v p_v^*\, \mathrm{d}r_v] - \sum_i \bar{p}_i^* s_i [\sum_v \partial X_i/\partial q_v p_v^*\, \mathrm{d}s_v]. \quad (36)$$

Assuming $m > 0$ the change in the set of taxes–subsidies will increase or decrease welfare as the right-hand side of eq. (36) is positive or negative.

Alternatively:

Proposition 7. Any pre-selected set of changes in taxes–subsidies will increase or decrease social utility as that part of the resulting change in total net revenue from all taxes–subsidies which is due to the change in the quantities of goods consumed and produced, is positive or negative.

The two double summations in eq. (36) represent the corresponding changes in total net revenue from taxes–subsidies on production and consumption respectively. Consider the total net revenue-payment from any consumption tax–subsidy. This is

$$T_i = \bar{p}_i^* r_i \psi_i(p_1, \ldots, p_n; y).$$

Hence,

$$\mathrm{d}T_i = \bar{p}_i^* r_i (\sum_j \partial\psi_i/\partial p_j \bar{p}_j^*\, \mathrm{d}r_j + \partial\psi_i/\partial y\, \mathrm{d}y) + \bar{p}_i^* C_i\, \mathrm{d}r_i. \quad (37)$$

Ignoring the last term and summing over all commodities gives the second term of eq. (15) or, multiplying by (m/U_0), the first term of eq. (36). Ohyama (1972, sect. VII) using set theory has also shown how the total net revenue change in this sense can be used to rank any two or more situations with different tax–subsidy regimes; but he does not consider the second-best tax–subsidy problem of sections 1 and 2 above nor the problems of this section, except to show that a uniform reduction in tariffs with no other distortions will improve welfare if the revenue change is positive. While the set theory method can deal readily with discrete changes the quantity changes which determine these revenue changes and the price elasticities which determine the quantity changes reflect the total adjustment simultaneously to all the prices which are varied as a result of the tax–subsidy changes. The determinants of these total elasticities are not revealed.[16] The form of eq. (36) has the advantage of exposing the demand and production determinants of the changes in net revenue and social utility. With caution one may use these expressions as approximations for discrete changes.

The case of uniform reductions in *all distortions* is perhaps the most interesting pre-selected change because, like that of a change in a single extreme distortion, it involves changes in instruments that appeal to common-sense and are easily put into practice. These policies do not require estimates of the degrees of complementarity and substitutability among commodities in production and consumption, as do the second-best taxes–subsidies. If there is an equal percentage reduction in all distortions, $dr_i/r_i = ds_i/s_i = \mu < 0$. The distortions themselves as defined in eqs. (1) and (2) were ad valorem distortions. Thus, we are considering what Foster and Sonnenschein (1970) called 'radial' changes in ad valorem distortions. In this case, eq. (36) becomes

$$\begin{aligned} m\,\mathrm{d}U &= \Big[\sum_{i\in A_1} \bar{p}_i^* r_i \sum_{v\in A_1} \partial C_i/\partial p_v \bar{p}_v^* r_v - \sum_{i\in A_2} \bar{p}_i^* s_i \sum_{v\in A_2} \partial X_i/\partial q_v \bar{p}_v^* s_v\Big]\mu \\ &= \Big[\sum_{i\in A_1}\sum_{v\in A_1} (p_i - \bar{p}_i^*)(p_v - \bar{p}_v^*)\partial C_i/\partial p_v\Big]\mu \\ &\quad - \Big[\sum_{i\in A_2}\sum_{v\in A_2} (q_i - \bar{p}_i^*)(q_v - \bar{q}_v^*)\partial X_i/\partial q_v\Big]\mu < 0. \end{aligned} \tag{38}$$

The first term in brackets is negative because of the strict convexity of the utility surface [Hicks (1939, p. 311)], given the linearity of real incomes in terms of foreign prices and domestic prices, $y = \sum p_i C_i$ and $y^* = \sum \bar{p}_i^* C_i$, which constrain utility maximisation. Similarly, the second term is negative.

Proposition 8. If the aggregate marginal propensity to consume evaluated at world prices is positive a sufficient condition for an increase in welfare is that there be a radial reduction in all distortions.

Moreover, a radial reduction in all production *or* all consumption distortions is sufficient because of the two-stage maximisation in this model. Earlier Foster and Sonnenschein (1970) had proved the same result for the more restricted case of no trade, a linear transformation surface and no inferior commodity. The condition of a positive marginal propensity to consume is implied by that of no inferiority. Bruno (1972) proved the result for the open economy case in which the only distorting instruments are tariffs. The proposition above is more general in that it encompasses any combination of positive and negative production and consumption distortions, though it is less general in that it applies locally whereas Bruno (1972) and Foster and Sonnenschein (1970) obtained global results using set theory.

[16]One can also define the second-best tax–subsidy set as that which maximises the expressions Ohyama (1972, eqs. (15″)–(17″)) gives for the change in revenue but this too does not reveal functional determinants.

The case of a radial reduction in all *prices* which are distorted produces a different result. In this case $|dr_i/(1+r_i)| = |\bar{p}_i^* \, dr_i/\bar{p}_i^*(1+r_i)| = |ds_i/(1+s_i)|$ for all commodities whose consumer or producer prices are distorted. From eq. (36) and using the Slutsky relation $\sum_{i=0}^{n} p_i \partial C_i/\partial p_v = 0$,

$$m\,dU = -[\sum_{i\in A_1} \bar{p}_i^* r_i (\sum_{v\notin A_1} \partial C_i/\partial p_v p_v^*(1+r_v))]\mu_i$$
$$+[\sum_{i\in A_2} \bar{p}_i^* s_i (\sum_{v\notin A_2} \partial X_i/\partial q_v p_v^*(1+s_v))]\mu_i^1,$$

where $\mu_i \lesseqgtr 0$ as $r_i \gtreqless 0$ and $\mu_i^1 \lesseqgtr 0$ as $s_i \gtreqless 0$. A sufficient condition for a welfare increase in this event is that the group of commodities whose consumer prices are distorted and the group whose producer prices are distorted be weighted average substitutes in consumption and production, respectively, for the groups of commodities whose consumer and producer prices are not distorted. Again a radial reduction in all consumer *or* all producer prices which were distorted will increase welfare if the corresponding groups of commodities whose prices are distorted are on average substitutes for the group of commodities whose prices are not distorted. Alternatively, these results may be looked upon as an application of Proposition 6 since the groups in this event are Hicks composite commodities.

4. Ranking of instruments

Meade (1955, Mathematical Supplement) had used the total differential method to compare pairs of instruments, and Bhagwati and Ramaswani (1963) had, using geometry, ranked several instruments in situations with certain distortions and externalities. With only two commodities in the model, Bhagwati, Ramaswami and Srinivasan (1969), derived the expression, in my symbols,

$$m\,dU_0 = (p_1^* - q_1)\,dX_1 - (p_1 - p_1^*)\,dC_1 + (X_1 - C_1)\,dp_1^*. \tag{39}$$

This is the two-commodity version of eq. (11) above, plus a term for the terms of trade effect since international prices were variable in their model. Among the cases they considered was that of a production externality and that of producers charging a premium over the cost of domestic and imported supplies. The former is analogous to a monopoly and the latter to a consumption tax. From eq. (39) they concluded that the first-best instrument to adjust for the former case was the production tax–subsidy and the second-best was a tax–subsidy on either trade or on input. In the latter case, they concluded that the first-best was a consumption tax–subsidy, the second-best a trade tax–subsidy and that a production or factor tax–subsidy were of no help.

These results can be generalised to the multi-commodity model using eq. (18),

$$m\,dU = \sum_i \bar{p}_i^* r_i \sum_j \partial C_i/\partial p_j \, dp_j - \sum_i \bar{p}_i^* s_i \sum_j \partial X_i/\partial q_j \, dq_j. \tag{18}$$

Consider the case where some relative producer prices are distorted. As with Bhagwati, Ramaswami and Srinivasan (1969) the first-best instrument, if it is available, is the production tax–subsidy. This coincides to Proposition 1. In deriving eq. (18) this possibility has been ruled out by considering that the distortions of the producer prices are unalterable. In this event, as established by Proposition 4, the second-best is a set of taxes–subsidies on the commodities substitutes–complements. This alternative was not considered by the previous authors because of the severe limitations of the two-commodity model. The third and only other available instrument in this situation is a set of taxes–subsidies on the trade of other commodities. This is clearly inferior to production taxes–subsidies which were calculated in section 2 because a tariff or import subsidy or export tax, being a tax–subsidy on both domestic production and domestic consumption, causes a welfare loss due to the additional distortion of prices to consumers which it creates and which partially offsets the benefits of correcting the distortions of production. The commodities which should be subject to the trade taxes–subsidies and the levels of these instruments can be obtained by setting $\mathrm{d}p_i = \mathrm{d}q_i = \mathrm{d}\tau_i$ in eq. (18). This yields the system of equations

$$\sum_i \bar{p}_i^*(r_i \partial C_i/\partial p_j - s_i \partial X_i/\partial q_j) = 0, \tag{40}$$

which has as many equations as there are trade taxes–subsidies which are considered variable. The solutions to these equations can be interpreted in much the same manner as the second-best levels of production and consumption taxes–subsidies considered in section 3. We should impose trade taxes (subsidies) on any commodity whose domestic production should be increased (decreased) or consumption decreased (increased). The solutions to the eq. (40) average the distortions in production and consumption, each weighted by the magnitude of the cross-price substitution and complementarity in production and consumption, respectively.

Using these methods all possible instruments can be ranked for different situations in this model or any other model.

Proposition 9. In any situation in which there are some unalterable distortions, it is possible to rank all of the alterable tax–subsidy instruments according to their effects on welfare.

It should be noted that these instruments are ranked by taking the effect on welfare for each instrument of the *best* level of that instrument. For example, in some situations the best level of a set of production subsidies may improve welfare more than the best level of the set of tariff-export subsidies which are considered adjustable, but some other higher or lower levels of these production subsidies may be inferior to the best level of tariff-export subsidies. This ranking therefore of alternative *instruments* still requires that we have an approximate idea at least of the magnitudes. One could if desired rank any number of different *levels* of each instrument using eq. (18).

5. Concluding remarks

These propositions have been established for a model whose behavioural assumptions are severely limited in many respects. However, the important point is that we have established the close links between several propositions concerning the best levels of taxes–subsidies or shadow prices, the effect on welfare of pre-selected tax–subsidy changes and the ranking of alternative instruments which have hitherto been considered separately. These rules for the choice of tax–subsidy instruments from among those which are variable and the best levels of these instruments or of shadow prices are important because they provide policy guidelines for the kind of situation where a government or policy-making authority has limited freedom to make changes which arises commonly in economic policy-making. Propositions 1, 3, 6, 7, 8 and 9 would carry over to more complex models with intermediate commodities, non-tradable commodities, variable international prices and some other variations.[17] The separation propositions 2, 4 and 5, would not carry over in their present form but they exemplify the general principle of confining intervention in the economy to commodities which are related in production and/or consumption to those whose prices are distorted.

[17]A few special cases of some of the propositions under more relaxed assumptions have been developed in the literature. In particular the terms of trade argument for tariffs in the presence of production and/or consumption taxes has been examined by Friedlaender and Vandendorpe (1968), Dornsbusch (1970) and Vandendorpe (1972), and in the presence of a divergence between the marginal rate of transformation and producer prices, by Ohyama (1972a). Many aspects of distortions in factor markets have been considered [see Magee (1973) for a survey] and Lloyd (1973) included taxes–subsidies on imported inputs in his model.

References

Bator, F.M., 1957, The simple analytics of welfare maximisation, American Economic Review 47, 22–59.

Baumol, W.J. and D.F. Bradford, 1970, Optimal departures from marginal cost pricing, American Economic Review 60, 265–283.

Bertrand, T.J. and J. Vanek, 1971, The theory of tariffs, taxes and subsidies: Some aspects of the second best, American Economic Review 61, 925–931.

Bhagwati, J., 1968, The theory and practice of commercial policy: Departures from unified exchange rates, Special Papers in International Economics, no. 8 (International Finance Section, Princeton University).

Bhagwati, J., 1971, The generalized theory of distortions and welfare, in: J. Bhagwati et al., eds., Trade, balance of payments, and growth: Papers in international economics in honor of Charles P. Kindleberger (North-Holland Amsterdam).

Bhagwati, J. and V.K. Ramaswami, 1963, Domestic distortions, tariffs and the theory of optimum subsidy, Journal of Political Economy 71, 44–50.

Bhagwati, J., V.K. Ramaswami and T.N. Srinivasan, 1969, Domestic distortions, tariffs and the theory of optimum subsidy: Some further results, Journal of Political Economy 77, 1005–1010.
Bruno, M., 1972, Market distortions and gradual reform, Review of Economic Studies 34, 373–383.
Davis, O. and A. Whinston, 1965, Welfare economics and the theory of second best, Review of Economic Studies 32, 1–14.
Diamond, P.A. and J.A. Mirrlees, 1971, Optimal taxation and public production: I, American Economic Review 61, 8–27.
Diamond, P.A. and J.A. Mirrlees, 1971, Optimal taxation and public production: II, American Economic Review 61, 261–278.
Dixit, A.K., 1970, On the optimum structure of commodity taxes, American Economic Review 60, 295–301,
Dornsbusch, R., 1971, Optimal commodity and trade taxes, Journal of Political Economy 79, 1360–1368.
Foster, E. and H. Sonnenschein, 1970, Price distortion and economic welfare, Econometrica 38, 281–296.
Friedlaender, A. and A. Vandendorpe, 1968, Excise taxes and the gains from trade, Journal of Political Economy 76, 1058–1068.
Graaff, J. v.d., 1957, Theoretical welfare economics (Cambridge University Press, Cambridge).
Green, H.A.J., 1961, The social optimum in the presence of monopoly and taxation, Review of Economic Studies 29, 66–78.
Hicks, J.R., 1939, Value and capital (Clarendon Press, Oxford).
Hicks, J.R. and R.G.D. Allen, 1934, A reconsideration of the theory of value, Economica N.S. 1, 52–76.
Kemp, M.C., 1962, The gain from international trade, Economic Journal 72, 803–819.
Kolm, S., 1971, La theorie des constraintes de valeur et ses applications (Dunod, Paris).
Leontief, W.W., 1947, Introduction to the theory of the internal structure of functional relationships, Econometrica 15, 361–373.
Lerner, A.P., 1970, On optimal taxes with an untaxable sector, American Economic Review 60, 284–294.
Lipsey, R.G. and K. Lancaster, 1956, The general theory of second best, Review of Economic Studies 24, 11–32.
Little, I.M.D., 1951, Direct versus indirect taxes, The Economic Journal 61, 577–584.
Lloyd, P.J., 1973, Optimal intervention in a distortion-ridden open economy, Economic Record, Sept., 377–393.
McManus, M., 1959, Comments on the general theory of second best, Review of Economic Studies 26, 209–224.
Magee, S.P., 1973, Factor market distortions, production and trade: A survey, Oxford Economic Papers 25, 1–43.
Meade, J., 1955, Trade and welfare (Oxford University Press, London).
Morishima, M., 1955/6, A note on definitions of related goods, Review of Economic Studies 23, 132–134.
Mosak, J.L., 1944, General equilibrium theory in international trade (The Principia Press, Bloomington, Ind.).
Negishi, T., 1961/2, Monopolistic firm competition and general equilibrium, Review of Economic Studies 28, 196–201.
Ohyama, M., 1972, Domestic distortions and the theory of tariffs, Keio Economic Studies 9, 1–14.
Ohyama, M., 1972, Trade and welfare in general equilibrium, Keio Economic Studies 9, 37–73.
Samuelson, P., 1950, The problem of integrability in utility theory, Economica N.S. 17, 355–385.
Samuelson, P., 1956, Social indifference curves, The Quarterly Journal of Economics 70, 1–22.
Sato, K., 1968, A two-level constant-elasticity-of-substitution production function, Review of Economic Studies 34, 201–218.

Sontheimer, K.C., 1971, The existence of international trade equilibrium with trade tax–subsidy distortions, Econometrica 39, 1015–1035.

Stiglitz, J. and P. Dasgupta, 1971, Differential taxation, public goods and economic efficiency, Review of Economic Studies 38, 151–174.

Vanek, J., 1964, Unilateral trade liberalization and global world income, The Quarterly Journal of Economics 78, 139–147.

Vanek, J., 1965, General equilibrium of international discrimination (Harvard University Press, Cambridge, Mass.).

Vandendorpe, A., 1972, Optimal tax structures in a model with traded and non-traded goods, Journal of International Economics 2, 235–256.

[9]

WELFARE EFFECTS OF TAX AND PRICE CHANGES

Avinash DIXIT*

University of Warwick, Coventry, Warwickshire, England

Received May 1974, revised version received September 1974

This paper studies a model of equilibrium in an economy without distributional problems but with distortions. The case where the distortions are due to specific taxes is examined in particular detail. A formula is derived to compare the utility levels in neighbouring equilibria corresponding to slightly different distortion levels. Several well known results in welfare economics and public finance are derived as corollaries, and other applications are suggested. An interpretation using consumers' and producers' surplus is given.

1. Introduction

It has long been known that policy changes which appear to be steps in the right direction, but stop short of attaining the full optimum, can actually reduce welfare. It is therefore important to look for ways of identifying partial welfare improvements, or in other words, seek particular solutions to the general problem of the second best. Several such attempts exist in the literature. One of the best known, that of Corlett and Hague (1953), actually antedates the discovery of the general problem by Lipsey and Lancaster (1956). Recent articles by Bertrand and Vanek (1971), Hatta (1973) and others follow Corlett and Hague in considering the effects of changing one distortion at a time. Foster and Sonnenschein (1970), Bruno (1972) and others consider equi-proportionate changes in all distortions. The conventional second best problem of Lipsey and Lancaster is to find the optimum values of one set of distortions when another set is fixed at given levels; Green (1961), Davis and Whinston (1965) and several others have analyzed such instances. The case where a fixed amount of revenue must be raised using distorting taxes has received a great deal of attention following Diamond and Mirrlees (1971), and Atkinson and Stern (1974) have studied the effects of small changes towards lump sum taxation in such a model.

*I am very grateful to Peter Diamond for several valuable discussions at an early stage of this research, to Tatsuo Hatta for detailed comments that saved me from some grievous errors, to James Mirrlees for suggesting simpler proofs of some results, and to Anthony Atkinson, Michael Bruno, Kunio Kawamata, Peter Lloyd, Michihiro Ohyama and two anonymous referees of this journal for useful comments. I am, of course, responsible for errors.

All these strands can be brought together by using an approach similar to that of Meade (1955), who develops a very general formula for welfare change and then applies it to obtain many particular results. In this paper I shall follow a similar line, with two important additions. I shall develop the general formula within stricter confines of general equilibrium than is done by Meade. Also, as in Hatta (1973), I shall use a dual formulation well suited to this problem. First, it yields all the results in a very compact form and with a minimum of effort. Next, it often enables me to relax the assumption of constant producer prices that has been necessary in much of previous work. Thirdly, the approach seems easy to extend to related problems like the provision of public goods, and to issues of trade and welfare. I shall point out such possibilities later.

Finally, the approach relates very well to ones used by earlier writers, including that of consumers' and producers' surpluses. In this connection, perhaps I should warn the readers that none of the ingredients of my method are novel, and most of the results are well known. It is the way in which the ingredients are assembled together that enables some unification and a simple exposition of large areas of welfare economics and public finance.

2. The model

There are $(n+1)$ commodities. The numéraire is labelled 0, and is best interpreted as leisure or minus labour. Its quantity is written as x_0; its price is of course 1. The other commodities are labelled $1, 2, \ldots, n$. The vector of their quantitites will be denoted by x, the vector of their prices facing consumers by q, that facing producers by p, and $t = q-p$, whether or not this difference arises from specific taxes.

The numéraire cost of producing x will be written $c(x)$; this is thus the transformation function of the economy solved out for the numéraire. By doing this I am assuming that there are no distortions within the production sector. Partial derivatives will be denoted by subscripts, and c_x will stand for the vector with components c_i, and c_{xx} for the matrix with elements c_{ij}. I shall assume that the matrix c_{xx} is positive semi-definite. This is almost like assuming that the technology is convex, but fixed costs are permissible so long as existence of equilibrium can be secured.

The demand side of the economy will be modelled assuming that there are no distributional problems. This is as if there is only one consumer, or community indifference curves exist, as discussed by Samuelson (1956). I shall obtain demand functions from an expenditure function. This approach is proving increasingly useful in economics, and its applications to the theory of public finance have been recently explained by Diamond and McFadden (1974). I shall state the essential properties very briefly. Write $E(1, q, u)$ for the minimum expenditure necessary for attaining the utility level u when prices are $(1, q)$. The function E is non-decreasing in all arguments and concave and homogeneous of degree one in $(1, q)$. Its partial derivatives with respect to prices give the compensated demand functions for the corresponding commodities. Using the subscript notation, we can write the demands as

$$\left.\begin{aligned} x_0 &= E_0(1, q, u) \\ x &= E_q(1, q, u) \end{aligned}\right\}. \tag{1}$$

As E is homogeneous of degree one and concave in $(1, q)$, the matrix of its second-order partial derivatives with respect to all prices will be negative semi-definite, but not negative definite. In absence of any further singularities in demand, E_{qq}, the matrix of second-order partial derivatives of E with respect to the prices of all commodities except the numéraire, will be negative definite. I shall assume this, but the condition can no doubt be relaxed using generalised inverses. Finally, each demand will be homogeneous of degree zero in all prices, and by Euler's theorem

$$E_{i0} + \sum_{j=1}^{n} q_j E_{ij} = 0, \qquad \text{for } i = 0, 1, 2, \ldots, n.$$

Using vector and matrix notation, and denoting the transpose of a matrix by $'$, these can be written

$$\left.\begin{aligned} E_{00} + q'E_{0q} &= 0 \\ E'_{q0} + q'E_{qq} &= 0 \end{aligned}\right\}. \tag{2}$$

The government will be supposed to act in such a way as to achieve command over a fixed amount G of the numéraire by levying commodity taxes, and possibly lump sum taxes T. Thus we have

$$t'x + T = G. \tag{3}$$

For the moment, the only specific assumption made about the behaviour of producers will be that their profit

$$P = p'x - c(x), \tag{4}$$

is distributed to the consumers in a lump sum fashion. There is no taxation of profits. As far as the general framework of this section is concerned, further details can be kept in the background, and any actions by producers that sustain the various equilibria considered are permissible. Particular behavioural assumptions will be brought in later for each specific case to ask which equilibria can be thus sustained, and to derive particular results.

Now suppose the consumer has an endowment Z of the numéraire. In the leisure interpretation, this could be 24 hours; in the labour interpretation, it would be zero. For all other commodities, define taxes and utility on his net trades. His budget constraint is

$$Z-T+P = E(1, q, u).$$

Substituting from (1), (3) and (4), this becomes

$$Z = G+E(1, q, u)-q'E_q(1, q, u)+c(E_q(1, q, u)). \tag{5}$$

Another way to derive this equation is to consider the equilibrium in the market for the numéraire, equating Z to the sum of the demands arising from the consumer, the government and the producers. This yields

$$Z = G+E_0(1, q, u)+c(E_q(1, q, u)). \tag{6}$$

Since E is homogeneous of degree 1 in $(1, q)$, the two are equivalent.

This completes the description of equilibrium in the model. For simplicity of exposition, I have cast it in a somewhat restrictive way, especially as regards the role of the numéraire. The consumer has no endowments of any other commodities, and the government is not interested in any of them. This asymmetry can be relaxed fairly easily. We can, of course, choose one untaxed commodity without loss of generality.

Eqs. (5) or (6) implicitly define the utility level in equilibrium as a function of consumer prices. Thus distortions arising from taxes or non-competitive behaviour of producers affect welfare only through the equilibrium prices faced by consumers. It is therefore of some interest to find out how utility depends on this price vector, independently of the underlying determinants of it. I shall confine the analysis to effects of small changes. In many cases, the results can be integrated to yield similar ones for finite changes. Ohyama (1972) uses a similar model to study issues of trade and welfare, and obtains all the well known results and some remarkable new ones, all for finite changes. Thus the approach is not inherently restricted to analysing small changes by calculus methods.

Suppose the equilibrium consumer price vector changes to $(q+\mathrm{d}q)$, and the utility to $(u+\mathrm{d}u)$. Taking total differentials of (5) or (6), we find

$$E_q'\,\mathrm{d}q-\mathrm{d}q'E_q-(q-c_x)'E_{qq}\,\mathrm{d}q+(E_{0u}+c_x'E_{qu})\,\mathrm{d}u = 0,$$

or, solving for du,

$$du = (q-c_x)'E_{qq}\,dq/(E_{0u}+c_x'E_{qu}). \tag{7}$$

I shall argue that it is reasonable to assume that the denominator is positive:

$$E_{0u}+c_x'E_{qu} > 0. \tag{8}$$

Each E_{iu} is the real income effect on the demand for a commodity, and the expression is the sum of these weighted by the corresponding marginal costs. Thus (8) will hold if all commodities are normal in demand. This is argued by Foster and Sonnenschein (1970), Bruno (1972) and Hatta (1973).

An even stronger argument comes from the following. Hold consumer prices fixed and examine the effect on utility of a change in the endowment of the numéraire. We have

$$du = dZ/(E_{0u}+c_x'E_{qu}). \tag{9}$$

Thus (8) holds if and only if an increase in the consumer's endowment at given prices increases welfare. Further, from (5) and (3) we see that an increase in Z is equivalent to an equal decrease in each of G and T. Thus another form of the condition is that an increase in government expenditure financed by lump sum taxes should lower utility. As G is not itself an argument of utility, this is surely reasonable. I shall assume (8) to hold in all that follows.

We can now conclude that the change in question increases welfare if and only if

$$(q-c_x)'E_{qq}\,dq > 0. \tag{10}$$

Writing $dx|_{comp} = E_{qq}\,dq$, the vector of changes in compensated demand quantities, (10) becomes

$$(q-c_x)'\,dx|_{comp} > 0. \tag{11}$$

The use of compensated demands opens up further fruitful lines of inquiry. Consider a compensated change in equilibrium, where consumer prices change to $(q+dq)$ as before, but the endowment is changed to $(Z+dZ)$ to keep utility at the previous level u. Differentiating (5), we have

$$dZ = -(q-c_x)'E_{qq}\,dq, \tag{12}$$

and (10) is equivalent to $dZ < 0$. In other words, provided the endowment and utility are positively related for each price vector, we can turn around the question of whether utility increases at a given endowment and ask the equivalent question of whether it is possible to attain a given utility level with less of the endowment. It is thus possible to think of a decrease in Z as a criterion of welfare increase.

This argument is just as valid for large changes, and enables me to relate the above method to conventional diagrammatic analyses. To illustrate, suppose there is only one good apart from the numéraire. Fig. 1 shows its marginal cost curve, and the compensated demand curve corresponding to the utility level in the initial equilibrium, which has a consumer price q and a producer price p.

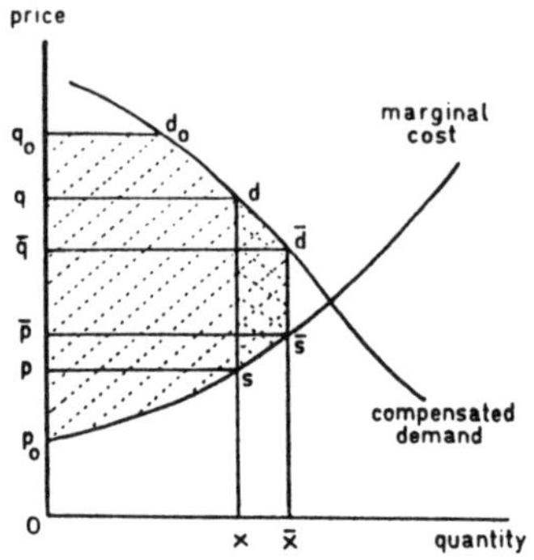

Fig. 1

It is now possible to represent various terms in (5) or (6) by areas in this figure. The cost term is simply the area under the marginal cost curve, $0p_0sx$. The revenue, $q'E_q$, is the rectangle $0qdx$. To interpret E, fix some q_0 which is larger than any consumer price being considered. We have

$$E(1, q_0, u) - E(1, q, u) = \int_q^{q_0} E_q(1, y, u)\,dy.$$

Thus we can represent $(-E)$ by the area qq_0d_0d, up to an additive constant. When we add all the terms with the correct signs, $(-Z)$ is represented, also up to an additive constant, by the area $p_0q_0d_0ds$, which is shaded once in the figure. This area has the standard interpretation as the sum of consumers' and producers' surpluses.

To compare this with an equilibrium which has the consumer price $\bar{q}$, we hold utility constant, and use $(-Z)$ as an index of welfare increase. The figure shows such a comparison, where the area $p_0q_0d_0\overline{ds}$ corresponding to the new equilibrium exceeds that for the old one by the area $s\overline{dds}$, shaded twice. The expression in (11) is simply the first-order rectangular approximation to this change in the surpluses. If the initial equilibrium is undistorted, the first-order approximation is zero, and we must carry the Taylor series for Z to second-order terms and find a quadratic approximation for the small triangle of loss, as is done by Harberger (1971). As I shall usually begin with a distorted equilibrium, this is not necessary for my present purpose.

It should be clear that my approach is very similar to the analysis of the dead-weight burden of taxation in Diamond and McFadden (1974). The difference is that I consider small changes from an arbitrary initial equilibrium, and use its utility level as the standard, while they refer back to the utility level in the undistorted equilibrium a finite distance away, thus producing an exact version of Harberger's criterion. I hope my analysis of the relation between endowment changes and utility changes makes it clear why such definitions of loss or surplus provide criteria for welfare improvement.

Of course for large changes care is necessary if we calculate surpluses for one commodity at a time and add. It is also important to remember that I have neglected considerations of distribution.

3. Specific taxes

Effects of price changes have an independent interest, but it is often desirable to look directly at the causes underlying these changes. I shall consider one such cause, namely specific taxes, in some detail. It is only when producer prices are constant that consumer price changes will be related to tax changes in a simple way. This is acceptable for a small economy which trades at given prices with the rest of the world, when the only distortions are excise taxes, as in Lloyd (1974a). But otherwise the assumption would be quite restrictive; we would need the non-substitution property, with constant returns to scale, no joint production, and only one scarce factor of production, to secure a transformation schedule in the shape of a hyperplane. It is thus important to relax the assumption of constant producer prices when possible.

Let the specific tax rates form a vector s. Suppose the economy is otherwise competitive, so producer prices equal the corresponding marginal costs. The condition for equilibrium is

$$s = q - c_x(E_q(1, q, u)). \tag{13}$$

It is possible to use this in (10) or (11), and I shall return to relate them, but it is instructive to consider the question afresh. We have equilibrium conditions (6) and (13), which define u and q as functions of Z and s. If this equilibrium is disturbed, we have by differentiation

$$\begin{bmatrix} \mathrm{d}Z \\ \mathrm{d}s \end{bmatrix} = \begin{bmatrix} E_{0u} + c_x' E_{qu} & -(q - c_x)' E_{qq} \\ -c_{xx} E_{qu} & I - c_{xx} E_{qq} \end{bmatrix} \begin{bmatrix} \mathrm{d}u \\ \mathrm{d}q \end{bmatrix}. \tag{14}$$

A great deal can be said about the partitioned matrix on the right-hand side, for sign patterns of its principal minors provide sufficient conditions for uniqueness of equilibrium, using a theorem due to Gale and Nikaido. [For an exposition, see Nikaido (1968, ch. VII).] It suffices to have all principal minors positive, or all negative with some subsidiary conditions, or odd and even order minors of alternating signs. Of these possible conditions, only the first is consistent with other reasonable economic requirements. First, the partial derivatives $\partial u/\partial Z$ and $\partial q_i/\partial s_i$ will all be ratios of n-by-n principal minors to the $(n+1)$-by-$(n+1)$ determinant of the whole matrix. If we allowed odd and even order minors to alternate in sign, all these ratios would be negative. Thus an increase in the endowment of the numéraire at given tax rates (not quite the same thing as given consumer prices) would lower utility. Further, an increase in each tax rate would lower the consumer price of that commodity: an Edgeworth-like paradox on a grand scale. Thus it is sensible to assume a condition which has all principal minors of the same sign. But the 1-by-1 minor in the top left corner has already been assumed positive.

I shall therefore assume that all principal minors of the matrix in (14) are positive. This is only a sufficient condition for uniqueness of equilibrium, and weaker requirements can be used at least while studying the effects of equi-proportionate changes in specific tax rates, as is done by Foster and Sonnenschein (1970) and Kawamata (1974).

There are well known formulae for calculating the determinants and inverses of partitioned matrices. [A reference easily accessible to economists is Johnston (1972, pp. 93–95).] We can use these to write the determinant as

$$\det(I-c_{xx}E_{qq})\cdot\det\,[(E_{0u}+c_x'E_{qu})-(-s'E_{qq})(I-c_{xx}E_{qq})^{-1}(-c_{xx}E_{qu})]$$
$$=\det(E_{qq}^{-1})\cdot\det(E_{qq}^{-1}-c_{xx})\cdot[E_{0u}+(c_x'-s'(E_{qq}^{-1}-c_{xx})^{-1}c_{xx})E_{qu}].$$

Now it is useful to introduce two notational abbreviations

$$H=E_{qq}^{-1}-c_{xx},\qquad J=(E_{qq}^{-1}-c_{xx})^{-1}. \tag{15}$$

As E_{qq} has been assumed to be negative definite and c_{xx} positive semi-definite, both H and J are negative definite. The condition for the determinant to be positive is then

$$E_{0u}+(c_x'-s'Jc_{xx})E_{qu}>0. \tag{16}$$

I shall write Ω for this expression. Now inverting the partitioned matrix, we find

$$\begin{bmatrix}\mathrm{d}u\\ \mathrm{d}q\end{bmatrix}=\begin{bmatrix}1/\Omega & s'J/\Omega\\ E_{qq}^{-1}Jc_{xx}E_{qu}/\Omega & E_{qq}^{-1}J[I+c_{xx}E_{qu}s'J/\Omega]\end{bmatrix}\begin{bmatrix}\mathrm{d}Z\\ \mathrm{d}s\end{bmatrix}. \tag{17}$$

In particular, $du = s'J\,ds/\Omega$, and since Ω has been assumed positive, we conclude that the tax change ds increases utility if and only if

$$s'J\,ds > 0. \tag{18}$$

The criterion is very similar to (10), and there is a very good reason for this. Consider a compensated change in the equilibrium. With u held constant, we have from (13)

$$ds = (I - c_{xx}E_{qq})\,dq|_{\text{comp}} = HE_{qq}\,dq|_{\text{comp}},$$

and the change in the compensated demand quantities is

$$dx|_{\text{comp}} = E_{qq}\,dq|_{\text{comp}} = J\,ds. \tag{19}$$

This explains the close parallel between (18) and (11).

We can also use (19) to interpret J: it yields the substitution effects of tax changes much as E_{qq} yields the substitution effects of price changes. If producer prices are constant, c_{xx} is identically zero, $dq = ds$, and the two substitution effects coincide, with $J = E_{qq}$. In general, the substitution effects of tax changes must include the general equilibrium interactions that work through the production side. We can therefore call J the generalised substitution matrix, and define concepts of generalised substitutes and complements in the obvious way: commodities i and j are substitutes or complements according as an increase in the tax rate on i increases or decreases the compensated demand for j. As J is a symmetric matrix, this definition is symmetric between commodities.

Bertrand and Vanek (1971) used a similar notion of generalised substitution, without however deriving an expression for the relevant matrix.

For later use, I shall derive an expression for the change in tax revenue that results from the change in tax rates. We have

$$\begin{aligned} d(s'x) &= ds'x + s'\,dx \\ &= ds'E_q + s'(E_{qq}\,dq + E_{qu}\,du) \\ &= E_q'\,ds + s'[J(I + c_{xx}E_{qu}s'J/\Omega)\,ds + E_{qu}s'J\,ds/\Omega] \\ &= E_q'\,ds + s'J\,ds[1 + (s'Jc_{xx}E_{qu} + s'E_{qu})/\Omega]. \end{aligned}$$

Using the expression for Ω, the equilibrium condition (13), and the fact that E_u is homogeneous of degree one in $(1, q)$, this reduces to

$$d(s'x) = E_q'\,ds + \Phi s'J\,ds, \tag{20}$$

where $\Phi = E_u/\Omega$ is a positive number.

4. Proportional changes

We can now prove some results concerning partial welfare improvement. The fact that E_{qq} is negative definite at once suggests the first result.

Theorem 1. A small movement of all consumer prices towards the corresponding marginal costs in proportion to the prevailing distortions, with lump sum taxes changed to keep government expenditure constant, increases welfare.

Thus, if we write $\mathrm{d}q = -(q-c_x)\,\mathrm{d}h$, where $\mathrm{d}h$ is a positive scalar (this will be the usage of $\mathrm{d}h$ throughout this paper), we have

$$(q-c_x)'E_{qq}\,\mathrm{d}q = -(q-c_x)'E_{qq}(q-c_x)\,\mathrm{d}h > 0.$$

This result is in a sense more general than the proportional change results in previous literature, as it requires knowledge only of the current marginal cost vector and not the optimum one. But this may not be very useful, as the underlying policy changes that will bring about such a price change will in general be quite complicated. But the generalised substitution matrix J is also negative definite, and this yields a corresponding result for specific taxes.

Theorem 2. If the technology is convex and the economy competitive, a proportional reduction in specific taxes, with offsetting changes in lump sum taxes to keep government expenditure constant, increases welfare.

This result is very similar to Lemma 1 of Foster and Sonnenschein (1970) and Corollary to Theorem 1 of Kawamata (1974). However, their results are somewhat more general, as they assume uniqueness of equilibrium directly, while I use a condition which is sufficient for uniqueness.

Let us turn to ad valorem taxes. These can be expressed as proportions of the marginal cost or of the consumer price, and equi-proportionate changes in one will not generally be equi-proportionate changes in the other. I shall begin with the former. Form a diagonal matrix A of the tax rates a_i as proportions of marginal costs. Then the equilibrium condition is

$$q = (I+A)c_x(E_q(1, q, u)). \tag{13'}$$

Suppose A changes to $(A+\mathrm{d}A)$. Reasoning exactly as was done for specific taxes we can calculate the change in quantities corresponding to the shift in the compensated equilibrium, and obtain

$$\mathrm{d}x|_{\text{comp}} = E_{qq}\,\mathrm{d}q = [E_{qq}^{-1}-(I+A)c_{xx}]^{-1}\,(\mathrm{d}Ac_x).$$

Continuing the analogy, we would like the matrix on the right-hand side to be negative definite, and for this it is sufficient to have $(I+A)c_{xx}$ positive definite. In general, this matrix need not even be symmetric. The simplest sufficient condition I have been able to think of is that c_{xx} be diagonal, i.e., $c(x)$ be additively separable. This is quite a restrictive condition. For example, it will be satisfied if there is no joint production and labour is the only factor of production which is shiftable between industries. If this is assumed, and the technology is convex, then $D = (I+A)c_{xx}$ will be a diagonal matrix with positive entries. The proportional change result will then follow at once; for $\mathrm{d}A = -A\,\mathrm{d}h$, we have

$$(q-c_x)'\,\mathrm{d}x\big|_{\text{comp}} = -(Ac_x)'[E_{qq}^{-1}-D]^{-1}(Ac_x)\,\mathrm{d}h > 0.$$

We have proved:

Theorem 3. If the technology is convex, there is no joint production, and only one factor of production is mobile, in a competitive economy, then a proportional reduction in ad valorem taxes expressed as proportions of marginal costs, with compensating changes in lump sum taxes, will increase welfare.

This theorem can be stretched and interpreted in terms of monopoly. Leaving aside the difficult problems of general equilibrium and game theory considerations, a major problem in forming a proper model of monopoly is that profit-maximisation with correct perception by the producers will involve derivatives of demand functions, i.e., second-order derivatives of the expenditure function. Comparative statics will then bring in third-order derivatives, and we will have little chance of obtaining any economically interesting results. But there is one particular misperception that is not too implausible. Suppose each monopolist believes that he faces a demand curve with a known and constant elasticity e_i, say from reading estimates of it in some economic journal. Then he will believe that his profits are maximised when

$$q_i(1-e_i^{-1}) = c_i,$$

and these equations define equilibrium. These are formally equivalent to (13′), with $(1+a_i) = 1/(1-e_i^{-1})$ for each i. We can then use Theorem 3 to obtain a comparative static result for a change in perceived monopoly power. Define the degree of monopoly power by $a = 1/(e-1)$. Note that this is not quite the conventional definition. Suppose the perceived degree of monopoly power for each commodity is reduced in the same proportion. The offsetting change in lump sum taxes simply corresponds to an altered sum of profit for distribution. Then Theorem 3 says that welfare will increase.

If ad valorem taxes are expressed as proportions a_i of the consumer prices, the relevant matrix will be

$$(I-A)E_{qq}^{-1}-c_{xx}.$$

The corresponding sufficient condition will be for E_{qq} to be diagonal, i.e., all compensated demands independent of other prices. This is even more restrictive than assuming no joint production.

Another important proportional change result concerns an economy in which the only distortions are trade taxes. This can be handled using a small modification of my approach. Suppose world prices are p, and are constant for the country in question. Suppose it levies specific trade taxes at a vector of rates r, so domestic prices both for consumers and for producers are $q = p+r$. Domestic output x is defined by $c_x(x) = q$, and imports of non-numéraire commodities are (E_q-x). For trade balance, exports of the numéraire must be $p'(E_q-x)$. The cost of production and trade activities together is $c(x)+p'(E_q-x)$, and this must replace $c(x)$ in (5) and (6). This describes an interior solution where all commodities are being produced domestically. It is in fact important to allow various corner solutions, for the regimes of specialisation pose some problems of relations between traded and non-traded goods. This is done by Bruno (1972), Hatta (1973, ch. VIII) and Ohyama (1972). I shall neglect these problems for sake of brevity.

Suppose trade taxes change by $\mathrm{d}r$. Then home prices change by $\mathrm{d}q = \mathrm{d}r$, and home production by $\mathrm{d}x$, where $c_{xx}\,\mathrm{d}x = \mathrm{d}q$. I shall assume that the technology is strictly convex (else non-specialisation breaks down completely). Then c_{xx} is positive definite, and $\mathrm{d}x = c_{xx}^{-1}\,\mathrm{d}q$. Let us now use the criterion $\mathrm{d}Z < 0$ of welfare increase. From (5), we have

$$\mathrm{d}Z = E_q'\,\mathrm{d}q-\mathrm{d}q'\,E_q-q'E_{qq}\,\mathrm{d}q+c_x'\,\mathrm{d}x+p'E_{qq}\,\mathrm{d}q-p'\,\mathrm{d}x.$$

On substituting and regrouping terms, the welfare increase criterion is

$$r'(E_{qq}-c_{xx}^{-1})\,\mathrm{d}r > 0.$$

As E_{qq} is negative definite and c_{xx} positive definite, this is satisfied for a proportional reduction in trade taxes, $\mathrm{d}r = -r\,\mathrm{d}h$. Thus we have

Theorem 4. If a competitive economy with a strictly convex technology facing constant world prices is in a completely non-specialised equilibrium under a system of trade taxes, then a proportionate reduction in these taxes, with offsetting changes in lump sum taxes, will increase welfare.

It is interesting to note that with a strictly convex technology, we can utilise duality in production as well. Define $\pi(1, q)$ to be the maximum profit achievable when prices are $(1, q)$; then it can be shown that supply functions of producers are the partial derivatives, $x = \pi_q(1, q)$ and $c(x) = -\pi_0(1, q)$. Then

$$Z = G + E_0 - \pi_0 + p'(E_q - \pi_q),$$

and Theorem 4 follows easily.

In conclusion, I should point out that although the proportional change results were proved for small changes, repeated small changes can be integrated in this case to yield the same results valid for finite changes.

5. Individual changes

In this section I shall discuss some non-proportional changes. I shall consider consumer prices without going into details of their determination for the most part. The case where producer prices are constant is of course easy; I shall point out some other possible generalisations.

The simplest example of this kind is one where the initial situation has equal proportional distortion in all sectors, i.e., when there is a scalar β such that $(q - c_x) = \beta q$. Now the criterion (10) for welfare increase becomes $\beta q' E_{qq}\,\mathrm{d}q > 0$, or using (2).

$$\beta E'_{q0}\,\mathrm{d}q < 0.$$

In the more common case where β is positive, we see that welfare is increased by a change in which $\mathrm{d}q_i$ and E_{i0} have opposite signs. The sign of E_{i0} tells us whether commodity i is a substitute or a complement to the numéraire, i.e., in our interpretation whether the compensated labour supply decreases or increases when the price of i rises. Thus we have the result

Theorem 5. If prices are initially above marginal costs by the same factor for all commodities except the numéraire, then welfare will be increased by slight increases in prices of commodities complementary to the numéraire and slight decreases in prices of those substitutes for it, with offsetting changes in lump sum taxes.

This result cannot be generalised for large changes, for the first small change destroys the special feature of equal proportional distortions.

If every E_{i0} is zero, then utility is not affected to first order by price changes, i.e., the initial situation with equal proportional distortion for all commodities satisfies the first-order conditions for first-best optimality. Of course if every E_{i0} is zero, then (2) says that E_{00} will be zero as well. In the interpretation I have been using, the compensated labour supply will then be completely inelastic. The result that equal proportional distortions, such as might arise from an equal degree of monopoly power in all sectors, do not affect welfare, is of course very well known.

When the whole vector E_{q0} is zero, (2) also tells us that the matrix E_{qq} is singular. This does not matter in the present context, since the derivation of (10) did not require its inverse.

Theorem 5 is similar to the result of Corlett and Hague (1953), but there is one important difference. I allow offsetting changes in lump sum taxes, while they require the revenue from commodity taxes to stay constant. Their result needs constant producer prices. Then $\mathrm{d}q = \mathrm{d}s$, $J = E_{qq}$, and the formula (20) for tax revenue change is simplified. Further using the initial condition $s = \beta q$, and (2), the tax revenue constraint is

$$(E_q - \beta\Phi E_{q0})'\,\mathrm{d}q = 0. \tag{21}$$

The welfare increase criterion can also be simplified using (2) and (21), and becomes

$$E_q'\,\mathrm{d}q < 0. \tag{22}$$

It is instructive to write these out explicitly. Note that $(1 \cdot E_{i0}/E_i)$ is the compensated elasticity of demand for commodity i with respect to the price of 0. The change in the price of the numéraire is of course interpreted as an equal and opposite proportional change in the price of all other commodities. Write θ_i for this elasticity. It may also be useful to note that $\theta_i = \pi_0\sigma_{0i}$, where π_0 is the budget share of the numéraire, and σ_{0i} the elasticity of substitution between the commodities 0 and i. Now the constraint can be written

$$\sum_{i=1}^{n} x_i(1-\beta\Phi\theta_i)\,\mathrm{d}q_i = 0 \tag{21'}$$

and, subject to it, welfare increases if

$$\sum_{i=1}^{n} x_i\,\mathrm{d}q_i < 0. \tag{22'}$$

If we make the standard assumption that an increase in each tax rate increases tax revenue, then all the $(1-\beta\Phi\theta_i)$ will be positive. Then, comparing tax reductions which have equal effects on revenue, their effects on welfare will be proportional to $1/(1-\beta\Phi\theta_i)$, i.e., for a positive β, increasing with θ_i. This gives the result of Corlett and Hague.

Theorem 6. In a competitive economy with constant producer prices and an initial equilibrium with equal proportional distortions, a small change in tax rates holding commodity tax revenue constant will increase welfare if all commodities whose prices are lowered are better substitutes for the numéraire than all those whose prices are raised.

This is of course sufficient but not necessary. The general price change that will increase welfare is easy to describe. It is more sensible to express the constraint as one requiring no decrease in tax revenue, i.e., to replace the equality in (21) by $\geqq$. Then the constraint defines a closed half-space in the n-dimensional space of the dq. The welfare-increasing directions are in an open half-space defined by (22). The permissible and welfare-increasing directions of price change then lie in the intersection of these two half-spaces. In general there are infinitely many such directions.

However, if all the θ_i are equal, the two half-spaces are disjoint. Utility to first order is unaffected by departures from proportionality satisfying the tax revenue constraint. Thus, subject to second-order conditions, a proportional tax structure is second-best optimum. This is very neatly discussed by Sandmo (1973) using weak separability of the direct utility function.

It is worth emphasising the difference between Theorems 5 and 6 on this point. The latter says that if all the θ_i are equal, then small deviations from proportionality satisfying the revenue constraint do not affect welfare to first order. The former says that if, in addition, the common value of the θ_i is zero, then welfare cannot be improved by bringing in lump sum taxes, either.

In the three commodity model of Corlett and Hague, the relation between $(q_i - c_i)/q_i$ and θ_i holds also at the optimum tax-levels subject to the tax revenue constraint, i.e.,

$$t_1/q_1 \gtrless t_2/q_2 \qquad \text{as} \qquad \theta_1 \lesseqgtr \theta_2,$$

[see Meade (1955, p. 29) and Diamond and Mirrlees (1971, p. 263)]. This does not appear to be the case with more commodities.

Finally, consider an arbitrary initial situation. Define

$$\beta_i = (q_i - c_i)/q_i, \qquad \text{for } i = 1, 2, \ldots n, \tag{23}$$

and arrange the commodities so that

$$\beta_1 \leqq \beta_2 \leqq \ldots \leqq \beta_n. \tag{24}$$

Consider the effect of changing the price of commodity j alone. Welfare will increase if

$$\sum_{i=1}^{n} \beta_i q_i E_{ij} \, \mathrm{d}q_j > 0. \tag{25}$$

Now write the homogeneity result (2) as

$$\beta_j\left[E_{0j}+\sum_{i=1}^{n}q_iE_{ij}\right]\mathrm{d}q_j = 0. \tag{26}$$

Subtracting (26) from (25), we have the welfare increase criterion

$$\left[\sum_{i=1}^{n}(\beta_i-\beta_j)q_iE_{ij}-\beta_jE_{0j}\right]\mathrm{d}q_j > 0. \tag{27}$$

Suppose the price of commodity j is initially above the marginal cost, and contemplate lowering the price slightly. We see that this will increase welfare if (a) $E_{ij} < 0$ for $i = (j+1), (j+2), \ldots, n$, (b) $E_{ij} > 0$ for $i = 1, 2, \ldots, (j-1)$ and (c) $E_{0j} > 0$. Thus we have proved

Theorem 7. Lowering the price of any one commodity towards its marginal cost will increase welfare if the commodity is complementary to all those with a greater proportional distortion and substitute for all others including the numéraire.

Corollary. Lowering the price of the commodity with the highest degree of distortion will increase welfare if it is a substitute for all other commodities.

This last result is due to Hatta (1973). An analogous result for an economy engaged in international trade at given prices but using distorting trade taxes is due to Bertrand and Vanek (1971). On piecing together small changes, all these results remain valid for large changes so long as the ranking in (24) is preserved.

Such results are useful not because we expect to find just the right combinations of complementarity and substitution in reality, but because they narrow down our zone of ignorance. The conditions are sufficient but not necessary, and it would be extremely useful to have stronger results for specific situations in this area.

6. Optimum taxes with a given revenue

Some of the discussion of the previous section touched on the question of the second-best optimum rates of commodity taxes raising a given amount of revenue. The first-order condition for optimality required the open half-space of welfare-increasing changes to be disjoint from the closed half-space of changes which conform to the revenue constraint. From (18) and (20), this requires the existence of a positive scalar α such that

$$s'J = -\alpha(E_q'+\Phi s'J),$$

or

$$s'J = -\gamma E_q', \tag{28}$$

where

$$\gamma = \alpha/(1+\alpha\Phi).$$

The revenue from commodity taxes is $(G-T)$, so

$$G-T = s'x = -\gamma x'Hx,$$

using

$$x = E_q \quad \text{and} \quad H = J^{-1}.$$

Substituting into (28), we have a formula for the optimum tax rates

$$s = (G-T)Hx/(x'Hx). \tag{29}$$

There is no need for me to repeat any of the well known properties of this, so I shall turn to a result obtained by Atkinson and Stern (1974) on partial welfare improvement related to optimum taxation. For this, the maximisation problem must be written down explicitly, with proper attention to the constraints so that we can be sure of the signs of the Lagrange multipliers. There are two constraints, that for equilibrium and the one on tax revenue. Thus we are to maximise u, when u and q are subject to the constraints

$$Z \geqq G+E_0(1,q,u)+c(E_q(1,q,u)), \tag{6'}$$

$$[q-c_x(E_q(1,q,u))]'E_q(1,q,u)+T \geqq G. \tag{3'}$$

Then there are non-negative multipliers λ and μ such that the Lagrange expression is, omitting arguments of functions for brevity,

$$L = u+\lambda(Z-G-E_0-c)+\mu[(q-c_x)'E_q+T-G]. \tag{30}$$

The optimum values of u and q are found by solving the first-order conditions $\partial L/\partial u = 0$ and $\partial L/\partial q_i = 0$ together with the constraints, and the implied tax rates are $(q_i - c_i)$. These yield conditions (29). What is of more interest now is the fact that the Lagrange multipliers are the effects of marginal relaxation of the respective constraints on the maximum value u^*. In particular, we have $\partial u^*/\partial T = \mu$, which proves

Theorem 8. A small move towards lump sum taxation increases welfare if for each level of lump sum taxes the rates of distorting taxes are chosen at their second-best optimum levels.

Atkinson and Stern also consider the question of the optimum level of government expenditure. To formulate this meaningfully in my framework, this level should be allowed to affect utility or production, i.e., G should be an argument of E or c. I shall leave this extension to the readers.

7. Theory of the second-best

The traditional analysis of the second-best assumes that the rates of taxes on some commodities are fixed, and then argues that even when lump sum taxes are available, the second-best optimum levels of taxes on the remaining commodities are not zero. This is very easy to express in my framework. Consider the case of specific taxes, and group the commodities into two classes, denoted by subscripts 'f' and 'v' corresponding to fixed and variable rates of tax. Partition all vectors and matrices accordingly. With offsetting lump sum taxation allowed, the effect on welfare of a small change $\mathrm{d}s_v$ in the variable tax rates will be proportional to

$$[s_f' \quad s_v'] \begin{bmatrix} J_{ff} & J_{fv} \\ J_{vf} & J_{vv} \end{bmatrix} \begin{bmatrix} 0 \\ \mathrm{d}s_v \end{bmatrix} = (s_f' J_{fv} + s_v' J_{vv})\, \mathrm{d}s_v. \tag{31}$$

If the variable taxes are at their optimum levels, this must be zero, i.e.,

$$s_f' J_{fv} + s_v' J_{vv} = 0.$$

Using symmetry of J and solving, we have

$$s_v = -J_{vv}^{-1} J_{vf} s_f. \tag{32}$$

In general, this is not very illuminating. One special case which is relatively simple is that of just one commodity with a variable tax rate. Then J_{vv} is a scalar. Choosing the commodity in question to be number n, we write (32) as

$$s_n = \sum_{i=1}^{n-1} (-J_{in}/J_{nn}) s_i. \tag{33}$$

Thus s_n should be a weighted sum of all remaining fixed tax rates, and we can include the numéraire in this by taking s_0 to be zero. Since $J_{nn} < 0$, the weight attached to s_i in this sum is positive if i and n are substitutes, and negative if they are complements.

This problem has been studied by Green (1961), assuming constant producer prices. Then $J = E_{qq}$, and we can use the homogeneity relations

$$\sum_{i=0} q_i E_{ni} = 0,$$

where of course $q_0 = 1$. Then (33) can be written as

$$\frac{s_n}{q_n} = \sum_{i=0}^{n-1}\left[-\frac{q_i E_{ni}}{q_n E_{nn}}\right]\frac{s_i}{q_i},$$

or

$$s_n/q_n = \sum_{i=0}^{n-1} \delta_i(s_i/q_i), \tag{34}$$

where the δ_i add to one, and are all non-negative if commodity n is a substitute for all other commodities. Then the proportional tax rate that can be varied should be a true weighted average of all the fixed proportional tax rates.

It is possible to use the inverse matrix H to derive an alternative form of (32). Partitioning H comformably and using obvious notation, we have

$$J_{vf}H_{ff}+J_{vv}H_{vf} = 0,$$

and, therefore,

$$-J_{vv}^{-1}J_{vf} = H_{vf}H_{ff}^{-1},$$

$$s_v = H_{vf}H_{ff}^{-1}s_f. \tag{35}$$

Obviously this is most useful in the opposite case where H_{ff} is a scalar, i.e., the tax rate on only one commodity, say the first, is fixed. Then the second-best optimum levels of the variable tax rates are

$$s_i = (H_{i1}/H_{11})s_1, \qquad \text{for } i = 2, 3, \ldots, n. \tag{36}$$

The general equilibrium version of the Hicks–Allen notion of complementarity or substitution between commodities enables us to interpret this. Commodities i and j are generalised Hicks–Allen substitutes if $H_{ij} < 0$ and complements if $H_{ij} > 0$. Since $H_{11} < 0$, we have the result that if the fixed tax rate is positive, the second-best optimum involves taxing commodities that are generalised Hicks–Allen substitutes for the commodity with the fixed tax, and subsidising its generalised Hicks–Allen complements. This approach is taken by Lloyd (1974b), who also combines the traditional second-best constraints with those of fixed revenue requirements. The problem has also been studied by Lispey and Lancaster (1956).

It is also instructive to look at the question from another angle. Suppose the tax rate on commodity 1 is fixeu and positive, and the initial situation has no taxes or subsidies on any other commodity. We can then look for small changes that increase welfare. This is how Haberler (1950) and others have posed the second-best problem. Using (31) we can answer it at once. The welfare increase criterion is

$$s_1 \sum_{i=2}^{n} J_{1i}\,ds_i > 0. \tag{37}$$

Thus we have

Theorem 9. Starting from an equilibrium where only one commodity is taxed, welfare will be increased by levying small taxes on its generalised substitutes and small subsidies on its generalised complements, with offsetting changes in lump sum taxation.

This result is the same as Theorem 5 with a change of numéraire, and allows variable producer prices.

If there are only two commodities besides the numéraire, then

$$J_{11}H_{12}+J_{12}H_{22} = 0.$$

Then H_{12} and J_{12} have opposite signs, and the Hicks–Allen definitions of complementarity and substitution agree with the usual Slutsky–Hicks ones. With more commodities this need not be so, and it is possible that while a small tax on a commodity yields a local welfare improvement, the second-best optimum requires a subsidy on it, or vice versa.

8. Concluding comments

I am fully aware that the method and the results of this paper leave the analysis of partial welfare improvement well short of its full optimum. Whether I have contributed to local progress remains to be seen. However, I hope I have succeeded in limiting the scope of the general problem of the second-best in the following sense. The problem is not that there are very few policies that lead to partial welfare improvement; at every point there is a whole half-space of such directions of change. Nor is it the case that partial welfare improvements are particularly difficult to characterise; there are many simple, specific and economically interesting results available. The real problem is that some particular rules that were at one time thought to be intuitively plausible by some economists turned out to be wrong, and this failure received a great deal of publicity. When seen from this angle, it appears that the pessimism generated about the possibility of fruitful piecemeal welfare economics has been greatly overdone.

References

Atkinson, A.B. and N.H. Stern, 1974, Pigou, taxation and public goods, Review of Economic Studies 41, 119–28.

Bertrand, T.J. and J. Vanek, 1971, The theory of tariffs, taxes and subsidies: Some aspects of the second best, American Economic Review LXI, 925–31.

Bruno, M., 1972, Market distortions and gradual reform, Review of Economic Studies 39, 373–83.

Corlett, W.J. and D.C. Hague, 1953, Complementarity and the excess burden of taxation, Review of Economic Studies 21, 21–30.

Davis, O.A. and A. Whinston, 1965, Welfare economics and the theory of second best, Review of Economic Studies 32, 1–14.

Diamond, P.A. and D.L. McFadden, 1974, Some uses of the expenditure function in public finance, Journal of Public Economics 3, 3–21.

Diamond, P.A. and J.A. Mirrlees, 1971, Optimal taxation and public production: I and II, American Economic Review LXI, 8–27 and 261–78.

Foster, E. and H. Sonnenschein, 1970, Price distortion and economic welfare, Econometrica 38, 281–97.

Green, H.A.J., 1961, The social optimum in presence of monopoly and taxation, Review of Economic Studies 29, 66–78.

Haberler, G., 1950, Some problems in the pure theory of international trade, Economic Journal LX, 223–40.

Harberger, A.C., 1971, Three basic postulates for applied welfare economics: An interpretative essay, Journal of Economic Literature 9, 785–97.

Hatta, T., 1973, A theory of piecemeal policy recommendations, unpublished Ph.D. dissertation (Johns Hopkins University, Baltimore, Md.).

Johnston, J., 1972, Econometric methods, 2nd ed. (McGraw-Hill, New York).

Kawamata, K., 1974, Price distortion and potential welfare, Econometrica 42, 435–460.

Lipsey, R.G. and K. Lancaster, 1956, The general theory of the second best, Review of Economic Studies 24, 11–32.

Lloyd, P.J., 1974a, A more general theory of price distortions in open economies, manuscript (Australian National University, Canberra).

Lloyd, P.J., 1974b, Optimal revenue taxes with some unalterable taxes and distribution effects, manuscript (Australian National University, Canberra, and University of Reading, Reading, Berks.).

Meade, J.E., 1955, Trade and welfare: Mathematical supplement (Oxford University Press, Oxford).

Nikaido, H., 1968, Convex structures and economic theory (Academic Press, New York).

Ohyama, M., 1972, Trade and welfare in general equilibrium, Keio Economic Studies 9, 37–74.

Samuelson, P.A., 1956, Social indifference curves, Quarterly Journal of Economics 70, 1–22.

Sandmo, A., 1973, A note on the structure of optimal taxation, American Economic Review, forthcoming.

[10]

A DYNAMIC QUANTITY ADJUSTMENT PROCESS IN A SMALL OPEN ECONOMY, AND WELFARE EFFECTS OF TARIFF CHANGES

Takashi FUKUSHIMA*

Southern Methodist University, Dallas, TX 75275, USA

Received June 1979, revised version received February 1981

Consider an n-good small open economy where the technology is strictly convex and ad valorem tariffs are imposed. In this world it is known that the tariff–utility relationship may be perverse. The fact is known as the Vanek–Bhagwati Paradox. The source of the perversity is found in aggregate income effects. The present paper shows that D-stability of our dynamic system implies non-perverse aggregate income effects, and hence the non-perverse tariff–utility relationship.

1. Introduction

It is well known that for a small country free trade is optimal. However, we *cannot* conclude from this fact alone that the higher the tariff the lower the level of utility. The fact is known as the Vanek–Bhagwati Paradox. The Paradox implies that we *cannot* draw the conclusion that a reduction of tariff rates improves the level of utility if it stops short of achieving free trade. We may end up with lower level of utility as a result of the tariff reduction. One way to rule out the possibility of the paradoxical outcome is to assume that all goods are normal. This assumption is sufficient to rule out the perverse tariff–utility relationship but not necessary, as Kemp (1968) points out. Recently, some careful studies on the tariff–utility relationship were made in a general n-commodity model.[1] The results, which are directly related to the present study, are provided in the next section in the form of two propositions. They show that the perverse utility–tariff relationship occurs if and only if the aggregated income terms evaluated by world price (AIW), to be defined later in the text, is negative.

The main issue of the present paper is to formulate a dynamic adjustment process in a general n-good open economy and prove that local D-stability

*I am indebted to Professors T. Hatta, W. W. Chang, two referees of this *Journal* for their helpful comments, and U.K. Goswami for making the paper more readable. The remaining errors are of course mine.

[1]See Dixit (1975), Hatta (1977b), and Fukushima (1979).

of the system implies the non-negativity of AIW. Our result thus shows that local D-stability rules out the possibility of the Vanek–Bhagwati Paradox. Of course, the discussion of stability and instability of an equilibrium is only meaningful under a specific dynamic process. The dynamic mechanism developed in this paper is a quantity adjusting process. This is because of the nature of the small open economy where the conventional price adjusting process does not make much sense since foreign prices are given. In addition, we have to note that consumption decisions and production decisions are made by different economic agents. Hence, we have to consider a suitable dynamic process for each sector.

2. The equilibrium model and preliminary results

In this section we present our equilibrium model briefly and state some conclusions which are necessary for our discussion.

(A.1). There are n goods in the economy and the economy has well behaved compensated demand functions[2]

$$c = f(p, u), \tag{1}$$

where c is the consumption vector associated with the price vector p and the utility level u.

(A.2). The economy has well behaved supply functions[3]

$$x = h(p), \tag{2}$$

where x is the output vector associated with the level of price vector p.

[2]For this to hold, we assume that there is only one consumer in the economy who has a well-behaved (increasing, strictly quasi-concave, and twice continuously differentiable) utility function $u = v(c_1, c_2, \ldots, c_n)$. Or alternatively, we may assume the existence of a well-behaved social welfare function. In any event, the first-order utility maximization (or expenditure minimization) yields

$$u_i = \lambda p_i, \qquad i = 1, 2, \ldots, n,$$

where $u_i = \partial u/\partial c_i$ and λ the Lagrangian multiplier. These n conditions, together with $u = v(c_1, \ldots, c_n)$, yield eq. (1).

[3]The production sector here is described by a well-behaved (increasing, strictly quasi-convex, twice continuously differentiable) production possibility frontier $T(x_1, x_2, \ldots, x_n) = 0$. If all producers are price takers and maximize their profits, we can obtain $n-1$ first-order conditions as

$$\frac{T_i}{T_j} = \frac{p_i}{p_j}, \qquad i, j = 1, 2, \ldots, n,$$

where $T_i = \partial T/\partial x_i$. These, together with the production possibility curve, give us eq. (2).

(A.3). All goods are tradables and ad valorem tariffs are imposed.

(A.4). The country concerned is small. From (A.3) and (A.4) we have

$$p=\begin{bmatrix}1+r_1 & & 0\\ & \ddots & \\ 0 & & 1+r_n\end{bmatrix}q, \tag{3}$$

where q is a vector of international price and r_i a tariff rate on commodity i.

(A.5). All tariff revenue is refunded to a consumer through a lump sum subsidy.

(A.6). International trade is always in balance

$$q'(c-x)=0. \tag{4}$$

Thus, eqs. (1), (2), (3) and (4) establish the full equilibrium of our economy and determine the equilibrium values of p, c, x, and u for a given level of r and q.

Note that $\partial f_i/\partial p_j$ ($\equiv f_{ij}$) and $\lambda \partial f_i/\partial u$ ($\equiv \lambda f_{iu}$, where λ is the marginal utility of income) are the substitution and income terms of the Hicks–Slutsky equation, respectively. We call the expression $\sum_{i=1}^{n} q_i f_{iu}$ the aggregate income terms evaluated by world price (AIW).

Within the framework of the model, we can establish the following propositions.[4]

Proposition 1. Suppose the commodities which have the highest tariff rate are substitutive to all other goods in both consumption and production. Then reducing all these highest tariffs up to the level of the next highest one improves (deteriorates) the level of utility if AIW is positive (negative).

Proposition 2. If AIW is positive (negative), then the proportional tariff reduction, which reduces all tariff rates by the same percentage, improves (deteriorates) the level of utility.

From these propositions we can see the importance of the sign of AIW. One obvious way to have positive AIW is to assume that there exists no inferior good. In what follows we will show that stability of the system incorporating a dynamic quantity adjustment mechanism implies the positivity of AIW.

[4]The propositions are proved by Hatta (1977b) and Fukushima (1979) in a model containing non-traded goods.

3. The dynamic adjustment mechanism

In order to formulate the dynamic adjustment mechanism, we have to note two essential characteristics in this economy. First we note that the economy is small so that world prices are given, which rules out the conventional price adjusting system. This problem can be resolved if we consider a quantity adjusting mechanism. Secondly, we have to note that the production point is different from the consumption point, and that both consumption and production adjust at the same time independently. Keeping these in mind we formulate our adjustment mechanism. To this end, consider the initial equilibrium state of the economy. As shown by the equilibrium model, consumption and production bundles are determined at a point on the budget line where MRS = MRT = domestic price ratio. If a tariff rate is changed, the domestic price ratio is no longer equal to the MRS (MRT). The consumers and producers find that they are no longer maximizing their objective functions and try to adjust their consumption bundles and production bundles towards a new equilibrium.

The situation is depicted in fig. 1. The point (c^1, x^1) shows the initial equilibrium of consumption and production, where the country imports food and exports clothing. At c^1, the MRS between food and clothing is equal to the initial price ratio which is the slope of the tangent line to the indifference curve u^1 at c^1. Similarly, at x^1 the MRT is equal to the price ratio. If the tariff rate on food is reduced, then the economy moves to the new equilibrium (c^2, x^2). The problem we are concerned with is to describe an adjustment process from (c^1, x^1) to (c^2, x^2).

3.1. Consumption adjustment

Consider the consumer at the initial equilibrium c^1. By the definition of MRS between clothing and food, he is indifferent to exchanging the MRS amount of food for one unit of clothing. On the other hand, the rate at which he is able to obtain food for a unit of clothing is given by the domestic price ratio p_c/p_f. Since at c^1 the MRS is equal to p_c/p_f, there is no incentive for the consumer to change the equilibrium consumption bundle.

Suppose now the tariff on food is reduced. We can assume, for the sake of simplicity, that it takes more time for production to adjust than consumption.[5] Production point remains at x^1 for a while. In this circumstance the consumer realizes that he can obtain more food for one unit of clothing in the market than he is willing to trade (MRS < new p_c/p_f). Thus, he is more than willing to give up clothing in exchange for food. Hence, more food is consumed in return for less clothing. Noting the budget constraint, the consumption point moves from c^1 toward c^* along the

[5]This assumption is not necessary. It is made purely for expository purposes.

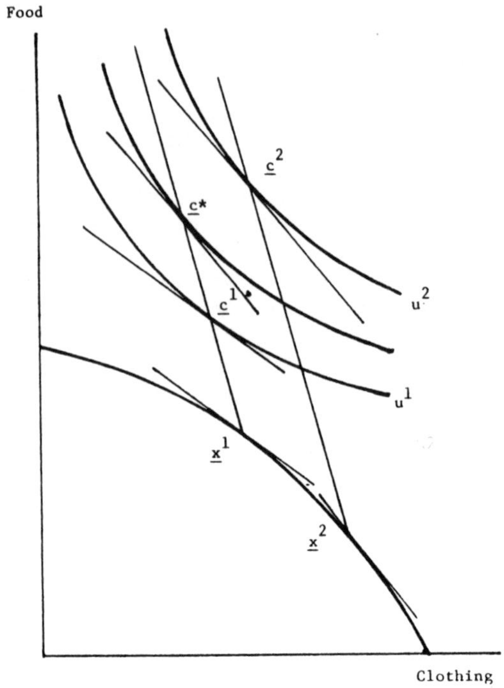

Fig. 1.

straight line passing through c^1 and x^1. This process continues until the consumption bundle reaches c^* where the new MRS is equal to the new domestic price ratio. This is the short-run consumption equilibrium point. The production point will eventually move from x^1 to x^2, as described below. Thus, the final consumption equilibrium will be achieved at c^2. In the n-commodity model, this process is formally stated as follows.

(A.7). Consumption of good i, c_i, adjusts in such a way that whenever the MRS between good j and good i is larger than the domestic price ratio, the consumption of the ith good is decreased and the consumption of the jth good is increased.

In view of this assumption, we can define z_i^j by

$$z_i^j = \frac{u_j}{u_i} - \frac{p_j}{p_i}, \qquad i,j = 1,2,\ldots,n, \tag{5}$$

where u_j/u_i is the marginal rate of substitution between the ith and the jth good defined by the utility function $u=v(c_1,c_2,\ldots,c_n)$. Then we can state (A.7) mathematically as follows:

$$\dot{c}_i = k_i a_i(z_i^1,\ldots,z^{i-1},z_i^{i+1},\ldots,z_i^n), \qquad i=1,2,\ldots,n, \tag{6}$$

where a_i is a function of $n-1$ variables z_i^j $(j=1,2,\ldots,n, j\neq i)$ and k_i is the speed of consumption adjustment in the ith market. Note that (A.7) implies

$$a_{ij}=\frac{\partial a_i}{\partial z_i^j}<0, \qquad i,j=1,2,\ldots,n, i\neq j. \tag{7}$$

3.2. Production adjustment

At the initial production equilibrium x^1, the MRT between food and clothing is equal to the initial domestic price ratio. Given the market prices this is the point where all the producers are maximizing their profit. At x^1, the marginal cost ratio is equal to the domestic price ratio since the MRT is equal to the marginal cost ratio. Hence, at the initial equilibrium there is no incentive for producers to change the level of output. If the domestic price of food is reduced due to a tariff reduction, the marginal cost ratio is no longer equal to the new domestic price ratio. The production of clothing is more profitable than that of food. Therefore producers shift the resources to the more profitable industry (clothing) from the less profitable industry (food).[6]

[6]Throughout the process the production is carried out on the production transformation surface. This may not be true in different frameworks such as the one presented by Kemp, Kimura, and Okuguchi (1977). They propose a process in which movements of the factors of production are induced sluggishly by the difference in factor rewards between sectors. This is indeed one way to describe factor movements, but not the only way. Suppose the price of a good is changed due to a tariff reduction. The connections between the price change and the resulting output change may be described stepwisely as follows.

(i) The producers find themselves out of the profit maximizing position following a change in price.

(ii) Each producer tries to find a new maximum profit output under the new price.

(iii) Each producer changes his demand for factors of production towards the new equilibrium.

(iv) The factor rewards change due to the changes of the derived demand.

(v) The factors of production move from one industry to the other according to factor reward differentials.

(vi) The output of each sector changes.

The sources of dynamics proposed by Kemp et al. are steps (iv) and (v). If the adjustments of the factors are slow, the factor reward differentials can be observed and the production point must be out of the efficient transformation surface. On the other hand, if adjustments (iv) and (v) are fast enough, the production can be carried out on the production transformation surface. Even in this case, the economy contains enough dynamics in steps (i), (ii), (iii) and (iv). Hence, our dynamic system is not in conflict with that of Kemp et al., but is complement to their formation.

Therfore the production point will move from x^1 to x^2. In general n-commodity model we assume the following.

(A.8). Production of good i, x_i, adjusts such that whenever the MRT between good i and good j is greater than the domestic price ratio p_j/p_i, the production of the ith good is increased and that of the jth good is reduced.

In view of this assumption, we can define y_i^j by

$$y_i^j = \frac{T_j}{T_i} - \frac{p_j}{p_i}, \qquad i,j = 1,2,\ldots,n, \tag{8}$$

where T_j/T_i is the marginal rate of transformation between the ith and the jth good defined by a production transformation curve $T(x_1, x_2, \ldots, x_n) = 0$. Then we can formally express the process as follows:

$$\dot{x}_i = k_{n+i} b_i(y_i^1, \ldots, y_i^{i-1}, y_i^{i+1}, \ldots, y_i^n), \qquad i = 1,2,\ldots,n, \tag{9}$$

where b_i is a function of $n-1$ variables y_i^j $(j = 1,2,\ldots,n,\ j \neq i)$ and k_{n+1} is the speed of production adjustment in the ith market. The assumption (A.8) implies that

$$b_{ij} = \frac{\partial b_i}{\partial y_i^j} > 0, \qquad i,j = 1,2,\ldots,n, \quad i \neq j. \tag{10}$$

In addition we make the following assumption on the functions a_i and b_i.

(A.9). If all $z_i^j = 0$, then $\dot{c}_i = 0$; and if all $y_i^j = 0$, then $\dot{x}_i = 0$.

This assumption shows that in equilibrium we have MRT = MRS = domestic price ratio. Note that eqs. (6) and (9) are homogeneous of degree zero with respect to vectors $(p_1, p_2, \ldots, p_n)$, $(u_1, u_2, \ldots, u_n)$, and $(T_1, T_2, \ldots, T_n)$ separately. Thus, we can choose one of the elements of each vector as a numeraire.

(A.10). The first commodity is chosen to be a numeraire so that we always measure u_i, T_i, and p_i $(i = 2,\ldots,n)$ in terms of U_1, T_1, and p_1, respectively. Specifically, we choose $u_1 = T_1 = p_1 = 1$.[7]

[7]Our result does not depend on the choice and value of the numeraire. If the ith commodity is chosen as a numeraire, we can always use $(u_1/u_i, u_2/u_i, \ldots, u_n/u_i)$ and rename them as $(u_2, u_3, \ldots, u_n)$. The same argument applies for $(p_1, \ldots, p_n)$ and $(T_1, \ldots, T_n)$. (A.10) is made to simplify the notation where we can use $u_i = p_i$ for $i = 2, 3, \ldots, n$ instead of $u_i/u_j = p_i/p_j$. Under this circumstance we can replace the condition $d(u_i/u_j) = d(p_i/p_j)$ simply by $du_i = dp_i$.

Finally, we assume

(A.11). International trade is always in balance and tariff revenue is refunded without any time lag.

This assumption shows that we always have eq. (4) satisfied, hence we have

$$\sum_{i=1}^{n} q_i \dot{c}_i = \sum_{i=1}^{n} q_i \dot{x}_i. \tag{11}$$

Assumptions (A.7)–(A.11) complete the description of our dynamic adjustment process. In what follows we will reduce this adjustment mechanism to an equivalent and more convenient system and consider the stability of the system. For this purpose, consider eq. (11) where we can always express $\dot{c}_1$ as a function of $\dot{c}_i$ $(i=2,\ldots,n)$ and $\dot{x}_j$ $(j=1,2,\ldots,n)$. Thus, we can eliminate one equation from (6) and consider altogether only $2n-1$ differential equations. In addition, note that z_j^i's are functions of u_i's. Therefore under (A.10) and eq. (6), $\dot{c}_i$ is expressed as a function of u_2, $u_3 \ldots$, and u_n. Let this function be written as

$$\dot{c}_i = k_i a_i^*(u_2,\ldots,u_n), \qquad i=2,\ldots,n. \tag{12}$$

Also using eq. (4), we obtain:

$$\begin{aligned} u_i &= v_i(c_1,\ldots,c_n) \\ &= v_i\left(-\frac{1}{q_1}\sum_{i=2}^{n} q_i c_i + \sum_{j=1}^{n} q_j x_j, c_2,\ldots,c_n\right) \\ &= w_i(c_2,\ldots,c_n,x_1,\ldots,x_n), \end{aligned} \tag{13}$$

where w_i is an implicitly defined function.

In view of (13), eq. (12) can be rewritten as

$$\dot{c}_i = k_i \phi_i(c_2,\ldots,c_n,x_1,\ldots,x_n), \qquad i=2,3,\ldots,n. \tag{14}$$

Similarly, in view of (8) and the fact that $T_i = T_i(x_1,\ldots,x_n)$, we can express $\dot{x}_j$ as a function of x_i's, that is

$$\dot{x}_j = k_{n+j}\psi_j(x_1,\ldots,x_n), \qquad j=1,2,\ldots,n. \tag{15}$$

Hence we have reduced our system to (14) and (15) which involve $2n-1$

equations and $2n-1$ unknowns: $\dot{c}_i$ ($i=2,\ldots,n$) and $\dot{x}_j$ ($j=1,\ldots,n$). We call the system given by (14) and (15) the original dynamic system. Sometimes it is convenient to consider the linearized system of the original dynamic system. For this purpose, we can write the linear approximation system as

$$\begin{pmatrix} \dot{c}^* \\ \dot{x}^* \end{pmatrix} = \left[\begin{array}{cccc|cccc} k_2 & & & & & & & \\ & k_3 & & & & & 0 & \\ & & \ddots & & & & & \\ & & & k_n & & & & \\ \hline & & & & k_{n+1} & & & \\ & 0 & & & & \ddots & & \\ & & & & & & & k_{2n} \end{array}\right] \left[\begin{array}{c|c} \Phi_c & \Phi_x \\ \hline 0 & \Psi_x \end{array}\right] \begin{pmatrix} c^* \\ x^* \end{pmatrix}. \tag{16}$$

where $c^*=c-c^e$, $x^*=x-x^e$; c^e and x^e are the equilibrium consumption and production bundles, respectively: and

$$\Phi_c = \left[\frac{\partial \phi_i}{\partial c_k}\right], \qquad i,k=2,\ldots,n,$$

$$\Phi_x = \left[\frac{\partial \phi_i}{\partial x_j}\right], \qquad i=2,\ldots,n,\ j=1,2,\ldots,n,$$

$$\psi_x = \left[\frac{\partial \psi_j}{\partial x_\ell}\right], \qquad j,\ell=1,2,\ldots,n.$$

We consider the implication of D-stability of the original system as well as of the linear system.[8] The following lemmas are essential to establish our results.

Lemma 1. Let a matrix Ω be defined as

$$\Omega = \left(\begin{array}{c|c} \Phi_c & \Phi_x \\ \hline 0 & \psi_x \end{array}\right).$$

If the original system given by (14) and (15) is locally D-stable, then all the pth order principal minors of Ω evaluated at the equilibrium have the same sign as $(-1)^p$ with possibility of zero.

[8]A dynamic system is said to be D-stable if it is stable for any positive speed of adjustment. We consider the stability problem of the original system as well as the linear system since local stability of the original system does not necessarily imply stability of linear system.

Proof. The stability of the original system implies that all of the characteristic roots of the Jacobian matrix, i.e. the matrix of speed of adjust times Ω, have non-positive real parts. On the other hand, the characteristic equation of the Jacobian matrix can be expressed as an nth degree polynomial with real coefficients:

$$\lambda^n + m_1\lambda^{n-1} + m_2\lambda^{n-2} + \dots + m_n = 0.$$

The solutions of this equation are the characteristic roots of the matrix and, moreover, we can write the coefficient m_p $(p=1,2,\dots,n)$ as

$$m_p = (-1)^p \times \text{(sum of all the } p\text{th order principal minors of the Jacobian matrix).}$$

It is readily seen that the non-positivity of the real part of the characteristic roots implies non-negativity of the coefficients $m_1, m_2, \dots, m_n$. Notice that m_p contains speed of adjustment coefficients and the local D-stability requires that m_p be non-negative for any positive adjustment coefficients. It follows that all the pth order principal minors of Ω have the sign $(-1)^p$ with the possibility of zero. Q.E.D.

Lemma 2. If the linear system givien by (16) *is D-stable, then all the pth order principal minors of Ω have the same sign as $(-1)^p$ with the possibility of zero. In addition, at least one non-zero principal minor exists for every p.*

Lemma 2 follows immediately from the Routh–Hurwitz Theorem.[9] As we can expect, D-stability of the linear system implies a stronger condition than that of the non-linear system. In addition to these, we need the following which is due to Hatta (1977a).

Lemma 3. Let us denote f_u and F by.

$$f_u = \begin{pmatrix} f_{1u} \\ \vdots \\ f_{nu} \end{pmatrix} \quad \text{and} \quad F = \begin{bmatrix} f_{12} & \cdots & f_{1n} \\ \vdots & & \\ f_{n2} & \cdots & f_{nn} \end{bmatrix}.$$

where f_{ij} is a partial derivative of the compensated demand function (1).

Suppose that the utility function is increasing, twice continuously differentiable, strictly quasi-concave and that the bordered Hessian does not

[9]See Quirk and Saposnik (1968, pp. 165–166).

vanish.[10] *Then we have*

$$(-1)^n |f_u \ F| > 0. \tag{17}$$

Now we are in the position to state and prove our main theorem.

Theorem 1. If the economy described by (14) *and* (15) *is locally D-stable, then AIW is non-negative around the full equilibrium.*

Proof. In view of lemma 1, we have

$$(-1)^{n-1} |\Phi_c| \geqq 0, \tag{18}$$

since $|\Phi_c|$ is one of the $(n-1)$th order principal minors of Ω.

Let a_{ij}^* and w_{ij} be partial derivatives of the functions defined by (12) and (13), respectively, i.e. $a_{ij}^* \equiv \partial a_i^* / \partial u_j$ and $w_{ij} \equiv \partial w_i / \partial c_j$. We can define matrices A^* and W as follows:

$$A^* = \begin{bmatrix} a_{22}^* & \cdots & a_{2n}^* \\ \vdots & & \\ a_{n2}^* & \cdots & a_{nn}^* \end{bmatrix}; \qquad W = \begin{bmatrix} w_{22} & \cdots & w_{2n} \\ \vdots & & \vdots \\ w_{n2} & \cdots & w_{nn} \end{bmatrix}.$$

Note that we have

$$\Phi_c = A^* W. \tag{19}$$

In view of (18) and (19) we have

$$(-1)^{n-1} |A^*| \, |W| \geqq 0. \tag{20}$$

We will prove the theorem by first establishing $|A^*| > 0$ and secondly by reducing $|W|$ into the expression which contains the expression $q'f_u$ (AIW).

(i) *Positivity of* $|A^*|$. In view of eqs. (5), (6), and (12) we have

$$a_{ij}^* = \begin{cases} \dfrac{1}{u_i} a_{ij} & \text{if} \quad i \neq j, \\ -\dfrac{1}{u_i} \displaystyle\sum_{k=1}^{n} \left(\dfrac{u_k}{u_i} \right) a_{ik}, & \text{if} \quad i = j. \end{cases} \tag{21}$$

[10] A careful reading of Hatta's proof shows that these assumptions are implicitly made and that inequality (17) holds strictly.

Notice that $a_{ii}^*>0$ and $a_{ij}^*<0$ $(i \neq j)$ because of inequality (7). Let us now define e_{ij} by

$$e_{ij}=\left(\frac{u_j}{u_i}\right)a_{ij}. \tag{22}$$

In view of eqs. (21) and (22), we have

$$A^*\begin{bmatrix} u_2 & 0 \\ 0 & u_n \end{bmatrix} = \begin{bmatrix} -\sum\limits_{k=2}^{n} e_{2k} & e_{23} & \cdots & e_{2n} \\ e_{32} & -\sum\limits_{k \neq 3}^{n} e_{3k} & \cdots & e_{3n} \\ \vdots & \vdots & \ddots & \vdots \\ e_{n2} & e_{n3} & \cdots & -\sum\limits_{k \neq n} e_{nk} \end{bmatrix}, \tag{23}$$

where $\sum_{k \neq i}^{n}$ shows the summation on k from 1 to n except for i.

Expression (23) implies that we have

$$u_i|a_{ii}^*| > \sum_{j \neq i} u_j|a_{ij}^*|, \quad \text{for} \quad i=2,3,\ldots,n. \tag{24}$$

Therefore we have established that A^* has (a) the dominant diagonal,[11] (b) positive diagonal elements, and (c) negative off diagonal elements. Conditions (a) and (b) imply that the real parts of all the characteristics roots of A^* are positive,[12] and this fact and (c) imply all successive minors of A^* are positive.[13] Therefore, we get $|A^*|>0$. In view of (20) we obtain

$$(-1)^{n-1}|W| \geqq 0. \tag{25}$$

(ii) *Alternative expression of* $|W|$. Noting (A.10), differentiating (1) totally, we obtain

[11]An $n \times n$ matrix is said to have a dominant diagonal if there exists n positive numbers d_j such that

$$d_i|a_{ii}| > \sum_{j \neq i} d_j|a_{ij}|, \qquad i=1,2,\ldots,n.$$

See McKenzie (1959) and Takayama (1974).

[12]Takayama (1974, theorem 4.C.2, p. 382).

[13]Takayama (1974, theorem 4.C.8, p. 386).

$$\begin{pmatrix} dc_1 \\ \vdots \\ dc_n \end{pmatrix} = \left[\begin{array}{c|ccc} f_{1u} & f_{12} & \cdots & f_{1n} \\ \vdots & & \cdots & \\ f_{nu} & f_{n2} & \cdots & f_{nn} \end{array}\right] \begin{pmatrix} du \\ dp_2 \\ \vdots \\ dp_n \end{pmatrix}. \tag{26}$$

Thus, we have

$$\begin{pmatrix} du \\ dp_2 \\ \vdots \\ dp_n \end{pmatrix} = [f_u \,|\, F]^{-1} \begin{pmatrix} dc_1 \\ \vdots \\ dc_n \end{pmatrix}. \tag{27}$$

Since we are interested in obtaining the expression $\partial u_i/\partial c_j$ defined by eq. (13) as the (i,j)th element of W $(i,j=2,3,\ldots,n)$, we can keep the x_j's constant and differentiate eq. (4) to obtain

$$dc_1 = -\sum_{i=2}^{n} \frac{q_i}{q_1} dc_i. \tag{28}$$

Premultiply an $(n-1)\times n$ matrix $[0 \,|\, I_{n-1}]$ to eq. (27), and noting eqs. (28) and (A.10), we get

$$\begin{pmatrix} du_2 \\ \vdots \\ du_n \end{pmatrix} = [0 \,|\, I_{n-1}][f_u \,|\, F]^{-1} \left[\frac{-q'_*}{I_{n-1}}\right] \begin{pmatrix} dc_2 \\ \vdots \\ dc_n \end{pmatrix}$$

$$= M \begin{pmatrix} dc_2 \\ \vdots \\ dc_n \end{pmatrix}, \tag{29}$$

where $q'_* = (q_2/q_1, q_3/q_1, \ldots, q_n/q_1)$, and M is defined implicitly from eq. (29). Thus, we can conclude:

$$M = W. \tag{30}$$

In view of inequality (25), this implies

$$(-1)^{n-1}|M| \geqq 0. \tag{31}$$

Using (31) and lemma 3, we obtain

$$|M|\,|f_u \vdots F| \geqq 0. \tag{32}$$

The l.h.s. of (32) can be written as the determinant of the following expression:[14]

$$E = \left[\begin{array}{c|c|c} 0_{(n-1)(n-1)} & \mathbf{0} & -I_{n-1} \\ \hline -q'_* & & \\ \cline{1-1} I_{n-1} & f_u & F \end{array}\right].$$

E is a $(2n-1)\times(2n-1)$ matrix, and in particular in this case we have

$$|E| = \det \left[\begin{array}{c|c|c} -I_{n-1} & 0 & \mathbf{0} \\ \hline & -q'_* & \\ \cline{2-2} F & I_{n-1} & f_u \end{array}\right]$$

$$= \det \left[\begin{array}{c|c} f_u & -q'_* \\ \cline{2-2} & I_{n-1} \end{array}\right]$$

$$= \frac{1}{q_1} q' f_u \geqq 0, \tag{33}$$

where the last inequality follows from (32). Q.E.D.

Thus, we have proved that if our dynamic system is stable for any positive speed of adjustment, AIW must be non-negative. This theorem, however, does not exclude the possibility of zero AIW. We can exclude this possibility by reasonably assuming that our equilibrium model given by (1), (2), (3), and (4) satisfies the conditions of the implicit function theorem. In this event we are sure that the Jacobian of the system is non-vanishing and hence AIW is non-zero. The other way is to assume the D-stability of linear approximation system (16). For this case we have the following theorem.

Theorem 2. *AIW is positive if the linear system is D-stable.*

Proof. In view of lemma 2, we have

$$(-1)^{n-1}|\Phi_c| \geqq 0 \tag{34}$$

since $|\Phi_c|$ is one of the $(n-1)$th order principal minors of Ω.

[14]The determinant of a partitioned matrix can be written as

$$\det\left[\begin{array}{c|c} A & B \\ \hline C & D \end{array}\right] = |A - BD^{-1}C|\,|D|,$$

where A and D are square and D is non-singular. See Johnston (1972, p. 95).

In addition, we have

$$(-1)^{2n-1}\begin{vmatrix}\Phi_c & \Phi_x \\ 0 & \psi_x\end{vmatrix}>0. \tag{35}$$

Expression (35) holds with strict inequality since this is the only $(2n-1)$th order principal minor of Ω. Thus, this expression shows that $|\Phi_c| \neq 0$. Therefore (34) holds with strict inequality. This implies all inequalities (20), (25), (31), (32), and (33) hold with strict inequalities. Q.E.D.

4. A geometric interpretation

We can interpretate our result in the usual two-commodity diagram. In fig. 2, (x^0, c^0) is the equilibrium position. EE is the Engel curve passing through

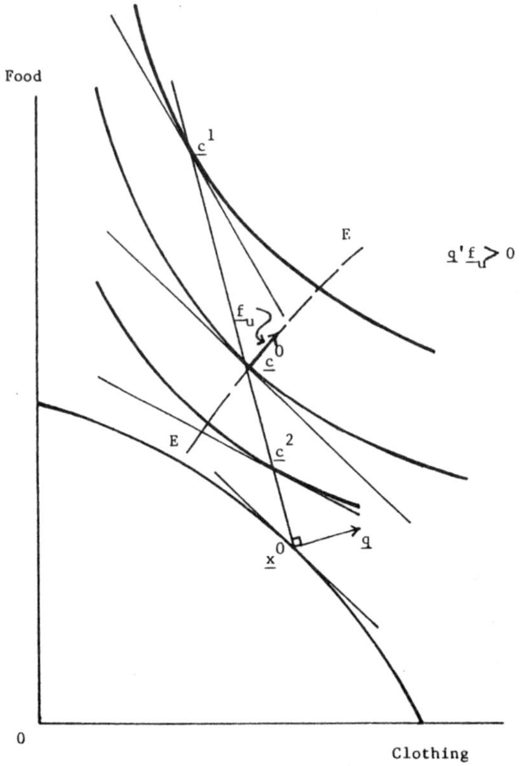

Fig. 2.

c^0. This figure shows the stable equilibrium. For if a consumption bundle happens to be at c^1, the MRS at c^1 is larger than that at c^0. It follows that more clothing will be demanded in return for food under our consumption adjustment process. Hence, the consumption bundle will move towards c^0. If consumption is at c^2, then by the similar process it moves towards c^0. This is true because EE passes through c^0 from inside to outside. The shape of the EE curve and the stability of the system is closely related. For example, in fig. 3, EE passes through c^0 from outside to inside. If we conduct the same experiment as before, we realize that c^0 is unstable. The relationship between the stability and the sign of AIW can be seen as follows. The vector q is a normal vector to the line c^0x^0. The vector f_u is, by definition, on EE starting from c^0. Hence, their inner product $q'f_u$ is positive if the angle between the two vectors q and f_u is less than $\Pi/2$ and it is negative if it is larger than $\Pi/2$. Clearly, the stable equilibrium corresponds to the former case and unstable equilibrium fits into the latter. This explains the relationship between the sign of AIW and stability of the system in the diagram.

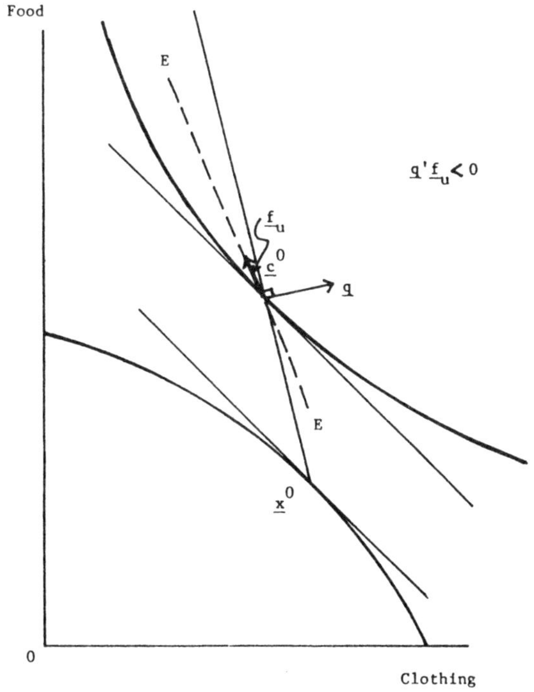

Fig. 3.

5. Concluding remarks

Our method and results are closely related to the work of Kemp (1968) who uses the consumption adjustment process in a two-commodity world; of Amano (1968) who shows a production adjustment process in a two-good economy; and of Hatta (1977a) who utilizes a similar adjustment mechanism in a constant cost closed economy. Our model is essentially an extension of these models and provides a dynamic process of an n-good small open economy.

The adjustment process presented in this paper may be called Marshallian mechanism.[15] We proved that the stability of the equilibrium rules out the perverse tariff utility relationship. In other words, the stability of the system provides a restriction on the magnitude of income effects. There are several other cases in trade theory which require analogous restrictions such as in the case of the customs union. Our analysis might be extended to apply in these cases also. Furthermore, since the perverse tariff and utility relationship is somewhat related to the uniqueness of equilibrium, the positivity of AIW may prove sufficient for the uniqueness. However, these are beyond the scope of the present paper.

[15]It may be unfair for Marshall that the quantity adjustment is labeled 'Marshallian' since he considered both quantity and price adjusting processes. However, many times it is customary to call the type of adjustment process 'Marshallian'.

References

Amano, A., 1968, Stability conditions in the pure theory of international trade: A rehabilitation of the Marshallian approach. Quarterly Journal of Economics 82, 327–339.

Bhagwati, J., 1968, The gains from trade once again, Oxford Economic Papers 20, 137–148.

Dixit, A., 1975, Welfare effects of tax and price changes, Journal of Public Economics 4, 103–123.

Fukushima, T., 1979, Tariff structure, non-traded goods and theory of piecemeal policy recommendations, International Economic Review 20, 427–435.

Hatta, T., 1977a, A theory of piecemeal policy recommendations, Review of Economic Studies 136, 1–21.

Hatta, T., 1977b, A recommendation for a better tariff structure, Econometrica 45, 1859–1869.

Johnston, J., 1972, Econometric methods, 2nd edn. (McGraw-Hill, New York).

Kemp, M.C., 1968, Some issues in the analysis of trade gains, Oxford Economic Papers 20, 149–161.

Kemp, M.C., Y. Kimura and K. Okuguchi, 1977, Monotonicity properties of a dynamical version of the Heckscher–Ohlin model of production, Economic Studies Quarterly 28, 249–253.

McKenzie, L., 1959, Matrices with dominant diagonals and economic theory, in: Arrow, Karlin and Suppes, eds., Mathematical methods in social sciences (Stanford University Press) ch. 4.

Quirk, J. and R. Saposnik, 1968, Introduction to general equilibrium theory and welfare economics (McGraw-Hill, New York).

Takayama, A., 1974, Mathematical economics (The Dryden Press, Hinsdale, Ill.).

Vanek, J., 1965, General equilibrium of international discrimination. The case of customs unions (Harvard University Press, Cambridge, Mass.).

Part III
Results on Reform and National Welfare

[11]

The Theory of Tariffs, Taxes, and Subsidies: Some Aspects of the Second Best

By TRENT J. BERTRAND AND JAROSLAV VANEK*

The purpose of this paper is twofold. First, we establish three theorems defining the relationship between the gross and net production possibilities sets when production possibilities are bounded by the fixed supply of primary factors in the economy. We prove that the normal assumption of a strictly convex efficient surface on the gross production possibility set yields a strictly convex efficient surface on the net production possibility set. Furthermore, it is shown that perfect competition will lead to production on the efficient surface of the gross production possibility set where the marginal rate of transformation is equated to the ratios of unit values added and that the corresponding solution in terms of net outputs is characterized by equality of the marginal rate of transformation on the efficient surface of the net production possibility surface and the ratio of product prices. These results of profit maximizing behavior in a perfectly competitive economy provide constraints to the normative problems set out in Sections II and III.

The second and principal purpose of this paper is to examine the second best solutions corresponding to prescribed levels of some tariffs, taxes, or subsidies and variable levels of others. The interest of such an examination is perhaps obvious. Governments often are under obligation—owing to domestic pressure groups, international agreements, or legal commitments—to preserve tariffs or subsidies on some commodities. If this is so, our analysis then tells us what levels of protection should be selected for those commodities where no rigid commitments are present.

Based on a model with intermediate products, our analysis is also relevant to the newly developing general equilibrium theory of effective protection. By and large, concern in recent papers has focused on questions of the quantitative impact of effective protection.[1] Questions of second best for which a general equilibrium approach is so well suited have largely been neglected.

In Section II, it is proved that under certain conditions a welfare maximizing policy requires the elimination of extreme distortions which are within the control of policy makers when the existence of distortions outside their control prevent the attainment of a first best solution. In Section III, it is shown that the consumption possibilities facing a community may be increased by a similar elimination of extreme distortions in a model where the distortions are defined in terms of *effective* or value added distortions rather than nominal distortions.

I. The Production Possibility Sets

The economy consists of n commodities, X_i $(i=1 \dots n)$, and m factors, v_h $(h=1 \dots m)$. Technology is defined by production functions permitting substitution of primary factors in a neoclassical manner and the input of intermediate products in fixed proportions, that is;

$$(1)\quad X_i = \min\left[f^i(v_1^i, \dots, v_m^i), \frac{X_1^i}{a_{1i}}, \dots, \frac{X_n^i}{a_{ni}}\right]$$

where a_{ji} $(j=1, \dots, n)$ is the fixed amount

* Assistant professor at the Johns Hopkins University and professor at Cornell University, respectively. We are indebted to Bela Balassa, Frank Flatters, Peter Newman, Hugh Rose, Alan Kirman, and a referee for helpful comments. Tatsuo Hatta has been especially helpful in several discussions of the methodology and results of this study, while Hajime Hori is responsible for pointing out several errors in an earlier draft.

[1] See, for instance, W. M. Corden, V. K. Ramaswami and T. N. Srinavasan, Roy Ruffin, Balassa and S. F. Guisinger. For an excellent exception dealing with the second best with different constraints than studied here, see A. H. H. Tan.

of commodity j used in the production of one unit of commodity i ($a_{ij}=0$ if $i=j$), v_h^i is the amount of the hth factor used in production of the ith commodity, and X_j^i is the total amount of the jth commodity used in producing the ith commodity.

We assume that the effective constraint on production is always the availability of primary factors,[2] so that (1) may be rewritten as (1′):

$$(1') \qquad X_i = f^i(v_1^i, \ldots, v_m^i)$$

The gross production possibility set T,

$$(2) \qquad T(X_1, \ldots, X_n) \leq 0$$

is bounded due to a fixed endowment of primary factors. The relationship between gross and net outputs is defined in relation (3);

$$(3) \qquad [I - A]X = x$$

where I is the identity matrix, A is the nxn matrix of input-output coefficients, X is a vector of gross outputs, and x is a vector of net outputs. The net production possibility set τ is therefore[3]

$$(4) \quad \tau\left(X_1 - \sum_j a_{1j}X_j, \ldots, X_n - \sum_j a_{nj}X_j\right) = \tau(x_1, \ldots, x_n) \leq 0$$

and is obtained by subtracting outputs used as intermediate inputs from the gross outputs.

Preliminary to our analysis of protection, we establish three theorems concerning the gross and net production possibility sets.

THEOREM 1. *If the gross production possibility set is strictly convex, then the net production possibility set will be strictly convex.*

PROOF:

Choose any two points X' and X'' in the gross output set T and let X be a strictly convex linear combination of these points. Then by the strict convexity of T, we can choose $\overline{X}$ such that;

$$(5) \qquad \overline{X} > X = \rho X' + (1 - \rho)X''$$

where $0<\rho<1$, and $X \in T$. Premultiplying the right-hand side of inequality (5) by $[I-A]$, and by definition of τ, we have:

$$(6) \qquad x = \rho x' + (1 - \rho)x''$$

where $x \in \tau$, and x, x', and x'' are the net output vectors corresponding to X, X', and X'', respectively. Let δ be a strictly positive vector of arbitrarily small net outputs. Then τ is strictly convex if $(x+\delta) \in \tau$. But $(x+\delta) \in \tau$ if $(X+[I-A]^{-1}\delta) \in T$. By the Hawkins-Simon condition,[4] $[I-A]^{-1}$ is a matrix of positive elements so that we have

$$(7) \qquad X + [I - A]^{-1}\delta > X$$

But since $[I-A]^{-1}\delta$ may be made arbitrarily small by the appropriate selection of δ, we choose δ such that,

$$(8) \qquad \overline{X} > X + [I - A]^{-1}\delta$$

which means by (5), that $X+[I-A]^{-1}\delta \in T$ and therefore, we have $(x+\delta) \in \tau$.

THEOREM 2:[5] *Profit maximizing behavior with perfectly competitive product and factor markets will lead to production on the gross production possibility surface where the marginal rate of transformation is equated to the ratio of values added.*

PROOF:

Situated on the boundary of T, we consider the possibility of reallocating one unit of any factor of production from the ith to the jth industry. The total cost of production for the jth industry is;

$$(9) \qquad TC_j = \sum_h w_h v_h^j + \sum_i P_i^d a_{ij} X_j$$

and for the ith industry;

$$(10) \qquad TC_i = \sum_h W_h v_h^i + \sum_j P_j^d a_{ji} X_i$$

where P_i^d is the domestic price of the ith

[2] This assumption has been used previously by Vanek (1963).

[3] Summations, unless otherwise specified, are over all commodities or factors.

[4] The Hawkins-Simon conditions assure that the economy is not self-consuming.

[5] A direct proof of the equality of relative prices to the marginal rates of transformation along τ is provided for the two-product case in Vanek (1963).

commodity. Differentiating (9) and (10) with one factor v_* variable and noting that profit maximizing behavior under perfect competition implies marginal cost pricing, we obtain;

$$(11) \quad MC_j = \frac{dTC_j}{dX_j} = w_* \frac{dv_*^j}{dX_j} + \sum_i P_i^d a_{ij} = P_j^d$$

and

$$(12) \quad MC_i = \frac{dTC_i}{dX_i} = w_* \frac{dv_*^i}{dX_i} + \sum_j P_j^d a_{ji} = P_i^d$$

Since v_* is reallocated from the ith to the jth industry, $dv_*^j = -dv_*^i$ and since w_* is the same for both industries, we obtain from (11) and (12);

$$(13) \quad -\frac{dX_i}{dX_j} = \frac{T_j^*}{T_i^*} = \frac{P_j^d - \sum_i a_{ij}}{P_i^d - \sum_j P_j^d a_{ij}} = \frac{\pi_j^d}{\pi_i^d}$$

where $\pi_i^d = P_i^d - \sum_j P_j^d a_{ji}$ is the domestic value added (or net price) of commodity i. The slope defined in relation (13) is the marginal rate of transformation along a production possibility surface, T^*, constrained by the immobility of factors other than v_*. Since we are evaluating this slope at a point on the boundary of T which (by definition) cannot be intersected by T^*, it must be equal to the slope of the unconstrained production possibility surface, that is

$$(14) \quad \frac{T_j}{T_i} = \frac{T_j^*}{T_i^*} = \frac{\pi_j^d}{\pi_i^d}$$

THEOREM 3: *If the marginal rates of transformation of gross outputs are equated to the ratios of value added, the marginal rates of transformation between net outputs will be equated to the ratio of their prices.*

PROOF:

Differentiating equation (4) and setting all changes in gross output except for the ith and jth industry equal to zero, we obtain;

$$(15) \quad (\tau_i - \sum_j a_{ji}\tau_j)\, dX_i + (\tau_j - \sum_j a_{ij}\tau_i)\, dX_j = 0$$

$$(16) \quad -\frac{dX_i}{dX_j} = \frac{\tau_j - \sum_i a_{ij}\tau_i}{\tau_i - \sum_j a_{ji}\tau_j} = \frac{1 - \sum_i a_{ij}\frac{\tau_i}{\tau_j}}{\frac{\tau_i}{\tau_j} - \sum_j a_{ji}}$$

Equating (16) to π_j^d/π_i^d and solving for τ_i/τ_j, we obtain;

$$(17) \quad \frac{\tau_i}{\tau_j} = \frac{P_i^d}{P_j^d}$$

The correspondence between the net output and gross output production possibility sets defined by these three theorems not only proves useful in this paper but makes possible the extension of many theorems concerning the effects of nominal tariffs (which distort prices) on net outputs to the effect of effective tariffs (which distort values added) on gross outputs.

II. Distortions through Tariffs and Subsidies on Trade[6]

We now consider the conditions for improving community welfare in a small country facing fixed terms of trade when the first best solution of zero or equal tariffs and subsidies is not possible either in the sense that all tariffs cannot be immediatly equated due to time constraints involved in changing commercial policy or because some tariffs cannot be altered because of political infeasibility. It is assumed in the analysis that tariff revenue is redistributed to the community.

With the nth commodity having an extreme distortion ($t_n >$ or $< t_i$), policy author-

[6] A simplification of an earlier treatment of this section was suggested by Tatsuo Hatta.

ities seek to improve community welfare by varying t_n while holding all other tariffs constant. It is assumed that the preferences of the community are represented by a convex nonintersecting preference map given by relation (18);

$$(18) \qquad u = u(C_1, \ldots, C_n)$$

where C_i is the consumptions of the ith commodity.

The budget constraint facing the community with tariff revenue redistributed is given in relation (19);

$$(19) \qquad \begin{aligned} \sum_i P_i C_i &= \sum_i P_i X_i - \sum_i \sum_j P_j a_{ij} X_j \\ &= \sum_j P_i X_i \end{aligned}$$

where P_i is the fixed international price of the ith commodity, and which shows that the value of the consumption bundle in equilibrium is constrained by the value of net output, both evaluated at world prices.

Net production possibilities are given in relation (20) and the conditions for profit maximization and consumer utility maximization are given in relations (20), (21), and (22), respectively;

$$(20) \quad \tau(x_1, \ldots, x_n) = 0$$

$$(21) \quad \frac{\tau_i}{\tau_j} = \frac{P_i(1+t_i)}{P_j(1+t_j)} \quad (i=1, \ldots, n, \; j=1, \ldots, n)$$

$$(22) \quad \frac{u_i}{p_i}(1+t_i) = A \quad (i=1, \ldots, n)$$

where t_i is the percentage price distortion due to the imposition of a tariff or trade subsidy and A is the marginal utility of income.

By differentiating (18), we have the change in social welare as;[7]

$$(23) \qquad du = \sum_i u_i dC_i$$

[7] Relations (23)–(27) define the welfare index applicable to the open economy with interindustry flows. This relation has been derived and discussed by T. J. Bertrand. See also the related papers by Vanek (1970).

which, by relation (22) may be rewritten as;

$$(24) \quad \begin{aligned} du &= A \sum_i P_i(1 + t_i) dC_i \\ &= \{ \sum_i P_i dC_i + \sum_i P_i t_i dC_i \} \end{aligned}$$

which, by differentiating (19) and substituting in (24) gives;

$$(25) \quad \begin{aligned} du &= A\{ \sum_i P_i dx_i + \sum_i P_i t_i dC_i \} \\ &= A\{ \sum_i P_i(1 + t_i) dx_i \\ &\quad - \sum_i P_i t_i dx_i + \sum_i P_i t_i dC_i \} \end{aligned}$$

Differentiating relation (20) and using relation (21), it is seen that

$$(26) \qquad \sum_i P_i(1 + t_i) dx_i = 0$$

which can be substituted into (25) to obtain

$$(27) \quad \begin{aligned} du &= A\{ - \sum_i P_i t_i dx_i + \sum_i P_i t_i dC_i \} \\ &= A\{ \sum_i P_i t_i dE_i \} \end{aligned}$$

where $E_i(=C_i - x_i)$ is the excess demand of the community for the ith commodity.

Letting e denote the commodity with extreme distortions, we have;

$$(28) \quad du = A\{ t_e P_e dE_e + \sum_j P_j t_j dE_j \}$$

where the j subscript denotes the $n-1$ other commodities. But by differentiating the budget constraint, we have;

$$(29) \qquad P_e dE_e = - \sum_j P_j dE_j$$

which when substituted into (28) gives relation (30).

$$(30) \qquad \frac{du}{dt_e} = A \left\{ \sum_j P_j(t_j - t_e) \frac{\partial E_j}{\partial t_e} \right\}$$

It defines the change in community welfare when t_e is varied but all other distortions are held constant. Equation (30) is central to our analysis.

First, we define commodity i as a complement of commodity j if excess demand for commodity i decreases with an increase in the domestic price of commodity j, i.e., if $\partial E_i/\partial t_j<0$ $(i\neq j)$. Note that this definition differs from the Hicksian definition as it is not based on income compensated price terms but on changes in excess demand due to changes in price distortions with real income not fixed but constrained by the production possibilities and the structure of price distortions.

Noting that if complementarity between commodities does not occur ($\partial E_j/\partial t_e<0$ for all commodities) and that t_e is extreme (either $t_e>$ or $<t_j$, the distortion on all other commodities), it is immediately seen from equation (30) that community welfare improves when a) t_n is increased if $t_n<t_j$ and b) t_n is decreased if $t_n>t_j$.

This establishes Theorem 4:

THEOREM 4: *In a multi-commodity model with no complementarity, it is necessary in order to achieve a second best solution and sufficient for an increase in welfare that variable extreme distortions be eliminated.*

Since the one by one reduction of extreme distortions unambiguously improves welfare in a world with some unchangeable tariffs, the overall second best solution (with all variable tariffs optimally adjusted) must be characterized with no variable tariffs which are extreme.

Theorem 4 is the central finding of our second best analysis.[8] It provides a general guideline to policy formulation in a world where first best conditions cannot be immediately attained. These guidelines have two aspects. First, a general rule to reduce extreme distortions as far as possible—that is, until all distortions which are variable are intermediate to the highest and lowest distortions that cannot be altered. Second, if a policy of trade liberalization is to be carried out, even when all tariffs are variable, it may not be feasible to carry out all the required changes in commercial policy simultaneously. In these circumstances, policy authorities can follow the general rule of eliminating extreme distortions until the first best solution is eventually attained.

Theorem 4 is also applicable to the analysis of production taxes or subsidies which have no effect on consumers behavior. A change in the excess demand will occur solely due to the production effect. Thus, if it is assumed that an increase in the producer's price of a particular product increases the output of that good and reduces the output of all others, all variable extreme production taxes or subsidies should be eliminated, i.e., reduced or raised until they are no longer extreme.

It should be noted that Theorem 4 can remain valid even if complementarity exists between some commodities. All that is required is that the term in equation (30) for the noncomplementary commodities dominate those for the complements.

Finally, equation (30) is a generalized form of the Meade welfare index. The economic rationale of Theorem 4 is that changes in the extreme tariff will tend to reallocate expenditures towards products where the excess of the value to consumers over the real cost to the economy (defined by the fixed world prices) is greatest or reallocate resources away from industries where the excess of domestic over real costs (again defined by fixed world prices) is greatest.

III. Distortions through Taxes and Subsidies on Production

The theorems established in the preceding section are conditional on the effects of price changes on excess demands. It is also interesting to consider the problem when protection for industries is defined by the degree of distortion of value added. This is important because the profitability of different industries depends on value added or net prices rather than prices per se and sophisticated pressure groups may seek to maintain effective rather than nominal protection. We therefore consider the situation where value added distortions, brought about by

[8] Theorems of this nature have been derived by R. G. Lipsey and R. K. Lancaster for a three-commodity model, by Vanek (1964) for trade liberalization in a multi-country world, and by Hatta for welfare improvements in a single country where consumption and production distortions cause a divergence between marginal rates of transformation and substitution for different producers and consumers.

taxes and subsidies imposed on the production process, are fixed for some industries and variable for others.

The distortions we are concerned with may be defined as the policy induced percentage change of value added from that given by the international prices. That is, where $\bar{t}_i$ is the tax ($\bar{t}_i<0$) or subsidy ($\bar{t}_i>0$) rate for individual commodities, the *effective* rate of tax or subsidy, f_i, is defined as;

$$(31)\quad \begin{aligned} f_i &= \frac{P_i(1+\bar{t}_i) - \sum_j P_j(1+\bar{t}_j)a_{ji}}{P_i - \sum_j a_{ji}P_j} - 1 \\ &= \frac{P_i\bar{t}_i - \sum_j \bar{t}_j a_{ji}}{P_i - \sum_j a_{ji}P_j} \end{aligned}$$

where P_i is again the internationally determined price.

Since consumption distortions do not arise with taxes or subsidies in production, the welfare of the community is maximized when the consumption possibilities available to the community are maximized. The consumption possibilities are given by the budget constraint as

$$(32)\quad \begin{aligned} \sum_i P_iC_i &= \sum_i P_iX_i - \sum_i \sum_j P_i a_{ji} X_j \\ &= \sum_i \pi_i X_i \end{aligned}$$

The gross production possibility set is

$$(33)\quad T(X_i, \ldots, X_n) = 0$$

and the profit maximizing condition is

$$(34)\quad \frac{T_i}{T_j} = \frac{\pi_i(1+f_i)}{\pi_j(1+f_j)} \quad (i+1, \ldots, n\; j=1, \ldots, n)$$

Since the consumption distortion does not arise here due to the use of subsidies or distortion offsetting consumption taxes, the equilibrium condition for consumers is now

$$(35)\quad \frac{u_i}{P_i} = A \quad (i = 1, \ldots, n)$$

From (18), (35), and (32), we have

$$(36)\quad \frac{du}{A} = \sum_i P_i dC_i = \sum_i \pi_i dX_i$$

By (33), we have (37)

$$(37)\quad \sum_i T_i dX_i = 0$$

which, in conjunction with (34), yields,

$$(38)\quad \sum_i \pi_i(1+f_i)dX_i = 0$$

substituting (38) into (36), we have

$$(39)\quad \begin{aligned} \frac{du}{A} &= \sum_i P_i dC_i = -\sum_i \pi_i f_i dX_i \\ &= -\pi_e f_e dX_e - \sum_j \pi_j f_j \partial X_j \end{aligned}$$

where f_e is an extreme effective rate and j denotes all other commodities. But from the budget constraint (32), we obtain

$$(40)\quad f_e \pi_e dX_e = f_e \sum_i P_i dC_i - f_e \sum_j \pi_j dX_j$$

Using (40) in (39), we have for a change in f_e

$$(41)\quad \begin{aligned} \frac{1}{A}\frac{du}{df_e} &= \sum_i P_i dC_i \\ &= \frac{\sum_j (f_e - f_j)}{(1+f_e)} \pi_j \frac{dX_j}{\partial f_e} \end{aligned}$$

Since $1+f_e>0$ for produced commodities, after defining X_j as a complement in production with X_i if $\partial X_j/\partial f_i>0$, we establish a theorem closely related to Theorem 4.

THEOREM 5: *In the multi-commodity model with no complementarity in production, it is necessary in order to achieve a second best solution and sufficient for an increase in welfare that variable extreme distortions be eliminated.*

Note that Theorem 5 is directly relevant to the theory of effective tariff rates if the objective is to maximize the consumption possibilities set available to the community. Even if consumption distortions cannot be ignored or offset by consumption taxes, as this would imply, these findings are still relevant to the analysis of the production effects of effective tariffs.

REFERENCES

B. Balassa, "Tariffs, Intermediate Goods, and Domestic Protection: Comment," *Amer. Econ. Rev.*, Dec. 1970, *60,* 968–69.

T. J. Bertrand, "Welfare Indexes with Interindustry Flows: Comment," *J. Polit. Econ.*, forthcoming.

W. M. Corden, "Effective Protection Rates in a General Equilibrium Model: A Geometric Approach," *Oxford Econ. Pap.*, July 1969, *21,* 135–41.

S. E. Guisinger, "Negative Value Added and the Theory of Effective Protection," *Quart. J. Econ.*, Aug. 1969, *83,* 415–35.

T. Hatta, "A Critical Analysis of Welfare Economics," M.A. Thesis (Japanese), International Christian Univ., Tokyo 1968.

R. G. Lipsey, and R. K. Lancaster, "The General Theory of Second Best," *Rev. Econ. Stud.*, 1956, *24,* No. 1, 11–32.

V. K. Ramaswami and T. N. Srinavasan, "Tariff Structure and Resource Allocation in the Presence of Factor Substitution," in *J. Bhagwati et al., eds., Trade, Balance of Payments and Growth,* Amsterdam 1971.

R. J. Ruffin, "Tariffs, Intermediate Goods, and Domestic Protection," *Amer. Econ. Rev.*, June 1969, *59,* 261–69.

A. H. H. Tan, "Imported Material, Inter-Industry Flows, Non-Traded Goods and Optimal Trade Policies," unpublished paper, Aug. 1968.

J. Vanek, "Variable Factor Proportions and Interindustry Flows in the Theory of International Trade," *Quar. J. Econ.*, Feb. 1963, *77,* 129–42.

———, "Unilateral Trade Liberalization and Global World Income," *Quart. J. Econ.*, Feb. 1964, *78,* 139–47.

———, "The Derivation of Professor Meade's Second Best Index for the Case Where Interindustry Flows are Present," *J. Polit. Econ.*, Mar.-Apr. 1971, *79,* 345–50.

———, "Welfare Indexes with Interindustry Flows: Reply," mimeo. Dec. 1970.

[12]

A RECOMMENDATION FOR A BETTER TARIFF STRUCTURE[1]

By Tatsuo Hatta

Consider a small country with a strictly convex production possibility set, where non-traded goods as well as traded goods are produced. Suppose that tariffs are the only causes of the distortions in this economy. In the present paper, we will prove that in this economy reduction of the highest tariff rate to the level of the second highest rate will improve welfare if (i) inferior goods do not exist, (ii) the good on which the highest tariff rate is imposed is substitutive to all the other goods both in consumption and in production, and (iii) the non-traded goods are substitutive to all the other goods both in consumption and in production.

1. INTRODUCTION

The theory of the second best revealed that a reduction in a distortion of an economy with multiple distortion may reduce the welfare.

In the present paper, we will consider the welfare effect of a tariff reduction in an open economy with a strictly convex production possibility set where tariffs are the only cause of the distortions. Specifically, we will prove that the policy which reduces the highest tariff rate to the level of the second highest rate will improve welfare if (i) inferior goods to not exist, (ii) the good on which the highest tariff rate is imposed is substitutive to all the other goods both in consumption and in production, and (iii) the non-traded goods are substitutive to all the other goods both in consumption and in production. This result is a generalization of Theorem 1 in Hatta [**12**], which was proved under a stringent condition upon technology. Our approach of equating the highest distortion to the level of the "second highest" rather than to the level of the "second best" has clear practical advantages.[2]

2. THE MODEL OF THE T-ECONOMY

The following notation will be used for construction of the model: u is utility level; c_i is quantity demanded of good i; x_i is quantity supplied of good i; $z_i = c_i - x_i$; p_i is the domestic price of good i that both consumers and producers face; q_i is foreign price of good i; r_i is tariff rate for good i; m is total number of imported goods; t is total number of traded goods (namely, imported goods plus exported goods); n is total number of goods. In addition, $\boldsymbol{c}$, $\boldsymbol{x}$, $\boldsymbol{z}$, $\boldsymbol{p}$, and $\boldsymbol{q}$ are vectors of order n whose ith elements are c_i, x_i, z_i, p_i and q_i, respectively. Symbols f and h represent the compensated demand and supply functions, respectively.

We assume that the economy satisfies the following conditions.

[1] This paper is taken from the author's Ph.D. dissertation [**10**] presented at the Johns Hopkins University. He is indebted to Professors Peter Newman, Carl Christ, Trent Bertrand, Hirofumi Shibata, and Peter Diamond for invaluable comments on earlier drafts. This study was supported by the Brookings Research Fellowship during 1971–1972. The author alone is responsible for the remaining errors.

[2] See Hatta [**12**, Section B].

1. *There is only one consumer in the economy. He is a price taker and has a well-behaved utility function.*

Let his utility function be $u = v(\boldsymbol{x})$. The utility function v is said to be well behaved if it is (i) increasing in each argument, (ii) strictly quasi-concave, and (iii) twice continuously differentiable. Let the *compensated demand function* associated with v be

$$\text{(1)} \qquad \boldsymbol{c} = \boldsymbol{f}(\boldsymbol{p}, u) \quad \text{or}$$

$$c_i = f_i(\boldsymbol{p}, u) \qquad (i = 1, \ldots, n).$$

The commodity bundle $\boldsymbol{f}(\boldsymbol{p}, u)$ minimizes the expenditure under the given $\boldsymbol{p}$ among the bundles that attain the given utility level u. The function $\boldsymbol{f}$ is continuously differentiable, since v is assumed to be twice continuously differentiable. Let $f_{ij} = \partial f_i / \partial p_j$, $f_{iu} = \partial f_i / \partial u$, and $\lambda =$ the marginal utility of income. It is readily seen that f_{ij} and λf_{iu} are respectively the substitution and income terms of the pertinent Slutsky equation. A pair of goods (i, j) is said to be *substitutive* (*complementary*) *in consumption* if f_{ij} is positive (negative). Good i is said to be *superior* (*inferior*) if f_{iu} is positive (negative).

2. *The production possibility frontier of the economy is well behaved.*

Let the production possibility frontier of this economy be implicitly represented by $g(\boldsymbol{x}) = 0$. The production possibility frontier is said to be *well behaved* if the function g is (i) increasing in each argument, (ii) strictly quasi-convex, and (iii) twice continuously differentiable. Condition (ii) guarantees that the production possibility frontier is strictly concave to the origin.

3. *Producers maximize their profit regarding prices as given.*

Since the production possibility frontier is well behaved, under the present assumption the economy as a whole will produce a unique output bundle $\boldsymbol{x}$ for the given price. This relationship defines a function

$$\text{(2)} \qquad \boldsymbol{x} = \boldsymbol{h}(\boldsymbol{p}) \quad \text{or}$$

$$x_i = h_i(\boldsymbol{p}) \qquad (i = 1, \ldots, n).$$

Namely the bundle $\boldsymbol{h}(\boldsymbol{p})$ maximizes the value of the economy's production evaluated at $\boldsymbol{p}$ among those bundles that are on the production possibility frontier.

The function $\boldsymbol{h}$ may be called the *compensated supply function.*[3] It is continuously differentiable since the function g is assumed to be twice continuously differentiable. Let $h_{ij} = \partial h_i / \partial q_j$ for $i, j = 1, \ldots, n$. A pair of goods (i, j) is said to be *substitutive (complementary) in production* if h_{ij} is negative (positive).

4. *Both consumers and producers face the same price.*

This means there is no excise tax or monopoly that creates domestic distortions. This was already implicitly assumed in equations (1) and (2), since single price vector $\boldsymbol{p}$ appears in both of them.

5. *The country concerned is small.*

It faces a fixed foreign price vector $\boldsymbol{q}$.

6. *Trading with foreign countries requires no transaction cost.*

7. *Ad valorem tariffs are imposed.*

Let r_i be the tariff rate for good i specified in terms of the foreign price. Then at equilibrium we have $p_i = (1 + r_i)q_i$ if good i is imported; and $p_i = q_i$ if good i is exported. Assuming $r_i = 0$ for all exported goods, the above two conditions can be summarized as:

(3) $p_i = (1 + r_i)q_i$ if good i is traded.

Index the goods in the economy as $1 \leqslant i \leqslant m$ for imported goods, $m < i \leqslant t$ for exported goods, $t < i \leqslant n$ for non-traded goods.[4] We can express (3) as

(4) $\boldsymbol{p}_T = \boldsymbol{R}_T \boldsymbol{q}_T,$

[3] Two points regarding our terminology "compensated supply function" are in order. First, the compensated supply function is different from the ordinary long-run supply function in that when any price is changed, the total amount of resources is fixed in the former, while it is not fixed in the latter. As a result, the elasticity of supply is finite in the case of the compensated supply function, while it is infinite in the case of the ordinary long-run supply function. Secondly, the compensated supply function defined in our way is not formally symmetric to the compensated demand function. A precise symmetry would require the production possibility frontier to be represented by a function of the form $g(\boldsymbol{x}) = k$, and the corresponding compensated supply function to be represented by a function of the form $\boldsymbol{x} = \boldsymbol{h}(\boldsymbol{q}, k)$ where k denotes the total amount of the single resource, say labor, in the economy. However, we may regard $g(\boldsymbol{x}) = 0$ as a suppressed form of the production function $g_*(\boldsymbol{x}, \boldsymbol{z}) = 0$, where the input vector $\boldsymbol{z}$ is fixed. Thus, we would have to sacrifice in economic content if we kept a formal symmetry between the compensated demand and supply functions (the symbols k and $\boldsymbol{z}$ will be given completely different interpretations outside of the present footnote).

[4] Non-traded goods here include (i) intrinsically non-tradable goods like barber's service, (ii) goods with prohibitive transportation costs, and (iii) goods with prohibitive tariff rates. (If a prohibitive tariff is imposed on good i, $q_i \leqslant p_i \leqslant (1 + r_i)q_i$ must hold.)

where[5]

$$(5)\qquad p_T = \begin{Bmatrix} p_1 \\ \cdot \\ \cdot \\ \cdot \\ p_t \end{Bmatrix}, \quad q_T = \begin{Bmatrix} q_1 \\ \cdot \\ \cdot \\ \cdot \\ q_t \end{Bmatrix}, \quad \text{and} \quad R_T = \begin{bmatrix} 1+r_1 & & 0 \\ & \ddots & \\ 0 & & 1+r_t \end{bmatrix}.$$

8. *All government revenue from the tariffs is refunded to consumers through a lump sum subsidy.*

9. *The economy is in equilibrium; the balance of trade is zero, and the domestic demand and supply for the non-traded goods are equal.*

Let

$$(6)\qquad z_i \equiv c_i - x_i \qquad (i = 1, \ldots, n).$$

We call z_i the *net demand* of the country for the ith good.[6] Define z_T and z_N by

$$(7)\qquad z_T = \begin{Bmatrix} z_1 \\ \cdot \\ \cdot \\ \cdot \\ z_t \end{Bmatrix} \quad \text{and} \quad z_N = \begin{Bmatrix} z_{t+1} \\ \cdot \\ \cdot \\ \cdot \\ z_n \end{Bmatrix}.$$

Since by Assumption 8 there is no demand from the public sector for any good, the private sector is the only source of demand. Thus Assumption 8 implies

$$(8)\qquad q_T' z_T = 0,$$

$$(9)\qquad z_N = \mathbf{0}.$$

The economy described above will be called the T-economy (reminiscent of *t*rade). When (1), (2), (4), (6), (8), and (9) are all satisfied, we say that the T-economy is in full equilibrium.

In view of (1), (2), and (6), the net demand z of a country is a function of the price vector p and the utility level u:

$$(10)\qquad z = f(p, u) - h(p) \equiv s(p, u).$$

In terms of this notation, the T-economy is in full equilibrium if and only if it satisfies the following system:

$$(11)\qquad q_T' z_T = 0,$$

[5] Note that in matrix R_T we have $r_i = 0$ for all $i = m+1, \ldots, t$.

[6] Note that z_i is *not* the excess demand that causes the change in the price. At the equilibrium z_i could well be positive or negative, so long as it is offset by an equal amount of import or export. We may also call z_i the import demand for good i.

$$s(R_T q_T, p_N, u) - \left\{ \frac{z_T}{0} \right\} = \mathbf{0}. \tag{12}$$

Note that p_N, z_T, and u are endogeneous and that q_T and R_T are exogeneous in this system.

3. A THEOREM OF PIECEMEAL POLICY IN THE OPEN ECONOMY

Suppose that in a full equilibrium of the T-economy a tariff rate (say r_i) is changed while keeping all the other rates (r_j; $j \neq 1$) constant. Will the utility level be increased or decreased when the economy reaches the new equilibrium? The comparative static approach for solving this problem is to take the total differential of equations (11) and (12), and solve for $\partial u/\partial r_i$. In order to state this result we need additional notation.

Let f_i, h_i, and s_i be the ith elements of f, h, and s; namely

$$\begin{aligned} s_i &= s_i(p, u) \\ &= f_i(p, u) - h_i(p) \qquad (i = 1, \ldots, n). \end{aligned}$$

Let

$$s_{iu} = \frac{\partial}{\partial u} s_i(p, u) = \frac{\partial}{\partial u} f_i(p, u),$$

$$s_{ij} = \frac{\partial}{\partial p_j} s_i(p, u),$$

$$s_u = \begin{Bmatrix} s_{1u} \\ \vdots \\ s_{nu} \end{Bmatrix}, \quad s_j = \begin{Bmatrix} s_{1j} \\ \vdots \\ s_{nj} \end{Bmatrix}, \quad \text{and} \quad S = \begin{bmatrix} s_{11} & \cdots & s_{1n} \\ \vdots & & \vdots \\ s_{1n} & \cdots & s_{nn} \end{bmatrix}.$$

Then the matrix S has the following properties.[7]

[7] Define the substitution matrices, F and H, of the compensated demand and supply functions by

$$F = \begin{bmatrix} f_{11} & \cdots & f_{1n} \\ \cdots & \cdots & \cdots \\ f_{n1} & \cdots & f_{nn} \end{bmatrix} \quad \text{and} \quad H = \begin{bmatrix} h_{11} & \cdots & h_{1n} \\ \cdots & \cdots & \cdots \\ h_{n1} & \cdots & h_{nn} \end{bmatrix}.$$

Then F and H satisfy the following celebrated properties:
Symmetry Condition: $F = F'$, $H = H'$.
Homogeneity Condition: $Fp = \mathbf{0}$, $Hq = \mathbf{0}$.
Non-positive Definiteness Condition:

$$y'Fy \begin{cases} = 0 & \text{if } y = kp \text{ for some } k, \\ < 0 & \text{otherwise.} \end{cases} \qquad -y'Hy \begin{cases} = 0 & \text{if } y = kq \text{ for some scalar } k \\ < 0 & \text{otherwise.} \end{cases}$$

Since $S = F - H$, the matrix S has properties similar to those of F and H.

The three properties of F are proved in Samuelson [**17**, pp. 113–115]. Hicks [**13**] calls the homogeneity and non-positive definiteness conditions the third and the fourth demand rules, respectively. The properties of H can be similarly proved. For an exact statement of the non-positive definiteness condition, see Hatta [**11**].

Symmetry condition:

$$(13) \qquad S = S'.$$

Homogeneity condition:

$$(14) \qquad S\boldsymbol{p} = \mathbf{0}.$$

Non-positive definiteness condition:

$$(15) \qquad \boldsymbol{y}'S\boldsymbol{y} \begin{cases} =0 & \text{if } \boldsymbol{y} = k\boldsymbol{p} \text{ for some } k, \\ <0 & \text{otherwise.} \end{cases}$$

Let S be partitioned as

$$S = \left[\begin{array}{c|c} S_{TT} & S_{TN} \\ \hline S_{NT} & S_{NN} \end{array} \right],$$

where S_{TT} and S_{NN} are $t \times t$ and $(n-t)\times(n-t)$, respectively. It is readily seen that $S_{TN} = S_{NT}$. Also the non-positive definite condition implies that S_{NN} is negative definite, and $|S_{NN}| \neq 0$. Thus, we can define a $t \times n$ matrix Z and an $n \times 1$ vector $\boldsymbol{q}_*$ by

$$Z = [I \,|\, -S_{TN}S_{NN}^{-1}], \quad \text{and}$$

$$\boldsymbol{q}_*' = \boldsymbol{q}_T'Z,$$

where I is a $t \times t$ identity matrix.

The following lemma shows the solution for $\partial u/\partial r_i$.

LEMMA (Basic Equation): *At the full equilibrium of the T-economy, the following holds:*

$$(16) \qquad \frac{\partial u}{\partial r_i} = -q_i \frac{\boldsymbol{q}_*'\boldsymbol{s}_i}{\boldsymbol{q}_*'\boldsymbol{s}_u}.$$

PROOF: Taking the total differential of equations (12) and (13), we have

$$\left[\begin{array}{c|c|c} 0 & \boldsymbol{q}_T' & \mathbf{0}' \\ \hline \boldsymbol{s}_u & I & S_{TN} \\ \hline & 0 & S_{NN} \end{array} \right] \left\{ \begin{array}{c} du \\ \hline -d\boldsymbol{z}_T \\ \hline d\boldsymbol{p}_N \end{array} \right\} = -q_i \left\{ \begin{array}{c} 0 \\ \hline \boldsymbol{s}_i \\ \\ \end{array} \right\} dr_i.$$

It follows that

$$\frac{du}{dr_i} = -q_i \frac{\alpha}{\beta},$$

where

$$\alpha \equiv \begin{vmatrix} 0 & \boldsymbol{q}_T & \boldsymbol{0}' \\ \boldsymbol{s}_i & I & S_{TN} \\ & 0 & S_{NN} \end{vmatrix} \quad \text{and}$$

$$\beta \equiv \begin{vmatrix} 0 & \boldsymbol{q}_T & \boldsymbol{0}' \\ \boldsymbol{s}_u & I & S_{TN} \\ & 0 & S_{NN} \end{vmatrix}.$$

Since

$$\begin{vmatrix} I & S_{TN} \\ 0 & S_{NN} \end{vmatrix} = |S_{NN}| \neq 0,$$

we get[8]

$$\beta = (\boldsymbol{q}_T \vdots \boldsymbol{0}'') \begin{bmatrix} I & S_{TN} \\ 0 & S_{NN} \end{bmatrix}^{-1} \{\boldsymbol{s}_u\} |S_{NN}|.$$

Noting that

$$\begin{bmatrix} I & S_{TN} \\ 0 & S_{NN} \end{bmatrix}^{-1} = \begin{bmatrix} I & -S_{TN}S_{NN}^{-1} \\ 0 & S_{NN}^{-1} \end{bmatrix},$$

we have

$$\beta = \boldsymbol{q}'_* \boldsymbol{s}_u |S_{NN}|.$$

Similarly, we obtain

$$\alpha = \boldsymbol{q}'_* \boldsymbol{s}_i |S_{NN}|.$$

Therefore, $du/dr_i = -q_i(\boldsymbol{q}'_*\boldsymbol{s}_i/\boldsymbol{q}'_*\boldsymbol{s}_u)$. *Q.E.D.*

We say that the commodity pair (i, j) is *net substitutive* (net complementary) if s_{ij} is positive (negative). Note that pair (i, j) is net substitutive if the pair is substitutive in both consumption and production.[9]

We are finally in a position to recommend a tariff reduction policy in the situation where the government can alter the tariff rates of only a certain number of goods at one time.

THEOREM: *Suppose the T-Economy satisfies the following:* (i) *there is no inferior good;* (ii) *the good on which the highest tariff rate is imposed is net substitutive to all*

[8] Let A, D, and E be square matrices and let E be partitioned as

$$E = \begin{bmatrix} A & B \\ C & D \end{bmatrix}.$$

Then $|E| = |A - BD^{-1}C| \cdot |D|$, provided $|D| \neq 0$. See Dhrymes [6, p. 570] for the proof.

[9] The converse of this proposition does not hold.

the other goods; (iii) *the non-traded goods are net substitutive to all the other goods. Then the utility level of the economy will be raised if the highest tariff rate is reduced to the level of the next highest one.*

PROOF: Assume that the highest tariff is imposed on the first good. Then the theorem may be formally stated as follows:

Suppose (a) $\boldsymbol{s}_u > \mathbf{0}$, (b) $\boldsymbol{s}_1 = (-, +, \dots, +)'$, (c) $S_{TN} > 0$, (d) all the off-diagonal elements of S_{NN} are positive, and (e) $r_1 > r_i$ for all $i = 2, \dots, t$. Then $\partial u/\partial r_1 < 0$.

From the Homogeneity Condition (14), we have

$$(17) \qquad \boldsymbol{p}_T' S_{TN} + \boldsymbol{p}_N' S_{NN} = \mathbf{0}'.$$

Since $\boldsymbol{p}_T' S_{TN} > 0$ from (c), this implies $\boldsymbol{p}_N' S_{NN} < 0'$. On the other hand, (15) implies that $s_{ii} < 0$ for all $i = 1, \dots, n$. Thus, in view of (d), we have[10] $-S_{NN}^{-1} > 0$. This, together with condition (d) and the definition of Z, yields

$$(18) \qquad Z > 0.$$

Thus it follows from the definition of $\boldsymbol{q}_*$ and from condition (a) that

$$(19) \qquad \boldsymbol{q}_*' \boldsymbol{s}_u = \boldsymbol{q}_T' Z \boldsymbol{s}_u > 0.$$

Since (17) implies

$$\boldsymbol{p}_N' = -\boldsymbol{p}_T' S_{TN} S_{NN}^{-1},$$

we have

$$\boldsymbol{p}' = \boldsymbol{p}_T' Z$$
$$= \boldsymbol{q}_T' R_T Z.$$

This and (14) yield

$$\boldsymbol{q}_T' R_T Z \boldsymbol{s}_1 = 0.$$

From this and the definition of $\boldsymbol{q}_*$, we have

$$(20) \qquad (1 + r_1)\boldsymbol{q}_*' \boldsymbol{s}_1 = (1 + r_1)\boldsymbol{q}_T' Z \boldsymbol{s}_1$$
$$= \boldsymbol{q}_T' W Z \boldsymbol{s}_1,$$

where $W = [(1 + r_1)I - R_T]$.

From condition (e) and from (18) we have $WZ \geqslant 0$. Moreover, the first column of matrix WZ is a zero vector, because the matrix consisting of the first t columns of WZ are identical with W, whose first column is a zero vector. Thus, from (b) we get $WZ\boldsymbol{s}_1 > \mathbf{0}$, and $\boldsymbol{q}_T' WZ \boldsymbol{s}_1 > 0$. Hence, it follows from (20) that $\boldsymbol{q}_*' \boldsymbol{s}_1 > 0$. This, together with (16) and (19), proves the theorem. *Q.E.D.*

[10] If (a) all the diagonal elements of an $n \times n$ matrix A are positive and all the off-diagonal elements are negative, and (b) $A\boldsymbol{x} > \mathbf{0}$ for some $n \times 1$ positive vector $\boldsymbol{x}$, then $A^{-1} > 0$. This immediately follows from Theorem 3 and its lemma in Debreu and Herstein [**5**, p. 602]. Note that the matrix A in our Theorem 2 is indecomposable from (a).

4. NOTE ON THE LITERATURE

Green [**9**] is one of the first works to have studied the relationship between the distortion change and Hicksian complementarity. He showed that in an n-commodity economy with the constant cost technology where excise taxes cause the distortions, the internal second best solution of one tax rate must be within the highest and the lowest fixed tax rates if the good whose tax rate is variable is substitutive in the Hicksian sense to all the other goods. Clearly, our result is closely related to his. However, since the focus of his work is the characterization of the second best solution, rather than the analysis of reduction in a tax rate, inferiority did not come into the picture.

Vanek [**18**] and Bhagwati [**3**] first revealed that a reduction in the price distortion in the two commodity world can reduce the welfare in the presence of the inferior goods. Kemp [**14**], Foster and Sonnenschein [**8**], and Bruno [**4**] extended their works and analyzed the relationship between the uniform distortion reduction and inferiority. Our result synthesizes the work of this work and that of Green in the situation where distortions are caused by tariffs.[11]

Bertrand and Vanek [**2**] proved the following proposition in a model similar to ours.[12]

BERTRAND AND VANEK'S THEOREM: *The utility level of the economy will be raised when the highest tariff rate is reduced to the level of the next highest one, if this tariff reduction causes a decrease in the amount imported of every other import good and an increase in the amount exported of every export good.*

Despite similarities in other respects, this theorem of Bertrand and Vanek (hereafter B-V theorem) and our Theorem 2 belong to different trends of the literature. First, the assumption of non-inferiority is not required in the B-V theorem. Second, the B-V theorem makes assumptions as to the direction of the actual (uncompensated) change in the equilibrium commodity bundle. In this sense the B-V theorem is an extension of pp. 120–121 of Meade [**16**] and Section V of Lipsey and Lancaster [**15**]. Assumptions in our Theorem 2, on the other hand, are made in terms of (compensated) substitutability in the Hicksian sense, as in Green [**9**].

One significant advantage of the B-V theorem is that after the tax rate is actually reduced it is directly observable, by comparing the commodity bundles of the old and the new equilibria, whether or not their condition is satisfied. Since the conditions of our Theorem 2 are based on the properties of the utility function and the production possibility surface, they are not directly observable.

On the other hand, our theorem may have an advantage in *prediction*. If we want to know from the B-V theorem the welfare effect of a tax reduction before the tax is actually reduced, we have to predict the direction in which the equilibrium

[11] Dixit [**7**] and Hatta [**12**] synthesize the two trends in closed-economy situations.

[12] Theorem 4, Bertand and Vanek [**2**, p. 929]. Their definition of "complementarity," which is different from Hicks', is given in the paragraph on pp. 928–929.

bundle changes. This is a difficult task, unless the tariff rate of the good whose rate is to be lowered has been reduced under almost the same structures of distortions and foreign prices. This is because the direction in the change of the equilibrium bundle is dependent upon the particular combination of the functional form of the utility function, the shape of the production surface, and the structure of the foreign prices and distortions in a complicated way.

The only conditions required by our Theorem 2, however, are information about certain direct properties of the utility function and the production possibility surface. This information has a high degree of autonomy and is estimatable from the market data as long as foreign prices have changed often enough to give sufficient numbers of observations. Note that it is estimatable, even if the tariff rate of the good whose rate is to be reduced was never changed before.

Saitama University
and
The Johns Hopkins University

Manuscript received February, 1975; revision received October, 1976.

REFERENCES

[1] ARROW, K., AND F. HAHN: *General Competitive Analysis.* San Francisco: Holden-Day, 1971.

[2] BERTRAND, T., AND J. VANEK: "The Theory of Tariffs, Taxes and Subsidies: Some Aspects of the Second Best," *American Economic Review*, 61 (1971), 925–931.

[3] BHAGWATI, J.: "The Gains from Trade Once Again," *Oxford Economic Papers*, 20 (1968), 137–148.

[4] BRUNO, MICHAEL: "Market Distortions and Gradual Reform," *The Review of Economic Studies*, 39 (1972), 373–383.

[5] DEBREU, G., AND I. N. HERSTEIN: "Nonnegative Square Matrices," *Econometrica*, 21 (1953), 597–607. Reprinted in *Readings in Mathematical Economics*, ed. by P. Newman, Vol. 1. Baltimore: John Hopkins Press, 1968.

[6] DHRYMES, P. J.: *Econometrics: Statistical Foundations and Applications.* New York: Harper and Row, 1970.

[7] DIXIT, A.: "Welfare Effects of Tax and Price Changes," *Journal of Public Economics*, 4 (1975), 103–123.

[8] FOSTER, E., AND H. SONNENSCHEIN: "Price Distortion and Economic Welfare," *Econometrica*, 38 (1970), 281–297.

[9] GREEN, J.: "The Social Optimum in the Presence of Monopoly and Taxation," *Review of Economic Studies*, 29 (1961), 66–77.

[10] HATTA, T.: *A Theory of Piecemeal Policy Recommendations*, Ph.D. Dissertation, The Johns Hopkins University, 1973.

[11] ———: "A Note on a Theorem in 'Value and Capital'," *Western Economic Journal*, 11 (1973), 164–166.

[12] ———: "A Theory of Piecemeal Policy Recommendations," *Review of Economic Studies*, 44 (1977), 1-21.

[13] HICKS, J. R.: *Value and Capital*, 2nd ed. London: Oxford University Press, 1946.

[14] KEMP, M.: "Some Issues in the Analysis of Trade Gains," *Oxford Economic Papers*, 20 (1968), 149–61.

[15] LIPSEY, R., AND K. LANCASTER: "The General Theory of Second Best," *Review of Economic Studies*, 24 (1956), 11–32.

[16] MEADE, J. E.: *The Theory of Customs Unions.* Amsterdam: North-Holland Publishing Co., 1955.

[17] SAMULESON, P. A.: *Foundations of Economic Analysis.* Cambridge, Massachusetts: Harvard University Press, 1947.

[18] VANEK, J.: *General Equilibrium of Internation Discrimination: The Case of Customs Unions.* Cambridge, Massachusetts: Harvard University Press, 1965.

[13]

INTERNATIONAL ECONOMIC REVIEW
Vol. 20, No. 2, June, 1979

TARIFF STRUCTURE, NONTRADED GOODS AND THEORY OF PIECEMEAL POLICY RECOMMENDATIONS*

BY TAKASHI FUKUSHIMA[1]

1. INTRODUCTION

The theory of the second best revealed the difficulty in the formulation of piecemeal policy. However, several attempts were made recently to find out a set of sufficient conditions under which piecemeal policy enables us to attain higher level of welfare. Among those are Bertrand and Vanek [1971], Foster and Sonnenschein [1970] and more recently Hatta [1973, 1977]. The results which are especially relevant to ours are Hatta [1977a]. He proved in a n-good economy that the reduction of the highest tariff rate to the level of the next highest one improves the level of utility under substitutability and no inferior conditions. His analysis was focused on the "single" tariff reduction. If several commodities share the highest tariff rate, the policy formulation is no longer possible in the very strict sense.

In this present paper, on the other hand, we deal with the simultaneous change of several tariffs in a n-good open economy where nontraded goods exist. First we show that the result of Hatta [1977a] can be extended to the situation where several commodities share the highest tariff rate. Secondly we prove that the *uniform tariff change*, which moves all the tariff rates proportionally to a given rate, will improve the level of utility. The proportional tariff reduction, which reduces all the tariff rates proportionally to zero, is the special case of the uniform tariff change.

2. THE MODEL

There are n goods in the economy and there is only one consumer in the economy who has a well behaved compensated demand function[2]

$$\underline{c} = \underline{f}(\underline{p}, u)\,, \tag{1}$$

where $\underline{c}$ is a consumption vector, $\underline{p}$ a price vector and u a utility level.[3] Let $f_{ij} = \frac{\partial f_i}{\partial p_j}$ and $f_{iu} = \frac{\partial f_i}{\partial u}$, and λ = marginal utility of income. It is readily seen

* Manuscript received October 12, 1976; revised November 7, 1977.

[1] I am indebted to Professors Takao Fukuchi and Tatsuo Hatta for their comments and suggestions. Helpful comments by a referee are also gratefully acknowledged. The remaining errors are of course mine.

[2] See Arrow and Hahn [1971, p. 104].

[3] Underlined small case letter represents a vector.

that f_{ij}, and λf_{iu} are the substitution and income terms of the Hicks-Slutsky equation, respectively. We say that the good i and the good j are *substitutes* (*complements*) in consumption if f_{ij} is positive (negative), and the good i is *superior* (*inferior*) if f_{iu} is positive (negative). Let F denote the matrix whose ij-th element is f_{ij}. Then F is negative semi-definite with $F\underline{p}=\underline{0}$ and has rank $n-1$.

The economy has a well behaved compensated supply function.[4]

$$\underline{x} = \underline{h}(\underline{p}), \tag{2}$$

where $\underline{x}$ is the output level for the given price $\underline{p}$. Let $h_{ij}=\partial h_i/\partial p_j$. We say that the good i and the good j are *substitutes* (*complements*) in production if h_{ij} is negative (positive). Let H denote the matrix whose ij-th element is h_{ij}. It is well known that the matrix H is positive semi-definite with $H\underline{p}=\underline{0}$ and has rank $n-1$.

We also assume the following: Consumer and producer face the same price; all tariff revenue is refunded to consumer through a lump sum subsidy; ad valorem tariffs are imposed and country concerned is small; the commodities are indexed so that first t goods are traded goods and others are nontraded goods.

Let $\underline{q}$ and $\underline{r}$ be the foreign price vector and the tariff rate vector, then $\underline{q}$ is invariant by the county's commercial policy and in equilibrium we have[5]

$$\underline{p}_T = Q_T(\underline{1} + \underline{r}_T) \tag{3}$$

where

$$Q_T = \begin{bmatrix} q_1 & & 0 \\ & \ddots & \\ 0 & & q_t \end{bmatrix} \quad \underline{1} + \underline{r}_T = \begin{pmatrix} 1 + r_1 \\ \vdots \\ 1 + r_t \end{pmatrix} \quad \underline{p}_T = \begin{pmatrix} p_1 \\ \vdots \\ p_t \end{pmatrix}.$$

Similarly, the vectors $\underline{c}$, $\underline{x}$, $\underline{f}$, $\underline{h}$, $\underline{p}$, and $\underline{q}$, are partitioned into two parts, the one corresponding to traded goods and the other to nontraded goods. We denote these vectors by subscripts T and N, which stand for traded goods and nontraded goods, respectively.

The economy is in equilibrium. The balance of trade is zero and domestic demand and supply for the nontraded goods are equal.

$$\underline{q}'_T(\underline{c}_T - \underline{x}_T) = 0 \tag{4}$$

$$\underline{c}_N = \underline{x}_N. \tag{5}$$

Thus equations (1), (2), (3), (4) and (5) establish the full equilibrium of our economy and determine the equilibrium levels of $\underline{c}$, $\underline{x}$, and $\underline{p}_N$, and u for the given levels of Q_T and $\underline{r}_T$.

[4] See Hatta [1977a] for the remarks of this terminology.

[5] r_i can be negative. For instance, $r_i<0$ for import good means positive subsidy for import good. The similar remark also applies to export good.

Let a function $\underline{s}$ be defined by

$$\underline{s}(\underline{p}, u) = \underline{f}(\underline{p}, u) - \underline{h}(\underline{p}).$$

The function $\underline{s}$ can be partitioned into $\underline{s}_T$ and $\underline{s}_N$. Let a matrix S be defined by $S \equiv F - H$, then S is negative semidefinite with $S\underline{p} = \underline{0}$ and has rank $n-1$. Let S be partitioned as

$$S = \begin{bmatrix} S_{TT} & S_{TN} \\ S_{NT} & S_{NN} \end{bmatrix}$$

then we can easily see that the condition implies S_{NN} is negative definite and thus we have $|S_{NN}| \neq 0$. Note that $s_{iu} = f_{iu}$ and $s_{ij} = f_{ij} - h_{ij}$. We say that the good i and the good j are *net substitutes* (*net complements*) if s_{ij} is positive (negative). Clearly, if they are substitutes (complements) in both consumption and production, then they are net substitutes (complements).

In terms of this notation, our model can be reduced to the following system of equations.

$$q_T' \underline{s}_T(Q_T(\underline{1} + \underline{t}_T), \underline{p}_N, u) = 0 \tag{6}$$

$$\underline{s}_N(Q_T(\underline{1} + \underline{t}_T), \underline{p}_N, u) = \underline{0}. \tag{7}$$

The equations (6) and (7) determine the equilibrium values of u and $\underline{p}_N$ for the given values of Q_T and $\underline{t}_T$. By virtue of implicit function theorem, there exists a continuously differentiable function g in the neighborhood of the equilibrium and we can state[6]

$$u = g(\underline{t}_T). \tag{8}$$

3. THE BASIC LEMMA

In this section we present and prove the basic lemmas which are used for the proof of our theorems of policy recommendation.

LEMMA 1. *Let*

$$D = [S_{TT} - S_{TN}S_{NN}^{-1}S_{NT}] \qquad \underline{s}_u = \begin{pmatrix} \underline{s}_{Tu} \\ \underline{s}_{Nu} \end{pmatrix}$$

$$Z = [I \,\vdots\, - S_{TN}S_{NN}^{-1}]$$

then for the change of $\underline{t}_T$, *we have*

$$\left(\frac{du}{d\underline{t}_T}\right)' = -\frac{1}{q_T' Z \underline{s}_u} q_T' D Q_T.$$

[6] Therefore our results in this paper are local results. This is not because our method depends on differentiation, but because the function g is only assured to exist in the neighborhood of the equilibrium. If we adopt the assumption that $g(\underline{t}_T)$ is a globally well defined function on some global domain D, as was done by Foster and Sonnenschein [1970], we can extend our results on the global domain D without much change of the argument.

Proof. Differentiate (6) and (7) totally, we have

$$\begin{bmatrix} \underline{q}'_T \underline{s}_{Tu} & \underline{q}'_T S_{TN} \\ \underline{s}_{Nu} & S_{NN} \end{bmatrix} \begin{pmatrix} du \\ d\underline{p}_N \end{pmatrix} = - \begin{pmatrix} \underline{q}'_T S_{TT} Q_T d\underline{t}_T \\ S_{NT} Q_T d\underline{t}_T \end{pmatrix}. \tag{9}$$

By Cramer's rule we can solve (9) as $du = -B/A$, where

$$A = \underline{q}'_T(\underline{s}_{Tu} - S_{TN}S_{NN}^{-1}\underline{s}_{Nu})|S_{NN}|$$

$$B = \underline{q}'_T(S_{TT} - S_{TN}S_{NN}^{-1}S_{NT})Q_T d\underline{t}_T |S_{NN}|.$$

Therefore, we get

$$\left(\frac{du}{d\underline{t}_T}\right)' = -\frac{\underline{q}'_T(S_{TT} - S_{TN}S_{NN}^{-1}S_{NT})Q_T}{\underline{q}'_T(\underline{s}_{Tu} - S_{TN}^{-1}S_{NN}\underline{s}_{Nu})}. \tag{10}$$

Equation (10), together with the definitions of D, Z, and $\underline{s}_u$, proves the lemma.

Q. E. D.

Lemma 2. *Let D be the matrix defined by Lemma 1, then for any number τ, we have*[7]

$$\underline{q}'_T D Q_T = \frac{1}{1+\tau}(\underline{\tau}' - \underline{t}'_T)Q_T D Q_T$$

where

$$\underline{\tau}' = (\tau, \tau, \ldots, \tau).$$

Proof. From Homogeneity of S, we have

$$S_{TT}\underline{p}_T + S_{TN}\underline{p}_N = \underline{0}_T \tag{11}$$

$$S_{NT}\underline{p}_T + S_{NN}\underline{p}_N = \underline{0}_N. \tag{12}$$

Since $|S_{NN}| \neq 0$, there exists S_{NN}^{-1}, then from (12) we have

$$\underline{p}_N = -S_{NN}^{-1}S_{NT}\underline{p}_T. \tag{13}$$

By substituting (13) into (11), we obtain $D\underline{p}_T = \underline{0}_T$. Noting that D is a $(t \times t)$ symmetric matrix, and applying (3), it becomes

$$(\underline{1}' + \underline{t}'_T)Q_T D = \underline{0}'_T. \tag{14}$$

On the other hand for any number τ, we have

$$(1+\tau)\underline{q}'_T D Q_T = (\underline{1}' + \underline{\tau}')Q_T D Q_T$$
$$= (\underline{\tau}' - \underline{t}'_T)Q_T D Q_T$$

[7] $\tau \neq -1$. In fact we only consider $\tau > -1$ in order to assure the positivity of domestic price vector.

where the last equality follows from (14). Q. E. D.

LEMMA 3. *Let Z be the matrix defined by Lemma 1. Suppose* (i) $S_{TN}>0$, *and* (ii) *all the off diagonal elements of S_{NN} are positive, then $Z \geq 0$.*

PROOF. See Hatta [1977a].[8]

LEMMA 4. *Let D, Z be the matrices defined by Lemma 1, and S be the substitution matrix. Then the following relation holds.*

$$D = ZSZ'$$

PROOF. Form ZSZ' in the partitioned form and straightforward calculation yields the result. Q. E. D.

4. THE MAIN THEOREMS

In this section we consider two types of piecemeal policy. In order to proceed we need an additional notation. Let a function $\underline{w}$ represent tariff reform program with a parameter α indicating the stage of the reform program, that is

$$\underline{r}_T = \underline{w}(\alpha)\,. \tag{15}$$

In view of equation (8), we have

$$\frac{du}{d\alpha} = \left(\frac{du}{d\underline{r}_T}\right)'\left(\frac{d\underline{w}}{d\alpha}\right).$$

As shown below, it is convenient to give a specific policy by a system of differential equations $d\underline{r}_T/d\alpha$, which is a vector of the t-th order.

Now we are in the position to state and prove the following theorems.

THEOREM 1 (SELECTED TARIFF CHANGE). *Suppose* (i) *there is no inferior good,* (ii) *the goods which share the highest (lowest) tariff rate are net substitutable for all other goods, and* (iii) *nontraded goods are net substitutable for all other goods. Then the policy of reducing (increasing) all the highest (lowest) tariffs to the level of next highest (lowest) one improves the level of utility.*

PROOF. Suppose the traded goods are indexed so that the last $t-m$ commodities share the highest tariff rate, that is

$$r_1 \leqq r_2 \leqq \cdots \leqq r_m < r_{m+1} = \cdots = r_t$$

The policy of reducing the highest tariff rate is formally stated as

$$\frac{dr_i}{d\alpha} = 0 \qquad \text{for} \quad 1 \leqq i \leqq m$$

[8] The essence of the proof is to establish the positivity of $-S_{NN}^{-1}$.

$$\frac{dr_i}{d\alpha} = -1 \qquad \text{for} \quad m+1 \leqq i \leqq t.$$

The theorem will be proved if we establish $\frac{du}{d\alpha}>0$. In view of Lemma 1 and 2, we get

$$\frac{du}{d\alpha} = -\frac{1}{\underline{q}'_T Z \underline{s}_u} \frac{1}{1+\tau}(\underline{\tau}' - \underline{r}'_T) Q_T D Q_T\left(\frac{d\underline{r}_T}{d\alpha}\right).$$

Lemma 3, together with the condition (i), yields

$$\underline{q}'_T Z \underline{s}_u > 0. \tag{16}$$

Let us denote the highest tariff rate r_h. Choose $\tau = r_h$, then we have

$$\begin{aligned} &-\frac{1}{1+\tau}(\underline{\tau}' - \underline{r}'_T) Q_T D Q_T\left(\frac{d\underline{r}_T}{d\alpha}\right) \\ &= \frac{1}{1+r_h}(q_1(r_h - r_1), \ldots, q_m(r_h - r_m)) D_t^m \begin{pmatrix} q_{m+1} \\ \vdots \\ q_t \end{pmatrix} \end{aligned} \tag{17}$$

where

$$D_t^m = \begin{bmatrix} d_{1,m+1} & d_{1,m+2} \cdots & d_{1,t} \\ \vdots & \vdots & \vdots \\ d_{m,m+1} & d_{m,m+2} \cdots & d_{m,t} \end{bmatrix}$$

Since $r_h - r_i > 0$ $(i=1, \ldots, m)$, and $q_i > 0$, it remains to show $D_t^m > 0$. By the proof of Lemma 3, we know that $-S_{NN}^{-1} > 0$. The condition (iii) of the theorem implies that S_{TN} and S_{NT} are the positive matrices. Thus we have

$$-S_{TN} S_{NN}^{-1} S_{NT} > 0.$$

On the other hand the condition (ii) of the theorem implies that the corresponding elements of S_{TT} to D_t^m are positive. As a result we get $D_t^m > 0$. This, together with the equation (16), establishes the case of reducing the highest tariff rates. The case of increasing the lowest tariff rates can be proved in the same manner.

Q. E. D.

We note that the theorem holds if net substitutability condition is replaced by the substitutability in both consumption and production. The theorem is applicable to the following situation. Suppose $r_1 < r_2 < \cdots < r_t$, then to attain higher level of welfare we should reduce r_t to r_{t-1}, then for the next step r_t and r_{t-1} should be reduced to r_{t-2}. In this way we can attain higher level of utility step by step provided the conditions of substitutability and no inferiority.

THEOREM 2 (UNIFORM TARIFF CHANGE). *Suppose* (i) *there exists no inferior good, and* (ii) *nontraded goods are substitutable for all other goods, then the policy which moves all the tariffs proportionally to a given number* τ *always improves the level of utility.*

PROOF. The policy can be written by[9]

$$\frac{d\underline{r}_T}{d\alpha} = \underline{\tau} - \underline{r}_T .$$

In view of Lemma 1, Lemma 2, and Lemma 4, we obtain

$$\frac{du}{d\alpha} = -\frac{1}{\underline{q}'Z\underline{s}_u}\frac{1}{1+\tau}(\underline{\tau}' - \underline{r}_T')Q_T ZSZ'Q_T(\underline{\tau}-\underline{r}_T) > 0,$$

where the last inequality follows from (16) and negative semi-definiteness of S.

If we set $\tau=0$, then this policy may be called "proportional tariff reduction", which is an obvious corollary to Theorem 2.

COROLLARY (PROPORTIONAL TARIFF REDUCTION). *Suppose* (i) *there exists no inferior good, and* (ii) *nontraded goods are net substitutable for all other goods, then proportional tariff reduction always increases the level of utility.*

In order to shed some light on the relationships between Theorem 1 and Theorem 2, we can take up a simple case where all goods are traded goods. Without loss of generality, we can assume $r_i > r_j$ whenever $i > j$. Then the change of utility is

$$\frac{du}{d\alpha} = \sum_{j=1}^{n} \frac{\partial u}{\partial r_j}\frac{dr_j}{d\alpha} .$$

We know $\frac{\partial u}{\partial r_n}\frac{dr_n}{d\alpha} > 0$ under the conditions of Theorem 1. Also from the same theorem we may have $\frac{\partial u}{\partial r_i}\frac{dr_i}{d\alpha} < 0$ if $i < n$. Theorem 2 on the other hand shows if $\frac{dr_i}{d\alpha}$'s are chosen equal to $-r_i$'s, then in combination $\frac{du}{d\alpha} > 0$. We note further that $\frac{\partial u}{\partial r_i}$'s are derived within the model. Hence we come up to a conclusion that it is the speed of reduction of each tariff rate $\frac{dr_i}{d\alpha}$ that determines a rise or fall of the level of utility. In fact by Lemma 1, we can obtain

$$\frac{du}{d\alpha} = \sum_i \sum_j -\frac{1}{\underline{q}'\underline{f}_u(1+r_j)} q_i q_j s_{ij}(r_j - r_i)\frac{dr_j}{d\alpha}$$

[9] This does not imply that all the tariffs become the rate τ instantaneously. Rather it says that if we choose an arbitrary number τ, we can calculate the deviation from τ by

$$\underline{e} = \underline{r}_T - \underline{\tau} .$$

Our policy implies that for each i

$$\frac{de_i}{e_i} = -d\alpha$$

where $-d\alpha < 0$ and common to all the traded goods. Therefore our policy is to reduce the deviation from τ by the same percentage. Clearly, if $\tau=0$, then it implies that all tariffs are reduced by the same percentage. Needless to say, it is not equivalent to abolish all the tariffs.

$$= \sum_i \sum_{j<i} \frac{1}{q'f_u} q_i q_j s_{ij}(r_i - r_j)\left(\frac{1}{1+r_j}\frac{dr_j}{d\alpha} - \frac{1}{1+r_i}\frac{dr_i}{d\alpha}\right),$$

where the last expression is derived using the fact that $s_{ij}=s_{ji}$ and $\sum_i \sum_j m_{ij} = \sum_i \sum_{j<i} (m_{ij}+m_{ji})$ if $m_{ii}=0$. Hence under the conditions of Theorem 1, we can state that a piecemeal policy is successful if it is $r_i > r_j$ and $\frac{1}{1+r_j}\frac{dr_j}{d\alpha} - \frac{1}{1+r_i}\frac{dr_i}{d\alpha} > 0$ whenever $i > j$. Notice that $-\frac{1}{1+r_j}\frac{dr_j}{d\alpha}$ is a percentage reduction in price distortion $(1+r_i)$. This result can be summarized as follows.

PROPOSITION. *Under the conditions of Theorem* 1, *if* (i) *the percentage reduction in distortion of the higher-tariff-rate commodity is higher and* (ii) *the relative ranking of distortion is unchanged under new tariff rate, then the piecemeal policy gives higher level of utility.*

Finally we note that both Theorem 1 and Theorem 2 follow this general rule. The difference is the lack of substitutability condition in Theorem 2. In case of proportional tariff reduction, we can regard the whole export goods as one commodity and import goods as the other. Then essentially we are in two-commodity world where two goods are necessarily substitutes. This may explain intuitively why we do not need substitutability condition.

Southern Methodist University., U.S.A.

REFERENCES

AMANO, A., "Nontraded Goods and the Effects of Devaluation," *Economic Studies Quarterly*, 23 (August, 1972), 1–9.

ARROW, K. J. AND F. HAHN, *General Competitive Analysis* (San Francisco: Holden Day, 1971).

BERTRAND, T. J. AND J. VANEK, "The Theory of Tariffs, Taxes, and Subsidies; Some Aspect of the Second Best," *American Economic Review*, 61 (December, 1971) 925–931.

BRUNO, M., "Market Distortion and Gradual Reform," *Review of Economic Studies*, 39 (July, 1972), 373–383.

CORLETT, W. J. AND D. C. HAGUE, "Complementarity and Excess Burden of Taxation," *Review of Economic Studies*, 21 (1953), 21–30.

DHRYMES, P. J., *Econometrics: Statistical Foundations and Applications* (New York: Harper and Row, 1970).

DIXIT, A., "Welfare Effects of Tax and Price Changes," *Journal of Public Economics*, 4 (February, 1975), 103–123.

FOSTER, E. AND H. SONNENSCHEIN, "Price Distortion and Economic Welfare," *Econometrica*, 38 (March, 1970), 281–297.

GREEN, H. A. J., "The Social Optimum in the Presence of Monopoly and Taxation," *Review of Economic Studies*, 29 (October, 1961), 66–77.

HATTA, T., "Theory of Piecemeal Policy Recommendations," Ph. D. Dissertation, The Johns Hopkins University, 1973.

———, "Theory of Piecemeal Policy Recommendations," *Review of Economic Studies*, 44 (February, 1977) 1–22.

———, "A Recommendation for a Better Tariff Structure," *Econometrica*, 45 (November,

1977a), 1859–1869.

HICKS, J. R., *Value and Capital*, 2nd ed. (London: Oxford University Press, 1946).

LIPSEY, R. G. AND K. LANCASTER, "The General Theory of Second Best," *Review of Economic Studies*, 24 (October, 1956), 11–32.

———, "McManus on Second Best", *Review of Economic Studies*, 26 (June, 1959), 225–226.

MCMANUS, M., "Comments on 'The General Theory of Second Best'," *Review of Economic Studies*, 26 (June, 1959), 209–224.

NEGISHI, T., *General Equilibrium Theory and International Trade* (Amsterdam: North Holland, 1972).

PONTRYAGIN, L. S., *Ordinary Differential Equations* (Reading, Mass: Addison-Wesley, 1962).

SAMUELSON, P. A., *Foundations of Economic Analysis* (Cambridge: Harvard University Press, 1967).

[14]

Piecemeal trade reform in presence of producer-specific domestic subsidies

John C. Beghin
North Carolina State University, Raleigh NC, USA

Larry S. Karp
University of California at Berkeley, Berkeley CA, USA
University of Southampton, Southampton, UK

Received 16 September 1991
Accepted 4 January 1992

We extend the theory of unilateral piecemeal tariff reforms by considering both economy-wide (tariffs) and sector-specific (production subsidies) distortions. Sufficient conditions for welfare-improving policy reforms involve both tariffs and sector-specific distortions changes and require stronger assumptions on goods' substitutability and the structure of distortions.

1. Introduction

The theory of second-best trade distortions has concentrated on two types of problems. The first problem is the optimality of alterable trade distortions when other distortions are fixed [Dixit and Newbery (1985), Beghin and Karp (1989, 1992), Dixit and Norman (1980)]. The second type is the determination of sufficient conditions for reforms such as a decrease of the most extreme distortion or proportional reduction of all tariffs to be welfare improving [Hatta (1977), Fukushima (1979), Bertrand and Vanek (1971)]. The latter authors have established the chief results for unilateral tariff reforms, which have been generalized to multilateral reforms [Hatta and Fukushima (1979), Fukushima and Kim (1989), Turunen-Red and Woodland (1991)] and to quota piecemeal reforms [Corden and Falvey (1985), and Falvey (1988)].

This paper extends the unilateral tariff piecemeal reform results to the case of producer-specific price vectors. Each producer or sector may face both tariffs and a vector of sector-specific subsidies/taxes. We consider two cases: a proportional decrease of all tariffs and a reduction of extreme tariffs. For both cases, tariff changes have to be coupled with reforms of the sector-specific subsidies in order to ensure that the reforms increase welfare.

The results on proportional reduction of tariffs is extended intuitively to all distortions, i.e., a proportional decrease of both tariffs and firm-specific distortions is welfare-improving. However, to

Correspondence to: John C. Beghin, Department of Agricultural and Resource Economics, North Carolina State University, Box 8109, Raleigh, NC 27695, USA.

ensure that the reduction of the most extreme distortion is welfare improving requires stronger assumptions on the structure of the firm-specific distortions as well as on commodities' substitutability.

The next section presents the assumptions and two sets of results. The concluding comments relate the results to trade negotiations involving domestic distortions as well as trade barriers. An appendix contains the proofs of the propositions and lemmas.

2. The theoretical model

The theoretical model follows Fukushima (1979) and Beghin and Karp (1992) and derives the sufficient conditions for two piecemeal reforms: proportional reduction of tariffs and reduction of the most extreme tariffs. Because sector-specific subsidies/taxes are used, producers in different sectors may face different price vectors. For simplicity, we suppose that the economy is divided into two sets of sectors: one faces the price vector $\boldsymbol{p}^{\mathrm{a}} = (\boldsymbol{1} + \boldsymbol{t} + \boldsymbol{s})Q$ and the other set faces price $\boldsymbol{p}^{\mathrm{b}} = (\boldsymbol{1} + \boldsymbol{t})Q$; $\boldsymbol{1}$ is a row vector of 1's; $\boldsymbol{t}$ and $\boldsymbol{s}$ are row vectors of ad valorem tariffs and subsidies, respectively; and Q is a diagonal matrix of world prices. Hereafter, we refer to the two sets of sectors as firm a and firm b. We ignore consumption taxes, so that consumers face price $\boldsymbol{p}^{\mathrm{b}}$. We assume that nontradables are not taxed; the price of nontradables is the vector $\boldsymbol{p}^{\mathrm{N}}$. There are T traded and N nontraded goods.

The representative individual has the compensated demand system $\boldsymbol{c}(\boldsymbol{p}^{\mathrm{b}}, \boldsymbol{p}^{\mathrm{N}}, u)$ where the column vector $\boldsymbol{c}$ is partitioned with the first T elements being traded goods and the last N elements being nontraded; u is the level of utility. The (column) output vectors of the two firms are $\boldsymbol{y}^{\mathrm{a}}(\boldsymbol{p}^{\mathrm{a}}, \boldsymbol{p}^{\mathrm{N}})$ and $\boldsymbol{y}^{\mathrm{b}}(\boldsymbol{p}^{\mathrm{b}}, \boldsymbol{p}^{\mathrm{N}})$. They are partitioned in the same manner as $\boldsymbol{c}$. The vector of excess demand is $\boldsymbol{z}(\boldsymbol{p}^{\mathrm{a}}, \boldsymbol{p}^{\mathrm{b}}, \boldsymbol{p}^{\mathrm{N}}, u) = \boldsymbol{c} - \boldsymbol{y}^{\mathrm{a}} - \boldsymbol{y}^{\mathrm{b}}$. The equilibrium in the balance of payments is expressed as

$$\boldsymbol{1}Q\boldsymbol{z}_T = 0. \tag{1}$$

The equilibrium in the nontraded sector requires

$$\boldsymbol{z}_N = 0, \tag{2}$$

where $\boldsymbol{z}_T$ and $\boldsymbol{z}_N$ denote the first T and the last N elements of z, respectively. We define the Jacobian of z as the matrix Z, i.e.,

$$\frac{\partial z}{\partial(\boldsymbol{p}^{\mathrm{T}} \mid \boldsymbol{p}^{\mathrm{N}})} = \begin{bmatrix} Z_{TT} & Z_{TN} \\ Z_{NT} & Z_{NN} \end{bmatrix}.$$

The vector $\boldsymbol{p}^{\mathrm{T}}$ is the price of tradables, $\boldsymbol{p}^{\mathrm{a}}$, or $\boldsymbol{p}^{\mathrm{b}}$. For example,

$$Z_{TT} = \frac{\partial c_T}{\partial p^{\mathrm{b}}} - \frac{\partial y_T^{\mathrm{a}}}{\partial p^{\mathrm{a}}} - \frac{\partial y_T^{\mathrm{b}}}{\partial p^{\mathrm{b}}}.$$

By differentiating (2), we obtain

$$\mathrm{d}\boldsymbol{p}^{\mathrm{N}\prime} = -Z_{NN}^{-1}(\boldsymbol{c}_{Nu}\,\mathrm{d}u + Z_{NT}Q\,\mathrm{d}\boldsymbol{t}' - Y_{NT}^{\mathrm{a}}Q\,\mathrm{d}\boldsymbol{s}'), \tag{3}$$

in which the Jacobian of y^a, Y^a, is defined as

$$\frac{\partial y^a}{\partial(p^T \mid p^N)} = \begin{bmatrix} Y^a_{TT} & Y^a_{TN} \\ Y^a_{NT} & Y^a_{NN} \end{bmatrix} = Y^a,$$

and where the vector c_{Nu} (respectively, c_{Tu}) is the vector of the partial derivatives with respect to u of the demand for nontradables (respectively, tradables).

We differentiate (1) and then substitute (3) into the result. This yields

$$-B\,du = 1Q(DQ\,dt + D^a + Q\,ds), \tag{4}$$

with the following definitions:

$$B = 1Q(c_{Tu} - Z_{TN}Z_{NN}^{-1}c_{Nu}), \qquad D = Z_{TT} - Z_{TN}Z_{NN}^{-1}Z_{NT},$$

$$D^a = -Y^a_{TT} + Z_{TN}Z_{NN}^{-1}Y^a_{NT}.$$

To establish the piecemeal trade reform results, we also use the homogeneity in prices of z_T and y_t^a, which gives [1]

$$1QD = -tQD - sQD^{a\prime}. \tag{5}$$

To obtain comparative statics results, multiply (4) by $(1+\tau) > 0$ and substitute (5) into the result to rewrite (4) as

$$(1+\tau)B\,du = [(t-\boldsymbol{\tau})QDQ + sQD^{a\prime}Q]\,dt' - (1+\tau)QD^aQ\,ds', \tag{6}$$

where $\boldsymbol{\tau} = \tau 1$, with $\tau \neq -1$.

We adopt the following:

Assumption 1. (i) There are no inferior goods. (ii) The goods that share the highest (lowest) tariff rate are substitutable for all other goods in firm a and in net consumption for the rest of the economy $(c - y^b)$. (iii) Nontradable goods are substitutable for all other goods in firm a and in net consumption for the rest of the economy $(c - y^b)$.

Conditions (ii) and (iii) are stronger than the corresponding conditions in Theorem 1 of Fukushima (1979); the latter require net substitutability in excess demand, rather than substitutability in firm a and in net consumption in the rest of the economy. The welfare effects of the reforms depend on the sign of

$$du/d\alpha = (du/dt')(dt/d\alpha) + (du/ds')(ds/d\alpha).$$

We have the following first results concerning proportional reductions of distortions.

Proposition 1. Under Assumptions 1(i) and (iii), a policy reform moving all tariffs proportionally towards a given rate τ, *and reducing all sector-specific subsidies proportionally is welfare improving, i.e.,* $(dt/d\alpha) = (\boldsymbol{\tau} - t)'$; $ds/d\alpha = -s'$ *implies* $du/d\alpha > 0$.

[1] This derivation is shown in the appendix with eq. (A.3).

Proof. See appendix.

This proposition extends Fukushima's Theorem 2 intuitively to all distortions (economy-wide and sector-specific); moving all distortions towards uniformity is welfare improving. We have the obvious corollary for $\tau = 0$.

Corollary 1. Under Assumptions 1(i) and (iii) a proportional reduction of both tariffs and sector-specific distortions is welfare-improving; i.e., $\mathrm{d}\boldsymbol{t}/\mathrm{d}\alpha = -\boldsymbol{t}'$, $\mathrm{d}\boldsymbol{s}/\mathrm{d}\alpha = -\boldsymbol{s}'$ *implies* $\mathrm{d}u/\mathrm{d}\alpha > 0$.

Proof. See appendix.

The second set of results addresses the reduction of the most extreme tariff distortions. Next assume that sectors are ranked by order of decreasing tariff, i.e., $(t_1 > t_2 \ldots > t_T)$. We have the following proposition:

Proposition 2. Suppose that Assumption 1 holds, and that when the highest (smallest) tariff, t_1, *is decreased (increased) up to the next highest (smallest) tariff,* t_2, *the subsidy* s_1 *is either increased (decreased) by the same amount or is chosen optimally. If* $\boldsymbol{s} < \mathbf{0}$ *(respectively,* $\boldsymbol{s} \geq \mathbf{0}$*) after the policy change, the change is welfare improving, i.e.,*

$$\text{let} \quad \tau = t_1,\ \mathrm{d}t_i/\mathrm{d}\alpha = \begin{cases} -1 & \text{if } i = 1 \\ 0 & \text{otherwise} \end{cases}, \quad \text{and either } \mathrm{d}\boldsymbol{s}/\mathrm{d}\alpha = -\mathrm{d}\boldsymbol{t}/\mathrm{d}\alpha, \text{ or } \mathrm{d}u/\mathrm{d}\boldsymbol{s}' = 0,$$

$$\text{then if } \boldsymbol{s} \leq 0,\ \mathrm{d}u/\mathrm{d}\alpha > 0.$$

Proof. See appendix.

Proposition 2 has a straightforward interpretation in the case where only the first good has a subsidy, i.e., $s_1 \neq 0$, $s_j = 0$ for $j \geq 2$. A reduction in t_1 reduces the nominal distortion on commodity 1 facing consumers and firm b. If $\mathrm{d}s_1 = \mathrm{d}t_1$, the nominal distortion on commodity 1 in firm is a unchanged; if $s_1 < 0$, firm a faces a smaller distortion than consumers and firm b, so a reduction in t_1 does represent a 'harmonization' of distortions. If, on the other hand, $s_1 > 0$, a reduction in t_1 does represent a 'harmonization' of distortions. If on the other hand, $s_1 > 0$, a reduction in t_1 may fail to be welfare improving for much the same reason that the reduction of an arbitrary (i.e., not the largest) distortion may fail to improve welfare when holding other distortions constant.

Following Proposition 2, we have

Corollary 2. Under Assumption 1, if s_1 *is chosen optimally or* $\mathrm{d}s_l = -\mathrm{d}t_1$, *and there are no nontraded goods, a reduction (increase) of the largest (smallest) tariff up to the next highest (smallest) tariff improves welfare, i.e.,*

$$\tau = t_1,\ \mathrm{d}t_i/\mathrm{d}\alpha = \begin{cases} -1 & \text{if } i = 1 \\ 0 & \text{otherwise} \end{cases}, \quad \text{and either } \mathrm{d}\boldsymbol{s}/\mathrm{d}\alpha = -\mathrm{d}\boldsymbol{t}/\mathrm{d}\alpha, \text{ or } \mathrm{d}u/\mathrm{d}\boldsymbol{s}' = 0,$$

$$\text{then } \mathrm{d}u/\mathrm{d}\alpha > 0.$$

Proof. See appendix.

3. Concluding remarks

The welfare effects of changing tariffs alone in the presence of sector-specific domestic distortions are ambiguous. Hence, the outstanding implication of introducing sector-specific price distortions is the requirement of involving both types of distortions (economy-wide and sector-specific) in the reform package.

Another implication is the stronger assumptions on substitutability among goods and domestic distortion structure required to establish the sufficient conditions of welfare-improving reductions of the most extreme tariff. The two sets of results obtained above demonstrate the contrasting degree of robustness of the chief results derived by Fukushima (1979) and Hatta (1977) with respect to the assumption of a unique price vector faced by all producers. The importance of our results is illustrated by recent trade agreements and negotiations that include both border measures ad domestic production distortions. For instance, in the Uruguay round of the GATT negotiations, agricultural distortions (both domestic programs and trade barriers) were central to the negotiations. In the U.S. and E.C. many farm programs make different industries face different price structures. Our results validate the inclusion of domestic distortions in a trade liberalization package but also shed light on the conditions required by different types of reforms to be welfare-improving. Since the result on proportional decrease of all distortions relies on fewer assumptions, this is an additional motivation to favor the latter type of reform, i.e., to include all commodities and programs in the negotiations.

Appendix

The appendix presents lemmas used in the proofs, the homogeneity conditions used to derive eq. (5) and the proofs of the propositions.

1. Lemmas

For the proofs, we rely on the following lemmas based on Hatta (1977), Beghin and Karp (1992), and Fukushima (1979).

Lemma 1. *Given Assumption 1, the off-diagonal elements in the column of* $D - D^{a}$, *which correspond to the first tariff, are positive;* $Y^{a}_{TN} Z^{-1}_{NN} (Z_{NT} + Y^{a}_{NT})$ *is a positive matrix; and* $B > 0$.

Lemma 2. (Fukushima's Lemma 3). *Let K be the matrix* $[I - Z_{TN} Z^{-1}_{NN}]$, *then* $D = KZK'$.

Proof. See Fukushima (1979, p. 431).

2. Homogeneity conditions

Homogeneity conditions in price of consumption and production vectors are used to derive eq. (5) as follows. Homogeneity in price is expressed for net consumption ($\boldsymbol{c} - \boldsymbol{y}^{a} - \boldsymbol{y}^{b}$):

$$\boldsymbol{p}^{b} Z_{TT} + \boldsymbol{p}^{N} Z_{NT} - \boldsymbol{s} Q Y^{a}_{TT} = 0, \quad \text{and} \tag{A.1}$$

$$\boldsymbol{p}^{N} Z_{NN} + \boldsymbol{p}^{b} Z_{TN} - \boldsymbol{s} Q Y^{a}_{TN} = 0. \tag{A.2}$$

The system (A.1), (A.2) is solved for $\boldsymbol{p}^{\mathrm{N}}$ to yield

$$\boldsymbol{p}^{\mathrm{N}} = -\boldsymbol{p}^{\mathrm{b}} Z_{TN} Z_{NN}^{-1} + \boldsymbol{s} Q Y_{TN}^{\mathrm{a}} Z_{NN}^{-1}, \quad \text{and}$$

$$\boldsymbol{p}^{\mathrm{b}} Z_{TT} - \boldsymbol{s} Q Y_{TT}^{\mathrm{a}} - \boldsymbol{p}^{\mathrm{b}} Z_{TN} Z_{NN}^{-1} Z_{NT} + \boldsymbol{s} Q Y_{TN}^{\mathrm{a}} Z_{NN}^{-1} Z_{NT} = 0, \quad \text{or} \tag{A.3}$$

$$\boldsymbol{p}^{\mathrm{b}} D + \boldsymbol{s} Q D^{\mathrm{a}\prime} = 0 \quad [\text{eq. (5)}].$$

Similarly, $\boldsymbol{p}^{\mathrm{N}}$ is substituted into the homogeneity condition in production of firm a to yield

$$\boldsymbol{p}^{\mathrm{a}} Y_{TT}^{\mathrm{a}} + \left(-\boldsymbol{p}^{\mathrm{b}} Z_{TN} Z_{NN}^{-1} + \boldsymbol{s} Q Y_{TN}^{\mathrm{a}} Z_{NN}^{-1}\right) Y_{NT}^{\mathrm{a}} = 0, \quad \text{or} \tag{A.4}$$

$$\boldsymbol{p}^{\mathrm{b}} D^{\mathrm{a}} - \boldsymbol{s} Q\left(Y_{TT}^{\mathrm{a}} + Y_{TN}^{\mathrm{a}} Z_{NN}^{-1} Y_{NT}^{\mathrm{a}}\right) = 0. \tag{A.5}$$

3. *Proofs of propositions*

Proof of Proposition 1 and its Corollary

Proof of Proposition 1. The reform $[\mathrm{d}\boldsymbol{t}/\mathrm{d}\alpha = (\boldsymbol{\tau} - \boldsymbol{t})$, and $\mathrm{d}\boldsymbol{s}/\mathrm{d}\alpha = (-\boldsymbol{s})']$ is substituted into (6) to yield

$$(1+\boldsymbol{\tau}) B \; \mathrm{d}u/\mathrm{d}\alpha = \left[(\boldsymbol{t}-\boldsymbol{\tau}) Q D Q + \boldsymbol{s} Q D^{\mathrm{a}\prime} Q\right](\boldsymbol{\tau}-\boldsymbol{t})' + (\boldsymbol{1}+\boldsymbol{\tau}) Q D Q^{\mathrm{a}} \boldsymbol{s}'. \tag{A.6}$$

Using homogeneity of $\boldsymbol{z}$ [eq. (A.5)] we have $(\boldsymbol{1}+\boldsymbol{t})QD = -\boldsymbol{s}QD^{\mathrm{a}\prime}$ and $DQ(\boldsymbol{1}+\boldsymbol{t})' = -D^{\mathrm{a}}Q\boldsymbol{s}'$; which yields

$$\begin{aligned}(1+\boldsymbol{\tau}) B \; \mathrm{d}u/\mathrm{d}\alpha &= \left[(\boldsymbol{t}-\boldsymbol{\tau}) Q D Q - (\boldsymbol{1}+\boldsymbol{t}) Q D Q\right](\boldsymbol{\tau}-\boldsymbol{t})' - (\boldsymbol{1}+\boldsymbol{\tau}) Q D Q (\boldsymbol{1}+\boldsymbol{t})' \\ &= -(\boldsymbol{1}+\boldsymbol{\tau}) Q D Q (\boldsymbol{1}+\boldsymbol{\tau})',\end{aligned} \tag{A.7}$$

which is positive since D is negative definite because of Lemma 2 and because Z is negative definite. Q.E.D.

Proof of the Corollary. Set $\boldsymbol{\tau} = 0$ into (A.6). Q.E.D.

Proof of Proposition 2 and its Corollary

Proof of Proposition 2. We add $\boldsymbol{\tau} Q D^{\mathrm{a}}$ to each side of eq. (A.5) to obtain

$$(\boldsymbol{1}+\boldsymbol{\tau}) Q D^{\mathrm{a}} = (\boldsymbol{\tau}-\boldsymbol{t}) Q D^{\mathrm{a}} + \boldsymbol{s} Q\left(Y_{TT}^{\mathrm{a}} + Y_{TN}^{\mathrm{a}} Z_{NN}^{-1} Y_{NT}^{\mathrm{a}}\right). \tag{A.8}$$

We can substitute (A.8) into (6) to obtain

$$\begin{aligned}(1+\boldsymbol{\tau}) B \; \mathrm{d}u &= \left[(\boldsymbol{t}-\boldsymbol{\tau}) Q D Q + \boldsymbol{s} Q D^{\mathrm{a}\prime} Q\right] \mathrm{d}\boldsymbol{t}' \\ &\quad - \left[(\boldsymbol{\tau}-\boldsymbol{t}) Q D^{\mathrm{a}} + \boldsymbol{s} Q\left(Y_{TT}^{\mathrm{a}} + Y_{TN}^{\mathrm{a}} Z_{NN}^{-1} Y_{NT}^{\mathrm{a}}\right) Q\right] \mathrm{d}\boldsymbol{s}'.\end{aligned} \tag{A.9}$$

If $\mathrm{d}s = -\mathrm{d}t$, and if we set $\tau = t_1$, we obtain

$$(1+t_1)B\,\mathrm{d}u/\mathrm{d}\alpha = \left[-(t_1 - t)Q(D - D^{\mathrm{a}})Q + sQY^{\mathrm{a}}_{TN}Z^{-1}_{NN}(Z_{NT} + Y^{\mathrm{a}}_{NT})Q\right]\mathrm{d}t'/\mathrm{d}\alpha. \tag{A.10}$$

If, on the other hand, s_1 is chosen optimally the necessary condition is that $1QD^{\mathrm{a}}Q\,\mathrm{d}s' = 0$ [see (6)]; this implies that $1QD^{\mathrm{a}}Q\,\mathrm{d}t' = 0$ since t_1 is the only tariff being changed. Adding this expression to (6), using the optimality of s_1 and the definition in (A.8), results in an equation with the same form as (A.10). The right-hand side of the equation is evaluated at a different point, however, since the optimal s_1 and the s_1 obtained by offsetting the change in t_1 are not the same in general. If t_1 is the largest (respectively, smallest) tariff and $\mathrm{d}t/\mathrm{d}\alpha \leq 0$ (respectively, $\mathrm{d}t/\mathrm{d}\alpha \geq 0$), Lemma 1 guarantees that $-(t_1 - t)(D - D^{\mathrm{a}})Q\,\mathrm{d}t'/\mathrm{d}\alpha > 0$ and that the elements of $QY^{\mathrm{a}}_{TN}Z^{-1}_{NN}(Z_{NT} + Y^{\mathrm{a}}_{NT})Q\,\mathrm{d}t'/\mathrm{d}\alpha$ are negative (respectively, positive). Therefore, if s is a negative (positive) vector, $\mathrm{d}u/\mathrm{d}\alpha > 0$. Q.E.D.

Proof of the Corollary. In the absence of nontraded goods, the second term on the right-hand side of (A.10) vanishes and the first term is positive by Lemma 1. Q.E.D.

References

Beghin, J.C. and L.S. Karp, 1992, Tariff reform in the presence of sector-specific distortions, Canadian Journal of Economics 25.

Beghin, J.C. and L.S. Karp, 1989, Do nonagricultural distortions justify the protection of U.S. agriculture?, in: B. Greenshields and M. Bellamy, eds., Government intervention in agriculture (Gower, Brookfield) 189–196.

Bertrand, T.J. and J. Vanek, 1971, The theory of tariffs, taxes, and subsidies: Some aspects of the second best, American Economic Review 61, 925–931.

Corden, W.M. and R.E. Falvey, 1985, Quotas and the second best, Economics Letters 18, 67–70.

Dixit, A.K. and D.M.G. Newbery, 1985, Setting the price of oil in a distorted economy, Economic Journal 95, 71–82.

Dixit, A.K. and V. Norman, 1980, Theory of international trade (Cambridge University Press, Cambridge, UK).

Falvey, R.E., 1988, Tariffs, quotas and piecemeal policy reform, Journal of International Economics 25, 173–183.

Fukushima, T., 1979, Tariff structures, nontraded goods, and the theory of piecemeal policy recommendations, International Economic Review 20, 427–435.

Fukushima, T. and N. Kim, 1989, Welfare improving tariff changes: A case of many goods and countries, Journal of International Economics 26, 383–388.

Hatta, T., 1977, A recommendation for a better tariff structure, Econometrica 45, 1859–1869.

Hatta, T. and T. Fukushima, 1979, The welfare effect of tariff rate reductions in a many country world, Journal of International Economics 9, 503–511.

Turunen-Red, A. and A.D. Woodland, 1991, Strict Pareto-improving multilateral reforms of tariffs, Econometrica 59, 1127–1152.

[15]

On the Theory of Piecemeal Tariff Reform: The Case of Pure Imported Intermediate Inputs

By RAMÓN LÓPEZ AND ARVIND PANAGARIYA*

What is the effect of a tariff reduction that applies only to a subset of commodities subject to tariffs? This important question was addressed systematically for the first time by James Meade (1955 Ch. 13) in his classic work *Trade and Welfare*. After a careful analysis, Meade concluded, "[T]here is more likely to be a gain in economic welfare if the rate of duty is high on the primary imports which will come in in increased volume and is low on the secondary imports which will come in in reduced volume" (p. 208).[1]

This result was proved formally by Trent J. Bertrand and Jaroslav Vanek (1971), who demonstrated that, in a small open economy, if the highest tariff rate is reduced to the next highest one, welfare will rise provided the import demand for the good with the highest tariff exhibits gross substitutability with respect to all other goods.[2] Subsequently, following a different strand of the literature as exemplified in John Green (1961), Tatsuo Hatta (1973, 1977) and Peter Lloyd (1974) independently proved similar results in terms of Hicksian substitutability.[3]

In deriving their results, Bertrand and Vanek allowed for the use of final goods as intermediate inputs (i.e., interindustry flows).[4] However, neither they nor the subsequent writers (including Hatta and Lloyd) allowed for the existence of "pure" imported intermediate inputs that are not produced domestically. Therefore, a natural question is whether the piecemeal policy prescription derived by them remains valid in the presence of pure imported intermediates.

This question is particularly important for developing countries for two reasons. First, by far the bulk of the imports of developing countries are intermediate and capital goods. According to the World Bank, during the period 1975–1985 50 percent of developing countries' imports were accounted for by intermediate inputs, and an additional 30 percent were capital goods. A sizable proportion of both capital and intermediate goods are neither produced nor directly consumed in these countries.

Second, the Meade-Bertrand-Vanek-Hatta-Lloyd result has been the cornerstone of trade policy reform in many developing countries, especially during the last decade. In most countries, trade reform has been based on the so-called "concertina" approach, under which the highest tariffs are reduced to the next highest ones and then to the next highest ones, and so on. Thus,

*López: Professor, Department of Agricultural and Resource Economics, University of Maryland, College Park, MD 20742, and consultant, Trade Policy Division, World Bank, 1818 H Street, N.W., Washington, DC 20433; Panagariya: Senior Economist, Trade Policy Division, World Bank, 1818 H Street, N.W., Washington, DC 20433, and Professor, Department of Economics, University of Maryland, College Park, MD 20742. The findings, interpretations, and conclusions in this paper are entirely those of the authors. They do not necessarily represent the views of the World Bank, its Executive Directors, or the countries they represent. The authors are indebted to two referees and Tatsuo Hatta for valuable comments on an earlier draft.

[1] In this quotation, "primary imports" refers to the goods on which tariffs are reduced, while "secondary imports" refers to other importables subject to tariffs.

[2] Robert Lipsey and Kelvin Lancaster (1956) had proved the basic result of Bertrand and Vanek in a one-factor, three-good model with a Cobb-Douglas utility function.

[3] More recently, Takashi Fukushima (1979) has proved the validity of the Hatta-Lloyd result when the highest tariff is shared by several commodities, while Rodney Falvey (1988) has done the same in the presence of quantitative restrictions on imports.

[4] Although Hatta (1973, 1977) did not allow explicitly for interindustry flows, his results can also be shown to be valid in the presence of such flows.

trade reforms in Chile during the 1970's and those in Guatemala, Costa Rica, Tanzania, Indonesia, and Venezuela in recent years provide the purest examples of the concertina method (e.g., Michael Michaely et al., 1991; Vinod Thomas et al., 1991). According to the detailed study of trade liberalization in developing countries by Michaely et al., many other countries have carried out reforms that combine the concertina method with elements of across-the-board proportionality rules.

In this paper, we revisit the basic Meade result (henceforth, the "concertina theorem") in a model with a pure imported input that is not produced domestically. We demonstrate that when such an input is present, it may be impossible to satisfy the substitutability condition of the concertina theorem. At most, one can assume that final goods exhibit substitutability with respect to each other. As long as the Rybczynski relationship holds with respect to the imported input—and it necessarily does for most of the standard models of international trade —a rise in the price of the input (which is equivalent to a decline in the total supply of the input) will be accompanied by an expansion of at least one final good. That is to say, the required substitutability condition between the imported input and all final goods is impossible to satisfy.

We demonstrate that any one of the following cases is sufficient to give rise to complementarity between the pure imported input and at least one final good: (i) the imported input is used in fixed proportions; (ii) the number of inelastically supplied primary factors equals the number of produced final goods, as in the Heckscher-Ohlin model; or (iii) there is one commonly shared factor and one specific factor in each sector, as in the Ricardo-Viner model, and not all goods use the imported input. Observe that in case (i), substitution is allowed among primary factors of production, while in cases (ii) and (iii) substitution is allowed among all factors including the imported input.

Assuming case (i) and that *final* goods exhibit substitutability with respect to each other, we also derive two specific results. First, if the highest tariff rate applies to the imported input, a decrease in it will be unambiguously welfare-reducing, provided the final importables enjoy positive effective protection and the least protected good also uses the imported input least intensively. Even if this latter condition is not satisfied, a reduction in the tariff is not necessarily welfare-improving. Second, if the highest tariff applies to a final importable, a reduction in it will not be necessarily welfare-improving. An unambiguous improvement in welfare requires the additional condition that the good with the highest nominal tariff also be subject to the highest effective rate of protection.[5]

At this point, it is useful to relate the present paper to the literature on pure imported inputs. This literature includes inter alia V. K. Ramaswami and T. N. Srinivasan (1968), López and Dani Rodrik (1990), and Panagariya (1992). Our paper is related to Panagariya (1992), in which some tariff reform issues are analyzed in the presence of a revenue constraint. Panagariya (1992) does not question the validity of the concertina theorem; indeed, that paper assumes that the theorem is valid, and its primary concern is whether a country continues to gain from a reduction in the highest tariff when it has to offset the resulting revenue loss by an increase in the lowest tariff applicable to imported inputs.[6] By contrast, our concern in the present paper is with a more fundamental point, namely, that the concertina

[5]The results described in this paragraph will also obtain, albeit under slightly different conditions, in cases (ii) and (iii). Thus, the assumption of fixed proportions with respect to the imported input simplifies the exposition but is not necessary to obtain the results.

[6]It is of utmost importance to note that the effects of a reduction in the highest tariff and those of an increase in the lowest tariff are not symmetric. More explicitly, given substitutability, a reduction in the highest tariff is welfare-improving, but an increase in the lowest tariff need not be. Therefore, the increase in the lowest tariff rate to maintain a constant revenue can counter the welfare gain from the reduction in the highest tariff. Panagariya (1992) derives conditions under which an increase in the lowest tariff rate does not lead to a welfare loss in the case when the lowest tariff applies to inputs. The results of Panagariya (1992) are entirely consistent with the concertina theorem.

theorem itself may be invalid in the presence of imported inputs.

The paper is organized as follows. In Section I we outline the model, while in Section II we demonstrate that the existence of pure imported inputs must give rise to complementarity in a variety of models. In Section III we impose the assumption of fixed-coefficients technology with respect to the imported input and analyze the case when the highest tariff applies to the imported input. In Section IV we consider the case when the good subject to the highest tariff is a final importable. Finally, conclusions are presented in Section V.

I. The Model

Consider a small open economy consuming and producing three final goods: 1, 2, and 3. Goods 1 and 2 are importables, while good 3 is exportable. All three goods are produced with primary factors and an imported input not produced at home. We assume perfect competition in all markets. In order to rule out the possibility of complete specialization, we assume that there are three or more primary factors available in fixed supply and that world prices are such that an internal production equilibrium exists. We denote the vector of primary inputs by $\mathbf{z}$. As the country is small, we can set the world prices of all goods including the input equal to unity. The ad valorem tariff on the ith importable is denoted t_i $(i=1,2)$, and the tariff on the imported input is τ. The domestic prices of final importables, the exportable, and the imported input will be $1+t_1$, $1+t_2$, 1, and $1+\tau$, respectively.

Assuming that tariff revenue is redistributed among consumers in a lump-sum fashion, the economy's budget constraint may be written

$$(1)\quad E(1+t_1,1+t_2,1;\mu) = \pi(1+t_1,1+t_2,1,1+\tau;\mathbf{z}) - \tau\pi_\tau + t_1(E_1-\pi_1) + t_2(E_2-\pi_2)$$

where $E(\cdot)$ is the standard expenditure function, $\pi(\cdot)$ is the revenue function, and $\mathbf{z}$ is the factor-endowments vector. We assume that $E(\cdot)$ and $\pi(\cdot)$ have all the standard properties (Avinash Dixit and Victor Norman, 1980 Ch. 2). E_i and π_i $(i=1,2,3)$ represent the first partials of the expenditure and revenue functions, respectively, with respect to the ith argument. As usual, E_i is the quantity demanded, and π_i is the quantity supplied of good i; π_τ is the first partial of the revenue function with respect to $1+\tau$ and equals the negative of the total quantity of the imported input used in the production of final goods. Finally, μ stands for the level of utility.

We will first demonstrate the importance of the substitutability assumption for the concertina theorem.[7] To highlight the importance of the imported input, we assume that τ is the highest tariff rate. Differentiating (1) with respect to τ and solving for the change in μ, we obtain

$$(2)\quad N(d\mu/d\tau) = -(t_1\pi_{1\tau} + t_2\pi_{2\tau} + \tau\pi_{\tau\tau})$$

where $N \equiv E_\mu - t_1E_{1\mu} - t_2E_{2\mu}$, E_μ is the first partial of $E(\cdot)$ with respect to μ, and $E_{i\mu}$ $(i=1,2)$ is the partial effect of a change in utility on the demand for good i. Following Hatta (1973, 1977), we rule out inferiority in consumption, which guarantees $N>0$. By the convexity of the revenue function, $\pi_{\tau\tau}$ is positive. Moreover, if we assume that the imported input exhibits complementarity with *all* the other importables subject to tariffs, we have $\pi_{1\tau}, \pi_{2\tau} > 0$. In this case, a reduction in τ will be unambiguously welfare-improving. Intuitively, the tariff reduction expands imports of all goods subject to tariffs, a change which brings the economy closer to the efficient (free-trade) equilibrium.

This result has not played much of a role in the literature. The reason is that the

[7]Throughout the paper, goods i and j are defined as substitutes if a rise in the price of i leads to an increase in the compensated excess demand (i.e., demand minus supply) for good j. In the case of the pure imported input, the excess demand coincides with the input demand in production.

assumption of complementarity across all goods subject to tariffs is not very realistic. Therefore, theorists have focused more on the substitutability case. Inspection of (2) shows that if one or more goods subject to tariffs exhibit substitutability with respect to the imported input, the effect of a reduction in the tariff on the latter will be ambiguous in general. It is at this point that the conditions of the concertina theorem come into play.

Making use of the property that $\pi_\tau(\cdot)$ is homogeneous of degree 0 in all prices, we can transform (2) into

$$(2') \quad N(d\mu/d\tau) = [1/(1+\tau)] \times [(\tau - t_1)\pi_{1\tau} + (\tau - t_2)\pi_{2\tau} + \tau\pi_{3\tau}].$$

If we assume that τ is the highest tariff rate and that the imported input exhibits net substitutability with all other goods implying $\pi_{i\tau} < 0$ $(i = 1,2,3)$, a reduction in τ will necessarily improve welfare.

Intuitively, imports of the good that is liberalized (the input in the present case) rise, and given substitutability, imports of other goods subject to tariffs fall. The former change is welfare-increasing, while the latter change is welfare-reducing. The net effect depends on which of the two effects dominates. Substitutability across all goods implies that the tariff reduction will increase exports. As trade is balanced, expansion of exports implies a net expansion of imports (valued at world prices) as well. In other words, imports of the good that is liberalized rise more than the decline in the imports of other goods subject to tariffs. This result and the fact that the good that is liberalized is subject to the highest tariff imply that the welfare-increasing effect of the tariff reduction must dominate the welfare-reducing effect.[8]

II. Can All Goods Be Substitutable with the Imported Input?

We are now in a position to address the question that is central to this paper: can all goods exhibit substitutability with respect to the imported input? We now demonstrate that, in most of the plausible cases, all goods cannot exhibit substitutability with the imported input. We consider first the case in which the imported input is used in fixed proportions but substitution is permitted among primary factors.

A. *Fixed Coefficients with Respect to the Imported Inputs*

In this case, the production function for good i is written

$$(3) \quad x_i = \min\{G^i(\mathbf{z}_i), m_i/a_i\} \qquad i = 1,2,3$$

where x_i is the output of good i, $\mathbf{z}_i$ is the vector of primary factors, m_i is the quantity of imported input, and a_i is the imported-input-to-output coefficient. Function $G_i(\mathbf{z}_i)$ is linearly homogeneous in $\mathbf{z}_i$ and may be interpreted as value added in sector i.

Given (3), the economy's revenue function may be written

$$(4) \quad R = R(\nu_1(\mathbf{q}), \nu_2(\mathbf{q}), \nu_3(\mathbf{q}); z) = R(\boldsymbol{\nu}(\mathbf{q}); \mathbf{z}),$$

where $\mathbf{q} \equiv (1+t_1, 1+t_2, 1, 1+\tau)$ and $\nu_i(\mathbf{q}) \equiv 1 + t_i - a_i(1+\tau)$, is the unit value added in industry i $(i = 1,2)$ (Panagariya, 1992). We have also defined $\boldsymbol{\nu}(q) \equiv [\nu_1(q), \nu_2(q), \nu_3(q)]$ for compactness. We assume that all $\nu_i(\mathbf{q})$ are positive.

Given that $R(\boldsymbol{\nu}(\mathbf{q}); \mathbf{z})$ is linearly homogeneous in $\boldsymbol{\nu}$, it will also be linearly homogeneous in $\mathbf{q}$. As $R_\tau(\cdot)$ is the first partial of

[8] More explicitly, let M_i $(i = 1,2)$ be the imports of good i, and let m be the imports of the input. Then, given balanced trade, $dM_1 + dM_2 + dm > 0$, because a tariff cut must increase exports by the substitutability assumption. This inequality, along with the facts that $dm > 0$ and that $dM_1, dM_2 < 0$, implies that $t_1\,dM_1 + t_2\,dM_2 + \tau\,dm > 0$ if the highest tariff is cut.

$R(\cdot)$ with respect to $1+\tau$ which is an element in $\mathbf{q}$, this partial derivative must be homogeneous of degree 0 in $\mathbf{q}$. Finally, as is easily verified, $R_\tau(\cdot)$ must also be homogeneous of degree 0 in $\boldsymbol{\nu}$. We immediately have

$$(5) \qquad \nu_1 R_{\tau 1} + \nu_2 R_{\tau 2} + \nu_3 R_{\tau 3} = 0.$$

This equation implies that at least one $R_{\tau i}$ must be positive; that is, it is impossible to rule out complementarity.[9]

An important question is whether the assumption of a fixed-coefficients technology with respect to the imported input is the driving force behind this strong result. We demonstrate below, however, that the result remains valid for a wide class of models when the production technology is non-Leontief.

B. *The Heckscher-Ohlin Framework*

Consider the case when the number of primary factors equals the number of produced goods, (i.e., $\mathbf{z}$ is 1×3). Under the usual long-run competitive equilibrium conditions, prices of primary factors depend solely on the exogeneously given prices, $\mathbf{q}$. Indeed, it is easily shown that these prices are linearly homogeneous in $\mathbf{q}$. Letting $\mathbf{w}(\mathbf{q})$ be the 1×3 vector of primary-factor prices the imported-input-to-output ratio may be written $a_i(\mathbf{w}(\mathbf{q}), 1+\tau)$ where $a_i(\cdot)$ is homogeneous of degree 0 in $\mathbf{w}(\mathbf{q})$ and $1+\tau$ or, equivalently, in $\mathbf{q}$. Moreover, all $a_i(\cdot)$ functions are independent of output levels.

For a given $\mathbf{q}$, the $a_i(\mathbf{w}(\mathbf{q}), 1+\tau)$ are thus constant. Therefore, as we demonstrate formally in the Appendix, the revenue function in the present case exhibits the same properties with respect to the elements of vector $\mathbf{q}$ as in the fixed-coefficients case, and the substitutability condition of the concertina theorem fails to hold.

C. *The Ricardo-Viner Framework*

Finally, let us consider a Ricardo-Viner type of model in which each sector employs one specific and one common factor and technology is of a general form. In addition, assume that at least one sector, say sector 3, does not use the imported input.

Consider now a rise in the tariff on the imported input. This change reduces the demand for labor in sectors 1 and 2, which use the imported input, but leaves the demand in sector 3 unchanged. The wage rate declines, and sector 3 expands by making use of cheaper labor. That is to say, good 3 exhibits complementarity with respect to the imported input.

This model can also be used to illustrate the importance of the assumption that the input is not produced domestically. Thus, suppose that of the three goods, good 1 is the input. Then, an increase in τ will increase demand for labor in sector 1 and lower the demand for labor in sector 2. If we impose the additional assumption that the former effect is stronger, the net effect of the increase in τ will be to increase the total demand for labor in the economy. In this instance, output of good 1 (the imported input) will expand, while outputs of other goods will contract; the substitutability conditions of the concertina theorem can be satisfied.

In the present section, we have shown that if there is an imported input that is neither consumed nor produced domestically, the substitutability condition of the concertina theorem is impossible to satisfy for a wide class of models. Recalling, however, that the substitutability condition is sufficient but not necessary for welfare improvement following a reduction in the highest tariff, the question remains whether we can still rely on the concertina method for piecemeal tariff reform to yield higher levels of welfare. In the following sections, we provide two examples to demonstrate that extreme caution is necessary in this regard and that under plausible circum-

[9]As an example, suppose that the input is used in goods 2 and 3 only. Then a reduction in t_1 which causes sector 1 to contract and sectors 2 and 3 to expand will lead to an increase in the use of the input. That is to say, good 1 and the input are complements.

stances it is altogether possible for welfare to decline when the highest tariff is lowered. For clarity of exposition and tractability, these examples assume that the imported input is used in fixed proportions as in Subsection II-A above. We note, however, that the basic message of the ensuing analysis will hold for the cases considered in Subsections II-B and II-C, where substitution is allowed among all inputs.

III. Welfare Effects of a Tariff Reduction When the Highest Tariff Applies to the Input

We first consider the case when the highest tariff applies to the imported input. Observe that this case is not a mere theoretical curiosity and may, indeed, have substantial policy relevance. Many developing countries tax imported inputs heavily. In some of these countries, trade taxes constitute a major source of government revenue, and imports of most final consumption goods are essentially banned or controlled via quantitative restrictions. Therefore, the burden of trade taxes falls most heavily on imported inputs. For example according to the World Bank, in Brazil, electrical communications equipment and machinery were subject to ad valorem nominal tariffs of 71 percent and 48 percent, respectively, during 1980–1981. The only sector that was subject to a higher tariff than these sectors was pharmaceuticals (97 percent). Similarly, in Argentina, capital goods were subject to the second-highest nominal tariff (32 percent) in the year 1987. The same basic story applies to India, where in 1987 the average tariff for intermediate goods was higher than the average tariff for consumer goods. In several other major developing countries, such as Bangladesh, China, and Mexico, overall tariffs on intermediate and capital goods, are not significantly lower than those on consumption goods. Observe that even if tariffs on imported inputs are not the highest but second- or third-highest, as the process of reforms progresses, the issue of lowering them must be confronted.

Assuming a fixed-coefficients technology with respect to the imported input, the relevant revenue function is given by equation (4). The economy's budget constraint may be written

$$(6)\quad E(1+t_1,1+t_2,1;\mu) = R(\nu_1(\mathbf{q}),\nu_2(\mathbf{q}),\nu_3(\mathbf{q});\mathbf{z}) + t_1(E_1-R_1)+t_2(E_2-R_2) + \tau(a_1R_1+a_2R_2+a_3R_3).$$

In the remainder of this section, we will assume that the imported input is not used in the production of the exportable. We make this assumption for simplicity; none of our results is affected by it. The effect of a change in τ on welfare can be written as

$$(7)\quad E_\mu\frac{d\mu}{d\tau} = t_1\frac{dM_1}{d\tau}+t_2\frac{dM_2}{d\tau}+\tau\frac{dm}{d\tau} = (t_1-a_1\tau)\frac{dM_1}{d\tau}+(t_2-a_2\tau)\frac{dM_2}{d\tau}$$

where M_1, M_2, and m stand for imports of goods 1, 2, and the input, respectively. We assume that the final importables are subject to positive effective protection. This assumption implies that the terms in parentheses in the second equality of (7) are positive. Then, a reduction in τ will improve welfare if it increases final imports. Intuitively, however, a reduction in τ works like a production subsidy on goods 1 and 2 at different rates. Other things equal, a production subsidy on good i expands production, lowers M_i, and hence reduces welfare.

Further insight into the effects of a change in τ can be obtained by substituting for $dM_1/d\tau$ and $dM_2/d\tau$ in terms of the revenue and expenditure functions and making use of the homogeneity property of the revenue function. After some simplifications, we obtain

$$(7') \quad N\frac{d\mu}{d\tau} = -(1+t_1)(1+t_2) \times A\frac{\nu_1^*\nu_2^*}{\nu_1\nu_2}\left(\frac{\nu_1}{\nu_1^*} - \frac{\nu_2}{\nu_2^*}\right)R_{12} - \left[a_1\left(\frac{\nu_1-\nu_1^*}{\nu_1}\right)R_{13} + a_2\left(\frac{\nu_2-\nu_2^*}{\nu_2}\right)R_{23}\right]$$

where N was defined in the context of equation (2) and is positive. In addition, ν_i^* $(\equiv 1-a_i)$ is obtained by setting $t_i = \tau_i = 0$ in ν_i and $A \equiv a_1/(1+t_1) - a_2/(1+t_2)$. Intuitively, ν_i^* is the unit value added in industry i under free trade. As an example, consider the special case when $a_2 = t_2 = 0$. In this case, good 1 is the only protected good. A reduction in τ, working like a production subsidy to good 1, causes that good to expand and, given substitutability among final goods, causes other goods to contract. All of these changes move the economy further away from the Pareto-efficient allocation and worsen welfare.

In order to interpret (7′), let us assume that the input is subject to the highest tariff $(\tau > t_i)$ and that both final importables are protected relative to the exportable $(\nu_i - \nu_i^* > 0)$.[10] Observe that since $\nu_i - \nu_i^* = (1+t_i) - a_i(1+\tau) - (1-a_i) = t_i - a_i\tau$, these assumptions are both satisfied if $a_i/t_i > \tau > t_i$. Then, if good 1 is protected more than good 2 $(\nu_1/\nu_1^* - \nu_2/\nu_2^* > 0)$, (7′) implies that a small reduction in the highest tariff, τ, will lead to (i) an unambiguous decline in welfare if $A > 0$ and (ii) an ambiguous effect on welfare if $A < 0$. That is to say, the concertina result that a reduction in the highest tariff to the next highest one must increase welfare does not hold. If good 2 is more protected than good 1, a reduction in τ will worsen welfare if $A < 0$ and will have an ambiguous effect if $A > 0$.

These results can be best understood by thinking of the reduction in τ as a production subsidy to goods 1 and 2 at different rates. Remembering that the domestic price of the ith importable is $1+t_i$ initially, a reduction in τ equal to $d\tau$ implies an ad valorem production subsidy of $a_i\,d\tau/(1+t_i)$ to good i. If $A > 0$, the rate of subsidy will be higher on good 1 than on good 2 $(a_1\,d\tau/[1+t_1] > a_2\,d\tau/[1+t_2])$. If good 1 is protected more than good 2 initially and if both importables are protected relative to the exportable, this reduction in τ will make the existing distortion worse, and welfare will decline unambiguously. In the case when $A < 0$, the production subsidy via a reduction in τ is lower on good 1 than on good 2. To the extent that both importables are protected initially, a further production subsidy to them is welfare-reducing. However, since good 1 is protected more initially and the rate of implicit production subsidy is lower on this good, the reallocation effect between the two importables works in the opposite direction. Thus, the net effect on welfare is ambiguous.

How does this explanation of our result relate to the conditions of the concertina theorem? Recall that the substitutability condition of the concertina theorem requires that, in order for welfare to improve unambiguously, the decline in τ must lead to a contraction in the compensated excess demand for *every* other good. As the decline in τ is not accompanied by a change in any final goods prices, this condition is equivalent to the condition that outputs of all final goods expand. However, as we have seen, this is impossible in the cases considered above, for a decline in τ necessarily leads to a contraction of the exportable. Formally, letting $R_{3\tau}$ be the partial of R_3 with respect to τ, we can verify that, given $a_3 = 0$,

$$(8) \quad R_{3\tau} = -(a_1R_{31} + a_2R_{32}) > 0$$

[10] Equation (7′) applies in general when tariff rates are not subject to these restrictions. Indeed, it can be shown that at $\tau = 0$ and $t_1, t_2 > 0$, the right-hand side is necessarily positive.

where the sign of the right-hand side follows from the assumption that $R_{31}, R_{32} < 0$.

IV. The Highest Tariff Applies to a Final Good

We now turn to the case in which the highest tariff applies to a final importable. We revert to the assumption that a_3 is positive. We assume that the highest tariff applies to good 1 (i.e., $t_1 > t_2, \tau$). We are then interested in the effect of a change in t_1 on welfare. Differentiating (6) with respect to t_1 and making use of the linear homogeneity property of $E(\cdot)$ and $R(\cdot)$, we obtain

$$(9)\quad N\frac{d\mu}{dt_1} = -\frac{1}{1+t_1}[(t_1-t_2)E_{12}+t_1E_{13}] + \left[\frac{\nu_1^*\nu_2^*}{\nu_1}\left(\frac{\nu_1}{\nu_1^*}-\frac{\nu_2}{\nu_2^*}\right)R_{12} + \frac{\nu_3}{\nu_1}(\nu_1-\nu_1^*)R_{13}\right]$$

(recall that ν_i is the price of value added in the presence of tariffs and ν_i^* is the price under free trade).

Given $t_1 > t_2$ and net substitutability in demand, the first term on the right-hand side of (9) is negative. Therefore, if we lower t_1, this term will contribute positively to welfare. The sign of the second term is ambiguous in general, however. Therefore, the effect of a change in t_1 on welfare is also ambiguous in general. For concreteness, assume as before (and in conformity with the concertina theorem) that R_{12} and R_{13} are negative. Also assume that the effective protection on good 1 is less than that on good 2 ($\nu_1/\nu_1^* - \nu_2/\nu_2^* < 0$) and that ν_3 is small ($a_3[1+\tau]$ is close to 1). Then, the second term on the right-hand side will be negative, and the welfare effect of a change in t_1 will be ambiguous. A sufficient condition for concertina cuts to improve welfare is that the sector with the higher nominal tariff also has the higher effective tariff.

Intuitively, given $E_{12}, E_{13} > 0$ and $t_1 > t_2$, a reduction in t_1 necessarily reduces consumption distortions. However, if good 1 enjoys lower effective protection than good 2, a reduction in t_1 has an ambiguous effect on production distortions. To the extent that a contraction of good 1 induces an expansion of the exportable, the change is beneficial; but to the extent that the contraction leads to an expansion of good 2 (the most highly protected good), the change is harmful. The lower the value added per unit in the exportable relative to good 2, the smaller is the contribution of the former effect relative to that of the latter. Therefore, the lower the value of ν_3 relative to ν_1, the more likely it is that the latter (harmful) effect will dominate.

As in the previous section, we can relate this result to the substitutability condition of the concertina theorem. Observe first that there is no difficulty in satisfying the substitutability requirement among final goods. The difficulty arises with respect to the imported input. Substitutability requires that a decline in t_1 be accompanied by a decline in the use of the input. However, if the input is used mostly in goods 2 and 3 and not in good 1 (i.e., if a_2 and a_3 are large but a_1 is small), a decline in t_1 which causes good 1 to shrink and causes goods 2 and 3 to expand may well lead to an *increase* in the use of the input.[11] Formally, we know that

$$(10)\quad R_{\tau 1} = -[a_1R_{11} + a_2R_{12} + a_3R_{13}].$$

Clearly, if $a_1 = 0$, and $R_{12}, R_{13} < 0$, $R_{\tau 1}$ must be positive.

The usefulness of the concertina theorem declines sharply as we increase the number of importable commodities. To illustrate, consider the case when there are K final importable goods and one exportable (the

[11] Note that a low value of a_1 and high value of a_2 is consistent with a lower effective protection for good 1 than for good 2 even when $t_1 > t_2$.

$[K+1]$th). Expression (9) generalizes to

$$(11)\quad N\frac{d\mu}{dt_j} = -\frac{1}{1+t_j} \times \left[\sum_{k \neq j}^{K} (t_j - t_k)E_{kj} + t_j E_{K+1,j}\right] + \frac{1}{\nu_j}\left[\sum_{k \neq j}^{K} \nu_j^* \nu_k^* \left(\frac{\nu_j}{\nu_j^*} - \frac{\nu_k}{\nu_k^*}\right) R_{kj}\right] + \frac{\nu_{K+1}}{\nu_j}(\nu_j - \nu_j^*) R_{K+1,j}.$$

Thus, if $t_j > t_k$ $(k = 1,\dots,K; k \neq j)$ net substitutability is sufficient for a decrease in t_j to reduce consumption distortions. This is reflected in the negative sign of the first right-hand-side term of (11). However, production distortions are not necessarily diminished by a reduction in t_j, even if $R_{kj} < 0$ for all $k \neq j$, and $R_{K+1,j} < 0$. The sufficient condition is that $\nu_j/\nu_j^* - \nu_k/\nu_k^*$ be positive for all $k = 1,\dots K$ $(k \neq j)$. That is, the final good with the highest import tariff should also be subject to the highest effective rate of protection. This result considerably reduces the usefulness of the concertina method of tariff reform. Thus, suppose we start from the most favorable situation such that the above condition is satisfied at the initial equilibrium by good j. As we reduce the tariff of good j, welfare improves. After the tariff on good j has been reduced to the level of the second-highest tariff (say, good i), we would like to reduce the tariffs on both good j and good i. However, for this to be welfare-improving unambiguously, we need the effective protection on both goods i and j to be higher than that on any other good in the new equilibrium, and so on. Thus, as the tariff reform based on the concertina method proceeds, the sufficiency condition is progressively more likely to be violated.

V. Conclusion

The principal conclusion of this paper is that the key assumption of substitutability required by the concertina theorem of piecemeal tariff reform is not consistent with the Rybczynski relationship in the presence of pure imported intermediates. We have shown that for three popular models of international trade the substitutability condition between the imported input and all final goods is impossible to satisfy.

Thus, the presence of imported inputs considerably limits the usefulness of the concertina method of tariff reform. In the case when the highest tariff applies to a final good, one of the sufficiency conditions requires that the good(s) subject to the highest nominal tariff also be subject to the highest effective protection.[12] This is a rather stringent requirement. In the case when the highest nominal tariff applies to an imported input, we are unable even to spell out a meaningful set of sufficiency conditions for welfare improvement in response to a reduction in this tariff. Ironically, the sufficiency conditions for a decline in welfare turn out to be straightforward in this case.

The lack of applicability of the concertina theorem in this latter case is serious because, as indicated in Section III, imports of intermediates and capital goods in several of the largest developing countries are subject to very high tariffs. In these countries, the prime instruments to protect final goods are import prohibitions or quantitative restrictions, not tariffs, and thus the highest tariffs affect intermediates rather than final goods. Moreover, even if the highest tariffs affect a final good, as the concertina method is implemented, very soon a point is reached where an imported input is subject to the highest tariff.

Appendix

We show here that in the context of the Heckscher-Ohlin framework, the revenue

[12] Incidentally, the estimates of the correlation coefficient between nominal and effective rates of protection usually range between 0.85 and 0.9. The conditions for the breakdown of the concertina theorem may appear to be less stringent than is argued here. However, the effective-rate measures include interindustry flows but not pure imported inputs, so it is not clear how relevant they are in the present context.

function can be expressed in terms of value-added prices ($\boldsymbol{\nu}$), satisfying the same properties with respect to the elements of $\mathbf{q}$ as in the fixed-coefficients case. Long-run competitive equilibrium implies that output prices equal average costs:

$$\text{(A1)} \quad p_i = c^i(\mathbf{w}, 1+\tau) \qquad i = 1,2,3$$

where $p_1 = 1 + t_1$, $p_2 = 1 + t_2$, and $p_3 = 1$ are the domestic prices of the three outputs, $\mathbf{w} = (w_1, w_2, w_3)$ is the vector of the three primary-factor prices, and $1+\tau$ is the domestic price of the imported input. In this "even" case, one can solve (A1) for the primary-factor prices and obtain $\mathbf{w} = \tilde{\mathbf{w}}(\mathbf{p}, 1+\tau) = \mathbf{w}(\mathbf{q})$, where $\mathbf{q} = (1+t_1, 1+t_2, 1, 1+\tau)$ is the vector of exogenous prices.

Using Shephard's lemma, we obtain the cost-minimizing level of the vector of primary factors and imported inputs for each industry. We have

$$\text{(A2)} \quad \mathbf{z}_i / x_i = c^i_{\mathbf{w}}(\mathbf{w}, 1+\tau) \equiv \alpha_i(\mathbf{q})$$

$$m_i / x_i = c^i_{\tau}(\mathbf{w}, 1+\tau) \equiv a_i(\mathbf{q})$$

$$i = 1,2,3$$

where x_i is output of industry i, $\mathbf{z}_i$ is the vector of primary factors used by industry i, and m_i is the level of the imported input used in industry i. Note that $\alpha_i(\cdot)$ and $a_i(\mathbf{q})$ are homogeneous of degree 0 in $\mathbf{q}$.

The economy's revenue function can now be defined as

$$\text{(A3)} \quad R = \max_{\mathbf{z}_i, m_i} \left[\sum_i p_i F^i(\mathbf{z}_i, m_i) - (1+\tau) \times \sum_i m_i + \lambda\left(\mathbf{z} - \sum_i \mathbf{z}_i\right) \right]$$

where $F^i(\cdot)$ is the constant-returns-to-scale production function of industry i, and λ is the Lagrangian multiplier.

Using the linear homogeneity condition of the function $F^i(\cdot)$, expression (A3) can be expressed as

$$\text{(A4)} \quad R = \max_{m_i} \left[\sum_i p_i m_i f^i(\beta_i(\mathbf{q})) - (1+\tau) \sum_i a_i(\mathbf{q}) m_i f^i(\beta_i(\mathbf{q})) + \lambda\left(\mathbf{z} - \sum_i \beta_i(\mathbf{q}) m_i\right) \right]$$

where $\beta_i(q) \equiv \alpha_i(q)/a_i(q)$ is also homogeneous of degree 0. Collecting terms, we obtain

$$\text{(A5)} \quad R = \max_{m_i} \left\{ \sum_i [p_i - (1+\tau) a_i(\mathbf{q})] f_i(\beta_i(\mathbf{q})) m_i + \lambda\left(\mathbf{z} - \sum_i \beta_i(\mathbf{q}) m_i\right) \right\}$$

which yields the following expression for the revenue function:

$$\text{(A6)} \qquad R = R(\boldsymbol{\nu}(\mathbf{q}), \boldsymbol{\beta}(\mathbf{q}); \mathbf{z})$$

where $\boldsymbol{\nu}$ is a vector of value-added prices [i.e., $\nu_i = p_i - (1+\tau) a_i(\mathbf{q})$] and $\boldsymbol{\beta}(\mathbf{q})$ is the vector of the $\beta_i(\mathbf{q})$ ($i = 1,2,3$). We note again that the $\beta_i(\mathbf{q})$ are homogeneous of degree 0 in $\mathbf{q}$, while the $\nu_i(\mathbf{q})$ are homogeneous of degree 1 in $\mathbf{q}$. This revenue function is thus of the same structure as the one defined by (4) in the text, the only difference being that the a_i coefficients are not fixed, but rather a function of the vector of output prices and the price of the imported input. By inspection of (A5) it is clear that $R(\cdot)$ is linearly homogeneous in $\boldsymbol{\nu}$ and that, since each of the $\nu_i(\mathbf{q})$ functions is also linearly homogeneous in $\mathbf{q}$, it satisfies all the properties of the revenue function defined in the imported-input fixed-coefficients case.

REFERENCES

Bertrand, Trent J. and Vanek, Jaroslav, "The Theory of Tariffs, Taxes, and Subsidies: Some Aspects of the Second Best,"

American Economic Review, October 1971, *61*, 925–31.

Dixit, Avinash and Norman, Victor, *Theory of International Trade*, Welwyn: Nisbets, Welwyn, 1980.

Falvey, Rodney E., "Tariffs, Quotas and Piecemeal Policy Reform," *Journal of International Economics*, August 1988, *25*, 177–83.

Fukushima, Takashi, "Tariff Structure, Nontraded Goods and Theory of Piecemeal Policy Recommendations," *International Economic Review*, June 1979, *20*, 427–35.

Green, H. A. John, "The Social Optimum in the Presence of Monopoly and Taxation," *Review of Economic Studies*, October 1961, *29*, 66–78.

Hatta, Tatsuo, *A Theory of Piecemeal Policy Recommendations*, Ph.D. dissertation, Johns Hopkins University, 1973.

______, "A Recommendation for a Better Tariff Structure," *Econometrica*, November 1977, *45*, 1859–69.

Lipsey, Robert and Lancaster, Kelvin, "The General Theory of Second Best," *Review of Economic Studies*, October 1956, *24*, 11–32.

Lloyd, Peter J., "A More General Theory of Price Distortions in Open Economies," *Journal of International Economics*, November 1974, *4*, 365–86.

López, Ramón and Rodrik, Dani, "Trade Restrictions with Imported Intermediate Inputs: When Does the Trade Balance Improve?" *Journal of Development Economics*, November 1990, *34*, 329–38.

Michaely, Michael, Papageorgiou, Demetris and Choksi, Armeane, *Liberalizing Foreign Trade: Lessons of Experience in the Developing World*, Oxford: Blackwell, 1991.

Meade, James, *Trade and Welfare*, London: Oxford University Press, 1955.

Panagariya, Arvind, "Input Tariffs, Duty Drawbacks and Tariff Reform," *Journal of International Economics*, 1992 (forthcoming).

Ramaswami, V. K. and Srinivasan, T. N., "Optimal Subsidies and Taxes when Some Factors Are Traded," *Journal of Political Economy*, July/August 1968, *76*, 569–82.

Thomas, Vinod, Nash, John, Edwards, Sebastian, Hutcheson, Thomas, Keesing, Donald, Matin, Kazi, Pursell, Garry and Yeats, Alexander, *Best Practices in Trade Policy Reform*, New York: Oxford University Press, 1991.

Part IV
World Welfare and Trade Reform

[16]

UNILATERAL TRADE LIBERALIZATION AND GLOBAL WORLD INCOME

Jaroslav Vanek

I

Meade [1] and Ozga,[2] both writing in 1955, consider the effects on world income of a unilateral trade liberalization. Both arrive at the conclusion that such a liberalization in a world where other countries impose trade restrictions can be detrimental to total world income and welfare. The conclusion is consistent with the theory of "second best," as expounded by Meade,[3] and Lancaster and Lipsey.[4]

Meade does not provide a rigorous proof of the proposition, rather he points out the conditions which will tend to make such an outcome more likely, using his customary criteria of second best evaluation. Ozga, on the other hand, presents a set of lengthy concrete examples, based on such restrictive assumptions as constant (marginal) opportunity costs and strict proportionality of consumption of all products. Both Meade's and Ozga's analyses require adding the gains of some with losses of others in arriving at an index of global world income. Ozga's study, moreover, may leave some readers with the impression that the result depends crucially on his assumption of proportionality.

The first task of the present paper is to reiterate the analysis of the problem at hand, relying exclusively on ordinal (rather than cardinal) preferences and on the compensation criterion (rather than on that of interpersonal comparability of cardinal utilities). It will be shown that using this method, the same results as those of Meade and Ozga can be obtained.

Our second task is to show that a good deal more can be said about the situation at hand than merely that loss of world income is

1. J. Meade, *Trade and Welfare* (London: Oxford University Press, 1955), Chap. 31.
2. S. A. Ozga, "An Essay in the Theory of Tariffs," *Journal of Political Economy*, LXIII (Dec. 1955), 489–99.
3. J. Meade, *op. cit.*
4. R. G. Lipsey and R. K. Lancaster, "The General Theory of Second Best," *Review of Economic Studies*, XXIV (1956–57), 11–32.

possible. Under certain well-defined conditions, indeed, no such loss can occur.

Finally, the third task of our analysis is to derive a certain number of fairly significant policy conclusions with respect to unilateral trade liberalization.

For convenience of exposition, we shall start by stating the results without proof using the customary tool of utility possibility functions. This we shall do in the following section. In Section III, we present the proof of a "fundamental proposition" whereon the results of Section II are based, as well as some subsidiary proofs. In Section IV, finally, we shall turn to the conclusions of the inquiry, consideration of some special cases, and to policy implications.

II

We assume that there are three countries: country one, country two and country three. For simplicity, we further assume that outputs of each are given and invariant. Each country produces one or two products, x and y. Preferences of each country have all the properties of a single individual's preference map and can otherwise be of any kind, except for one thing: for *no* combination of outputs and for *no* relative prices can there be Giffen's paradox present. Because we are able to draw utility possibility curves only for two of the three countries, we assume throughout satisfaction of one country, say, country three, constant; that is, $\bar{u}_3 =$ constant. But it will be apparent that whatever propositions are shown for that level of u_3 will also hold true for any other level of u_3. Finally, we assume that all three countries continuously trade with one another, and that differences in relative prices in the different countries can arise only from a tariff being imposed by one country or another. Let us refer henceforward to the three relative prices in the three countries as p_1, p_2, and p_3 respectively.

If the three countries are permitted to trade freely, an optimum allocation of world resources (i.e., optimum income) will be attained. For a given level of satisfaction on the part of country three, $\bar{u}_3$, available output can be distributed among the three countries in such a way as to yield the Pareto-optimal combination of utilities of country one and country two illustrated by F° in Figure I. This is the situation where, with free trade, p_1, p_2 and p_3 are all equal.

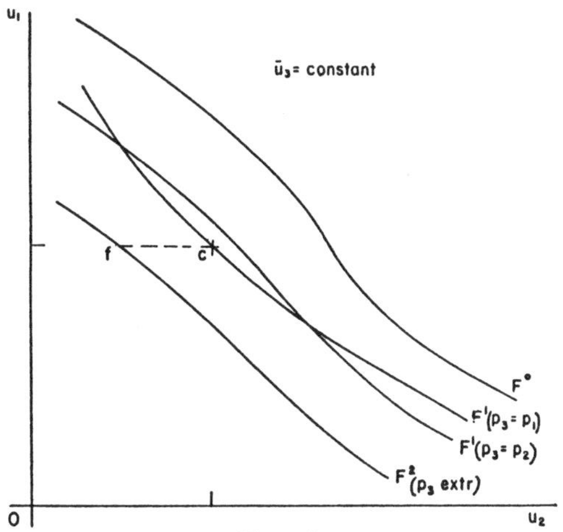

Figure I

Now suppose that all three countries impose a tariff on their respective imports (redistributing tariff revenue to the private sector) so that none of the three prices p_1, p_2 and p_3 is equal to the international terms of trade t. With international trading two of the prices must be greater than t and one smaller than t, or vice versa. Moreover, let us assume that as a result of equal rates of ad valorem tariff, the two prices on one side of t, say, p_3 and p_1, are equal. Again, with a given level of utility in country three, $\bar{u}_3$, a unique utility possibility function for u_1 and u_2 is defined by these conditions. It is illustrated in Figure I by $F^1_{(p_3=p_1)}$. For the opposite case where $p_3 = p_2$ (a case possible for a different allocation of different countries' outputs), there is defined another utility possibility function, illustrated by $F^1_{(p_3=p_2)}$. As indicated in the diagram, the two loci can intersect.

Let us now focus our attention on the first of the two utility possibility curves, i.e., $F^1_{(p_3=p_1)}$. Suppose that conditions of production and trading consistent with that locus prevail, but p_3 is greater than p_1, if p_1 is greater than t, or p_3 is smaller than p_1 if p_1 is smaller than t. In other words, among the four relevant price ratios, p_1, p_2, p_3 and t, p_3 assumes an extreme value. To this situation then corresponds a new utility possibility contour, $F^2_{(p_3\ \mathrm{extr})}$, in Figure I. It must be entirely to the left and below $F^1_{(p_3=p_1)}$.

This is the important proposition to be proven in the following section.

The interpretation of this result is as follows. If country three trades in the same direction (exports and imports the same products) as country one, but has a higher tariff than country one, then reduction of its tariff will necessarily move the world to higher and higher utility possibilities, up to the point where tariffs of country one and country two are equal. Further reductions of tariffs by country three, placing p_3 between p_1 and p_2, may or may not improve further total (potential) world welfare. The latter is the case discussed by Meade and Ozga. At the point where trade of country three is completely liberalized, p_3 will be equal to t, differing from p_1 and p_2 precisely by the amounts of the ad valorem tariffs of the two restricting countries.

Some information as to whether complete trade liberalization will or will not improve the state of world welfare beyond that of $F^1_{(p_3=p_1)}$ can be obtained, in the case where protection by countries one and two is of comparable intensity, from the comparative positions of the two F^1 loci in the relevant region.[5] Indeed, we know that with p_3 equal to p_1 the allocation of utilities of the first two countries will be somewhere on F^1 defined by those two price ratios, and for p_3 equal to p_2, on the other F^1 locus. With free trade p_3 must be between p_1 and p_2, and the corresponding point in the ordinal $u_1 - u_2$ plane is likely, assuming a certain regularity of the indifference maps, to be in the area enclosed by the two contours F^1.

So far we have discussed the case where p_3 initially assumes an extreme value and is on the same side of the world terms of trade, t, as p_1. It is immediately apparent that a perfectly analogous argument pertains for the case where p_3 initially assumes an extreme value, and is on the same side of t as p_2.

The results are more clear-cut if p_3 assumes an extreme value, and is on one side of t, while p_1 and p_2 are both on the other side. In other words, country three is trading the same products with both other countries. In this case, the situation described by the F^1 loci can never be attained by liberalization of trade by country three, save, of course, in the limiting case where either of the two other countries practices free trade. Consequently, gradual liberalization of trade by country three *will uniformly lead to higher and higher* levels of world welfare, the maximum being attained in the free-trade case where t is equal to p_3.

5. However, the exact answer to this question must be derived using the method shown in the following section.

III

The fundamental proposition underlying the preceding analysis is that as long as relative prices of one country (in a two-commodity three-country world) assume an extreme value, reduction of trade restrictions by that country will necessarily improve the utility possibility of the world as a whole. To prove this proposition, let us turn to Figure II.

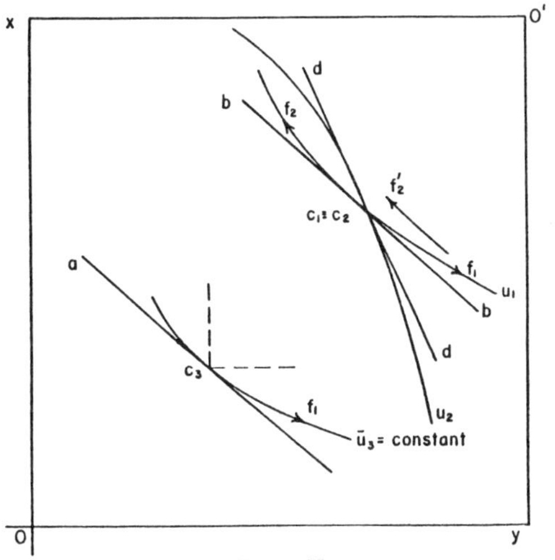

Figure II

The rectangle defined by O and O' in that diagram represents total world output; it is constant as are the outputs of the three countries. The situation illustrated in the box corresponds to point c on $F^1_{(p_3=p_1)}$. First of all, we observe the contour (indifference curve) $\bar{u}_3$, and a point of optimal consumption c_3 on it, corresponding to domestic prices p_3 indicated by the slope of aa. The contour u_1 is an indifference curve of country one, and represents the level of satisfaction corresponding to c in Figure I. It measures levels of consumption of country one in a plane with its origin placed at c_3 in Figure II. As required by $F^1_{(p_3=p_1)}$, relative prices within country one are the same as within country three, and thus the equilibrium point of consumption in country one is at c_1, where the slope of u_1 is the same as that of aa. Point c_1 coincides with point c_2 on u_2, the indifference curve of country two measuring levels of consumption of that country from origin O'.

Let us now hold the levels of satisfaction of country one and country three unchanged, and ask ourselves whether country two can attain the same level of satisfaction as before, if the price ratio p_3 assumes an extreme value, that is, if *aa* becomes flatter than *bb*, the ratio of the slopes of *bb* and *dd* remaining unchanged.

To a prescribed divergence between p_3 and p_1 will generally correspond a single solution, indicating the equilibrium levels of consumption of the three countries, and (with unchanged u_3 and u_1) the corresponding level of u_2. It is our task here to show that the new point such as $c_1 \equiv c_2$ must lie to the right of the contour u_2 in Figure II.

Excluding the possibility of Giffen's paradox, the adjustment to a new equilibrium solution with a new *aa* flatter than a new *bb* will be attained through a movement of c_3 along $\bar{u}_3$ towards a point such as f_1, and a movement of c_1 along u_1 to the left and upwards to a point such as f_2. As the origin of the consumption-plane of country one is placed at c_3 (wherever that may be), the new position of c_1, f'_2, will be found as a result of a composite movement, $c_1f'_1$, and $f'_1f'_2$. Each of these arcs, drawn in the diagram, are merely transpositions of portions of the invariant indifference contours $\bar{u}_3$ and u_1, c_3f_1 and c_1f_2. It will be observed that as required, the slope of $f'_1f'_2$ at f'_2 is greater than that of *bb*, and the slope of $c_1f'_1$ at f'_1 smaller than that of *aa*. Moreover, it will be remembered that, by definition, the slope of an indifference curve of country two at the solution point f'_2 must be in the original constant proportion to the slope of $f'_1f'_2$ at f'_2, corresponding to the degree of trade restriction by countries one and two. It then follows that the slope of the indifference curve of country two at f'_2 must be steeper than that of *dd*.

Under these conditions, could the solution point f'_2 ever lie to the left of u_2 in the diagram? On our assumptions it definitely could not. Observing from the construction that the solution point f'_2 must be above *bb*, a solution point in the area enclosed by *bb* and u_2 — recalling what was said above about the equilibrium marginal rate of substitution in country two at f'_2 — would necessarily imply a possibility of Giffen's paradox.

The careful reader may ask himself the question whether the two arcs, representing the movement from one to the other equilibrium point, could not point in the same direction, and thus lead to a solution yielding a gain in utility for country two. As long as the assumption of "no Giffen's paradox" is made, the answer is negative. Consider for example, the limiting case where the arc $c'_1f'_1$

would be reduced to zero (that is, point c_3 remains in its original position). The arc $f'_1f'_2$ must now point in the northwest direction, because the tariff in country three is increased (p_3 becomes extreme). But this is impossible, because the solution point f'_2 would have to imply existence of Giffen's paradox.

Reinterpreted in terms of Figure I, the important proof presented so far can be stated as follows: Starting from a point such as c on $F^1_{(p_3=p_1)}$, a change in commercial policy by country three leading to an extreme value of p_3 will necessarily lead to a lower level of satisfaction by country two, with unchanged satisfactions of countries three and one, at a point such as f. Vice versa, reduced protection will necessarily lead to an increased world utility possibility as long as the liberalizing country's domestic price ratio assumes an extreme value before, and is equal to its nearest price ratio after liberalization.

Actually, it can be shown that the utility possibility will be a uniformly increasing function of reduced protection by a country assuming an extreme domestic price ratio. The proof of this proposition is analogous to that just produced (see Figure II), with the exception that the initial slopes of *aa* and *bb* are not identical. Consequently, as the reader may verify, the slopes of the arcs analogous to $c_1f'_1$ and $f'_1f'_2$ in such a proof will also be different at their respective starting points (i.e., c_1 and f'_1). But this, loosely speaking, can only make more important the losses of world welfare resulting from strengthened protection.

Finally, let us at least indicate the proof of the Meade-Ozga proposition: namely, that liberalization can worsen aggregate world income, or, in terms of our analysis, can move to an inferior utility possibility. From what precedes, we know already that this can happen only if after liberalization the price ratio of the liberalizing country, p_3, assumes a nonextreme value. Such a value necessarily will be assumed by p_3 in the situation described in our diagram, where p_3 is on the same side of t as p_1, and where trade of country three is fully liberalized.

The technique of the proof is the same as that of our fundamental proposition, except that, with the marginal rate of substitution in country three moving to some value between p_1 and p_2, the arc analogous to $c_1f'_1$ will point, starting from c_1, in the northwest direction, and the arc analogous to $f'_1f'_2$ in the southeast direction. The resulting allocation point f'_2, then can be located either to the left, or to the right of u_2 (whose position is unchanged) in

Figure II. If the former is the case, the total world welfare can increase, and if the latter, the world's utility (actually, in our case utility of country two with incomes of countries one and three unchanged) will be reduced.

To make our argument complete, it ought to be pointed out that if Giffen's paradox can be present for some outputs and some price ratios, then a loss to world utility possibility, resulting from unilateral reductions of extreme tariffs to other extreme levels, cannot be excluded on the grounds of our analysis. But we can be quite confident that for any real situations this case is of very little relevance.

As an extension of the theory of second-best to the case of many individuals (in our case, many countries) with ordinal preferences, it will be observed that there will be some value of p_3, necessarily between p_1 and p_2, for which the welfare of country two is maximized, given constant levels of satisfaction of countries one and three. In other words, referring to the situation discussed in this section, if country three proceeds to reduce its tariff below the level of the tariff of country one, possibly going as far as free trade or even an import subsidy, it must reach some point where the level of social welfare of country two is maximized. It is clear from our construction that such an optimal adjustment of the internal price ratio of country three will be different for different preassigned levels of utility of countries three and one, and generally will not correspond to the free-trade situation.

IV

Using the customary tools of ordinal utility analysis, we have shown in this paper that while it is possible that unilateral trade liberalization could reduce world income in a tariff-ridden world, there are important ranges of possible situations where a unilateral trade liberalization could not have any such effects. In particular, translating our analysis into concrete terms, a country with highest barriers will not be likely to reduce the world's utility possibility as long as it reduces tariffs to the level of the next-highest tariff country. But even if such a country proceeded further towards a complete trade liberalization, the losses to total world income that this might cause would not be important, if they occurred at all.

A number of further results and generalizations can be derived directly from our analysis. First, if two countries impose tariffs and trade with each other, while any number of other countries practice free trade, then any reduction of tariffs by either or both countries must increase the world's potential welfare. This follows from the fact that in this situation both restricting countries must have extreme domestic price ratios. An even simpler and more straightforward proposition is that if only one country imposes tariffs while all other countries adhere to free trade, then any degree of trade liberalization will improve the world's utility possibility. In these two cases the passage from a three-country to an n-country situation is justified because all the free-trade countries, in the context of our analysis, can be taken as a single country, characterized by a single "collective" indifference curve corresponding to a given fixed level of satisfaction of each country.

Realizing that in our analysis one of the three countries can be made arbitrarily small, it further follows that in a two-country world any liberalization of tariffs will improve the potential world welfare. But this is known from other types of analysis.

Keeping in mind that at this point we are moving away from the sphere of rigorous theory, formulation of some policy implications of our analysis may be in order. First, it is possible to argue that there exists a path of gradual trade liberalizations, leading eventually to perfectly free trade, each step of which would be connected with some positive gain in total world utility possibility. Such a path is one where the most protectionist countries keep adjusting their barriers to the levels of their second-most protectionist trading partners.[6] Besides having the stated desirable welfare property, there even seems to be justification for such a process on grounds of equity; those doing the most harm repenting first.

Alternatively, on grounds of our analysis it can be argued that a unilateral trade liberalization on the part of industrialized countries vis-à-vis the rest of the world would be a desirable policy. Indeed, in terms of our analysis, this would correspond approximately to an adjustment of extreme domestic prices p_3 to the level of international terms of trade t, in the case (discussed in Section II) where p_3 is extreme, and alone on one side of t. As we have noted, in this particular case, no losses in total world income are possible. The redistributional effect of such a policy, that might lead to reduced real income of the advanced countries, could then supplement economic assistance to less advanced nations.

6. Of course, to the extent that more than one country would fit the description "most protectionist" an agreement on collective action would be necessary.

HARVARD UNIVERSITY

[17]

THE WELFARE EFFECT OF TARIFF RATE REDUCTIONS IN A MANY COUNTRY WORLD

Tatsuo HATTA*

The Johns Hopkins University, Baltimore, MD 21218, USA

Takashi FUKUSHIMA

Southern Methodist University, Dallas, TX 75222, USA

Received September 1978, revised version received April 1979

Consider a two-commodity *n*-country model without inferior goods where import tariffs are the only trade barriers. In this paper we establish that the world's welfare is improved if the country with the highest tariff rate unilaterally reduce its rate to the level of the second highest country or if all the countries of the world reduce tariff rates proportionally. The second rule serves as a theoretical justification of the Kennedy and Tokyo Round Tariff Reductions.

1. Introduction

When several countries are imposing tariffs on their imports, an arbitrary reduction of the tariff rates by some countries may *decrease* the welfare of the world as a whole. The celebrated 'theory of the second best' revealed such perverse welfare effects of a distortion reduction.

However, a tariff reduction can increase the welfare, if it is done under some rule rather than arbitrarily. In this paper we present two rules of tariff reduction that improve the welfare in a two-commodity *n*-country world, where each country has a strictly convex production possibility set and import tariffs are the only trade barriers. First, we establish that if there is no inferior good, a unilateral reduction of tariff rate by the country with the highest tariff rate to the level of the second highest country can improve the welfare of the world.[1] Secondly, we prove that if no inferior good exist, a proportional reduction of tariff rates by all the countries of the world improves the world welfare. This part serves as a theoretical justification of the Kennedy Round and the Tokyo Round Tariff Reductions.

Recently piecemeal policies in price-distorted economies have been extensively studied by Foster and Sonnenschein (1970), Bertrand and Vanek

*We are indebted to two anonymous referees of the Journal for their helpful comments and suggestions.

[1]For a three-country model with a *fixed output bundle* of the world, Vanek (1964) showed the effectiveness of this rule by a graphical method.

(1971), Kawamata (1974, 1977), Bruno (1972), Dixit (1975), Hatta (1977a, 1977b), and Fukushima (1979). An essential difference exists, however, between the models of this group and the present one. In the former models all consumers face the same price vector, and distortions exist between consumers' and producers' price vectors. In the present model, however, consumers of different countries face different price vectors due to tariffs; distortions exist among consumers' prices in different countries. In the former models the assumption of a representative consumer gives basic insight into the welfare effects of distortion changes. In the present model, it is impossible to make such an assumption because the type of distortions with which the present paper is concerned cannot exist under such an assumption. This forces us to employ the expansion of the world's utility possibility set as the criterion of welfare improvement.

2. The model

(1) *There are two goods x and y.*

(2) *There are n countries in the world.*

(3) *There is only one consumer in each country.*[2] *He is a price taker and has well behaved compensated demand functions for goods x and y.*

The compensated demand function of country i for good j may be written as

$$c_j^i = f_j^i(p_x^i, p_y^i, u^i), \qquad i=1,\dots,n; \quad j=x,y, \tag{1}$$

where

c_j^i = quantity demanded of good j by country i,
p_j^i = domestic price of good j in country i, and
u^i = utility level of country i.

(4) *The production possibility frontier of each country is smooth and concave to the origin.*

(5) *The producers in each country maximize their profits regarding prices as given.*

Let a_j^i be the output level of good j in country i. Then we have

$$a_j^i = h_j^i(p_x^i, p_y^i), \qquad i=1,\dots,n; \quad j=x,y, \tag{2}$$

[2]Alternatively, we can assume that there exist many consumers in each country and that their utility levels are represented by Scitovsky's community indifference curves. In this event, the utility levels of all but one consumer within a country are fixed by using lump sum income taxes and transfers.

where h_j^i is the compensated supply function of the jth good in the ith country.[3]

(6) *Both the consumers and producers in each country face the same prices.*

This assumption is implicitly used in eqs. (1) and (2). Let z_j^i denote the net import demand for the jth good in the ith country, i.e. $z_j^i \equiv c_j^i - a_j^i$. By virtue of eqs. (1) and (2), z_j^i is a function of p_x^i, p_y^i and u^i:

$$\begin{aligned} z_j^i &= f_j^i(p_x^i, p_y^i, u^i) - h_j^i(p_x^i, p_y^i) \\ &\equiv s_j^i(p_x^i, p_y^i, u^i). \end{aligned} \tag{3}$$

We call s_j^i the net demand function. This is the compensated demand function for the system of trade indifference curves of Meade (1952). Note that s_j^i, like f_j^i and h_j^i, is positively homogeneous of degree zero with respect to p_x^i and p_y^i; for any positive number m, we have

$$s_j^i(p_x^i, p_y^i, u^i) = s_j^i(mp_x^i, mp_y^i, u^i). \tag{4}$$

(7) *Each country is small and takes the world prices p_x and p_y of the two goods as given.*[4]

(8) *No country imports or exports both goods.*

(9) *Each country imposes an ad valorem tariff for the imported good.*

Suppose country i imports good x and imposes the tariff rate τ_x^i on this good. Then the domestic prices are

$$p_x^i = (1 + \tau_x^i)p_x \quad \text{and} \quad p_y^i = p_y.$$

We assume that $\tau_j^i = 0$ if good j is exported by country i. Then we can write

$$p_j^i = t_j^i p_j, \qquad i = 1, \ldots, n; \quad j = x, y,$$

where

$$t_j^i = (1 + \tau_j^i).$$

Note that t_j^i is positive, and it is equal to or greater than one according as country i exports commodity j or imports commodity j. Thus, by virtue of eqs. (3) and (4) we can write

$$z_j^i = s_j^i(t_x^i, t_y^i p, u^i), \qquad i = 1, 2, \ldots, n, \tag{5}$$

[3]See Hatta (1977b, p. 1861) for the compensated supply function.

[4]This assumption differs from the well-known small country assumption employed by Viner's customs union model, which assumes a fixed world price level under tariff changes. In our model, the world price level is an endogenous variable.

where $p \equiv p_y/p_x$.

(10) *Total demand for x and y are equal to the total supply of goods x and y.*

Let z^i_j denote the net demand for the jth good in the ith country. The assumption implies that we have

$$\sum_{i=1}^{n} z^i_j = 0, \qquad j = x, y. \tag{6}$$

Substituting (5) into (6) we have

$$\sum_{i=1}^{n} s^i_j(t^i_x, t^i_y p, u^i) = 0, \qquad j = x, y. \tag{7}$$

This system of equations represents the equilibrium condition for the demand and supply of the world as a whole for goods x and y. The system involves two equations and $n+1$ variables, $u^1, \ldots, u^n$, and p; so the model is not quite complete.[5]

In order to complete the model we have to introduce a welfare criterion. In a multinational world, the efficiency can be said to have improved if the utility possibility set of the world expands in the new situation. In this paper we choose this criterion for the improvement of the world welfare; we show that when $u^1, \ldots, u^{n-1}$ are kept constant at the arbitrary original levels, u^n is increased in the new situation under certain change in the tariff structure. This criterion is, of course, originally due to Samuelson (1950).

Fixing $u^1, \ldots, u^{n-1}$ regarding only u^n as the variable leaves only two variables, p and u^n, in the two-equation system [eq. (7)]. This enables us to examine the effect of a change in the tax structure upon the utility level of country n when the utility levels of all the other countries are fixed.

(11) *Among the utility levels of all the countries, only that of country n is treated as a variable*

$$u^i = \bar{u}^i, \qquad i = 1, \ldots, n-1. \tag{8}$$

When u^n is increased while keeping other u^i's constant at arbitrary levels,

[5]If we were to construct a *positive* rather than a *normative* model of international trade, we would have to specify the budget condition in each country. Accordingly, the utility level of each country may be expressed as:

$$u^i = g^i(t^i_x, t^i_y, p), \qquad i = 1, \ldots, n.$$

We would then have $n+2$ equations and $n+1$ variables. These and Walras's law would complete the positive model.

we say the *welfare of the world is improved.*[6]

The system of eqs. (7) and (8) completes our normative model, and determines the equilibrium values of p and u^n for given values of t_x^i, t_y^i, and $\bar{u}^i$.

3. Basic lemma

Let a parameter r denote the stage of the reform program of the international tariff structure, and let the reform program itself be represented by the following system of equations:

$$\tau_j^i = w_j^i(r), \qquad i=1,\dots,n; \quad j=x,y.$$

Substituting this for τ_j^i in the definitional equation of t_j^i, we can express t_j^i as a function of r. For brevity, we write this function as

$$t_j^i = t_j^i(r), \qquad i=1,\dots,n; \quad j=x,y. \tag{9}$$

The lemma in this section gives the expression that represents the welfare effect of a change in r upon the level of u^n when u^i are kept constant for $i=1,\dots,n-1$.

In deriving this result, we use a few properties of the function s_j^i. Let $s_{jk}^i \equiv \partial s_j^i/\partial p_k^i$, $s_{ju}^i \equiv \partial s_j^i/\partial u^i$ and $\lambda^i \equiv$ marginal utility of income in the ith country. It is readily seen that $s_{jk}^i \equiv f_{jk}^i - h_{jk}^i$ and $s_{ju}^i \equiv f_{ju}^i$, and that f_{jk}^i, h_{jk}^i and $\lambda^i f_{ju}^i f_j$ are the Hicksian substitution and income terms, respectively.[7] Thus, the own net substitution term s_{jj}^i is negative and the following well-known properties hold.[8]

Homogeneity condition:

$$\begin{aligned} &s_{xx}^i p_x^i + s_{xy}^i p_y^i = 0, \\ &s_{yx}^i p_x^i + s_{yy}^i p_y^i = 0, \qquad i=1,\dots,n. \end{aligned} \tag{10}$$

Symmetry condition:

$$s_{xy}^i = s_{yx}^i, \qquad i=1,\dots,n. \tag{11}$$

Lemma. At an equilibrium described by (7) *and* (8) *the following holds:*

$$\frac{\partial u^n}{\partial r} = \frac{\beta}{\alpha},$$

[6]Note that we do not lose generality by choosing the utility level of the nth country as the variable. After all, we can call any country the nth country by rearranging the indices.

[7]See Arrow and Hahn (1971, p. 105).

[8]See Hatta (1977b, pp. 1863–1864).

where

$$\alpha \equiv \sum s^i_{yy} t^i_y (s^n_{xu} + p s^n_{yu} t^i), \tag{12}$$

$$\beta \equiv -p^2 \sum_i^n \sum_j^n s^i_{yy} s^j_{yy} t^j_y (t^i - t^j)\left(t^i \frac{\mathrm{d}t^i_x}{\mathrm{d}r} - \frac{\mathrm{d}t^i_y}{\mathrm{d}r}\right), \tag{13}$$

and

$$t^i \equiv \frac{t^i_y}{t^i_x}.$$

Proof. Substitute (8) into (7) and differentiate it with respect to r. We have

$$\begin{bmatrix} s^n_{xu} & \sum s^i_{xy} t^i_y \\ s^n_{yu} & \sum s^i_{yy} t^i_y \end{bmatrix} \begin{pmatrix} \dfrac{\partial u^n}{\partial r} \\ \dfrac{\partial p}{\partial r} \end{pmatrix} = -\begin{pmatrix} \sum\left(s^i_{xx} \dfrac{\mathrm{d}t^i_x}{\mathrm{d}r} + p s^i_{xy} \dfrac{\mathrm{d}t^i_y}{\mathrm{d}r}\right) \\ \sum\left(s^i_{yx} \dfrac{\mathrm{d}t^i_x}{\mathrm{d}r} + p s^i_{yy} \dfrac{\mathrm{d}t^i_y}{\mathrm{d}r}\right) \end{pmatrix}.$$

From the definitions of p and t^i, we obtain

$$p^i_y / p^i_x = t^i p.$$

Taking this into account, the homogeneity condition (10) may be rewritten as follows:

$$s^i_{yx} = -p s^i_{yy} t^i,$$

and

$$s^i_{xx} = p^2 s^i_{yy} (t^i)^2, \qquad i = 1, \ldots, n.$$

Applying these and noting the symmetry condition (11), we get

$$\begin{bmatrix} s^n_{xu} & -p \sum s^i_{yy} t^i_y t^i \\ s^n_{yu} & \sum s^i_{yy} t^i_y \end{bmatrix} \begin{pmatrix} \dfrac{\partial u^n}{\partial r} \\ \dfrac{\partial p}{\partial r} \end{pmatrix} = -\begin{pmatrix} p^2 \sum s^i_{yy} t^i \left(t^i \dfrac{\mathrm{d}t^i_x}{\mathrm{d}r} - \dfrac{\mathrm{d}t^i_y}{\mathrm{d}r}\right) \\ -p \sum s^i_{yy} \left(t^i \dfrac{\mathrm{d}t^i_x}{\mathrm{d}r} - \dfrac{\mathrm{d}t^i_y}{\mathrm{d}r}\right) \end{pmatrix}.$$

Thus, by the Cramer's rule we have

$$\frac{\partial u^n}{\partial r} = \frac{\beta}{\alpha},$$

where

$$\alpha = \begin{vmatrix} s^n_{xu} & -p\sum s^i_{yy}t^i_y t^i \\ s^n_{yu} & \sum s^i_{yy}t^i_y \end{vmatrix}$$

and

$$\beta = \begin{vmatrix} -p^2\sum_i^n s^i_{yy}t^i\left(t^i\dfrac{dt^i_x}{dr}-\dfrac{dt^i_y}{dr}\right) & -p\sum_j^n s^j_{yy}t^j_y t^j \\ p\sum_i^n s^i_{yy}\left(t^i\dfrac{dt^i_x}{dr}-\dfrac{dt^i_y}{dr}\right) & \sum_j^n s^j_{yy}t^j_y \end{vmatrix}.$$

This proves the lemma. Q.E.D.

4. Unilateral tariff reduction

Now we are in a position to prove a welfare proposition concerning the unilateral tariff reduction.

Theorem 1. Suppose neither x nor y is an inferior good in any country of the world. Then a unilateral reduction of the tariff rate by the country with the highest tariff rate to the level of the second highest country improves the welfare of the world.

Proof. Without loss of generality, we can assume that the first country imposes the highest tariff rate on x. Hence we have

$$t^1_x > t^i_x, \qquad i = 2, 3, \ldots, n.$$

This, together with the definition of t^i, implies

$$t^1 < t^i, \qquad i = 2, 3, \ldots, n. \tag{14}$$

The unilateral tariff reduction of the first country may be formally stated as

$$dt^i_j/dr = \begin{cases} -1, & \text{if } i = 1 \text{ and } j = x, \\ 0, & \text{otherwise.} \end{cases} \tag{15}$$

This assumption implies that as r is increased, the first country reduces its tariff rate while other countries keep their rates fixed.

The theorem will be proved if we establish $\partial u^n/\partial r = \beta/\alpha > 0$ under assumptions (14) and (15). The negativity of α immediately follows from (12) since an own substitution term s^i_{yy} is always negative and s^n_{xu} and s^n_{yu} are non-negative owing to our noninferiority assumption.

Noting (15) we have

$$\beta = -p^2 \sum s^1_{yy} s^j_{yy} t^j_y (t^1 - t^j) t^1 < 0,$$

where the last inequality follows from (14). Hence $\partial u^n/\partial r > 0$ follows.

Q.E.D.

5. The multilateral tariff reduction

We now analyze the welfare effect of a simultaneous reduction of tariff rates by all the countries of the world. As we indicated in the introduction, the arbitrary reduction of the tariff rates may lead us to a lower level of utility. The following theorem establishes, however, that a proportional reduction of all the tariffs, as intended by the Kennedy Round and the Tokyo Round Tariff Reductions, generally improves the welfare of the world.

Theorem 2. Suppose neither x nor y is an inferior good in any of the countries, then the proportional reduction of the tariff rates of all the countries improves the world welfare.

Proof. The proportional reduction of all the tariff rates may be formally stated as

$$\mathrm{d}t^i_j/\mathrm{d}r = 1 - t^i_j, \qquad i = 1, 2, \ldots, n; \quad j = x, y. \tag{16}$$

The theorem will be proved if we establish $\partial u^n/\partial r = \beta/\alpha > 0$ under assumptions $s^i_{xu} > 0$, $s^i_{yu} > 0$, and (16). From the proof of theorem 1, we already know that α is negative owing to the noninferiority assumption. In what follows we establish the negativity of β.

Without loss of generality, we can index the n countries in such a way that the following holds:

$$t^1_x \geqq t^2_x \geqq \ldots \geqq t^{k-1}_x > t^k_x = \ldots = t^n_x = 1$$

and (17)

$$1 = t^1_y = t^2_y = \ldots = t^{k-1}_y < t^k_y \leqq \ldots \leqq t^n_y.$$

From the lemma and eq. (16) we get

$$\beta = -p^2 \sum_i \sum_j s^i_{yy} s^j_{yy} (t^i - t^j)(t^j_y t^i - t^j_y)$$

$$= -p^2 \sum_i \sum_{j<i} s^i_{yy} s^j_{yy} (t^i - t^j)\{(t^j_y t^i - t^i_y t^j) + (t^i_y - t^j_y)\},$$

where the last expression follows from the fact that

$$\sum_i \sum_j m_{ij} = \sum_i \sum_{j<i} (m_{ij} + m_{ji}), \quad \text{if } m_{ii} = 0 \text{ for } i = 1, \ldots, n.$$

Thus, we have

$$\beta = -p^2 \sum_i \sum_{j<i} \theta_{ij}, \tag{18}$$

where

$$\theta_{ij} \equiv s^i_{yy} s^j_{yy} (t^i - t^j)\{t^i t^j (t^j_x - t^i_x) + (t^i_y - t^j_y)\}.$$

Inequalities (17) imply that $t^j_x \geqq t^i_x$, $t^i_y \geqq t^j_y$, and $t^i \geqq t^j$ whenever $j < i$, where strict inequalities hold at least when $j \leqq k-1$ and $k \leqq i$. Thus, we have

$$\theta_{ij} > 0, \quad \text{if } j < i.$$

This proves $\beta < 0$, and the theorem is proved. Q.E.D.

References

Arrow, Kenneth and Frank Hahn, 1971, General competitive analysis (Holden Day, San Francisco).

Bertrand, Trent and Jaroslav Vanek, 1971, The theory of tariffs, taxes and subsidies: Some aspects of the second best, American Economic Review 61, no. 5, 925–931.

Bruno, Michael, 1972, Market distortions and gradual reform, Review of Economic Studies 39, no. 4, 373–383.

Dixit, Avinash, 1975, Welfare effects of tax and price changes, Journal of Public Economics 4, 103–123.

Foster, Edward and Hugo Sonnenschein, 1970, Price distortion and economic welfare, Econometrica 38, no. 2, 281–297.

Fukushima, Takashi, 1979, Tariff structure, nontraded goods and theory of piecemeal policy recommendations, International Economic Review 20, no. 2, 361–369.

Hatta, Tatsuo, 1977a, A theory of piecemeal policy recommendations, Review of Economic Studies 44, 1–21.

Hatta, Tatsuo, 1977b, A recommendation for a better tariff structure, Econometrica 45, 1859–1869.

Hicks, John R., 1946, Value and capital, 2nd edn. (Oxford University Press, London).

Kawamata, Kunio, 1974, Price distortion and potential welfare, Econometrica 42, 435–460.

Kawamata, Kunio, 1977, Price distortion and the second best optimum, Review of Economic Studies 44, 23–30.

Meade, James E., 1952, A geometry of international trade (George Allen and Unwin, London).

Samuelson, Paul A., 1950, Evaluation of real national income, Oxford Economic Papers (New Series) II, 1–29.

Vanek, Jaroslav, 1964, Unilateral trade liberation and global world income, Quarterly Journal of Economics 78, 139–147.

[18]

Trade Negotiations and World Welfare

By CARSTEN KOWALCZYK*

Trade subsidies have recently received top billing in the political debate as the largest industrialized nations have engaged in heated disputes over direct and indirect policies of trade inducement.

The theoretical issues raised by trade subsidies are twofold. One line of inquiry, which has been pursued by, among others, James Brander and Barbara Spencer (1984), and Jonathan Eaton and Gene Grossman (1986), is to attempt to rationalize subsidization as an optimal trade policy from the perspective of the individual nation. Another line, and the one to be followed in the present paper, is to investigate the nature of trade negotiations when trade can not only be taxed but also subsidized. In particular, the question of what happens to world welfare as global free trade is approached is addressed.

Since a nation rejects any proposal that inflicts a loss upon it, only proposals that satisfy the Pareto criterion as applied to all of the trading community have any chance of constituting a final agreement; thus the concern with world welfare. In addition, particular attention will be paid to reforms aiming at free trade as a desirable terminal state. This is not only because of the free trade doctrine's considerable appeal to practical men, but also because of its theoretical prominence. In his survey of the normative theory of trade Max Corden (1984) thus summarizes the received wisdom: "The central proposition of normative trade theory is that there are gains from trade and, more specifically, that given certain assumptions, not only is free trade Pareto-superior to autarky but it is also Pareto-efficient, being superior to various degrees of trade restrictions." (1984, p. 69)

The earlier literature confined itself to initial equilibria of nonnegative import taxes. Thus Jaroslev Vanek (1964), in a two-good, three-country model, showed that a tariff reduction by the country with the highest rate to the level of the next highest rate raises world welfare. He showed also, that a reduction of the tariff, which is neither the highest nor the lowest, may be detrimental to world welfare; a result which he attributed to James Meade (1955) and S. A. Ozga (1955). Tatsuo Hatta and Takashi Fukushima (1979) allowed for an arbitrary number of countries while maintaining the assumption of two goods, and they showed that a proportionate reduction of all tariff rates improves world welfare.

This paper shows that approaching free trade may reduce world welfare when both tariffs and subsidies are involved. In particular, a reform of proportionate reductions may do so when falling short of free trade.[1]

To investigate the nature of this paradox it is useful to consider as an intermediate, and auxiliary, variable the price distortion. For competitive environments, Edward Foster and Hugo Sonnenschein (1970) showed

*Department of Economics, Dartmouth College, Hanover, NH 03755. This paper is based upon a chapter of my dissertation at the University of Rochester. I have greatly benefited from advice by Ronald Jones, and from comments by an anonymous referee. I am also grateful for discussions with Robert Baldwin, Ken Chan, John Chipman, Carl Davidson, Motoshige Itoh, Laurence Kranich, Rachel McCulloch, Peter Neary, Ping Wang, John Weymark, and seminar participants at Rochester, the Midwest International Economics Conference in Madison, Konstanz, Florida, Rutgers, and the Institute for International Economic Studies in Stockholm. The responsibility for any errors remains mine. Financial support from the University of Copenhagen and the Danish Social Science Research Council, Grant No. 14-3986, is gratefully acknowledged.

[1]Although only one of several possible rate-cutting schemes, the proportionate rule is appealing in two respects: the country that inflicts the most damage by being further away from free trade reduces its rate by more; in addition, the path of proportionate reductions is the shortest route to free trade. As is, however, evident from the body of the paper, there exist other rate-reducing paths with negative welfare outcomes.

that welfare monotonically falls as an appropriate measure of distortions takes values further from the one obtained at free, or, more generally, undistorted trade. This holds the implication that the best line of attack is to develop an appropriate measure of distortions and then investigate how it behaves as the reform unfolds. Any paradox must be due to this distortion measure changing in a counter-intuitive fashion.

Section I presents the model and the distortion measure for *ad valorem* rates, while Section II investigates the behavior of this measure as a function of reforms of tariffs and subsidies. A concluding discussion is offered in Section III, and an Appendix contains some of the derivations.

I. Welfare and *Ad Valorem* Distortions

Let there be two goods, x and y, with world market prices p_x^e and p_y^e as quoted in some arbitrary monetary unit. The world market relative price of good y in terms of good x is then given by $p^e = p_y^e/p_x^e$. There are two countries, home and foreign, where variables pertaining to the former (latter) are superscripted by an "H" ("F"). Goods x and y are demanded by price-taking consumers and offered by price-taking producers with constant returns to scale technologies in both countries. Assuming that country i $(i = H, F)$ quotes an *ad valorem* rate in terms of the world price of good j, to be denoted by τ_j^i,[2] agents in country i face the prices,

$$(1)\quad p_j^i = \left(1+\tau_j^i\right)p_j^e;\; i = H, F;\; j = x, y.$$

It shall prove useful to define the variable t_j^i by,

$$(2)\qquad t_j^i = 1+\tau_j^i,$$

where the assumption of strictly positive prices implies that $t_j^i > 0$.

The utility level of the representative consumer in country i is denoted by u^i, and the corresponding expenditure function by e^i, while r^i is the national income function, and v^i the vector of factor endowments in country i. The derivative of the expenditure (revenue) function in country i with respect to the jth price is denoted by $e_j^i(r_j^i)$; by Hotelling's lemma this derivative is the compensated demand (supply) function for good j. The compensated import demand function of country i for good j can then be written as,

$$(3)\quad m_j^i\left(p_x^i, p_y^i, u^i\right) = e_j^i\left(p_x^i, p_y^i, u^i\right) - r_j^i\left(p_x^i, p_y^i, v^i\right).$$

The home country will be assumed to import good y, and the foreign country good x, thus $m_y^H > 0$, and $m_x^F > 0$. Clearing of commodity markets implies that,

$$(4)\qquad m_j^H(\;\;) + m_j^F(\;\;) = 0,$$

which constitutes two equations in the three unknowns: p^e, u^H, and u^F. The welfare measure to be employed is that of the potential Pareto criterion. This implies that the model is closed by fixing one of the two utility levels, say the foreign, at its initial value, $u^F = \bar{u}^F$, whereupon (4) is solved for u^H and p^e. If u^H increases (falls), then world welfare is said to increase (fall). In the remaining part of the paper u rather than u^H will denote world welfare.

For the special case of two endowment economies, the workings of this criterion can be illustrated by use of the Edgeworth box diagram. Thus consider Figure 1, where W_1 denotes the initial endowment point and E_1 is the competitive equilibrium supported by the price line p_1^e. The tangency between the foreign indifference curve labeled i^F, which corresponds to the utility level $\bar{u}^F$, and p_1^e at E_1 reflects that the initial situation is one in which the foreign country has no tariff or subsidy in place. On the other hand, the home country indifference curve i_1^H is flatter than p_1^e at E_1 as implied by an initial, positive home tariff.

[2] A remark on specific rates is contained in fn. 5.

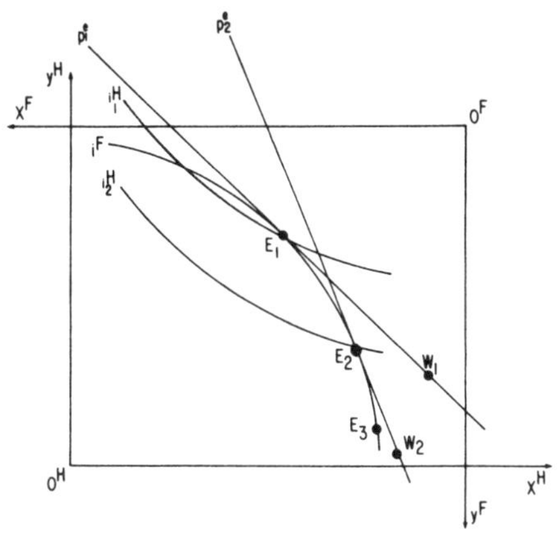

FIGURE 1

Suppose that the home country decides to further increase its tariff rate. The assumption that foreign consumers be compensated implies that the new equilibrium lies on i^F. If the foreign country, furthermore, remains a free trader, the new price line must be tangent to i^F at some new equilibrium point E_2. This point is found by searching along i^F for the point at which the ratio of the marginal rate of substitution along the home country's indifference curve and the price line equals $1+\tau_y^H$, where τ_y^H is the post-change value of the home country's tariff rate.

The price line p_2^e implicitly defines the transfer of goods required for E_2 to materialize as a competitive equilibrium. For example, the transfer from W_1 to W_2, together with the increase in τ_Y^H, induces the equilibrium E_2. The implied transfer is, of course, not unique: any endowment point on p_2^e supports E_2 as a competitive equilibrium.

Should the foreign country follow suit by levying a tariff τ_x^F, then the final equilibrium would no longer be E_2 but rather some point on i^F below E_2, say E_3, where the ratio of the marginal rate of substitution along i^F and the price line equals $1/(1+\tau_x^F)$ in addition to the above requirement regarding the relationship between the home country's marginal rate of substitution and the slope of the world price line.

Define the domestic relative price by $p^i = p_y^i/p_x^i$, and let a circumflex (^) denote a relative change in a variable (for example, $\hat{z} = dz/z$). Then total differentiation with respect to u, p^e, and tariff rates yields, after some manipulation,[3] the following expression for how domestic price changes affect world welfare,

$$du = B\left(p^H - p^F\right)\{\hat{p}^H - \hat{p}^F\}. \quad (5)$$

As is shown in the Appendix, B is negative and is given as $B = (1/|A|)p^H m_{yy}^H m_{yy}^F$, where $|A|$ is the negative-valued determinant of the coefficient matrix, and m_{yy}^i is the negative-valued compensated own-price derivative of import demand for good y in country i. The larger is either of these derivatives in absolute value, the larger is the welfare impact from a given policy change.

Let $B^* = p^F B$, and define α to be the ratio of domestic relative prices as given by,

$$\alpha = p^H/p^F. \quad (6)$$

Expression (5) can then be rewritten as,

$$du = B^*(\alpha - 1)\hat{\alpha}, \quad (7)$$

where $\hat{\alpha} = \hat{p}^H - \hat{p}^F$ is the relative change in the ratio p^H/p^F.

By the first welfare theorem, world welfare is maximized when domestic prices are equalized, and thus α is one. Given that B^* is negative, it furthermore follows from (7), that world welfare monotonically falls as this ratio moves away from unity in either direction. The import of this result by Foster and Sonnenschein (1970) is that it is sufficient for a welfare assessment of a reform to investigate how α changes relative to unity as rates vary.

II. Welfare and Reform

A reform is, most generally, defined to be any sequence of changes of countries' trade policy variables. The following discussion

[3]The derivation is provided in the appendix.

will, however, be restricted to reforms where countries are not allowed to change the bases in terms of which they quote their rates. Thus, if a country initially quotes a tariff or a subsidy as a percentage of the world price of its import good, it is required to quote all subsequent rates as percentages of the emanating sequence of world prices of that good.

It will be demonstrated, that the combination of bases chosen by the countries critically determines the welfare properties of reforms. Specifically, it will be shown that world welfare can fall from the proportionate reduction of a tariff and a subsidy if countries quote rates on the same good, but one quotes on the world price and the other on its domestic price, or if countries quote rates on different goods, but both quote either in terms of world prices or domestic prices.

In order to develop this result, the discussion proceeds by considering reforms in two environments that differ by their combination of bases. This is followed by a general characterization of how the countries' choices of bases affect the welfare consequences of reform.

Consider first the case where both countries quote rates in terms of the world price of their import goods, the rates in question being τ_y^H and τ_x^F. From (6), the initial relative wedge is then,

$$\alpha = t_y^H t_x^F. \tag{8}$$

It follows from (7), that world welfare stays constant if α does not change. Rewriting (8) in terms of t_x^F thus yields the equation for a world welfare indifference curve in (t_y^H, t_x^F)-space as,

$$t_x^F = \alpha / t_y^H, \tag{9}$$

where α is to be interpreted as a distortion parameter.

Consider the implied world welfare indifference curve map in Figure 2. For α equal to one, trade is undistorted and the corresponding indifference locus CC goes through the free trade point (1,1). As α deviates from one, lower-valued indifference curves are traced out: For values of α exceeding one,

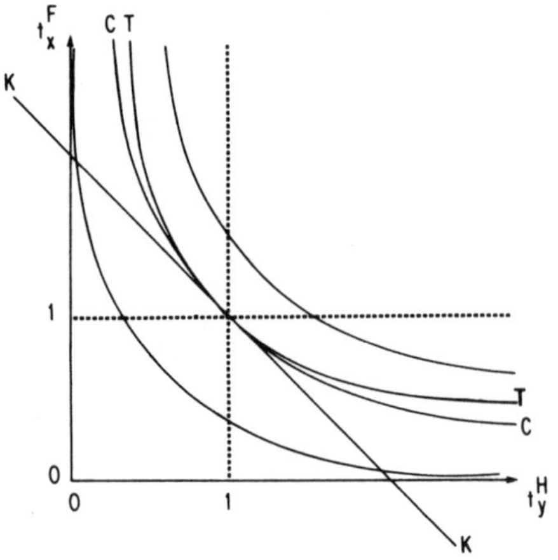

FIGURE 2

trade is restricted and indifference curves above CC are implied, while trade is excessive when α falls short of one, corresponding to indifference curves below CC.

A reform can now be illustrated as a path, where a particular step raises world welfare if it moves the world's tariff/subsidy point from a lower-valued to a higher-valued indifference curve. The set of directions of welfare-improving reforms is thus given by the half-space between the indifference curve through the initial point and CC.

Consider the reform of reducing rates in proportion, which, diagrammatically, shifts the tariff and/or subsidy point along the line connecting the initial point with the free trade point. If both countries initially levy tariffs or subsidies, then world welfare increases at each step of the reform until free trade is reached.[4] If one country taxes and

[4] In the case of tariffs, this result is a special case of that derived by Hatta and Fukushima (1979), who considered two goods but arbitrarily many countries. Figure 2 also permits a two-country version of the three-country result shown by Vanek (1964), that reducing the highest tariff to the next highest rate raises world welfare: When τ_y^H exceeds τ_x^F, a horizontal shift of the tariff point toward the line through the free trade point with slope one traverses higher-valued indifference curves, as does a vertical shift of the tariff point when τ_x^F exceeds τ_y^H.

the other subsidizes trade, then a reform of proportionate rate reductions will raise world welfare from any initial equilibrium on or below *KK*, which is drawn through the free trade point with slope minus one. Locus *TT* is constructed, in a manner analogous to the offer curve, by connecting all the points of tangency between rays from the free trade point and welfare indifference curves. It follows, that proportionate rate reductions from any initial point on or above *TT* also raise world welfare.

This leaves only points between *KK* and *TT* as consistent with the welfare paradox. For any initial equilibrium between *CC* and *TT*, a reform of proportionate rate reductions lowers world welfare until the reform reaches *TT*, whereupon welfare increases until the reform halts at free trade. Furthermore, although a proportionate reduction from an initial equilibrium between *KK* and *CC* at first raises welfare, it paradoxically begins to fall after *CC* has been reached and continues to do so until *TT* is traversed.

It is shown, in the Appendix, that *TT* is given by the expression,

$$t_x^F = 1/\left(2-\left(1/t_y^H\right)\right). \tag{10}$$

Therefore, the condition that a point lies between *CC* and *TT* is that,

$$1/t_y^H < t_x^F < 1/\left(2-\left(1/t_y^H\right)\right). \tag{11}$$

Some values for the part of this region, where the home country taxes and the foreign country subsidizes, are given in the following table:

τ_y^H percent:	10	25	100	200
$-\tau_x^F$ percent:	8–9	17–20	33–50	40–67

The rapid increase in the likelihood of a paradox as the absolute values of the rates increase is noteworthy. Since negotiations are frequently initiated in environments of deteriorating trade relations, this should support the practical relevance of the paradox. And, of course, these values only characterize the region between *CC* and *TT*, and not the one between *KK* and *CC*, which, as previously argued, leads to a paradox at later stages of the reform.

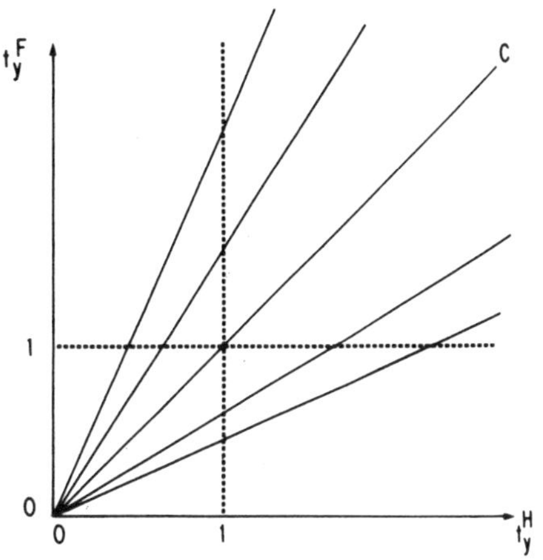

FIGURE 3

To illustrate the importance of how rates are quoted, suppose that both countries quote rates on the world price of good *y*, such that $\tau_y^H > 0$ is a home tariff, and $\tau_y^F > 0$ is a foreign subsidy. From (6), the relative wedge is then given by $\alpha = t_y^H/t_y^F$, which, in turn, defines the equation for a world welfare indifference locus in (t_y^H, t_y^F)-space as,

$$t_y^F = t_y^H/\alpha. \tag{12}$$

As is shown in Figure 3, the implied indifference loci are lines emanating from (0,0) with slope $1/\alpha$. Line *OC*, which corresponds to α equal to one, defines all the points of maximum world welfare, while lower-valued indifference lines are implied for all other values of α. The diagram reveals that, for any initial point not on *OC*, a reform of proportionate rate reductions improves world welfare—no paradox is possible.

In order to develop a general characterization of which combinations of bases can lead to the paradox, it is useful to look at α as the ratio of two wedges, each being between a domestic price and the world market relative price. Thus dividing and multiplying

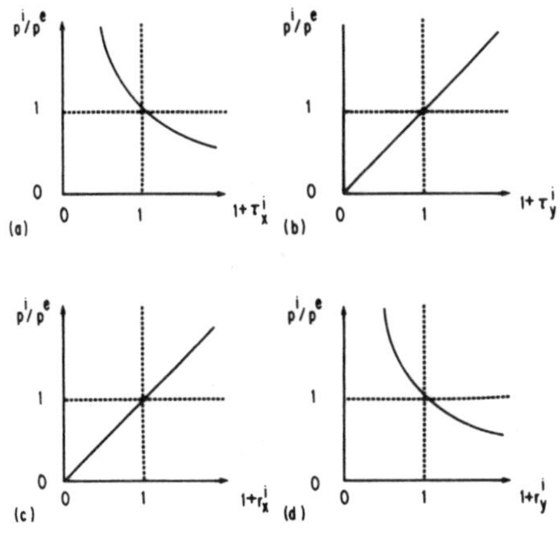

FIGURE 4

expression (6) by p^e yields,

$$\alpha = (p^H/p^e)/(p^F/p^e). \tag{13}$$

For any country, the relationship between domestic and world relative price depends upon how a rate is quoted. If quoted in terms of the world price, then the price equation is (1), restated here as (14),

$$p_j^i = (1+\tau_j^i)p_j^e. \tag{14}$$

This, in turn, implies that the relative wedge, p^i/p^e (where p^i equals $(p_y/p_x)^i$), is either a hyperbola or a line as a function of the policy rate, which is illustrated in panels (a) and (b) of Figure 4.

Were country i instead to quote the rate in terms of its domestic price of either commodity, the price equation would be,

$$p_j^i(1+r_j^i) = p_j^e, \tag{15}$$

where r_j^i is the *ad valorem* rate when a domestic price base is used. In Figure 4, the implied relative wedge (p^i/p^e) is illustrated in panels (c) and (d) for the two possible base choices.

The two cases previously discussed were the one where the home country chooses panel (b) and the foreign country panel (a), and the one where both countries choose panel (b). More generally, the possibility of a welfare paradox from a proportionate reform arises when one country's base choice implies that the wedge between its domestic relative price and the world market relative price is a hyperbola while, simultaneously, the other country's base choice implies a linear wedge. Hence a paradox may occur if (*i*) one country quotes its rate in terms of a world price and the other country quotes its rate in terms of its domestic price of the same good (combines panels (a) and (c), and panels (b) and (d), respectively); or if (*ii*) countries quote rates on different goods but both quote either in terms of world prices or domestic prices (panel (a) with panel (b), and panel (c) with panel (d)).[5]

III. Conclusion

This paper has investigated tariff reforms as motivated by the recent emergence of subsidization as an important trade policy. A two-country, two-commodity model has been analyzed and, to further keep matters simple, it has been assumed that there exists a mechanism, that allows for costless income transfers between countries.

The basic insights of the analysis would remain unaltered from increased dimensionality. It is also of comfort that the nonmonotonicity of the ratio of domestic prices is independent of any considerations regarding the determination of the terms of trade and hence market structure. Although free trade generally might not be optimal from the perspective of world welfare under imperfect competition, paradoxes from reforms could still very much be a possibility. The same cannot as easily be said if lump-sum transfers were ruled out. The merit of the approach taken here is, however, that it isolates, relative to the most extensively analyzed model in international trade, any new features that subsidization would imply.

[5]When rates are specific, the distortion measure is $p^H - p^F$. In this case, indifference curves can be drawn without solving for p^e only when both countries quote their rates on good y.

In these, final, remarks shall be emphasized two policy implications with very different tenors: one of activism, one of caution.

The activist chord follows from a corollary which, although not stressed in the analysis, deserves attention: If a country subsidizes trade, her trade partner should respond with a positive tariff—she should, in particular, not allow for unilateral free trade.

The reason for this is twofold. First, a subsidy does not invalidate the Bickerdike-van Graaf optimum tariff argument. Simple offer curve geometry reveals that, if the optimum tariff is positive under free trade, it is so if the other country subsidizes. Second, as the tariff rate increases relative to unilateral free trade, the domestic relative prices move closer together and world welfare improves. That the tariff rate, which maximizes world welfare, falls short of the unilaterally optimal tariff rate is irrelevant for the common implication: In the standard trade model, any optimality of unilateral free trade must be rejected under foreign subsidization. This is hardly a surprising result, and is but a restatement of Richard Lipsey and Kelvin Lancaster's (1956–57) celebrated theorem of the second best.

What is, perhaps, more surprising is the main result of the paper, which strikes a note of caution: Reforms of proportionate rate reductions have an intrinsic appeal since they specify the shortest route to free trade. It has been shown that this appeal is deceptive.

APPENDIX

(*i*) *Derivation of Equation* (5). Define m^H_{ju} to be the marginal propensity to consume good j ($k = x, y$) in the home country, and let m^i_{jk} ($i = H, F$; $j = x, y$) be the derivative of import demand for good j in country i with respect to the kth price holding utility constant. Then total differentiation with respect to u, p^e, and tariff rates (expressed in terms of t^i_j's) yields,

$$\text{(A1)} \qquad \underbrace{\begin{bmatrix} m^H_{xu} & \Sigma m^i_{xy} t^i_y \\ m^H_{yu} & \Sigma m^i_{yy} t^i_y \end{bmatrix}}_{A} \begin{bmatrix} du \\ dp^e \end{bmatrix} = -\begin{bmatrix} \Sigma m^i_{xx} dt^i_x + p^e \Sigma m^i_{xy} dt^i_y \\ \Sigma m^i_{yx} dt^i_x + p^e \Sigma m^i_{yy} dt^i_y \end{bmatrix}.$$

Let $|A|$ be the determinant of the matrix A. Assuming non-inferiority of both goods, m^H_{xu} and m^H_{yu} are both positive. Since m^H_{xy} is positive and m^H_{yy} is negative, $|A|$ is negative. From the homogeneity conditions,

$$\text{(A2)} \qquad m^i_{jk} p^i_k + m^i_{jj} p^i_j = 0; \qquad j, k = x, y;\ j \neq k;\ i = H, F,$$

the cross-substitution terms m^i_{jk} and the own-substitution terms m^i_{xx} can be eliminated. Finally, assuming that $\tau^H_x = \tau^F_y = 0$, (A1) implies the following welfare expression,

$$\text{(A3)} \qquad du = (1/|A|)\, p^H m^H_{yy} m^F_{yy} \times (p^H - p^F)\{\hat{t}^H_y + \hat{t}^F_x\}.$$

Since $p^H/p^F = t^H_y p^e/((1/t^F_x)p^e)$, $\hat{t}^H_y + \hat{t}^F_x = \hat{p}^H - \hat{p}^F$ Substituting this into (A3), together with $B = (1/|A|)p^H m^H_{yy} m^F_{yy}$, yields equation (5) of the text.

(*ii*) *Derivation of TT-Locus*: The schedule *TT* is constructed by connecting all points of tangency between rays from the free trade point and welfare indifference curves. Its equation is found by simultaneously solving the following equations for some given α,

$$\text{(A4)} \qquad 1 + k(t^H_y - 1) = 1/(\alpha t^H_y)$$

and,

$$\text{(A5)} \qquad k = -1/(\alpha (t^H_y)^2).$$

Expression (A4) is the condition that a ray from the free trade point with slope k intersects the indifference curve of distortion α, while (A5), in addition, equates their slopes. The solution can be found to be $2t^H_y t^F_x - t^H_y - t^F_x = 0$, or

$$\text{(A6)} \qquad t^F_x = 1/(2 - (1/t^H_y)),$$

which is expression (10) of the paper. It should be noticed that this locus has $t^H_y = 1/2$ and $t^F_x = 1/2$ as asymptotes.

REFERENCES

Brander, James A. and Spencer, Barbara J., "Trade Warfare: Tariffs and Cartels," *Journal of International Economics*, May 1984, *16*, 227–42.

Corden, W. Max, "The Normative Theory of International Trade," in Ronald W. Jones and Peter B. Kenen, eds., *Handbook of*

International Economics, Vol. 1, Amsterdam: North-Holland Publishing Company, 1984.

Eaton, Jonathan and Grossman, Gene M., "Optimal Trade and Industrial Policy under Oligopoly," *Quarterly Journal of Economics*, May 1986, *51*, 383–406.

Foster, Edward and Sonnenschein, Hugo, "Price Distortion and Economic Welfare," *Econometrica*, March 1970, *38*, 281–97.

Hatta, Tatsuo and Fukushima, Takashi, "The Welfare Effect of Tariff Rate Reductions in a Many Country World," *Journal of International Economics*, November 1979, *9*, 503–511.

Lipsey, Richard G. and Lancaster, R. Kelvin, "The General Theory of Second Best," *Review of Economic Studies*, October 1956, *24*, 11–32.

Meade, James, *Trade and Welfare*, London: Oxford University Press, 1955.

Ozga, S. A., "An Essay in the Theory of Tariffs," *Journal of Political Economy*, December 1955, *63*, 489–99.

Vanek, Jaroslev, "Unilateral Trade Liberalization and Global World Income," *Quarterly Journal of Economics*, February 1964, *78*, 139–47.

[19]

WELFARE IMPROVING TARIFF CHANGES

A Case of Many Goods and Countries

Takashi FUKUSHIMA

State University of New York at Albany, Albany, NY 12222, USA

Namdoo KIM*

Trade Policy Division, Korea Institute for Economics and Technology, Seoul 131-010, Korea

Received April 1987, revised version received June 1988

In a model of many goods and countries with specific tariffs and subsidies, the paper proves that a proportional reduction (a radial contraction) of all tariff/subsidy rates improves the world's potential welfare. This generalizes a result obtained in a two-good economy by Hatta and Fukushima (1979).

1. Introduction

One of the central themes developed in the literature on piecemeal tariffs and tax reform is that a radial distortion reduction improves economic efficiency. The idea first appeared in Foster and Sonnenschein (1970). Since then various authors such as Hatta (1977), Dixit (1975), Fukushima (1979), and Diewert, Turunen and Woodland (1984) have presented variations of this distortion reduction theme. In this journal, Hatta and Fukushima (1979) proved a theorem which states that a proportional ad valorem tariff rate reduction of all countries in the world improves the world's potential welfare in a two-good and n-country model.

In the present note, we attempt to extend their analysis in two important directions. First, we treat the problem in a fully general $(n+1)$-good and m-country model. Second, our model allows the countries to have tariffs and subsidies on all goods, which is contrasted with the model with only import tariffs in the Hatta–Fukushima model. In turn, we assume specific tariffs and

*We are grateful for the comments by two anonymous referees. The remaining errors are ours.

subsidies.[1] We show that a proportional reduction of all tariff/subsidy rates of the world improves world potential welfare.[2]

2. The model

We consider a model with m countries and $n+1$ goods. Let $p=(p_0, p_1, \ldots, p_n)'$ denote the vector of world prices. Let $\tau^i=(\tau_0^i, \tau_1^i, \ldots, \tau_n^i)'$ be the tariff/subsidy vector of country i in specific rates. Then the domestic price vector of country i can be written as

$$p^i = p + \tau^i, \quad i=1,2,\ldots,m. \tag{1}$$

Suppose the compensated demand function of country i is given by $f^i(p^i, u^i)$, and the supply function by $h^i(p^i)$. Then we can define a compensated import demand function by

$$s^i(p, \tau^i, u^i) = f^i(p+\tau^i, u^i) - h^i(p+\tau^i), \quad i=1,2,\ldots,m. \tag{2}$$

Using (2) we can define an aggregated compensated import demand function by

$$s(p, \tau^1, \tau^2, \ldots, \tau^m, u^1, \ldots, u^m) = \sum_{i=1}^{m} s^i(p, \tau^i, u^i). \tag{3}$$

Then the international market equilibrium is described by

$$s(p, \tau^1, \tau^2, \ldots, \tau^m, u^1, \ldots, u^m) = 0. \tag{4}$$

Let us normalize the world price vector with $p_0=1$. Then the equilibrium condition (4) contains n relative world prices and m utility levels to be determined. Following Hatta and Fukushima, we adopt[3]

$$u^i = \bar{u}^i, \quad i=2,3,\ldots,m. \tag{5}$$

[1]This is a small price we pay for the purpose of generalization. The difficulties of using ad valorem tariff/subsidy rates are demonstrated by Kowalczyk (1986). He showed that a proportionate ad valorem tariff/subsidy reduction may reduce world potential welfare even though all goods are net substitutes and no inferiority exists.

[2]Actually, a proportional tariff/subsidy reduction is a special case of our theorem. See section 4.

[3]Needless to say, we need to spell out m balance of trade conditions to construct a positive model of international trade. Then we can determine m utility levels and n relative prices. However, for the purpose of normative analysis we can fix all but one level of welfare. From the point of view of balance of trade constraints, this can be done by international transfers so as to keep the $(m-1)$ utility levels constant. Note that the actual international transfer is not necessary for the analysis of *potential* world welfare.

Then our $(n+1)$ equilibrium conditions given by (4) determine n relative prices and u^1 for given values of τ^i $(i=1,2,\ldots,m)$.

3. Some preliminary results

Define matrices S^i and S by $\partial s^i/\partial p$ and $\partial s/\partial p$, respectively. We assume that a sufficient substitutability exists in production and consumption in each country so that the rank of S^i is n.

For this model we can prove the following lemmas.

Lemma 1. Suppose that S is partitioned by

$$S=\left[\begin{array}{c|c} s_{OO} & s_{ON} \\ \hline s_{NO} & S_{NN} \end{array}\right].$$

Then for the model described by (4) *and* (5), *we have*

$$\mathrm{d}u^1=\frac{-1}{(s^1_{Ou}-s_{ON}S^{-1}_{NN}s^1_{Nu})}(1,\,-s_{ON}S^{-1}_{NN})\sum_{i=1}^{m} S^i\,\mathrm{d}\tau^i,$$

where

$$\left[\begin{array}{c} s^1_{Ou} \\ \hline s^1_{Nu} \end{array}\right]\equiv s^1_u\equiv\frac{\partial s^1}{\partial u^1}.$$

Proof. Total differentiation of (4) gives us

$$s^1_u\,\mathrm{d}u^1+S\,\mathrm{d}p=-\sum_{i=1}^{m} S^i\,\mathrm{d}\tau^i.$$

Thus, we get

$$\left[\begin{array}{c|c} s^1_u & \begin{array}{c} s_{ON} \\ \hline S_{NN} \end{array} \end{array}\right]\left[\begin{array}{c} \mathrm{d}u^1 \\ \hline \mathrm{d}p_N \end{array}\right]=-\sum S^i\,\mathrm{d}\tau^i,$$

where $p_N=(p_1,p_2,\ldots,p_n)'$. Cramer's rule and a straightforward calculation[4] gives us the desired result. □

[4]The determinant of a partitioned matrix can be written as

$$\det\left[\begin{array}{c|c} A & B \\ \hline C & D \end{array}\right]=|A-BD^{-1}C||D|,$$

where A and D are square and D is non-singular. See Johnston (1972, p. 95).

Lemma 2. $|S|=0$ *if* $p^i=k^{ij}p^j$ *for all pairs* $(i,j)(i,j=1,\ldots,m)$ *and for some scalar* k^{ij}, *and* $|S|\neq 0$ *otherwise.*

Proof. Since $y'Sy=y'(\sum S^i)y$, it is obvious under our assumption on the rank of S^i and its negative semidefiniteness that for a non-zero vector y, $y'Sy=0$ if $p^i=k^{ij}p^j$ for all pairs (i,j) and for some scalar k^{ij}, and $y'Sy<0$ otherwise. □

Lemma 3.

$$s_{00}-s_{0N}S_{NN}^{-1}s_{N0}\leqq 0,$$

where the strict inequality holds if there exists at least one pair (i,j) *such that* $p^i\neq k^{ij}p^j$ *for any scalar* k^{ij}.

Proof. Since

$$\det\left[\begin{array}{c|c} s_{00} & s_{0N} \\ \hline s_{N0} & S_{NN}\end{array}\right]=(s_{00}-s_{0N}S_{NN}^{-1}s_{N0})|S_{NN}|,$$

the inequality follows from the fact that S *and* S_{NN} are negative definite matrices with order $(n+1)\times(n+1)$ and $n\times n$, respectively, and the strict inequality must hold by virtue of Lemma 2 if there is a pair p^i and p^j such that one is not proportional to the other. □

4. The theorem

Now we are ready to prove the following theorem.

Theorem. Suppose either (*a*) *there is no inferiority and no complementarity either in consumption or production in any country* or (*b*) *a small increase in the endowment of the numeraire is potentially Pareto improving.*[5] *Then world potential welfare is increased by moving all specific tariff and subsidy rates proportionately towards* βp, *where* β *is a scalar and* $\beta>-1$.[6]

Proof. Let σ represent the stage of the progress of the prescribed policy. Then our policy can be written as $d\tau^i=(\beta p-\tau^i)\,d\sigma$. Use Lemma 1 to get

[5] Needless to say, the rank condition mentioned in section 3 is assumed to hold.

[6] Notice that if $\beta=0$ it is the proportionate tariff/subsidy reduction, and that if the tariff/subsidy rate vector equals βp, there is no distortion in this economy. Thus, the tariff/subsidy change towards βp is a move toward less distortion.

$$\frac{du^1}{d\sigma}=\frac{-1}{(s^1_{0u}-s_{0N}S^{-1}_{NN}s^1_{Nu})}(1,\,-s_{0N}S^{-1}_{NN})\sum_i S^i(\beta p-\tau^i). \tag{6}$$

Using (1) and the homogeneity condition $S^i p^i=0$, we get

$$\begin{aligned}(1,\,-s_{0N}S^{-1}_{NN})\sum_i S^i(\beta p-\tau^i)&=(1,\,-s_{0N}S^{-1}_{NN})\sum_i S^i\{(1+\beta)p-p^i\}\\ &=(1+\beta)(1,\,-s_{0N}S^{-1}_{NN})Sp\\ &=(1+\beta)(1,\,-s_{0N}S^{-1}_{NN})\begin{bmatrix}s_{00} & s_{0N}\\ s_{N0} & S_{NN}\end{bmatrix}p\\ &=(1+\beta)(s_{00}-s_{0N}S^{-1}_{NN}s_{N0},\,0)p\\ &\leqq 0,\end{aligned}$$

where, by virtue of Lemma 3, the strict inequality holds whenever there is a pair of price vectors p^i and p^j such that one is not proportional to the other.

On the other hand, if condition (a) of the theorem holds, then $s^i_u>0$ and $-S^{-1}_{NN}\geq 0$.[7] Thus, the denominator of the RHS of (6) is positive. As for condition (b), suppose dε represents an increase in the endowment of the numeraire. Then we have

$$\frac{du}{d\varepsilon}=\frac{1}{(s^1_{0u}-s_{0N}S^{-1}_{NN}s^1_{Nu})},$$

and the positivity of the expression proves the result. □

5. Concluding remarks

The potential world welfare improvement defined in the text should be distinguished from the actual welfare improvement. As we mentioned in footnote 3, we need international lump-sum transfers in order to actually realize the Pareto improvement. Therefore, if our policy is applied, it may reduce some country's welfare level if there is no transfer. However, if such efficiency improvements are seen, one may argue that such efficiency gains should be captured and equity considerations should be made by other means.

[7]Our assumption on substitutability implies that all the off-diagonal elements of $-S_{NN}$ are negative. In addition, all the successive principal minors of $-S_{NN}$ are positive since it is a positive definite matrix. Therefore the well-known Hawkins–Simon condition is satisfied. Therefore we have $-S^{-1}_{NN}\geq 0$. See Takayama (1974, pp. 383–384) for details.

Similar arguments appear frequently in public economics where there are trade-offs between efficiency and equity .

Our net substitutability condition (a) of the theorem imposes a restriction upon the utility or production function. It can be made somewhat weaker since it is obvious from our proof that all that is required is that the aggregate substitution matrix S has non-negative off-diagonal elements. In other words, every country's utility and production functions need not satisfy this restriction. Yet, it is a condition stronger than one may wish. The alternative condition (b), on the other hand, is a very mild one. It is an economically plausible condition and does not impose the restrictions on the utility function. However, from a purely theoretical point of view the latter condition is something to be proved rather than assumed. Thus, it is more desirable to find weaker restrictions on the utility function sufficient to prove the result. The theorem holds either under (a) or under (b). Some variations of these conditions may be found.

References

Diewert, W.E., A.H. Turunen and A.D. Woodland, 1984, Productivity and Pareto improving changes in taxes and tariffs, University of British Columbia, Department of Economics, Discussion paper 84-06.

Dixit, A.K., 1975, Welfare effects of tax and price changes, Journal of Public Economics 4, 103–123.

Dixit, A.K. and V.D. Norman, 1980, Theory of international trade (Cambridge University Press, Cambridge).

Foster, Edward and Hugo Sonnenschein, 1970, Price distortion and economic welfare, Econometrica 38, no. 2, 281–297.

Fukushima, Takashi, 1979, Tariff structure, nontraded goods and theory of piecemeal policy recommendations, International Economic Review 20, 361–369.

Hatta, Tatsuo, 1977, A theory of piecemeal policy recommendations, Review of Economic Studies 44, 1–21.

Hatta, Tatsuo and Takashi Fukushima, 1979, The welfare effect of tariff rate reductions in a many country world, Journal of International Economics 9, 503–511.

Johnston, J., 1972, Econometric method, 2nd ed. (McGraw-Hill, New York).

Keen, Michael, 1986, Welfare effects of commodity tax harmonization, Journal of Public Economics (forthcoming).

Kowalczyk, Carsten, 1986, Trade distortions and world welfare, Mimeo. (University of Rochester).

Takayama, Akira, 1974, Mathematical economics (The Dryden Press, Hinsdale, IL).

[20]

MULTILATERAL TAX AND TARIFF REFORM*

By MICHAEL KEEN

1. Introduction

One of the central principles to emerge from the analysis of piecemeal tax and tariff reform is the presumption that a radial contraction of all distortions improves efficiency. The main purpose of this paper is to present a result that generalises some of the main variants on this theme. It is shown that in a standard competitive model of a world with two countries and many commodities (both tradeable and non-tradeable)—and in the absence of transfer-type paradoxes—a multilateral uniform proportionate reduction of all domestic consumption taxes and all tariffs is strictly potentially Pareto-improving.

This result, it should be emphasised, requires the reduction of both taxes *and* tariffs. In discussing its significance and antecedents, however, it is convenient to focus on each set of instruments in turn.

In its implications for internal taxation the present result extends the familiar proposition that a radial contraction of consumption taxes increases welfare in the single-consumer closed economy (Foster and Sonnenschein (1970)). This extension—to the case of trading partners with differing initial tax structures—is intended to be of more than technical interest, having some relevance to the debate on indirect tax harmonisation in the European Community; a debate firmly revived by the European Commission's current ambitious proposals for the 'approximation' of Member States' internal taxes by 1993. For large countries which—like those Member States—are unable to use tariffs against one another will typically have some incentive to use internal consumption taxes as a protective device (Friedlander and Vandendorpe (1968)). In the European Community, there is reason to suppose that this does indeed happen: the UK, for instance, has been required on these grounds to lower its domestic tax on wine relative to that on beer. This suggests that there may be an efficiency argument for harmonization as a collective response to tax-induced trade distortions. In practice, the multilateral tax reform envisaged by the Commission is most accurately characterised as one of convergence towards a non-zero average of Member States' initial tax structures (the welfare implications of which are considered in Keen (1987, 1989)), rather than as one of convergence towards the origin. Nevertheless, to the extent that the perceived rationale for a policy of tax coordination is to counter the nationalistic incentive to levy internal taxes not for revenue-raising but purely for reasons of protection, the

* The first version of this paper was written during a stimulating and enjoyable stay at the Kyoto Institute of Economic Research, whose support and hospitality it is a pleasure to acknowledge. I am also grateful to Tatsuo Hatta, Takashi Fukushima and two referees for their comments and suggestions. Errors and opinions remain my own.

present conclusion that convergence towards the complete elimination of distorting taxes is potentially improving has some importance for the evaluation of that policy.

The tariff part of the result—that is, the corollary obtained by taking all internal taxes to be zero—generalises a proposition of Hatta and Fukushima (1979), who show that a multilateral radial contraction of tariffs is potentially improving when there are only two goods (and both are normal in demand). That proposition has recently also been extended by Fukushima and Kim (1987),[1] who deal with the case in which there are many tradeable goods but (in contrast to the present result) no non-tradeables. These results provide some welfare-theoretic support for the tariff reductions of the Kennedy and Tokyo rounds, though that proved here also emphasises the importance for the evaluation of tariff reform of the interaction with domestic distortions induced by internal taxation.

Section 2 sets out the model. The result is then derived in Section 3, a necessary detail being verified in an appendix. Section 4 concludes.

2. The Model

There are T tradeable commodities and N non-tradeables (including, perhaps, variable factor supplies) in each of the two countries that together constitute the world.[2] Consumer prices in the 'home' (upper case) country are denoted by Q, a $(T + N)$-dimensional column vector, and may differ from home producer prices P as a result of destination-based consumption taxation at the specific rates Γ:

(1) $Q = P + \Gamma.$

Similarly for the foreign (lower case) country:

(2) $q = p + \gamma.$

Numbering commodities so that the tradeables come first, price vectors are partitioned between tradeables and non-tradeables in obvious notation as, for instance, $P = (P'_T, P'_N)'$: here P_N denotes the producer prices of non-tradeables in the home country and a prime indicates transposition. Producer prices for tradeables are related to world prices R as

(3) $P_T = R + \Pi,\ p_T = R + \pi$

where Π and π denote the vectors of tariffs imposed by the home and foreign countries respectively; in the usual way, $\Pi_i > 0$ indicates an import tax if the i-th good is imported by the home country and an export subsidy if it is exported. Though they are not explicitly represented in (1)-(3), the result to be derived below is also applicable to production subsidies: as discussed in Dixit (1985), these are simply equivalent to tariffs (or, for non-tradeables, increased producer prices) combined with matching consumption subsidies.

Note too that the analysis and results are cast in terms of specific taxes and tariffs rather than (as in Hatta and Fukushima (1979), for instance) ad valorem ones. These two forms of distortion are of course precisely equivalent in terms of the characterisation of a competitive equilibrium, but in the context of the present comparative statics exercise—as in others—the specific formula-

1) I am grateful to Takashi Fukushima for bringing this paper to my attention.

2) Apart from notation, there would be no difficulty in allowing many countries (so long as all participate in the reform) with differing numbers of non-tradeables.

tion leads to sharper insights: see Kowalczyk (1986).

The preferences of the representative consumer in the home country are described by an expenditure function $E(Q, U)$, U denoting utility. By Hotelling's Lemma, compensated commodity demands are then given by the vector of price derivatives $E_Q = (E'_T, E'_N)'$. Differentiating again, the matrix of Slutsky substitution effects is partitioned as

$$(4)\quad E_{QQ} = \begin{bmatrix} E_{TT} & E_{TN} \\ E_{NT} & E_{NN} \end{bmatrix}$$

where E_{TN}, for instance, is the $(T \times N)$-matrix containing the derivatives of the compensated demands for tradeable goods with respect to the prices of the non-tradeables. Concavity of the expenditure function implies that E_{QQ} is negative semi-definite. Linear homogeneity implies that

$$(5)\quad E_{QQ}\cdot Q = O_{T+N},$$

where O_K denotes the K-vector of zeros, and (4) then gives

$$(6)\quad E_{TT}\cdot Q_T + E_{TN}\cdot Q_N = O_T;\ E_{NN}\cdot Q_N + E_{NT}\cdot Q_T = O_N.$$

Firms behave as perfect competitors, enabling the production side to be characterised by a GNP (or, synonymously, revenue) function $G(P)$. Outputs are then $G_P = (G'_T, G'_N)'$. The matrix of substitution effects in production, G_{PP}, is partitioned exactly as in (4) above. By convexity, G_{PP} is positive semi-definite. By linear homogeneity

$$(7)\quad G_{PP}\cdot P = O_{T+N}$$

and hence, from the partitioned form,

$$(8)\quad G_{TT}\cdot P_T + G_{TN}\cdot P_N = O_T;\ G_{NN}\cdot P_N + G_{NT}\cdot P_T = O_N.$$

It is also convenient to define

$$(9)\quad S = E_{QQ} - G_{PP} = \begin{bmatrix} S_{TT} & S_{TN} \\ S_{NT} & S_{NN} \end{bmatrix}$$

which is the (symmetric) matrix of price derivatives of compensated excess demands in the home country, and at least negative semi-definite.

The characterisation of the foreign country is precisely analogous, with small letters replacing large. It is assumed throughout that there is enough substitutability to ensure that E_{QQ}, G_{PP}, e_{qq} and g_{pp} all have rank $T + N - 1$ (see for instance Dixit and Norman (1980), p. 130).

Turning to the equilibrium conditions, market-clearing requires

$$(10)\quad E_T(Q, U) + e_T(q, u) - G_T(P) - g_T(p) = O_T$$

for tradeables, and

$$(11)\quad E_N(Q, U) - G_N(P) = O_N$$

$$(12)\quad e_N(q, u) - g_N(p) = O_N$$

for non-tradeables. To identify potential Pareto-improvements, it is assumed that an amount Z_1 of commodity 1 is transferred between the two countries; this will later be varied so as to leave the foreign country indifferent to reform. With tax and tariff revenue returned to the consumer as a lump-sum, the national income-expenditure identities are then

$$(13)\quad E(Q, U) - G(P) - \Pi'\cdot\{E_T(Q, U) - G_T(P)\} - \Gamma'\cdot E_Q(Q, U) + R_1 Z_1 = 0$$

$$(14)\quad e(q, u) - g(p) - \pi'\cdot\{e_T(q, u) - g_T(p)\} - \gamma'\cdot e_q(q, u) - R_1 Z_1 = 0,$$

where R_1 denotes the world price of the first commodity. The homogeneity properties noted earlier imply that the system (10)-(14) is undisturbed by multiplying any of P, Q, p, q or R by a positive scalar.[3] Without loss of generality, commodity 1 can therefore be taken to bear no tax or tariff, and its world price normalised at unity. To preclude trivialities, it will be assumed that the initial equilibrium is distorted: that is, at least one of the equalities

(15) $P_T = p_T$; $Q = P$; $q = p$

does not hold. As a final preliminary, note that (13) and (14) amount only to a single budget constraint; and this, by Walras' Law, we can choose to ignore. The analysis will thus focus on the $T + 2N$ equations in (10)-(12). Taxes, tariffs and foreign utility are regarded as parametric, so that the unknowns are U, P_N, p_N and $T - 1$ components of R; a total of $T + 2N$.

3. Multilateral Tax and Tariff Reduction

Consider then some (small) reform of taxes and/or tariffs, described by $[d\Pi, d\pi, d\Gamma, d\gamma]$. With foreign utility held constant by adjusting the transfer to or from the home country, the reform is potentially Pareto-improving if and only if home utility is increased. Thus the first task is to solve for dU. To do so, begin by noting that perturbing (11) and (1) gives the effect on home producer prices for non-tradeables as

(16) $dP_N = -(S_{NN})^{-1}[E_{NU}dU + S_{NT}\cdot dP_T + E_{NQ}d\Gamma]$,

where E_{NU} denotes the N-vector of utility derivatives of compensated demands for non-tradeables, $E_{NQ} = [E_{NT} | E_{NN}]$, and the existence of the inverse is assured by the earlier rank assumptions. From (12), and since $du = 0$, one similarly finds

(17) $dp_N = -(s_{NN})^{-1}[s_{NT}dp_T + e_{NQ}\cdot d\gamma]$.

Perturbing (10), using the price relations in (1)-(3) and substituting from (16) and (17) then gives

(18) $\{E_{TU} - S_{TN}(S_{NN})^{-1}E_{NU}\}dU + \Sigma.dR + \delta = 0_T$,

in which we have defined the $T \times T$ matrix

(19) $\Sigma = S_{TT} - S_{TN}(S_{NN})^{-1}S_{NT} + s_{TT} - s_{TN}(s_{NN})^{-1}s_{NT}$

and the T-vector $\delta = \delta_H + \delta_F$, where δ_F is the foreign analogue to

(20) $\delta_H = \{S_{TT} - S_{TN}(S_{NN})^{-1}S_{NT}\}d\Pi + \{E_{TQ} - S_{TN}(S_{NN})^{-1}E_{NQ}\}.d\Gamma$.

By normalisation, the world price of the first commodity is unaffected by the reform: $dR = (0, (dR^*)')'$, say. Partitioning Σ as

$$\Sigma = \begin{bmatrix} \sigma_{11} & \sigma_{j1}' \\ \sigma_{j1} & \Sigma^* \end{bmatrix}$$

where Σ^* is $(T - 1) \times (T - 1)$, and $E_{TU} - S_{TN}(S_{NN})^{-1}E_{NU}$ correspondingly, (18) can thus be written

3) For the income-expenditure conditions, this is most easily seen by using linear homogeneity to rewrite (13), for instance, as (omitting arguments)

$$P_N'(E_N - G_N) + R'\cdot(E_T - G_T) + R_1Z_1 = 0$$

and noting from (11) that the first term vanishes at an equilibrium.

$$\begin{bmatrix} E_{1U} - S_{1N}(S_{NN})^{-1}E_{NU} & \sigma'_{j1} \\ E_{jU} - S_{jN}(S_{NN})^{-1}E_{NU} & \Sigma^* \end{bmatrix} \begin{bmatrix} dU \\ dR^* \end{bmatrix} = -\delta.$$

Using a standard result on the determinant of a partitioned matrix (see for example Proposition 30 of Dhrymes (1978)), it then follows from Cramer's rule that

(21) $$dU = [\alpha.\, \text{Det}\,(\Sigma^*)]^{-1}\, \text{Det} \begin{bmatrix} -\delta & \begin{matrix} \sigma'_{j1} \\ \Sigma^* \end{matrix} \end{bmatrix}$$

where

(22) $$\alpha = E_{1U} - S_{1N}(S_{NN})^{-1}E_{NU} - \sigma'_{j1}(\Sigma^*)^{-1}\{E_{jU} - S_{jN}(S_{NN})^{-1}E_{NU}\}.$$

The existence of the denominator in (21) obviously requires that neither α nor Det (Σ^*) vanish. Proposition 2 below gives conditions under which α is strictly positive. That Det (Σ^*) $\neq 0$ is implied by the observation—which will be crucial to the argument below—that Σ (and hence also Σ^*) is negative definite. This is readily proved when there are no non-tradeables. For in this case it is immediate from the definitions that Σ is simply the sum of four negative semi-definite matrices, and can fail to be negative definite (if and) only if there exists some non-null x such that

$$E_{QQ}.x = G_{PP}.x = e_{qq}.x = g_{pp}.x = 0.$$

But in view of the homogeneity restrictions (5) and (7) the rank conditions would then imply that $x = Q = P = q = p$ (up to a scalar multiple), so contradicting the assumption that the original position is distorted. The proof is more involved when non-tradeables are present, but no more instructive; it is therefore consigned to an appendix.

Equation (21) is valid for an arbitrary change in taxes and tariffs. Here we are concerned with the particular reform in which all taxes and tariffs in both countries are moved closer to zero by the same proportion of their initial values; that is,

(23) $$[d\Pi, d\pi, d\Gamma, d\gamma] = [-b\Pi, -b\pi, -b\Gamma, -b\gamma]$$

where b is a small positive scalar. For this we have:

Proposition 1: *If $\alpha > 0$, a multilateral uniform proportionate reduction of all taxes and tariffs (in the sense of (23)) is strictly potentially Pareto-improving.*

Proof: Note first that for this reform

(24) $$\delta = b\Sigma.R.$$

This is derived by substituting from (23) into (20) and then using (1), (3) and the relationships between the components of the partitioned forms of S, E_{QQ} and G_{PP} implied by (9) to find

(25) $$\begin{aligned} -\delta_H/b = {} & \{E_{TT}.Q_T + E_{TN}.Q_N\} - S_{TN}(S_{NN})^{-1}\{E_{NN}.Q_N + E_{NT}.Q_T\} \\ & -\{G_{TT}.P_T + G_{TN}.P_N\} + S_{TN}(S_{NN})^{-1}\{G_{NN}.P_N + G_{NT}.P_T\} \\ & -\{S_{TT} - S_{TN}(S_{NN})^{-1}S_{NT}\}.R. \end{aligned}$$

By the homogeneity conditions in (6) and (8), the first four terms in (25) vanish. Arguing in the same way for δ_F, one arrives at (24).

Substituting from (24), the numerator of (21) is in this case

$$\text{Det}\left[-b\Sigma.R\left|\begin{matrix}\sigma'_{j1}\\ \Sigma^*\end{matrix}\right.\right] = -b.\text{Det}\left[\Sigma.R\left|\begin{matrix}\sigma'_{j1}\\ \Sigma^*\end{matrix}\right.\right]$$
$$= -b.\text{Det}\,(\Sigma),$$

the second equality reflecting the normalisation $R_1 = 1$ combined with the fact that the determinant of a matrix is unaffected by adding to any of its columns a linear combination of the others (see for example Hadley (1969), p. 94). Thus (21) becomes

$$dU = \frac{-b.\text{Det}\,(\Sigma)}{\alpha.\text{Det}\,(\Sigma^*)}.$$

Both Σ and Σ^* are negative definite, as noted earlier, but of orders T and $T-1$ respectively; their determinants are therefore of opposite sign. With b strictly positive by definition, it follows that $dU > 0$ if $\alpha > 0$. (Q.E.D.)

The limitations of this result should be emphasised: each country is required to reduce both taxes and tariffs, and they are required to do so by the same proportion.

It remains to consider the circumstances in which α will indeed be positive:

Proposition 2: *It is*

(a) Sufficient for $\alpha > 0$ that all goods be strictly normal in home demand and strict net substitutes in each country's compensated excess demand,

(b) Necessary and sufficient for $\alpha > 0$ that an increase in the world's endowment of commodity 1 be strictly potentially Pareto-improving.

Proof: (a) The first step is to note that if $B = [b_{ij}]$ is an $M \times M$ negative definite matrix with all off-diagonal elements strictly positive then $-B^{-1} > 0$ (*i.e.* all elements of $-B^{-1}$ are strictly positive). To see this, choose some $\mu > \max_k \{|b_{kk}|\}$ and define $A = \mu I_M + B$. It is easily shown that A is positive, indecomposable and (from the negative definiteness of B) that its dominant eigenvalue is strictly less than μ. Hence

$$(\mu I_M - A)^{-1} = -B^{-1} > 0$$

by the Frobenius-Perron theorem (as stated, for instance, in Theorem 64 of Heal, Hughes and Tarling (1974)).

With $E_U = [E_{1U}, E'_{JU}, E'_{NU}]' > 0$ by normality and $S_{TN} = [S'_{1N} | S'_{JN}]' > 0$ by substitutability, it therefore suffices (from (22) and since σ_{j1} consists of off-diagonal elements of Σ) to show that both S_{NN} and Σ are negative definite with positive off-diagonal elements. The first of these follows from substitutability and the rank assumptions. Negative definiteness of Σ is proved in the appendix[4]; recalling (19), positivity of its off-diagonal elements follows from that of S_{NT}, $-S_{NN}^{-1}$, the off-diagonal elements of S_{TT} and their foreign analogues.

(b) This requires a lengthy but routine comparative statics exercise, details of which are available from the author. (Q.E.D.)

The sufficient conditions in part (a) of this proposition are familiar from previous results on uniform tariff reduction, such as that of Fukushima (1979) for the small economy. Note too that

4) That proof rests on the maintained assumption that the initial equilibrium is distorted; see footnote 6) for the case in which it is not.

in the two good case of Hatta and Fukushima (1979) the substitutability condition is automatically satisfied (unless all substitution effects—and hence also the welfare cost of distortions—are zero). The necessary and sufficient conditions in part (b) provide a deeper interpretation of the requirement that α be strictly positive, showing that it serves precisely to rule out troublesome paradoxes of a kind well-known from the transfer literature.[5] For if $\alpha < 0$, in which case an increase in the world's endowment of the numeraire would actually reduce its welfare, then the very concept of a potentially improving reform would become problematic: even a tax/tariff reform that in itself lowered welfare in both countries could emerge as a potential improvement if these direct effects were to be offset by beneficially throwing away part of the world's endowment in the process of compensation. Such difficulties cannot arise at an undistorted equilibrium, since it is then straightforward to show that the positivity of α is implied by non-satiation.[6] But this observation—analogous to the general proposition on transfer paradoxes of Bhagwati, Brecher and Hatta (1985)—is of little comfort in the present context. In particular, it seems that in the many good case non-inferiority alone is not enough: α may fail to be positive, and apparent paradoxes arise, even if all goods are normal.

4. Concluding Remarks

There is no novelty of principle in the result proved here. In this respect the purpose has simply been to verify some natural conjectures. The analysis does though serve to highlight the comparatively neglected possibilities of trade distortion through internal taxation. As experience with the taxation of whisky in Japan illustrates, the gradual reduction of tariff barriers seems likely to mean that such effects will become as pronounced in other parts of the world—and the issues they raise as sensitive—as they currently are within Europe.

Appendix

The purpose here is to show that Σ, defined in (19), is negative definite. For this, begin by defining

$$\bar{S}_{TT} = S_{TT} - S_{TN}(S_{NN})^{-1}S_{NT}$$

and the foreign analogue $\bar{s}_{TT}$, so that $\Sigma = \bar{S}_{TT} + \bar{s}_{TT}$. Recalling the partitioned structure of S in (9), note that[7]

$$\bar{S}_{TT} = D'_H.S.D_H$$

where $D'_H = [I_T | -S_{TN}(S_{NN})^{-1}]$, and similarly for $\bar{s}_{TT}$. It follows from this and the negative semi-definiteness of S that Σ will be negative definite unless there exists some $x \neq 0_T$ such that $x.\bar{S}_{TT}.x = 0 = x.\bar{s}_{TT}.x$. Suppose, for a contradiction, that such an x exists. One would then have

5) See also Theorem 2 of Turunen-Red and Woodland (1988), which shows that the conditions of part (a) preclude the existence of Pareto-improving international transfers.

6) One then has $\alpha = E_U$. The proof of this is somewhat lengthy—and details are available from the author—but relies on the observations that $E_U = Q' \cdot E_{QU}$ (by linear homogeneity) and that, in the absence of distortions, $R^* + (\Sigma^*)^{-1}\sigma_{J1} = 0_{T-1}$.

7) This is Lemma 4 of Fukushima (1979).

(26) $S.y_H = 0_{T+N} = s.y_F$,

where $y_H = D_H.x$ and $y_F = D_F.x$ are both non-null. Since S is the sum of the negative semi-definite matrices E_{QQ} and $-G_{PP}$, the first of the equalities in (26) can hold only if $E_{QQ}.y_H = 0_T = G_{PP}.y_H$. By the homogeneity conditions in (5) and (7), the assumption that both E_{QQ} and G_{PP} have rank $T + N - 1$ then implies that y_H is collinear with both Q and P. From the normalisation, this in turn implies that $Q = P$. Applying the same argument to the second equality in (26) gives $q = p$. Since the first T elements of y_H and y_F are identical (being just x), it follows too that $P_T = p_T$. Thus all of the equalities in (15) are met, violating the assumption that the initial equilibrium is distorted.

(*University of Essex*)

REFERENCES

Bhagwati, J. N., R. A. Brecher and T. Hatta (1985) "The Generalized Theory of Transfers and Welfare: Exogenous (Policy-Imposed) and Endogenous (Transfer-Induced) Distortions," *Quarterly Journal of Economics*, Vol. 100, pp. 697–714.

Dhrymes, P. J. (1978) *Mathematics for Econometrics*, New York: Springer-Verlag.

Dixit, A. (1985) "Tax Policy in Open Economies," in A. Auerbach and M. S. Feldstein, eds., *Handbook of Public Economics*, Vol. 1, pp. 313–374, Amsterdam: North-Holland.

_______ and V. Norman (1980) *Theory of International Trade*, Cambridge, Mass.: Cambridge University Press.

Foster, E. and H. Sonnenschein (1970) "Price Distortion and Economic Welfare," *Econometrica*, Vol. 38, pp. 281–297.

Friedlander, A. F. and A. L. Vandendorpe (1968) "Excise Taxes and the Gains from Trade," *Journal of Political Economy*, Vol. 76, pp. 1058–1068.

Fukushima, T. (1979) "Tariff Structure, Nontraded Goods and Theory of Piecemeal Policy Recommendations," *International Economic Review*, Vol. 20, pp. 427–435.

_______ and N. Kim (1987) "Welfare Improving Tariff Changes: A Case of Many-Good and Many-Country," *mimeo*, State University of New York at Albany.

Hadley, G. (1969) *Linear Algebra*, Reading, Mass.: Addison-Wesley.

Hatta, T. and T. Fukushima (1979) "The Welfare Effect of Tariff Rate Reductions in a Many Country World," *Journal of International Economics*, Vol. 9, pp. 503–511.

Heal, G., G. Hughes and R. Tarling (1974) *Linear Algebra and Linear Economics*, London: Macmillan.

Keen, M. J. (1987) "Welfare Effects of Commodity Tax Harmonisation," *Journal of Public Economics*, Vol. 33, pp. 107–114.

_______ (1989) "Pareto-Improving Indirect Tax Harmonisation," *European Economic Review*, Vol. 33, pp. 1–12.

Kowalczyk, C. (1986) "Trade Distortions and World Welfare," *mimeo*, University of Rochester.

Turunen-Red, A. H. and A. D. Woodland (1988) "On the Multilateral Transfer Problem," *Journal of International Economics*, Vol. 25, pp. 249–269.

Part V
Coalitions, Welfare, and Trade Reform

[21]

THE PARTIAL FREEING OF TRADE: (2) DISCRIMINATORY AND PREFERENTIAL TARIFF REDUCTIONS

IN the preceding chapter we discussed the effect upon economic welfare of a unilateral non-discriminatory reduction in A's import duties when the rest of the world is made up not of one country but of a number of other countries, B, C, etc. In this chapter we wish to discuss the effect upon economic welfare of a unilateral discriminatory reduction in A's duties on, say, imports from B without a corresponding reduction in duties on imports from the rest of the world—which may be constituted either of a single third country C or of a number of other countries, C, D, E, etc. This analysis can, however, readily be extended to cover the case where A's discriminatory reduction in duties on imports from B is accompanied by a discriminatory reduction of B's duties on imports from A. In other words, the analysis can be applied to the problem of the formation of a preferential trading area or, in the extreme case, a full customs union between a limited number of trading countries.

In order to isolate certain particular issues for examination we shall make three basic assumptions in this chapter. First, we assume that the distributional weight attached by the policy-makers to the income of each citizen is the same for every citizen regardless of the country in which he resides or the source of his income. In other words, we shall be concerned with the problem of economic efficiency and not of economic equity; and we shall be looking at it from an international point of view and not from the point of view of the interests solely of the countries which give each other preferential treatment or of any other limited group of countries.

Second, we shall assume that within each country a policy of modified laissez-faire is successfully adopted so that there are no divergences between marginal social values and marginal social costs in the domestic trade of any country. This means that no marginal changes in domestic trade which are caused by any change in duties on international trade will add anything to, or subtract anything from, total economic welfare. Changes in domestic trade may be omitted from our calculus of gain and loss.

Third, we shall assume that there are taxes but no subsidies on various parts of the trade in products between the various countries. This means that anything which leads to an expansion of these elements of international trade will add to economic welfare, whereas anything which causes these elements of international trade to contract will reduce economic welfare.

Let us start with the simplest possible case of a three-country world in which the authorities in A make a small reduction in A's duties on certain imports from B without any change in the level of A's duties levied on imports from C. We want to know whether, on the three basic assumptions mentioned in the last paragraph, this is likely to lead to an increase or to a decrease in economic welfare.

The analysis which is necessary to answer this question is merely a particular application of the analysis which we have already carried out at great length in Chapter XIII. Accordingly in this chapter we shall not develop the analysis in great detail, but will merely refer to the ways in which the analysis may be applied in the present three-country case. As was pointed out in Chapter XIII, we may take it for granted that the reduction in the duty on A's imports of, say, blankets from B will cause a primary increase in economic welfare because it will increase the amount of blankets sent from B to A on which there is an excess of marginal value over marginal cost equal to the existing rate of tax on the trade. This primary gain will be the greater, (i) the greater is the expansion in the volume of trade caused by the reduction in the duty (i.e. the greater are the elasticities of A's demand for imported blankets and of B's supply of exported blankets), and (ii) the greater is the initial rate of duty on the trade and so the greater is the initial excess of marginal value over marginal cost in this trade.

But, as was argued in Chapter XIII, there may be important secondary repercussions on the flows of international trade resulting from the primary increase in the export of blankets from B to A. These possibilities may be enumerated under the following eight heads.

(1) A's imported blankets may compete very closely in A's markets with some other imports of A, in which case there will be some secondary reduction in A's imports of these competing products.

(2) A's imported blankets may be complementary in A's markets with some other imports of A, in which case there will be some secondary increase in A's imports of these complementary products.

(3) A's imported blankets may compete in A's markets with products which A exports, in which case there will be some secondary increase in the export of these products from A.

(4) A's imported blankets may be complementary in A's markets with products which A exports, in which case there will be some secondary reduction in the amount of these products which A exports.

(5) B's exported blankets may compete in B's markets with other products which B exports, in which case there will be some secondary reduction in B's exports of these other products.

(6) B's exported blankets may be complementary in B's markets

with other products which B exports, in which case there will be some secondary increase in B's exports of these other products.

(7) B's exported blankets may compete in B's markets with some products which B imports, in which case there will be some secondary increase in B's imports of these competing products.

(8) B's exported blankets may be complementary in B's markets with some products which B imports, in which case there will be some secondary decrease in B's imports of these complementary products.

Now there is only one formal difference between the analysis of the problem discussed in Chapter XIII and the analysis of the problem under discussion in this chapter. In the former case all the secondary repercussions on A's trade (items 1–4 above) were necessarily secondary repercussions on A's imports from B or on A's exports to B; but in the present case these secondary repercussions on A's trade may be secondary repercussions on A's imports from C as well as from B or on A's exports to C as well as to B. Similarly, the secondary repercussions on B's trade (items 5–8) may now fall upon B's import or export trade with C as well as upon her import or export trade with A. But the principle is exactly the same. We must add to the gain of economic welfare from the primary increase of trade any secondary gain due to a secondary increase in A's or B's import or export trade either with each other or with C and we must deduct any secondary loss due to a secondary decrease in A's or B's import or export trade either with each other or with C.

But the fact that we are now dealing with a reduction of a duty by A which applies to B's products and not to C's products may considerably affect the type of secondary repercussion which will in fact take place in A's and B's trade. If A imports, as she may well do, some of the product concerned from C as well as from B, then A's imports from C may be practically perfect substitutes for A's imports from B. If, then, A's authorities reduce a duty on imports of B's products without reducing the corresponding duty on the import of identical or very closely substitutable products from C, a large part of the effect of the tariff reduction will be merely to divert A's imports from purchase in C's to purchase in B's market. There would be a large element of secondary import trade destruction in A (item 1 in the list on p. 522).

Exactly similar considerations may be applied to B's exports. B may well export the same product to C as well as to A. The reduction in A's import duty on B's products without any corresponding reduction in C's import duty on B's product might well have a major effect in diverting B's exports away from sale in C's markets to sale in A's markets. In so far as this is likely to be the normal case it much increases the chance that the main secondary repercussion in B will be one of secondary export trade destruction (item 5 in the list on p. 522).

Now it is not possible to lay down any *a priori* principle on these matters. Each case needs special consideration to determine its probable secondary repercussions. It might be that a reduction in the United Kingdom's duty on French wines (all other duties, including duties on other wines, remaining constant) would have a marked effect by increasing the total supply of wine in the United Kingdom in shifting consumers in the United Kingdom away from the consumption of whiskey on to that of wine, thus releasing more whiskey for export from the United Kingdom to the United States. And it might at the same time be the case that in France the export of additional quantities of wine made wine scarcer in France and caused the French consumer to shift to the consumption of beer, thus stimulating the import of German beer into France. In this case the secondary gains from the United Kingdom's additional exports of whiskey (item 3) and from France's additional imports of beer (item 7 in the list on pp. 522–523) would have to be taken into account.

But a more probable and direct reaction might be that the lowered duty on French wines, while it caused some net increase in the consumption of wine in the United Kingdom, to a very large extent merely caused people to purchase French wines instead of, say, German wines. In France it may very well be that wines are sold to the United States as well as to the United Kingdom. A reduction in the duty in the United Kingdom market may induce the French wine merchants to increase their total export of wine to some extent; but a more marked effect may be that they now have an inducement to sell their wines in the United Kingdom rather than in the United States. In this case there might be a marked secondary loss of economic welfare due to the secondary decrease in the United Kingdom's imports of German wine (item 1) and the second decrease in France's exports of wine to the United States (item 5 on the list on p. 522).

Consider a three-country world made up of countries A, B, and C, in which A reduces a duty on blankets from B without reducing her duties on any other products. Then in order to get the extreme case of secondary import trade destruction which we have just examined we must assume that A imports blankets from C as well as from B. And in order to get the extreme case of secondary export trade destruction we must simultaneously assume that B exports blankets to C as well as to A. In this case C would be importing blankets from B and exporting them to A, which might appear improbable. Indeed, it would be an impossible situation if C were a single country with no problems of transport cost. But if we allow for the fact that C, the rest of the world, may stand for many countries or at least for many regions between which there are important and differing costs of transport, the proposition is not so unrealistic. Indeed, if the United Kingdom is an importer of wines it is most probable that she will import some from other countries (say, Germany) as well as from France; and if France is an exporter of wines, it is most probable that she will export them to other countries (such as the United States) as well as to the United Kingdom.

But this consideration does suggest one important way in which the secondary loss of economic welfare due to this secondary destruction of import trade in A and of export trade in B may itself in turn be mitigated by a series of secondary secondary repercussions. To revert to the particular example which we have just used, if the United Kingdom reduces discriminatorily a duty on French wines, this may divert United Kingdom imports away from German wines on to French wines; and it may divert French wine exports away from the United States to the United Kingdom market. But this leaves the United States citizens short of wine and the German wine merchants looking for markets for wine. The obvious result may be a secondary secondary stimulation of the export of wine from Germany to the United States.[1] We would then have:

(1) an increased sale of French wine to the United Kingdom;
(2) a decreased sale of German wine to the United Kingdom;
(3) a decreased sale of French wine to the United States; and
(4) an increased sale of German wine to the United States.

If all the trade flows are subject to duties, then there is a gain on elements 1 and 4 above and a loss on elements 2 and 3. The amount of gain and loss will depend upon the size of the change of trade in each of these four cases and upon the rate of divergence between marginal value and cost (i.e. the rate of duty levied) in each case. But it is quite clear that the change might lead to a net loss of economic welfare.

Let us take a case in which there is likely to be a large net loss of economic welfare. Suppose that there are no initial duties in the trade between Germany and the United States, which are merely different regions of one large pre-existing free-trade area—our single country C. Then there is no gain from any series of marginal increments in the trade between Germany and the United States, because there is no

[1] While this is the most probable form of the secondary secondary reaction it is by no means the only possible one. The United States might be exporting some commodity to Germany (say, beer) which both in Germany and the United States was a close substitute for wine. The shortage of wine in the United States might encourage the consumption of beer there and so reduce the United States exports of beer, and the glut of wine in Germany might discourage the consumption and import of beer there. In this case the secondary secondary repercussion might take the form of a *reduction* in the flow of beer from the United States to Germany instead of an *increased* flow of wine from Germany to the United States. If this were so and if the beer were subject to an export duty in the United States or an import duty in Germany, it would lead to a secondary secondary loss of economic welfare, since there would be a reduction of the trade in beer in which, because of the duty, the marginal value in Germany exceeded the marginal cost in the United States.

divergence between marginal costs and values in such trade. There is no gain from element 4 above. But suppose at the same time that the reduction in the United Kingdom's duty on French wine causes a little, but very little, expansion in the total export of French wines or in the total import of wine into the United Kingdom. It causes primarily a shift of United Kingdom imports from German to French wines and of French exports from the United States to the United Kingdom market. Then each of elements 2 and 3 above taken separately is almost as large as element 1. The secondary destruction of trade is almost twice as large as the primary creation of trade, since for each additional bottle of wine sent from France to the United Kingdom, one less is sent from France to the United States and one less from Germany to the United Kingdom. If the initial rates of duty, and so the rates of divergence between marginal values and costs, were the same on all these three channels of trade, the secondary loss of economic welfare would be almost twice as large as the primary gain.

But in other cases the discriminatory reduction of the United Kingdom's duty on French wines might well increase total economic welfare. This would be the case where there was quite a large increase in the total import of wine into the United Kingdom (because the reduced duty on imported French wine made it compete much better with home-made drinks in the United Kingdom) and quite a large increase in the total export of wine from France (because the reduced difficulty of selling in the United Kingdom market expanded the domestic production or restricted the domestic consumption of wine in France). In this case element 1 on p. 525 would be considerably greater than element 2 or 3 taken separately. Suppose at the same time that the reduced sale of French wine in the United States is almost entirely replaced by an increased sale of German wine in the United States (element 4 on p. 525 is almost as great as element 3), and that there are duties on the trade between the United States and Germany of about the same level as between the other countries. Then the gain from element 4 would almost offset the loss from element 3; and the gain from element 1 would be much greater than the loss from element 2. There might be a substantial net gain.[1]

[1] In order to make a complete account of the effects of the reduction of a particular duty by one country upon economic welfare, one ought properly to take into account the tertiary changes in the flows of trade. It is almost certain that the combined primary and secondary changes will leave some countries with a deficit and some with a surplus on the balance of payments. The deficit countries will then have to reduce their money prices, costs, and incomes relatively to those of the surplus countries either by a depreciation of the exchange value of the currencies of the deficit countries in terms of those of the surplus countries or by an internal deflation in the deficit and inflation in the surplus countries. This will expand the exports and contract the imports of the deficit countries. Allowance should be made for the effect of these adjustments on economic welfare, since to the extent that the trade is taxed and therefore

All this analysis can be applied very directly to the case of a mutual preferential reduction of duties on the trade between the members of a limited group of countries. Suppose that the authorities of countries A, B, and C all agree to reduce their import duties on each other's products without any reduction of the duties which they levy on imports from outside countries D, E, and F. Is such an arrangement likely to lead to a net improvement or a net worsening of world economic efficiency? The following is a list of the considerations which will determine the answer to this question.

(1) First, there is more likely to be a net increase in economic welfare if the initial rates of duty (and so the initial excesses of marginal values over marginal costs) were high in the case of the trade between A, B, and C which is now allowed to flow with greater freedom.

(2) Second, there is more likely to be a net increase in economic welfare if the elasticities of the demands for the imports on which the duties are reduced are very high in each of the members of the preferential group, A, B, and C, provided that these high elasticities of demand for imports are due to the fact that these imports compete closely with other home-produced products in these member countries, A, B, and C. In such a case there is likely to be a relatively large expansion in the volume of trade in these commodities between the member countries A, B, and C without anything like so large a diversion of imports into A, B, and C away from purchases in the outside world on to purchases from within the preferential area. But if the elasticities of demands for imports of the products on which the duties are reduced are high in the member countries A, B, and C simply because they compete largely with similar imports from outside countries D, E, and F, then the large primary expansion of the trade between A, B, and C will be offset by an almost equally large secondary reduction in imports into A, B, and C from D, E, and F.

(3) Third, in a similar way there is more likely to be a net increase in economic welfare if in the case of the products on which the duties are reduced the elasticities of supply of exports from countries A, B, and C to each other are high, provided that this is due to the fact that these products compete with other lines of home production in A, B,

---

subject to an excess of marginal value over marginal cost the expansion of the exports of the deficit countries will increase economic welfare and the contraction of the exports of the deficit countries will reduce economic welfare. But there is no reason to believe that these tertiary adjustments will have a very significant effect upon economic welfare unless there is special reason to think *either* (i) that in the adjustment of the balances of payments the expansion of the exports of the deficit countries will be of a different order of magnitude than the contraction of their imports, *or else* (ii) that the rates of duty and so the rates of divergence between marginal values and costs which apply to the exports of the deficit countries are very different from the rates which apply to their imports. (See Chapter XIII, pp. 218–223.)

and C and not merely to the fact that they can now be sold in smaller volume in the other export markets of D, E, and F.

(4) Fourth, there is more likely to be a net increase in economic welfare if the rates of duty (and so the excess of marginal values over marginal costs) are low in the case of the trade between A, B, or C on the one hand and D, E, or F on the other hand in the products on which A, B, and C have reduced their duties to each other. For, as we have seen, there is in the case of these products likely to be some diversion of imports to A, B, and C away from sources of supply in D, E, and F on to sources of supply within A, B, and C; and there is likely to be some diversion of exports from A, B, and C away from sales to D, E, and F towards sales within A, B, and C. On this diverted trade there will be a loss of welfare; but the loss will be the smaller, the smaller is the rate of duty and so the excess of marginal value over marginal cost in this trade.

(5) There is more likely to be a net increase in economic welfare if each member of the preferential group, A, B, C, reduces its duties on the import of those products of which the other members of the group are its principal suppliers and/or for which it provides the principal outlet for the exports of the other members. In this case there will be only a small amount of trade between A, B, and C on the one hand and D, E, and F on the other which is capable of being directly diverted from the preferential tariff reductions within A, B, and C.

(6) There is more likely to be a net increase in economic welfare if the elasticity of demand for imports in D, E, and F and the elasticity of supply of exports from D, E, and F is low in the case of those products on which A, B, and C reduce their duties on a preferential basis. An inelasticity of the supply of exports or of the demand for imports of these products in D, E, and F will mean that there is not so great a reduction in the amount of the trade in the products between A, B, C on the one hand and D, E, F on the other. There will thus be less loss from secondary trade destruction.

(7) There is more likely to be a net increase in economic welfare if the rates of duty are high on the trade between D, E, and F in the case of those products on which A, B, and C grant each other preferential reductions of duty. For, as we have seen (p. 525), any secondary reduction in the trade in these products between A, B, C on the one hand and D, E, F on the other is likely to cause a secondary secondary increase in the trade in these products between D, E, and F. The higher are the rates of duty on this trade (i.e. the greater the excess of marginal values over marginal costs in this trade), the greater the contribution to economic welfare caused by any given stimulation of this trade.

The arguments which are developed in the preceding paragraphs strictly apply only to the effects of small marginal changes in rates of duty. If the seven conditions listed above are favourable, this means that, given the initial rates of all duties and the other relevant circumstances, a small marginal reduction of the duties under examination would increase rather than decrease economic welfare. But the analysis can be extended to cover the case of large structural changes in trade taxes.

Let us consider the most extreme example of this, namely the formation of a complete customs union between our countries A, B, and C. Starting from a given structure of duties, including substantial duties on the trade between A, B, and C, these three countries decide totally to remove all duties on the trade between themselves without altering at all the duties levied on imports from other countries, D, E, and F.[1]

This large change in the structure of their import duties can be examined as if it took place by a number of successive small changes. Suppose A, B, and C all had duties initially of 100 per cent on all the products which they imported from each other. They then abolish these duties, all other duties remaining unchanged. The effect of this on economic welfare can be regarded as the sum of the effects of 100 successive marginal adjustments, in the first of which all these duties were reduced from 100 to 99 per cent, in the second of which they were reduced from 99 to 98 per cent, and so on until the duties have disappeared.

Now if the seven conditions mentioned on pp. 527–528 are initially favourable, then the early stages in this successive reduction in the duties on trade between A, B, and C will add to economic welfare; and if the seven conditions remain favourable throughout the process of removal of the duties, the final full customs union will increase economic welfare. Conversely the seven conditions may be initially unfavourable and may remain unfavourable throughout the successive stages of reductions of duties by A, B, and C. In such a case the formation of the customs union clearly reduces economic welfare.

[1] The arrangement described in the text might perhaps be more appropriately described as a 'free-trade area' rather than as a 'customs union', since A, B, and C are not assumed to have drawn up a common tariff schedule for their imports from the outside countries, D, E, and F. The free-trade area has its own peculiar administrative problems. Thus suppose that initially A has a 50 per cent and B only a 10 per cent duty on imports of, say, drugs, which are a principal export of D. If A and B remove all duties on trade between themselves and leave their duties on imports from D unchanged, then drugs could be imported into B for a 10 per cent duty and from B to A without duty. Unless transport costs were heavy, there would be a strong tendency for importers of drugs in A to purchase them from D *via* B and thus pay an import duty of only 10 per cent instead of 50 per cent on them. Unless further steps are taken or unless transport costs are heavy for these indirect flows of trade, the formation of a free-trade area would tend in effect to reduce the effective rates of duty on imports into the area from outside to the lowest import duty imposed by an individual member of the area on the import of that class of product. This sort of difficulty means that in fact the rules of the free-trade area would not be able to extend the free movement of trade to all products moving between the member countries, but would have to confine it to the free movement between the member countries of products which had been manufactured in those countries.

But there are two rather more complicated cases. First, it might be that initially the seven conditions were unfavourable, so that the early stages of tariff reductions reduced economic welfare; but it is possible that in the later stages the conditions would be favourable, so that the later stages would raise economic welfare again. Now whether or not the formation of a complete customs union would cause a net rise or a net fall in economic welfare in this case would clearly depend upon whether the improvement in economic welfare during the last stages of tariff reduction outweighed the deterioration in economic welfare during the first stages of the process. Second, it is possible that the early stages of tariff reduction would lead to some rise in economic welfare while the later stages would lead to some fall. In this case, to judge the desirability of the complete customs union, one would have to balance the gain from the early stages of tariff reduction against the loss from the later stages.

Now there is very good reason for believing that the first of these two cases is a most improbable one, whereas the second is a very likely case. The reason for this is simple. The reduction of duties on the trade between A, B, and C will cause a direct primary increase in that trade. On this there is a gain in economic welfare. But this primary gain depends upon two factors—the amount of the increase in the trade which is caused by the tariff reduction and the rate of excess of marginal value over marginal cost (i.e. the *ad valorem* rate of duty) on that trade. Now the further we have gone through the stages of reduction of duties on the trade between A, B, and C, the lower will be the existing *ad valorem* rates of duty and so the excesses of marginal value over marginal cost in respect of the primary trade created by further tariff reductions. But there is no such reason why in the later stages of the process any secondary loss should be lower than in the early stages. A secondary loss may result, as we have seen, because A, B, and C may divert their import demands away from the products of D, E, and F when the duties on purchasing among themselves are reduced and may divert their exports away from D, E, and F's markets on to each other's markets when entry into their own markets is made easier. The loss on this diversion of trade in turn depends upon two things—the volume of trade so diverted and the rate of excess of marginal value over marginal cost in respect of the trade. This rate of excess is equal to the *ad valorem* rate of import and export duties in A, B, and C on the one hand and in D, E, and F on the other hand on the trade between these two groups. But *ex hypothesi* these rates are unchanged. Thus as the stages of tariff reduction proceed the gain of economic welfare on any given amount of primary trade creation becomes smaller and smaller, while the loss of economic welfare on any given amount of secondary trade destruction remains unchanged. There is thus very good reason to believe that the earliest stages of the process of tariff reductions in the direction of a customs union will be much more useful in raising (or much less pernicious in reducing) economic welfare than the later stages. A very normal outcome may be that the first stages in the process raise, while the last stages in the process lower, economic welfare.

A very simple illustration may help to make this argument clear, though the reader is asked to remember that the argument is of much wider scope than the following example, which takes a very special simple case merely to illustrate the principle.

Suppose (i) that the United Kingdom is the only consumer of wines, (ii) the consumption of wine in the United Kingdom is quite inelastic so that the total amount consumed is fixed, (iii) the United Kingdom, France, and Germany all produce identically the same wines under conditions of increasing cost, and (iv) that the United Kingdom protects her wine-producing industry by means of a 100 per cent *ad valorem* duty on imports from France and Germany. The United Kingdom then by a process of successive small reductions removes the duty on wines imported from France without altering the duty on wines imported from Germany. It will be noted that we have set a problem in which the gain in economic welfare can be simply measured by the reduction in the cost of producing a given fixed world output of wine. Moreover, we have only to consider two elements: (i) the primary gain due to the fact that French wine production may expand at the expense of the United Kingdom production, which at the margin will be more costly than the French by the amount of the duty on imports of French wines into the United Kingdom; and (ii) the secondary loss due to the fact that the French wine production may expand at the expense of the German, which at the margin will be cheaper to produce than the French by the excess of the United Kingdom duty on German wine over the United Kingdom duty on French wine.

Suppose that the conditions of supply (the elasticities of supply) of wine in Germany and the United Kingdom are such that when the French wine producers are enabled by the reduction of the duty to replace German and United Kingdom producers in the United Kingdom market, the German and United Kingdom production is reduced by the same amount. In other words, when the French put two more bottles on the market the Germans and the United Kingdom producers each put on one less.

Consider now the starting point for the United Kingdom's preferential tariff reduction in favour of France. If United Kingdom production of wine at the margin costs \$100, the French and German production at the margin will cost \$50 in both cases, since \$50 with a 100 per cent *ad valorem* import duty is just equal to the marginal cost of $100 of the domestic wine in the United Kingdom. If now a small reduction in duty enables France to produce two more bottles, one at the expense of German and one at the expense of United Kingdom production, there will be a net saving of cost. One bottle will be produced in France at $50 instead of in the United Kingdom at $100, and on this there is a saving of $50 of cost. The other bottle will be produced in France at $50 instead of in Germany at $50 and on this there is no gain or loss. At the starting point there is therefore pure gain offset by no loss. This is illustrated in row 1 of Table XXXVI.

Suppose now that the United Kingdom duty on French wine has already been reduced to 50 per cent, the duty on German wine remaining at 100 per cent. The production of wine in the United Kingdom and Germany will have been restricted at the expense of an expansion of French production; the marginal cost will have fallen in the United Kingdom and Germany and will have risen in France. These changes in marginal costs must be such that the marginal costs in the United Kingdom must still be 100 per cent higher than in Germany (since there is still a 100 per cent duty on the import of German wine) and they must now be 50 per cent higher than in France (since there is now a 50 per cent duty on the import of French wine). Row 2 of Table XXXVI gives a possible example where the price of wine in the United Kingdom (owing to increased French competition) has fallen to $90 with the marginal cost in Germany having fallen to $45 and in France having risen to $60. Now a further small reduction of duty would still increase economic welfare. If such a reduction enabled two more bottles to be produced in France, one at the expense of United Kingdom and the other at the expense of German production, there would be a saving of cost of $30 on the bottle which was produced in France at a cost of $60 instead of in the United Kingdom at a cost of $90, and against this it would be necessary to set a loss of only $15 on the bottle which was produced in France at $60 instead of in Germany at $45.

Row 3, however, shows a case where the duty on French wine has already been reduced so far (namely to 10 per cent) that any further reduction in it would cause a net loss of economic welfare. The price and marginal cost in the United Kingdom has now fallen to $77 because of the increased competition of French wines; the price and cost in Germany has fallen to $38·5 (since $38·5 plus a duty of 100 per cent is equal to the United Kingdom price of $77); and the price and marginal cost in France has risen to $70 (since $70 plus a duty of 10 per cent is equal to the United Kingdom price of $77). If now a further reduction of the duty on French wines enabled the French to produce two more bottles, one at the expense of the United Kingdom and one at the expense of Germany, there would be a net increase in the total

TABLE XXXVI

A Discriminatory Tariff Reduction

	Ad valorem rate of duty imposed in the United Kingdom on imports of wine from		Domestic price and marginal cost of wine in		
	Germany	France	United Kingdom	Germany	France
	%	%	$	$	$
(1)	100	100	100	50	50
(2)	100	50	90	45	60
(3)	100	10	77	38·5	70
(4)	100	0	75	37·5	75

cost of producing the given output of wine. One more would be produced at $70 in France instead of at $77 in the United Kingdom, a saving of $7; but one more would also be produced in France at $70 instead of in Germany at $38·5, an increase in cost of $31·5. The use of the world's resources would be made less economic by reason of the tariff reduction.

Row 4 of the table simply shows how when the duty on French wines has been wholly removed, there must be a net gain in raising it somewhat again. The price in the United Kingdom is now $75; it must therefore be $37·5 in Germany (on whose wines there is a 100 per cent duty) and $75 in France as well as in the United Kingdom. If the final small reduction in duty to zero increased French output by two bottles at the expense of one bottle in the United Kingdom and one bottle in Germany, then it caused a pure loss offset by no gain. One bottle was produced in France at $75 instead of in the United Kingdom at $75, i.e. without gain or loss; but one bottle was produced in France at $75 instead of in Germany at $37·5, a loss of $37·5.

These considerations suggest that there is more likely to be a case for a partial reduction rather than for a complete elimination of duties on a preferential basis, provided, of course, that in neither case are rates of duties raised against the trade with outsiders when the preferential reductions of duties are made among the member countries. There is, however, one way in which this argument for a system of partial preferences rather than for a full customs union may need to be modified. It has been pointed out [1] that when countries form a full customs union they must automatically reduce all duties on all trade with their partners to zero, whereas in the formation of a partial preferential group they can pick and choose the products on which they will make the tariff reductions as well as the extent to which they will reduce each duty. Now the example which we have just used of the import of German and French wines into the United Kingdom will help to show the distinction between a preferential tariff reduction which is in effect primarily a protective device (which may, therefore, be expected to reduce economic efficiency) and one which is primarily a movement towards free trade (which may be expected to raise economic efficiency). If the main effect of the reduction of the duty in the United Kingdom on French wines is to enable the French producers to undercut the previously protected producers in the United Kingdom, then the reduction of duty will be a significant move towards the most efficient free-trade position in which the low-cost French producers would largely replace the high-cost producers in the United Kingdom. But if the main effect of the reduction in the United Kingdom duty was to enable the French producers who enjoyed the preferential treatment in the United Kingdom to undercut the German producers who did not enjoy this preference, then the preferential tariff reduction would represent in the main a method of protecting the relatively high-cost French industry against competition from the relatively low-cost German industry in the United Kingdom market. Suppose that in return for such a preferential treatment of French wines in the United Kingdom market, the French government agrees to reduce a duty preferentially on some particular United Kingdom product which competes in the French market with similar German products rather than with French products. Then the mutual preferential arrangement between France and the United Kingdom would be essentially an arrangement for increasing the protection of certain industries in the two countries against German competition.

The argument on pp. 531–533 must, therefore, not be taken to represent a straightforward argument in favour of partial preferential arrangements as opposed to a customs union. The argument is more limited in scope. It states merely that if there is a choice between (*a*) a partial preferential reduction of certain duties, and (*b*) the total removal of those same duties on the same discriminatory basis as between countries, then there is a greater chance that course *a* will raise economic welfare than course *b*.[2]

[1] Professor Jacob Viner, *The Customs Union Issue* (New York, Carnegie Endowment for International Peace, 1950), pp. 50–1.

[2] Note that the argument does not maintain that course *a* will do more good than course *b*. On the contrary, circumstances can be imagined in which the

It is of some interest to examine a little more thoroughly this choice of products on which countries might give each other preferential tariff reductions. The first point to note is that any preferential tariff reduction which causes a secondary destruction of trade with outside countries is likely to help to turn the terms of trade in favour of the countries forming the preferential group. Thus suppose that when the United Kingdom reduces a duty on French wines there is a substantial reduction in the United Kingdom's demand for German wines (secondary import trade destruction in the United Kingdom). The reduced demand for German wines will probably cause some reduction in the price at which such wines are sold to the United Kingdom and there will thus be some movement in the terms of trade of the Anglo-French area with Germany. Or suppose that when the United Kingdom reduces its duty on French wines there is a substantial reduction in the amount of wine which the French producers are prepared to continue to send to the United States (secondary export trade destruction in France). The reduced supply of French wines in the United States will probably cause some rise in the price which can be charged for them in that market, and there is thus likely to be some improvement in the terms on which the Anglo-French area can trade with the United States. And conversely any secondary repercussions of a preferential tariff arrangement which caused the members to increase either their demand for imports from the outside world or their exports to the outside world would be liable either to raise the price of what they bought from the outside world or else to lower the price of what they sold to the outside world, and thus to cause a deterioration in their terms of trade with the outside world.

But while trade destruction, whether it be of imports or of exports, is likely to move the terms of trade in favour of the members of the preferential area, secondary import trade destruction and secondary export trade destruction may have very different effects upon the balance of payments of the countries forming the preferential area. Thus, suppose that as a result of a preferential reduction of a duty on French wines the United Kingdom reduces its imports of German wines significantly (secondary import trade destruction). Then the amount spent by the United Kingdom on imports of German products will be reduced, and to this extent there will be an improvement in the balance of payments of the Anglo-French area with the outside world. But suppose that the reduction in the United Kingdom duty on French wines causes the French wine exporters to sell significantly less in the United States

later stages of tariff reduction as well as the earlier stages will raise economic welfare. In this case course *b* will do more good than course *a*. But what is true is that the early stages of preferential tariff reduction are likely to do more good (or less harm) than the later stages.

(secondary export trade destruction). Then, provided that the elasticity of demand for imports of French wines in the United States is greater than unity, the value of French exports to the United States will go down, and the balance of payments of the Anglo-French area with the rest of the world will deteriorate.[1]

If, therefore, a group of countries wish to form a preferential area for the purpose of extending the protection of their own domestic industries, they are most likely to select for preferential tariff reductions those imports from each other of which important supplies are simultaneously imported from the outside world. This is likely to protect the industries of the area from the outside competition of these products, to induce the outside world to trade these products on terms which are more favourable to the members of the preferential area, and by reducing the total expenditure on imports from the outside world to improve the balance of trade of the preferential area with the outside world.

The formation of a preferential area or a full customs union between A, B, and C may therefore turn the terms of trade favourably to ABC and against the outside countries DEF by reducing the demand in ABC for the products of DEF or by reducing the supply in DEF for the products of ABC. But there is a second way in which the formation of a preferential arrangement between A, B, and C—particularly if it takes the form of a full customs union—may improve the terms of trade of ABC; it is likely to increase the bargaining power in trade negotiations of the members of the preferential area with outside countries. Thus, consider the possibility of one member of the area, say A, obtaining a trade concession from an outside country, say D, before the formation of the customs union between A, B, and C. The authorities in A may threaten to raise an import duty on some export of D to A unless the authorities in D grant some concession to A's trade with D. This threat may be of little importance if D can find alternative markets for her exports in other countries. Now if B and C are important alternative markets for D's exports, a joint threat by A, B, and C that the whole ABC customs union will raise its import duty on D's exports unless D makes some concession would clearly be of very much greater weight than a similar threat by A alone.

Similarly with A's exports to D. The authorities in A might threaten D with the imposition of a duty on A's exports to D unless the authorities in D granted some concession on A's trade with D. Even if the export in question is a product which it is essential for D to import, the threat may not be a very grave one if D can import it from other sources

[1] If the elasticity of demand for imports of French wines in the United States is less than unity, then the United States will pay a greater total amount of money for a smaller quantity of imports. In this case secondary export trade destruction will also improve the balance of trade of the preferential area with the outside world.

of supply. Now if B and C were important alternative sources of supply of the import for D, then a threat by the combined customs union ABC to impose a tax on the export of the product in question to D would be a much more serious matter for D and would be much more likely than a threat by A alone to wring some trade concession out of D.

Thus by increasing the bargaining power of the independent constituent members, the formation of a customs union may be the means of inducing outside countries to reduce duties on imports from the constituent members of the customs union (thus raising the price available for their products in the outside world) or to reduce duties on exports of the outside world to the constituent members of the customs union (thus lowering the price payable by them for imports from the outside world).

Moreover, the governments of A, B, and C in combination need have much less hesitation than any one of them alone in raising a duty on imports from D. If A raised a duty on imports from D, exporters in D would be free to sell the products to B and C instead. But if A, B, and C simultaneously raise a duty on the same product, D's alternative markets are much more restricted and there is therefore a much greater chance that D's exporters will have to cut the price at which they sell the product to A, B, and C. Similarly, if A alone imposed an export duty on a product sold to D, D could purchase from B or C instead. But if A, B, and C simultaneously tax the export of this product to D, it is much less easy for D to obtain alternative supplies, and it is, therefore, more probable that importers in D will have to be willing to pay a higher price for imports of the products.

In all these ways the formation of a full customs union between A, B, and C, by enabling them to carry out a single joint commercial policy *vis-à-vis* the rest of the world, is likely to enable them to turn the terms of trade with the rest of the world in their favour. Thus the formation of a preferential area or of a full customs union is likely to do something to redistribute income away from the rest of the world and in favour of the citizens of the preferential area, first, simply by reason of the secondary import or export trade destruction which it may occasion even if the duties levied on trade with outsiders remain unchanged and, second, by increasing the bargaining power of the area *vis-à-vis* the rest of the world so that it can more freely raise its own duties on trade with the outside world and can induce outsiders to reduce their duties on their trade with the area.[1] Whether or not this redistribution in favour

[1] The increased bargaining power of the preferential area will improve the area's terms of trade whether it results in an increase in the duties levied by the area on its trade with outsiders or in a decrease in the duties levied by outsiders on their trade with the area. But from the point of view of efficiency as opposed to equity the two results will, of course, be very different. The former result will raise duties and restrict trade between the area and the outside world; the

of the citizens of the preferential area is to be counted as increasing or decreasing economic welfare will depend upon whether a higher distributional weight should be allotted to the citizens of the preferential area or to those of the outside world.

---

latter result will lower duties and expand trade. They will have opposite effects upon efficiency, there being a strong presumption that the former will reduce and the latter will raise world economic efficiency.

[22]

WELFARE AND INTEGRATION*

By Carsten Kowalczyk[1]

Tufts University, U.S.A.

This article argues that the terms-of-trade and volume-of-trade taxonomy from the theory of tariffs constitutes an attractive alternative to Viner's trade diversion and creation effects for the analysis of preferential trading arrangements. In applications of the alternative approach, the article establishes that results by Lipsey and Riezman on large versus small preunion trade flows for choice of partners are not "contradictory" and that under some conditions a small country's optimal strategy is to seek membership of multiple free-trade areas.

1. INTRODUCTION

As international integration redraws the map, the fundamental questions of coalition formation are as important as ever: Who collude, and how? And how does the formation or expansion of coalitions affect the welfare of individual countries, whether members or outsiders, of groups of them, and of the global trading community?

One of the oldest literatures in economics on coalition formation considers the customs union, a group of countries agreeing on internal free trade while setting common tariffs on trade with nonmember nations.[2] This literature is voluminous and indeed has grown in recent years. Yet it still contains a relatively small number of results, and analyses are cast in a language that is not shared with any other branch of economics.[3] The contention of this article remains, therefore, the same as when it appeared in 1990 as an NBER working paper, namely, that the ability to analyze these issues, and hence provide answers, is hampered by difficulties with the standard analytical approach used for this problem.

A seminal contribution to the integration literature is Viner's (1950) *The Customs Union Issue*, in which he proposed that the formation of a customs union involves

* Manuscript received November 1996; revised August 1998.

[1] This paper was previously entitled "Welfare and Customs Unions." I thank anonymous referees for comments. I am grateful also to Leonard Cheng, Patrick Conway, James Dana, Jr., Ronald Jones, Prakash Loungani, and Raymond Riezman for discussions of earlier drafts.

[2] The following analysis applies not only to customs unions but also, more generally, to preferential trading arrangements, including free-trade areas, which are defined by free internal trade with individual tariffs on nonmember trade. It applies also to the reverse process of economic disintegration.

[3] Corden (1984), Pomfret (1986), and Kowalczyk (1990) survey the literature on customs unions under perfect competition. Baldwin and Venables (1995) stress imperfect competition and scale effects. Lawrence (1996) and Frankel (1997) contain extensive references to the literature.

two fundamental effects: a change in location of production of imports from a lower-cost nonmember country to a higher-cost member country and a change in location of production from higher-cost domestic producers to lower-cost producers in the member country. Viner claimed that the former effect, which he labeled "trade diversion," reduces welfare, and that the latter effect, which he called "trade creation," raises welfare. Viner argued that trade diversion can exceed trade creation and that the formation of a customs union, which represents a liberalization of international trade, therefore in paradoxical fashion may reduce world welfare. With this result Viner anticipated the later work by Lipsey and Lancaster (1956) on the second best.

While Viner's insight that a customs union may reduce welfare is of vast theoretical and practical significance, there are, unfortunately, some difficulties with his methodologic approach. First, and as pointed out by Gehrels (1956) and Lipsey (1957), trade diversion need not reduce welfare. Second, Viner's terminology is not exhaustive, since effects that cannot be characterized as either trade diversion or creation can occur, even in a simple competitive setting. Finally, and in part because of these reasons, it is difficult to conduct empirical research based on Viner's approach. Despite these difficulties, Viner's concepts have remained the pliers with which theorists and empirical researchers have attempted to solve the customs union problem.

This article argues that the theory of tariffs and their reform offers an attractive alternative approach to the analysis of integration. I present my argument by reviewing, in Section 2, Viner's approach and by demonstrating, in Section 3, how the alternative approach, that of terms-of-trade and volume-of-trade effects, immediately resolves two outstanding difficulties in integration theory: an apparent contradiction between results by Lipsey (1957) and Riezman (1979) and what is the best trade policy strategy of a small country in a world of many free-trade areas. Section 4 concludes that since forming customs unions is nothing but a particular type of multicountry tariff reform, it would be surprising if the analysis of customs unions should have its own language in the first place.

2. TRADE DIVERSION AND CREATION AND AN ALTERNATIVE CALCULUS

Consider Figure 1, and suppose that there are two goods, 1 and 2, and three countries, a, b, and c. Suppose, further, that country a specializes in the production of its export good 1 and that it purchases good 2 from country b at $(p^e)_2^b$ or from country c at $(p^e)_2^c$, where both prices are expressed in units of good 1. Assume that costs are such that $(p^e)_2^c$ exceeds $(p^e)_2^b$. If country a initially applies a nondiscriminatory tariff, then it trades exclusively with country b to point A. If countries a and c then form a customs union, and if country a's tariff reduction on imports from country c is sufficient to overcome the cost differential between countries b and c, then country a will obtain its imports from country c. Point C illustrates country a's trade flows after forming this customs union.

A comparison of points A and C raises three issues, each of which illustrates an important difficulty with the trade diversion and trade creation approach. First, and as demonstrated originally by Gehrels (1956) and Lipsey (1957), trade diversion need

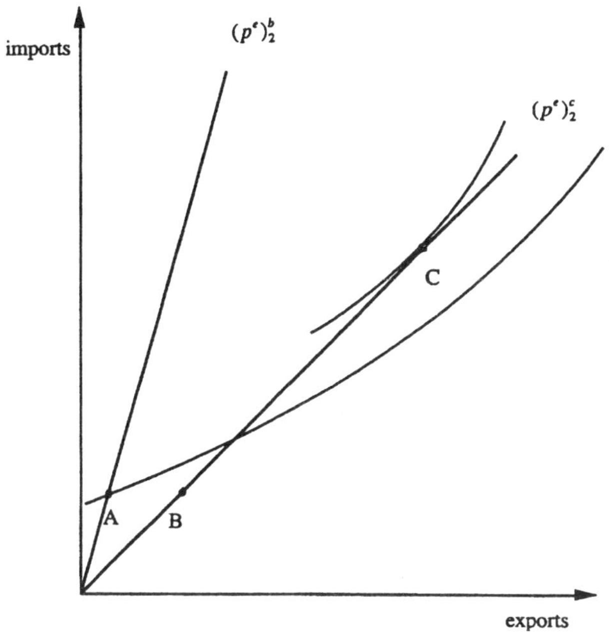

FIGURE 1

not reduce welfare. Country a was assumed to specialize in production both before and after joining the customs union; thus no trade creation has taken place. However, since country a has switched to a more expensive supplier of its imports, it has experienced trade diversion, and yet point C supports a higher-valued trade indifference curve than does point A. Hence a trade-diverting customs union can raise welfare.[4]

Second, in a setting with more countries and more goods than in Figure 1, the trade diversion and trade creation terminology will not, in general, be exhaustive. For example, the formation of a customs union could raise rather than lower demand for certain imports from the rest of the world due to complementarity between such goods and increased intraunion trade or as higher income of the union members raises demand for normal goods.[5] Such effects are neither trade diversion nor trade creation as defined by Viner. Nor do Viner's terms incorporate the possible effects from changes in world prices of goods traded with the rest of the world due to the formation of the union. In other words, use of trade diversion and

[4] Bhagwati (1971, 1973), Kirman (1973), and Michaely (1976) offered interpretations of what Viner "really had in mind." Kemp (1969) equated trade diversion and trade creation with reduced and increased trade volumes, respectively, and Collier (1979) introduced several consumption and production effects. None of these interpretations or amendments has gained general acceptance.

[5] Such possibilities are considered in Kowalczyk and Wonnacott (1992).

trade creation requires the introduction of additional concepts to describe effects not captured by Viner's terminology.[6]

Third and finally, since the formation of a customs union has the potential for causing changes that have opposing effects on welfare, the welfare consequences for a country joining a particular preferential trading arrangement would depend on the magnitudes of these effects and would hence become an empirical issue.[7] A direct measure of the shift from A to C in Figure 1, i.e., of trade diversion, apparently could be obtained by a simple comparison of the corresponding trade volumes. However, it is possible to envision an alternative Figure 1 that leaves everything as drawn except that the trade indifference curve through point A never intersects $(p^e)_2^c$. The changes in country a's trade flows between points A and C would be the same as in the authentic Figure 1, but country a's welfare would fall. Determining trade diversion empirically by estimating changes in trade volumes without considering price effects could thus lead to erroneous welfare conclusions.[8] Add to this that the terminology is not exhaustive, and it follows that Viner's approach does not present a complete menu of effects to be estimated, even for the simplest competitive environments. These difficulties make it a puzzle why Viner's terminology has remained in such wide use.

Points A and C lead us to the alternative strategy. Thus the shift from A to C can be decomposed into a move from A to B, which is welfare-worsening because it captures the effect from a higher import price due to the change of trade partners, and a move from B to C, which is welfare-improving because of increased imports of a good that commands a higher domestic price in country a than the price at which it can be obtained in world markets. These are examples of the terms-of-trade and volume-of-trade effects from the theory of tariffs that I will demonstrate constitute a useful alternative approach to Viner's for analysis of customs unions.[9]

Consider a country k inhabited by price-taking consumers and firms operating under constant returns to scale. Assuming balanced trade in up to N goods, the change in country k's real income $d\eta^k$, as measured in units of a numeraire good, is given by

$$d\eta^k = -m^k dp^e + (p^k - p^e)\, dm^k \tag{1}$$

[6] Meade (1955b, p. 34) recognized this problem: "[Viner's] analysis is in my opinion in some respects incomplete; and when an attempt is made to complete it, it no longer remains as simple in its application as may at first sight appear to be the case." Johnson's (1960) discussion is a case in point. Besides trade diversion and trade creation, he adds, as basic terms, trade expansion, changes in producers' and consumers' surplus, changes in tariff revenue, terms-of-trade effects, and cost-differential effects. Not surprisingly, this quickly becomes unwieldy.

[7] Of course, the effects need not be opposing. They could be mutually reinforcing instead.

[8] Indeed, the following discussion will reveal that estimates of changes in trade volume must be supplemented with estimates of price effects to have meaningful welfare implications.

[9] The terminology originates with Meade (1955a) and was analyzed by Jones (1969). Dixit and Norman (1980) and Bond (1990), among others, derive Equation (1) for a nation trading many goods. Ohyama (1972) and Grinols and Wong (1991) derive the corresponding expression for finite rather than infinitesimal changes. The weights differ, and the expression contains additional (nonnegative) terms for substitution in consumption and production.

where m^k is a column vector with N elements listing country k's net imports, p^e denotes the N-element column vector of tariff-exclusive prices at which country k trades internationally, p^k is the N-element column vector of domestic prices in country k, and dp^e and dm^k are changes in prices and trade volumes. The first term is the terms-of-trade effect as given by the inner product of net imports and changes in tariff-exclusive prices. The second term is the volume-of-trade effect as given by the inner product of the tariff wedge and the change in net imports.[10] If tariffs are specific, $p^k = p^e + t^k$, where t^k is an N-column vector whose components are per-unit tariff (or subsidy) rates. If rates are *ad valorem*, $p^k = (1+\tau^k)p^e$, where $(1+\tau^k)$ is an $N \times N$ diagonal matrix.[11]

Expression (1) applies whether country k joins a customs union (or any other type of preferential trading club) or, and important, stands on the sideline as other nations engage in a preferential trading arrangement. In the former case, changes in p^e and m^k are induced by changes in both foreign and country k's tariffs, while in the latter case, only the reform of foreign tariffs causes country k's terms of trade and volume of trade to change.[12] As shown in Ohyama (1972), the approach also allows for welfare expressions for coalitions of countries and thus, if their trading partners' offer surfaces are known, for derivation of these coalitions' optimal tariffs.[13] Finally, when integrated over the range of changes or when expressed in its discrete form, Expression (1) offers an appealing strategy for empirical work. The vector of initial trade flows m^k and the vector of initial price wedges $(p^k - p^e)$ can

[10] As mentioned in Kowalczyk (1990), the other standard decomposition in the theory of tariffs breaks the change in a nation's welfare into a change in *producers' and consumers' surplus* and a change in *tariff revenue*, i.e., $d\eta^k = -m^k\,dp^k + d[(p^k - p^e)m^k]$. Harrison et al. (1993) suggest that this approach is useful for customs union analysis. They do not, however, present any results on customs unions or free-trade areas.

[11] More generally, country k's domestic and tariff-exclusive prices are given by the $N \times (K-1)$-dimensional matrices $\mathbf{P}^k$ and $\mathbf{P}^e$ permitting for the possibility that some good i commands different prices and tariff rates depending on origin or destination. If country k neither taxes nor subsidies its exports, if all its export markets are perfectly competitive, and if k is not quantity-constrained in any of them (the latter ensures that k will not be selling the same good to two different destinations at two different tariff-exclusive prices), the domestic price matrix $\mathbf{P}^k$ reduces to the N-component vector discussed in the text. These assumptions do not imply that $\mathbf{P}^e$ reduces in similar fashion, since country k might import good i from different trading partners, j and l, whose costs differ, as long as k's differential tariffs are such that $p_i^k = (1+\tau_i^{kj})(p^e)_i^{kj} = (1+\tau_i^{kl})(p^e)_i^{kl}$.

[12] Kowalczyk and Wonnacott (1992) contains a discussion.

[13] Let S constitute the set of coalition partners, with s and s' being indices for the members of S, and let R be the set of nonmembers represented by index r. Assuming that income transfers are feasible between coalition members, the potential Pareto criterion applies to the coalition and yields the welfare expression $d\mu = \Sigma_s \Sigma_{s'} (p^c - p^e)\,dm^{ss'} + \Sigma_s \Sigma_r [-m^{sr} d(p^e) + (p^s - p^e)\,dm^{sr}]$. This states that the coalition's welfare is affected through terms-of-trade and volume-of-trade effects on trade with nonmembers but only through volume-of-trade effects on intracoalition trade. For changes in world welfare, all terms-of-trade effects vanish. Hence, if k and k' are indices over the members of K, the set of the world's trading nations, the change in world welfare is $d\omega = \Sigma_k \Sigma_{k'} (p^k - p^e)\,dm^{kk'}$. Kowalczyk (1992) derives some results on integration by use of the latter expression.

be inferred from national trade statistics and tariff schedules, while changes in prices and trade volumes can be estimated.[14,15]

3. TWO APPLICATIONS

A complete assessment of whether a proposed preferential trading arrangement will be beneficial or not requires estimates of trade and price responses in a fully specified general equilibrium model of the world economy. Often, a decision whether to integrate or not must be based on less complete information, such as, for example, initial trade flows or rates of protection, and the answer to the question with whom to integrate thus becomes a search for "back-of-the-envelope" indicators of positive welfare effects from integration.

Particularly interesting, and controversial, is whether large or small initial trade flows between potential members indicate that a welfare-improving trade arrangement can be made. Two results in the literature have received particular attention: Lipsey established that "[a] customs union is more likely to raise welfare, *given the total volume of imports of the country*, the larger is the proportion of these imports obtained from the country's union partners and the less is the proportion devoted to imports from the outside world" (Lipsey, 1970, p. 56, his italics); Riezman demonstrated that "two countries can benefit from a customs union provided that their mutual trade is initially small" (Riezman, 1979, p. 342).[16] Starting with Lloyd (1982), the conventional view has become that these results are "contradictory."[17]

I will now put forth that the statements by Lipsey and Riezman are not contradictory. For this, return to the case of three countries, and express Equation (1) for country a in a fashion stressing its initial sources of trade:

$$d\eta^a = -m^{ab}\,dp^e + (p^a - p^e)\,dm^{ab} - m^{ac}\,dp^e + (p^a - p^e)\,dm^{ac} \tag{2}$$

Suppose a customs union between countries a and c causes country a to eliminate imports from country b and instead obtain them from country c. Country a then suffers a terms-of-trade worsening of size $(-m^{ab}\,dp^e)$, where dp^e equals the

[14] Hamilton and Whalley (1995) present some CGE estimates of terms-of-trade effects from integration. See also Kose and Riezman (1997).

[15] In his later writings on customs unions, Johnson (1974, 1975) proposed that Viner's trade diversion be interpreted as the shift from point A to point B in Figure 1 and that the shift from point B to point C be incorporated into the trade-creation effect. Johnson's suggestion still begs the question of how to denominate price and quantity effects in a more general case where some nation experiences an improvement in its terms of trade or a reduction in its trade volume. It seems to me that it would be advantageous to have a simple terminology that allows in a straightforward manner for analysis of price and quantity changes regardless of which directions such changes might take.

[16] While not reflected in this quote, Riezman (1979, p. 349) actually shows that each of the members benefits.

[17] "Yet, after the conditions have been expressed in comparable forms, there remain many distinctions, and some propositions still appear contradictory; for example, the Riezman proposition has a *small* intraunion trade as a sufficient condition for a welfare increase (in both countries), whereas the Lipsey proposition has a *large* intraunion trade as a sufficient condition," (Lloyd, 1982, p. 43, his italics.)

cost differential between countries b and c. This is smaller the smaller is m^{ab} or, for given total volume of trade $m^a = m^{ab} + m^{ac}$, the larger is m^{ac}, which establishes Lipsey's result.[18] If, instead, the customs union between countries a and c causes world prices to change such that country a experiences a terms-of-trade improvement on its initial trade with country c of the size $(-m^{ac}\,dp^e)$, then union partner c suffers a terms-of-trade worsening of the same size equal to $(-m^{ca}\,dp^e)$. The more these countries trade before forming a customs union, the larger is this loss for country c, and the more likely will country c lose from entering into a customs union with country a, which is Riezman's result.

Had Lipsey not stressed the total volume of trade, he would not have needed to assume a larger volume of initial intraunion trade in order to reduce initial extraunion trade. He could instead have taken the direct route of stating a small initial extraunion volume of trade, in which case Lipsey's and Riezman's statements are consistent. They would then combine to the intuitive proposition, contained in Lipsey (1960), that a customs union is more likely to be beneficial the closer to autarky are its members, i.e., the higher are the two countries' initial duties.

Consider next the question of what is a small country's optimal trade policy strategy in a world of free-trade areas. Conventional theory has that the small country's best policy is unilateral free trade, leading some to argue that a small country can gain nothing from a customs union that it cannot obtain from a unilateral tariff reduction.[19] But changes in a trading partner's tariffs can affect even the small country's terms of trade.[20] Standard tariff theory, which does not consider discriminatory policies, defines as a small country one that cannot affect world market prices or, equivalently, one unable to affect its own terms of trade. Preferential tariffs create segmentation of markets, which allows nations to discriminate among their trading partners. Thus, even though world market prices are constant, the small country can influence its terms of trade through its integration strategy.

Suppose that small country a exports goods 1 and 2 and imports goods 3 and 4 at tariff-exclusive prices $(p^e)_i$ $(i = 1, \ldots, 4)$. Drop superscript a for convenience, and let y denote a's income, let $m_{iy} \equiv \partial m_i / \partial y$ be its marginal income propensity to import good i, and let $m_{ij} \equiv \partial m_i / \partial p_j$ be the effect on compensated import demand for good i from a change in the price of good j. Define $I = 1 - \Sigma_{i=3,4} \tau_i (p^e)_i m_{iy}$, which is positive if no good is inferior in consumption or if a gift of real income raises utility.[21] Finally, let $d\vartheta = I\,d\eta$ be the implied change in country a's welfare. Expres-

[18] Assuming perfect substitutes permits the most direct proof of Lipsey's statement and comparison with Riezman's. If a's imports from b and c are imperfect substitutes, then Lipsey's statement requires that large initial imports from c induce a large increase in (welfare increasing) imports from c [the fourth term in Equation (2)] relative to any (welfare reducing) reduction in imports from b [the second term in Equation (2)]. See also Ju and Krishna (1997) and Panagariya (1996).

[19] See, for example, Berglas (1979).

[20] See Wonnacott and Wonnacott (1981).

[21] See Bruno (1972).

sion (1) can then, after differentiation of the trade volumes and rearranging terms, be written as

$$d\vartheta = \sum_{i=1,2}\left[-m_i + \sum_{j=3,4}\tau_j(p^e)_j m_{ji}\right]d(p^e)_i + \sum_{j=3,4}\tau_j(p^e)_j\left[\sum_{h=3,4} m_{jh}(p^e)_h\,d\tau_h\right] \tag{3}$$

The first bracketed term on the right-hand side identifies the two channels through which changed export prices affect welfare: the terms-of-trade effect and an effect via tariff revenue due to substitution toward or away from taxed imports (maintaining the assumption of no taxes or subsidies on exports). The second bracketed term captures the effect from changing *a*'s own tariffs through their effect on tariff revenue. It is possible that improved export prices or a reduction of own tariffs in paradoxical fashion can lower small country *a*'s welfare.[22,23] It may matter, therefore, how markets are accessed.

Suppose that all countries in the world except small country *a* are members of large free-trade areas *b* or *c* that have tariffs on their mutual trade, and suppose that country *a* accedes simultaneously to *b* and *c* through a process of mutual equiproportionate tariff reductions. Assume that $p_1^b > p_1^c$ and $p_2^c > p_2^b$ and that initial *ad valorem* tariffs in *b* and *c* are such that country *a* exports good 1 to area *b* and good 2 to area *c*.[24] Denoting by a circumflex the rate of change of a variable ($\hat{z} \equiv dz/z$), an equiproportionate reduction of tariff rates, where $\lambda > 0$ is the agreed rate of reduction, can be written as

$$\hat{\tau}_3^a = \hat{\tau}_4^a = \hat{\tau}_1^b = \hat{\tau}_2^c = -\lambda \tag{4}$$

Since $(p^e)_1 = p_1^b/(1+\tau_1^b)$ and $(p^e)_2 = p_2^c/(1+\tau_2^c)$, country *a*'s export prices change by

$$(\hat{p}^e)_1 = (\tau_1^b/1+\tau_1^b)\lambda \quad \text{and} \quad (\hat{p}^e)_2 = (\tau_2^c/1+\tau_2^c)\lambda \tag{5}$$

22 Woodland (1982) discusses how a higher price of good 1 can reduce country *a*'s welfare if exports of good 1 are small and if good 1 is a strong complement to high-tariff imports. [He shows also that the paradox of a larger terms-of-trade improvement being worse for a free-trading small country than a smaller terms-of-trade improvement, originally discussed by Krueger and Sonnenschein (1967), vanishes if the weights of price indices are adjusted continuously as prices change.] A reduction in an own tariff such as τ_4 can reduce welfare if *a*'s initial tariffs are high and if good 4 is a strong substitute relative to other (high-taxed) imports.

23 It is important to recognize that the case considered here, where the small country experiences a terms-of-trade improvement through access to large foreign markets, differs from Viner's case of welfare-reducing trade diversion, where the small country's terms of trade worsen.

24 These assumptions imply that country *a* will want to accede to both free-trade areas and that trade patterns do not change.

Substituting Equations (4) and (5) into Equation (3) and manipulating then yields

$$(6)\quad d\vartheta/\lambda = -m_1(p^e)_1(\tau_1^b/1+\tau_1^b) - m_2(p^e)_2(\tau_2^c/1+\tau_2^c)$$
$$+\tau_3(p^e)_3\big[m_{31}(p^e)_1(\tau_1^b/1+\tau_1^b) + m_{32}(p^e)_2(\tau_2^c/1+\tau_2^c)$$
$$-m_{33}(p^e)_3\tau_3 - m_{34}(p^e)_4\tau_4\big]$$
$$+\tau_4(p^e)_4\big[m_{41}(p^e)_1(\tau_1^b/1+\tau_1^b) + m_{42}(p^e)_2(\tau_2^c/1+\tau_2^c)$$
$$-m_{43}(p^e)_3\tau_3 - m_{44}(p^e)_4\tau_4\big]$$

With λ positive, the welfare contribution from the first two terms (which are the terms-of-trade effects when substitution is ignored) is positive (since m_1 and m_2 are both negative). The first two terms on each of the next lines capture the substitution from export price changes. If each of exports 1 and 2 is a substitute with respect to each of the imports, implying that m_{31}, m_{32}, m_{41}, and m_{42} are positive, their welfare contributions are positive. The only remaining possibility for welfare to fall then lies with the last two terms on the second and third lines. But they are the terms for a small country's unilateral equiproportionate *ad valorem* tariff reduction, which Fukushima (1979) showed to be positive when goods are substitutes. Hence we have shown

PROPOSITION. *If all nations but a single small country are members of one of two free-trade areas, and if goods are substitutes, then the small country gains from accessing both free-trade areas through mutual equiproportionate tariff rate reductions.*[25,26]

Would a large trading partner (or large bloc) be willing to extend the privilege of free trade to a small country? Absent other considerations, the answer in this model is "No," since such an agreement does not change domestic prices in the large country and hence, from the welfare expression in footnote 10, only has a welfare-reducing loss-of-tariff-revenue effect. However, since joint welfare of the small and large nations increases by the positive volume-of-trade effect in the small country (the large country's lost tariff revenue is transferred to the small country as a terms-of-trade improvement), there exists a sidepayment from the small country to each of the large countries not less than their lost tariff revenues which, if paid, will

[25] This result extends Fukushima's (1979) to the case where a small country is affected by improved export prices in addition to its own tariff reduction. The result extends also the analysis in Kowalczyk (1993) by providing an explicit formula for welfare-improving tariff reductions.

[26] A hub-and-spoke system is created with the small country as the hub and its large partners as its spokes. This is contrary to the conventional view that hub countries will be large. Expression (6) reveals further that if country *a* is already in a free-trade agreement with *b* but maintains a tariff on imports from free-trade area *c*, then *a* would want to join area *c* through equiproportionate tariff reductions if the good country *a* exports to *c* (good 2) is a substitute relative to *a*'s imports from *c* (good 4). Equation (6) shows also that even if goods are substitutes, it may be harmful for country *a* to join one but not both free-trade areas.

make all countries better off.[27,28] Other linkages include (1) that the small country exerts political influence over the large country, e.g., in a multilateral trade negotiation requiring unanimity, (2) a desire to stem migration between the countries, or (3) a desire to reduce political or military conflict.

4. CONCLUSION

This article has offered a critique of Viner's trade diversion and trade creation approach and has argued that an alternative methodology, that of terms-of-trade and volume-of-trade effects, has attractive properties. It is exhaustive, it has empirical implications, and it can generate results easily and transparently. This article demonstrates, as examples of the latter, that results by Lipsey and Riezman are not "contradictory" and that the small country's first best trade policy, under some conditions, is to seek membership of all free-trade areas.

The formation or expansion of trading blocs is nothing but an exercise in multicountry tariff reform. It would be a surprise, therefore, if the customs union problem should require its own language. One of the purposes of this article is to bring the analysis of customs unions back into the mainstream of international trade economics.

REFERENCES

BALDWIN, R., AND A. J. VENABLES, "Regional Economic Integration," in G. M. Grossman and K. Rogoff (eds.), *Handbook of International Economics*, Vol. 3 (Amsterdam: North Holland, 1995).

BERGLAS, E., "Preferential Trading Theory: The n Commodity Case," *Journal of Political Economy* 87 (1979), 315–31.

BHAGWATI, J. N., "Trade Diverting Customs Unions and Welfare-Improvement: A Clarification," *Economic Journal* 81 (1971), 580–87.

———, "A Reply to Professor Kirman," *Economic Journal* 83 (1973), 895–7.

BOND, E. W., "The Optimal Tariff Structure in Higher Dimensions," *International Economic Review* 31 (1990), 103–16.

BRUNO, M., "Market Distortions and Gradual Reform," *Review of Economic Studies* 39 (1972), 373–83.

COLLIER, P., "The Welfare Effects of Customs Union: An Anatomy," *Economic Journal* 89 (1979), 84–95.

CORDEN, W. M., "The Normative Theory of International Trade," in R. W. Jones and P. B. Kenen (eds.), *Handbook of International Economics*, Vol. 1 (Amsterdam: North Holland, 1984).

[27] Kowalczyk and Sjöström (1994) show how such payments would tend to go from those with much to gain to those with little to gain from integration or from small country a to large partners b and c.

[28] Examples of preferential arrangements between large and small countries include several agreements involving the European Union. Israel, with its free-trade agreements with the United States, the European Union, and EFTA, and Chile, with its free-trade agreement with Mercosur and application for entry into NAFTA, are examples of small countries that have pursued the integration strategy derived in this article.

DIXIT, A., AND V. NORMAN, *Theory of International Trade* (Cambridge, England: Cambridge University Press, 1980).
FRANKEL, J. A., *Regional Trading Blocs in the World Trading System* (Washington: Institute for International Economics, 1997).
FUKUSHIMA, T., "Tariff Structure, Nontraded Goods and Theory of Piecemeal Policy Recommendations," *International Economic Review* 20 (1979), 427–35.
GEHRELS, F., "Customs Union from a Single-Country Viewpoint," *Review of Economic Studies* 24 (1956), 61–4.
GRINOLS, E., AND K. WONG, "An Exact Measure of Welfare Change," *Canadian Journal of Economics* 24 (1991), 428–49.
HAMILTON, B., AND J. WHALLEY, "Geographically Discriminatory Trade Arrangements," *Review of Economics and Statistics* 67 (1995), 446–55.
HARRISON, G., T. RUTHERFORD, AND I. WOOTON, "An Alternative Decomposition for Customs Unions," *Canadian Journal of Economics* 26 (1993), 961–8.
JOHNSON, H. G., "The Economic Theory of Customs Unions," *Pakistan Economic Journal* 1 (1960), 14–32.
———, "Trade-Diverting Customs Unions: A Comment," *Economic Journal* 84 (1974), 618–21.
———, "A Note on Welfare-Increasing Trade Diversion," *Canadian Journal of Economics* 8 (1975), 117–23.
JONES, R. W., "Tariffs and Trade in General Equilibrium: Comment," *American Economic Review* 59 (1969), 418–24.
JU, J., AND K. KRISHNA, "Evaluating Trade Reform Using Ex-Post Criteria," National Bureau of Economic Research working paper no. 6152, 1997.
KEMP, M. C., *A Contribution to the General Equilibrium Theory of Preferential Trading* (Amsterdam: North Holland, 1969).
KIRMAN, A. P., "Trade Diverting Customs Unions and Welfare Improvement: A Comment," *Economic Journal* 83 (1973), 890–3.
KOSE, A., AND R. RIEZMAN, "Understanding the Welfare Implications of Preferential Trade Agreements," mimeo, University of Iowa, 1997.
KOWALCZYK, C., "Welfare and Customs Unions," National Bureau of Economic Research working paper no. 3476, 1990.
———, "Paradoxes in Integration Theory," *Open Economies Review* 3 (1992), 51–9.
———, "Integration in Goods and Factors," *Regional Science and Urban Economics* 23 (1993), 355–67.
——— AND T. SJÖSTRÖM, "Bringing GATT into the Core," *Economica* 61 (1994), 301–67.
——— AND R. WONNACOTT, "Hubs and Spokes, and Free Trade in the Americas," National Bureau of Economic Research working paper no. 4198, 1992.
KRUEGER, A., AND H. SONNENSCHEIN, "The Terms of Trade, the Gains from Trade and Price Divergence," *International Economic Review* 8 (1967), 121–7.
LAWRENCE, R. Z., *Regionalism, Multilateralism, and Deeper Integration* (Washington: The Brookings Institution, 1996).
LIPSEY, R. G., "The Theory of Customs Unions: Trade Diversion and Welfare," *Economica* 24 (1957), 40–6.
———, "The Theory of Customs Unions: A General Survey," *Economic Journal* 70 (1960), 496–513.
———, *The Theory of Customs Unions: A General Equilibrium Analysis* (London: Weidenfeld and Nicholson, 1970).
——— AND R. K. LANCASTER, "The General Theory of Second Best," *Review of Economic Studies* 24 (1956), 11–32.
LLOYD, P. J., "3 × 3 Theory of Customs Unions," *Journal of International Economics* 12 (1982), 41–63.
MEADE, J., *Trade and Welfare* (London: Oxford University Press, 1955a).
———, *The Theory of Customs Unions* (Amsterdam: North Holland, 1955b).
MICHAELY, M., "The Assumptions of Jacob Viner's Theory of Customs Unions," *Journal of International Economics* 6 (1976), 75–93.
OHYAMA, M., "Trade and Welfare in General Equilibrium," *Keio Economic Studies* 9 (1972), 37–73.

PANAGARIYA, A., "The Meade Model of Preferential Trading: History, Analytics, and Policy Implications," Center for International Economics working paper no. 21, University of Maryland, 1996.

POMFRET, R., "The Theory of Preferential Trading Arrangements," *Weltwirtschaftliches Archiv* 122 (1986), 439–99.

RIEZMAN, R., "A 3 × 3 Model of Customs Unions," *Journal of International Economics* 37 (1979), 47–61.

VINER, J., *The Customs Union Issue* (New York: Carnegie Endowment for International Peace, 1950).

WONNACOTT, P., AND R. WONNACOTT, "Is Unilateral Tariff Reduction Preferable to a Customs Union? The Curious Case of the Missing Foreign Tariffs," *American Economic Review* 71 (1981), 704–14.

WOODLAND, A., *International Trade and Resource Allocation* (Amsterdam: North Holland, 1982).

Part VI
Quotas, Tariffs, and Reform

[23]

QUOTAS AND THE SECOND BEST

W. Max CORDEN and Rodney E. FALVEY

Australian National University, Canberra, ACT 2601, Australia

Received 28 September 1984

This note makes two observations about trade restrictions on subgroups of commodities. First, unlike tariffs, unalterable quotas provide no second-best justification for general restrictions. Second, the optimal allocation of intra-subgroup trade depends on the form of restraint imposed.

1. Introduction

This note makes two related points concerning quantitative restrictions and the second best. The first is that unalterable quota restrictions on a subgroup of traded commodities provide no second best justification for general trade restrictions. This contrasts sharply with the implications of unalterable tariff restrictions, and provides a unifying perspective for several of the tariff-quota non-equivalence results that have appeared in the literature. The second point relates to the growing tendency for quantitative trade controls to be applied to aggregates of differentiated products. The optimal intra-restraint trade allocation then depends on the form in which the restraint is specified, and effectively requires a uniform specific tax for a restraint expressed in physical units, and a uniform ad valorem tax for a restraint in value terms. Provided these optimal intra-restraint policies are available, no restrictions outside the aggregate are implied.

These points are likely to be of increasing relevance for policy-making as quantitative restraints become the dominant instrument through which trade is 'managed', and given that much of this trade intervention is justified on second-best grounds (at least implicitly).

2. Product quotas: An anti-agnostic proposition

For simplicity, attention is confined to a small country, although the optimal policies for a large country simply involve the addition of the standard optimal taxes to the policies derived below. Suppose the home government wishes to maximize a social welfare function, $W(C_0, C_1, \ldots, C_n)$, possessing the usual properties and defined over aggregate consumption of $n+1$ commodities; subject to the following familiar constraints:

Production Feasibility:	$F(X_0, X_1, \ldots, X_n) = 0,$
Market Clearing:	$C_i = X_i + M_i, \quad i = 0, \ldots, n,$
Balance of Trade:	$\sum_{i=1}^{n} P_i^* M_i = 0,$

where C_i, X_i and M_i are aggregate consumption, output and imports (exports if negative) respectively of commodity i, and P_i^* is the given world relative price of commodity i ($i = 1,\ldots,n$) in terms of the numeraire (0). The first-order conditions from this undistorted maximization then yield the familiar equation of marginal rates of substitution in production and consumption with relative world prices, i.e.,

$$\frac{W_i}{W_0} = \frac{F_i}{F_0} = P_i^*, \qquad i = 1,\ldots,n. \tag{1}$$

Now suppose unalterable trade restrictions exist on some commodities (not including the numeraire). What do these imply for the optimal trade policies on the remainder? The answer is obtained by examining the first-order condition for a welfare maximizing solution, namely

$$\frac{\mathrm{d}W}{W_0} = \sum_{i=1}^{n} (P_i - P_i^*)\mathrm{d}M_i = 0, \tag{2}$$

where P_i is the domestic relative price of commodity i and equals the corresponding domestic marginal rates of substitution in production and consumption, since only trade distortions are considered.

If the unalterable distortions involve tariffs, then $P_i = (1 + t_i)P_i^*$ for commodities in the restricted subgroup (S), and free trade will not be optimal for the remaining commodities [i.e., setting $P_i = P_i^*$ for all $i \notin S$ will not satisfy (2)]. The point is that the unalterable tariffs reduce the volume of imports of some goods below their optimal levels. By taxing (subsidizing) trade in the substitutes (complements) of these goods, their import volumes can be increased, thus partially offsetting the adverse consequences of the unalterable distortions, albeit by creating others. It has been shown that the second-best policy in this case involves imposing tariffs on the remaining goods which are a weighted average of the unalterable rates, including any zero rates [Lloyd (1974)]. Only for a good which is unrelated to those in the trade distorted group will free trade be optimal.

The clear implication is that even for a small country, when trade is unalterably tariff-distorted in some commodities, free trade cannot be presumed to be optimal for the remainder. This is a particular case of the essentially agnostic conclusion of Lipsey and Lancaster (1956, p. 17) that 'to apply to only a small part of an economy welfare rules which would lead to a Paretian optimum if they were applied everywhere, may move the economy away from, not toward, a second best optimum position'.

Here we wish to emphasize that unalterable quantitative restrictions do not have the same policy implication favouring agnosticism about the optimality of free trade for undistorted markets. Taxing trade in substitutes cannot increase import volumes that are already at their permitted maxima, and would merely introduce costly distortions with no offsetting gain. Since $\mathrm{d}M_i = 0$ for all quantitatively restricted commodities ($i \notin S$), (2) then reduces to

$$\frac{\mathrm{d}W}{W_0} = \sum_{i \notin S} (P_i - P_i^*)\mathrm{d}M_i = 0, \tag{2'}$$

which is satisfied by free trade ($P_i = P_i^*$) for all $i \notin S$. Thus *unalterable quantitative restrictions on a subgroup of products do not provide a possible second-best justification for trade restrictions on other products*.

Specific instances of this notion that quota distortions do not 'spill over' into other markets do appear in the literature. Thus, in contrast to tariffs, preferential trading arrangements amongst countries with quantitative trade restrictions are not trade diverting [Meade (1955)], growth under a quota regime will not be immiserizing [Alam (1981)], and smuggling will not be welfare reducing when legal trade is quantitatively restricted [Falvey (1978)].

This notion can also be found in the literature on cost-benefit analysis for the open economy. Assume no distortions other than trade restrictions. Suppose a cost-benefit exercise is being carried out for a project in industry X which would have to draw to some extent on labor currently used in tradeable-good industry Y. If industry Y benefits from a tariff, the shadow price of this labour to industry X will be below its market price, since, as shown by Little and Mirrlees (1969), output of industry Y should be valued at world prices and not at its tariff-distorted domestic price. On the other hand Joshi (1972) has shown that if industry Y were protected by a non-redundant quota, a marginal withdrawal of labor from that industry would have no effect on the value of imports. Product Y would be just like a non-tradeable, and labor withdrawn from it should be valued at its market price (given no distortion other than the quota).

We have therefore a range of special cases – from customs union theory, the welfare economics of growth, the economics of smuggling, and cost-benefit analysis – which illustrates the much more general *anti-agnostic proposition*.

3. Category quotas

The preceding section specifically considered unalterable quantitative restrictions on individual products. Our anti-agnostic conclusions will also carry over to restraints applied to a category of products, as long as the intra-restraint allocation is made optimally. Suppose an importing country has committed itself to restraining total imports in some product category. It then faces the problem of determining a policy instrument that will yield the optimal intra-category composition of imports while satisfying this total restraint.

The restraint itself can take one of two forms. The first restricts the *value* (at world prices) of total imports in this sub group to equal $\bar{V}$, i.e.,

$$\sum_{i \in S} P_i^* M_i = \bar{V}. \tag{3}$$

The second restricts the total *quantity* of imports in this subgroup to equal $\bar{Q}$. Such a restriction is only applicable if the products in the subgroup have comparable units, of course, and can then be expressed as

$$\sum_{i \in S} M_i = \bar{Q}. \tag{4}$$

Reperforming the welfare maximization under these alternative constraints (and assuming the numeraire is not in S), yields (1) as before for $i \notin S$ under both constraints. With the value restraint,

$$\frac{W_i}{W_0} = \frac{F_i}{F_0} = P_i^*(1 + t) \quad \text{for all } i \in S, \tag{5}$$

while with the quantity restraint,

$$\frac{W_i}{W_0} = \frac{F_i}{F_0} = P_i^* + T \quad \text{for all } i \in S. \tag{6}$$

As has been noted in the literature, the optimal policy to meet a value restraint is a *uniform ad valorem tariff* on all commodities in the subgroup, with no restrictions on other goods [Vandendorpe (1974)]. The same outcome can be achieved if the government auctions import permits specified in value terms totalling the appropriate amount ($\bar{V}$). But for a quantity restraint the optimal policy is a *uniform specific tariff* on the subgroup [or the auctioning of import licences specified in quantity terms of the appropriate amount ($\bar{Q}$)]. This difference in optimal policies reflects the differing trade-offs between products under the two constraints – involving value units in one case and physical units in the other. Thus whether a restraint is imposed in value or quantity terms makes a difference to the optimal import composition and hence to the optimal instrument to meet the restraint.

In practice such intra-category allocation problems are more likely to characterize the administration of voluntary export restraints. Typically these result from pressure by an importing country which induces an exporter to restrain 'voluntarily' its total exports in some product category to a level acceptable to the importer, but leaves the exporter free to administer the restraint and hence to determine the intra-category trade allocation. The policy problem facing the exporter is then formally equivalent to that examined for the importer above. Under a value restraint the optimal policy will be a uniform ad valorem export tax of the appropriate magnitude, while for a quantity restraint it will be a uniform specific tax. Thus, given the same restraint, both importers and exporters will apply identical policies, implying that the question of who administers the restraint is of more significance for the inter-country distribution of quota rents than for the intra-category allocation of trade.

Finally, relating the two parts of this note, it can be shown that no spillover effects will occur outside the subgroup of restricted products, as long as each restraint is met in the optimal way. [See Ray (1974) for the value-restraint.] But if neither the appropriate uniform tariffs nor the marketing of appropriate licenses is permitted then second-best restrictions outside the category will be implied along the lines noted for the unalterable tariffs in section 1.

References

Alam, M.S., 1981, Welfare implications of growth under quotas, Economics Letters 8, 177–180.

Falvey, R.E., 1978, A note on preferential and illegal trade under quantitative restrictions, Quarterly Journal of Economics, 175–178.

Joshi, V., 1972, The rationale and relevance of the Little-Mirrlees criterion, Bulletin 34 (Oxford University Institute of Economics and Statistics, Oxford) 3–32.

Lipsey, R.G. and K. Lancaster, 1956, The general theory of the second-best, Review of Economic Studies 24, 11–32.

Little, I.M.D. and J.A. Mirrlees, 1969, Manual of industrial project analysis for developing countries, Vol. II, Social cost-benefit analysis (OECD Development Centre, Paris).

Lloyd, P.J., 1974, A more general theory of price distortions in open economics, Journal of International Economics 4, 365–386.

Meade, J.E., 1955, The theory of customs unions (North-Holland, Amsterdam).

Ray, A., 1974, A general theorem on uniform versus differentiated tax-subsidy structures, Journal of Economic Theory.

Vandendorpe, A.L., 1974, On the theory of non-economic objectives in open economies, Journal of International Economics 4, 15–24.

[24]

TARIFFS, QUOTAS AND PIECEMEAL POLICY REFORM

Rodney E. FALVEY*

Research School of Pacific Studies, Australian National University, Canberra, ACT 2601, Australia

Received September 1986, revised version received July 1987

This paper extends recent results on the welfare implications of piecemeal tariff adjustments to include cases where the initial trade distortions involve *both* tariffs and quotas. It shows that the standard prescriptions for piecemeal tariff reform are largely unaffected by the presence of unalterable quotas on other goods. Prescriptions for piecemeal quota reform are also derived, although they are constrained by the presence of unalterable tariffs.

1. Introduction

The welfare implications of piecemeal tariff adjustments have received some attention in the trade policy literature [the results and references are provided in Woodland (1982, ch. 11), and in Dixit (1985)]. This paper extends this analysis to cases where the initial trade distortions involve *both* tariffs *and* quantitative restrictions. It makes three basic points. First, the standard prescriptions for piecemeal tariff reform are largely unaffected by the presence of unalterable quotas on other goods. Second, if the only distortions present are the result of quantitative restrictions on trade, then the loosening or removal of *any* of these restrictions will be welfare improving. Third, while the presence of unalterable tariff distortions implies some structure of quota restrictions on the tariff-free items will be (second-best) optimal in general, prescriptions for piecemeal quota reform can still be derived. These prescriptions are now constrained by the magnitudes of the unalterable tariffs, however.

2. The welfare effects of policy changes

To make the presentation both simple and familiar, the structure adopted is essentially that used by Hatta (1977) and Fukushima (1979). Consider a small country, with all goods tradable, no government consumption, only trade (tariff and quota) distortions, all tax revenues redistributed by lump-sum transfers, and, for welfare purposes, a single consumer. With the

*I would like to thank Max Corden and a referee for helpful comments.

exception of the last two, relaxing these assumptions merely requires some reinterpretation of the results. For simplicity attention is limited to import tariffs and quotas, since export taxes and quotas, consumption and production taxes and subsidies, etc. can be treated analogously. There are then two categories of goods to be considered: those goods subject to (possibly zero) import tariffs (indexed by T and including the numeraire); and those goods subject to quantitative restrictions (indexed by R). The trade balance constraint for this country can be written as

$$r^{\mathrm{T}}S_{\mathrm{T}}+r^{\mathrm{R}}S_{\mathrm{R}}=0, \tag{1}$$

while market clearing for the quota-restricted commodities requires:

$$S_{\mathrm{R}}=Q. \tag{2}$$

In the equations the $S_i(p^{\mathrm{T}},p^{\mathrm{R}},U)$ are the compensated commodity excess demand functions, Q is the vector of quantitative restraints, U denotes the consumer's welfare level, and $p=(p^{\mathrm{T}},p^{\mathrm{R}})$ and $r=(r^{\mathrm{T}},r^{\mathrm{R}})$ are the domestic and world price vectors, respectively.

As long as there is some substitutability between the tariff-restricted and quota-restricted tradables (so that the substitution matrix S_{RR} is negative definite), (2) can be solved for

$$\mathrm{d}p^{\mathrm{R}}=S_{\mathrm{RR}}^{-1}[\mathrm{d}Q-S_{\mathrm{R}U}\,\mathrm{d}U-S_{\mathrm{RT}}\,\mathrm{d}p^{\mathrm{T}}]. \tag{3}$$

Totally differentiating (1), and using (3) to substitute for $\mathrm{d}p^{\mathrm{R}}$, and the homogeneity of S_p, one can show that

$$m\,\mathrm{d}U=[(p^{\mathrm{T}}-r^{\mathrm{T}})S_{\mathrm{TT}}-v^{\mathrm{R}}S_{\mathrm{RT}}]\,\mathrm{d}p^{\mathrm{T}}+(p^{\mathrm{R}}-r^{\mathrm{R}}+v^{\mathrm{R}})\,\mathrm{d}Q, \tag{4}$$

where $v^{\mathrm{R}}=(p^{\mathrm{T}}-r^{\mathrm{T}})S_{\mathrm{TR}}S_{\mathrm{RR}}^{-1}$ and $m=[r^{\mathrm{T}}S_{\mathrm{T}U}+(p^{\mathrm{R}}+v^{\mathrm{R}})S_{\mathrm{R}U}]$. The coefficient m has a standard interpretation as the 'marginal propensity to spend' evaluated at 'shadow prices' and should be positive for stability [see Fukushima (1981)]. The welfare effects of tariff and quota policy changes can then be determined directly from (4).

3. Piecemeal tariff reform

Suppose one contemplates piecemeal *tariff* reform from an initial equilibrium possibly distorted by *both* arbitrary tariffs and quotas. Substituting for v^{R} in (4), and setting $\mathrm{d}Q=0$, one has:[1]

$$m\,\mathrm{d}U=(p^{\mathrm{T}}-r^{\mathrm{T}})[S_{\mathrm{TT}}-S_{\mathrm{TR}}S_{\mathrm{RR}}^{-1}S_{\mathrm{RT}}]\,\mathrm{d}p^{\mathrm{T}}. \tag{5}$$

[1] Fukushima's Lemma 1 (1979) and Hatta's Lemma (1977) give essentially the same result as (5) for the special case where $Q=0$.

Two new results emerge directly from (5). First, if there are no tariff distortions in the initial equilibrium ($p^T = r^T$), then none should be introduced. The distortions created by the existence of binding quantitative restrictions do not spill over into other markets [Corden and Falvey (1985)]. This property of quotas is important for the subsequent results. Second, the structure of the coefficient matrix on dp^T becomes familiar once one recognizes that the fixed quotas effectively render the corresponding tradables 'non-traded' at the margin. As Hatta (1977) and Fukushima (1979) have shown, the standard piecemeal tariff reform recommendations continue to be valid in the presence of non-tradables provided the latter are net substitutes for all other goods. Thus, if the quota-restricted goods are net substitutes for all other goods, an equiproportionate reduction in all tariffs raises welfare [Fukushima (1979, Theorem 2)], and if, in addition, the good(s) with the highest (lowest) tariff is a net substitute for all other goods, then reducing (increasing) the highest (lowest) tariff to the level of the next highest (lowest) tariff will raise welfare [Fukushima (1979, Theorem 1)].

4. Piecemeal quota reform

Alternatively, suppose attention is restricted to piecemeal *quota* reform. Then (4) reduces to

$$m\,\mathrm{d}U = [(p^R - r^R) + (p^T - r^T)S_{TR}S_{RR}^{-1}]\,\mathrm{d}Q. \tag{6}$$

One significant feature that is immediately apparent from (6) is that, although the coefficient on each $\mathrm{d}Q_i$ contains all the explicit tariffs ($p^T - r^T$) in general, the only 'implicit' tariff it contains is that on commodity i itself ($p_i^R - r_i^R$). While the entire quota structure is important in determining the structure of implicit tariffs, the direction in which a particular quota should be adjusted, if any, is independent of the implicit distortions in the other quota-restricted markets. This again is an implication of the absence of spillovers from quota distortions. Thus, in the absence of explicit tariffs, (6) reduces to

$$m\,\mathrm{d}U = \sum_{i \in R} (p_i^R - r_i^R)\,\mathrm{d}Q_i,$$

which implies that a loosening of *any* binding quota leads to an increase in domestic welfare.

In the presence of explicit tariffs, the prescriptions for piecemeal quota reform are less straightforward. Suppose, initially, there are no quotas ($p^R = r^R$). In general, the matrix $S_{TR}S_{RR}^{-1}$ may have a complex sign pattern depending on the substitution and complementarity relationships both within the quota-restricted group and between those goods and the tariff-restricted items. As in the tariff case, however, definite results are forthcoming in special cases. In particular, suppose the quota-restricted goods are net substitutes both for each other and for the tariff-restricted goods. Then $S_{RR}^{-1} < 0$ [Hatta (1977, p. 1866)], $S_{TR} > 0$, and consequently the elements of $S_{TR} S_{RR}^{-1}$ are all negative. The imposition of binding quotas ($dQ < 0$) on all goods within the quota group will then be welfare improving.

To interpret (6) further, it is useful to break the coefficient matrix down and to rewrite it in terms of ad valorem tariffs (both implicit and explicit). Dealing with the case of a change in one quota only, this yields:

$$m\,dU = p_i^R [t_i^R - \sum_{k \in T} a_{ki} t_k^T]\, dQ_i, \tag{7}$$

where $t_i = (p_i - r_i)/p_i$ denotes the ad valorem tariff on commodity i expressed in terms of domestic prices:[2]

$$a_{ki} = -\sum_{j \in R} (p_k^T / p_i^R) s_{kj} s_{ji}^{-1},$$

and s_{ij} and s_{ij}^{-1} are the ijth elements of S_{TR} and S_{RR}^{-1}, respectively. One can readily show that $\sum_{k \in T} a_{ki} t_k^T$ is a weighted average of the explicit ad valorem tariffs (including any zero tariffs), with $\sum_{k \in T} a_{ki} = 1$.[3] Whether a quota should then be applied to i depends [from (7)] on the sign of $-\sum_{k \in T} a_{ki} t_k^T$. These expressions have familiar interpretations in terms of substitutes and complements. The kith element of the matrix $S_{TR} S_{RR}^{-1}$ captures the effects of a tightening of the quota on good i ($i \in R$) on the compensated excess demand

[2] The use of domestic prices is simply for convenience. One obtains the same rankings for individual distortions whether they are expressed in terms of domestic or world prices, and only the rankings are important in this context.

[3] One can rewrite

$$\sum_{k \in T} a_{ki} = -\sum_{j \in R} \left(\sum_{k \in T} (p_k^T s_{kj} / p_i^R) \right) s_{ji}^{-1}.$$

From the homogeneity of the S_p matrix, one has that

$$\sum_{k \in T} p_k^T s_{kj} = -\sum_{k \in R} p_k^R s_{kj} \quad \text{for all } j.$$

Substituting this and rearranging yields:

$$\sum_{k \in T} a_{ki} = \sum_{j \in R} (p_j^R / p_i^R) \left(\sum_{h \in R} s_{jh} s_{hi}^{-1} \right).$$

The definition of matrix inverse requires that

$$\sum_{h \in R} s_{jh} s_{hi}^{-1} \begin{cases} 1, & \text{if } i = j \\ 0, & \text{otherwise,} \end{cases}$$

and hence

$$\sum_{k \in T} a_{ki} = p_i^R / p_i^R = 1.$$

for good k ($k \in \mathrm{T}$), when the prices of all the quota-restricted goods are allowed to adjust to clear their markets. Thus,

$$a_{ki} = -\frac{p_k^{\mathrm{T}}}{p_i^{\mathrm{R}}} \cdot \frac{\mathrm{d}S_k}{\mathrm{d}Q_i} = -\frac{p_k^{\mathrm{T}}}{p_i^{\mathrm{R}}} \cdot \sum_{h \in R} \frac{\partial S_k}{\partial p_h} \cdot \frac{\partial p_h}{\partial Q_i}, \quad k \in \mathrm{T},\ i \in \mathrm{R}.$$

As an illustration, consider the special case where only good k is subject to a tariff, then (7) reduces to

$$m\,\mathrm{d}U = (p_k - r_k)\frac{\partial S_k}{\partial p_i} \cdot \frac{\partial p_i}{\partial Q_i}\mathrm{d}Q_i. \tag{8}$$

Since $\partial p_i/\partial Q_i < 0$, (8) implies that the quota on i should be tightened ($\mathrm{d}Q_i < 0$) if $\partial S_k/\partial p_i$ is positive – that is if k and i are net substitutes. Of course if k and i are net complements, (8) implies the quota on i should be loosened, but this is unattainable since there is no binding quota initially (a minimum import quota would have to be introduced).[4] Thus, the existence of a tariff on k implies a gain from restricting (expanding) imports of i if k and i are 'substitutes' ('complements') in the sense that $\mathrm{d}S_k/\mathrm{d}Q_i < (>) 0$.

Setting the coefficients in (7) equal to zero allows one to express the second-best optimal implicit tariffs on the quota-restricted items as weighted averages of the explicit tariffs [Green (1961)], i.e.,

$$t_i^0 = \sum_{k \in \mathrm{T}} a_{ki} t_k^{\mathrm{T}}, \quad i \in \mathrm{R}. \tag{9}$$

Though all the explicit tariffs in (9) are positive, their weights may have either sign in general, and hence t_i^0 may be positive or negative. Naturally, a negative implicit tariff cannot be achieved by an import quota, so that the full structure of second-best optimal implicit tariffs may not be attainable. However, as noted above, in the important case where all commodities are net substitutes these weights are all non-negative. The optimal implicit tariffs are then positively weighted averages of the explicit tariffs, and must therefore lie between the latter's largest and smallest values [cf. Lloyd (1974, Proposition 3)].

The net substitutes case also yields a useful proposition for piecemeal quota reform in the presence of unalterable tariffs. If all commodities are net

[4] Guesnerie and Roberts (1984) provide a general microeconomic analysis of the potential gains from imposing quantity controls (rationing or redistribution-in-kind) in a second-best equilibrium involving price distortions. As an alternative to the treatment here, one could extend their analysis towards the derivation of prescriptions for piecemeal quota reform from an initial equilibrium involving an arbitrary set of price and quantity distortions. Their structure is not designed for this purpose, however, and while more general, it is also both less familiar and considerably more complex than those employed to analyze piecemeal trade reform in the past.

substitutes, $\sum_{k\in T} a_{ki}t_k^T$ is a positively weighted average of the explicit tariffs, and hence lies between their maximum and minimum values. Thus, if the implicit tariff on commodity i is greater (less) than the highest (lowest) explicit tariff, one knows immediately that the coefficient on dQ_i in (7) is unambiguously positive (negative). Hence:

Proposition. If all commodities are net substitutes, then a loosening (tightening) of any quota whose implicit tariff is higher (lower) than the highest (lowest) explicit tariff will increase welfare.

5. Conclusion

One can summarize these results as follows. Suppose trade is restricted by a combination of explicit tariffs on some goods and quotas on others. Then, if the quota-restricted goods are net substitutes for all other goods, the standard prescriptions for piecemeal policy reform continue to apply to the explicit tariffs even if the quotas remain untouched. Furthermore, if all goods are net substitutes, then a loosening (tightening) of any quota whose implicit tariff is above (below) the highest (lowest) explicit tariff will raise welfare, even if the explicit tariffs remained unchanged.

Finally, one further interesting implication of these results for trade liberalization is worth noting. It is now almost a standard recommendation that a country intent on trade liberalization should, as a preliminary, convert all of its quantitative restrictions to ('equivalent') tariffs, and only then begin the process of liberalization itself along the general lines of piecemeal tariff reform noted above. But if one disregards for the moment the other well-known objections to quotas as trade-restricting devices (lack of transparency, difficulties with quota allocation, potential for corruption, etc.), the preceding analysis does suggest that a process of piecemeal policy reform which begins from a position where all distortions are quantitative is considerably less constrained than one beginning from a position where all distortions are due to tariffs. Since quantitative distortions do not spill over into other markets, they have the advantage that loosening any restriction will raise welfare. With tariffs on the other hand, one runs the risk that an inappropriate piecemeal adjustment may reduce welfare and thus threaten the prospects for further liberalization.

References

Corden, W.M. and R.E. Falvey, 1985, Quotas and the second best, Economics Letters 18, 67–70.
Dixit, A., 1985, Tax policy in open economies. Chapter 6, in: A.J. Auerbach and M. Feldstein, eds., Handbook of public economics (North-Holland, Amsterdam).

Fukushima, T., 1979, Tariff structure, nontraded goods and theory of piecemeal policy recommendations, International Economic Review 20, 427–435.
Fukushima, T., 1981, A dynamic quantity adjustment process in a small open economy, and welfare effects of tariff changes, Journal of International Economics 11, 513–529.
Green, H.A.J., 1961, The social optimum in the presence of monopoly and taxation, Review of Economic Studies 29, 66–78.
Guesnerie, R. and K. Roberts, 1984, Effective policy tools and quantity controls, Econometrica 52, 59–86.
Hatta, T., 1977, A recommendation for a better tariff structure, Econometrica 45, 1859–1869.
Lloyd, P.J., 1974, A more general theory of price distortions in open economies, Journal of International Economics 4, 365–386.
Woodland, A., 1982, International trade and resource allocation (North-Holland, Amsterdam).

[25]

TRADE REFORM WITH QUOTAS, PARTIAL RENT RETENTION, AND TARIFFS

BY JAMES E. ANDERSON AND J. PETER NEARY[1]

Quotas are the predominant means of protection in developed countries, with quota rents commonly shared between exporter and importer. This paper derives shadow prices appropriate to evaluating trade reform under these circumstances, and provides a number of useful sufficient conditions for welfare-improving "piecemeal" reform. In doing so, we apply the distorted (quantity-constrained) expenditure function, and use implicit separability to derive more powerful results than have previously been available.

KEYWORDS: Piecemeal trade reform, quotas, shadow price.

QUOTAS ARE THE PREDOMINANT MEANS of protection in developed countries. The evaluation of trade reform in the presence of quotas is complicated by two features: quotas typically coexist with tariffs and quota rents are commonly shared between exporter and importer.[2] The first objective of this paper is to develop a general approach to evaluating trade reform in these circumstances. Our analysis of quota reform proceeds by identifying the general equilibrium shadow prices of quotas under various assumptions and then characterizing the admissible welfare-improving reforms. We provide a number of useful sufficient conditions for welfare-improving unilateral quota reform and extend the standard tariff reform results to allow for fixed quotas.

As a by-product we are able to unify existing results on quota and tariff reform. In the literature, the case of "pure" quotas (where all rent is retained at home) offers a puzzling contrast to tariff reform. On the one hand, much stronger results are available for quota reform than for tariff reform: any quota increase is always welfare-improving for a small country (Corden and Falvey (1985)), whereas a selective tariff cut for a small country may reduce welfare because of the loss of tariff revenue on other imported goods. On the other hand, intuition suggests that tariffs and quotas are duals, so that the structure of reform should preserve a kind of equivalence. Our more general structure

[1] An earlier version of this paper was delivered to the Midwest International Economics meetings, Minneapolis, April, 1988, and to the Econometric Society European meetings in Bologna, August, 1988. We are grateful to Ron Jones and other participants for helpful comments. The current version has improved greatly due to the many excellent suggestions of the referees.

[2] By contrast, previous analysts have considered only "pure quotas" where all rents are retained at home, and "pure" voluntary export restraints (VER's) where all rents are awarded to foreigners. VER's are the most commonly used type of quantitative restriction in developed countries but in practice there appears to be considerable reverse transfer of rents. For example, the U.S. markup on Japanese autos under the VER of 1981–85 gave substantial rent to U.S. dealers. Also, in many cases (such as textiles and apparel) VER's coincide with substantial domestic import tariffs which retain a portion of the rent. Even apparently pure import quota systems such as the U.S. cheese import control structure generate significant rent sharing due to their allocation to very fine commodity-by-country categories, so that bilateral monopoly is approximately the norm. (See Hornig, Boisvert, and Blandford (1988) for evidence.)

reveals the precise sense in which equivalence is preserved and why it breaks down.

We now outline the main results of the paper. Section 1 develops a general approach to calculating the general equilibrium shadow price of quotas. This yields in Section 2 a rich harvest of new results on partial quota reform.[3] The "piecemeal reform" literature has generally considered only "reforms" which are liberalizations: all distortions are cut, as for example in the cited result of Corden and Falvey. In contrast, we define *reform* to include a mixture of increases and decreases in distortions, which is the case for actual VER negotiations such as those occurring in the Multi-Fiber Arrangement. Welfare improves under unilateral quota reform for a small country if and only if the reform is such that quota changes are positively associated with quota shadow prices. With "pure" import quotas (full rent retention), we show in Section 2.1 that the shadow price of a quote is the rent premium; hence a reform raises welfare if it raises normalized quota rent.

In Section 2.2 we initiate formal consideration of intermediate rent retention. With fixed rent shares (defended below), equivalent to fixed shares of licenses awarded to foreigners, we offer quota relaxation (reform with no tightening permitted) analogues of the standard tariff reform results: any quota expansion in proportion to existing quota levels is welfare-improving, and if constrained goods are "substitutes" in a sense developed below, all quota expansions are welfare improving. Net substitutability of all goods turns out to be sufficient for "constrained substitutability." As an alternative restriction on preferences, which is independent of net substitutability and in some ways less restrictive, we consider the case of implicit separability with respect to the partition between quota constrained goods and other goods. This turns out to permit much stronger results. Quota reform (with some tightening permitted) raises welfare if it raises normalized quota rent and also raises the expenditure on imports in foreign prices under the assumption of uniform rent retention and no tariffs.

In Section 2.3 tariffs on non-quota-constrained goods are admitted. Quota reform in the presence of tariffs is amended by the loss of tariff revenue as expenditure flows to the constrained goods and reduces the benefit of reform, but the previous simple quota reform theorem holds under implicit separability with either of two added conditions which are likely to be met in developed countries. Section 2.4 sketches how the results may be extended to incorporate the terms of trade effect facing a large country. Section 2.5 takes up consideration of the determinants of the rent share, and shows that, in two important cases, the previous reform theorems are essentially unaltered.

Turning to the treatment of unilateral reform of tariffs in the presence of quotas in Section 3, the shadow quantity corresponding to a change in a tariff is the value of the distorted trade displaced by the tariff change, or the marginal

[3] The reforms considered are infinitesimal, as is typical of the literature, which in the context of quota reform is subject to an additional and well-known qualification that finite policy changes must be sufficiently small that the mix between binding and non-binding quotas is not altered.

tariff burden. With quotas, the marginal effect of a tariff change has an additional term equal to the change in the value of the quota-constrained trade. Lowering tariffs tends to reduce the demand pressure on quota-constrained markets, thus reducing the rent transferred abroad. For implicit separability or net substitutability and uniform rent retention, the set of welfare-improving tariff reforms is increased by the fixed quota effect. Indeed, small import and export subsidies are welfare-increasing.

1. THE SHADOW PRICE OF QUOTAS

The analysis throughout is of a competitive open economy with no distortions other than those in trade. A representative agent maximizes revenue in production and minimizes expenditure in consumption. The government distorts trade and redistributes revenues in lump-sum fashion. Explicitly, all goods are tradable, but nontraded goods are implicit, since they may be interpreted as quota-constrained goods whose quota levels are set at zero. The economy is usually assumed to be small (price-taking), but Section 2.4 relaxes this assumption.

1.1. *Expenditure Functions*

We begin with the *trade expenditure function* $E(p,\pi,u)$:

$$(1.1) \qquad E(p,\pi,u) = \min_{Q,Z}\{p'Q + \pi'Z | U(Q,Z) = u\},$$

where U is a Meade trade utility function defined over the trade vectors Q and Z, and p and π are the price vectors facing the domestic representative agent. E has the standard properties of an expenditure function: it is concave in (p,π) and its derivatives with respect to prices are the economy's excess demand functions; $E_p = Q$, $E_\pi = Z$.[4]

The trade expenditure function (1.1) is the appropriate tool of analysis when tariffs are the only form of trade restriction. By contrast, in this paper we wish to allow for a very general class of trade policies, whereby some goods are subject to quantitative controls and the remainder are subject to tariffs.[5] Let Q be the permitted trade volumes in the quota-restricted product group, with foreign prices p^*. We shall ordinarily interpret Q as an import quota, but a symmetric interpretation is immediate for export quotas. For the unrestricted group, Z is the trade quantity and π is the domestic price vector, equal to $\pi^* + t$, where π^* and t are world prices and specific tariffs respectively. (For an export tax, t is negative.) Expenditure on the unrestricted product group is

[4] This function embodies both consumer and producer behavior, since it equals the difference between a standard expenditure function, $e(p,\pi,u)$, and a GNP or revenue function, $g(p,\pi)$. This is why its derivatives with respect to prices equal the economy's excess demand functions (with negative values corresponding to exports).

[5] Unrestricted goods and goods subject to export taxes may be included in the latter category, with zero and negative values of t, respectively.

based on minimizing behavior as in (1.1), which leads us to the *distorted trade expenditure function*:

$$(1.2) \qquad \tilde{E}(Q,\pi,u) = \min_{Z}\{\pi' Z | U(Q,Z) = u\}.$$

Alternatively, and more conveniently,

$$(1.3) \qquad \tilde{E}(Q,\pi,u) = \max_{p}\{E(p,\pi,u) - p'Q\}.$$ [6]

(1.3) is a well behaved maximization problem, since E is concave in p. Mechanically, the first order conditions solve for the price p which equates demand $E_p(p,\pi,u)$ with Q, the supply. p is also the shadow price for Q which maximizes the value of the Lagrangean function for the choice problem (1.2). The first derivative properties of $\tilde{E}$ are straightforward from (1.3):

$$(1.4) \qquad \tilde{E}_{\pi}(Q,\pi,u) = Z,$$

$$(1.5) \qquad \tilde{E}_{Q}(Q,\pi,u) = -p.$$

The first property follows from Shephard's Lemma. The second is less familiar, with the intuition that a relaxation of the quota by one unit reduces expenditure on the unconstrained group by $\pi' Z_Q$, which equals $-p$. This gives the economy's marginal willingness to pay for, or the "virtual price" of consumption of the quota-constrained goods.[7] $\tilde{E}$ is concave in π and convex in Q, by its minimum in Z and maximum in p properties. Where the important derivative matrix $p_Q = -\tilde{E}_{QQ} = E_{pp}^{-1}$ exists, it is negative definite.

1.2. *The Budget Constraint and the Shadow Price of Quotas*

Now consider the internal and external payment constraints facing the economy (which is assumed until Section 2.4 to be small, so that world prices p^*

[6] (1.3) follows from a formal consideration of the full program behind (1.2):

$$(1.2') \qquad \min_{Q'',Z}\{\pi Z | U(Q'',Z) - u \geq 0, \quad Q'' - Q \leq 0\}.$$

Here, Q'' is the decision variable, and Q is the quota level. The Lagrangean for (1.2′) is

$$\max_{\lambda,p}\min_{Q'',Z}\{\pi Z - \lambda[U(Q'',Z) - u] + p[Q'' - Q]\}.$$

This may be rearranged to form

$$\max_{p}\left\{\max_{\lambda}\min_{Q'',Z}\{\pi Z + pQ'' - \lambda[U(Q'',Z) - u]\} - pQ\right\},$$

which upon using the Lagrangean for (1.1) yields (1.3).

[7] See Neary and Roberts (1980). In contrast to their paper, the virtual price is directly observable, since it equals the domestic price. $\tilde{E}(Q,\pi,u)$ offers a simpler derivation of the Neary and Roberts conditional expenditure function, equal to $\tilde{E} + \bar{p}Q$, where $\bar{p}$ is the fixed consumer price of the constrained goods.

and π^* are given). All tariff revenue $t'Z$ is retained at home. By contrast, a fraction ω of quota rents accrues to foreigners. This is consistent with awarding the fraction ω of all quota licenses to foreigners, or with VER's where foreigners return a fraction $(1-\omega)$ of the rents to domestic residents, or with a tariff on quota-controlled imports at specific rate $(1-\omega)(p-p^*)$. For concreteness we will use the former convention. We will also assume that ω is uniform across commodities[8] and fixed by a process invariant to Q or t.[9]

In terms of external prices the budget constraint is therefore:[10]

$$(1.6) \qquad \pi^{*\prime}Z + p^{*\prime}Q + \omega[p-p^*]'Q = 0,$$

where the first two terms give the total net imports valued at world prices and the third term represents the transfer to foreigners via the gift of quota licenses. The total rent is $(p-p^*)'Q$. Each element in the sum is nonnegative. For a typical import quota on good i, $p_i - p_i^*$ is positive and Q_i is positive. For a typical export quota, $p_j - p_j^*$ is negative and Q_j is negative. Straightforward manipulation of (1.6) gives the budget constraint expressed in domestic prices:[11]

$$(1.7) \qquad \tilde{E}(Q,\pi,u) + p'Q = t'Z + (1-\omega)(p-p^*)'Q.$$

Here, the left-hand side equals net domestic expenditure on all goods (recall the definition of $\tilde{E}$ in (1.2)); and in equilibrium this must equal the revenue from trade restrictions retained at home, given by the right-hand side.

To derive the welfare effects of different policy changes, we now need to differentiate equation (1.7). This yields initially (using (1.4) and (1.5) to simplify):

$$(1.8) \qquad \tilde{E}_u\, du = t'\,dZ + (1-\omega)(p-p^*)'\,dQ - \omega Q'\,dp - (p-p^*)'Q\,d\omega.$$

The left-hand side is the change in utility measured in expenditure units (since $\tilde{E}_u$, which equals E_u, is the inverse of the marginal utility of income). This equals, first, the effects of changes in the volume of trade in both categories of goods (that in Q dampened by the loss in rents); next, the effect of a rise in home prices of quota-constrained goods, which raises rents lost (provided $\omega > 0$) and so tends to lower welfare; and finally, the effect of a rise in the rent transfer coefficient ω itself, which naturally tends to lower welfare.

To proceed further, we must recognize that the variables Z and p are themselves functions of (Q,π,u) from (1.4) and (1.5). Differentiating these

[8] The case where ω varies across commodities will be considered in footnotes.

[9] Alternative ways of relaxing this assumption are considered in Section 2.5. Note that rent-seeking behavior can lead to social rent loss fractions which exceed one.

[10] No borrowing or other transfer is permitted for simplicity. If it is introduced, the constraining value in (1.6) becomes nonzero.

[11] With differential rent retention, the second term on the right-hand side becomes $(p-p^*)'(I-\Omega)Q$, where I is the identity matrix and Ω is a diagonal matrix with the commodity-specific rent transfer shares ω_i on the diagonal.

equations, substituting in (1.8), and collecting terms yields:[12]

$$(1.9)\qquad \mu^{-1}\tilde{E}_u\, du = \chi'\, dt + \rho'\, dQ - (p - p^*)'Q\, d\omega,$$

where

$$(1.10)\qquad \mu^{-1} = \tilde{E}_u^{-1}\left(\tilde{E}_u - t'Z_u + \omega Q'p_u\right)$$

$$= 1 - t'\tilde{Z}_I - \omega Q'E_{pp}^{-1}Q_I,$$

$$(1.11)\qquad \chi' = t'Z_\pi - \omega Q'p_\pi,$$

$$(1.12)\qquad \rho' = t'Z_Q - \omega Q'p_Q + (1-\omega)(p - p^*)'.$$

The coefficients χ and ρ are the *marginal cost of tariff increases* and the *shadow prices of quotas* respectively, and their interpretation is the objective of Sections 2 and 3. As for the coefficient of $\tilde{E}_u$ on the left-hand side of (1.9), μ is the *shadow price of foreign exchange*. (See (A3) and (A6) in the Appendix for the derivation of the terms in this expression.) Intuitively, a one dollar gift from abroad is worth more than a dollar to the extent that it increases demand for tariff-constrained goods and so raises imports closer to their free trade levels, but less than a dollar to the extent that it raises demand for quota-constrained goods, driving up their domestic prices, and raising rents transferred to foreigners. Following standard practice, we assume that this term is positive.[13]

1.3. *The Separable Case*

A number of the critical terms in the expressions for χ and ρ are considerably simplified in the case of *implicit separability* between the quota-constrained goods and all other goods. Separability in one form or another is ubiquitous in empirical work, so propositions assuming it can be applied to the trade reform models in use. Implicit separability has the extremely useful property that the form of separability is the same in the primal and the dual. Thus dual aggregate

[12] Equations (1.9)–(1.12) can alternatively be derived from (1.6) by defining and then differentiating the constrained balance of payments function:

$$B(Q,t,\omega,u) \equiv \pi^{*\prime}Z(Q,\pi^*+t,u) + p^{*\prime}Q + \omega[p(Q,\pi^*+t,u) - p^*]'Q,$$

$$B_u = u^{-1}\tilde{E}_u,$$

$$B_Q = -\rho,$$

$$B_t = -\chi.$$

See the Appendix for details on the structure in (1.10)–(1.12).

[13] The first two terms in the denominator of μ, $1 - t'\tilde{Z}_I$, represent the "tariff multiplier" (Jones (1969)). A sufficient condition for this to be positive is that all goods be normal in demand. The third term, $-\omega Q'E_{pp}^{-1}Q_I$, is presumptively positive; a sufficient (though over-strong) condition for this is homothetic tastes and uniform import shares within the category of quota-constrained goods. Homothetic tastes imply that $Q_I = Q^c/I$ where Q^c is consumption of quota-constrained goods; hence $Q_I = \alpha(Q/I)$ where α equals Q^c/Q. Hatta (1977a) shows that normality and Hicksian substitutability between each quota good and all other goods also suffice. Stability arguments can be used to defend the assumption that μ is positive (see Hatta (1977b) and Fukushima (1981)).

price and quantity subindices are readily defined. For this reason it serves to provide sharp results in the subsequent analysis of trade reform.

Under implicit separability, the trade expenditure function becomes[14]

$$(1.13)\qquad E(p,\pi,u)=\xi[\phi(p,u),\eta(\pi,u),u].$$

The function ξ is concave and homogeneous of degree one in the subgroup price indices ϕ and η, and each of them is concave and homogeneous of degree one in the appropriate price vector, so that[15]

$$(1.14)\qquad \phi_p'p=\phi,\quad \eta_\pi'\pi=\eta.$$

The first implication of implicit separability concerns the critical term $Q'p_Q$ in expression (1.12) for the shadow price of quotas, which measures the change in rents on existing imports following a marginal relaxation of quota levels. This

[14] There are many conceivable assumptions sufficient to yield implicit separability of the trade expenditure function. One empirically important case is: (i) implicit separability of the expenditure and revenue functions, and (ii) the Armington assumption. The Armington assumption is that imports and domestically produced goods are imperfect substitutes in consumption or production. Also, exports are imperfect substitutes for domestically consumed goods. Such differentiation is empirically well founded and is rationalized as due to packaging and safety requirements, etc. The Armington structure may be seen as the general case, with perfect substitutes emerging as its limiting specialization.

Any trade expenditure function is a reduced form, with nontraded goods in the background, contributing to the substitution and real income effect structure. Prices of nontraded goods are determined by a reduced form function of the prices of traded goods. In the present context the reduced form is implicitly separable if the structural revenue and expenditure functions are implicitly separable with respect to the partition between traded and nontraded goods.

Formally, let the expenditure function be $e(\phi^1(p^1,u),\eta^1(\pi^1,u),q,u)$ and the revenue function be $r(\phi^2(p^2),\eta^2(\pi^2),q)$, where q is the nontraded goods price vector. p^1 and p^2 are disjoint price vectors, as are π^1 and π^2. Market clearance implies $e_q=r_q$, and the equilibrium price has a reduced form solution $q(\phi^1,\phi^2,\eta^1,\eta^2,u)$. The implicitly separable trade expenditure function is

$$\xi(\phi^1,\phi^2,\eta^1,\eta^2,u)\equiv e(\phi^1,\eta^1,q(\phi^1,\phi^2,\eta^1,\eta^2,u),u)$$
$$-r(\phi^2,\eta^2,q(\phi^1,\phi^2,\eta^1,\eta^2,u)).$$

Equation (1.13) follows under the further simplifying assumption that either ϕ^1 or ϕ^2 is null; i.e., quota constraints are placed either on intermediate inputs or on final consumption, but not both.

The (mild) consequence of relaxing the last assumption is that (1.22) below becomes

$$(1.22')\qquad p_QQ=\begin{pmatrix} p^1/\varepsilon^1 \\ p^2/\varepsilon^2 \end{pmatrix},$$

while (1.28) becomes:

$$(1.28')\qquad t'Z_Q=\begin{pmatrix} -\bar{\tau}^1p^1 \\ -\bar{\tau}^2p^2 \end{pmatrix}.$$

In (1.22′) the inverse elasticities ε^i are specific to the quota constrained groups, and in (1.28′) the average *ad valorem* tariffs $\bar{\tau}^i$ are trade-weighted average final consumption and intermediate input tariffs (or export tariffs) respectively. These collapse to (1.22) and (1.28) in the special case of $\bar{\tau}^1=\bar{\tau}^2$ and $\varepsilon^1=\varepsilon^2$. Generally, in the applications which follow, Theorems 4–6 can be restated in terms of an average inverse elasticity and an average of the two tariffs.

[15] See Deaton and Muellbauer (1980, pp. 130–135) for further discussion.

term is negative when Q is a scalar but need not be so in general. However, we have the following result:

LEMMA 1: *Under implicit separability, the term $Q'p_Q$ is negative.*

PROOF: From (1.13) the demand functions for quota-constrained goods are

$$Q = E_p = \xi_\phi \phi_p. \tag{1.15}$$

Moreover, E_p is homogeneous of degree zero in p and π:

$$E_{pp}p + E_{p\pi}\pi = 0, \tag{1.16}$$

and ξ_ϕ is homogeneous of degree zero in ϕ and η:

$$\xi_{\phi\phi}\phi + \xi_{\phi\eta}\eta = 0. \tag{1.17}$$

Hence, from (1.16):

$$p = -E_{pp}^{-1}\phi_p \xi_{\phi\eta}\eta'_\pi \pi, \tag{1.18}$$

$$= -E_{pp}^{-1}\phi_p \xi_{\phi\eta}\eta \qquad (\text{from } (1.14)), \tag{1.19}$$

$$= E_{pp}^{-1}\phi_p \xi_{\phi\phi}\phi \qquad (\text{from } (1.17)), \tag{1.20}$$

$$= p_Q Q \frac{\xi_{\phi\phi}\phi}{\xi_\phi} \qquad (\text{from (A4) and } (1.15)). \tag{1.21}$$

Hence,

$$p_Q Q = p/\varepsilon, \tag{1.22}$$

where

$$\varepsilon \equiv \frac{\xi_{\phi\phi}\phi}{\xi_\phi} < 0, \tag{1.23}$$

the elasticity of demand for the quota-constrained group with respect to its aggregate price. *Q.E.D.*

Two other results follow from the assumption of implicit separability.

LEMMA 2: *Under implicit separability the term $t'Z_Q$ is negative and equals the import weighted average tariff times minus p.*

PROOF: Consider the jth row of the matrix Z_Q, denoted Z_{Q_j} (i.e., the vector of changes in demand for the Z goods following an increase in the quota on good j). Recalling from (1.5) that $\tilde{E}_Q = -p = \pi' Z_Q$, and using $\hat{\pi}$ to denote a diagonal matrix with the elements of the Z price vector π on the principal diagonal, we obtain

$$(1.24)\qquad Z_{Q_j} = -\hat{\pi}^{-1}\frac{\hat{\pi} Z_{Q_j}}{\pi' Z_{Q_j}} p_j = -\hat{\pi}^{-1}\theta^j p_j.$$

Here θ^j is a vector of weights, the typical element of which is $\theta_{ij} = \pi_i Z_{iQ_j} / \Sigma_h \pi_h Z_{hQ_j}$. Equation (1.24) is always true, but with implicit separability the weights are the trade shares, common across j. This follows from using (1.4) and (1.13):

$$(1.25)\qquad Z = \tilde{E}_\pi(Q,\pi,u) = E_\pi[p(Q,\pi,u),\pi,u]$$
$$= \xi_\eta[\phi(p\{Q,\pi,u\},u),\eta(\pi,u),u]\eta_\pi(\pi,u).$$

Differentiating the ith element of this with respect to Q_j, and replacing η_{π_i} by Z_i/ξ_η,

$$(1.26)\qquad Z_{iQ_j} = \frac{\xi_{\eta\phi}}{\xi_\eta}\phi'_p p_{Q_j} Z_i.$$

Substituting (1.26) into the expression for θ_{ij} and canceling the common terms in numerator and denominator allows us to rewrite (1.24) as

$$(1.27)\qquad Z_Q = -\hat{\pi}^{-1}\theta p',$$

where θ denotes the common vector of weights $\theta_i = \pi_i Z_i / \Sigma_h \pi_h Z_h$. Now pre-multiply by the tariff vector t and denote by τ the vector of tariff rates (i.e., $\tau_i = t_i/\pi_i$) to obtain

$$(1.28)\qquad t' Z_Q = -t'\hat{\pi}^{-1}\theta p' = -\tau'\theta p' = -\bar{\tau} p',$$

where $\bar{\tau}$ denotes the import-share-weighted average tariff. *Q.E.D.*

LEMMA 3: *Under implicit separability, $Q' p_\pi$ is positive.*

PROOF: From symmetry, $-Q' p_\pi$ equals $(Z_Q Q)'$. Post-multiplying (1.27) by Q,

$$(1.29)\qquad Z_Q Q = -\hat{\pi}^{-1}\theta p' Q.$$

Under implicit separability, every element of this vector is clearly nonpositive and so the same is true for every element of $-Q' p_\pi$. *Q.E.D.*

2. QUOTA REFORM

We now turn to evaluate (1.12) under various assumptions. In Section 2.1, we evaluate pure quota reform. In Sections 2.2 and 2.3 we consider less than 100% rent retention, and tariffs on non-quota-constrained goods. Section 2.4 develops the extension to the large open economy case, and Section 2.5 briefly considers two alternative approaches to endogenizing the rent retention share.

2.1. *Pure Quota Reform*

It is well known that a unilateral tariff reduction need not improve the welfare of a small country. In contrast, any relaxation of binding quotas in the absence of tariffs is always welfare-improving. (See Corden and Falvey (1985) and Neary (1988).) For binding import quotas, Q_i is positive, $p_i - p_i^*$ is positive, and a *relaxation* is a rise in Q_i. For binding export quotas, Q_j is negative, $p_j - p_j^*$ is negative, and a *relaxation* is an algebraic decrease in Q_j. In this subsection, we extend the latter result to show that any quota *reform* (which may include both quota increases and decreases) which increases normalized quota rent (in a sense to be described) is welfare-improving.

Consider any trade reform which results in a small change in restricted imports or exports dQ. Since we have not chosen any commodity as numeraire, the shadow prices, ρ, are determined only up to a factor of proportionality. It is therefore legitimate, and it turns out to be very convenient, to normalize shadow prices by the shadow quota rent.[16] This implies that $Q'\,d\rho = 0$, so that the change in normalized shadow quota rents equals $\rho'\,dQ$:

$$(2.1) \qquad d(\rho' Q) = Q'\,d\rho + \rho'\,dQ = \rho'\,dQ.$$

This immediately implies the following lemma.

LEMMA 4: *With a positive shadow price of foreign exchange, any quota reform is welfare improving if and only if it raises normalized shadow quota rent.*

Note that the condition of the lemma is necessary and sufficient, so it provides a *complete* characterization of the directions of welfare-improving reform: locally, all moves about Q^0 in the half-space above the budget line formed by $\rho' Q = \rho' Q^0$ are welfare improving.

We now flesh out the meaning of the lemma with a series of special cases in the remainder of this section. With fixed world prices, zero tariffs, and full rent retention, from (1.9) and (1.12), with $\omega = t = 0$, utility changes by

$$(2.2) \qquad \tilde{E}_u\,du = [\,p - p^*\,]'\,dQ.$$

The shadow prices are equal to the quota premia, $p - p^*$.

THEOREM 1: *With fixed world prices, zero tariffs, and full rent retention, any quota reform is welfare-improving if and only if it raises normalized quota rent.*

Theorem 1 provides a very simple test for evaluating any reform in which some quotas are tightened and others are relaxed. Moreover, this test is part of the sufficient conditions in the more complex cases below.

One special case of the theorem has an especially neat interpretation. In (2.2) multiply the element of dQ by p^* and divide the elements of $[\,p - p^*\,]$ by p^* to

[16] A more thorough defense of this procedure is offered in Anderson and Neary (1990).

obtain

$$(2.3)\qquad \mu^{-1}\tilde{E}_u\, du = [p - p^*]'[\hat{p}^*]^{-1}\hat{p}^*\, dQ,$$

where $\hat{p}^*$ denotes a diagonal matrix with the elements of p^* along the diagonal. Now suppose that the trade reform is constrained to have zero balance of trade implications, as is often a side constraint in actual trade negotiations. This implies that $p^{*\prime}\, dQ$ is zero. Then the inner product of the vector of ad valorem tariff (or export tax) equivalents and the algebraic changes in the foreign exchange value of trade is a covariance, since the second vector has zero mean. Formally we have the following corollary.

COROLLARY: *Welfare improves with quota reform under a neutral trade balance impact if the correlation of trade value changes and the ad valorem tariff equivalent is nonnegative.*

2.2. *Rent Sharing*

From (1.12) with no tariffs, the shadow price of quotas is $\rho = (1-\omega)[p - p^*] + (-\omega p_Q Q)$. For imports, this is a weighted average of the implicit tariffs (which measure the total welfare gain on marginal imports) and the change in rents (which measure the total welfare gain on intramarginal imports), the weights being the shares of rents accruing to home and foreign residents. The export goods interpretation is symmetric to that for imports, so we shall stick to the more intuitive import good interpretation for most of the discussion.[17] The first term arises because the global value of more imports, $p - p^*$, is shared with foreigners, only $(1-\omega)$ percent being retained at home. The second term arises because the benefit of lower prices, which in the pure import quota case is a transfer from domestic license holders to domestic consumers, is now partly a transfer from foreign license holders.

What can be said about the sign of the shadow prices of quotas in this case? For a single good the second term, $-\omega p_Q Q$ is necessarily positive. For more goods $-p_Q$ is positive definite, but this does not allow us to sign $-\omega p_Q Q$ for arbitrary quota changes and preferences. Thus, for $\omega > 0$, quota reform is just as prone to multi-commodity complications as is tariff reform.[18] Nevertheless we can state two results which provide parallels with the tariff reform literature.

THEOREM 2: *With a positive shadow price of foreign exchange, fixed world prices, zero tariffs, and intermediate rent retention, all quota relaxations which are proportionate to existing quota levels are welfare improving.*

[17] For exports, the negative first term, multiplied by minus one to denote a rise in exports (Q_j becomes more negative), measures the total welfare gain on marginal exports. The negative second term (export supply elasticities normally being expected to be positive), multiplied by minus one to denote a rise in exports, measures the welfare gain on intramarginal exports.

[18] This was noted for the case of pure VER's ($\omega = 1$) in Neary (1988).

PROOF: Under the condition, $dQ = \kappa Q$, where $\kappa > 0$. Then from (1.12)

$$\rho' \, dQ = \kappa\{1-\omega\}[p - p^*]'Q - \kappa\omega Q' p_Q Q \tag{2.4}$$

where $Q'p_QQ$ is negative. Then $\rho' \, dQ > 0$. *Q.E.D.*

Note that the theorem is restricted to radial relaxations (increases for imports, algebraic decreases for exports) in trade. This result is very similar to the familiar uniform-radial-cut in taxes rule (see Foster and Sonnenschein (1970)), and arises for essentially the same reason.[19] For the nonuniform rent retention case a similar proposition holds.[20]

The other main result on gradual tariff reform is the "concertina" rule: provided all goods are net substitutes, welfare improves if we cut the highest tax first. (See Bertrand and Vanek (1971), Lloyd (1974), and Hatta (1977a).) Following Hatta (p. 1866) we note that net substitutability among the quota group (which is analytically equivalent to the nontraded group of Hatta) suffices for p_Q, equal to E_{pp}^{-1}, to be a negative matrix. This condition guarantees that $-\omega p_Q Q$ is nonnegative; hence we have the much stronger result for the quota case that all quota relaxations are welfare improving.[21]

THEOREM 3: *With a positive shadow price of foreign exchange, fixed world prices, uniform rent retention, and zero tariffs, if quota goods are net substitutes for each other and all tradable goods, all quota relaxations are welfare improving.*

It is also possible to state a version of Theorem 3 which uses "constrained Antonelli substitutes" in place of net substitutes.[22] Theorem 3 is far more general than the corresponding "concertina" reform theorem for tariffs, because it allows the entire trade orthant[23] instead of a single path. This generality arises because the relevant substitution effects all have the same sign, whereas in tariff reform the critical matrix E_{pp} has negative diagonal and positive off-diagonal elements.

Theorem 3 is nevertheless still quite restrictive, being provided mainly to connect with the tariff reform literature. To move to quota reforms (which allow

[19] Whereas tariff reform works if the reform permits a Hicksian composite commodity, quota reform requires that a composite Leontief commodity be constructed.

[20] Let Ω be the diagonal matrix with the rent transfer shares ω_i on the diagonal. Then we can show the following theorem.

THEOREM 2′: *With a positive shadow price of foreign exchange, fixed world prices, and zero tariffs, all quota relaxations in proportion to ΩQ, the existing transferred quota levels, are welfare improving.*

The proof follows the lines of that for Theorem 2, using the relaxation rule $dQ = \kappa\Omega Q$ and noting that $(\Omega Q)'p_Q(\Omega Q)$ must be negative.

[21] Theorem 3 also holds for the nonuniform rent retention case, since $-p_Q\Omega Q \geqslant 0$.

[22] The theorem in terms of Antonelli substitutes requires that the group of non-quota-constrained goods be "constrained Antonelli substitutes" for each quota-constrained good, while not restricting the substitution effects among the quota-constrained goods. Space does not permit a full development, but the structure of $\tilde{E}$ can be related to a distance function in Q space. Details will be supplied by the authors on request.

[23] For export quotas it is the negative orthant.

some quotas to tighten), as opposed to relaxations, we take up the case of implicit separability developed in Section 1.4. Complementarities among the Q's are possible, but on average the Q's substitute for the Z's. We can now show the following theorem.

THEOREM 4: *With a positive shadow price of foreign exchange, fixed world prices, uniform rent retention, and zero tariffs, welfare improves under implicit separability with any quota reform which (i) raises normalized rent, and (ii) raises the external value of controlled trade.*[24]

PROOF: Welfare rises if $\rho' dQ > 0$, where in this case $\rho = (1-\omega)(p-p^*) - (\omega/\varepsilon)p$, from (1.12) and (1.22). The first part of $\rho' dQ$, $(1-\omega)[p-p^*]' dQ$ is positive by condition (i). Then $p' dQ > p^{*\prime} dQ > 0$ where the second inequality follows by condition (ii). Then $p' dQ > 0$ which means $-(\omega/\varepsilon)p' dQ > 0$. *Q.E.D.*

2.3. *Quota Reform with Tariffs*

When quotas are relaxed in the presence of tariffs, there is a third effect (additional to those considered in the last two subsections) given by the term $t'Z_Q$ in (1.12). This arises from the change in tariff revenue as changes in quota-constrained imports spill over to affect demands for tariff-constrained imports. If the two categories of goods are "constrained substitutes," in the sense that the elements of Z_Q are negative, then this effect tends to reduce welfare. (See the expression for Z_Q in (A1).) Our results may be compared with those of Falvey (1988), building on Hatta (1977b), who shows that if all goods are net substitutes, then Z_Q is negative. Based on this, he offers a quota relaxation theorem (see below). Our alternative route to signing Z_Q is via implicit separability, which is arguably less restrictive than net substitutability, since it restricts cross-effects between groups of substitution effects rather than the sign of every cross-effect. It has independent interest in any event.

From Lemmas 1 and 2 in Section 1.3, the shadow price of quotas under implicit separability becomes:

$$(2.5) \qquad \rho = (1-\omega)(p-p^*) - \frac{\omega}{\varepsilon}p - \bar{\tau}p.$$

The additional term $-\bar{\tau}p$ acts in the "wrong" direction: quota reform causes a switch in spending away from tariff-ridden goods, thus reducing their import levels still further below the first-best. Nevertheless, in plausible circumstances this is likely to be outweighed by the first two terms. In particular, Theorem 4 may be extended to give the following result.

THEOREM 5: *With a positive shadow price of foreign exchange, fixed world prices, and uniform rent retention, any quota reform improves welfare under*

[24] The normalized rent is $[p-p^*]'Q/p'Q$.

implicit separability provided (i) normalized rent rises, (ii) the external value of controlled trade rises, and (iii) $\bar{\tau} \leqslant -(\omega/\varepsilon)$; *i.e., the average tariff rate is not greater than the rent share deflated by the elasticity of quota-constrained goods with respect to their own average price.*

As always, reform denotes mixtures in which some quotas may be tightened. It may be noted that average tariffs are very low in developed countries, that elasticities of demand for quota constrained goods such as textiles are typically below unity in absolute value, and that some form of separability is almost always used in empirical work on the evaluation of trade reform. The implication is that the third condition of Theorem 5 is met since likely values of ω exceed $-\varepsilon\bar{\tau}$. Theorem 5 also suggests that an important task for empirical work is to develop information on ω.

An alternative condition which avoids any assumptions about ω is available from manipulating (2.5):[25]

THEOREM 6: *With a positive shadow price of foreign exchange, fixed world prices, and uniform rent retention, any quota relaxation improves welfare under implicit separability provided the average tariff rate* $\bar{\tau}$ *is not greater than: (i) the implicit tariff on every quota-constrained good,* $(p_i - p_i^*)/p_i$, *and (ii) the inverse of the elasticity of demand for quota-constrained goods with respect to their average price,* $-1/\varepsilon$.

Note that Theorem 6 is more restrictive than Theorem 5 in no longer allowing some quotas to decrease; this was the price of doing away with any restriction on ω. Nevertheless, the entire positive orthant is admissible, as in Corden and Falvey. Both conditions of Theorem 6 appear to be met in developed countries, where average tariffs are below five per cent while quota premia on actively negotiated categories such as textiles and steel are much higher.

It is also noteworthy that (2.5) implies that, for less developed countries whose exports are subject to VER's, under implicit separability *all export quota increases are welfare improving*. This follows from (2.5): (i) $p < p^*$ for an export quota, and (ii) $\varepsilon > 0$, so $\rho < 0$. An increase in an export quota is a reduction in Q algebraically, so all export quota increases imply $\rho' dQ > 0$.

Perspective on the value-added of our results is gained by reviewing Falvey (1988). He offers a quota reform theorem in the case of full rent retention under

[25] For any shadow price i,

$$\frac{\rho_i}{p_i} = (1-\omega)\frac{p_i - p_i^*}{p_i} - \frac{\omega}{\varepsilon} - (1-\omega)\bar{\tau} - \omega\bar{\tau}$$

$$= (1-\omega)\left(\frac{p_i - p_i^*}{p_i} - \bar{\tau}\right) + \omega\left(-\frac{1}{\varepsilon} - \bar{\tau}\right),$$

which is greater than or equal to zero if the implicit tariff rate exceeds the average tariff, and the inverse elasticity exceeds the average tariff rate in absolute value.

the assumption that all goods are net substitutes. In our notation, he shows that the shadow price of the ith quota, ρ_i, is $p_i - p_i^* - \tau_i p_i$, where τ_i is a positive-weighted average of the explicit ad valorem tariffs on the unconstrained goods, with the weights being dependent on the identity of the quota, i. His proposition is immediate: *a relaxation is welfare-improving if the implicit tariff on good i is greater than any explicit tariff on the unconstrained group*. Theorem 6 is able to be less restrictive because implicit separability permits the messy τ_i term, which depends on complex weights, to be collapsed into the readily observable import-weighted average tariff $\bar{\tau}$, independent of i.[26]

2.4. *The Large Country Case*

Now we turn to the extension of the small country results to the large country case. This gives perspective on how our previous conditions must be amended to incorporate terms of trade effects. The new difficulty is that p^*, π^* are dependent on Q. At the optimal quota, the effects via p^*, π^* vanish by the envelope theorem. Here we explore restrictions on the trade reform and substitution effects similar to those in previous subsections such that welfare is guaranteed to rise from arbitrary initial quotas.

Suppose first for simplicity that π^* (and hence π) is invariant to Q, but p^* is not. The domestic price p is a reduced form function of Q and $\pi = \pi^* + t$. Welfare is determined by (1.9) as before. Then by obvious steps a version of Theorem 1 is available for the case of zero tariffs when the shadow price of quotas vector equals $\rho' = (p - p^*)' - Q'p_Q^*$.[27]

THEOREM 7: *With a positive shadow price of foreign exchange, π^* constant, zero tariffs, and full rent retention, under implicit separability a quota reform is welfare-improving if (i) quota rent increases and (ii) evaluated at initial domestic prices, the average absolute value of trade rises.*

PROOF: Quota rent rises by $dR = (p - p^*)'\,dQ + Q'(dp - dp^*)$. Rearranging terms,

$$(2.6)\qquad dR - Q'p_Q\,dQ = (p - p^*)'\,dQ - Q'p_Q^*\,dQ$$
$$= \rho'\,dQ.$$

Under implicit separability, $-Q'p_Q\,dQ = -(1/\varepsilon)p'\,dQ$, so under the conditions both terms on the left of (2.6) are positive. *Q.E.D.*

[26] We may extend Falvey's proposition to the case of rent-sharing, understanding that "implicit tariff" rate is now taken to mean $(1-\omega)(p-p^*)/p$. This follows because under net substitutability the term $-\omega Q'p_Q$ is positive.

[27] ρ' equal to zero implies the optimal quota, when $p = p^* + (p_Q^*)'Q$, which yields the inverse elasticity formula.

Condition (ii) means that on average, import quotas and export quotas must be relaxed.

Now consider the relation of the large country case to our earlier results. The conditions are pleasingly similar, indicating the same controlling logic. Theorem 7 implies Theorem 1 when p_Q^* is zero, since in that case (2.6) means that normalized quota rent increases under the conditions. The added implicit separability assumption plus condition (ii) is needed to take care of a "leakage" involving terms of trade effects, once these are admitted. This is similar to the leakage involving domestic terms of trade effects under the small country assumption when some rent is transferred. It should be noted, however, that the test (i) in Theorem 7, unlike our others, is an *ex post* test (becoming an *ex ante* test when the external price is fixed). Finally, suppose that π can vary as a function of Q. The effect is to add a component to the marginal cost of imports, $(\pi_Q^*)'Z$. Theorem 7 is easily amended. Mixed tariff and quota reform with rent sharing can also be handled as a routine exercise using the steps of Theorems 2 to 6 amended to measure correctly the marginal cost of imports.

2.5. *The Rent Retention Share*

So far, the rent retention share has been assumed to be invariant to the quota setting process. Here we provide a model of the determination of the rent share which suffices for invariance, and provide an important model of endogenous rent share under which previous results still obtain.

First, a Nash bargaining model of dividing the total rents is sufficient for the rent share to be invariant to the size of the total rent. This is appropriate for situations of bilateral monopoly, which are likely to be prevalent in quota-constrained situations due to narrow quota definitions. Suppose the total quota rent R, equal to $[p-p^*]'Q$, is divided in a Nash bargaining game between the importer and the exporter. If the parties do not agree, R is zero and hence both parties' utility is zero. This is the "threat point." If the utility of income is a concave homogeneous function of income for each party, the Nash bargaining share ω is the solution to

$$(2.7) \qquad \max_{\omega}((1-\omega)R)^{1-\alpha}(\omega R)^{1-\alpha^*}\frac{1}{(1-\alpha)(1-\alpha^*)},$$

where $1/\alpha$ and $1/\alpha^*$ are the home and foreign elasticities of intertemporal substitution. The first order condition yields the Nash bargain ω as the solution to $(1-\omega)(1-\alpha^*)=\omega(1-\alpha)$, which is independent of R and hence of the size of the quota. The more impatient party (the one with the lower elasticity of intertemporal substitution) receives the lower share of R. With symmetry, the rent is divided equally.

Next, consider the simplest case of endogenous rent retention, which arises when the government awards all licenses to competitive foreigners but taxes quota-constrained imports at a specific rate q to retain some rent.[28] The rent retention share, $1-\omega$, is equal to $q'Q/[p-p^*]'Q$, which is generally a function of Q. Nevertheless, the shadow price of the quota vector is essentially the same as in (1.12), with subsequent specializations applicable. The budget constraint in domestic prices under the tax vector q becomes instead of (1.7):

$$(2.8) \qquad \tilde{E}(Q,\pi,u)+p'Q=t'Z+q'Q.$$

Following the same chain of substitutions which led to (1.12), the shadow price of the quota vector is

$$(2.9) \qquad \rho'=t'Z_Q+q'-Q'p_Q.$$

Here, the role of $(1-\omega)[p-p^*]$ is taken by q, while the reverse transfer term $-Q'p_Q$ has a coefficient of unity rather than ω. The implication of (2.9) is that *when a tariff is the means of rent retention, we can use the uniform rent retention reform Theorems 2–6*. This is true even though rent retention is generally not uniform and its rate in each sector is endogenous. This is a handy result of some practical importance.

3. TARIFF REFORM IN THE PRESENCE OF QUOTAS

We now turn to the evaluation of tariff reform. Rewriting (1.9) with $dQ=d\omega=0$ and using (1.11), welfare rises with a tariff reform according to

$$(3.1) \qquad \mu^{-1}\tilde{E}_u\,du=(t'Z_\pi-\omega Q'p_\pi)\,dt.$$

The interpretation is straightforward: raising tariffs has the usual direct welfare cost of $t'Z_\pi$. The form of this expression (though not its magnitude) is unaffected by the presence of quotas, as long as all rents are retained at home. (See Neary (1989).) In addition, if any rents are lost, there is an extra effect arising from the induced changes in the prices of quota-constrained goods. Loosely speaking, the latter is a cost if the goods are substitutes, since the presumption is that the p's must rise. The new effect of a tariff increase in the second term is negative because the prices of quota-constrained goods are driven up by substitution away from the tariff-ridden goods, which lowers welfare through the increased rent transfer to foreigners.

Under net substitutability a rise in π will raise p, since Z_Q is negative as noted earlier (following Falvey (1988)), and since Z_Q is equal to $-p_\pi^{\mathrm{T}}$. For the case of implicit separability the p's also rise with a rise in tariffs. Specifically, from (1.29),

$$(3.2) \qquad \mu^{-1}\tilde{E}_u\,du=\left(t'Z_\pi-(\omega p'Q)\theta'\hat{\pi}^{-1}\right)dt,$$

$$(3.3) \qquad =\left(t'Z_\pi-\frac{\omega p'Q}{\pi'Z}Z'\right)dt.$$

[28] The *ad valorem* tariff case is essentially identical.

For the case of a tariff reform in the presence of quotas, the new term arising from interaction with quotas thus presumably acts to increase the set of welfare improving reforms, *for practical purposes making further cuts in tariffs for developed countries welfare-increasing*. Falvey (1988) extends the two basic results on tariff reform to the presence of quotas: uniform radial cuts in tariffs and concertina cuts when all goods are net substitutes will improve welfare in the presence of full rent retention quotas (ω equal to zero). This continues to hold with less-than-full rent retention and, in addition, evaluating (3.1) at a zero tariff level, we obtain the following theorem.

THEOREM 8: *With a positive shadow price of foreign exchange, fixed world prices, and uniform rent retention, tariff cuts below zero (import and export subsidies) on unconstrained goods are welfare-improving in the presence of the transfer of import or export quota rent under either net substitutability or implicit separability.*

The intuition of Theorem 8 is that the import and/or export subsidy induces agents to shift away from quota-constrained imports or exports, reducing the leakage to foreigners. The second-best optimal ad valorem subsidy vector for the case of implicit separability is, setting (3.3) equal to zero,

$$(3.4) \qquad \tau^* = \frac{\omega p'Q}{\pi'Z}(\hat{\pi}^{-1}Z_{\pi}^{-1}\hat{Z})1,$$

where 1 is the vector of ones, the circumflex denotes a diagonal matrix, and the term in brackets is the familiar inverse elasticity matrix. If all unconstrained goods are net substitutes, by Hatta's (1977a) argument, the elasticities are negative for imports and positive for exports; and thus *every* unconstrained trade must be subsidized. Note in particular that this implies that *developing countries with exports subject to VER's should subsidize their unconstrained exports*.

4. CONCLUSION

In this paper we have derived a variety of results which can be used to evaluate trade reform in the realistic context where trade is restricted by *both* tariffs and quotas and where some (but typically not all) quota rents accrue to foreign residents. We have presented a variety of results which are in the tradition of the "piecemeal policy reform" approach of Foster and Sonnenschein (1970), Bertrand and Vanek (1971), Bruno (1972), Dixit (1975), Hatta (1977), Fukushima (1979), and Falvey (1988). Thus we have derived a number of sufficient conditions for welfare-improving reforms under a range of assumptions concerning the policy environment and the structure of technology and preferences. Our main innovations are (i) to introduce consideration of rent-sharing, (ii) to make use of the distorted expenditure function, and (iii) to show how implicit separability can produce much more powerful results than the previously exploited assumption of net substitutability.

Rather than summarizing our results in detail (which is done in the introduction) we conclude by noting that our results point in the direction of several desirable investigations. (i) The importance of the rate of quota rent retention for the theoretical results suggests that effort should be devoted to measuring it. (ii) The welfare analysis of policy changes with quotas is directly applicable to the analysis of welfare in a model of nontraded goods or elastically supplied domestic factors. Thus the evaluation of changes in quotas using our methods is applicable to such reforms as project evaluation of nontradables, immigration policy, and changes in public goods in an open economy.

Department of Economics, Boston College, Chestnut Hill, MA 02167, U.S.A.
and
Department of Economics, University College Dublin, Dublin, Ireland

Manuscript received October, 1989; final revision received December, 1990.

APPENDIX

Derivatives of the Import Demand and Domestic Price Functions

Throughout the paper, we make extensive use of the derivatives of the direct demand functions for unconstrained imports, $Z(Q, \pi, u)$, and the *inverse* demand functions for quota-constrained imports, $p(Q, \pi, u)$. These can be expressed in terms of the derivatives of either the distorted trade expenditure function $\tilde{E}(Q, \pi, u)$ or the standard trade expenditure function $E(p, \pi, u)$. The former simply involves differentiating (1.4) and (1.5) while the latter involves differentiating the direct demand functions for both goods and inverting the total differential of $E_p = Q$ to solve for dp. (See Neary and Roberts (1980) and Neary (1989) for further details and discussion.) Equating corresponding terms yields:

(A1) $$Z_Q = \tilde{E}_{\pi Q} = E_{\pi p} E_{pp}^{-1},$$

(A2) $$Z_\pi = \tilde{E}_{\pi\pi} = E_{\pi\pi} - E_{\pi p} E_{pp}^{-1} E_{p\pi},$$

(A3) $$Z_u = \tilde{E}_{\pi u} = E_{\pi u} - E_{\pi p} E_{pp}^{-1} E_{pu}$$
$$= \tilde{Z}_I \tilde{E}_u = \left(Z_I - E_{\pi p} E_{pp}^{-1} Q_I\right) E_u,$$

(A4) $$p_Q = -\tilde{E}_{QQ} = E_{pp}^{-1},$$

(A5) $$p_\pi = -\tilde{E}_{Q\pi} = -E_{pp}^{-1} E_{p\pi},$$

(A6) $$p_u = -\tilde{E}_{Qu} = -E_{pp}^{-1} E_{pu} = -E_{pp}^{-1} Q_I E_u.$$

Here, we have used Z_I and Q_I to denote the income derivatives of Marshallian demand in the absence of quotas and $\tilde{Z}_I$ to denote the income derivatives of demand for unconstrained goods in the presence of quota constraints.

REFERENCES

Anderson, J. E., and J. P. Neary (1990): "The Coefficient of Trade Utilization: Back to the Baldwin Envelope," in *The Political Economy of International Trade: Essays in Honor of Robert E. Baldwin*, ed. by R. W. Jones and A. O. Krueger. Oxford: Basil Blackwell, pp. 49–72.

BERTRAND, T. J., AND J. VANEK (1971): "The Theory of Tariffs, Taxes, and Subsidies: Some Aspects of the Second Best," *American Economic Review*, 61, 925–931.

BRUNO, M. (1972): "Market Distortions and Gradual Reform," *Review of Economic Studies*, 39, 373–383.

CORDEN, W. M., AND R. E. FALVEY (1985): "Quotas and the Second Best," *Economics Letters*, 10, 67–70.

DEATON, A., AND J. MUELLBAUER (1980): *Economics and Consumer Behavior*. Cambridge: Cambridge University Press.

DIXIT, A. K. (1975): "Welfare Effects of Tax and Price Changes," *Journal of Public Economics*, 4, 103–123.

FALVEY, R. E. (1988): "Tariffs, Quotas, and Piecemeal Policy Reform," *Journal of International Economics*, 25, 177–188.

FOSTER, E., AND H. SONNENSCHEIN (1970): "Price Distortion and Economic Welfare," *Econometrica*, 38, 281–297.

FUKUSHIMA, T. (1979): "Tariff Structure, Non-traded Goods, and Theory of Piecemeal Policy Recommendations," *International Economic Review*, 20, 427–435.

——— (1981): "A Dynamic Quantity Adjustment Process in a Small Open Economy, and Welfare Effects of Tariff Changes," *Journal of International Economics*, 11, 513–529.

HATTA, T. (1977a): "A Recommendation for a Better Tariff Structure," *Econometrica*, 45, 1859–1869.

——— (1977b), "A Theory of Piecemeal Policy Recommendations," *Review of Economic Studies*, 44, 1–21.

HORNIG, E., R. N. BOISVERT, AND D. BLANDFORD (1988): "Quota Rents and Subsidies: The Case of U.S. Cheese Import Quotas," Cornell University.

JONES, R. W. (1969): "Tariffs and Trade in General Equilibrium: Comment," *American Economic Review*, 59, 418–424.

LLOYD P. J. (1974): "A More General Theory of Price Distortions in Open Economies," *Journal of International Economics*, 4, 365–386.

NEARY, J. P. (1988): "Tariffs, Quotas, and VERs with and without International Capital Mobility," *Canadian Journal of Economics*, 21, 714–735.

——— (1989): "Trade Liberalisation and Shadow Prices in the Presence of Tariffs and Quotas," Working Paper No. 89/4, Centre for Economic Research, University College, Dublin.

NEARY, J. P., AND K. W. S. ROBERTS (1980): "The Theory of Household Behavior under Rationing," *European Economic Review*, 13, 25–42.

Part VII
Reform with Government Production and Revenue

[26]

TARIFF REFORM IN A SMALL OPEN ECONOMY WITH PUBLIC PRODUCTION*

By Kenzo Abe[1]

This paper examines the welfare effects of the reduction of the highest tariffs and the uniform change of all the tariffs in a small open economy with public production. Using the restricted GNP and expenditure functions, we show that such tariff reforms can improve the welfare of the economy if the public production is initially abundant. A change in the public production as well as a change in the distortion of tariff structures is shown to affect the welfare of the economy.

1. Introduction

A development of the theory of tariff reform has supported an argument for tariff reduction. It is well known that a tariff reduction does not always improve the welfare of the economy initially distorted by taxes or tariffs.[2] The class of tariff reform which improves the welfare, however, has been derived by Foster and Sonnenschein (1970), Bertrand and Vanek (1971), Bruno (1972), Lloyd (1974), etc. In particular, Hatta (1977) showed that the reduction of the highest tariff rate is the welfare improving policy for a small open economy under the conditions of the normality in consumption and the substitutability between the commodity under the tariff reform and the other commodities. Fukushima (1979) also showed that the uniform change of all the tariffs improves the welfare of the economy under the normality condition. All of them, however, assumed implicitly that the tariff revenue is transferred to the consumers in a lump-sum fashion. Thus, they have ignored the distortion due to the spending of the tariff revenue. Diewert, Turunen and Woodland (1989) have recently criticized that feature of their models.

The purpose of this paper is to examine the theory of tariff reform in a small open economy where the tariff revenue is spent on the public production of a good.[3] Examining such a model, we try to answer a question: whether tariff reforms proposed by former authors improve a welfare or not, even when a change in the tariff revenue increases or decreases the supply of a publicly produced good. In

* Manuscript received August 1988; revised February 1991.

[1] I am indebted to an anonymous referee and Professor Tatsuo Hatta for their helpful suggestions. I am also grateful to the participants in seminars at Osaka, Nagoya City, Kwansei-gakuin, Chukyo, Doshisha, and Nagoya-gakuin Universities, and the second annual Southeastern International Economics Meeting at University of Florida. This study is supported by the Research Administration Grant of Ritsumeikan University.

[2] See Vanek (1965), Bhagwati (1968) and Kemp (1968).

[3] Diewert, Turunen and Woodland (1989) also examined the welfare effects of tariff reforms in the model without a lump-sum transfer where the tariff revenue is spent on the government's purchase of fixed amounts of private goods. In the optimal tariff theory, Boadway, Maital and Prachowny (1973) and Feehan (1988) incorporate the production of a public good financed by a tariff revenue.

considering the economy of countries whose government revenue depends largely on tariffs, a change in the tariff revenue due to a tariff reform would closely relate to the welfare of the countries.

In this paper, using the restricted GNP and expenditure functions, we will show that the policy of the reduction of the highest tariffs or the uniform change of all the tariffs improves the welfare of an economy if a publicly produced good is initially over supplied. Moreover, we will decompose the welfare effects of the tariff reform into two parts. One is the welfare change due to the improvement in the distortion of the tariffs, and the other is the welfare change due to the improvement in the distortion of the supply of the publicly produced good. Using the decomposition, we make clear the reasons for the tariff reforms mentioned above to improve the welfare of the economy. In addition, we derive the situation where such tariff reforms reduce the welfare of the economy.

This paper is organized as follows. Next section presents the model of a small open economy with public production. In Section 3 we derive the equation of the welfare change and give an important definition. Propositions on the welfare improving reforms of tariffs are presented in Section 4. In addition, we also decompose the welfare effects of the tariff reform not only to interpret the results but also to derive the conditions under which such tariff reforms reduce the welfare. The final section gives concluding remarks.

2. A SMALL OPEN ECONOMY WITH PUBLIC PRODUCTION

We consider a small open economy with n private goods, m factors of production, and one publicly produced good. All the private goods except the factors of production are internationally traded.

2.1. *The Private Production.* First we consider the structure of private production. All the private goods are produced by the use of m factors of production, and all the markets of the private goods and the factors of production is perfectly competitive. Once we give the amount of factors available to the private sectors, the information on the private production is drawn from the following GNP function,

$$G^*(p, v^p) \equiv \max_y \{p'y | y \in F(v^p)\},$$

where p and v^p are the domestic price vector of the private goods and the vector of factors of production available to the private sectors, respectively. $F(v^p)$ is the production possibility set of the private goods when v^p is the vector of factors available to the private production. The properties of this GNP function are listed in Appendix. In particular, the gradient vector $G^*_p(p, v^p)$ represents the production vector of the private goods, and the factor price vector w is expressed as,

$$w = G^*_v(p, v^p), \tag{1}$$

where the subscript on the function, throughout this paper, represents the partial derivative with respect to the element (or the vector), i.e., $G^*_p(p, v^p) \equiv \partial G^*/\partial p$.

2.2. *The Demand for the Private Goods.* There is a representative consumer in the economy. The utility level of the consumer depends upon not only the private goods but also the publicly produced good. The consumer can use the publicly produced good free of charge, and considers it to be a parameter in the decision of demand for the private goods. Then, the expenditure function can be defined as,

$$E(p, g, u) \equiv \min_x \{p'x | U(x, g) \geq u\},$$

where g and x are the amount of the publicly produced good and the consumption vector of the private goods, and $U(x, g)$ is the utility function of the consumer. Then the gradient vector $E_p(p, g, u)$ gives the demands for the private goods.[4]

2.3. *The Government.* The government imposes specific tariffs on the private goods. Then the domestic price vector of private goods p is,

$$p = q + t, \tag{2}$$

where q and t are the world price vector of private goods and the vector of specific tariffs on the private goods, respectively.

The government utilizes its tariff revenue to produce a good which is supplied through the nonmarket system instead of transferring the revenue to consumers in a form of lump-sum transfer. The good is publicly produced by the use of m factors of production and supplied free of charge for the consumers. The good is called a publicly produced goods in this paper. The cost of production is assumed to be minimized. Let $C^g(w)$ denote the unit cost function of the public production. Then the budget constraint of the government is,

$$C^g(w)g = t'\{E_p(p, g, u) - G_p^*(p, v^p)\}. \tag{3}$$

From the property of the unit cost function, the government's demand vector for factors of production v^g is,

$$v^g = C_w^g(w)g. \tag{4}$$

2.4. *The Full Employment and the Balance of Trade.* We assume the full employment of the factors of production. Since the factors of production are employed either in the private sectors or in the public sector, the full-employment condition is,

$$v^p + v^g = v, \tag{5}$$

[4] The publicly produced good can be regarded as the public good in many consumers' economy. In the case, the demand for the ith consumer can be written as $x^i = E_p^i(p, g, u^i)$. Then, the total demand is expressed as $\Sigma E_p^i(p, g, u^i)$. In the many-consumer economy, however, there are two types of welfare criteria. One is the potential improvement of welfare which utilizes a lump-sum transfer to exclude the distributional effects of tariff reforms, and the other is the actual improvement of welfare which allows for no lump-sum transfer to exclude the distributional effects of them. The latter approach is difficult to analyze even in the economy without a public good. For example, Diewert, Turunen and Woodland (1989) obtain the existence theorem of welfare-improving tariff reforms but do not obtain the practical formula of tariff reforms.

where v is the vector of factor endowments in the economy.

Since the world price vector of the private goods is given by q and no other good is traded in the economy, the condition of trade balance is,

$$q'\{E_p(p, g, u) - G_p^*(p, v^p)\} = 0. \tag{6}$$

The $3m + n + 2$ equations from (1) to (6) describe the full equilibrium in our model. There are $3m + n + 2$ endogenous variables: u, g, p, w, v^p, v^g, in the equations, while the exogenous variables are the tariffs t, the world prices q, and the factor endowments v. The economy described above is called *the small open economy with public production*.

3. PRELIMINARY ANALYSIS

In this section we will make some definitions which play an important role in the proof of our propositions and derive basic equations for the welfare change due to a tariff reform.

3.1. *The Restricted GNP Function.* There are a lot of equations which describe the equilibrium of the small open economy with public production, especially in the production side. Here we define *the restricted GNP function* which contains the information on the private and public production.

Substituting (1) into (4), and next (4) into (5), we obtain

$$v^p + C_w^g(G_v^*(p, v^p))g = v. \tag{7}$$

Solving (7) for v^p, we can get v^p as a function of p, g and v. Since the vector v is not changed in the following analysis, it is innocuous to define v^p satisfying (7) as,

$$v^p = v^p(p, g). \tag{8}$$

Substituting (8) into $G^*(p, v^p)$, we define the restricted GNP function $G(p, g)$ as,[5]

$$G(p, g) \equiv G^*(p, v^p(p, g)).$$

The following lemma gives the properties of the restricted GNP function.

LEMMA 1. *If* $G_{vv}^*(p, v^p) \equiv \partial^2 G^*(p, v^p)/\partial v^{p^2} = 0$, *then* $G(p, g)$ *has the following properties,*

(i) $G_p(p, g) = G_p^*(p, v^p)$,
(ii) $G_g(p, g) = -C^g(w)$,
(iii) $G(\alpha p, g) = \alpha G(p, g)$ *for any scalar* $\alpha \geq 0$,
(iv) $z'G_{pp}(p, g)z > 0$ *for any nonzero vector* $z \neq \alpha p$,

where $G_{pp}(p, g) \equiv \partial^2 G(p, g)/\partial p^2$.

[5] Notice that G^* or G only represents the market value of the private goods produced by the private industries. The intrinsic value of GNP in this economy is $G^* + C^g g$ since there are both private and public sectors producing goods.

PROOF. See the Appendix.

Let us consider the meaning of the condition $G^*_{vv} = 0$. Since G^*_v is the vector of factor prices as is shown by (2), the condition implies that the factor prices are never affected by the change in the factor endowments available for the private sectors. In the conventional Heckscher-Ohlin framework without a public sector, it is called the factor price equalization.[6] We assume that

Condition (F). $G^*_{vv} = 0$, is satisfied throughout this paper.

3.2. *The Basic Equation for a Welfare Change.* Let us define $S(p, g, u)$ as,

$$S(p, g, u) \equiv G(p, g) - E(p, g, u).$$

From the properties of the restricted GNP function and the expenditure function, $S(p, g, u)$ is linear homogeneous and convex in p, and $S_p = G^*_p - E_p$.

Now we derive the reduced equations which represent the equilibrium of the small open economy with public production. Noticing the definition of $S(p, g, u)$ and the property (ii) of the restricted GNP function, equations (6) and (3) are respectively expressed as,

$$q'S_p(p, g, u) = 0, \tag{9}$$

$$t'S_p(p, g, u) - G_g(p, g)g = 0. \tag{10}$$

The system (1) through (6) reduces to those equations (9) and (10) as well as (2). Equations (9) and (10) contain two endogenous variables u and g, while the exogenous variables are t and q.

Since the world price vector is kept constant in our analysis, the solution function of u from (9) and (10) can be written as a function of t,

$$u = u(t). \tag{11}$$

Let σ denote the stage of the tariff reform program. Then we can express the tariff structure as the function of the parameter σ, that is,

$$t = t(\sigma). \tag{12}$$

In view of (11) and (12), we have

$$\frac{du}{d\sigma} = \left(\frac{du}{dt}\right)' \cdot \left(\frac{dt}{d\sigma}\right). \tag{13}$$

The tariff reform program gives the explicit expression of $dt/d\sigma$, and we will specify it in the next section. On the other hand, the total differentiation of (9) and (10) gives the explicit expression of (du/dt).

[6] The conditions for the factor price equalization in the conventional Heckscher-Ohlin model with many goods and factors are surveyed in Woodland (1983) and Ethier (1984). In particular, the number of goods should not be less than that of factors.

LEMMA 2. *Suppose that the condition (F) is satisfied in the small open economy with public production. We have*

$$\left(\frac{du}{dt}\right)' = J^{-1}\{E_g \cdot q'S_{pp} + q'S_{pg} \cdot (S_p - G_{pg} \cdot g)'\},$$

$$J \equiv E_g \cdot q'E_{pu} + q'S_{pg} \cdot E_u,$$

where $S_{pg} \equiv \partial^2 S/\partial p \partial g$, $G_{pg} \equiv \partial^2 G/\partial p \partial g$, *and* $E_{pu} \equiv \partial^2 E/\partial p \partial u$.

PROOF. From (1) and the property (ii) of the restricted GNP function, we have

$$G_g(p, g) = -C^g(G_v^*(p, v^p(p, g)).$$

Then, the condition (F) yields

$$G_{gg} = -(C_w^g)'G_{vv}^* v_g^p = 0.$$

Noticing this fact, the differentiation of (9) and (10) gives the lemma. Q.E.D.

3.3. *The Over Supply and Under Supply of the Publicly Produced Good.* We present a definition which is essential to the proof of our propositions.

DEFINITION. *We say that the publicly produced good is initially* under supplied *when* $q'S_{pg} > 0$, *and* over supplied *when* $q'S_{pg} < 0$.

Note that the sign of $q'S_{pg}$ relates to the welfare change resulting from an additional unit of g financed by nondistortionary means. From the definition of $S(p, g, u)$, we have $q'S_{pg} = (-q'E_{pg}) - (-q'G_{pg})$. The first term $(-q'E_{pg})$ represents the marginal benefit of g valued by the world price of the private goods. It is the value, evaluated by the world price, of the compensated consumption of the private goods to the additional one unit of g. On the other hand, the second term $(-q'G_{pg})$ is the marginal cost or the shadow price of g valued by the world price of the private goods. It is the value, evaluated by the world price, of the decrease in the production of the private goods which is brought about by the additional production of g financed by nondistortionary means. Therefore, the inequality $q'S_{pg} > 0$ implies that the marginal benefit of g financed by nondistortionary means is larger than the marginal cost of it, and the additional unit of g would increase the welfare of the economy. In fact, if an additional unit of g were financed by nondistortionary means, p could be held constant in equation (9). Then the additional unit of g would produce an increase in the trade surplus by $q'S_{pg}$, which implies that the welfare of the country could be increased if there is no inferior private good. On the other hand, the publicly produced good is said to be over supplied when $q'S_{pg} < 0$ from the same reasoning.

This criterion relates to the shadow price of nontraded goods in an open economy. Little and Mirrlees (1974), Findlay and Wellisz (1976), and Srinivasan and Bhagwati (1978) examined an appropriate factor shadow prices in a small open economy and proposed that governments should adopt a public project if it increases the national income valued at world prices. Recently Smith (1987, p. 60) showed that, under our condition (*F*), a public project defined as a public production of private goods should be evaluated by the world price of the private goods. Our definition of over and under supply of a publicly produced good indicates that we should evaluate the cost and benefit of the public good by the opportunity cost and benefit valued by their world prices of private goods.

4. THE WELFARE EFFECTS OF TARIFF REFORMS

4.1. *The Selected Tariff Change.* First, we consider the reduction of the highest tariffs in the small open economy with public production. Before the formal analysis, we define the complementarity between the private good and the publicly produced good.

DEFINITION. *We say that the i-th private good is* complement to the publicly produced good in production *when* $G_{p_i g} \equiv \partial^2 G/\partial p_i \partial g > 0$ *where* p_i *is the domestic price of the i-th private good.*

Since G_{p_i} represents the production of the *i*-th private good, the condition $G_{p_i g} > 0$ means that the supply of the *i*-th private good increases when the amount of the publicly produced good is increased with the prices of the private goods kept constant hypothetically.

The complementarity between the publicly produced good and the private good in production can occur, even if the resources available to the private sectors are reduced by an increase in the public production. Consider the case where there are two private goods, two factors and one publicly produced good in the small open economy. Let the two factors be labor and capital, and assume that the public sector uses capital more intensively than the factor endowment ratio of capital. In this case, an increase in the public production reduces the capital-labor ratio of the resources available to the private sectors. Then, the output of the private sector which is more labor intensive in the private sectors can increase by "Rybczynski" effect.[7]

Then, we have the following proposition.

PROPOSITION 1. *Suppose that the condition (F) and the following conditions are satisfied in the small open economy with public production where the tariffs are imposed only upon the imported goods.*

(i) *The publicly produced good is initially over supplied.*
(ii) *The private goods on which the highest tariff rate is imposed are complement to the publicly produced good in production.*
(iii) *There is no inferior private good.*
(iv) *The private goods on which the highest tariff rate is imposed are net substitutable for all the other private goods.*

[7] The figure in Shibata and Shibata (1987) implies this possibility.

Then, the reduction of all the highest tariffs improves the welfare of the small open economy with public production.

PROOF. Suppose that the private goods are indexed such that the first k commodities share the highest tariff rate. That is, let t_i denote the specific tariff on the ith private good and

$$t_1/q_1 = t_2/q_2 = \cdots = t_k/q_k > t_{k+1}/q_{k+1} \geq t_{k+2}/q_{k+2} \geq \cdots \geq t_n/q_n = 0,$$

where the tariff rate for the exported goods is set equal to 0. The reduction of the highest tariff rate is formally expressed as,

$$dt_i/d\sigma = -1 \text{ for } 1 \leq i \leq k, \text{ and } dt_i/d\sigma = 0 \text{ for } k+1 \leq i \leq n.$$

Notice that $E_g < 0$ and $E_u > 0$. We have $J < 0$, since the conditions (i) and (iii) imply that $q'S_{pg} < 0$ and $q'E_{pu} > 0$, respectively.

From the homogeneity of S, we have $(1+\tau)q'S_{pp} = (\tau q' - t')S_{pp}$ for any number τ. Setting τ equal to t_1/q_1, we obtain

$$\text{(14)} \quad q'S_{pp}\left(\frac{dt}{d\sigma}\right)$$
$$= -(1 + t_1/q_1)^{-1}(t_1 q_{k+1}/q_1 - t_{k+1}, \cdots, t_1 q_n/q_1 - t_n)S_{pp}^{\bar{k}k} > 0,$$

where $S_{pp}^{\bar{k}k}$ is the matrix which is composed of the last $n-k$ rows and the first k columns of S_{pp}. The last inequality follows from the initial structure of tariffs and the condition (iv).

Since the tariffs are imposed on the imported goods, the condition (ii) yields

$$\text{(15)} \quad (S_p - G_{pg}\cdot g)'\left(\frac{dt}{d\sigma}\right) = -\left\{\sum_{i=1}^{k}(S_{p_i} - G_{p_i g}\cdot g)\right\} > 0,$$

Thus, inequalities (14) and (15), together with (13) and Lemma 2, yield $du/d\sigma > 0$. Q.E.D.

The model of Hatta (1977) incorporates the nontraded private goods and the conditions of the highest tariff reduction to improve the welfare contains the net substitutability between the nontraded private goods and the other private goods. On the other hand, in our model we substitute the publicly produced good for the nontraded private goods. In the case, we assume the complementarity between the nontraded publicly produced good and some traded private goods for the improvement of the welfare. This makes a sharp contrast between the small open economy only with private goods and that with public production.

4.2. *The Uniform Tariff Change.* Next we consider the uniform change of all the tariffs in the small open economy with public production. The reform program is expressed as,

$$\frac{dt}{d\sigma} = \beta q - t \text{ for any } \beta > -1.$$

This reform of tariffs indicates the proportional squeezing of all the tariffs toward a certain level βq.[8] If β is set equal to zero, we call it the proportional tariff reduction.

Then, we have the following proposition.

PROPOSITION 2. *Suppose that the condition (F) and the following conditions are satisfied in the small open economy with public production.*

(i) *The publicly produced good is initially over supplied.*

(ii) *The marginal cost of public production evaluated by the world price of private goods is positive, i.e.,* $-q'G_{pg} > 0$.

(iii) *There is no inferior private good.*

Then, the uniform change of all the tariffs toward any target βq $(\beta > -1)$ *always improves the welfare of the small open economy with public production.*

PROOF. Conditions (i) and (iii) yield $J < 0$.

Noticing $p'S_{pp} = (0, 0, \ldots, 0)$, we have

$$(16) \qquad q'S_{pp}\left(\frac{dt}{d\sigma}\right) = q'S_{pp}(\beta q - t)$$
$$= q'S_{pp}\{(1 + \beta)q - p\}$$
$$= (1 + \beta)q'S_{pp}q > 0.$$

Homogeneity of $S(p, g, u)$ and $G(p, g)$, we have $p'S_p = S$ and $p'G_{pg} = G_g$. Noticing (9) and $S - G_g g = 0$,[9] we obtain under the condition (ii)

$$(17) \qquad (S_p - G_{pg}g)'\left(\frac{dt}{d\sigma}\right) = (S_p - G_{pg}g)'(\beta q - t)$$
$$= \{(1 + \beta)q - p\}'(S_p - G_{pg}g)$$
$$= (1 + \beta)q'(S_p - G_{pg}g)$$
$$= (1 + \beta)(-q'S_{pg})g > 0.$$

From equations (16), (17), and Lemma 2, we get $du/d\sigma > 0$. Q.E.D.

Comparing the proposition with the result of Fukushima (1979), we have newly imposed the conditions (i) and (ii). The condition (ii) holds when the factors used in the public production are proportional to the factor endowments. In this case, an

[8] Note that we have $D_q^{-1}(dt/d\sigma) = \beta e - D_q^{-1}t$, where D_q is the diagonal matrix whose diagonal elements are composed of q, and e is the unit vector. Therefore, this type of tariff reforms means the policy of squeezing all the ad valorem tariff rates proportionally toward the common target rate β.

[9] Adding (9) and (10), we have $p'S_p - G_g g = S - G_g g$, which implies the budget constraint of the consumer.

increase in the public production, while keeping the commodity prices fixed, reduces all the productions of the private goods by the "Rybczynski" effect.

4.3. *The Decomposition of Welfare Effects.* Proposition 2 may be somewhat surprising, since it shows the possibility that a policy of raising all the tariffs may increase the welfare of the economy even if the publicly produced good is initially over supplied. This subsection will clarify the sources of welfare gain from the tariff reform in the small open economy with public production.

From equation (9), u is solved for given t and g. Let $u^*(t, g)$ be its solution function of u. Moreover, equations (9) and (10) yield the solution function of g for given t. We write the solution function of g as $g(t)$. Noticing (11) and (12), we obtain

$$u(\sigma) = u^*(t(\sigma), g(t(\sigma))). \tag{18}$$

Differentiating (18) with respect to σ, we have

$$\frac{du}{d\sigma} = \left[\left(\frac{\partial u^*}{\partial t}\right)' + \left(\frac{\partial u^*}{\partial g}\right) \cdot \left(\frac{dg}{dt}\right)'\right]\left(\frac{dt}{d\sigma}\right). \tag{19}$$

The first term in the brace of (19) represents the welfare effect of the tariff reform satisfying the balance of trade while the amount of g is hypothetically kept constant. This is the very effect that appears in the small open economy without public production. Since this effect is caused by the change in the degree of the distortion due to the inefficient tariffs, we call it the *t-effect*.

The second term in the brace of (19) represents the welfare effect of the tariff reform due to the change in the supply of g. This effect is the newly appearing impact of the tariff reform in the small open economy with public production. Since this effect is caused by the change in the distortion due to the inefficient supply of g, we call it the *g-effect*.

The explicit expressions of $\partial u^*/\partial t$ and $\partial u^*/\partial g$ can be obtained from equation (9). On the other hand, the total differentiation of (9) and (10) yields the explicit form of dg/dt. Then, we have

$$\left(\frac{du}{d\sigma}\right) = \left[\frac{q'S_{pp}}{q'E_{pu}} + \frac{q'S_{pg}}{q'E_{pu}} \cdot \left(\frac{dg}{dt}\right)'\right]\left(\frac{dt}{d\sigma}\right), \tag{20}$$

where

$$\left(\frac{dg}{dt}\right)' = J^{-1}\{-E_u \cdot q'S_{pp} + q'E_{pu} \cdot (S_p - G_{pg} \cdot g)'\}. \tag{21}$$

Equation (20) shows us what determines the sign of each effect. Under the normality condition ($q'E_{pu} > 0$), the conventional t-effect depends upon the substitutability among the private goods. On the other hand, the g-effect depends upon the initial level of publicly produced good and the change in the supply of the publicly produced good due to the tariff reform.

The g-effect is ambiguous under the conditions assumed in Propositions 1 and 2, while the t-effect on the welfare is positive from (14) and (16). Since the propositions assume the normality of the private goods and the over supply of the publicly produced good, equation (20) shows that the g-effect becomes positive if those tariff reforms decreases the supply of g. The tariff reforms, however, may increase the supply of g under the conditions in Propositions 1 and 2. This is due to the fact that we have $-J^{-1}E_u q' S_{pp}(dt/d\sigma) > 0$ in (21) for the highest or the uniform tariff reductions.

A closer examination, however, shows that t-effect more than offsets the g-effect in those cases. Thus, regardless of the ambiguity of the g-effect, the reduction of the highest tariffs or the uniform change of all the tariffs improves the welfare of the economy under the conditions listed in each proposition.

4.4. *An Argument Against Tariff Reduction.* The decomposition of welfare effects of the tariff reform makes clear the case where the highest or the uniform change of tariffs is harmful to the small country with public production.

Let us introduce the adjustment process whose stability condition is utilized in the following proposition. We assume that the economy always satisfies the condition of trade balance (9). Then, we consider the adjustment process,

$$\dot{g} = -t' S_p(p, g, u^*(t, g)) - C^g(G_v^*(p, v^p(p, g)))g, \tag{22}$$

where "·" indicates the derivative with respect to time, and the functions G_v^* and v^p are given by (1) and (8) respectively. In view of the government's budget constraint (10), the adjustment process (22) states that the public production is increased (decreased) if there is government's surplus (deficit).

Then, we have the following.

PROPOSITION 3. *Suppose that the condition (F) and the following conditions are satisfied in the small open economy with public production.*

(i) *The publicly produced good is initially under supplied.*

(ii) *The marginal cost of public production evaluated by the world prices of private goods is positive, i.e.,* $-q' G_{pg} > 0$.

(iii) *There is no substitutability among the private goods in the production and consumption, i.e.,* $S_{pp} = 0$.

(iv) *The equilibrium is locally stable under the adjustment process (22).*

(v) *There is no inferior private good.*

Then the uniform change of all the tariffs always reduces the welfare of the small open economy with public production.

PROOF. From (21) and the assumption (iii) we have

$$\left(\frac{dg}{dt}\right)' = J^{-1} \cdot q' E_{pu} \cdot (S_p - G_{pg} \cdot g)'. \tag{23}$$

Noticing $p' S_{pg} = S_g = G_g - E_g = -C^g - E_g$ and $p' E_{pu} = E_u$, the stability condition requires

$$(d\dot{g}/dg) = -t'\{S_{pg} - E_{pu} \cdot (\partial u^*/\partial g)\} - C^g$$

$$= (q - p)'\{S_{pg} - E_{pu}(q'S_{pg}/q'E_{pu})\} - C^{\dot{g}}$$
$$= J/q'E_{pu} < 0.$$

Thus, we obtain $J^{-1} \cdot q'E_{pu} < 0$ under the condition (iv).

In addition, the assumption (ii) yields the inequality (17), that is, $(S_p - G_{pg} \cdot g)'(dt/d\sigma) > 0$. Thus, from (23), we have $(dg/dt)'(dt/d\sigma) < 0$.

Since there appears only the g-effect from the assumption (iii), we have $du/d\sigma < 0$ from (20) and the assumptions (i) and (v). Q.E.D.

We can also get the similar result on the highest tariff reduction. This proposition shows the situation where we should not recommend the tariff reforms proposed by former authors. Roughly speaking, the highest tariff reduction or the uniform change of tariffs may be harmful to the small open economy where (i) the publicly produced good is scarce due to the small tariff revenue, and (ii) the production and consumption of private goods are inflexible to the price changes.

5. CONCLUDING REMARKS

This paper has examined the welfare change in the small open economy with public production due to the tariff reforms proposed by Hatta (1977) and Fukushima (1979). By making clear the factors which affect the welfare of the economy from the decomposition we proposed, we have derived the conditions under which the highest tariff reduction or the uniform reduction of tariff increases or decreases the welfare.

We should notice, however, the applicability of our propositions to the real economy. First, we have made the assumption of the factor price equalization. This assumption requires, in the conventional Heckscher-Ohlin model with many goods and many factors, that the number of goods should be not less than that of factors. Thus, this assumption may restrict the situations where we can apply our propositions. Second, the publicly produced good we consider is the consumption type. There is the other type of publicly produced goods, i.e., public inputs such as an infrastructure for the private sectors.[10] Although the production of public inputs is more important for the developing countries, incorporating the public inputs into the model may make the welfare analysis of tariff reforms so complex that we cannot derive clear results.

Osaka City University, Japan

APPENDIX

In this Appendix we will prove Lemma 1. First, note that $G^*(p, v^p)$ has the following properties,

[10] Recently, trade theories and welfare economics with the production of public inputs have been developed by several authors. See, for example, Manning and McMillan (1979), Tawada and Abe (1984), and Abe (1990) for the pure theories of international trade with the public intermediate good. Diewert (1986) and Tsuneki (1987) developed the welfare measures in the economy with public good production.

$$G_p^*(p, v^p) = y,$$

$$G_v^*(p, v^p) = w,$$

$$G^*(\alpha p, v^p) = \alpha G^*(p, v^p), \text{ for any scalar } \alpha \geq 0,$$

$$z' G_{pp}^*(p, v^p) z > 0 \text{ for any nonzero vector } z \neq \alpha p,$$

where y and w are the production vector of the private goods and the factor price vector respectively.

Furthermore, from the definition of $v^p(p, g)$ we have

$$v_p^p(p, g) \equiv \partial v^p / \partial p = -C_{ww}^g \cdot G_{vp}^* \cdot g,$$

$$v_g^p(p, g) \equiv \partial v^p / \partial g = -C_w^g,$$

under the condition (F).

Then from the definition of $G(p, g)$, we obtain

(A1) $$G_p = G_p^* + (v_p^p)' G_v^* = G_p^* - G_{pv}^* \cdot C_{ww}^g \cdot w \cdot g = G_p^*,$$

where the last equality follows from the homogeneity of $C^g(w)$. In addition, we have

(A2) $$G_g = (G_v^*)' v_g^p = -w' C_w^g = -C^g(w),$$

where the last equality follows from the homogeneity of $C^g(w)$.

Since G^* is homogeneous of degree one in p and C_w^g is homogeneous of degree zero in w, we have

$$v^p + C_w^g(G_v^*(\alpha p, v^p))g = v^p + C_w^g(\alpha G_v^*(p, v^p))g$$
$$= v^p + C_w^g(G_v^*(p, v^p))g,$$

which implies that $v^p(\alpha p, g) = v^p(p, g)$. Thus we obtain

(A3) $$G(\alpha p, g) = G^*(\alpha p, v^p(\alpha p, g))$$
$$= \alpha G^*(p, v^p(p, g)) = \alpha G(p, g).$$

Finally, from (A1), we have

$$G_{pp} = G_{pp}^* + G_{pv}^* \cdot v_p^p = G_{pp}^* - G_{pv}^* \cdot C_{ww}^g \cdot G_{vp}^* \cdot g.$$

Since G_{ww}^g is negative definite for any nonzero vector $z \neq \alpha w$, we obtain

(A4) $$z' G_{pp} z = z'[G_{pp}^* - G_{pv}^* \cdot C_{ww}^g \cdot G_{vp}^* \cdot g] z > 0,$$

for any nonzero vector $z \neq \alpha p$. The equalities and inequality from (A1) to (A4) prove Lemma 1.

REFERENCES

ABE, K., "A Public Input as a Determinant of Trade," *Canadian Journal of Economics* 23 (1990), 400–407.

BHAGWATI, J. N., "The Gains from Trade Once Again," *Oxford Economic Papers* 20 (1968), 137–148.

BOADWAY, R., S. MAITAL AND M. PRACHOWNY, "Optimal Tariffs, Optimal Taxes and Public Goods," *Journal of Public Economics* 2 (1973), 391–403.

BERTRAND, T. J. AND J. VANEK, "The Theory of Tariffs, Taxes, and Subsidies: Some Aspects of the Second Best," *American Economic Review* 61 (1971), 925–931.

BRUNO, M., "Market Distortion and Gradual Reform," *Review of Economic Studies* 39 (1972), 373–383.

DIEWERT, W. E., *The Measurement of the Economic Benefits of Infrastructure Services* (Berlin: Springer-Verlag, 1986).

———, A. H. TURUNEN, AND A. D. WOODLAND, "Productivity- and Pareto-Improving Changes in Taxes and Tariffs," *Review of Economic Studies* 56 (1989), 199–216.

ETHIER, W. J., "Higher Dimensional Issues in Trade Theory," in R. W. Jones and P. B. Kenen, eds., *Handbook of International Economics*, Vol. 1 (Amsterdam: North-Holland, 1984), 131–184.

FEEHAN, J. P., "Efficient Tariff Financing of Public Goods," *Journal of International Economics* 24 (1988), 155–164.

FINDLAY, R. AND W. WELLISZ, "Project Evaluation, Shadow Prices, and Trade Policy," *Journal of Political Economy* 84 (1976), 543–552.

FOSTER, E. AND H. SONNENSCHEIN, "Price Distortion and Economic Welfare," *Econometrica* 38 (1970), 281–297.

FUKUSHIMA, T., "Tariff Structure, Nontraded Goods and Theory of Piecemeal Policy Recommendations," *International Economic Review* 20 (1979), 427–435.

HATTA, T., "A Recommendation for a Better Tariff Structure," *Econometrica* 45 (1977), 1859–1869.

KEMP, M. C., "Some Issues in the Analysis of Trade Gains," *Oxford Economic Papers* 20 (1968), 149–161.

LITTLE, I. M. D. AND J. A. MIRRLEES, *Project Appraisal and Planning for Developing Countries* (New York: Basic Books, 1974).

LLOYD, P. J., "A More General Theory of Price Distortions in Open Economies," *Journal of International Economics* 4 (1974), 365–386.

MANNING, R. AND J. MCMILLAN, "Public Intermediate Goods, Production Possibilities, and International Trade," *Canadian Journal of Economics* 12 (1979), 243–257.

SHIBATA, H. AND A. SHIBATA, "Rent Redistribution through Provision of Public Goods," in A. M. El-Agraa, ed., *Protection, Cooperation, Integration and Development* (London: Macmillan, 1987), 268–284.

SMITH, A., "Factor Shadow Prices in Distorted Open Economies," in H. Kierzkowski, ed., *Protection and Competition in International Trade: Essays in Honor of W. M. Corden* (Oxford: Basil Blackwell, 1987), 54–67.

SRINIVASAN, T. N. AND J. N. BHAGWATI, "Shadow Prices for Project Selection in the Presence of Distortions: Effective Rate of Protection and Domestic Resource Costs," *Journal of Political Economy* 86 (1978), 97–116.

TAWADA, M. AND K. ABE, "Production Possibilities and International Trade with a Public Intermediate Good," *Canadian Journal of Economics* 17 (1984), 232–248.

TSUNEKI, A., "The Measurement of Waste in a Public Goods Economy," *Journal of Public Economics* 33 (1987), 73–94.

VANEK, J., *General Equilibrium of International Discrimination* (Cambridge: Harvard University Press, 1965).

WOODLAND, A. D., *International Trade and Resource Allocation* (Amsterdam: North-Holland, 1982).

[27]

Revenue Enhancing Tariff Reform

By

Rod Falvey

I. Introduction

Trade policy reform has been an important component of policy packages designed to increase "outward-orientation" and promote structural adjustment in many developing countries. In general these trade reforms have been undertaken on a "piecemeal" or "gradual" basis, proceeding in stages over several years, rather than as abrupt "one-shot" affairs. The design of appropriate programmes of piecemeal trade policy reform has also received attention in the trade theory literature. The standard approach, which is also followed here, has been to examine piecemeal reforms as a one-off comparative statics exercise and to focus on finding reform packages that improve the welfare of a "representative individual". Underlying this approach is an implicit assumption that reform packages that are welfare improving at each stage will have greater credibility and are more likely to be sustainable.

Beginning with the pioneering work of Hatta [1977] and Fukushima [1979] who concentrated on tariff reform in a small country, this literature has been extended subsequently to encompass many households. Dixit [1987], Diewert et al. [1991]; many countries, Hatta and Fukushima [1979], Fukushima and Kim [1989], Turunen-Red and Woodland [1991]; quotas, Falvey [1988], Anderson and Neary [1992], Lahiri and Raimondos [1993]; producer-specific interventions, Beghin and Karp [1992]; pure imported intermediate goods, Lopéz and Panagariya [1992]; duty-drawback provisions, Panagariya [1992]; and public production financed by tariff revenue, Abe [1992].

In the small country, representative individual context, two main welfare improving tariff reform structures emerge (see Fukushima

---

Remark: I am grateful to Norman Gemmell, David Greenaway, Jim Markusen, Alasdair Smith, two referees and to participants at the 1993 IESG Conference and seminars at the Universities of Essex and Nottingham for helpful comments and suggestions.

[1979] for details). The first is a *proportional* reform, where *all* trade taxes are reduced in the same proportion. The second is a *concertina* reform, under which the highest (and/or lowest) tariffs are reduced (raised) to the next highest (lowest) at each step. These reforms are discussed in more detail below.

One important constraint facing tariff reformers in developing countries, however, is those countries' relatively heavy reliance on trade taxes as a source of government revenue [Heady and Mitra, 1987; Greenaway and Milner, 1991].[1] Although the tax structure may not have been "chosen" primarily with revenue in mind, the revenue implications of tariff reform proposals have been raised as a major concern by many governments. While trade taxes may have a much smaller fiscal role in the post reform economy, it takes time for alternative sources of revenue to be established. In the early stages of reform at least, a tariff reform package that is both *welfare improving* and *revenue enhancing* (hereafter a WIRE reform) will be more attractive to reforming governments and also appear more credible to their populations. Moreover, where tariff reform is part of an agreement with multilateral donors, a revenue enhancing reform will reduce the likelihood of "slippage" against agreed conditions due to government budgetary difficulties.

This paper therefore seeks to answer three questions. First, when will a WIRE reform exist? Second, when, if ever, will the welfare improving proportional and concertina reforms also be revenue enhancing? Finally, what alternative WIRE reforms are available?

In outline the remainder of this paper is as follows. Section II sets up the framework and determines the conditions under which no WIRE reform will exist. Single tax reforms are then considered in Section III, and multi-tax reforms in Section IV. Conclusions are presented in the final section.

II. A Framework for Evaluating Tariff Reform

Consider a perfectly competitive general equilibrium model of a small open economy producing and consuming n internationally tradeable goods. The government of this economy intervenes at the

[1] Burgess and Stern [1993, p. 779] note that foreign trade taxes account for 5.1 per cent of GDP and for 29.4 per cent of toal tax revenue in developing countries. They also list trade tax revenue as a percentage of GDP for individual developed and developing countries.

border through specific taxes and subsidies. There are no other domestic distortions. The domestic price vector (p) is then given by

$$p = p^* + t \tag{1}$$

where p^* is the given world price vector and t is the vector of trade taxes/subsidies.

The government has a net revenue target (T), but for simplicity it is assumed that this revenue is then redistributed to consumers in a lump sum fashion.[2] Since trade taxes are not "first-best" for achieving a revenue target, in general, the following analysis is conducted within a "second-best" framework [Dixit, 1985]. Subsequent steps in the reform programme may involve moving towards first-best taxes.

Domestic demand can be represented using the economy's expenditure function $E(p, u)$ where u denotes the welfare of a "representative individual".[3] The derivatives with respect to prices yield the compensated demand vector $E_p(p, u)$. Domestic supply can similarly be represented using the economy's Gross National Product function $G(p, V)$ where V is the vector of factor endowments.[4] The derivatives of this function with respect to prices yield the economy's supply vector $G_p(p, V)$. The net import vector, M, can then be expressed as[5]

$$M(p, u, V) = E_p(p, u) - G_p(p, V).$$

The balance of trade constraint for this small country is

$$B(t, u) = p^* M = 0 \tag{2}$$

[2] This minimizes the difference between our framework and that used elsewhere in the piecemeal reform literature, and avoids the complications of explicitly treating public production and distribution [see Abe, 1992]. Since our objective is to find tariff reforms that are at worst revenue neutral, the level of public activity could be included, but held constant, in what follows with any increases in revenue redistributed lump sum.

[3] The expenditure function is concave and linearly homogeneous in prices and increasing in utility. It is also assumed to be twice continuously differentiable.

[4] The GNP function is convex and linearly homogeneous in prices and is assumed to be twice continuously differentiable. The number of factors is assumed to be at least as great as the number of products so that problems of production indeterminacy do not arise. If public production were included, G would denote private sector output, and V the net factor supplies available to the private sector. The level of publically provided output would then enter, as a parameter, into the private expenditure or GNP functions, depending on whether public production is a consumer or producer good. Abe [1992] discusses the implications of public provision of a consumption good for welfare improving tariff reform.

[5] The net import vector is homogeneous of degree zero in prices, i.e. $p M_p = 0$.

and net tax revenue is

$$T(t,u) = t\,M = (p - p^*)\,M\,. \tag{3}$$

If good j is an importable ($M_j > 0$), then $t_j > (<) 0$ if imports of j are taxed (subsidized). If good j is an exportable ($M_j < 0$), then $t_j > (<) 0$ if exports of j are subsidized (taxed). Thus $t_j M_j > (<) 0$ as trade in j is taxed (subsidized).

Units of goods are chosen so that all world prices are unity. No distinction need then be made between specific and ad valorem tariffs. It is useful to retain the notation p^*, however. Given this normalization, the tariff vector remains arbitrary up to a constant – i.e. tariff vector $t' = t + a$, where a is a scalar, generates the same tariff revenue as t.[6] We therefore follow standard practice in this area and fix the tax on some arbitrary good, say good 1, at zero [Auerbach, 1985, p. 89].

From (2), (3) can be rewritten in the sometimes more convenient form

$$T(t,u) = p\,M\,. \tag{3'}$$

Our reform problem, then, is to find a welfare improving ($\mathrm{d}u > 0$), revenue enhancing ($\mathrm{d}T \geq 0$) trade reform package ($\mathrm{d}t$) that continues to satisfy constraints (2) and (3′). Totally differentiating these constraints we have

$$p^*\,M_u\,\mathrm{d}u - t\,M_p\,\mathrm{d}t = 0\,, \tag{4}$$

$$p\,M_u\,\mathrm{d}u + M\,\mathrm{d}t = \mathrm{d}T, \tag{5}$$

where we have used the homogeneity of net imports in prices (i.e. $p\,M_p = 0$, so that $p^*\,M_p = -(p - p^*)\,M_p = -t\,M_p$).

Our discussion of reforms can be greatly simplified if we employ the concept of the *compensated radial elasticity* (CRE) of a tax base [Fane, 1991]. The CRE of good j (denoted e_j) is defined as the proportionate reduction in net purchases of product j with respect to a common proportionate increase in all taxes, holding utility constant. Thus if we let $\mathrm{d}t_i = t_i\,\mathrm{d}\alpha$, for all i, where α is some scalar, then, recalling that $M_{ij} = M_{ji}$,

$$e_j \equiv -\frac{1}{M_j}\frac{\partial M_j}{\partial \alpha} = -\frac{\sum_i M_{ji}\,t_i}{M_j} = -\frac{\sum_i t_i\,M_{ij}}{M_j}\,.$$

[6] That is $t'\,M = t\,M + a\,M = t\,M$ since $a\,M = a\,p^*\,M = 0$ when p^* is the unit vector.

We can then write $t M_p = -e M$, where $e M$ is a vector whose j^{th} element is $e_j M_j$. Substituting these expressions into (4), and rewriting (4) and (5) in matrix notation gives

$$\begin{bmatrix} E_u^* & 0 \\ E_u & -1 \end{bmatrix} \begin{bmatrix} \mathrm{d}u \\ \mathrm{d}T \end{bmatrix} + \begin{bmatrix} e M \\ M \end{bmatrix} \mathrm{d}t = \begin{bmatrix} 0 \\ 0 \end{bmatrix}, \tag{6}$$

where E_u^* $(= p^* M_u)$ and E_u $(= p M_u)$ are the domestic aggregate "marginal propensities to spend" evaluated at world and domestic prices respectively [Lloyd, 1974]. Both these terms are assumed to be positive.[7, 8]

A WIRE reform will exist if system (6) can be solved for some $\mathrm{d}t$ such that $\mathrm{d}u > 0$ and $\mathrm{d}T \geq 0$. Let us refer to this as the *primary* problem. A general statement of the necessary and sufficient conditions for the existence of a solution to the primary problem can be obtained using Motzkin's Theorem of the Alternative.[9] This Theorem states that *either* the primary problem has a solution *or* the *alternative*

$$[E_u^* \quad E_u] \begin{bmatrix} \lambda_B \\ \lambda_T \end{bmatrix} > 0; \quad [0 \quad -1] \begin{bmatrix} \lambda_B \\ \lambda_T \end{bmatrix} \geq 0;$$

$$[e M \quad M] \begin{bmatrix} \lambda_B \\ \lambda_T \end{bmatrix} = 0_{n-1},$$

---

[7] That E_u^* is positive is sometimes referred to as the "Hatta normality condition", and is a necessary and sufficient condition for a transfer of income to this small open economy to increase welfare [Turunen-Red and Woodland, 1991]. Note that one can write $E_u = E_u^*(1 + \delta)$, where $\delta = \sum_i t_i M_{iu} / \sum_i p_i^* M_{iu}$ represents the distortion in the "marginal cost of living" as a result of the tax system. This distortion can be positive or negative depending on the mix of import taxes and export subsidies (which tend to raise domestic prices above world prices) versus export taxes (which tend to lower domestic prices).

[8] If the government purchases a fixed basket of goods (g) on the world market, and finances the resulting expenditure ($p^* g$) from tariff revenue ($T = t M$), then the balance of trade constraint, including both private and public purchases, becomes $p^* M + p^* g = 0$ or $p^* M + T = 0$, and the private budget constraint is $p M = 0$. Totally differentiating these constraints and making the same substitutions as above yields system

$$\begin{bmatrix} E_u^* & 1 \\ E_u & 0 \end{bmatrix} \begin{bmatrix} \mathrm{d}u \\ \mathrm{d}T \end{bmatrix} + \begin{bmatrix} e M \\ M \end{bmatrix} \mathrm{d}t = \begin{bmatrix} 0 \\ 0 \end{bmatrix},$$

which has the same general solution and structure as that in the text.

[9] See Mangasarian [1969, p. 34]. Similar applications of Motzkin's Theorem are given in Dixit [1987] and Turunen-Red and Woodland [1991].

where λ_B and λ_T are scalars and 0_{n-1} is an $n-1$ dimensional vector of zeroes, has a solution but *not both*. Thus the general conditions for the existence of a WIRE reform reduce to the general conditions for the non-existence of a solution to the alternative.

Expanding the alternative provides a system of $n+1$ equations in 2 variables i.e.

$$\lambda_B E_u^* + \lambda_T E_u > 0 \tag{7 A}$$

$$\lambda_T \leq 0 \tag{7 B}$$

$$\lambda_B e_j + \lambda_T = 0 \quad \text{for each } j. \tag{7 C}$$

Equations (7 A) and (7 B) imply that $\lambda_B > 0$. Let $\lambda = -\lambda_T/\lambda_B \geq 0$. Then equations (7 A) and (7 C) can be rewritten as

$$E_u^*/E_u > \lambda \geq 0 \tag{7 A'}$$

and

$$e_j = \lambda \quad \text{for each } j, \tag{7 C'}$$

respectively.

To interpret these conditions, suppose a solution to the alternative exists. Then substituting from (7 C') into the primary problem

$$E_u^* \, \mathrm{d}u = -\lambda M \, \mathrm{d}t \quad \text{and} \quad \mathrm{d}T = \{(1/\lambda) - (E_u/E_u^*)\} \lambda M \, \mathrm{d}t.$$

But from (7 A'), $1/\lambda > E_u/E_u^*$, so that any reform that raises welfare reduces revenue and vice versa.

For the alternative to have a solution, and no WIRE reform to exist, two general conditions must be met. First, the existing *structure* of tariffs must be such that the CREs are equal for all tax bases (from (7 C')). As noted in Section IV below, this implies that no welfare improvement can be obtained from adjusting individual tariffs while maintaining their "average level". Second, given their structure, the overall *level* of tariffs must not be "too high" (from (7 A')). To see this, consider a radial reduction in all tariffs (i.e. $\mathrm{d}t = -t\,\mathrm{d}\alpha$, where α is a scalar and $\mathrm{d}\alpha > 0$), from an existing position where all CREs are equal (to λ). Then

$$E_u^* \, \mathrm{d}u = \lambda T \, \mathrm{d}\alpha > 0 \quad \text{and} \quad \mathrm{d}T = -\{(1/\lambda) - (E_u/E_u^*)\} \lambda T \, \mathrm{d}\alpha.$$

Welfare and revenue move in opposite directions only if $\lambda < E_u^*/E_u$. Even with the correct "structure" of taxes a WIRE reform may still be available if the "level" of taxes is at or above the revenue maximum.

One (obvious) case in which the alternative will have a solution, is when the trade taxes are set at their (revenue) constrained optimal levels. At this optimum the CRE of each tax base is equalized [Fane, 1991], i.e.

$$e_j = \beta E_u^* / (1 + \beta E_u) \quad \text{for each } j, \tag{8}$$

where β denotes the gain in welfare from a marginal reduction in the revenue constraint.[10] Comparing (8) with (7 C′) and (7 A′) we see that the alternative is solved if $E_u^*/E_u > \beta E_u^*/(1 + \beta E_u)$ which is satisfied as long as $\beta > 0$, i.e. the optimal "level" is below the revenue maximum.

In general, if all taxes can be varied, then the constrained optimum will be the only case in which the alternative has a solution. Where only a subset of taxes may be varied, however, then it may be the case that for each tax (t_j) in the subset du/dt_j and dT/dt_j have opposite signs.[11]

Naturally, simply knowing that some WIRE reform exists when the alternative has no solution does not single out specific WIRE reforms. The remainder of the paper therefore considers cases where specific WIRE reforms can be identified.

III. Reform of Single Taxes

Suppose policymakers are contemplating a change in the intervention on one product only (say product j) at the first stage of the reform. Which tax/subsidies can be identified as generating a potential WIRE reform in this instance?

---

[10] Consider the optimal tax problem of max u subject to $p^* M = 0$ and $pM = T$. Forming the Lagrangian $L = u + \alpha p^* M + \beta [pM - T]$ and maximising, yields first order conditions $1 + \alpha E_u^* + \beta E_u = 0$ and $e_j = -(\beta/\alpha)$ for each j. The first condition yields $\beta/\alpha = -\beta E_u^*/(1 + \beta E_u)$.

[11] For example, consider the special case where all cross price effects, other than those with the unrestricted "numeraire" (good 1) are zero. Then, excluding its first row and column, M_p is a diagonal matrix, and (8) can be solved for the constrained-optimal tax on good $j(\tilde{t}_j)$ as

$$\tilde{t}_j = [\beta E_u^*/(1 + \beta E_u)](M_j/M_{jj}).$$

Thus $\tilde{t}_j \gtrless 0$ as $M_j \gtrless 0$, i.e. trade in all goods, other than good 1, is taxed. Consider then a reform that changes t_j only. From (9 A) and (9 B) below, we have in this special case,

$$E_u^*\, du = t_j M_{jj} dt_j \quad \text{and} \quad dT = \{(E_u/E_u^*) t_j M_{jj} + M_j\} dt_j.$$

Assuming, without loss of generality, that $t_j > 0$ and $M_j > 0$, we know that $t_j M_{jj} < 0$, indicating that a cut in t_j would raise welfare. But for this also to raise revenue we require that $t_j > (-E_u^*/E_u)(M_j/M_{jj})$. Since this lower bound is itself strictly greater than $\tilde{t}_j$, there is a range of $t_j \neq \tilde{t}_j$ for which no WIRE reform (of t_j) can be found.

Substituting (4) in (5), the primary constraints for such a limited reform are

$$E_u^* \, du = \sum_i t_i M_{ij} dt_j = -e_j M_j dt_j \tag{9A}$$

and

$$\begin{aligned} dT &= \{(E_u/E_u^*) \sum_i t_i M_{ij} + M_j\} dt_j \\ &= \{1 - (E_u/E_u^*) e_j\} M_j dt_j . \end{aligned} \tag{9B}$$

The necessary and sufficient condition for a WIRE reform to exist in this case is that the coefficients on dt_j in (9 A) and (9 B) have the same sign, i.e. that $-e_j$ and $1-(E_u/E_u^*)e_j$ have the same sign. A sufficient condition for a WIRE reform to exist is that $e_j < 0$, which requires that $\sum_i t_i M_{ij}$ and M_j have the same sign. We can consider the standard concertina reform recommendations in the light of this condition.

While the sign of $\sum_i t_i M_{ij}$ is unknown in general, it can be determined in important special cases. Using $\sum_i p_i M_{ij} = 0$, we can transform[12]

$$\sum_i t_i M_{ij} = \sum_{i \neq j} (M_{ij}/p_j)(t_i - t_j) . \tag{10}$$

If we assume that j is a net substitute for all other goods (i.e. $M_{ij} \geq 0$ for all $i \neq j$), then a sufficient condition for $\sum_i t_i M_{ij} > (<) 0$ is that $t_j \leq (\geq) t_i$ for all $i \neq j$, with a strict inequality for at least one i. This result forms the theoretical basis for the concertina reform package.

Recall that if j is imported, $t_j > (<) 0$ if imports are taxed (subsidized), while if j is exported, $t_j > (<) 0$ if exports are subsidized (taxed). To limit the options to the empirically most relevant cases, suppose that while some exports may be taxed and others subsidized, no imports are subsidized. Four subcases can then be distinguished depending on whether j is imported (M) or exported (X) and whether $t_i \leq t_j$, so that (10) is negative (−) or $t_i \geq t_j$ so that (10) is positive (+), for all $i \neq j$, with strict inequality for some i. Recall that trade in at least

[12] $\sum_j p_i M_{ij} = 0$ implies that $M_{jj} = -\sum_{i \neq j} (p_i/p_j) M_{ij}$. Hence

$$\sum_i t_i M_{ij} = t_j M_{jj} - \sum_{i \neq j} t_i M_{ij} = \sum_{i \neq j} p_i M_{ij} [(t_i/p_i) - (t_j/p_j)] = \sum_{i \neq j} (M_{ij}/p_j)[t_i - t_j],$$

since $p_i = (1 + t_i)$ for all $i = 1, \ldots, n$.

one product is not taxed or subsidized (e.g. $t_1 \equiv 0$). We consider each of these four cases in turn[13]

$(M+)$ where j is an untaxed import, which is a net substitute for all other goods, and there are no export taxes;

$(M-)$ where j is the import taxed at the highest rate, which is a net substitute for all other goods, and there are no export subsidies at higher rates;

$(X+)$ where j, the most highly taxed export, is a net substitute for all other goods;

$(X-)$ where j, the most highly subsidized export, is a net substitute for all other goods, and there are no import tariffs at higher rates.

In cases $(M-)$ and $(X-)$, the coefficient on dt_j in (9A) is negative, and a small cut in the import tariff in $(M-)$, or a small cut in the export subsidy in $(X-)$, so that $dt_j < 0$ in each case, would result in a welfare improvement. In cases $(M+)$ and $(X+)$, the coefficient on dt_j in (9A) is positive and imposing a small import tariff in $(M+)$ or a small cut in the export tax (or introducing a small export subsidy if there is no tax on j initially) in $(X+)$, so that $dt_j > 0$ in each case would result in a welfare improvement.

Recall that our sufficient condition for a WIRE reform is that $\sum_i t_i M_{ij}$ and M_j have the same signs, that is both are positive for an import and negative for an export. Once the revenue enhancing condition is included, $(M+)$ and $(X-)$ both fairly obviously meet the sufficient condition for a WIRE reform. In the other two cases $(M-)$ and $(X+)$ welfare improves, but one would have to empirically check that $(E_u/E_u^*)e_j > 1$ to determine if revenue is enhanced.

One additional piece of evidence that may be available is whether or not a tax is at or above its revenue maximum level, ceteris paribus. From (9)

$$dT/dt_j = [E_u \, du/dt_j + M_j]. \qquad (11)$$

Suppose j is a taxed import ($M_j > 0$), then if t_j is at or above its revenue maximum level ($dT/dt_j \leq 0$) it must be the case that $du/dt_j < 0$ from (11) and a cut in t_j will result in a WIRE reform. If j is a taxed export (i.e. $t_j < 0$ and $M_j < 0$), then $dt_j < 0$ corresponds to an increase in the export tax, and an export tax at or beyond the revenue maximizing

[13] Note that not all of these cases can occur at any one time.

level is one for which $\mathrm{d}T/\mathrm{d}t_j \geq 0$, which requires $\mathrm{d}u/\mathrm{d}t_j > 0$ from (11). A cut in this export tax ($\mathrm{d}t_j > 0$) will then be a WIRE reform. Thus cutting any tax above its revenue maximum level will result in a WIRE reform.

There is an analogous signal for an export subsidy. If an increase in an export subsidy on product j does not reduce revenue, then since $M_j < 0$, $\mathrm{d}T/\mathrm{d}t_j \geq 0$ requires $\mathrm{d}u/\mathrm{d}t_j > 0$ from (11), and an increase in this export subsidy also raises welfare.

IV. Reform of Several Taxes

In general one would expect that the possibility of adjusting two or more taxes at one time should increase the opportunities for a WIRE reform. Some combinations of welfare increasing but revenue decreasing tax adjustments with those that are revenue enhancing but welfare reducing may yield a WIRE outcome on balance, for instance.

At first glance the standard *proportional* reduction in all interventions would seem an unlikely candidate as a WIRE reform. While such a reform is known to be welfare increasing, the direct effect on revenue will be negative if all taxes and subsidies are cut in the same proportion, given positive net revenue in the first place. A revenue reduction need not be the overall outcome, however.

As before, a proportional reduction in all trade interventions can be written as $\mathrm{d}t = -t\,\mathrm{d}\alpha$, where $\mathrm{d}\alpha$ is a positive scalar. From (4)

$$E_u^*\,\mathrm{d}u = -t\,M_p\,t\,\mathrm{d}\alpha > 0\,, \tag{12}$$

since M_p is a negative definite substitution matrix. A proportional reduction in all interventions therefore clearly improves welfare. Substituting (12) in (5) gives the change in revenue

$$\mathrm{d}T = -[(E_u/E_u^*)\,t\,M_p\,t + t\,M]\,\mathrm{d}\alpha\,. \tag{13}$$

The first term in parenthesis in (13) is negative while the second term, which is equal to net tax revenue (T), is positive. The potential for revenue enhancement depends on the expenditure effect from the increase in welfare dominating the direct effect of the reduction in taxes on revenue. If it does, this implies that the overall "tariff level" is initially above the corresponding revenue maximum, given the tariff structure.

Turning to non-proportional adjustments, it is useful to define an *ex ante revenue neutral* (EARN) reform as a change in the tax structure such that $M\,\mathrm{d}t = 0$. Since M is observable in the initial equilibrium, the adjustments in tax rates requires to achieve an EARN reform can be calculated directly. For an EARN reform (5) reduces to

$$\mathrm{d}T = E_u \mathrm{d}u\,. \tag{14}$$

Thus so long as an EARN reform is directly welfare improving it will also be ex post revenue enhancing.[14]

Clearly there are many potential EARN reforms. The underlying principles can most easily be demonstrated by first considering the simple case where only two taxes are to be changed – on products j and k. The EARN constraint then requires that

$$M_k \mathrm{d}t_k = -M_j \mathrm{d}t_j. \tag{15}$$

Applying the same procedure as for equation (9 A), only this time for changes in both t_j and t_k, and then substituting from (15) we have:

$$E_u^* \mathrm{d}u = [e_k - e_j]\, M_j \mathrm{d}t_j. \tag{16}$$

If the CREs differ on two goods, then welfare (and revenue) can be increased by reducing the tax on the base with the relatively high CRE and raising the tax on the base with the lower CRE [Fane, 1991, p. 269]. So if k and j are both imported, and $e_k > e_j$, then welfare is improved if $\mathrm{d}t_j > 0$.

Performing the same transformations as for (10) equation (16) can be expanded into

$$\begin{aligned} E_u^* \mathrm{d}u = \{ & \sum_{i \neq j} (M_{ij}/p_j)[t_i - t_j] \\ & - (M_j/M_k) \sum_{i \neq k} (M_{ik}/p_k)[t_i - t_k]\}\, \mathrm{d}t_j. \end{aligned} \tag{17}$$

As long as the coefficient on $\mathrm{d}t_j$ is not zero, a WIRE reform can be found.

Again there are circumstances under which the sign of this coefficient can be determined. Basically it is composed of two terms of the form found in (10), and hence its sign can be determined under similar conditions. As before there are four cases to be considered (j and k are assumed to be net substitutes for all other goods in each case):

$(M+, M-)$ where j is an untaxed import, k is the highest taxed import, any export subsidies are at lower rates and there are no export taxes. In this case imposing a tax on

[14] At the (revenue) constrained optimal taxes $\mathrm{d}u = [-\beta/(1+\beta E_u)]\, M\,\mathrm{d}t$ and $\mathrm{d}T = [1/(1+\beta E_u)]\, M\,\mathrm{d}t$, confirming that $\mathrm{d}u = 0$ for any EARN reform.

$j\,(\mathrm{d}t_j > 0)$ and reducing the tax on $k\,(\mathrm{d}t_k < 0)$ in an EARN fashion will result in a WIRE reform.

$(X+, X-)$ where j is the most highly taxed export, k is the most highly subsidized export and any import taxes are at lower rates. In this case cutting the tax on $j\,(\mathrm{d}t_j > 0)$ and reducing the subsidy on $k\,(\mathrm{d}t_j < 0)$ in an EARN fashion yields a WIRE reform.

$(M+, X+)$ where j is an untaxed import, k is an unsubsidized export and there are no export taxes. In this case imposing a tax on $j\,(\mathrm{d}t_j > 0)$ and a subsidy on $k\,(\mathrm{d}t_k > 0)$ in an EARN fashion will result in a WIRE reform.

$(M-, X-)$ where j is the most highly taxed import, k is the most highly subsidized export, and these tax and subsidy rates are the same. In this case a cut in the tax on $j\,(\mathrm{d}t_j < 0)$ and a corresponding EARN reduction in the subsidy on $k\,(\mathrm{d}t_k < 0)$ is a WIRE reform.

In seeking to find a more general formula for WIRE reforms, in particular one that can be applied to reform of any subset of taxes, it is useful to begin with the observation that as long as CREs are not identical across products, a welfare improving reform can be found. From equation (16) a reform package that reduces taxes with relatively high CREs, and raises taxes with relatively low CREs will raise welfare. If this is simultaneously an EARN reform, then revenue will increase also.

This suggests a general reform formula of the form:

$$\mathrm{d}t_j = a\,[(\bar{e} - e_j)/M_j]\,, \tag{18}$$

where a is a positive constant, and $\bar{e}$ is a constant to be determined below, for all j in the reform set (i.e. the set of products whose tax rates are being altered). To be an EARN reform we require that

$$\sum_j M_j \mathrm{d}t_j = a \sum_j (\bar{e} - e_j) = 0\,.$$

To satisfy this constraint, $\bar{e}$ must be the average of the CREs in the reform set, i.e. $\bar{e} = \sum_j e_j / n_r$, where n_r is the number of products in the reform set.

From (9 A) above, we have

$$E_u^* \,\mathrm{d}u = -\sum_j e_j M_j \mathrm{d}t_j\,. \tag{19}$$

Exploiting the constraint on an EARN reform, we have $\bar{e}\sum_j M_j \mathrm{d}t_j = 0$, which can be added to (19) to yield

$$E_u^* \mathrm{d}u = \sum_j (\bar{e} - e_j) M_j \mathrm{d}t_j .$$

Substituting from (18), we then have

$$E_u^* \mathrm{d}u = \sum_j (\bar{e} - e_j)^2 > 0 .$$

Thus a reform that satisfies (18), where $\bar{e}$ is the average CRE of those taxes in the reform set, will be a WIRE reform.

Of course the main practical difficulty in implementing (18) will be knowledge of the CREs in the initial equilibrium.[15] Where only the CREs for some products are known, then reform could be confined to these products in the first instance, otherwise one can fall back on combinations of concertina reforms.

V. Concluding Comments

While the structure of protection in most developing countries may have evolved primarily in response to non-revenue considerations, the potential loss of revenue when tariff reform is contemplated has been a source of major concern to their governments. This paper has therefore examined piecemeal reforms that are both welfare improving and revenue enhancing. We have shown that, as long as the tariff structure is such that the compensated radial elasticities of all tariffs in the reform set are not equal, then a reform that is both welfare improving and revenue enhancing exists. Even where there are no gains arising from adjustments to the tax "structure" (i.e. the CREs are all equal), a WIRE reform may still exist if the overall tax "level" is at or beyond the revenue maximum.

---

[15] Note that both the CREs and their underlying compensated excess demand elasticities are variables whose values depend on where they are evaluated. Indeed the revenue-constrained optimal trade tax structure is one which sets all the CREs to the same value. If we let ε_{ij} denote the elasticity of the compensated excess demand for product i with respect to the price of product j $(i,j = 1, \ldots, n)$ and suppose that the matrix of these elasticities can be estimated at the initial equilibrium, then $e_j = -\sum_i t_i M_i \varepsilon_{ij}/p_j M_j$ can also be evaluated. But it is likely that the values of these elasticities (both the ε_{ij}s and the e_js) will change quite significantly as tariffs change, even where the underlying product and utility functions are say constant elasticity of substitution in form. It is therefore problematic whether the initial values of the e_js should be used in scheduling later steps in the reform, which may occur far from the initial equilibrium.

Reforms involving adjustment of a single tax obviously face the greatest constraints. Of the piecemeal reforms, only those which involve raising the lowest tax or cutting the highest subsidy are clearly WIRE reforms. For the others, their implications for revenue must be checked. Those taxes above their revenue maximizing levels should be cut, and any subsidy whose net effect is to raise revenue should be increased.

In considering general tax reform, it was useful to apply the notion of an ex ante revenue neutral reform. If such reforms are welfare improving, they also raise revenue ex post. This option allows combinations of the concertina reform to be adopted, as noted in Section IV. A general formula for reform was also demonstrated, based on deviations of CREs from the average in the reform set.

Naturally, the discussion above has focussed on only a narrow aspect of the trade policy reform process. Other aspects of reform will also impact on revenue (and welfare). The substitution of tariffs for quantitative restrictions will divert rents to the government. The removal of tariff exemptions on imports by certain categories of user will also have positive revenue implications. These types of reforms can also be included in the preceding analysis, at least in principle.

References

Abe, Kenzo, "Tariff Reform in a Small Open Economy with Public Production." *International Economic Review*, Vol. 33, 1992, pp. 209–222.

Anderson, James E., J. Peter Neary, "Trade Reform with Quotas, Partial Rent Retention and Tariffs." *Econometrica*, Vol. 60, 1992, pp. 57–76.

Auerbach, Alan J., "The Theory of Excess Burden and Optimal Taxation." In: Alan J. Auerbach, Martin Feldstein (Eds.), *Handbook of Public Economics, Vol. I.* Amsterdam 1985, Chapter 2.

Beghin, John C., Larry S. Karp, "Piecemeal Trade Reform in Presence of Producer-Specific Domestic Subsidies." *Economic Letters*, Vol. 39, 1992, pp. 65–71.

Burgess, Robin, Nicholas Stern, "Taxation and Development." *Journal of Economic Literature*, Vol. 31, 1993, pp. 762–830.

Diewert, W. Erwin, Arja H. Turunen-Red, Alan D. Woodland, "Tariff Reform in a Small Open Multi-Household Economy with Domestic Distortions and Non-Traded Goods." *International Economic Review*, Vol. 32, 1991, pp. 937–957.

Dixit, Avinash, "Tax Policy in Open Economics." In: Alan J. Auerbach, Martin Feldstein (Eds.), *Handbook of Public Economics, Vol.* I. Amsterdam 1985, pp. 313–374.

–, "On Pareto-Improving Redistributions of Aggregate Economic Gains." *Journal of Economic Theory*, Vol. 41, 1987, pp. 133–153.

Falvey, Rod, "Tariffs, Quotas and Piecemeal Policy Reform." *Journal of International Economics*, Vol. 22, 1988, pp. 177–183.

Fane, George, "Piecemeal Tax Reforms and the Compensated Radial Elasticities of Tax Bases." *Journal of Public Economics*, Vol. 45, 1991, pp. 263–270.

Fukushima, Takashi, "Tariff Structure, Non-traded Goods and Theory of Piecemeal Policy Recommendations." *International Economic Review*, Vol. 20, 1979, pp. 427–435.

–, **Nandoo Kim,** "Welfare Improving Tariff Changes: A Case of Many-Goods and Countries." *Journal of International Economics*, Vol. 26, 1989, pp. 383–388.

Greenaway, David, Chris Milner, "Fiscal Dependence on Trade Taxes and Trade Policy Reform." *Journal of Development Studies*, Vol. 27, 1991, pp. 95–132.

Hatta, Tatsuo, "A Recommendation for a Better Tariff Structure." *Econometrica*, Vol. 45, 1977, pp. 1859–1869.

, **Takashi Fukushima,** "The Welfare Effect of Tariff Rate Reductions in a Many Country World." *Journal of International Economics*, Vol. 90, 1979, pp. 503–511.

Heady, Christopher J., Pradeep K. Mitra, "Distributional and Revenue Raising Arguments for Tariffs." *Journal of Development Economics*, Vol. 26, 1987, pp. 77–101.

Lahiri, Sajal, Pascalis Raimondos, On the Correction of Trade Distortions in a Small Open Economy. University of Essex, 1993, mimeo.

Lloyd, Peter, "A More General Theory of Price Distortions in Open Economics." *Journal of International Economics*, Vol. 4, 1974, pp. 365–386.

Lopéz, Ramon, Arvind Panagariya, "On the Theory of Piecemeal Tariff Reform: The Case of Pure Imported Intermediate Inputs." *The American Economic Review*, Vol. 82, 1992, pp. 615–625.

Mangasarian, Olvi L., *Nonlinear Programming*. New York 1969.

Panagariya, Arvind, "Input Tariffs, Duty Drawbacks and Tariff Reforms." *Journal of International Economics*, Vol. 32, 1992, pp. 131–147.

Turunen-Red, Arja A., Alan D. Woodland, "Strict Pareto-Improving Multilaterial Reform of Tariffs." *Econometrica*, Vol. 59, 1991, pp. 1127–1152.

* * *

Abstract: Revenue Enhancing Tariff Reform. – Programmes of gradual trade policy reform have been included in most of the structural adjustment packages adopted by developing countries. So far the literature on piecemeal trade policy reform has concentrated on finding reform programmes that improve the welfare of a representative individual. Yet trade taxes are an important source of government revenue in many developing countries. This paper therefore examines tariff reform programmes that are both welfare improving and revenue enhancing. It first determines general conditions under which such a reform will exist and then considers specific reforms of both single tariffs and groups of tariffs. The standard welfare improving reform programmes – proportional and concertina reforms – are also discussed. *JEL No. F13*

*

Zusammenfassung: Aufkommenserhöhende Reform von Zolltarifen. – In den meisten Paketen von Maßnahmen zur strukturellen Anpassung, die von Entwicklungsländern angenommen wurden, sind Programme einer allmählichen Reform der Handelspolitik enthalten. Bisher hat sich die Literatur über solche Reformen darauf konzentriert, Programme zu ermitteln, die die Wohlfahrt eines repräsentativen Wirtschaftssubjekts erhöhen. Aber die Zölle sind in vielen Entwicklungsländern eine wichtige Einnahmequelle der Regierung. Deshalb werden in diesem Aufsatz Programme zur Reform der Zolltarife untersucht, die sowohl die Wohlfahrt erhöhen als auch die Einnahmen steigern. Zuerst werden die allgemeinen Bedingungen bestimmt, unter denen eine solche Reform möglich ist, und dann werden bestimmte Reformen sowohl einzelner Zollsätze als auch einer Gruppe von Zollsätzen behandelt. Die üblichen wohlfahrtserhöhenden Reformprogramme werden ebenfalls diskutiert, so die Reform, bei der alle Handelsabgaben in demselben Verhältnis reduziert werden, und die Reform, bei der die höchsten (und/oder niedrigsten) Zollsätze bei jedem Schritt auf das nächsthöhere (-niedrigere) Niveau gesenkt (erhöht) werden.

Part VIII
Reform in Multi-Household Economies

[28]

ON THE DIRECTION OF TAX REFORM

Roger GUESNERIE*
CEPREMAP and CNRS, Paris 13e, France

Received February 1975, revised version received July 1976

1. Introduction

Despite the rapid growth and recent achievements of the optimal taxation literature, the methods and approach of this line of research have been criticized on several grounds. Criticism comes either from contributors to this field aware of its shortcomings – 'internal' criticism – or from specialists who doubt the whole approach – 'external' criticism. 'Internal' criticism puts the emphasis on the fact that the knowledge of optimal taxes may be useless for practical purposes since 'actual changes are slow and piecemeal' [Feldstein (1975)] and that 'policy changes which appear to be steps in the right direction but stop short of attaining the full optimum can reduce welfare' [Dixit (1975)]. 'External' criticism expresses skepticism about the use of a social welfare function which does not 'exist, independently of the mutual adjustment process itself'[Buchanan (1975)] and correlatively stresses that the optimal taxation framework ignores the existing tax system, the conflicts about changes, and the considerations of horizontal equity which have been an important topic of the previous public finance literature [see Musgrave (1959)]. Such objections are clearly exposed in Buchanan (1975) who advocates returning to a previous 'Wicksellian' theoretical tradition.

Both 'internal' and 'external' critiques could to some extent agree with Feldstein's (1975) proposition aimed at shifting the emphasis from 'tax design,' which is the topic of the optimal taxation literature, to 'tax reform' which 'takes as its starting point, the existing tax system and . . . consider the position of each individual before as well as after any proposed change.' This paper does not aim at exploring all dimensions of the question of tax reform – whose intricacies have been analyzed in Feldstein (1975) – but rather to focus the

*This paper is a revised version of an internal CEPREMAP paper of February 1975. I thank an anonymous referee for helpful comments. Valuable discussions with A.B. Atkinson, P. Champsaur, F. Fogelman, J. Mirrlees, M. Quinzi helped me to clarify the issue of temporary inefficiencies. Comments of J.P. Laffargue and Y. Younes are also gratefully acknowledged.

attention on the simple problem of the direction of tax reform which can be formulated as follows: given an existing tax system, what are the characteristics of the 'small' moves of taxes which are both feasible and satisfactory (relatively to a given criterion)?

Thus, the topic we are considering has aims – the search for desirable directions of tax changes – and requires techniques – the comparison of neighbour equilibria – which contrast with the aims and techniques of studies on optimal taxation. Similar approaches seems to have been more frequent in international trade theory [see for example Negishi (1971)] than in the public finance literature (the work of Dixit (1975) is a recent and noticeable exception).

The specific concern of this note is to consider the problem of the direction of tax reform in the framework of the Diamond–Mirrlees model, the most well-known model of the optimal taxation literature, with the goal of carefully considering the relationship between the 'tax design' and the 'tax reform' point of view. So, the attention will successively be focused on the following points:

(1) First, the tax reform problem as defined above will be analysed. Starting from a given equilibrium corresponding to the existing tax system, one will explore neighbour equilibria in order to exhibit directions of tax reform which are *both feasible and satisfactory* in a Pareto sense, i.e. satisfactory for all agents. Where such directions actually exist, they will be characterized in a way allowing an effective computation of the corresponding change in taxes. A striking result will appear, making clear that *temporary inefficiencies in the production sector may be desirable* in the process of tax reform in spite of the 'efficiency' property which holds for optimal tax design.

(2) Second, the complementarity between the 'tax reform' and the 'optimal taxation' points of view will be stressed; it will be argued that a better understanding of the latter can be gained from the former. Characterization of second-best optimal taxes will be derived from the analysis of the direction of tax reform, providing incidentally a proof of classical results which does not refer to any social welfare function nor directly to Kuhn–Tucker techniques.

In the next section all elements of the problem – model and notations, the starting point, some preliminary results, and definitions – will be presented. In section 3 feasible moves of taxes and Pareto improving moves will be characterized. The results will be commented on in section 3.3.

2. Presentation of the problem and preliminary work

2.1. Model and notation

We will adopt notation similar to that used by Diamond–Mirrlees (1971). In the economy, there are H households indexed by $h = 1, \ldots, H$ and n commodities indexed by $k = 1, \ldots, n$. Commodities are specialized in the sense that commodities 1 to n_1 can only be consumed in negative quantities (or supplied) and commodities n_1+1 to n can only be consumed in positive quantities (or demanded) – this being true for each household.

This can be formalized through the definition of adequate consumption sets Ω_h. Assumptions on Ω_h that will be made in the following are gathered in (H1).

(H1) Ω_h is such that commodities can be partitioned in two specialized sets: $(1, \ldots, n_1)$, $(n_1+1, \ldots, n)$. Furthermore Ω_h is convex and bounded below. Each household has preferences on Ω_h, represented by a utility function u_h which satisfies (H2).

(H2) u_h is a strictly quasi-concave function, and u_h is monotonic (i.e. $x_h > x'_h \Rightarrow u_h(x_h) > u_h(x'_h)$) and differentiable.

Faced with the price system[1] $q \in \mathbf{R}^n_+ - \{0\}$ (q is the consumer price system), household h, which has no other source of income than labor income, determines his consumption choice by solving the program

$$\text{Max } u_h(x_h)\{x_h \in \Omega_h,\ q \cdot x_h \leqq 0\}.$$

(H1) and (H2) assure that the solution of this program is unique and that at the optimum the budgetary constraint is tight.

Let us call this solution $x_h(q)$; it is the demand vector of household $h \cdot x_h$: $(\mathbf{R}^n_+ - \{0\}) \rightarrow \mathbf{R}^n$) *is the demand function of household h*. It is homogeneous of degree zero and such that $q \cdot x_h(q) = 0$.

$V_h(q) = u_h(x_h(q))$ is the indirect utility function. The aggregate net demand is $X(q) = \sum_{h=1}^{H} x_h(q)$.

The production sector has production possibilities described through the production function $G(y) \leqq 0$.

(H3) G is a strictly quasi convex function defined on $\mathbf{R}^n$ and G is monotonic: $y > y' \Rightarrow G(y) > G(y')$.

Given a production price system $p \in \mathbf{R}^n_+ - \{0\}$ the competitive supply of the production sector is determined by solving

$$\text{Max } p \cdot y\{y | G(y) \leqq 0\}.$$

From (H3), when this program has a solution, this solution is unique and at the optimum the constraint is tight.

Let us call $\eta(p)$ this solution, $\eta(p)$ is the supply vector of the production

[1]In the following, unless otherwise explicitly stated, price vectors will be line vectors and quantity vectors will be column vectors. A^T will denote the transposed of A (A being a vector or matrix). The complementary of the set X will be denoted CX. If a and b are vectors, $a \geqq b \Leftrightarrow a_i \geqq b_i \forall_i$, $a > b \Leftrightarrow a_i \geqq b_i$ and $a \neq b$.

sector when production prices are p, and $\eta: N \subset \mathbf{R}^n_+ - \{0\} \to \mathbf{R}^n$ is the *supply function*. It is homogeneous of degree zero.

Let us remark that the above formulation rests upon a rough treatment of production since it only describes a regular aggregate constraint for consumption commodities and evades the study of the production of intermediate goods in several firms. However, a more sophisticated description of the production possibilities would not basically modify the line of argument presented in what follows.

2.2. *The starting point*

Let us consider an initial position (at time zero) of the economic system:

the production price system is $p(0)$,
the consumption price system is $q(0)$,
the tax vector is then $T(0) = q(0) - p(0)$,
the consumption vector of household h is $x_h(0)$,
the aggregate production plan is $y(0)$.

Moreover, this initial position is supposed to be an equilibrium – relative to the tax system $T(0)$ – in the sense that

$$x_h(0) = x_h(q(0)), \tag{1}$$

$$y(0) = \eta(p(0)), \tag{2}$$

$$\sum_{h=1}^{H} x_h(0) \leqq y(0). \tag{3}$$

More precisely, one will suppose that constraints corresponding to (3) are met:

$$\sum_{h=1}^{H} x_h(0) = y(0). \tag{4}$$

When (1), (2) and (4) are met, we say that the corresponding equilibrium is *tight*. If (3) holds and (4) does not hold, the equilibrium will be *nontight*.

Let us observe that the implementation of such an equilibrium requires that the government be able to separate consumption and production prices through consumption taxes and to operate a 100% taxation of pure profits. These implicit assumptions on the set of policy tools have been lengthily discussed elsewhere, and we will limit ourselves to this brief recall. A second remark concerning this definition is that $T(0)$ is considered as a data. Another approach would have consisted in considering a set of given initial taxes $\bar{T}$ and wondering whether an equilibrium can be reached given these fixed taxes (existence problem). For such a problem a positive answer cannot be expected whatever $\overline{T}$. It follows that the tax vector $T(0)$ associated with our initial equilibrium position cannot be any vector T, but we are not interested here in discovering the restrictions on $T(0)$ which make it compatible with an equilibrium.

One can now state additional assumptions. These assumptions are local assumptions, in the sense that they only concern characteristics of the system in a neighbourhood of the initial situation. In order to be distinguished from global assumptions, they will be denoted not by numbers but by greek letters:

(Hα) x_h is continuously differentiable in a neighbourhood of $q(0)$, $\forall\, h$.
(Hβ) η is continuously differentiable in a neighbourhood of $p(0)$.

If all x_h are differentiable, X, the aggregate demand function, is also differentiable. We will denote by $\partial X^{=}(0)$, the $(n\times n)$ matrix whose element in the lth line, and the kth column is

$$\left(\frac{\partial X_l}{\partial q_k}\right)_{(q(0))}.$$

Similarly $\partial\eta^{=}(0)$ will denote the $(n\times n)$ matrix whose element in the lth line, and the kth column is

$$\left(\frac{\partial \eta_l}{\partial p_k}\right)_{(p(0))}.$$

One knows that $\partial\eta^{=}(0)$ is a symmetric matrix such that $p(0)\cdot\partial\eta^{=}(0) = 0$. It follows that $\partial\eta^{=}(0)$ is at most of rank $n-1$.

Assumption (Hγ) can now be stated:

(Hγ) $\partial\eta^{=}(0)$ is of rank $(n-1)$.

(Hα), (Hβ) and (Hγ) are not, strictly speaking, implied by (H2) and (H3). Nevertheless they do not introduce severe restrictions in addition to (H2) and (H3).[2]

2.3. *A preliminary lemma*

(Hβ)–(Hγ) allow us to prove the following useful lemma

Lemma 1. Let us consider $V(0) = \{u\in \mathbf{R}^n | p(0)\cdot u = 0\}$. *Then* $\partial\eta^{=}(0)$ *defines a one to one correspondence from* $V(0)$ *onto* $V(0)$ *denoted* $\partial\tilde{\eta}(0)$.

[2]The problem of differentiability of demand function has been discussed extensively elsewhere [see Debreu (1972)]. This discussion could be transposed to supply functions. In case of demand functions, the only serious disturbing nondifferentiabilities occur at prices in the neighbourhood of which the consumption of some commodity changes from zero to a positive quantity.

Proof. As $\partial\eta^{=}(0) = (\partial\eta^{=}(0))^T$, $\partial\eta^{=}(0)\cdot p(0)^T = 0$. This means that $p(0)^T$ belongs to the kernel of the linear mapping defined by $\partial\eta^{=}(0)$. But since $\partial\eta^{=}(0)$ is of rank $(n-1)$, the kernel is of dimension 1 and $\partial\eta^{=}(0)$ defines a one to one correspondence from a supplementary of the kernel – as is $V(0)$ – onto its image (Im). It remains to prove that Im $V(0) = V(0)$; which results from the fact that dim. Im $V(0) = n-1$ and that $\partial\eta^{=}(0)\cdot u \in V(0)$ since $p(0)\cdot\partial\eta^{=}(0) = 0$.

Q.E.D.

Hence $\partial\tilde{\eta}(0): V(0) \to V(0)$, the restriction of $\partial\eta^{=}(0)$ to $V(0)$ has an inverse which will be denoted $\partial\tilde{\eta}^{-1}(0)$.

The intuitive content of the argument of the proof and of the consequence of lemma 1 must be emphasised: $\partial\eta^{=}(0)\cdot p(0)^T = 0$ means that any small move of production prices in the direction of the actual production prices does not modify the supply vector (a consequence of the homogeneity property). $\partial\eta^{=}(0)\cdot u \in V(0)$ means that any small move of production prices leads to moves in supply, the direction of which defines a vector normal to $p(0)$ (an obvious geometric property).

The fact that $\partial\tilde{\eta}(0)$ has an inverse means *that any small move in supply, the direction of which is normal to* $p(0)$, *can be obtained through a small modification of production prices, whose direction can be chosen normal to* $p(0)$ (see fig. 1). The fact that $\partial\tilde{\eta}(0)$ is one to one means that the correspondence between directions of small moves in supply normal to $p(0)$ and directions of production prices associated with such moves and normal to $p(0)$ is one to one. As soon as one is aware of the normalization rule $\|p\| = C^{ste}$ implicit to the choice of production price changes normal to $p(0)$, the two latter properties become intuitively appealing.

2.4. More preliminary definitions

In order to discuss the directions of tax reform we will introduce the following sets: $K(0)$, $\mathring{K}(0)$ and $\mathring{Q}(0)$,

$$K(0) = \{a \in \mathbf{R}^n | a\cdot x_h(0) \leqq 0,\ h = 1, \ldots, H\}.^3$$

Intuitively $K(0)$ is the set of price systems for which the cost of all consumption bundles $x_h(0)$ is smaller than or equal to zero. Obviously any $a = \lambda q(0)$ belongs to $K(0)$ $\forall\, \lambda \geqq 0$.

$\mathring{K}(0)$ will designate the interior of $K(0)$, i.e. the set of price systems for which the cost of all consumption bundles is strictly smaller than zero,

$$\mathring{K}(0) = \{a \in \mathbf{R}^n | a\cdot x_h(0) < 0,\ h = 1, \ldots, H\}.$$

[3] a is by definition a line vector, hence a^T is a column vector.

From (H1) it is clear that whatever the bundles $x_h(0)$, $\mathring{K}(0)$ is not empty (in order to lower the cost of all bundles (from $q(0)$) it suffices to raise the price of any 'supplied commodity' or to lower the price of any 'demanded commodity').

Finally, let us consider $Q(0)$, its interior $\mathring{Q}(0)$ and its frontier Fr $Q(0)$:

$$Q(0) = \{a \in \mathbf{R}^n | p(0) \cdot \partial X^{=}(0) \cdot a^T \leqq 0\},$$

$$\mathring{Q}(0) = \{a \in \mathbf{R}^n | p(0) \cdot \partial X^{=}(0) \cdot a^T < 0\},$$

$$\text{Fr } Q(0) = \{a \in \mathbf{R}^n | p(0) \cdot \partial X^{=}(0) \cdot a^T = 0\}.$$

$Q(0)$ can be given two related interpretations:

(1) Let us consider a small change of consumption prices in the direction of a^T. The induced change in consumption is proportional to $\partial X^{=}(0) \cdot a^T$. The value of this change expressed with production prices is $p(0) \cdot \partial X^{=}(0) \cdot a^T$. So $Q(0)$ is *the set of directions of consumption prices changes which imply changes in consumption whose value expressed in production prices is negative.*

(2) Let us consider the budget surplus Δ as a function of p and q: $\Delta(p, q) = (q-p) \cdot X(q) + p \cdot \eta(p)$ (Δ is the sum of receipts coming from consumption taxes and profit tax). One can check that $\Delta(p(0), q(0)) = 0$: in the initial equilibrium state, the government budget is balanced. Let us consider, however, a small move of consumption prices – production prices are assumed to remain constant (generally this does not define a feasible state). Taking into account $q \cdot X(q) = 0$, it comes out $\mathrm{d}\Delta = -p \cdot \mathrm{d}X$. Thus, $Q(0)$ also appears as the set of directions of tax changes, which *ceteris paribus* would preserve the budget equilibrium.

Let us notice, before continuing that the knowledge of $K(0)$ and $Q(0)$ requires information of different nature. $K(0)$ is known as soon as the consumption bundles are known, when $Q(0)$ depends on the set of all price elasticities of the *aggregate* demand function, the evaluation of which requires sophisticated investigation.

In the following, the sets K and Q will sometimes be not indexed by time (here zero) but considered functions of production and consumption price vectors. In this way, without introducing additional notations, $K(q)$ will designate $\{a \in \mathbf{R}^n | a \cdot x_h(q) \leqq 0, \forall h = 1, \ldots, H\}$ (so that $K(0)$ is a notation for $K(q(0))$) and $Q(p, q)$ will be $\{a \in \mathbf{R}^n | p \cdot \partial X^{=}(q) \cdot a^T \leqq 0\}$ (so that $Q(0)$ is a notation for $Q(p(0), q(0))$).

All the elements of the model are now presented, and we are in a position to give a more precise formulation of the problem studied here. Loosely speaking, our aim is to exhibit small tax changes which are, first, feasible and, second, satisfactory in a Pareto sense or Pareto improving. For that, one will reason with infinitesimal moves (a natural idealisation of 'small' moves) of the system.

Relating these infinitesimal moves with infinitesimal moves of an exogenous variable called time – and denoted dt – allows defining directions of moves of the variable z as dz/dt and leads to formal definitions of 'feasible' and 'Pareto improving' directions of tax reform.

The direction of a move of consumption prices denoted dq/dt, and the direction of move of production prices denoted dp/dt will be said to be *equilibrium preserving* if

$$\sum_{h=1}^{H} \frac{\mathrm{d}x_h}{\mathrm{d}t} \leqq \frac{\mathrm{d}y}{\mathrm{d}t},$$

with

$$\frac{\mathrm{d}x_h}{\mathrm{d}t} = \partial x_h^{=}(0)\cdot\left(\frac{\mathrm{d}q}{\mathrm{d}t}\right)^T,$$

$$\frac{\mathrm{d}y}{\mathrm{d}t} = \partial\eta^{=}(0)\cdot\left(\frac{\mathrm{d}p}{\mathrm{d}t}\right)^T.$$

The direction of move of prices dq/dt and dp/dt will be said to be *tight equilibrium preserving if*

$$\sum_{h=1}^{H} \frac{\mathrm{d}x_h}{\mathrm{d}t} = \frac{\mathrm{d}y}{\mathrm{d}t},$$

with

$$\frac{\mathrm{d}x_h}{\mathrm{d}t} = \partial x_h^{=}(0)\cdot\left(\frac{\mathrm{d}q}{\mathrm{d}t}\right)^T,$$

$$\frac{\mathrm{d}y}{\mathrm{d}t} = \partial\eta^{=}(0)\cdot\left(\frac{\mathrm{d}p}{\mathrm{d}t}\right)^T.$$

Thus, a tight equilibrium preserving direction of change tends to maintain the equality between demand and supply and not only assures the inequality.

Similarly, directions of moves of consumption and production prices at time zero dq/dt and dp/dt will be said *strictly Pareto improving* if:

(1) dq/dt and dp/dt are equilibrium preserving,

(2) $$\frac{\mathrm{d}V_h}{\mathrm{d}t} = \left(\frac{\partial V_h}{\partial q}\right)(0)\cdot\left(\frac{\mathrm{d}q}{\mathrm{d}t}\right)^T > 0, \quad \forall\, h = 1,\ldots, H,$$

where V_h is the indirect utility function and

$$\left(\frac{\partial V_h}{\partial q}\right)(0) = \left[\cdots \frac{\partial V_h}{\partial q_k} \cdots\right]_{q(0)}.$$

Hence price changes in a strictly improving direction tend to increase the welfare of all individuals.

3. Statement of results

Feasible and Pareto improving moves of prices are characterized in sections 3.1 and 3.2. Results are commented on in section 3.3.

3.1. Feasible directions of price changes

We assume that (H1), (H2), (Hα), (Hβ) and (Hγ) are true.

Proposition 1. For any direction of consumption price changes $\mathrm{d}q/\mathrm{d}t$ *belonging to* $Q(0)$, *there is at least one direction of production price changes* $\mathrm{d}p/\mathrm{d}t$ *such that* $(\mathrm{d}q/\mathrm{d}t,\ \mathrm{d}p/\mathrm{d}t)$ *is equilibrium preserving. Moreover, if* $\mathrm{d}q/\mathrm{d}t \in \mathrm{Fr}\ Q(0)$, *the associated direction of change of production prices is unique and* $(\mathrm{d}q/\mathrm{d}t,\ \mathrm{d}p/\mathrm{d}t)$ *is tight equilibrium preserving.*

Proof. Let $\mathrm{d}q/\mathrm{d}t \in \mathrm{Fr}\ Q(0)$ be

$$\frac{\mathrm{d}X}{\mathrm{d}t} = \partial X^{=}(0)\cdot\left(\frac{\mathrm{d}q}{\mathrm{d}t}\right)^T$$

and

$$p(0)\cdot\frac{\mathrm{d}X}{\mathrm{d}t} = p(0)\cdot\partial X^{=}(0)\cdot\left(\frac{\mathrm{d}q}{\mathrm{d}t}\right)^T = 0\,.$$

Hence, $\mathrm{d}X/\mathrm{d}t \in V(0)$ and, from lemma 1, there exists $\mathrm{d}p/\mathrm{d}t = \partial\tilde{\eta}^{-1}(0)\cdot(\mathrm{d}X/\mathrm{d}t)$ It follows that

$$\frac{\mathrm{d}y}{\mathrm{d}t} = \partial\eta^{=}(0)\cdot\left(\frac{\mathrm{d}p}{\mathrm{d}t}\right)^T = \partial\eta^{=}(0)\cdot\partial\tilde{\eta}^{-1}(0)\,\frac{\mathrm{d}X}{\mathrm{d}t} = \frac{\mathrm{d}X}{\mathrm{d}t}\,.$$

If $\mathrm{d}q/\mathrm{d}t \in \operatorname{Int} Q(0)$,

$$\frac{\mathrm{d}X}{\mathrm{d}t} = \partial X^{=}(0)\cdot\left(\frac{\mathrm{d}q}{\mathrm{d}t}\right)^{T}$$

is such that $p(0)\cdot \mathrm{d}X/\mathrm{d}t < 0$.
One can take $U \in (\mathrm{d}X/\mathrm{d}t) + \mathbf{R}^n_+$ such that $p(0)\cdot U = 0$.
Using the same argument as above, it can be seen that $\mathrm{d}q/\mathrm{d}t$, $\mathrm{d}p/\mathrm{d}t = \partial\tilde{\eta}(0)\cdot U$ is equilibrium preserving but not tight equilibrium preserving. Q.E.D.

Proposition 1 has a strong intuitive content: with respect to the discussion above it means that if a small move of consumption prices is such that the value of the associated consumption changes, measured with the production prices, does not increase – or equivalently is such that the State Budget be not affected in the way indicated above – then the equilibrium of the system can be maintained through an adequate change of the production price system. It is worth noting that the fact of belonging to $Q(0)$ for a direction of change only removes one degree of freedom for the possible movements of the consumption price vector. As such a vector is a vector of $\mathbf{R}^{n-1}$ (taking into account the homogeneity of demand functions), it can be stressed that proposition 1 implies, loosely speaking, that from any equilibrium the *system can move in* $(n-2)$ *directions*.

Proposition 2 completes proposition 1 by establishing the existence of small finite moves associated with tight equilibrium preserving directions of moves.

Proposition 2. If $Q(0) \neq \mathbf{R}^n$, *for any* $a(0) \in \operatorname{Fr} Q(0)$ *there exists* t_0 *and paths of prices* $p(t)$, $q(t)$, $t \leqq t_0$, *such that*

$$\left(\frac{\mathrm{d}q}{\mathrm{d}t}\right)_{t=0} = a(0)\,,$$

where $p(t)$, $q(t)$, $x_h(q(t), \eta(p(t))$ *define tight equilibria* $\forall\, t \leqq t_0$.

Proof. Let us consider Fr (Q) as a function of p and q (cf. section 2.4) and let $v(p,q)$ be the projection of $a(0)$ on the hyperplane Fr $Q(p,q)$.[4]

Let the differential system be

$$\frac{\mathrm{d}q}{\mathrm{d}t} = v(p,q)\,, \tag{1}$$

$$\frac{\mathrm{d}p}{\mathrm{d}t} = \partial\tilde{\eta}^{-1}(p)\cdot\partial X^{=}(q)\cdot v(p,q)\,. \tag{2}$$

With (Hα) and (Hβ) the second member of (1) and (2) is continuously differen-

[4]For p, q close to $p(0)$, $q(0)$, $Q(p,q) \neq \mathbf{R}^n$.

tiable. Hence a standard argument of existence [cf. Dieudonne (1969)] allows to assert that the system has locally a solution, hence the conclusion. Q.E.D.

3.2. The direction of Pareto-improving price changes

The directions of Pareto improving directions of move of prices can be characterized through propositions 3 and 4.

Proposition 3. For any direction of consumption price changes $\mathrm{d}q/\mathrm{d}t$ *belonging to* $\mathring{K}(0) \cap Q(0)$, *one can find at least one direction of production price changes* $\mathrm{d}p/\mathrm{d}t$ *such that* $(\mathrm{d}q/\mathrm{d}t, \mathrm{d}p/\mathrm{d}t)$ *is strictly Pareto improving. Moreover, if* $\mathrm{d}q/\mathrm{d}t \in \mathring{K}(0) \cap \mathrm{Fr}\, Q(0)$, $\mathrm{d}p/\mathrm{d}t$ *is unique and* $(\mathrm{d}q/\mathrm{d}t, \mathrm{d}p/\mathrm{d}t)$ *is tight equilibrium preserving.*

Proof. Given proposition 2, it is enough to prove that $\mathrm{d}V_h/\mathrm{d}t > 0\ \forall\, h = 1, \ldots, H$, where

$$\frac{\mathrm{d}V_h}{\mathrm{d}t} = \left(\frac{\partial V_h}{\partial q}\right)(0) \cdot \left(\frac{\mathrm{d}q}{\mathrm{d}t}\right)^T .$$

But our assumptions assure that

$$\left(\frac{\partial V_h}{\partial q}\right)(0) = -\lambda_h x_h(0) ,$$

where λ_h is a strictly positive number which can be interpreted as the individual value of income of h; conclusions follow. Q.E.D.

The content of proposition 3 is intuitively clear if one remembers that any direction of price change belonging to $\mathring{K}(0)$ *tends to decrease the cost of consumption bundles of all individuals.*

Proposition 4 gives a condition for the existence of strictly Pareto improving price changes, in terms of the position of the vector $p(0) \cdot \partial X^{=}(0)$ – the vector of production costs associated with lowering all consumption prices one 'small' unit – and of the cone generated by consumption vectors.

Proposition 4. Let $\Lambda(0)$ *be the cone generated by the consumption vectors* $x_h(0)$,

$$\Lambda(0) = \{x | x = \sum_{h=1}^{H} \lambda_h x_h(0), \text{ for some } \lambda_h \geqq 0\}.$$

If $[p(0)\partial X^{=}(0)]^T = 0$, *the existence of strictly Pareto improving directions of price changes depends upon the position of* $[p(0)\cdot\partial X^{=}(0)]^T$ *relative to* $\Lambda(0)$, according to the following rules:[5]

(a) $[p(0)\cdot\partial X^{=}(0)]^T \in -\Lambda(0)$: there does not exist strictly Pareto improving directions of prices changes,

(b) $[p(0)\cdot\partial X^{=}(0)]^T \in +\Lambda(0)$: there exist Pareto improving directions of prices changes but none of them is tight equilibrium preserving,

(c) $[p(0)\cdot\partial X^{=}(0)]^T \in C(\Lambda(0)U-\Lambda(0))$: there exist strictly Pareto improving directions of prices changes which are tight equilibrium preserving.

Proof. According to the separation theorem given in the appendix, $\mathring{K}(0) \cap Q(0) = \emptyset$ is equivalent to the fact that there exist $\lambda_h \geqq 0$ and $\mu \geqq 0$ such that

$$\sum_h \lambda_h x_h(0) + \mu[p(0)\cdot\partial X^{=}(0)]^T = 0.$$

Let us note that, then, μ is strictly positive (if not, by the same theorem, one would have $\mathring{K}(0) = \emptyset$, which is excluded by the assumptions).
So,

$$[p(0)\cdot\partial X^{=}(0)]^T \in -\Lambda(0) \Leftrightarrow \mathring{K}(0) \cap Q(0) = \emptyset.$$

In the same way one can prove that

$$[p(0)\cdot\partial X^{=}(0)] \in \Lambda(0) \Leftrightarrow \mathring{K}(0) \cap \overline{C(Q(0))} = \emptyset.$$

Then: if $[p(0)\cdot\partial X^{=}(0)]^T \in \Lambda(0)$, $\mathring{K}(0) \cap Q(0) \neq \emptyset$ and $\mathring{K}(0) \cap \text{Fr } Q(0) = \emptyset$, which together with proposition 3 proves (b); if $[p(0)\cdot\partial X^{=}(0)] \in C(\Lambda(0)U-\Lambda(0))$, $\mathring{K}(0) \cap \text{Fr } Q(0) \neq \emptyset$, which together with proposition 3 proves (c); (a) results from the first above equivalence and from the fact that any dq/dt associated with a Pareto improving direction of price changes necessarily belongs to $\mathring{K}(0) \cap Q(0)$. Q.E.D.

The different cases (c), (b) and (a) are illustrated in figs. 2, 3 and 4 for a 3-commodity 2-household world. The plane in which those figures are drawn is the budget hyperplane $\{x|q(0)\cdot x = 0\}$.

The implications of the proposition 4 for small but finite moves are given by proposition 5.

[5]One has $q(0)\cdot[p(0)\cdot\partial X^{=}(0)]^T = 0$ (as the reader will easily check) so that $[p(0)\cdot\partial X^{=}(0)]^T$ is a vector belonging to the budget hyperplane (common to all consumers).

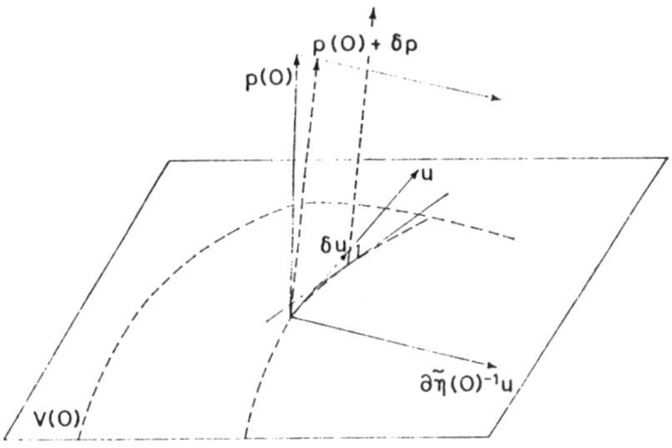

Fig. 1

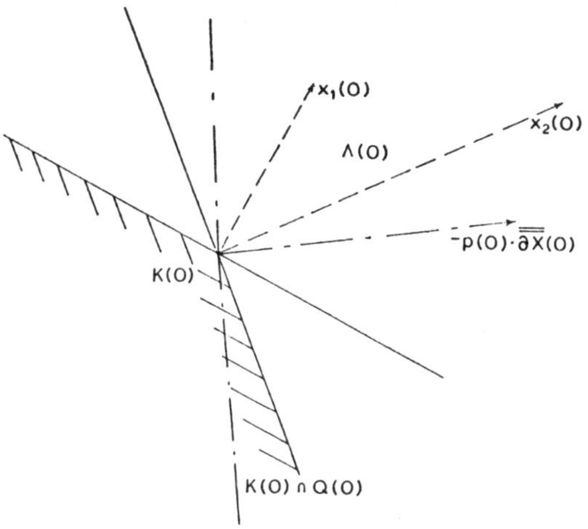

Fig. 2. $p(0)\cdot\partial X^{=}(0)\in C(\Lambda(0)\,U-\Lambda(0))$: there exist tight equilibrium preserving and Pareto improving directions of price changes.

Proposition 5. If $[(p(0)\cdot\partial X^{=}(0)]^T\notin\Lambda(0)U-\Lambda(0)$, *there exists a small but finite Pareto improving move which is tight equilibrium preserving. If* $[p(0)\cdot\partial X^{=}(0)]^T\in\mathring{\Lambda}(0)$ *there exists a finite Pareto improving move.*

Proof. One knows that the assumptions imply that $\mathring{K}(0)\cap\mathrm{Fr}\,Q(0)\neq\emptyset$. Let $a(0)\in\mathring{K}(0)\cap\mathrm{Fr}\,Q(0)$. One can apply proposition 2 above and consider along the equilibrium path $p(t)$, $q(t)$ (starting from $p(0), q(0)$ with $\mathrm{d}q/\mathrm{d}t(0)=a(0)$), the quantities $(x_h(p(t))\cdot(\mathrm{d}q/\mathrm{d}t)(t),\ h=1,\ldots,H)$. From the continuity of functions

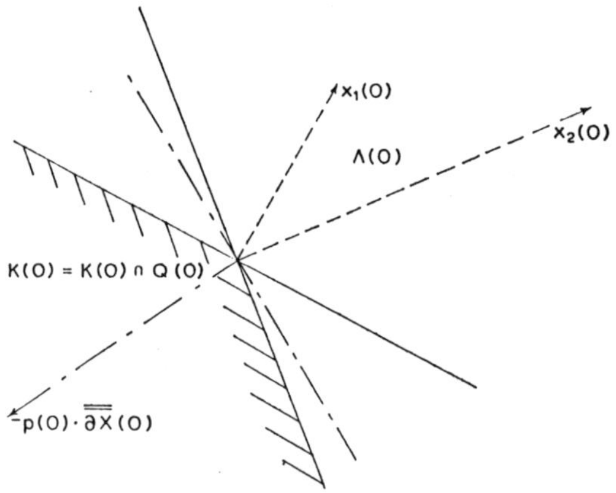

Fig. 3. $+p(0)\cdot\partial X^{=}(0)\in\Lambda(0)$: there exist Pareto improving directions of price changes but none are tight equilibrium preserving.

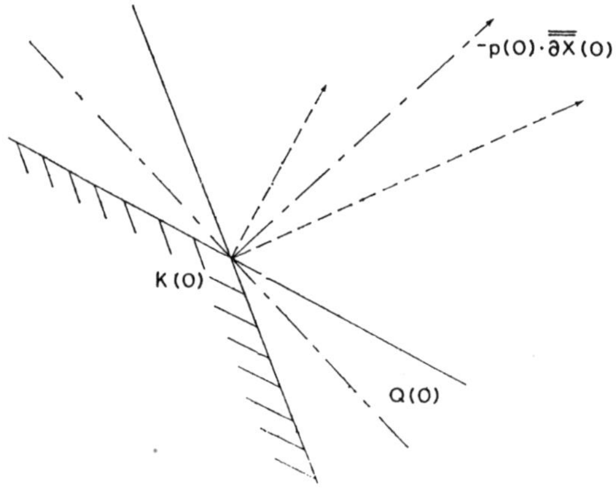

Fig. 4. $-p(0)\cdot\partial X^{=}(0)\in\Lambda(0)$: there do not exist Pareto improving directions of changes.

$x_h(p)$, $p(t)$ and $\mathrm{d}q/\mathrm{d}t(t)$, one can conclude that for t small enough, all these quantities remain strictly negative. It follows that the utilities of all individuals strictly increase.

The second part of the proposition has to be proven without reference to proposition 2 by taking $a(0)\in\mathring{K}(0)\cap\mathring{Q}(0)$ and considering the path $q(t)=$

$q(0)+a(0)t$. The reader will check that it is possible to choose t small enough so that $q(t) \in \mathring{K}(t)$ and $G(X(q(t))) < 0$.[6]

3.3. *Comments and complements*

We will successively consider the implications of the above statements on four questions:

(1) the characterization of second-best Pareto optima;
(2) the computation of the direction of tax reform;
(3) the temporary inefficiencies issue;
(4) the implementation of finite changes of taxes.

(A) The above analysis gives criteria – (b) and (c) of proposition 4 – for determining whether a given equilibrium can be improved upon in the Pareto sense through 'small' manipulations of the tax system. Testing this criterion in a given situation requires the knowledge of prices (production prices), quantities (consumption bundles of all individuals) – which are directly observable – and elasticities of aggregate demand – which are not directly observable. (It is worth noting that the knowledge of elasticities of individual demand are not needed. Elasticities of supply are not needed for testing the criterion but only for computing the effective tax change.)

On the other hand, those equilibria which cannot be improved upon in the Pareto sense by any tax manipulation – either small or large – necessarily correspond to case (a) of proposition 4: as a consequence of proposition 5, they cannot fall in case (b) or (c). Characteristics of such states which are second-best Pareto optimal states according to the usual vocabulary appear as a joint product of the analysis in corollary 1.

Corollary 1. In any second-best equilibrium, $-[p(0)\cdot\partial X^{=}(0)] \in \Lambda(0)$. Equivalently, there exists $\lambda_h \geqq 0$ s.t.

$$-[p(0)\cdot\partial X^{=}(0)] = \sum_{h=1}^{H} \lambda_h x_h(0).$$

These conditions are well known since Diamond–Mirrlee's seminal article (1971, eg. 66). Besides providing another proof, this makes it clear that such conditions do not rest on the use of a social welfare function, a concept foreign to the analysis attempted here. The analysis also provides an understanding of the phenomena underlying second-best Pareto optimality. Some conjectures can for example be derived from the geometrical features of the problem.

[6]The argument is slightly more technical: one can for example tax ε small enough such that $\|p-p(0)\| \leqq \varepsilon$ and $\|B-\partial X^{=}(0)\| \leqq \varepsilon \Rightarrow p\cdot B \in \mathring{\Lambda}(0)$, and then choose t so that $x_h(q(t))\cdot a(0) < 0$, and the above conditions on p and $B = \partial X^{=}(t)$ are satisfied.

The fact that $[p(0)\cdot\partial X^{=}(0)]^T \in -\Lambda(0)$ seems unlikely to occur when the number of consumers is smaller than the number of commodities minus two (this corresponds to $\Lambda(0)$ being of measure zero in the hyperplane $\{x|q(0)\cdot x = 0\}$. This suggests that under these circumstances the set of Pareto equilibria be of 'measure zero' in the set of equilibria. Obviously giving a precise meaning to such a conjecture, and *a fortiori* proving it, is outside the scope of this note.

In the case where the number of consumers is greater than the number of commodities minus one, tight equilibria with $p(0)$ 'close enough' to $q(0)$ would be second-best equilibria. The argument supporting this conjecture is that if $T(0)$ were small enough, $p(0)\cdot\partial X^{=}(0)$ would be close to $q(0)\cdot\partial X^{=}(0)$. Hence, it would belong to $-\Lambda(0)$ so that there would not exist Pareto improving directions of prices changes. However, some difficulties appear in an attempt of obtaining a formal proof: considering it is outside the scope of this note.

(B) If proposition 4 gives a criterion for determining whether unanimously advantageous 'directions of tax reform' exist, proposition 3 allows exhibition of such directions by selecting directions of consumption price moves in $\mathring{K}(0) \cap Q(0)$ and adapting correspondingly the production price system. Three remarks will be made:

(1) Giving an operational representation of the set $K(0)$ raises computational problems which are also slightly different according to whether the number of households is smaller or greater than the number of commodities. A view of these problems is provided in the appendix.
(2) Voluntarily, the attention has not been focused here on normalization problems. If productions prices are modified according to the implicit and specific normalization rule $\|p\| = Cste$, consumption prices movements are not governed by any *a priori* normalization constraint; so that taxes – in the ordinary meaning of the term – are not unambiguously fixed. It is clear that the normalization rule for production prices could be modified and that a normalization rule for consumption prices could be imposed in order to meet any *a priori* requirement in this matter, without affecting the basic line of argument (For example, assuming the existence of an untaxed commodity – 'labor' – leads to economically meaningful interpretations). Additional insights on the tax system could possibly have been gained from such a normalization convention. They remain outside the scope of this study.
(3) Raising a similar problem in a different – and simpler – context (one consumer, lump sum transfers feasible), Dixit (1975) in a systematic investigation was able to obtain strong results: he exhibited moves of the tax system (in terms of specific as well as *ad valorem* taxes), which where both (in some sense) 'distortions-reducing' and desirable. The reader will easily convince himself from examination of $K(0) \cap Q(0)$ and proposition 3 that results of a similar type are quite unlikely to be obtained in this model, both be-

cause lump sum transfers are excluded and because of the distributional problems appearing in a many-agents economy. This reinforces Dixit's conclusion that the real problem is not 'that there are few policies leading to partial welfare improvements . . . nor . . . that partial welfare improvements are particularly difficult to characterize . . .' but 'that some particular rules that were thought to be intuitively plausible by some economists turned out to be wrong.' Let us add that familiarity with the analysis of direction of tax reform could be an appropriate way of developing correct intuitions in this field.

(C) From proposition 3, when $p(0)\cdot\partial X^{=}(0) \in \Lambda(0)$, any Pareto improving direction of prices changes tends to lead to a nontight equilibrium. It follows that small finite Pareto improving moves of prices, starting from such initial situations, possibly yield nontight equilibria, i.e. in the Diamond–Mirrlees vocabulary to inefficient equilibria. It must first be noticed that such a phenomenon does not contradict the so-called efficiency property which here straightforwardly holds in any second-best equilibrium (cf. (H1)). It only means that in spite of the need for efficiency at the final stage, *temporary inefficiencies may be necessary and unavoidable in the process of tax reform* when the process is astrained to be monotone in terms of utility. One must then make sure that situations where $p(0)\cdot\partial X^{=}(0) \in \Lambda(0)$ – which govern the possibility of temporary inefficiencies – can actually occur. Examples of such equilibria are given in the appendix in an economy with 3 commodities and 3 households, which make it clear that the property derives from the distortion created by taxes in the price system and does not rest on pathological features of preferences. Especially the second example shows that the property may hold without inferior goods.

Now one can wonder whether in a given economy the set of equilibria such that $p\cdot\partial X^{=} \in \Lambda$ is 'big' or not and consequently to have some idea about the 'frequency' of the temporary inefficiencies phenomena in the process of tax reform. A complete and satisfactory answer to this question would probably require lengthy developments. However some useful qualitative remarks which can be drawn from our analysis shed some light on this problem.

(1) Temporary inefficiencies are not very likely to occur when you are close to a second-best equilibrium. This intuition is based on the fact that in order to enter $-\Lambda$, the vector $p\cdot\partial X^{=}$ must leave Λ, unless it goes through zero, which is 'unlikely'.
(2) If $p\cdot\partial X^{=}$ belongs to the interior of Λ relatively to $\mathbf{R}^{n-1}$ – this will be the case if $p\cdot\partial X^{=}$ belongs to the relative interior of Λ and if the number of consumers having linearly independent consumption bundles is greater than the number of commodities minus one – $p\cdot\partial X^{=}$ will remain in $\mathring{\Lambda}$ in some neighbourhood of p, q.
(3) At contrary when the number of consumers is strictly smaller than the number of commodities minus one, equilibria such that $p\cdot\partial X^{=} \in \Lambda$ are in

some sense very unlikely. Temporary inefficiencies probably become an insignificant phenomenon in such a context.

(D) The above analysis is a local analysis aimed at determining small moves of the tax pattern in the right direction and inducing small moves of the economy. However these small moves can be linked one with another in order to define changes of finite magnitude in the economic system. Such connected moves obey differential equations, which can be straightforwardly exhibited from the local approach.

Corollary 2. Let $p(t)$, $q(t)$ be paths of production and consumption prices starting from $p(0)$, $q(0)$, such that $\forall\, t \in [0, T]$,

$$\frac{\mathrm{d}q}{\mathrm{d}t} \in \mathring{K}(p, q) \cap \mathrm{Fr}\,(Q(p, q))\,,$$

$$\frac{\mathrm{d}p}{\mathrm{d}t} = \partial\tilde{\eta}^{-1}(p)\cdot\partial X^{=}(q)\cdot\frac{\mathrm{d}q}{\mathrm{d}t}\,.$$ [7]

Then, $x_h(q(t))$, $\eta(p(t))$, $q(t)$ define a tight equilibrium $\forall\, t \in [0, T]$ and $V_h(q(t))$ is a strictly increasing function of t, $\forall\, h = 1, \ldots, H$.

However, we have just noticed that paths such as those defined in corollary 2 can be stopped before that Pareto improving changes fail to exist (when such changes unavoidably lead to nontight equilibria).

In the general case, temporary inefficiencies must be allowed, which makes the differential system slightly more complicated. For example such a system is given by corollary 3.

Corollary 3. Let $p(t)$, $q(t)$ be paths of production and consumption prices and $\lambda(t)$ be a positive number depending upon t, such that $\forall\, t \in [0, T]$,

$$\frac{\mathrm{d}q}{\mathrm{d}t} \in \mathring{K}(p, q) \cap \tilde{Q}(p, q) \text{ with } \tilde{Q}(p, q) = \begin{cases} Q(p, q) & \text{if } \eta(p) = X(q)\,, \\ \mathbf{R}^n & \text{if } \eta(p) > X(q), \end{cases}$$

$$\frac{\mathrm{d}p}{\mathrm{d}t} = \partial\tilde{\eta}^{-1}(p)\cdot\left[\partial X^{=}(q)\cdot\frac{\mathrm{d}q}{\mathrm{d}t} - \frac{\mathrm{d}\lambda}{\mathrm{d}t}\,p - \lambda\,\frac{\mathrm{d}p}{\mathrm{d}t}\right],$$

$$\frac{\mathrm{d}\lambda}{\mathrm{d}t} = \frac{p\cdot\partial X^{=}(q)\cdot\dfrac{\mathrm{d}q}{\mathrm{d}t}}{\|p\|^2}\,.$$

[7] $\partial\tilde{\eta}$ is supposed to remain inversible along the path. For notational clarity, the signs T (transposed) are omitted in corollaries 2–3.

Then $x_h(q(t))$, $\eta(p(t))$, $p(t)$, $q(t)$ define equilibria which are tight if and only if $\lambda(t) = 0$; $V_h(q(t))$ is a strictly increasing function of t, $\forall\, h = 1, \ldots, H$.

The reader will check that if $p(\cdot)$, $q(\cdot)$ satisfy the above equations:

(a) $p \cdot \dfrac{dp}{dt} = 0$,

(b) Putting $\partial X^{=}(q) \cdot (dq/dt) - (d\lambda/dt)p - \lambda(dp/dt) = dX'/dt$, then $p \cdot (dX'/dt) = 0$,

(c) $\eta(p(t)) = X(q(t)) - \lambda(t)p(t), \quad \lambda(t) \leqq 0.$

It seems that such differential systems are worthy of careful study, with reference to the different contexts in which they may be relevant tools of analysis.

(1) In the so-called 'economic theory of socialism,' planning algorithms which have been proposed [see Heal (1972)] rest upon the hypothesis that lump sum transfers are feasible. Such an assumption remains questionable in a socialist economy. If it were given up, finding optimal taxes would be a part of the optimal planning problem. Differential equations of corollaries 2 and 3 could be considered idealised formalisations of a tatonnement planning procedure, where exchange of information between the Center and the agents would be intended to determine elasticities.

(2) In a market economy, if demand and supply functions are known not only locally but with some plausibility in a reasonably large interval (complete systems of demand functions such that those derived from the linear expenditure system of Stone – see for example Solari (1971) – are supposed to provide such a knowledge for demand functions), the above differential system would have to be solved by the government in order to implement a tax reform which would be not 'small'[8].

4. Conclusion

In conclusion, three possible extensions of the above analysis are as follows:

(1) Some parts of the analysis could be refined (introduction of a specific normalization rule for consumption prices, etc.; consideration of 'specific' or *ad valorem* taxes, etc.).

(2) The analysis could easily be extended in order to take into account one or several public goods. The differential systems of section 2.3.3 should be modified accordingly. As argued above, they would remain a topic of independent interest.

[8]Let us note that a nontatonnement interpretation of the differential system raises problems which have been carefully analyzed in Feldstein (1975).

(3) More generally, the principles of the method exposed here, distinguishing feasible from desirable moves, could fruitfully be applied to other second-best situations.

Appendix

1. Construction of the set $K(0) \cap \mathrm{Fr}\, Q(0)$

Let us consider the case in which $K(0) \cap \mathrm{Fr}\,(Q(0)) \neq \emptyset$ (equivalently $-[p(0)\cdot \partial X(0)]^T \notin \Lambda(0)$ and $[p(0)\cdot \partial X(0)]^T \notin \Lambda(0)$. Let π be the number of extreme directions of the cone $\Lambda(0)$ generated by vectors $x_h(0)$. Obviously $\pi \leqq H$.

In order to select directions in $K(0) \cap \mathrm{Fr}\, Q(0)$, we will make the additional requirement $q(0)\cdot a = 0$, a condition consistent with the normalization rule $\|q\| = C^{\text{ste}}$.

Let us put

$$p(0)\cdot \partial X^{=}(0) \overset{\text{def}}{=} W.$$

In constructing the set $K(0) \cap \mathrm{Fr}\, Q(0)$, two cases must be distinguished.

(1) In the case $\pi \geqq n-2$, extreme directions of this cone can be constructed as follows: taking any set (Hα) of n-3 indices chosen among π, one can consider C^{π}_{n-3} systems: $x_{h_l}\cdot a = 0 (h_l \in H_\alpha)$, $W\cdot a = 0$ and $q\cdot a = 0$.

Each such system has generally a one dimensional solution. Among these solutions some define half lines which are extreme directions of the polyhedron $K(0) \cap \mathrm{Fr}\, Q(0)$.

Any $a \in K(0) \cap \mathrm{Fr}\, Q(0)$ is a convex combination of these extreme directions.

(2) If $\pi < n$-2, the system $\{x_h\cdot a = 0, h = 1, \ldots, \pi, W\cdot a = 0, q\cdot a = 0\}$ defines a linear manifold of dimension n-π-2. The polyhedron has no extreme directions but only extreme faces. It can no longer be described in a systematic way. However, one can for example fix v coordinates of a ($v \geqq n$-π-2) and proceed as above for extracting elements of the cone.

The incidence of the relative number of commodities and consumers on the construction of the set $K(0) \cap \mathrm{Fr}\, Q(0)$ is not a pure mathematical problem: it reflects more or less the economic idea that the degree of freedom in finding Pareto improving changes in taxes increases when there are more tools.

2. Separation theorem (for cones of vertex 0)

Let $K_0, \ldots, K_{p-1}$ be p open convex cones and let K_p be a convex cone.

$$\bigcap_{0\ldots p} K_p = \emptyset$$

if and only if there exists $q_0, \ldots, q_i, \ldots, q_p$ (some of them nonzero) such that $\sum_{i=0}^{p} q_i = 0$, and $q_i \cdot x \leqq 0$, $\forall\, x \in K_i$.

3. Temporary Inefficiencies

Let us first remark on a straightforward example of temporary inefficiencies in an economy with two goods and one consumer (fig. 5). In fig. 5 the production set is limited by ACB and the demand curve of consumer goes through AEB.

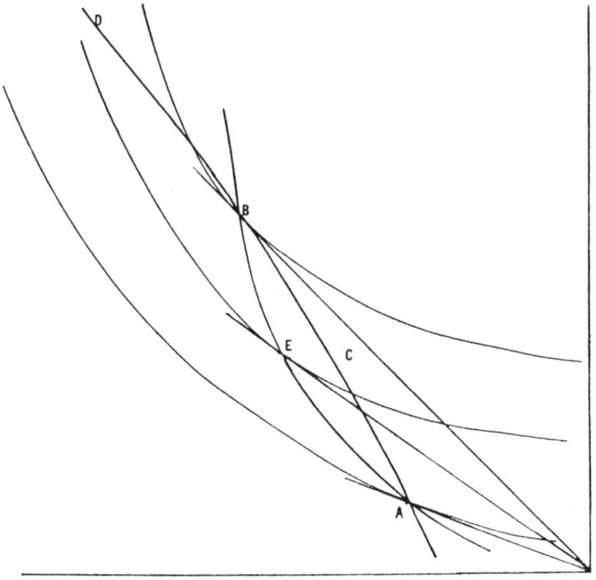

Fig. 5

Starting from A, a unique path of tax reform can be defined which goes to E and B, and all states between A and B are inefficient (B excluded). However it can be argued that this example is pathological since it rests upon the emptiness in A of the set of tight equilibrium preserving directions of price changes (a fact which only occurs with two goods).

Also, we could give, in a more convincing context, an example of a nondegenerate situation in which any small Pareto improving direction of price changes results in an inefficient (nontight) equilibrium.

The example is as follows.

There are three commodities (1, 2, 3) and three households (A, B, C), At time zero the following tight equilibrium prevails:

$$x_A(0) = \begin{pmatrix} 1 \\ 1 \\ -2 \end{pmatrix},$$

$$x_B(0) = \begin{pmatrix} 1.5 \\ 0.5 \\ -2 \end{pmatrix},$$

$$x_C(0) = \begin{pmatrix} 0.5 \\ 1.5 \\ -2 \end{pmatrix},$$

$$y(0) = \begin{pmatrix} 3 \\ 3 \\ -6 \end{pmatrix},$$

$$p(0) = (1, 2, 4), \quad q(0) = (1, 1, 1).$$

Furthermore, the local characteristics of demand of households are such that all consumers have the same matrix of compensated demand $(\partial X)^{U=\text{Cste}} = A$, but have different income effect vectors $\partial X/\partial R$:

$$\text{household A: } (\partial X_A^{=})^{U=\text{Cste}} = A, \quad \frac{\partial X_A}{\partial R} = \begin{pmatrix} 1 \\ 0 \\ 0 \end{pmatrix};$$

$$\text{household B: } (\partial X_B^{=})^{U=\text{Cste}} = A, \quad \frac{\partial X_B}{\partial R} = \begin{pmatrix} 1 \\ -9/16 \\ +9/16 \end{pmatrix};$$

$$\text{household C: } (\partial X_C^{=})^{U=\text{Cste}} = A, \quad \frac{\partial X_C}{\partial R} = \begin{pmatrix} 1 \\ 27/16 \\ -27/16 \end{pmatrix};$$

where A is a negative semi definite matrix,

$$A = \begin{pmatrix} -1 & 0.5 & 0.5 \\ 0.5 & -1 & 0.5 \\ 0.5 & 0.5 & -1 \end{pmatrix}.$$

One can then check that

$$\partial X^{=}(0) = \begin{pmatrix} -6 & -1.5 & 7.5 \\ 1.5 & -5.25 & 3.75 \\ 1.5 & 3.75 & -5.25 \end{pmatrix},$$

$$q(0)\cdot\partial X^{=}(0) = (-3 \quad -3 \quad 6),$$

and

$$p(0)\cdot\partial X^{=}(0) = (+3 \quad +3 \quad -6).$$

Then $p(0)\cdot\partial X^{=}(0) \in \Lambda(0)$. Hence there is no direction of price changes which is both tight equilibrium preserving and Pareto improving.

Particularly, one can check that if one either decreases the prices of consumption goods or increases the price of labor (which are obvious directions of Pareto improving movements) then the increase in labor demand from households is always greater than that needed to produce the increase in consumer goods demand.

The reader might object that such examples rely on the existence of inferior goods. Actually a slightly more complicated example can be given without inferior goods. $x_A(0)$, $x_B(0)$, $x_C(0)$, $y(0)$, $p(0)$ and $q(0)$ are as above. The local characteristics of demand of households are modified as follows:

household A: $(\partial X_A^{=})^{U=\mathrm{Cste}} = A, \quad \dfrac{\partial X_A}{\partial R} = \begin{pmatrix} 1 \\ 0 \\ 0 \end{pmatrix};$

household B: $(\partial X_B^{=})^{U=\mathrm{Cste}} = A, \quad \dfrac{\partial X_B}{\partial R} = \begin{pmatrix} 0 \\ 1 \\ 0 \end{pmatrix};$

household C: $(\partial X_C^{=})^{U=\mathrm{Cste}} = B, \quad \dfrac{\partial X_C}{\partial R} = \begin{pmatrix} 0.8 \\ 0.2 \\ 0 \end{pmatrix},$

where B is the following semi definite negative matrix,

$$B = \begin{pmatrix} -0.5 & 0 & 0.5 \\ 0 & -2 & 2 \\ 0.5 & +2 & -2.5 \end{pmatrix}.$$

Hence

$$\partial X^{=}(0) = \begin{pmatrix} -3.9 & -1.2 & 5.3 \\ -0.6 & -4.8 & 5.12 \\ 1.5 & +3 & -4.42 \end{pmatrix},$$

and

$$p(0)\cdot\partial X^{=}(0) = (0.9, \quad 1.2, \quad -2.1).$$

The latter vector is approximately 0.3 $(x_A(0)+x_B(0)+x_C(0))$ and is in the cone engendered by $x_A(0)$, $x_B(0)$, $x_C(0)$ (actually it is a convex combination of $x_B(0)$, $x_C(0)$).

References

Buchanan, J.M., 1975, Taxation in fiscal exchange, Journal of Public Economics 6, no. 1/2, 17–30.
Diamond, P.A. and J.A. Mirrlees, 1971, Optimal taxation and public production I and II, American Economic Review 61, 8–27 and 261–278.
Dixit, A., 1975, Welfare effects of tax and price changes, Journal of Public Economics 4, 103–123.
Dieudonne, J., 1969, Eléments d'analyse, Tome 1 (Gauthier–Vilars, Paris).
Feldstein, M., 1975, On the theory of tax reform, Journal of Public Economics 6, no. 1/2, 77–104.
Heal, G.M., 1972, The theory of economic planning (North-Holland, Amsterdam).
Laurent, P., 1972, Approximation et optimisation (Hermann, Paris).
Musgrave, R.A., 1959, The theory of public finance (McGraw–Hill, New York).
Negishi, T., 1971, General equilibrium and international trade (North-Holland, Amsterdam).
Solari, L., 1971, Le système linéaire de dépenses généralisé, Spécifications et estimations, Cahiers du Séminaire d'Econométrie.

[29]

OPTIMAL TAX PERTURBATIONS

W.E. DIEWERT*

University of British Columbia, Vancouver, B.C. V6T 1W5, Canada

Received July 1977, revised version received June 1978

The paper considers an economy with H households, $N+1$ commodities and M fixed factors with commodity taxes and government expenditures on goods and services. The paper studies under what conditions (small) Pareto improving tax changes exist, i.e., tax changes which increase the utility of each household in the economy. The basic analytical technique used is just the usual comparative statics apparatus, except that duality theory is used in order to simplify the computations. The paper derives both the changes in prices and in real incomes that are induced by (small) changes in exogenous tax variables (differential real income balanced budget incidence analysis).

1. Introduction

A considerable number of papers develop optimal taxation formulae [e.g. see Diamond and Mirrlees (1971), Mirrlees (1976), Sandmo (1976) and the references contained in these papers] but few policy applications of such formulae have yet occurred. There are a number of reasons for this state of affairs. (i) The formulae require information about the preferences of consumers and the technology of producers – information which is not readily available. (ii) Economic policy-makers are reluctant to implement the (possibly) large changes in taxes and expenditures that would be required by the application of an optimal tax formula. This caution is justified since our estimates of various elasticities describing consumer and producer behavior are tenuous at best, and moreover, large changes in taxes may take the economy outside of the regions where tastes and technology have been (partially) revealed to us using market data. (iii) Optimal tax formulae provide only *necessary* conditions for optimality, without telling us how to attain an optimum. Moreover, Harris (1975) has shown that it is extremely difficult to impose conditions on preferences or technology which will guarantee that the necessary conditions for optimality are also *sufficient*. (iv)

*This research has been supported by a Canada Council grant. I am indebted to C. Blackorby, A.K. Dixit, R. Guesnerie, J.A. Mirrlees, W. Schworm and J.A. Weymark for helpful comments and to A.B. Atkinson for useful suggestions. They are not to be held responsible for any remaining errors and deficiencies. My thanks also to V.M. Diewert for drawing the figures.

Finally, generally no single level of government has control of *all* of the tax and government expenditure decisions in the economy, which means that the usual optimal tax formulae, which assume that the 'government' can control all commodity taxes and expenditures, are not generally relevant to any single level of government.

Many of the above difficulties can be overcome if we consider only *perturbations* or small changes in a subset of taxes which a particular level of government has under its jurisdiction. Thus, in the present paper we take this *perturbation*, or *piecemeal*, or *tax reform approach* to taxation theory, an approach which is associated with Corlett and Hague (1953–54), Meade (1955), Atkinson and Stern (1974), Diamond and McFadden (1974), Dixit (1975), Feldstein (1976), Hatta (1977) and Guesnerie (1977).

We will also focus attention on small tax changes which increase the utility or real income for each class of consumer in the economy (if any such changes exist), using the tax instruments which are available to the government. Such tax changes are called *Pareto improving* tax changes; they have been discussed recently in the context of the Diamond–Mirrlees (1971) model of an economy by Hahn (1973), Guesnerie (1977), Harris (1978) and Weymark (1976).

Our basic method of analysis is just the usual comparative statics apparatus, where we have followed the example of Diamond and McFadden (1974), Dixit (1975) and Mirrlees (1976) in using duality theory (and the expenditure function in particular) in order to simplify the derivations. Our model of the economy is explained in section 2. It is quite similar to the Diamond–Mirrlees (1971) model with three major differences: (i) we assume that there are fixed inelastically supplied primary factors of production in the economy, (ii) we use expenditure functions instead of indirect utility functions in order to describe consumer's preferences, and (iii) we use a variable profit function[1] instead of a transformation function in order to describe technology.

In section 3 we linearize or totally differentiate the excess demand equations of our model, expressing changes in our target variables (household utilities) as functions of changes in the government's instruments (tax rates on consumer goods, labor supplies and fixed factors). We also derive the optimal tax perturbation, i.e. the direction of tax change that leads to the greatest rate of increase in the government's social welfare function.

In section 4, we derive criteria for the existence of (strict) Pareto improving tax changes, while in section 5 the same problem is studied when there are

[1]The terminology 'variable profit' function is used by Diewert (1973) (1974). The concept is due to Samuelson (1953–54, p. 20) who called it a national product function. Gorman (1968) and Lau (1976) use the alternative terminology 'gross profit' and 'restricted profit' function, respectively.

constraints on feasible changes in taxes, including one sided constraints where a tax can be decreased but not increased (or vice versa). Necessary conditions for Pareto optimality of the initial tax system are also derived. We also derive the Diamond–Mirrlees necessary conditions for optimality as a special case of our more general conditions.

In sections 6 and 7 we specialize our general formulae to the one and two household cases, while section 8 offers some concluding comments.

In spirit, our paper is similar to that of Guesnerie (1977); however, in detail, the papers differ somewhat. A useful reconciliation of the present paper with Guesnerie's is made by Weymark (1978).

2. The model

We assume that the number of finally demanded goods, intermediate goods and types of labor is $N+1$ (one of these goods will play the role of a numeraire good) and that there are M additional fixed factors ('land' and types of 'capital') in the economy. If the fixed factors are freely mobile between various industries during the Hicksian period under consideration, then there is no loss of generality in aggregating over all firms to obtain an aggregate production possibilities set $Y \equiv \sum_{j=1}^{J} Y^j$, where Y^j is the jth producer's production possibilities set.[2] Denote the M dimensional vector of fixed factors as $v \gg 0_M$.[3]

Define the *variable profit function* Π corresponding to Y as the solution to the following profit maximization problem:

$$\Pi(p,v) = \Pi(p_0, p_., v) \equiv \max_y \{p^{\mathrm{T}}y : (y,v) \in Y\},$$

where $p_0 > 0$ is the price of the zero-th finally demanded good, $p_. \equiv (p_1, \ldots, p_N)^{\mathrm{T}} \gg 0_N$ is an N dimensional vector whose components are the positive prices of other finally demanded (and supplied) goods which producers face, $p^{\mathrm{T}} \equiv (p_0, p^{\mathrm{T}}_.)$ and $y^{\mathrm{T}} \equiv (y_0, y^{\mathrm{T}}_.) \equiv (y_0, y_1, y_2, \ldots, y_N)$ is a vector of net outputs which the aggregate production sector can supply, given that it can utilize the vector v of fixed inputs. If $y_n > 0$, then the nth good is supplied by the production sector; if $y_n < 0$, then the nth good is an input

[2]On the other hand if certain fixed factors to the economy as a whole are not mobile between firms, then these inputs can be regarded as being firm specific and we can still aggregate over firms, at the cost of introducing a multiplicity of fixed factors. It should also be noted that the existence of sectoral technologies implies certain restrictions on the second order partial derivatives of the variable profit function Π introduced below: see Diewert and Woodland (1977) and the references within.

[3]Notation: $v \gg 0_M$ means that each component of the M dimensional vector v is positive; $v \geqq 0_M$ means each component of v is nonnegative; $v > 0_M$ means $v \geqq 0_M$ but $v \neq 0_M$ where 0_M is a vector of zeroes: $r^{\mathrm{T}}v \equiv \sum_{m=1}^{M} r_m v_m$ denotes the inner product of r and v.

into the production sector; if $y_n = 0$, then the nth good is an intermediate good, used by some firms and produced by others.

We assume that each producer's production possibilities set Y^j is subject to constant returns to scale and hence the aggregate production possibilities set Y also has this property. The assumption of constant returns to scale for each producer is not quite as restrictive as it might seem, since if some producer's production set is subject to decreasing returns to scale, we can simply introduce an ad hoc specific factor to which the pure profits of the firm are imputed. This device is due to McKenzie (1959) and is explained in more detail by Cass (1974, p. 276).

We make the following assumptions of a *global* nature on the aggregate production possibilities set Y: Y is a closed, nonempty, convex subset of R^{1+N+M}; Y is a cone (i.e. production is subject to constant returns to scale); Y has the property of free disposal; and for a given set of fixed inputs v, the set of variable output and inputs y such that $(y,v)\in Y$ is bounded from above. Under these conditions it can be shown [e.g. Gorman (1968) or Diewert (1973, pp. 291–294), (1974, pp. 134–141)] that the variable profit function $\Pi(p,v)$ is linearly homogeneous and convex in p and linearly homogeneous, concave and nondecreasing in v. Moreover, if the variable profit function is differentiable with respect to the components of the price vector p at a given point,[4] then by *Hotelling's* (1932, p. 594) *Lemma*, $\partial\Pi(p,v)/\partial p_n = y_n(p,v)$ for $n = 0,1,\ldots,N$, where $y_n(p,v)$ is the (variable) profit maximizing amount of output n [of input n if $y_n(p,v) < 0$] given variable good prices p and the vector of fixed inputs v. These relations can be summarized as

$$y = y(p,v) \equiv \nabla_p\Pi(p,v), \tag{1}$$

where $\nabla_p\Pi(p,v)$ denotes the column vector of first order partial derivatives of Π with respect to the components of p.

It can also be shown [e.g. see Diewert (1974, p. 140)] that if the variable profit function $\Pi(p,v)$ is differentiable with respect to the components of the vector of fixed inputs v, then the vector of competitive returns to the fixed inputs r is equal to

$$r = r(p,v) \equiv \nabla_v\Pi(p,v) > 0_M, \tag{2}$$

where $\nabla_v\Pi(p,v) \equiv [\partial\Pi(p,v_1,\ldots,v_M)/\partial v_1,\ldots,\partial\Pi(p,v_1,\ldots,v_M)/\partial v_M]^{\mathrm{T}}$ is the (column) vector of partial derivatives of Π with respect to the components of v.

[4]This is equivalent to the existence of single valued net supply functions for the aggregate production sector; see McFadden (1970) or Diewert (1973, p. 290).

In order to carry out a comparative statics analysis, we make the following assumption of a *local* nature on Y: $\Pi(p,v)$ is twice continuously differentiable with respect to its components at an initial point (p,v). Thus, eqs. (1) and (2) hold at this initial point.

The twice continuously differentiability and convexity of $\Pi(p,v)$ in p implies that the matrix of second order partial derivatives of Π with respect to $p_0, p_1, \ldots, p_N$,

$$\nabla^2_{pp}\Pi(p,v) \equiv \begin{bmatrix} \nabla^2_{p_0p_0}\Pi, & \nabla^2_{p_0p_.}\Pi \\ \nabla^2_{p_.p_0}\Pi, & \nabla^2_{p_.p_.}\Pi \end{bmatrix} \equiv \begin{bmatrix} \Pi_{00}, & \Pi_{0.} \\ \Pi_{.0}, & \Pi_{..} \end{bmatrix} = \begin{bmatrix} \Pi_{00} & \Pi_{0.} \\ \Pi_{.0} & \Pi_{..} \end{bmatrix}^{\mathrm{T}} \tag{3}$$

is a symmetric positive semidefinite $N+1$ by $N+1$ matrix. Note that by Hotelling's Lemma (1), the scalar Π_{00} equals $\partial y_0(p,v)/\partial p_0$, the row vector $\Pi_{0.}(=\Pi_{.0}^{\mathrm{T}})$ equals $[\partial y_0/\partial p_1, \ldots, \partial y_0/\partial p_N]$ and the matrix $\Pi_{..}$ has ijth element equal to $\partial y_i(p,v)/\partial p_j$ for $i,j = 1,2,\ldots,N$; i.e. the matrix $\nabla^2_{pp}\Pi(p,v)$ is the matrix of (net) supply responses to changes in the variable input and output prices p.

Using Euler's Theorem on homogeneous functions, it can be shown that

$$p^{\mathrm{T}}\nabla_p\Pi(p,v) \equiv p_0 y_0 + p_.^{\mathrm{T}} y_. = \Pi(p,v) \tag{4}$$

and

$$\nabla^2_{pp}\Pi(p,v)p \equiv \begin{bmatrix} \Pi_{00}, & \Pi_{0.} \\ \Pi_{.0}, & \Pi_{..} \end{bmatrix} \begin{bmatrix} p_0 \\ p_. \end{bmatrix} = \begin{bmatrix} 0 \\ 0_N \end{bmatrix}. \tag{5}$$

The linear homogeneity of $\Pi(p,v)$ in v (which is implied by our constant returns to scale assumption), Euler's Theorem on linearly homogeneous functions, and (1) and (2) imply the following identities [see Diewert (1974, pp. 142–146)]:

$$v^{\mathrm{T}}r \equiv v^{\mathrm{T}}\nabla_v\Pi(p,v) > 0, \tag{6}$$

$$v^{\mathrm{T}}\gamma_{v0} \equiv v^{\mathrm{T}}\nabla^2_{vp_0}\Pi(p_0,p_.,v) = \nabla_{p_0}\Pi(p_0,p_.,v) \equiv y_0, \tag{7}$$

$$v^{\mathrm{T}}\gamma_{v.} \equiv v^{\mathrm{T}}\nabla^2_{vp_.}\Pi(p_0,p_.,v) = \nabla_{p_.}\Pi(p_0,p_.,v) \equiv y_., \tag{8}$$

where $\gamma_{v0}^{\mathrm{T}} \equiv [\gamma_{10},\ldots,\gamma_{M0}] \equiv [\partial^2\Pi/\partial v_1\partial p_0,\ldots,\partial^2\Pi/\partial v_M\partial p_0] = [\partial r_1/\partial p_0,\ldots,\partial r_M/\partial p_0]$ and the mnth element of the M by N matrix $\gamma_{v.}$, $\gamma_{mn} \equiv \partial^2\Pi(p,v)/\partial v_m\partial p_n = \partial r_m(p,v)/\partial p_n$, measures the change in the competitive return to the mth fixed factor due to a change in the price of the nth variable good.

The above restrictions are utilized later in the paper.[5]

It should be noted that we use the variable profit function in this paper rather than the profit function, $\Pi^*(p,r) \equiv \max_{y,v}\{p^{\mathrm{T}}y + r^{\mathrm{T}}v : (y,v) \in Y\}$, which is used by Guesnerie (1977) for example, for two reasons: (i) the existence of fixed factors to the economy and the use of the variable profit function enable us to reduce the number of equations which have to be totally differentiated by M, and (ii) the profit function Π^* is extremely discontinuous (it equals either 0 or $+\infty$) when production is subject to constant returns to scale and thus is generally nondifferentiable at an initial equilibrium point.

We turn now to the household side of the model. We assume that there are H households in the economy, and that the hth household has preferences defined over the $N+1$ nonfixed commodities and types of labor which can be represented by the utility function $f^h(x^h)$ over a closed, bounded form below[6] consumption set $\Omega^h \subset R^{N+1}$ for $h = 1,2,\ldots,H$. We make the following *global* assumptions on each f^h: f^h is (i) continuous, (ii) nondecreasing, (iii) subject to local nonsatiation, and (iv) quasiconcave over Ω^h.

In the optimal tax literature, compensated demand functions are often introduced at a certain stage of the argument. We follow the example of Diamond–McFadden (1974), Dixit (1975) and Mirrlees (1976) by introducing these real income compensated or Hicksian [Hicks (1946, p. 331)] demand functions via the expenditure function. The hth household's *expenditure function* m^h is defined as the minimum net cost (labor supplies are indexed negatively) of achieving a given utility level:

$$m^h(u^h,q) \equiv \min_x \{q^{\mathrm{T}}x : f^h(x) \geqq u^h, \quad x \in \Omega^h\}, \tag{9}$$

where $(q_0, q_1, \ldots, q_N) \equiv q^{\mathrm{T}} \gg 0^{\mathrm{T}}_{N+1}$ are the positive prices consumers face, f^h is the hth household's utility function, and u^h belongs to the range of f^h, i.e. $u^h \in R[f^h]$. If f^h satisfies the global conditions listed above, then it can be shown[7] that m^h satisfies the following conditions: (i) $m^h(u^h,q)$ is defined for

[5]The γ_{mn} defined here are normalizations of the elasticities of intensity defined in Diewert (1974, p. 145) and they satisfy the additional restrictions $\gamma_{v0}p_0 + \gamma_{v.}p. = r$.

[6]If the nth good is demanded, the demand for that good is bounded below by 0; if the nth good is supplied, then (minus) the supply of that type of labour service is bounded from below by minus the number of hours that the household has available during the period.

[7]See Shephard (1953) (1970), Diamond and McFadden (1974), Diewert (1974), (1978), Blackorby and Diewert (1978), Blackorby, Primont and Russell (1978) and the references in these works. It can also be shown that if m^h satisfies conditions (i)–(iii) above (plus an additional assumption), then a direct utility function f^{h*} satisfying conditions (i)–(iv) above can be defined via the expenditure functions: $f^{h*}(x) \equiv \max_u\{u : m^h(u,q) \leqq q^{\mathrm{T}}x$ for every $q \gg 0_{NH}\}$, $x \in \Omega^h$. The additional assumption that we require is that m^h be such that f^{h*} is continuous over Ω^h. Moreover, f^{h*} will coincide with the original f^h. Finally, assumptions (ii) and (iv) on f^h can be dropped and m^h will satisfy the same regularity conditions. However, in this case f^{h*} will coincide with the free disposal convex hull of the original f^h.

all $u^h \in R[f^h]$, $q \gg 0_{N+1}$ and is continuous over this domain, (ii) $m^h(u^h, q)$ is increasing in u^h for fixed q, and (iii) for fixed u^h, $m^h(u^h, q)$ is linearly homogeneous and concave in q.

If m^h satisfies the above regularity conditions and in addition is differentiable with respect to the components of the price vector $q \equiv (q_0, q_1, \ldots, q_N) \equiv (q_0, q_.)$, then it can be shown [Hicks (1964, p. 331), Samuelson (1953–54, pp. 15–16), Shephard (1953, p. 11), Diamond and McFadden (1974, p. 4)] that the expenditure minimizing demand for the ith good needed to achieve utility level u^h is $x_i^h(u^h, q) = \partial m^h(u^h, q)/\partial q_i$, $i = 0, 1, 2, \ldots, N$ and $h = 1, 2, \ldots, H$. This result is analogous to Hotelling's Lemma and is sometimes called *Shephard's Lemma*. In vector notation, the above results can be summarized as

$$\begin{aligned} x_0^h &\equiv x_0^h(u^h, q) = \nabla_{q_0} m^h(u^h, q) \equiv \partial m^h(u^h, q)/\partial q_0, \\ x_.^h &\equiv x_.^h(u^h, q) = \nabla_{q_.} m^h(u^h, q); \qquad h = 1, 2, \ldots, H, \end{aligned} \tag{10}$$

where $x_.^h \equiv (x_1^h, \ldots, x_N^h)^{\mathrm{T}}$ and $\nabla_{q_.} m^h(u^h, q)$ is the vector of partial derivatives of m^h with respect to the N components of $q_. \equiv (q_1, q_2, \ldots, q_N)^{\mathrm{T}}$.

If m^h is twice continuously differentiable with respect to the components of q, then concavity of m^h in q implies that the matrix of Hicksian demand price derivatives

$$\begin{bmatrix} \nabla^2_{q_0 q_0} m^h, & \nabla^2_{q_0 q_.} m^h \\ \nabla^2_{q_. q_0} m^h, & \nabla^2_{q_. q_.} m^h \end{bmatrix} = \begin{bmatrix} \nabla_{q_0} x_0^h, & \nabla^{\mathrm{T}}_{q_0} x_.^h \\ \nabla_{q_0} x_.^h, & \nabla_{q_.} x_.^h \end{bmatrix} \equiv \begin{bmatrix} \sigma_{00}^h, & \sigma_{0.}^h \\ \sigma_{.0}^h, & \sigma_{..}^h \end{bmatrix} \tag{11}$$

is a negative semidefinite $1+N$ by $1+N$ symmetric matrix, and linear homogeneity of $m^h(u^h, q)$ in q implies that the following identity holds for each h:

$$\begin{bmatrix} \sigma_{00}^h, & \sigma_{0.}^h \\ \sigma_{.0}^h, & \sigma_{..}^h \end{bmatrix} \begin{bmatrix} q_0 \\ q_. \end{bmatrix} = \begin{bmatrix} 0 \\ 0_N \end{bmatrix}, \qquad h = 1, 2, \ldots, H. \tag{12}$$

Define the aggregate consumer substitution (or Slutsky) matrix as

$$\sigma \equiv \begin{bmatrix} \sigma_{00}, & \sigma_{0.} \\ \sigma_{.0}, & \sigma_{..} \end{bmatrix} \equiv \sum_{h=1}^{H} \begin{bmatrix} \sigma_{00}^h & \sigma_{0.}^h \\ \sigma_{.0}^h & \sigma_{..}^h \end{bmatrix}. \tag{13}$$

It is easy to verify that it too is a negative semidefinite symmetric matrix which satisfies the linear homogeneity restrictions given by (12).

In addition to assumptions (i)–(iii) above on m^h, we shall make the following *local* assumption on consumer preferences:[8] for $h = 1,2,\dots,H$, m^h is twice continuously differentiable with respect to its arguments at an initial equilibrium point (u^h, q), where $q \gg 0_{N+1}$. This means that the restrictions embodied in (11)–(13) above are valid.

We shall also make the following *local* assumptions on the derivatives of the expenditure functions with respect to the utility levels:

$$\frac{\partial m^h}{\partial u^h}(u^h,q) = 1, \qquad \frac{\partial^2 m^h}{\partial u^h \partial u^h}(u^h,q) = 0; \qquad h = 1,\dots,H. \tag{14}$$

The above restrictions simply provide convenient local cardinalizations of utility.[9] Some further implications of (14) can be obtained after we introduce some additional notation. Define for $h = 1,2,\dots,H$:

$$\begin{aligned} \eta_0^h &\equiv \partial x_0^h(u^h,q)/\partial u^h = \partial^2 m^h(u^h,q)/\partial q_0 \partial u^h, \\ \eta_\cdot^h &\equiv \partial x_\cdot^h(u^h,q)/\partial u^h = \nabla^2_{q_\cdot u^h} m^h(u^h,q), \end{aligned} \tag{15}$$

where the equalities in (15) follow from Shephard's Lemma (10), and where $\eta^h \equiv [\eta_1^h,\dots,\eta_N^h]^{\mathrm{T}}$. The η_i^h can be interpreted as ordinary income derivatives: define the income of the hth consumer as $y^h = m^h(u^h,q)$ and define his ith market demand function as $d_i^h(y^h,q)$ for $i = 0,1,\dots,N$. Then it can be verified [e.g. see Diewert (1978, p. 65)] that the following identities are true:

$d_i^h[m^h(u^h,q),q] = \partial m^h(u^h,q)/\partial q_i = x_i^h(u^h,q)$. Thus, upon differentiating both sides with respect to u^h, we get

$$\frac{\partial d_i^h}{\partial y^h}(y^h,q)\frac{\partial m^h}{\partial u^h}(u^h,q) = \frac{\partial d_i^h}{\partial y^h} = \frac{\partial^2 m^h}{\partial q_i \partial u^h}(u^h,q) \equiv \eta_i^h, \tag{16}$$

where the second equality in (16) follows using (14). Thus, η_i^h can be interpreted as the hth consumer's ordinary income derivative of demand for the ith commodity.[10] Since $\partial m^h(u^h,q)/\partial u^h$ is linearly homogeneous in q,

[8] Actually, the entire analysis can be undertaken making only local assumptions on preferences and technology; see Blackorby and Diewert (1978).

[9] They simply imply that (local) changes in real income are proportional to changes in nominal income when prices are held fixed at the initial equilibrium prices q. This type of scaling convention is consistent with the (global) scaling convention suggested by Samuelson (1974, p. 1262) and utilized by Berndt, Darrough and Diewert (1977, p. 655) in their empirical work on the estimation of Canadian consumer preferences.

[10] We should also mention that the market demand functions $d_i^h(y^h,q)$ satisfy the following Slutsky relations:

$$\sigma_{ji}^h = \sigma_{ij}^h = \partial d_i^h(y^h,q)/\partial q_j + d_j^h(y^h,q)\partial d_i^h(y^h,q)/\partial y^h = \partial d_i^h(y^h,q)/\partial q_j + x_j^h \eta_i^h$$

for $i,j,\dots,N$ and $h = 1,2,\dots,H$.

Euler's Theorem on homogeneous function plus the normalizations in (14) imply that the η_i^h satisfy the following additional restrictions:

$$1 = \frac{\partial m^h}{\partial u^h}(u^h, q) = \sum_{i=0}^{N} q_i \frac{\partial^2 m^h}{\partial u^h \partial q_i}(u^h, q) \equiv q_0 \eta_0^h + q_.^{\mathrm{T}} \eta_.^h, \qquad h = 1, \ldots, H. \tag{17}$$

We assume that the hth household owns the resource vector $v^h \geqq 0_M$ and that

$$\sum_{h=1}^{H} v^h = v \gg 0_M, \tag{18}$$

where v is the vector of fixed resources which appeared as an input into the aggregate production sector.

We assume that the government has the power to tax commodities and fixed factors. We assume that there are no tax distortions within the production sector, but that there are tax wedges between the prices producers face (p, r) and the prices consumers face (q, s). Specifically, assume that $q_i = (1 + t_i)p_i$ for $i = 0, 1, 2, \ldots, N$, where $p_i > 0$ is the ith producer price and $t_i > -1$ is the ad valorem tax on the ith good. If the ith good is being supplied by the production sector, then $t_i > 0$ $(t_i < 0)$ implies that the ith good is being taxed (subsidized) by the government, but if the ith good is being demanded by the aggregate production sector, then $t_i < 0$ $(t_i > 0)$ implies that the ith commodity, a type of labor service, is being taxed (subsidized) by the government. The relationship between producer and consumer prices can be summarized as

$$q_0 = (1 + t_0)p_0; \qquad q_. = (I_N + \hat{t}_.)p_., \tag{19}$$

where I_N is an $N \times N$ identity matrix and $\hat{t}_.$ is the vector of tax rates $t_. \equiv (t_1, t_2, \ldots, t_N)^{\mathrm{T}}$ diagonalized into a matrix.

Initially, one unit of the mth fixed factor earns a reward $r_m \geqq 0$, but the government taxes this reward at an ad valorem rate τ_m (subsidizes if $\tau_m < 0$) so that the after tax return to households is $s_m \equiv (1 - \tau_m)r_m$. Later in the paper, we will assume that $\tau_m \leqq 1$, so that fixed factors cannot be taxed at a rate exceeding 100 percent. Again we can summarize the relationship between producer and consumer prices using matrix notation as

$$s \equiv (I_M - \hat{\tau})r, \tag{20}$$

where $\hat{\tau}$ is the vector of tax rates $\tau \equiv (\tau_1, \tau_2, \ldots, \tau_M)^{\mathrm{T}}$ diagonalized into a matrix.

Note that we have not followed the usual procedure in the optimal tax literature where a single tax rate is set equal to zero. This is done for two reasons: (i) our results are *directly* applicable to economies where all goods are taxed (i.e. we do not have to 'rescale' empirical data in order to make it 'fit' our theoretical model) and (ii) we avoid the problems mentioned by Atkinson and Stern (1974), who note that some results of optimal taxation theory appear to depend in a nontrivial way on which tax rate is set equal to zero.[11]

We assume that the government spends its tax revenue on purchases of goods and services $(x_0^0, x_1^0, \ldots, x_N^0) \equiv (x_0^0, x_{.}^{0\mathrm{T}})$ in order to produce 'government services' or 'public goods', which are not listed as arguments in the household utility functions or the private production functions, since we hold x_0^0 and $x_{.}^0$ constant, in order to simplify our derivations. We assume that $x_i^0 \geq 0$ whether the ith commodity is being supplied or demanded by the aggregate private production sector for $i = 0, 1, \ldots, N$, with $x_i^0 > 0$ for at least one index i.

We can now list the basic demand equals supply equations in our model.

Household expenditure is equal to after tax income from fixed factors for each household and thus using eq. (2):

$$m^h(u^h, (1+t_0)p_0, (I_N+\hat{t}_{.})p_{.}) = v^{h\mathrm{T}}(I_M - \hat{\tau})\nabla_v \Pi(p_0, p_{.}, v), \qquad h = 1, 2, \ldots, H, \tag{21}$$

or $q^{\mathrm{T}}x^h = v^{h\mathrm{T}}s$ for $h = 1, 2, \ldots, H$ using eqs. (19) and (20). We also have consumer plus government net demand equals private producer net supply for goods 0 and 1 to N, and thus using eqs. (1) and (10):

$$\sum_{h=1}^{H} \nabla_{q_0} m^h(u^h, (1+t_0)p_0, (I_N+\hat{t}_{.})p_{.}) + x_0^0 = \nabla_{p_0}\Pi(p_0, p_{.}, v), \tag{22}$$

$$\sum_{h=1}^{H} \nabla_{q_{.}} m^h(u^h, (1+t_0)p_0, (I_N+\hat{t}_{.})p_{.}) + x_{.}^0 = \nabla_{p_{.}}\Pi(p_0, p_{.}, v). \tag{23}$$

The above equations can be rewritten as $\sum_{h=1}^{H} x^h + x^0 = y$. Finally, the government's budget constraint can be written as revenue from taxing goods 0 to N plus revenue from taxing fixed factors equals government expendi-

[11] See Munk (1976) for a more thorough discussion of normalization problems.

tures on goods and services valued at consumer prices:

$$p_0 t_0 \nabla_{p_0} \Pi(p_0, p, v) + p_.^{\mathrm{T}} \hat{t}_. \nabla_{p_.} \Pi(p_0, p, v) + v^{\mathrm{T}} \hat{\tau} \nabla_v \Pi(p_0, p_., v)$$
$$= p_0(1+t_0)x_0^0 + p^{\mathrm{T}}(I_N + \hat{t}_.)x^0. \qquad (24)$$

Eq. (24) may be rewritten in a more readily understandable form as $p^{\mathrm{T}}\hat{t}y + v^{\mathrm{T}}\hat{\tau}r = q^{\mathrm{T}}x^0$.

Eqs. (21)–(24) are the basic equilibrium relations of our model. We note that eqs. (21) could be used in order to solve for u^h as a function of the consumer prices q and the hth consumer's after tax income, $v^{h\mathrm{T}}(I_M - \hat{\tau})r \equiv y^h$ for each h. The resulting u^h functions (which are indirect utility functions) could be substituted into eqs. (22) and (23). However, the present system of eqs. (21)–(24) can conveniently be regarded as $H+N+2$ simultaneous equations in the following unknowns: H utility levels $u^1, u^2, \ldots, u^H : N+1$ producer prices $p_0, p_1, \ldots, p_N$; $N+1$ tax rates on variable commodities $t_0, t_1, \ldots, t_N$; M tax rates on fixed factors $\tau_1, \tau_2, \ldots, \tau_M$. It can be shown that not all of the $H+N+2$ equations are independent: any one of the equations can be derived from the others. Thus, we could drop one of the variable commodity demand equals supply equations, say (22), or the government budget constraint (24) without loss of generality. We shall choose to drop the government budget constraint.[12] Moreover [see Munk (1976)], there is no loss of generality in fixing one of the producer prices. In what follows we take the producer price $p_0 > 0$ to be our numeraire and express all other prices relative to p_0. This explains why we have introduced the notation $p_. \equiv (p_1, p_2, \ldots, p_N)^{\mathrm{T}}$ which is a vector of prices excluding good 0.

Thus, we are left with $H+N+1$ independent equations in $H+2N+1+M$ unknowns. We assume that the H utility levels $u \equiv (u^1, u^2, \ldots, u^H)^{\mathrm{T}}$, the N producer prices $p_. \equiv (p_1, p_2, \ldots, p_N)^{\mathrm{T}}$ and *one* of the tax rates can be determined implicitly as functions of the remaining $N+M$ tax rates, at least locally around the initial equilibrium. A sufficient condition for the existence of these implicit functions is that a certain matrix of size $H+N+1$ has a nonzero determinant.

We conclude this section by noting that a primal formulation of our model would involve an additional $H(N+1)$ household consumption and labor supply variables x_n^h, $N+1$ additional production sector net output variables y_n, and M additional prices r_m. Moreover, we would have additional equations generated by the first order conditions for the producer's profit

[12]In the first version of this paper (22) was dropped instead of (24), and this choice led to an extremely complicated comparative statics analysis. I am indebted to R. Guesnerie and J. Weymark for suggesting that the analysis would be much simpler if the government budget constraint (24) were dropped.

maximization problem and the household utility maximization problems,

$$\max_{x_0, x_.} \{f^h(x_0, x_.): q_0 x_0 + q_.^{\mathrm{T}} x_. = v^{h\mathrm{T}}(I_M - \hat{\tau})r, (x_0, x_.) \in \Omega^h\}.$$

The resulting system of equations and variables would be extremely large and unwieldy. Note that the properties of the expenditure functions m^h, (11) and (12), and the properties of the variable profit function Π, (3)–(8), already imbed the comparative statics properties of the household utility and producer profit maximization problems respectively.[13]

3. Optimal tax perturbations

Totally differentiate eqs. (21), (22) and (23) and we obtain the following system of equations which is approximately valid for small changes in the $M+N$ exogenous tax variables (one tax rate is endogenous):

$$A\Delta u = B_0 \Delta p_. + B_1 \Delta t_0 + B_2 \Delta t_. + B_3 \Delta \tau, \tag{25}$$

where

$$A \equiv \begin{bmatrix} 1, & 0, \ldots, & 0 \\ \vdots & & \vdots \\ 0, & 0, \ldots, & 1 \\ \eta_0^1, & \eta_0^2, \ldots, & \eta_0^H \\ \eta_.^1, & \eta_.^2, \ldots, & \eta_.^H \end{bmatrix}, \quad B_0 \equiv \begin{bmatrix} -x_.^{1\mathrm{T}}(I_N + \hat{t}_.) + v^{1\mathrm{T}}(I_M - \hat{\tau})\gamma_{v.} \\ \vdots \\ -x_.^{H\mathrm{T}}(I_N + \hat{t}_.) + v^{H\mathrm{T}}(I_M - \hat{\tau})\gamma_{v.} \\ -\sigma_{0.}(I_N + \hat{t}_.) + \Pi_{0.} \\ -\sigma_{..}(I_N + \hat{t}_.) + \Pi_{..} \end{bmatrix},$$

$$B_1 \equiv \begin{bmatrix} -x_0^1 p_0 \\ \vdots \\ -x_0^H p_0 \\ -\sigma_{00} p_0 \\ -\sigma_{.0} p_0 \end{bmatrix}, \quad B_2 \equiv \begin{bmatrix} -x^{1\mathrm{T}}\hat{p}_. \\ \vdots \\ -x^{H\mathrm{T}}\hat{p}_. \\ -\sigma_{0.}\hat{p}_. \\ -\sigma_{..}\hat{p}_. \end{bmatrix}, \quad B_3 \equiv \begin{bmatrix} -v^{1\mathrm{T}}\hat{r} \\ \vdots \\ -v^{H\mathrm{T}}\hat{r} \\ 0_M^{\mathrm{T}} \\ 0_{N \times M} \end{bmatrix},$$

and $\Delta u \equiv [\Delta u^1, \Delta u^2, \ldots, \Delta u^H]^{\mathrm{T}}$ is a vector of changes in utility levels, $\Delta p_. \equiv [\Delta p_1, \Delta p_2, \ldots, \Delta p_N]^{\mathrm{T}}$ is a vector of changes in the N variable commodity prices (recall that $\Delta p_0 \equiv 0$ since commodity 0 is the numeraire good), Δt_0 is the change in the tax rate for commodity 0, $\Delta t_. \equiv [\Delta t_1, \ldots, \Delta t_N]^{\mathrm{T}}$ is the vector of tax changes for (variable) commodities 1 to N, $\Delta \tau \equiv [\Delta \tau_1, \ldots, \Delta \tau_M]^{\mathrm{T}}$ is the

[13]However, A. Dixit and R. Guesnerie have reminded me that the use of duality methods has some drawbacks as well as advantages: for example, for use of the variable profit function precludes an examination of the production efficiency issue – producers will always be on the boundary of their production possibilities sets in our model.

vector of tax changes for the fixed factors, η_0^h and $\eta_.^h \equiv [\eta_1^h, \ldots, \eta_N^h]^T$ are the income derivatives of demand defined by (15), x_0^h and $x_.^{hT} \equiv [x_1^h, \ldots, x_N^h]$ are the initial consumer h demands (and labor supplies if $x_i^h < 0$) for the variable goods, $v^{hT} \equiv [v_1^h, \ldots, v_M^h]$ is the vector of initial holdings of the fixed factors by consumer h, σ_{00}, $\sigma_{0.} \equiv [\sigma_{01}, \sigma_{02}, \ldots, \sigma_{0N}]$ and $\sigma_{..} \equiv [\sigma_{ij}]$, $i,j = 1,2,\ldots,N$ are components of the aggregate consumer substitution matrix defined by (13) while $\Pi_{0.} \equiv [\Pi_{01}, \Pi_{02}, \ldots, \Pi_{0N}]$ and $\Pi_{..} \equiv [\Pi_{ij}]$, $i,j = 1,2,\ldots,N$ are components of the aggregate production substitution matrix defined by (3), $\gamma_{v.} \equiv [\gamma_{mn}]$, $m = 1,2,\ldots,M$, $n = 1,2,\ldots,N$ is the $M \times N$ intensity matrix defined below (8) [which tells us how the returns to fixed factors change as the variable commodity prices facing producers $(p_1, \ldots, p_N) \equiv p_.^T$ change], $0_{N \times M}$ is an $N \times M$ matrix of zeroes, 0_M is an M dimensional vector of zeroes, $t_. \equiv [t_1, \ldots, t_N]^T$ is the initial vector of tax rates on variable commodities 1 to N, $\tau \equiv [\tau_1, \ldots, \tau_M]^T$ is the vector of initial tax rates on the fixed factors, $r \equiv (r_1, \ldots, r_M)^T$ is the vector of initial pretax returns to the fixed factors and $\hat{t}_.$, $\hat{\tau}$, $\hat{p}_.$ and $\hat{r}$ denote diagonal matrices with the components of $t_.$, τ, $p_.$ and r on the main diagonals, respectively. We shall assume that the following inequality restrictions hold:

$$p_0 > 0; \quad q_0 = (1 + t_0)p_0 > 0; \quad p_. \gg 0_N; \quad q_. \equiv (I_N + \hat{t}_.)p_. \gg 0_N,$$

$$v \equiv \sum_{h=1}^{H} v^h \gg 0_M, \qquad r \gg 0_M. \tag{26}$$

The government's *optimal taxation problem* can be phrased as: maximize $f(u^1, u^2, \ldots, u^H)$ with respect to $u, p_., t_0, t_., \tau$ subject to the constraints (21), (22) and (23), where f is the government's (strictly increasing in the household utilities) social welfare function. Linearizing the objective function and the constraints of this constrained maximization problem around an initial equilibrium point satisfying the constraints (21)–(23) yields the following *optimal tax perturbation problem*:

$$\underset{\Delta u, \Delta p_., \Delta t_0, \Delta t_., \Delta\tau}{\text{maximize}} \quad \alpha^T \Delta u, \quad \text{subject to (25)},$$

where $\alpha^T \equiv (\alpha_1, \alpha_2, \ldots, \alpha_H) \equiv \nabla_u^T f(u) > 0_H$ is the vector of first order partial derivatives of the social welfare function f evaluated at the initial equilibrium utility levels.

In formulations of the optimal tax problem [for example, Stiglitz and Dasgupta (1971, pp. 152–160)], it is assumed that the government completely controls the production sector of the economy. We do not make this assumption; rather, we assume that the government controls only the tax rates $t_0, t_1, \ldots, t_N$, and $\tau_1, \ldots, \tau_M$. Of course, if the government chooses these $1 + N + M$ tax rates in a completely independent manner, then an equilibrium may not exist, i.e. with t_0, $t_.$ and τ independently determined, there may be no $u, p_.$ solution to eqs. (21)–(24). Put in another way, the government must choose tax rates so that the government budget constraint (24) is satisfied. Thus, in general the government will be able to choose only $N+M$ of the $1+N+M$ tax rates in an independent manner; the remaining tax rate becomes an endogenous variable. (It should also be noted that multiplying the $N+M$ independent tax rates by a scalar λ will leave equilibrium quantities unchanged.)

For the sake of definiteness, we assume that t_0 is the endogenous tax rate and thus $t_.$ and τ are the vectors of independent tax rates. Our differentiability assumptions plus the Implicit Function Theorem imply the existence of functions $u(t_., \tau)$, $p_.(t_., \tau)$ and $t_0(t_., \tau)$ in a neighborhood of the original equilibrium tax rates such that eqs. (21)–(24) are satisfied, provided that the following assumption is satisfied:

$$[A, -B_0, -B_1]^{-1} \text{ exists.} \tag{27}$$

Assuming (27), the *optimal tax perturbation problem* can be rewritten as the following unconstrained maximization problem in the independent government tax instruments $\Delta t_.$ and $\Delta\tau$:

$$\max_{\Delta t_., \Delta\tau} \quad \alpha^{\mathrm{T}}[I_H, 0_{H\times N}, 0_N][A, -B_0, -B_1]^{-1}[B_2, B_3]\begin{bmatrix}\Delta t_. \\ \Delta\tau\end{bmatrix}, \tag{28}$$

where I_H is an $H\times H$ identity matrix, $0_{N\times N}$ is an $H\times N$ matrix of zeroes, 0_H is an H dimensional column vector of zeroes, the matrices A, B_0, B_1, B_2, and B_3 are defined below (25), and $\alpha^{\mathrm{T}} \equiv (\alpha_1, \ldots, \alpha_H)$ is the vector of social welfare weights. From (25) it can be seen that $[A, -B_0, -B_1]^{-1}[B_2, B_3]$ is the $H+N+1$ by $N+M$ matrix of the first order partial derivatives of the implicit functions $u(t_., \tau)$, $p(t_., \tau)$ and $t_0(t_., \tau)$ with respect to the components of $t_.$ and τ. Thus, the coefficient vector in (28) (call it $\beta^{\mathrm{T}} \equiv [\beta_1, \ldots, \beta_N, \beta_{N+1}, \ldots, \beta_{N+M}]$) can be interpreted as the vector of partial derivatives of the government's social welfare function with respect to the independent tax instruments, $t_1, \ldots, t_N, \tau_1, \ldots, \tau_M$, evaluated at our initial equilibrium point. Hence, in order to find the *direction of tax change* [i.e. the directional derivative of the objective function in (28) with respect to the $N+M$ independent or exogenous tax parameters] which will lead to the greatest rate of increase in the objective function, we need to add the following normalization to (28):

$$\sum_{n=1}^{N} (\Delta t_n)^2 + \sum_{m=1}^{M} (\Delta\tau_m)^2 = 1. \tag{29}$$

It is straightforward to verify that the *optimal tax perturbation* [i.e. the solution to (28) and (29)] is $(\Delta t_{\cdot}^{\mathrm{T}}, \Delta \tau^{\mathrm{T}}) \equiv \beta^{\mathrm{T}}/(\beta^{\mathrm{T}}\beta)^{1/2}$ provided $\beta \neq 0_{N+M}$ where β^{T} is the coefficient vector in (28). However, it should be noted that the above optimal tax perturbation is not independent of the choice of the dependent tax rate.[14]

On the other hand, if $\beta = 0_{N+M}$, then the partial derivatives of the objective function with respect to the independent tax rates $t_1, \ldots, t_N$, $\tau_1, \ldots, \tau_M$ are all zeroes, i.e. the *first order necessary conditions for the initial set of taxes to be α optimal* are satisfied.[15]

It is possible to express these conditions for α optimality in some alternative ways which will prove to be convenient. Referring back to eqs. (25), it can be seen that we have the following *necessary condition for taxes to be α optimal*:

$$\text{if } z^1, z^2 \text{ is a solution to } Az^1 = Bz^2, \quad \text{then} \quad \alpha^{\mathrm{T}} z^1 = 0, \tag{30}$$

where $z^1 \equiv \Delta u$, $z^{2\mathrm{T}} \equiv [\Delta p_{\cdot}^{\mathrm{T}}, \Delta t_0, \Delta t_{\cdot}^{\mathrm{T}}, \Delta \tau^{\mathrm{T}}]$, $B \equiv [B_0, B_1, B_2, B_3]$ and the matrices A, B_0, B_1, B_2, B_3 are defined below (25). However, in order to rigorously justify (30), we require the following regularity condition which replaces (27):

$$[A, -B_0, -b]^{-1} \text{ exists,} \tag{31}$$

where b is *one* of the columns in the matrix $[B_1, B_2, B_3]$.[16]

Using Motzkin's Theorem of the Alternative,[17] it can be verified[18] that (30) is equivalent to the following *necessary condition for taxes to be α optimal*:

$$\text{there exists } w \text{ such that } w^{\mathrm{T}}B = 0_{N+1+N+M}^{\mathrm{T}} \quad \text{and} \quad w^{\mathrm{T}}A = \alpha^{\mathrm{T}}. \tag{32}$$

Note that the necessary conditions for α optimality, (30) or (32), both involve the matrix B_0 which contains various intensity and supply derivatives of the form $\gamma_{v,}$, $\Pi_{0.}$ and $\Pi_{..}$, which provides a contrast to the necessary conditions for α optimality derived by Diamond and Mirrlees (1971), which do not involve derivatives of supply functions. As we shall see in the next section, the difference in necessary conditions is due to Diamond and

[14]Dixit (1977) has considered alternative metrics, i.e. alternative normalizations to (29).

[15]Of course, this does not mean that taxes actually are α optimal – the objective function could be at a local maximum or minimum or at a saddle point.

[16]The tax rate which corresponds to b now becomes the endogenous tax rate in place of t_0. We assume (31) as a maintained hypothesis throughout the remainder of this paper.

[17]Either $Ex \gg \mathbf{0}$, $Fx \geqq \mathbf{0}$, $Gx = \mathbf{0}$ has a solution (where E is a nonvacuous matrix, F and G are matrices, and x is a vector of variables) *or* $y^{1\mathrm{T}}E + y^{2\mathrm{T}}F + y^{3\mathrm{T}}G = \mathbf{0}^{\mathrm{T}}$, $y^1 > \mathbf{0}$, $y^2 \geqq \mathbf{0}$ has a solution where y^1, y^2 and y^3 are vectors of variables. See Mangasarian (1969, p. 34).

[18]Let $E \equiv [\alpha^{\mathrm{T}}, 0_{N+1+N+M}^{\mathrm{T}}]$, $F \equiv 0$, $G \equiv [A, -B]$, $x^{\mathrm{T}} \equiv [z^{1\mathrm{T}}, z^{2\mathrm{T}}]$, $y^1 \equiv 1 > 0$, $y^{3\mathrm{T}} \equiv -w^{\mathrm{T}}$.

Mirrlees' implicit assumption that $\tau = 1_M$, i.e. that all fixed factors are taxed at a 100 percent rate.[19]

Inspection of problem (25) yields the following *sufficient condition for taxes to be a nonoptimal* (i.e. a direction of tax change leading to an increase in the objective function exists):

$$\text{there exists } z^1, z^2 \text{ such that } Az^1 = Bz^2 \quad \text{and} \quad a^T z^1 > 0 \tag{33}$$

Motzkin's Theorem of the Alternative shows that (33) is equivalent to the following *sufficient condition for taxes to be a nonoptimal:*[20]

$$\text{there is no solution } w \text{ to } w^T B = 0^T_{N+1+N+M} \quad \text{and} \quad w^T A = a^T. \tag{34}$$

Corollary. If the rank of B is $H + N + 1$, then the initial set of taxes is nonoptimal for any $a > 0_H$.

If the rank of B is $H + N + 1$, then the only solution to $w^T B = 0^T_{2N+1+M}$ is $w = 0_{H+1+N}$ and thus $w^T A = 0'_H \neq a^T$. The above corollary is quite useful in practice.

If some tax instruments cannot be changed, it is easy to see how the above conditions are modified: simply set the corresponding Δt_n or $\Delta \tau_m$ variables equal to zero, i.e. drop the corresponding columns from the B_1, B_2 or B_3 matrices.[21] In section 5 we will show how one sided constraints on tax changes can be modeled.

4. Pareto improving tax changes

Recall the matrices A and B defined below (25) in the previous section. One might think that a (small) Pareto improving tax change exists if a solution to $\Delta u > 0_H$ and $A[\Delta u] = B[\Delta p^T, \Delta t_0, \Delta t^T, \Delta \tau^T]^T$ exists, i.e. at least one utility change is positive while the others are nonnegative and at the same time the constraints of our model are satisfied for small shanges in the exogenous tax rates. However, this is not the case. Problems occur if a solution exists, but some components of Δ are equal to zero. The problem is that solutions to the system of equations $A\Delta u - B_0\Delta p - B_1\Delta t_0 = B_2\Delta t + B_3\Delta\tau$ cannot be rigorously interpreted as finite changes in utility levels, prices, etc. However, if assumption (27) is satisfied and the components of Δt, $\Delta\tau$ satisfy the normalization (29), then Δu, Δp and Δt_0 can be interpreted as *directional derivatives* of the implicit functions $u(t, \tau)$, $p(t, \tau)$ and $t_0(t, \tau)$

[19] This point is due to R. Guesnerie and J. Weymark.

[20] Conditions (33) and (34) both require that (31) hold. Also, it must be emphasized that (31) plus (33) or (31) plus (34) are only *sufficient* (and not *necessary*) conditions for a nonoptimality.

[21] Also the column b which occurs in assumption (31) must be one of the columns of B_1, B_2 or B_3 which has *not* been dropped

$\Delta\tau$. Thus, if $\Delta u > 0_H$ but it is not the case that $\Delta u \gg 0_H$, then although the *rate of change* of utility with respect to changes in the exogenous tax instruments is non-negative for all households, the *actual change* in utility for any finite change in taxes can be negative for those households where the rate of change of utility is zero.[22] In what follows we avoid these difficulties by using the concept of a *strict Pareto improving tax change*, where all households gain from the tax change. It is obvious that (27) plus the following condition is *sufficient for the existence of a strict Pareto improving tax change*:

$$\text{there exist } z^1, z^2 \text{ such that } z^1 \gg 0_H \quad \text{and} \quad Az^1 = Bz^2. \tag{35}$$

Corollary. If all of the columns of A are contained in the subspace generated by the columns of B, then a strict Pareto improving tax change exists.

Application of Motzkin's Theorem of the Alternative to (35) yields the following (second) *sufficient condition for the existence of a strict Pareto improving tax change*:

$$\text{there is no solution } w \text{ to } w^{\mathrm{T}}B = 0^{\mathrm{T}}_{N+1+N+M} \quad \text{and} \quad w^{\mathrm{T}}A > 0^{\mathrm{T}}_H. \tag{36}$$

Corollary. If the rank of B is $H+N+1$ (which is equal to the number of rows in B), then (36) is satisfied.

It is easy to modify the above criteria if some taxes cannot be changed: simply drop the corresponding columns from the B matrix. Thus, in an economy which had not been exposed to the virus of optimal taxation theory, in order to obtain the existence of a Pareto improving tax change, we generally require that the number of tax instruments that can be changed[23] be equal to or greater than $H+1$ [cf. Tinbergen's (1952) discussion of targets and instruments], where H is the number of households.

The negations of (35) and (36) yield the following *necessary conditions for the nonexistence of strict Pareto improving tax changes* which can be interpreted as *necessary conditions for the initial system of taxes to be Pareto optimal*:

$$\text{there is no solution } z^1, z^2 \text{ to } z^1 \gg 0_H \quad \text{and} \quad Az^1 = Bz^2; \tag{37}$$

$$\text{there exists } w \text{ such that } w^{\mathrm{T}}B = 0^{\mathrm{T}}_{N+1+N+M} \quad \text{and} \quad w^{\mathrm{T}}A > 0^{\mathrm{T}}_H. \tag{38}$$

[22] In other words, if $\partial u^1(t,\tau)/\partial t_1 = 0$, we cannot tell whether the function $u^1(t_1,\ldots,t_N,\tau_1,\ldots\tau_M)$ is increasing, decreasing or stationary with respect to t_1.

[23] If there are no restrictions on tax changes, this number is $1+N+M$. Thus, in general we will require that the number of taxable commodities be equal to or greater than the number of households (or homogeneous household groups) plus one.

Corollary. If (38) is satisfied, then the necessary condition for taxes to be α optimal (24) is satisfied for $\alpha^T \equiv w^T A$.

The above corollary is analogous to a result obtained by Guesnerie (1977, p. 193) in the context of the Diamond–Mirrlees (1971) model of an economy.

A geometric interpretation of the necessary condition for tax optimality (38) is that all of the columns of A lie on one side of the subspace spanned by the columns of B with at least one column of A not contained in this B spanned subspace. It can be seen that this is a natural dual interpretation to the primal condition (37). Thus, Motzkin's Theorem of the Alternative can be interpreted as a duality theorem.

We now proceed to use conditions (36) and (38) in order to prove a series of propositions with some economic content. Throughout, we assume (31) as a maintained hypothesis and we assume that there are no inequality restrictions on tax changes in this section. Propositions 1–4 below assume that all tax instruments can be changed while Propositions 5 and 6 assume that taxes on fixed factors cannot be varied.

Proposition 1. Suppose that $p_0(1+t_0)\Pi_{0.}+p_.^T(I_N+t_.)\Pi_{..} \equiv q_0\Pi_{0.}+q_.^T\Pi_{..} = = 0_N^T$. Then the necessary condition for Pareto optimality (38) is satisfied. Moreover, the necessary condition for α optimality (32) is satisfied for $\alpha \equiv 1_H$.

Proof. Define $w^T \equiv [0_H^T, q_0, q_.^T]$. Then using $q_0\Pi_0+q_.^T\Pi_{..} = 0_N^T$, (12) and (17), it can be verified that $w^T B = 0^T$ and $w^T A = 1_H^T > 0_H^T$, where 1_H is a vector of ones and A and B are defined below (25).

Q.E.D.

Corollary 1.1.[24] Suppose $t_0 = 0$, $t_. = 0_N$ so that the required government revenue is being raised by taxing only the fixed factors. Then the necessary condition for Pareto optimality (38) is satisfied.

Proof. If $t_0 = 0$, $t_. = 0_N$, then $q_0 = p_0$, $q_. = p_.$ and $p_0\Pi_{0.}+p_.^T\Pi_{..} = 0_N^T$ by (5).

Q.E.D.

Corollary 1.2.[25] Suppose that $t_. = 1_N t_0$ so that variable commodity taxes are proportional (this means that labor services are being subsidized if $t_0 > 0$). Then the necessary condition for Pareto optimality (38) is satisfied.

Proof. $q_0\Pi_{0.}+q_.^T\Pi_{..} = (1+t_0)(p_0\Pi_{0.}+p_.^T\Pi_{..}) = (1+t_0)0_N^T$ using (5).

Q.E.D.

[24]A similar result can be found in Hotelling (1932, p. 252) and for the one consumer case, in Stiglitz and Dasgupta (1971, p. 155).

[25]Related propositions have been proved by Atkinson and Stiglitz (1972, p. 105), Munk (1976, p. 6) and Sadka (1977). Sadka provides additional references.

Corollary 1.3. Suppose that the technology is Leontief so that $\Pi_{..} = 0_{N\times N}$.[26] Then the necessary condition for Pareto optimality (38) is satisfied.

Proposition 2. Suppose: (i) $p_0\sigma_{0.} + p_{.}^{\mathrm{T}}\sigma_{..} = 0_N^{\mathrm{T}}$ and (ii) $p_0\eta_0^h + p_{.}^{\mathrm{T}}\eta_{.}^h \geqq 0$ for $h = 1,2,\ldots,H$ with at least one strict inequality. Then the necessary condition for Pareto optimality (38) is satisfied.

Proof. Define $w^{\mathrm{T}} \equiv [0_H^{\mathrm{T}}, p_0, p_{.}^{\mathrm{T}}]$. Then $w^{\mathrm{T}}B = 0^{\mathrm{T}}$ and $w^{\mathrm{T}}A > 0_H^{\mathrm{T}}$.

Q.E.D.

Corollary 2.1. If consumer preferences are Leontief so that $\sigma_{..} = 0_{N\times N}$ (which implies also that $\sigma_{0.} = 0_N^{\mathrm{T}}$) and $p_0\eta_0^h + p_{.}^{\mathrm{T}}\eta_{.}^h \geqq 0$ for all h with at least one strict inequality, then (38) is satisfied.

Proposition 3. Suppose that: (i) the fixed factor endowment matrix $[v^1, v^2, \ldots, v^H]$ has rank H (so that the number of fixed factors M is equal to or greater than the number of households H),[27] (ii) $\sigma_{..}^{-1}$ exists, and (iii) $q_0\Pi_{0.} + q_{.}^{\mathrm{T}}\Pi_{..} \neq 0_N^{\mathrm{T}}$ Then the sufficient condition for the existence of a strict Pareto improving tax change (36) is satisfied.

Proof. It is easy to see that the rank of $B \equiv [B_0, B_1, B_2, B_3]$ is equal to the rank of $[B_0^*, B_1, B_2, B_3]$, where $B_0^{*\mathrm{T}} \equiv [\gamma_{v.}^{\mathrm{T}}(I_M - \hat{\tau})[v^1, \ldots, v^M], \Pi_{0.}^{\mathrm{T}}, \Pi_{..}^{\mathrm{T}}]$ (just add appropriate multiples of the columns of B_2 to the columns of B_0). Using (12), (19) and (21) it can be seen that B_1 is linearly dependent on the columns of B_2 and B_3, i.e. we have

$$B_1(1+t_0) + B_2(1_N + t_{.}) = B_3(1_M - \tau). \tag{39}$$

Furthermore, it can be seen that the rank of $[B_0^*, B_2, B_3]^{\mathrm{T}}$ is equal to the number of linearly independent rows in the three matrices: $[0_{H\times N}^{\mathrm{T}}, \sigma_{0.}^{\mathrm{T}}, \sigma_{..}^{\mathrm{T}}]$, matrix has rank H and its rows are linearly independent of the rows of the first matrix which has rank N by assumption (ii). Note by (12) that the rows of $[\sigma_{0.}^{\mathrm{T}}, \sigma_{..}^{\mathrm{T}}]$ are all orthogonal to $[q_0, q_{.}^{\mathrm{T}}]$. Thus, if (iii) above is satisfied, there is at least one row of $[0_{H\times N}^{\mathrm{T}}, \Pi_{0.}^{\mathrm{T}}, \Pi_{..}^{\mathrm{T}}]$ which is linearly independent from the rows of $[0_{H\times N}^{\mathrm{T}}, \sigma_{0.}^{\mathrm{T}}, \sigma_{..}^{\mathrm{T}}]$ and thus the rank of B is $H+N+1$. Now apply the corollary to (36).

Q.E.D.

[26] Using (5) we also have $\Pi_{0.} = -(p_0)^{-1}p_{.}^{\mathrm{T}}\Pi_{..} = 0_N^{\mathrm{T}}$.

[27] Dixit (1977) was the first investigator to employ an assumption of this type.

Proposition 4. Suppose that: (i) $[v^1, v^2, \ldots, v^H]$ has rank H, (ii) $\Pi_{..}^{-1}$ exists,[28] and (iii) $p_0\sigma_{0.} + p_.^{\mathrm{T}}\sigma_{..} \neq 0_N^{\mathrm{T}}$. Then the sufficient condition for the existence of a strict Pareto improving tax change (36) is satisfied.

The proof is analogous to the proof of Proposition 3, except that (5) is used in place of (12). Note that both Propositions 3 and 4 require that $t_. \neq 1_N t_0$, i.e. that variable commodity taxes be nonproportional.

We can specialize our model to the model used by Diamond and Mirrlees (1971) and Guesnerie (1977) if we assume that all fixed factors are taxed at 100 percent rates and that these rates are not changed, i.e. we need only assume that initially $\tau = 1_M$ and $\Delta\tau \equiv 0_M$.

Proposition 5. Suppose $\tau = 1_M$ and $\Delta\tau \equiv 0_M$. If there exist scalars $\lambda_0, \lambda_1, \ldots, \lambda_H$ such that

$$\sum_{h=1}^{H} x_.^h\lambda_h = \lambda_0[\sigma_{0.}p_0 + \sigma_{..}p_.] = -\lambda_0[\sigma_{.0}t_0p_0 + \sigma_{..}\hat{t}_.p_.], \tag{40}$$

$$\lambda_h \geqq \lambda_0[p_0\eta_0^h + p_.^{\mathrm{T}}\eta_.^h], \qquad h = 1, \ldots, H \tag{41}$$

with at least one strict inequality in (41), then the necessary condition for Pareto optimality of the initial system of taxes (38) is satisfied.[29]

Proof. Define $w^{\mathrm{T}} \equiv [-\lambda_1, \ldots, -\lambda_H, \lambda_0 p_0, \lambda_0 p_.^{\mathrm{T}}]$. Then using $\tau = 1_M$ (so that $\hat{\tau} = I_M$), (5) and (40), it can be verified that $w^{\mathrm{T}}B_0 = 0_N^{\mathrm{T}}$ and $w^{\mathrm{T}}B_2 = 0_N^{\mathrm{T}}$. Thus, using $\tau = 1_M$ and (39), $w^{\mathrm{T}}B_1 = 0$ also, which in turn can be rewritten as

$$\sum_{h=1}^{H} x_0^h\lambda_h = \lambda_0[\sigma_{00}p_0 + \sigma_{0.}p_.] = -\lambda_0[\sigma_{00}t_0p_0 + \sigma_{0.}\hat{t}_.p_.]. \tag{42}$$

Thus, $w^{\mathrm{T}}[B_0, B_1, B_2] = 0_{N+1+N}^{\mathrm{T}}$ and $w^{\mathrm{T}}A > 0_H^{\mathrm{T}}$ using (41).

Q.E.D.

We note that if in addition $[x^1, \ldots, x^H]$ has rank H (so that $N \geqq H$), then eqs. (40) and (41) cannot be satisfied if $\lambda_0 = 0$. Furthermore, if $\tau = 1_M$ and (40) holds, then the λ_h satisfy the following additional equalities:[30]

$$\sum_{h=1}^{H} p^{\mathrm{T}}x^h\lambda_h = -\sum_{h=1}^{H}[p_0t_0x_0^h + p_.^{\mathrm{T}}\hat{t}_.x^h]\lambda_h = \lambda_0 p^{\mathrm{T}}\sigma p, \tag{43}$$

[28]This assumption is employed by Guesnerie (1977) throughout his paper.

[29]Of course the matrix B is now equal to $[B_0, B_1, B_2]$, i.e. the columns of B_3 have been dropped from B since we are no longer optimizing with respect to taxes on the fixed factors. The second equality in (40) follows from (12) and (19). I owe this proposition to Guesnerie and Weymark.

[30]Add eqs. (42) to (40) and premultiply the resulting system by $[p_0, p_.^{\mathrm{T}}]$. (43) is a many consumer generalization of Diamond and Mirrlees (1971, p. 262), eq. (39).

where $p^{\mathrm{T}} \equiv [p_0, p_.^{\mathrm{T}}]$ and $p^{\mathrm{T}}\sigma p \leqq 0$ and σ is the $N+1$ by $N+1$ symmetric negative semidefinite aggregate substitution matrix defined by (13). Note that $p_0 t_0 x_0^h + p_.^{\mathrm{T}}\hat{t}_. x_.^h$ is the net revenue which the government is initially raising from the hth household by the taxation of variable commodities.

Corollary 5.1. Suppose $\tau = 1_M$ and $\Delta\tau \equiv 0_M$. Then the necessary condition for taxes to be α optimal (32) will be satisfied if there exist scalars $\lambda_0, \lambda_1, \ldots, \lambda_H$ such that *either*:

$$\sum_{h=1}^{H} x^h \lambda_h = \lambda_0 [\sigma_{.0} p_0 + \sigma_{..} p_.] \tag{44}$$

and

$$\lambda_h = \alpha_h + \lambda_0 [p_0 \eta_0^h + p_.^{\mathrm{T}} \eta_.^h],^{31} \qquad h = 1, 2, \ldots, H \tag{45}$$

or

$$\sum_{h=1}^{H} x_.^h \alpha_h = \lambda_0 \sum_{h=1}^{H} [(\sigma_{.0}^h - x_.^h \eta_0^h) p_0 + (\sigma_{..}^h - x_.^h \eta_.^{h\mathrm{T}}) p_.] \tag{46}$$

or

$$\sum_{h=1}^{H} \alpha_h x_.^h = -\lambda_0 \sum_{h=1}^{H} [(\sigma_{.0}^h - x_.^h \eta_0^h) t_0 p_0 + (\sigma_{..}^h - x_.^h \eta_.^{h\mathrm{T}}) \hat{t} p_. + x_.^h].^{32} \tag{47}$$

Proof. Define $w^{\mathrm{T}} \equiv [-\lambda_1, \ldots, -\lambda_H, \lambda_0 p_0, \lambda_0 p_.^{\mathrm{T}}]$. Then as before (44) plus $\tau = I_M$ implies $w^{\mathrm{T}}[B_0, B_1, B_2] = 0_{N+1+N}^{\mathrm{T}}$. Eqs. (45) imply $w^{\mathrm{T}} A = \alpha^{\mathrm{T}}$ and thus the necessary conditions for α optimality (32) are satisfied. (46) follows by substituting eqs. (45) into (44) and rearranging the terms. (47) follows from (46), and the identities (12), (19) and (17).

Q.E.D.

Corollary 5.2. Suppose $\tau = 1_M$, $\Delta\tau \equiv 0_M$ and $H = 1$ (*the one household case*). Then the necessary condition for Pareto optimality of the initial system of taxes (38) is satisfied if there exists scalar $\theta \neq [p_0 \eta_0^1 + p_.^{\mathrm{T}} \eta_.^1]$ such that

$$x_.^1(-\theta) = \sigma_{.0} t_0 p_0 + \sigma_{..} \hat{t} p_.^{\;33} \tag{48}$$

[31] These equations are essentially Mirrlees's (1976, p. 331) eqs. (10) and (8).

[32] This is essentially eq. (74) in Diamond and Mirrlees (1971, p. 268) or eq. (5) in Diamond (1975, p. 337) if we recall footnote 10 for the interpretation of the terms in the matrices $(\sigma_{..}^h - x_.^h \eta_.^{h\mathrm{T}})$.

[33] This is essentially (38) in Diamond and Mirrlees (1971, p. 262) except that we are missing the equation $x_0^1(-\theta) = \sigma_{00} t_0 p_0 + \sigma_{0.} \hat{t} p_.$ which can be derived from (48) if we recall eq. (42).

Proof. If (48) holds and $\theta > [p_0\eta_0^1 + p_{.}^{\mathrm{T}}\eta_{.}^1]$, then define $\lambda_1 \equiv \theta$, $\lambda_0 = 1$ and eqs. (40) and (41) will hold, which implies (38). If (48) holds and $\theta < [p_0\eta_0^1 + p_{.}^{\mathrm{T}}\eta_{.}^1]$, then define $\lambda_1 \equiv -\theta$, $\lambda_0 = -1$ and eqs. (40) and (41) will again hold.

Q.E.D.

Corollary 5.3. Suppose $\tau = 1_M$, $\Delta\tau \equiv 0_M$ and $N = 1$ (*the case of only two variable goods*). Then the necessary condition for Pareto optimality of the initial system of taxes (38) and the necessary condition for α optimality (32) will be satisfied for any $\alpha > 0_H$ if *either*

$$p^{\mathrm{T}}\sigma p + \sum_{h=1}^{H} [p_0 t_0 x_0^h + p_1 t_1 x_1^h][p_0\eta_0^h + p_1\eta_1^h] \neq 0 \tag{49}$$

or

$$\sum_{h=1}^{H} [(\sigma_{10}^h - x_1^h\eta_0^h)p_0 + (\sigma_{11}^h - x_1^h\eta_1^h)p_1] \neq 0, \tag{50}$$

where $p^{\mathrm{T}} \equiv [p_0, p_1]$, σ is the 2×2 aggregate Slutsky matrix defined by (13) and the terms $\sigma_{1i}^h - x_1^h\eta_i^h \equiv \partial d_i^h(y^h, q)/\partial q_1$, $i = 0, 1$ are interpreted in footnote 10.

Proof. When $N = 1$, (43) is equivalent to (44). Now substitute eqs. (45) into (43) and we obtain a single equation in λ_0 which can be solved for λ_0 if (49) is satisfied, irrespective of the value for α. Thus, eqs. (44) and (45) can be satisfied which in turn implies that the necessary condition for α optimality (32) can be satisfied for any α. In a similar manner, substitute eqs. (45) into (44) and we obtain a single equation in λ_0 which can be solved for λ_0 if (50) is satisfied. Thus, again (32) can be satisfied for any α.

Q.E.D.

Proposition 6. Suppose $\tau = 1_M$, $\Delta\tau \equiv 0_M$ and $N \geq H+1$. Sufficient conditions for the existence of a strict Pareto improving tax change are: (i) $\Pi_{..}^{-1}$ exists, (ii) $X \equiv [x^1, x^2, \ldots, x^H]$, the $N \times H$ matrix of initial consumptions and labor supplies (excluding commodity 0), has rank H, and (iii) there exists a vector z such that $z^{\mathrm{T}}X = 0_H^{\mathrm{T}}$ but $z^{\mathrm{T}}[\sigma_{.0}p_0 + \sigma_{..}p_{.}] \neq 0$.

Proof. As in the proof of Proposition 3, the rank of $[B_0, B_1, B_2]$ is equal to the rank of $[B_0^*, B_1, B_2]$, where $B_0^{*\mathrm{T}} \equiv [0_{H\times N}^{\mathrm{T}}, \Pi_{0.}^{\mathrm{T}}, \Pi_{..}^{\mathrm{T}}]$ when $\tau = 1_M$. Moreover, when $\tau = 1_M$, (39) implies that B_1 is linearly dependent on the columns of B_2. Thus the rank of $[B_0, B_1, B_2]$ is equal to the rank of $[B_0^*, B_2]$, which in turn is equal to the total number of linearly independent rows in the matrices $[0_{N\times H}, 0_N, \Pi_{..}]$ and $[X, \sigma_{.0}p_0 + \sigma_{..}p_{.}, \sigma_{..}]$. By assumption (i), there are N linearly independent rows in the first matrix, and by assumptions (ii) and (iii), there are an additional $H+1$ linearly independent rows in the second matrix. Thus, the rank of $[B_0, B_1, B_2]$ is $H+N+1$. Now apply the corollary to (36) and we obtain the existence of a strict Pareto improving tax change in this Diamond–Mirrlees world.

Q.E.D.

5. Pareto improving tax changes with inequality restrictions on tax instruments

Recall the basic constraints in our model (25), which can be rewritten as $Az^1 = Bz^2$, where the components of the vectors z^1 and z^2 are unrestricted in sign. Let us rewrite these constraints as

$$Az^1 = Bz^2 - Bz^4; \qquad z^2 \geqq 0_{2N+1+M}; \qquad z^3 \geqq 0_{2N+1+M}. \tag{51}$$

Now we can impose unfeasibility and inequality constraints on our tax instruments. If a tax rate cannot be changed at all, simply drop the corresponding column from the B and $-B$ matrices. If a tax instrument cannot be decreased, then drop the corresponding column from the $-B$ matrix; if a tax rate cannot be increased, drop the corresponding column from the B matrix. After dropping the appropriate columns, rewrite (51) as

$$Az^1 = B^*z^*, \qquad z^* \geqq 0. \tag{52}$$

The system of equations and inequalities (52) now represents the basic constraints on (small) changes in the variables of our model. It is evident (again use Motzkin's Theorem of the Alternative) that the following conditions are *sufficient for the existence of strict Pareto improving tax changes* under constraints on the tax instruments:[34]

$$\text{there exist } z^1, z^* \text{ such that } z^1 \gg 0_H, z^* \geqq 0 \quad \text{and} \quad Az^1 = B^*z^*; \tag{53}$$

$$\text{there does not exist } w \text{ such that } w^{\mathrm{T}}B^* \leqq 0^{\mathrm{T}} \quad \text{and} \quad w^{\mathrm{T}}A > 0_H^{\mathrm{T}}. \tag{54}$$

Note that if there are no constraints on tax changes, then $B^* = [B, -B]$ and $w^{\mathrm{T}}B \leqq 0^{\mathrm{T}}_{2(2N+1+M)}$ is equivalent to $w^{\mathrm{T}}B = 0^{\mathrm{T}}_{2N+1+M}$, so that in this case (54) reduces to (38).

The negations of (53) and (54) yield the following *necessary conditions for Pareto optimality* (or for the nonexistence of strict Pareto improving tax changes) under constraints on the tax instruments:

$$\text{there is no solution } z^1, z^* \text{ to } z^1 \gg 0_H, z^* \geqq 0 \text{ and } Az^1 = B^*z^*; \tag{55}$$

$$\text{there exists } w \text{ such that } w^{\mathrm{T}}B^* \leqq 0^{\mathrm{T}} \quad \text{and} \quad w^{\mathrm{T}}A > 0_H^{\mathrm{T}}. \tag{56}$$

[34]Throughout this section we still maintain the regularity condition (31) where the tax rate which corresponds to b can be changed in both directions.

A geometric interpretation of (56) may be helpful. The $H+1+N$ dimensional vector w is the normal vector to a hyperplane in R^{H+1+N} passing through the origin. $w^{\mathrm{T}}B^* \leqq 0^{\mathrm{T}}$ means that all of the columns of B^* lie on one side of this hyperplane (or lie on the hyperplane itself), while $w^{\mathrm{T}}A > 0_H^{\mathrm{T}}$ means that all of the columns of A lie on the other side of the hyperplane (or lie on the hyperplane itself), with at least one column of A lying strictly on the other side of the hyperplane. Thus, a strictly positive linear combination of the columns of A cannot lie in the set of vectors spanned by nonnegative linear combinations of the columns of B^*.

Note that the existence of one sided inequality restrictions on tax changes destroys the simple relationship between the existence of Pareto improving tax changes, and the existence of more tax instruments than households that was inherent in the corollary to (36).

We now turn to a more concrete application of the above rather abstract criteria. Suppose that all fixed factors are initially being taxed at 100 percent rates ($\tau = 1_M$) and that these tax rates cannot be increased ($\Delta\tau \leqq 0_M$) but that there are no other constraints on possible tax changes. Then if we recall the proof of Proposition 5, it is easy to verify that (56) translates into the following result.

Proposition 7. Suppose $\tau = 1_M$ and $\Delta\tau \leqq 0_M$. If there exist scalars $\lambda_0, \lambda_1, \ldots, \lambda_H$ such that (40), (41) and

$$v^1\lambda_1 + v^2\lambda_2 + \ldots + v^H\lambda_H \geqq 0_M \tag{57}$$

are satisfied, then the necessary condition for Pareto optimality of the initial system of taxes under inequality constraints (56) is satisfied.

Thus, the difference between Propositions 5 and 7 is the addition of the inequality constraints (57).

6. The one household, one consumption good, one type of labor, one fixed factor case

References on one consumer economies when there are taxes on profits are Stiglitz and Dasgupta (1971) and Munk (1976).

When $H = 1$, $N = 1$ and $M = 1$, the basic supply equals demand equations of our model, eqs. (21)–(24) become:

$$p_0(1+t_0)x_0^1 + p_1(1+t_1)x_1^1 = v_1^1(1-\tau_1)r_1, \tag{58}$$

$$x_0^1 + x_0^0 = y_0, \tag{59}$$

$$x_1^1 + x_1^0 = y_1, \tag{60}$$

$$p_0t_0y_0 + p_1t_1y_1 + v_1\tau_1r_1 = p_0(1+t_0)x_0^0 + p_1(1+t_1)x_1^0. \tag{61}$$

We assume that $t_0 > -1$, $t_1 > -1$, $x_0^1 > 0$, $x_1^1 < 0$, $y_0 > 0$, $y_1 < 0$, $x_0^0 > 0$, $x_1^0 \geqq 0$, $v_1^1 > 0$, $p_0 > 0$, $p_1 > 0$ and $r_1 > 0$. Thus, good 0 is a consumption good which is demanded by both the government and the single household, while good 1 is labor supplied by the household and demanded by the private sector (and by the government if $x_1^0 > 0$). From (5), $\Pi_{01} = -p_1\Pi_{11}/p_0$ (recall $\Pi_{11} \geqq 0$), and from (8), $v_1^1\gamma_{11} = y_1$. From (12) and (13), $\sigma_{00} = -p_1(1+t_1)\sigma_{01}/p_0(1+t_0)$ and $\sigma_{11} = -p_0(1+t_0)\sigma_{01}/p_1(1+t_1)$, where $\sigma_{01} \geqq 0$. From (17), $\eta_1^1 = (1 - p_0(1+t_0)\eta_0^1)/p_1(1+t_1)$. If we substitute these relations into (25) when $H = 1$, $N = 1$ and $M = 1$, add $p_0(1+t_0)/p_1(1+t_1)$ times the second row of (25) to the third row, then we find that (25) is equivalent to the following system of equations:

$$\begin{bmatrix} 1, & x_1^1(1+t_1)-(1-\tau_1)y_1, & x_1^1 p_1 \\ \eta_0^1, & \sigma_{01}(1+t_1)+p_1 p_0^{-1}\Pi_{11}, & \sigma_{01}p_1 \\ p_1^{-1}(1+t_1)^{-1}, & \Pi_{11}(t_0-t_1)/(1+t_1), & 0 \end{bmatrix} \begin{bmatrix} \Delta u^1 \\ \Delta p_1 \\ \Delta t_1 \end{bmatrix} = \begin{bmatrix} -x_0^1 p_0, & -v_1^1 r_1 \\ \sigma_{01}(1+t_1)p_1/(1+t_0), & 0 \\ 0, & 0 \end{bmatrix} \begin{bmatrix} \Delta t_0 \\ \Delta \tau_1 \end{bmatrix}. \tag{62}$$

We assume that the coefficient matrix on the left-hand side of (62) has an inverse, i.e. we assume that the determinant D of this matrix is nonzero:

$$D \equiv \{(1-\tau_1)\sigma_{01}(-y_1) + \Pi_{11}p_1 p_0^{-1}(-x_1^1) + (\eta_0^1 x_1^1 - \sigma_{01})\Pi_{11}(t_0-t_1)p_1\}/(1+t_1) \neq 0. \tag{63}$$

Note that the first two terms of D are nonnegative, since $y_1 < 0$ and $x_1^1 < 0$, but that the sign of the third term is indeterminate. Assumption (63) allows us to define u^1 (utility), p^1 (the price of labor) and t^1 (the tax rate on labor) as implicit functions of t_0 (the tax rate on the consumer good) and τ_1 (the tax rate on the fixed factor) in a neighborhood of the initial equilibrium point. The Implicit Function Theorem and Cramer's Rule allow us to calculate the partial derivatives of u^1, p^1, and t^1 with respect to t_0 and τ_1, evaluated at the initial equilibrium:

$$\partial u^1/\partial t_0 = (t_0-t_1)(1-\tau_1)\sigma_{01}\Pi_{11}p_1 v_1^1 r_1/(1+t_1)D, \tag{64}$$

$$\partial u^1/\partial \tau_1 = (t_0-t_1)\sigma_{01}\Pi_{11}p_1 v_1^1 r_1/(1+t_1)D, \tag{65}$$

$$\partial p_1/\partial t_0 = -(1-\tau_1)\sigma_{01}v_1^1 r_1/(1+t_0)(1+t_1)D, \tag{66}$$

$$\partial p_1/\partial \tau_1 = -\sigma_{01}v_1^1 r_1/(1+t_1)D, \tag{67}$$

$$\frac{\partial t_1}{\partial t_0}=\left\{\frac{(1-\tau_1)\sigma_{01}p_0y_0}{p_1(1+t_1)}+\frac{\Pi_{11}x_0^1}{1+t_1}-\frac{(t_0-t_1)\Pi_{11}p_0}{1+t_1}\right.$$
$$\left.\times\left[\eta_0^1x_0^1+\frac{\sigma_{01}p_1(1+t_1)}{p_0(1+t_0)}\right]\right\}\bigg/D, \qquad (68)$$

$$\partial t_1/\partial\tau_1=\{-(t_0-t_1)\eta_0^1\Pi_{11}v_1^1r_1$$
$$+[\sigma_{01}(1+t_1)+\Pi_{11}p_1p_0^{-1}]v_1^1r_1p_1^{-1}\}/(1+t_1)D. \qquad (69)$$

Note that if $\sigma_{01}>0$, then (67) provides us with a geometric interpretation for the sign of D: let u^1, t_1 and p_1 be endogenous variables and let τ_1 be an exogenous variable. Now increase τ_1 and calculate the new equilibrium, i.e. find the u^1, t_1 and p_1 which satisfy the basic balance equations (21)–(24), holding t_0 fixed. If p_1 increases then $D<0$ while if p_1 decreases, then $D>0$.

Proposition 8. If $H=1$, $M=1$ and $D\neq 0$ and any one of the following conditions is satisfied: (i) $t_0=t_1=0$ (commodity taxes are zero), (ii) $t_0=t_1$ (commodity taxes are proportional), (iii) $\Pi_{11}=\Pi_{01}=\Pi_{00}=0$ (the technology is Leontief) or (iv) $\sigma_{01}=\sigma_{11}=\sigma_{00}=0$ (consumer preferences are Leontief), then the necessary conditions for the initial system of taxes to be Pareto optimal with no restrictions on the tax instruments, $\partial u^1/\partial t_0=0$ and $\partial u^1/\partial\tau_1=0$, are satisfied.

Proof. Follows directly from eqs. (64) and (65). Q.E.D.

Proposition 9. If $H=1$, $N=1$, $M=1$, $D\neq 0$, $t_0\neq t_1$, $\Pi_{11}>0$ and $\sigma_{01}>0$, then utility can be increased by changing τ_1 [increase τ_1 if $(t_0-t_1)D>0$, decrease τ_1 if $(t_0-t_1)D<0$]. If in addition the fixed factor is not initially being taxed at a 100 percent rate (i.e. $\tau_1\neq 1$), then utility can be increased by changing the tax rate on the consumer good t_0 [increase t_0 if $(t_0-t_1)(1-\tau_1)D>0$, decrease t_0 if $(t_0-t_1)(1-\tau_1)D<0$].

Proof. Follows from eqs. (64) and (65) again. Q.E.D.

It should be noted that Proposition 8 is consistent with Propositions 1 and 2 (i.e. the condition $q_0\Pi_0+q_.^{\mathrm{T}}\Pi_{..}=0_N^{\mathrm{T}}$ reduces to $(t_0-t_1)\Pi_{11}=0$ when $N=1$ while the condition $p_0\sigma_{0.}+p_.^{\mathrm{T}}\sigma_{..}=0_N^{\mathrm{T}}$ reduces to $(t_0-t_1)\sigma_{01}=0$ when $N=1$) while Proposition 9 is consistent with Propositions 3 and 4 (i.e. the condition $\sigma_{..}^{-1}$ exists reduces to $\sigma_{01}>0$ when $N=1$ while the condition $\Pi_{..}^{-1}$ exists reduces to $\Pi_{11}>0$ when $N=1$, etc.). However, Proposition 9 and eqs. (64)–(69) give us more information than was contained in the earlier propositions in section 4: we can now tell precisely how the endogenous variables u^1, p_1 and t_1 change when the exogenous tax rates t_0 and τ_1 change. This is the major advantage of the brute force method for solving (25) which we adopted in this section. However, the present method is only practical when H, M and N are small.

Another reason for the present section is that we can provide geometric interpretations for some of the rather abstract propositions that we have stated earlier in the paper. Fig. 1 provides a geometric interpretation for

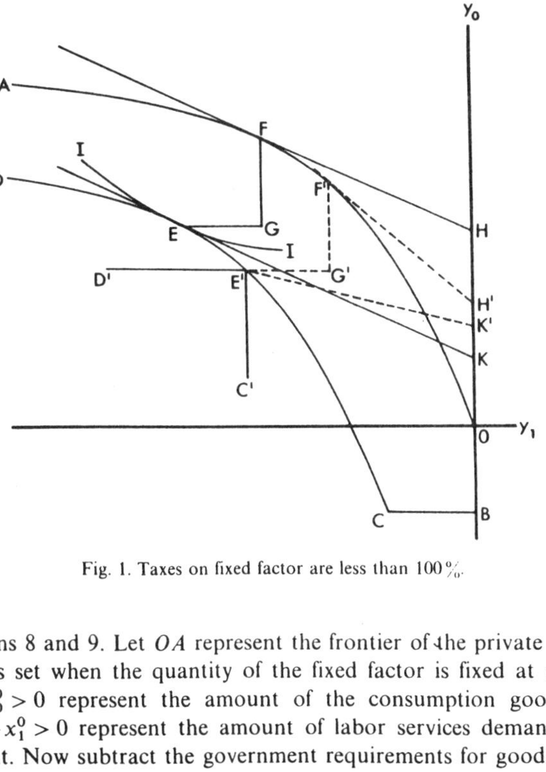

Fig. 1. Taxes on fixed factor are less than 100%.

Propositions 8 and 9. Let OA represent the frontier of the private production possibilities set when the quantity of the fixed factor is fixed at v_1^1. Let $OB = FG = x_0^0 > 0$ represent the amount of the consumption good and $BC = EG = -x_1^0 > 0$ represent the amount of labor services demanded by the government. Now subtract the government requirements for goods and labor from the private production frontier OA in order to obtain the after tax production frontier CD. I–I represents the highest consumer indifference curve which is tangent at the point E to this after tax frontier. FH is the price line facing producers[35] with slope $-p_1/p_0$, while EK is the parallel price line which faces consumers[36] with slope $-p_1(1+t_1)/p_0(1+t_0)$. Thus, if

[35]The equation which described this line is $p_0y_0 + p_1y_1 = r_1v_1^1$.

[36]The equation which describes this line is $p_0(1+t_0)x_0^1 + p_1(1+t_1)x_1^1 = (1-\tau_1)r_1v_1^1$.

the lines are parallel we must have $t_0 = t_1$. $OH = r_1 v_1^1/p_0$ represents producer profits or the return to the fixed factor before taxes, while $OK = (1 - \tau_1) r_1 v_1^1 / p_0(1+t_0)$ represents the consumer's after tax real income derived from his holdings of the fixed factor. The initial point of producer equilibrium is F while E is the initial point of consumer equilibrium. Note that $\tau_1 < 1$ in this example. i.e. taxes on the fixed factor are less than 100 percent. This initial equilibrium represents a Pareto optimal allocation of resources in an economy with government expenditures. Note that $OK/OH = (1-\tau_1)/(1+t_0)$, where τ_1 is the initial level of taxes on the fixed factor and t_0 is the initial level of taxes on the consumer good y_0.

Now look at the new equilibrium E', F'. E' is the new point of consumer equilibrium where the price line $E'K'$ is tangential to an indifference curve (not shown in the diagram) at the point E', while F' is the new point of producer equilibrium. Note that the new producer price line $F'H'$ is tangential to the before tax production possibilities curve AFO. Let us hold t_0 (and p_0) fixed as we move from the old equilibrium to the new equilibrium, but we allow u^1, p_1, t_1 and τ_1 to change. In moving from F to F', it is easy to see that p_1 has increased since $F'H'$ has a steeper slope than GH. Remember also that $OK'/OH' = (1-\tau_1')/(1+t_0)$ where τ_1' is the new equilibrium rate of fixed factor taxation. From fig. 1 we see that $OK'/OH' > OK/OH$ and thus τ_1 has *decreased* as p_1 has *increased* going from E, F to E', F'. Thus, recalling (67), we see that D defined by (63) must be positive when the relevant parameters in (63) are evaluated at the initial equilibrium E, F. The reader should now be able to redraw fig. 1 to illustrate the case where $D < 0$ (just redraw the price line $E'K'$ with a steeper slope and draw in an indifference curve tangent to this new price line at E').

Fig. 1 can also be used to show (cf. Proposition 8) that a Pareto optimal allocation of resources does *not* necessarily require that commodity taxes be proportional. For example. suppose that the after tax production frontier were $D'E'C'$ instead of DEC so that $\Pi_{11} = \Pi_{01} = \Pi_{00} = 0$. Then it is easy to see that the equilibrium represented by E', F' is Pareto optimal but $t_0 \neq t_1$. Similarly, if the indifference curve tangential to $E'K'$ were L shaped so that $\sigma_{01} = \sigma_{11} = \sigma_{00} = 0$ at the equilibrium E', F', then again we will have a Pareto optimal allocation of resources with $t_0 \neq t_1$.

The reader should be able to see why we required the hypotheses $\Pi_{11} > 0$ and $\sigma_{01} > 0$ in Proposition 9: we needed them in order to rule out these degenerate, no substitution economies.[37]

In fig. 2 we have reproduced the same after tax production frontier CD as in fig. 1, but consumer preferences have been shifted so that the highest

[37] It must be emphasized that $t_0 \neq t_1$, $\Pi_{11} > 0$ and $\sigma_{01} > 0$ is only a sufficient condition for the existence of a utility increasing tax change, and not a necessary and sufficient condition. The problem is that we could have $\Pi_{11} = 0$ but yet the production possibilities curve could look more like DEC than $D'E'C'$.

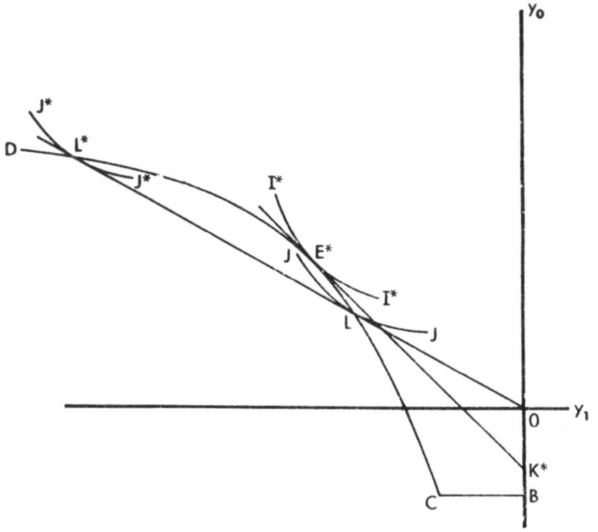

Fig. 2. Comparison of first and second best equilibria.

indifference curve just tangential (at the point E^*) to CD is I^*I^*. The price line facing consumers is now E^*K^*, which requires that $\tau_1 > 1$, i.e. that taxes on the fixed factor exceed 100 percent. Although a socialist economy could sustain the first best consumer equilibrium point E^*, it would be difficult for a decentralized market economy to do so. In fact, the best the consumer can do in a decentralized market economy is attain the utility level indexed by the indifference curve JJ (at the point L), which corresponds to a lower utility level than that indexed by the indifference curve I^*I^*. Note that the consumer price line OL, which is tangent to JJ at the point where the indifference curve JJ intersects the after tax production frontier CD, passes through the origin, which corresponds to $\tau_1 = 1$, i.e. taxes on the fixed factor are 100 percent. Thus, if we impose the inequality constraint on taxes, $\tau_1 \leqq 1$, then the second best equilibrium is attained at the point L where the consumer price line OL passes through the origin, and the point of tangency L to the indifference curve JJ also lies on the after tax production frontier. The following proposition provides the algebra behind the geometry of fig. 2.

Proposition 10. Let $D \neq 0$, $\tau_1 = 1$ (100 percent taxes on the fixed factor initially) and suppose that $\Delta\tau_1 \leqq 0$ (taxes on the fixed factor cannot be increased). Then the necessary conditions for Pareto optimality of the initial system of taxes under the constraint $\Delta\tau_1 \leqq 0$, $\partial u^1/\partial t_0 = 0$ and $\Delta\tau_1 \partial u^1/\partial\tau_1 \leqq 0$, are satisfied if and only if

$$(t_0 - t_1)\Pi_{11}\sigma_{01}\{(t_0 - t_1)(\eta_0^1 x_1^1 - \sigma_{01}) - p_0^{-1} x_1^1\} \geqq 0. \tag{70}$$

Proof. From (64) when $\tau_1 = 1$, $\partial u^1/\partial t_0 = 0$. From (65), $\partial u^1/\partial\tau_1 = (t_0 - t_1)\Pi_{11}\sigma_{01}p_1 v_1^1 r_1/(1+t_1)D$, and from (63) when $\tau_1 = 1$ we have

$$D = p_1 \Pi_{11}\{(t_0 - t_1)(\eta_0^1 x_1^1 - \sigma_{01}) - p_0^{-1} x_1^1\}/(1+t_1). \tag{71}$$

Now $\Delta\tau_1 \leqq 0$ and $\Delta\tau_1 \partial u^1/\partial\tau_1 \leqq 0$ is equivalent to $\partial u^1/\partial\tau_1 \geqq 0$ which in turn is equivalent to (70) using (65) and (71).

Q.E.D.

Condition (70) can also be derived using Proposition 7.

Note that $t_0 - t_1 > 0$ is equivalent to the inequality $(1+t_0) > (1+t_1)$ or $(1+t_1)p_1/(1+t_0)p_0 < p_1/p_0$ (assuming that $t_0 > -1$, $t_1 > -1$, $p_0 > 0$ and $p_1 > 0$). Thus, if $\tau_1 = 1$ and $t_0 - t_1 > 0$, then the absolute value of the slope of the consumer's price line $(1+t_1)p_1/(1+t_0)p_0$ is *less* than the absolute value of the slope of after tax production frontier, p_1/p_0, at the point where the price line intersects the frontier, which is the point L in fig. 2. Normally, we expect both the consumption good and labor to be taxed and thus normally $t_0 > 0$ and $-t_1 > 0$ so that $t_0 - t_1 > 0$.

What is the geometric interpretation of the case when $t_0 - t_1 < 0$? This case corresponds to a situation where the consumer's price line through the origin, OL, intersects the after tax production frontier CD at a point L^* where the absolute value of the slope of the price line is *greater* than the absolute value of the slope of the frontier, and an indifference curve J^*J^* is also tangential to the price line at the point L^*. If $t_0 < 0$, then consumption is being subsidized, while if $t_1 > 0$, then labor is being subsidized.

If we use our geometric interpretation for the sign of D developed earlier, it is straightforward to provide a geometric interpretation of condition (70). If we are at the initial equilibrium point L in fig. 2, then $t_0 - t_1 > 0$ and we wish to move *up* the after tax production possibilities frontier DC in order to attain a higher utility level, i.e. we wish to decrease p_1, but at the same time, τ_1 must not increase. Thus, if $\partial p_1/\partial\tau_1 > 0$ [which in view of (67) is equivalent to $D < 0$] and $t_0 - t_1 > 0$, we can find a new equilibrium by decreasing fixed factors taxes which will lead to a higher utility level. Similarly, if we are at the initial equilibrium point L^* in fig. 2, then $t_0 - t_1 < 0$ and we wish to move *down* the after tax production frontier in order to attain a higher utility level, and we can do so without increasing τ_1 if $D > 0$. In both cases, we require the condition $\Pi_{11}\sigma_{01}(t_0-t_1)D<0$ in order to obtain the existence of u utility increasing tax change that respects the constraint $\Delta\tau_1 \leqq 0$. Using (71) it can be seen that the negation of the condition $\Pi_{11}\sigma_{01}(t_0-t_1)D<0$ is equivalent to (70).

7. The two household, three good case

Key references on two household economies are Dasgupta and Stiglitz (1972), Mirrlees (1975) and Diamond (1975). As Dasgupta and Stiglitz (1972, p. 88) observe, a fundamental difficulty with the one household model is that it ignores the existence of a class of consumers who cannot (e.g. retired people) or will not (e.g. pure capitalists) supply labor services. For these people a 100 percent tax on fixed factor income would lead to starvation. Thus, in the present section we consider an economy that has two classes of households, the first class for simplicity we will assume holds no claims to fixed factors (workers), while the second class (capitalists) offers no labor services. We also assume that $M=1$, so that there is only one fixed factor, and $N=1$, so that there are only two variable goods. The first variable good is a consumer good while the second is labor. With these conventions, the basic balance equations (21)–(23) become

$$p_0(1+t_0)x_0^1+p_1(1+t_1)x_1^1=0, \tag{72}$$

$$p_0(1+t_0)x_0^2=(1-\tau_1)v_1^2r_1, \tag{73}$$

$$x_0^1+x_0^2+x_0^0=y_0, \tag{74}$$

$$x_1^1 \qquad +x_1^0=y_1. \tag{75}$$

We assume that $t_0>-1$, $t_1>-1$, $x_0^1>0$, $x_1^1<0$, $x_0^2>0$, $x_1^2=0$, $y_0>0$, $y_1<0$, $x_0^0>0$, $x_1^0\geqq 0$, $v_1^1=0$, $v_1^2>0$, $1-\tau_1>0$, $p_0>0$, $p_1>0$ and $r_1>0$. Since household 2 supplies no labor services, $\sigma_{01}^2=\sigma_{00}^2=\sigma_{11}^2=0$ [and thus $\sigma=\sigma^1$ where σ is the aggregate consumer substitution matrix defined by (13) and σ^1 is the laborer's substitution matrix], $\eta_1^2=0$, and from (17) $\eta_0^2=1/(p_0(1+t_0)$. We also have $\Pi_{01}=-p_1\Pi_{11}/p_0$ and $v_1^2\gamma_{11}=y_1$ using (5) and (8) again. Finally, from (12) and (13), $\sigma_{00}=-p_1(1+t_1)\sigma_{01}/p_0(1+t_0)$ and $\sigma_{11}=-p_0(1+t_0)\sigma_{01}/p_1(1+t_1)$. If we substitute these relations and (72) into (25) when $H=2$, $N=1$ and $M=1$, add $p_0(1+t_0)/p_1(1+t_1)$ times the third row of (25) to the fourth row, we find that (25) is equivalent to the following system of equations:

$$\begin{bmatrix} 1, & 0, & (1+t_1)x_1^1, & p_1x_1^1 \\ 0, & 1, & -(1-\tau_1)y_1, & 0 \\ \eta_0^1, & p_0^{-1}(1+t_0)^{-1}, & (1+t_1)\sigma_{01}^1+p_0^{-1}p_1\Pi_{11}, & p_1\sigma_{01}^1 \\ p_1^{-1}(1+t_1)^{-1}, & p_1^{-1}(1+t_1)^{-1}, & (t_0-t_1)(1+t_1)^{-1}\Pi_{11}, & 0 \end{bmatrix}$$

$$\times \begin{bmatrix} \Delta u^1 \\ \Delta u^2 \\ \Delta p_1 \\ \Delta t_1 \end{bmatrix} = \begin{bmatrix} (1+t_1)p_1x_1^1, & 0 \\ -(1-\tau_1)v_1^2r_1, & -v_1^2r_1 \\ (1+t_1)p_1\sigma_{01}^1, & 0 \\ 0, & 0 \end{bmatrix} \begin{bmatrix} \dfrac{\Delta t_0}{1+t_0} \\ \Delta\tau_1 \end{bmatrix}. \tag{76}$$

We assume that the coefficient matrix on the left-hand side of (76) has an inverse, i.e. we assume that the determinant D^* of this matrix is nonzero. Evaluating the determinant, we find that

$$D^* = D+(1+t_1)^{-1}(1-\tau_1)y_1x_1^1(\eta_0^1-\eta_0^2) \neq 0, \tag{77}$$

where D is defined by (63) (remember $\sigma_{01}^1 = \sigma_{01}$) and $\eta_0^2 \equiv p_0^{-1}(1+t_0)^{-1}$.

The Implicit Function Theorem and Cramer's Rule allow us to evaluate the partial derivatives of u^1 and u^2 with respect to the independent tax rates t_0 and τ_1 at the initial equilibrium point:

$$\frac{\partial u^1}{\partial t_0} = \frac{p_1x_1^1(1-\tau_1)v_1^2r_1\Pi_{11}}{p_0(1+t_0)(1+t_1)D^*}\left\{\frac{t_0-t_1}{1+t_0}-1\right\} = \frac{1-\tau_1}{1+t_0}\frac{\partial u^1}{\partial \tau_1}, \tag{78}$$

$$\frac{\partial u^2}{\partial t_0} = \frac{-(1-\tau_1)v_1^2r_1p_1\Pi_{11}}{(1+t_0)(1+t_1)D^*}\{(t_0-t_1)(\eta_0^1x_1^1-\sigma_{01}^1)-p_0^{-1}x_1^1\}$$

$$= \frac{1-\tau_1}{1+t_0}\frac{\partial u^2}{\partial \tau_1}, \tag{79}$$

where D^* is defined by (77).

Proposition 11. Let $H = 2$, $N = 1$, $M = 1$, make the assumptions listed below (75), assume that there are no restrictions on changing tax rates, let t_1 be the endogenous tax rate, and assume (77). Then a sufficient condition for the existence of a strict Pareto improving tax change is

$$\Pi_{11}\{(t_0-t_1)(\sigma_{01}^1-x_1^1\eta_0^1)+p_0^{-1}x_1^1\} > 0. \tag{80}$$

Proof. Since $(t_0-t_1)(1+t_0)^{-1}-1 = -(1+t_1)/(1+t_0) < 0$, $(1-\tau_1) > 0$, $p_1x_1^1 < 0$, $v_1^2r_1 > 0$, it can be seen from (78) that $\partial u^1/\partial t_0$ and $\partial u^1/\partial \tau_1$ have the sign of Π_{11}/D^* where $\Pi_{11} \geqq 0$. If (80) is satisfied then $\Pi_{11} > 0$, and from (79) $\partial u^2/\partial t_0$ and $\partial u^2/\partial \tau_1$ have the sign of Π_{11}/D^* also.

Q.E.D.

Corollary 11.1. If $D^* > 0$ ($D^* < 0$) and (80) holds, then the real incomes of both the laborer and the capitalist can be increased by increasing (decreasing) ***either*** the tax on the consumption good t_0 ***or*** the tax on the fixed factor τ_1.

Corollary 11.2. Under the above hypothesis, a necessary condition for the initial system of taxes to be Pareto optimal is the negation of (80):

$$\Pi_{11}\{(t_0-t_1)(\sigma_{01}^1-x_1^1\eta_0^1)+p_0^{-1}x_1^1\} \leqq 0. \tag{81}$$

Note that (81) is satisfied if $\Pi_{11}=0$ or if $t_0=t_1$ since $-p_0^{-1}x_1^1>0$. We also note that Proposition 11 and Corollary 11.2 can be proven using our general criteria (36) and (38), respectively, applied to (76). However, this latter approach does not allow us to obtain Corollary 11.1, which explains why we have used the present rather inelegant approach involving Cramer's Rule.

In order to provide an economic interpretation for (80) and (81), we need some additional facts and formulae. Denote the laborer's market demand function for good 0 as $d_0^1(y^1,q_0,q_1)$ and (minus) his supply of labor function as $d_1^1(y^1,q_0,q_1)$, where $y^1\equiv 0$ denotes his nonlabor income. Then, using footnote 10, the response of the laborer's demand for the consumer good to an increase in the after tax wage rate is $\partial d_0^1(y^1,q_0,q_1)/\partial q_1=\sigma_{01}^1-x_1^1\eta_0^1$ while the response of his supply of labor to an increase in the after tax wage rate is

$$\partial d_1^1(y^1,q_0,q_1)/\partial q_1=\sigma_{11}^1-x_1^1\eta_1^1 = -\{\sigma_{01}^1-x_1^1\eta_0^1+q_0^{-1}x_1^1\}q_0/q_1$$

where the second equality follows using the restrictions $0=\sigma_{11}^1q_1+\sigma_{01}^1q_0=0$ and $1=q_0\eta_0^1+q_1\eta_1^1$. If $\partial d_1^1/\partial q_1<0$, then work effort increases (becomes more negative) as the after tax wage rate, q_1, increases. If $\partial d_1^1/\partial q_1\neq 0$, then the slope of the worker's *offer curve* is

$$\frac{\partial d_0^1}{\partial q_1}\bigg/\frac{\partial d_1^1}{\partial q_1} = -\frac{p_1(1+t_1)(\sigma_{01}^1-x_1^1\eta_0^1)}{p_0(1+t_0)\{\sigma_{01}^1-x_1^1\eta_0^1+x_1^1/p_0(1+t_0)\}}. \tag{82}$$

Using Cramer's Rule and (76) we find that

$$\begin{aligned}\frac{\partial p_1}{\partial \tau_1} &= -\frac{v_1^2 r_1}{(1+t_1)D^*}\{\sigma_{01}^1-x_1^1\eta_0^1+x_1^1/p_0(1+t_0)\} \\ &= \frac{v_1^2 r_1 p_1}{p_0(1+t_0)D^*}\frac{\partial d_1^1}{\partial q_1} \qquad (83)\end{aligned}$$

where D^* is defined by (77). Finally, rewriting (78) we have

$$\partial u^1/\partial \tau_1 = p_1(-x_1^1)v_1^2 r_1 \Pi_{11}/p_0(1+t_0)D^*. \tag{84}$$

Thus, from (84) it can be seen that the sign of $\partial u^1/\partial \tau_1$ is equal to the sign of D^* if $\Pi_{11} > 0$ and from (83) if $\partial d_1^1/\partial q_1 < 0$, then the sign of $\partial p_1/\partial \tau_1$ is opposite to the sign of D^*.

The geometry of Proposition 11 is illustrated in fig. 3. AO represents the before tax and CD represents the after production frontier as usual while the

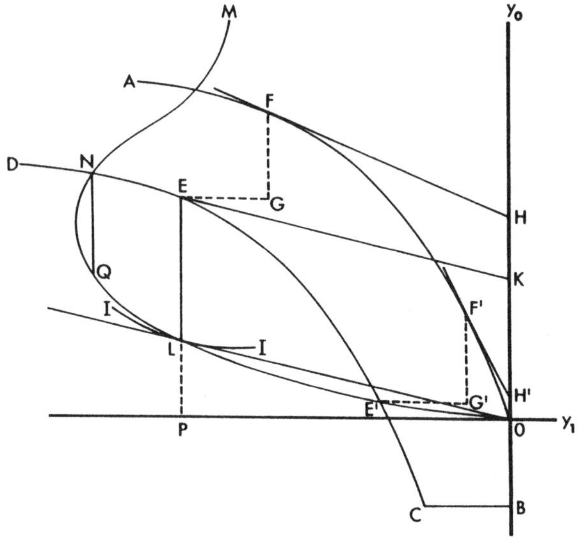

Fig. 3. Geometry of a two person economy.

curve OM represents the worker's offer curve. The price line OL is tangential to the consumer–worker's indifference curve I–I at the point L, where the worker consumes LP units of the consumption good y_0 and offers OP units of labor service. The capitalists' consumption turns out to be EL, the vertical distance between the after tax production frontier and the point L on the worker's offer curve. As in the previous section, we have $OK/OH = (1-\tau_1)/(1+t_0)$ where τ_1 is the fixed factor tax rate and t_0 is the consumption good tax rate at the L, E, F equilibrium. However, many other equilibria are possible. At the point E', the consumer–worker is taxed very heavily (i.e. $p_1/p_0 > q_1/q_0$ or equivalently, $t_0 - t_1 > 0$) so he works little, produces little and consumes little while the capitalist ends up consuming nothing, since $\tau_1 = 1$ at this E', F' equilibrium [here $K' \equiv 0$, so $OK'/OH' = (1-\tau_1)/(1+t_0) = 0$

which implies $\tau_1 = 1$]. As we move up the after tax production frontier to the point E, p_1/p_0 decreases, q_1/q_0 increases and the consumer–worker's utility increases as he moves up his offer curve to L, while τ_1 decreases and the capitalist's consumption increases to EL. As we move from E to N, the worker's utility continues to increase, but now the capitalist's consumption decreases to NQ.

All of this is consistent with the algebra developed above. We have $\partial d_1^1/\partial q_1 < 0$ and $\partial d_0^1/\partial q_1 > 0$ for any point on the worker's offer curve between E' and Q. Since the equilibrium p_1 and τ_1 both decrease as we move from E' to Q, from (83) and $\partial d_1^1/\partial q_1 < 0$, we see that D^* is negative along this range, and thus from (84) u^1 increases as τ_1 decreases.

It is obvious from fig. 3 that the capitalist's consumption will be maximal when the worker is at point L where the slope of the worker's offer curve is equal to the slope of the after tax production frontier at the point E, i.e. we have $(\partial d_0^1/\partial q_1)/(\partial d_1^1/\partial q_1)$ defined by (82) equal to $-p_1/p_0$ when we are at the L, E, F equilibrium. This last equality translates into the equality $(t_0 - t_1)(\sigma_{01}^1 - x_1^1\eta_0^1) + p_0^{-1}x_1^1 = 0$, which is consistent with the inequality (81). On the other hand, when the equilibrium is between E' and L the slope of the after tax production frontier $-p_1/p_0$ is more negative (or steeper) than the slope of the worker's offer curve. Since $\partial d_1^1/\partial q_1 < 0$, this inequality translates into $(t_0 - t_1)(\sigma_{01}^1 - x_1^1\eta_0^1) + p_0^{-1}x_1^1 > 0$, which is consistent with (80). Thus, if the economy's initial equilibrium is between E' and L, the utilities of both the worker and the capitalist can be increased by *either* decreasing the tax on the consumer good *or* by decreasing the tax on the fixed factor [see (84), (78) and (79) and remember that $D^* < 0$ and (80) holds].

Thus, if labor taxes are sufficiently large in magnitude (i.e. $-1 < t_1 < 0$ and t_1 large in absolute value), or if consumption taxes are sufficiently large (i.e. $t_0 > 0$ and large), $\Pi_{11} > 0$ so that there is some substitutability in production, and the laborer's demand for the consumer good increases sufficiently in response to an increase in his after tax wage rate (i.e. $\sigma_{01}^1 - x_1^1\eta_0^1 > 0$), then (80) will be satisfied and the real income of both classes of consumers can be increased by changes in government tax policy.

The above model is too simple to have an immediate empirical application but it does suggest that it is not implausible that strict Pareto improving tax changes exist for real life economies, especially those where labor income is heavily taxed.

8. Concluding remarks

We have not indicated explicitly how the *balanced budget incidence* of a change in a pair of taxes can be calculated, but it should be obvious: in eqs. (25), set all but *two* of the tax changes $\Delta t_0, \Delta t_1, \ldots, \Delta t_N, \Delta t_1, \ldots, \Delta t_M$ equal to zero and then simply solve the resulting system of equations for Δu, Δp and one of the nonzero tax changes in terms of the other nonzero tax change. This can be done if the appropriate coefficient matrix is nonsingular. Thus, our model can be viewed as an extension of the line of research pioneered by Harberger (1962) and extended by Mieszkowski (1969), Ballentine and Eris (1975), McClure (1975), Keller (1975) and Vandendorpe and Friedlaender (1976). The typical commodity incidence analysis [cf. McClure (1975, p. 137)] calculates changes in relative or nominal commodity prices due to a change in tax and expenditure policies that maintain a balanced budget [e.g. recall equations (66) and (67)]. Our analysis can be described as *differential real income balanced budget incidence analysis*: we derive not only the induced changes in commodity prices but we also derive directly the induced changes in utility of each household or consumer group in the economy [e.g. see eqs. (64) and (65) or (78) and (79)]. It should be mentioned, however, that these induced changes in utility and prices are, strictly speaking, valid only for infinitesimal changes in the exogenous tax variables. The question of how good are our formulae when infinitesimal changes in taxes are replaced by finite tax changes has been extensively discussed by Shoven and Whalley (1972), (1973), Whalley (1975) and Shoven (1976) in the context of several specific models. However, it should be noted that our comparative statics approach has some advantages of the more rigorous 'global' approach of Shoven and Whalley: (i) our 'local' approach is computationally simpler and (ii) we require only local information on preferences and technology – a decided advantage from an empirical point of view.[38]

There are some additional limitations of our analysis: (i) there is no foreign trade in our model, (ii) there is no optimization with respect to government expenditures (e.g. on public good production), (iii) there is no monopolistic behavior in our model,[39] and (iv) the complications of modeling a growing economy (savings and investment behavior) have been ignored. The first three limitations can be rectified, at least in theory, but the fourth limitation is a serious one. Some research on this last problem has been done by Diamond (1970), Dixit (1976), and Feldstein (1977). However, serious difficulties remain: it is difficult to define optimality in a Hicksian [Hicks (1946)] temporary equilibrium model where markets are incomplete.

It seems likely that the general equilibrium techniques outlined in sections 3–5 above will prove to be useful in more realistic models. In particular, the reader should note the computational advantages which occur when we use

[38]It is not difficult to use existing econometric techniques in order to estimate consumer preferences in a mannaer consistent with the normalizations (14); see Berndt, Darrough and Diewert (1977) for example. We note that the partial derivatives of the expenditure function can be calculated from a knowledge of the partial derivatives of the corresponding direct or indirect utility function; see Blackorby and Diewert (1978). Existing econometric techniques can also be used in order to estimate variable profit functions; for references see Diewert (1978).

[39]In an unpublished paper Guesnerie relaxes this limitation.

the alternative criteria for optimality which were derived using Theorems of the Alternative, i.e. it is often easier to check conditions (36) rather than (35).

To conclude: we have shown that it is quite easy to obtain sufficient conditions for (small) Pareto improving tax changes, and perhaps these conditions will prove to be more useful in practice than the necessary conditions for optimality which are prevalent in the literature.[40]

[40]This point has been made by Dixit (1975) and Hatta (1977).

References

Atkinson, A.B. and N.H. Stern, 1974, Pigou, taxation and public goods, Review of Economic Studies 41, 119–128.

Atkinson, A.B. and J.E. Stiglitz, 1972, The structure of indirect taxation and economic efficiency, Journal of Public Economics 1, 97–119.

Ballentine, J.G. and I. Eris, 1975, On the general equilibrium analysis of tax incidence, Journal of Political Economy 83, 633–644.

Berndt, E.R., M.N. Darrough and W.E. Diewert, 1977, Flexible functional forms and expenditure distributions: an application to Canadian consumer demand functions, International Economic Review 18, 651–675.

Blackorby, C. and W.E. Diewert, 1978, Expenditure functions, local duality and second order approximations, Econometrica (forthcoming).

Blackorby, C., D. Primont and R.R. Russell, 1978, Duality, separability and functional structure: Theory and economic applications (American Elsevier, New York).

Cass, D., 1974, Duality: A symmetric approach from the economist's vantage point, Journal of Economic Theory 7, 272–295.

Corlett, W.J. and D.C. Hague, 1953–54, Complementarity and the excess burden of taxation, Review of Economic Studies 21, 21–30.

Dasgupta, P. and J. Stiglitz, 1972, On optimal taxation and public production, Review of Economic Studies 39, 87–104.

Diamond, P., 1970, Taxation and public production in a growth setting, unpublished paper, Department of Economics, Massachusetts Institute of Technology, Cambridge, Massachusetts.

Diamond, P.A., 1975, A many-person Ramsey tax rule, Journal of Public Economics 4, 335–342.

Diamond, P.A. and D.L. McFadden, 1974, Some uses of the expenditure function in public finance, Journal of Public Economics 3, 3–22.

Diamond, P.A. and J.A. Mirrlees, 1971, Optimal taxation and public production I–II, American Economic Review 61, 8–27, 261–278.

Diewert, W.E., 1973, Functional forms for profit and transformation functions, Journal of Economic Theory 3, 284–316.

Diewert, W.E., 1974, Applications of duality theory, in: M.D. Intriligator and D.A. Kendrick, eds., Frontiers of quantitative economics, vol. II (North-Holland, Amsterdam).

Diewert, W.E., 1978, Duality approaches to microeconomic theory, Discussion Paper 78-09, Department of Economics, University of British Columbia, Vancouver, March.

Diewert, W.E. and A.D. Woodland, 1977, Frank Knight's theorem in linear programming revisited, Econometrica 45, 375–398.

Dixit, A., 1975, Welfare effects of tax and price changes, Journal of Public Economics 4, 103–124.

Dixit, A., 1976, Public finance in a Keynesian temporary equilibrium, Journal of Economic Theory 12, 242–258.

Dixit, A.K., 1977, Price changes and optimum taxation in a many-consumer economy, University of Warwick, October.

Feldstein, M., 1976, On the theory of tax reform, Journal of Public Economics 6, 77–104.

Feldstein, M., 1977, The surprising incidence of a tax on pure rent: A new answer to an old question, Journal of Political Economy 85, 349–360.
Gorman, W.M., 1968, Measuring the quantities of fixed factors, in: J.N. Wolfe, ed., Value, capital and growth: Papers in honour of Sir John Hicks (Aldine, Chicago).
Guesnerie, R., 1977, On the direction of tax reform, Journal of Public Economics 7, 179–202.
Hahn, F.H., 1973, On optimum taxation, Journal of Economic Theory 6, 96–106.
Harberger, A.C., 1962, The incidence of the corporate income tax, Journal of Political Economy 70, 215–240.
Harris, R., 1975, A note on convex-concave demand systems with an application to the theory of optimal taxation, unpublished paper, Department of Economics, Queen's University, Kingston, Canada.
Harris, R., 1978, Efficient commodity taxation, Journal of Public Economics, forthcoming.
Hatta, T., 1977, A theory of piecemeal policy recommendations, The Review of Economic Studies 44, 1–22.
Hicks, J.R., 1946, Value and capital, 2nd edn. (Clarendon Press, Oxford).
Hotelling, H., 1932, Edgeworth's taxation paradox and the nature of demand and supply functions, Journal of Political Economy 40, 577–616.
Keller, W.J., 1975, Tax incidence and general equilibrium: I, II and III, unpublished papers, Erasmus University, Rotterdam.
Lau, L.J., 1976, A characterization of the normalized restricted profit function, Journal of Economic Theory 12, 131–164.
Mangasarian, O.L., 1969, Nonlinear programming (McGraw-Hill, New York).
McLure, C.E. Jr., 1975, General equilibrium incidence analysis: The Harberger model after ten years, Journal of Public Economics 4, 125–162.
McFadden, D., 1970, Cost, revenue and profit functions, unpublished paper, Department of Economics, University of California, Berkeley.
McKenzie, L., 1959, On the existence of general equilibrium for a competitive market, Econometrica 27, 54–71.
Meade, J.E., 1955, Trade and welfare (Oxford University Press, London).
Mieszkowski, P.M., 1969, Tax incidence theory: The effects of taxes on the distribution of income, Journal of Economic Literature 7, 1103–1124.
Mirrlees, J.A., 1975, Optimal commodity taxation in a two-class economy, Journal of Public Economics 4, 27–83.
Mirrlees, J.A., 1976, Optimal Tax theory: A synthesis, Journal of Public Economics 6, 327–358.
Munk, K.J., 1976, A note on optimal taxation and public sector pricing, Discussion Paper 84, Department of Economics, University of Essex, June.
Sadka, E., 1977, A theorem on uniform taxation, Journal of Public Economics 7, 387–392.
Samuelson, P.A., 1953–54, Prices of factors and goods in general equilibrium, Review of Economic Studies 21, 1–20.
Samuelson, P.A., 1974, Complementarity – an essay on the 40th anniversary of the Hicks–Allen revolution in demand theory, The Journal of Economic Literature 12, 1255–1289.
Sandmo, A., 1976, Optimal taxation: An introduction to the literature, Journal of Public Economics 6, 37–54.
Shephard, R.W., 1953, Cost and production functions (Princeton University Press, Princeton, N.J.).
Shephard, R.W., 1970, Theory of cost and production functions (Princeton University Press, Princeton, N.J.).
Shoven, J.B., 1976, The incidence and efficiency effects of taxes on income from capital, Journal of Political Economy 84, 1261–1284.
Shoven, J.B. and J. Whalley, 1972, A general equilibrium calculation of the effects of differential taxation of income from capital in the U.S., Journal of Public Economics 1, 281–321.
Shoven, J.B. and J. Whalley, 1973, General equilibrium with taxes: A computational procedure and an existence proof, The Review of Economic Studies 60, 475–589.
Stiglitz, J.E. and P. Dasgupta, 1971, Differential taxation, public goods, and economic efficiency, Review of Economic Studies 38, 151–174.
Tinbergen, J., 1952, On the theory of economic policy (North-Holland, Amsterdam).

Vandendorpe, A.L. and A.F. Friedlaender, 1976, Differential incidence in the presence of initial distorting taxes, Journal of Public Economics 6, 205–230.
Weymark, J.A., 1976, Production efficiency in the absence of lump sum taxation, Department of Economics, University of Pennsylvania, Philadelphia, June.
Weymark, J.A., 1978, A reconciliation of recent results in optimal taxation theory, Department of Economics, Duke University, Durham, North Carolina, February.
Whalley, J., 1975, How reliable is partial equilibrium analysis?, The Review of Economics and Statistics 51, 299–310.

[30]

A RECONCILIATION OF RECENT RESULTS IN OPTIMAL TAXATION THEORY

John A. WEYMARK*

Duke University, Durham, NC 27706, USA

Received February 1978, revised version received July 1979

The recent papers by Guesnerie and Diewert on tax reforms are interpreted as contributions to the characterization of second-best optima. This paper demonstrates that when it is possible to achieve any feasible direction of change in supplies by a differential change in producer prices, there are unique producer support prices. Under these circumstances, the apparent differences between Guesnerie and Diewert are reconciled. Optimality conditions with nonunique support prices are also considered.

1. Introduction

One of the major concerns of optimal taxation theory is the presentation of conditions which characterize the Pareto optimal states of an economy which must operate with a limited set of tax instruments. Recently Diewert (1978) and Guesnerie (1977) have addressed themselves to the slightly different problem of analyzing tax reform proposals. Weymark (1978b) provides further results on tax reform. Diewert and Guesnerie consider whether it is possible to propose a set of marginal changes in the tax instruments so as to achieve a Pareto improvement. Necessary conditions for the nonexistence of Pareto-improving tax changes are necessary conditions for the initial allocation to be Pareto optimal. Consequently, it is possible to consider this aspect of Diewert's and Guesnerie's contributions in terms of the more traditional approach of characterizing optima.

Unfortunately, it is difficult to see the relationship between the conditions developed by Diewert and Guesnerie. To correspond with Guesnerie's model, Diewert's problem must be reformulated by replacing his ad valorem commodity taxes by specific taxes, by fixing profit tax rates at 100%, and by replacing compensated demand functions with ordinary demand functions.

*I have benefited from conversations with W.E. Diewert and R.A. Jones as well as written comments from A.K. Dixit, R. Guesnerie, and an editor of this *Journal*. I am particularly indebted to A.K. Dixit for suggestions which have simplified the presentation. Much of the research was carried out while visiting at the University of British Columbia.

However, applying Diewert's techniques to this respecified model yields conditions which appear to depend upon the derivatives of the aggregate supply function. This seems to contradict Guesnerie's conclusions, since his conditions do not contain terms of this sort. The main purpose of this paper is to reconcile this apparent difference.

In section 2 necessary conditions for second-best optimality are developed for an economy with specific commodity taxes and 100% profit taxation. These optimality conditions do not employ supply derivatives. Furthermore, the criteria derived in this section reduce to Guesnerie's results when it is assumed that the production vector has a unique support price. When this is the case, any feasible direction of change in supplies can be achieved by a differential change in producer prices, there is local controllability of the production sector. If the support prices are not unique, finite changes in producer prices are required to induce supply changes in some feasible directions.

In section 3, following Diewert (1978), feasible changes in supply are modelled by a linear approximation to the supply function at the initial prices. To use this technique only differential changes in the control variables can be considered, with the resulting criteria containing explicit reference to supply derivatives. However, when there are unique support prices this technique yields conditions identical to those found in section 2.

Section 4 briefly considers variable profit taxation. Dixit (1979) investigates this topic in some detail. The results of this section support the general conclusion that optimality conditions can be expressed without reference to supply derivatives if there is local controllability of the production sector, even if the optimality conditions are derived for differential changes in the control variables.

Section 5 presents conclusions. An appendix summarizes results on convex cones which are used in the text.

2. Second-best optimality

2.1. Statement of the problem

Given the preferences of consumers, the technologies of firms, and initial resource endowments, one of the central concerns of welfare economics is the establishment of conditions which characterize the Pareto optimal states of an economy. This characterization will, of course, depend upon the set of feasible allocations. In the first-best model an allocation is feasible if each consumption bundle belongs to the appropriate consumption set, each production plan is technically feasible, and the allocation satisfies a materials balance constraint. There is *no* requirement that consumer or firm decisions must be decentralized.

In the second-best literature some further constraints are imposed on the set of feasible allocations. In optimal taxation problems these constraints take the form of a requirement that private decision-making be decentralized and by a specification of the limited tax instruments available to the government.

The consumer sector consist of H households, indexed by $h=1,\ldots,H$, each with continuous strictly quasiconcave monotone utility functions $u^h=u^h(x^h)$, where x^h is an n-dimensional *net* consumption vector. The (net) consumption sets X^h are convex and bounded from below. Let $x=\Sigma_h x^h$ and $\hat{x}=(x_1,\ldots,x_H)$.

There are F private firms, indexed by $f=1,\ldots,F$, plus a government production sector indexed by $f=F+1$. Individual production possibilities sets Y_f contain typical elements y^f. It is assumed that these sets are closed, convex, contain the origin, and satisfy free disposability. Let $Y_P=\Sigma_{f=1}^F Y_f$ and $Y=Y_P+Y_{F+1}$. Y is assumed to be irreversible, i.e. $Y\cap(-Y)=\{0\}$.

The first-best problem may now be stated. Partially order by the Pareto criterion the set of all $\hat{x}\in c^1$ where

$$c^1=\{\hat{x}|x\in Y \quad \text{and} \quad x^h\in X_h \quad \text{for all} \quad h\}. \tag{1}$$

No behavioural constraints appear in c^1.

In the second-best problem considered in this section the additional constraints correspond to Guesnerie's (1977) model which in turn is based upon Diamond and Mirrlees (1971). All private decisions must be decentralized with all private firms behaving competitively. The government may use per unit (specific) commodity taxes and is required to use 100% profit taxation. Accordingly, consumers' incomes do not depend upon producers' prices. There is no lump-sum income.

Consumer prices are $q=(q_1,\ldots,q_n)^{\mathrm{T}}$, producer prices are $p=(p_1,\ldots,p_n)^{\mathrm{T}}$, and commodity taxes are $t=(t_1,\ldots,t_n)^{\mathrm{T}}$ with $p+t=q$. To simplify the exposition, boundary problems are avoided by assuming that $q\gg 0$ and $p\gg 0$.[1] Throughout, p and q will be used as control variables with t defined implicitly.

Consumer net demand functions are $x^h(q)$ which are assumed to be continuously differentiable. The indirect utility functions are $v^h(q)=u^h(x^h(q))$. One can easily demonstrate that each $v^h(q)$ is continuous, locally nonsatiated, quasiconvex, and homogeneous of degree zero in q. Differentiability of each $v^h(q)$ is assumed. Firm supply correspondences are denoted $y^f(p)$.

Using the Pareto criterion, the solution to the second-best problem is a partial ordering of the set of all $\hat{x}\in c^2$ where

[1]All vectors are column vectors unless superscripted with a transpose operator, T. Notation: $b\gg 0$ means $b_i>0$ for all i, $b>0$ means $b_i\geqq 0$ for all i with $b\neq 0$, and $b\geqq 0$ means $b_i\geqq 0$ for all i.

$$c^2 = \{\hat{x} | x \leqq y,\ y^f \in y^f(p) \text{ for some } p \text{ and, for that } p, \text{ for all } f = 1, \ldots, F,\ y^{F+1} \in Y_{F+1}, \text{ and } \hat{x} = \hat{x}(q) \text{ for some } q\}. \quad (2)$$

By construction all households face the same prices so there will be equality of marginal rates of substitution. Similarly, all *private* firms face common prices so production is on the frontier of Y_P (equality of marginal rates of transformation). However, in general $t \neq 0$ so the marginal rates of substitution do not equal the marginal rates of transformation.

2.2. *Production efficiency*

One of the major questions considered by the optimal taxation literature is whether it is desirable (i.e. whether it is a property of maximal elements of the Pareto partial ordering) for the government sector to determine its production vector so as to equate its marginal rates of transformation with those of the private sector. In other words, is aggregate production efficiency desirable? Given the assumptions on Y_{F+1} this is equivalent to asking if public production managers should act as profit maximizers with shadow prices equal to p.

To answer this question the concept of Pareto-improving (consumer) price changes is introduced.

Definition. For $\hat{x}(q)$, γ is a strictly Pareto-improving direction of (differential) price changes if and only if $\nabla v^h(q)^{\mathrm{T}}\gamma > 0$ for all h.

The use of strict Pareto improvements follows Diewert (1978) and Guesnerie (1977).[2] Employing the gradient vectors of the indirect utility functions in the evaluation of price changes involves the use of first-order approximations; when $\nabla v^h(q) \neq 0$ this is of negligible significance.[3] When $\nabla v^h(q) = 0$ the use of gradient vectors is inappropriate since any small finite change in prices makes the consumer better off while for differential changes no improvement is possible. Except for theorem 2, where it is unavoidable, zero gradients are excluded from consideration.

Now consider $\hat{x}(q^*)$, a Pareto optimal allocation, with corresponding aggregate net demand vector $x(q^*)$. Diamond and Mirrlees (1971) provided a methodology for determining whether $x(q^*)$ is on the frontier of Y. Suppose the contrary, $x(q^*) \in \operatorname{int} Y$, the interior of Y. If at $\hat{x}(q^*)$ there exists a strictly Pareto-improving direction of price changes, the induced change in demands

[2]Finite weak Pareto-improving changes are considered in Weymark (1978a).

[3]With $v^h(q)$ quasiconvex, if $\nabla v^h(q)^{\mathrm{T}}\gamma > 0$ then for all finite changes in the direction γ of sufficiently small magnitude the consumer is made better off while if $\nabla v^h(q)^{\mathrm{T}}\gamma = 0$ then for small finite changes in the direction γ the consumer is no worse off (and could be better off). Matthews (1978) considers the relationship between differential and small finite changes in some detail.

will be feasible (since $x(q^*) \in \text{int}\, Y$) which contradicts the assumption that $\hat{x}(q^*)$ is Pareto optimal.[4] Thus, $x(q^*)$ must be on the frontier of Y. Hence, if for all $\hat{x}(q)$ in c^2 it is possible to find a strictly Pareto-improving direction of price changes, then aggregate production efficiency is desirable in this second-best problem.

Let $T(q)$ be the set of all vectors orthogonal to q. Ignoring non-negativity constraints, for all consumers $T(q)$ is the net demands budget hyperplane. Since the demand functions are homogeneous of degree zero in prices, all price changes could be restricted to be orthogonal to q. Thus, $T(q)$ can also be viewed as the set of all possible directions of price changes. In fig. 1 the

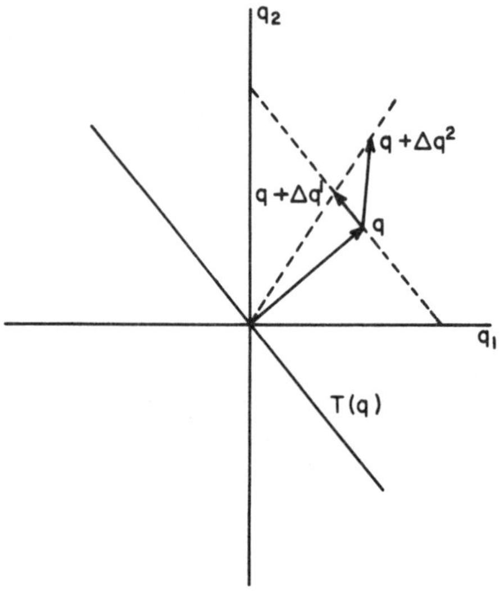

Fig. 1. The normalization procedure for price changes.

change in prices from q to $q+\Delta q^2$ results in the same demand behaviour as the change from q to $q+\Delta q^1$, where $\Delta q^1 \in T(q)$. Since only differential changes in prices are considered and $q \gg 0$, there is no need explicitly to consider non-negativity constraints. Henceforth all directions of change in consumer prices will be elements of $T(q)$.

Define

$$\Lambda(q)=\left\{\Lambda \middle| \Lambda=\sum_h \lambda_h x^h(q) \quad \text{for} \quad \lambda_h \geqq 0\right\}. \tag{3}$$

[4]By a suitable choice of p it is possible to induce private firms to produce any supply vector on the frontier of Y_p.

$\Lambda(q)$ is the cone generated by the net demand vectors and is contained in $T(q)$. Using Roy's Identity, $\nabla v^h(q)$ is proportional to $-x^h(q)$ so $-\Lambda(q)$ is the cone generated by the gradient vectors.

Let

$$P(q)=\{\gamma|\gamma\in T(q) \quad \text{and} \quad \Lambda^{\mathrm{T}}\gamma\leqq 0 \quad \text{for all} \quad \Lambda\in\Lambda(q)\}. \tag{4}$$

$P(q)$ is the negative polar cone to $\Lambda(q)$ (the positive polar cone to $-\Lambda(q)$).

Figure 2 illustrates these sets for the two-consumer three-good case. $T(q)$ is a plane which has been rotated to be coincident with the page. $\Lambda(q)$ is formed by drawing the rays from the origin through $x^1(q)$ and $x^2(q)$ and then taking all convex combinations of points on these rays. $P(q)$ is the intersection of the halfspace normal to $x^1(q)$ (which does not contain $x^1(q)$) with the corresponding halfspace for $x^2(q)$.

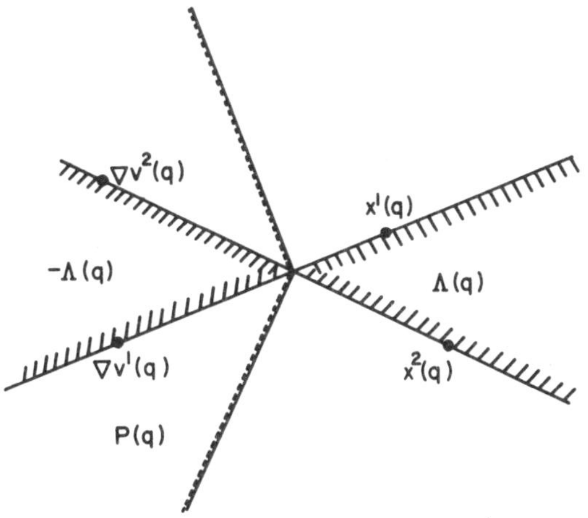

Fig. 2. Geometry of the two-person, three-good case.

Theorem 1. For $\hat{x}(q)$ with $x^h(q)\neq 0$ for all h, the set of directions of strictly Pareto-improving differential price changes is int $P(q)$[5] *which is nonempty iff $\Lambda(q)$ is pointed.*

Proof. The theorem is a trivial application of theorem A.1 and the corollary to theorem A.2 found in the appendix.

Since $P(q)$ is the positive polar cone to the cone generated by the gradient

[5]int $P(q)$ is the interior of $P(q)$ relative to $T(q)$.

vectors, it is intuitively clear that $\operatorname{int} P(q)$ is the set of Pareto-improving directions of price changes. An alternative interpretation of this result is provided by the fact that $P(q)$ is the negative polar cone to $\Lambda(q)$; $\operatorname{int} P(q)$ is the set of directions of price changes which reduce the value of all households' net demands.

Intuitively, if $\Lambda(q)$ is pointed there is some Hicksian composite good in net demand (or net supply) by all households. Lowering (raising) its 'price' makes all households better off. This generalizes the condition found in Diamond and Mirrlees (1971) that there be some good in net demand (or net supply) by all households. Guesnerie (1977) assumes that the Diamond and Mirrlees condition holds for all goods.

Returning to the efficiency question, the previous remarks may be summarized in the following theorem.

Theorem 2. If $\Lambda(q)$ is pointed for all q, then production efficiency is desirable.[6]

2.3. Motzkin's Theorem

As in Diewert (1978) optimality conditions are developed using Motzkin's Theorem of the Alternative. A theorem of the alternative states that either a system of homogeneous linear equations has a solution or, if not, a related system of inequalities does have a solution.

Motzkin's Theorem.[7] *For two matrices E and F containing the same number of columns, exactly one of the following holds:*

$$\exists b \text{ s.t. } Eb \geqq 0 \text{ and } Fb \gg 0, \quad \text{with } F \neq 0. \tag{5}$$

$$\exists w \text{ and } \exists \tilde{w} \text{ s.t. } w^{\mathrm{T}}E + \tilde{w}^{\mathrm{T}}F = 0^{\mathrm{T}}, \text{ with } w \geqq 0, \tilde{w} > 0. \tag{6}$$

The use of this theorem can be illustrated by reconsidering the existence of Pareto-improving price changes.

The (net) expenditure function for household h is defined as

$$m^h(u^h, q) = \min_{x^h} \{qx^h | u^h(x^h) \geqq u^h, x^h \in X_h\}. \tag{7}$$

[6]To rigorously establish theorem 2 it must be demonstrated that when $\Lambda(q)$ is pointed it is possible to make local Pareto improvements even if some $x^h(q)=0$. The conclusions of theorem 1 remain valid for $\hat{x}(q)$ with $x^h(q)=0$ for some h if attention is restricted to consumers with nonzero demands. Noting that $\nabla v^h(q)=0$ when $x^h(q)=0$, the earlier discussion suggested that any change in prices can be considered to be an improvement for this consumer.

[7]This is a special case of Motzkin's theorem. A closely related proposition is Tucker's theorem which has $Fb>0$ in (5) and $\tilde{w} \gg 0$ in (6). Tucker's theorem would be used to study weak Pareto-improving changes. Both theorems are discussed in Mangasarian (1969).

It is assumed that $m^h(u^h, q)$ is twice continuously differentiable. Use will be made of the fact that the compensated net demand functions are

$$x_i^h(u^h, q) = \partial m^h(u^h, q)/\partial q_i.$$

Household net expenditure must not exceed zero,

$$m^h(u^h, q) \leqq 0, \qquad h = 1, \ldots, H. \tag{8}$$

If initially (8) holds with equality, for differential changes

$$(-M, -X, 0)\begin{pmatrix} \mathrm{d}u \\ \mathrm{d}q \\ \mathrm{d}p \end{pmatrix} \geqq 0, \tag{9}$$

where M is a diagonal matrix with diagonal entries $\partial m^h/\partial u^h > 0$, X has rows x^{hT}, du is a vector with components du^h, etc. For later use, producer prices have been treated explicitly.

A strict Pareto improvement occurs if

$$(I, 0, 0)\begin{pmatrix} \mathrm{d}u \\ \mathrm{d}q \\ \mathrm{d}p \end{pmatrix} \gg 0, \tag{10}$$

where I is an identity matrix.

If initially (8) holds with equality, strictly Pareto-improving price changes exist if and only if (9) and (10) can be solved simultaneously. Using Motzkin's theorem, this occurs if and only if

$$\nexists (w \geqq 0 \quad \text{and} \quad \tilde{w} > 0) \ \text{ s.t. } \ w^{\mathrm{T}}(M, X, 0) = \tilde{w}^{\mathrm{T}}(I, 0, 0). \tag{11}$$

Since $\partial m^h/\partial u^h > 0$, if (11) has a solution with $\tilde{w} > 0$, then $w \neq 0$. Consequently, Pareto-improving price changes exist if and only if

$$\nexists w > 0 \ \text{ s.t. } \ \sum_h w_h x^h = 0. \tag{12}$$

If $x^h \neq 0$ for all h, by theorem A.3 in the appendix, (12) is equivalent to $\Lambda(q)$ being pointed. This is the result found in theorem 1.

2.4. Optimality conditions

Continuing on the assumption that production efficiency is desirable, it is possible to exhibit further properties of Pareto optimal allocations. The individual profit maximizing decisions of firms and the shadow profit maximizing decision of the government can be replaced by profit maximization on the aggregate production possibilities set Y resulting in the aggregate supply correspondence $y(p)$. The constraint set for the second-best problem may then be rewritten as c^3 where

$$c^3=\{\hat{x}|y\in y(p) \quad \text{for some} \quad p, \hat{x}=\hat{x}(q) \quad \text{for some} \quad q, \quad \text{and} \quad x(q)\leqq y\}. \tag{13}$$

If all production decisions were under central control the constraint set would be c^4:

$$c^4=\{\hat{x}|\hat{x}=\hat{x}(q) \quad \text{for some} \quad q \quad \text{and} \quad x(q)\leqq y \quad \text{for some} \quad y\in Y\}. \tag{14}$$

With this paper's production assumptions, c^3 and c^4 describe the same set of consumption allocations. Given any point on the frontier of Y, the closedness, convexity, and free disposability of Y ensures that there is some price vector that will support the choice of this supply vector. Thus, the requirement that production decisions be decentralized places no additional restriction on the problem if the materials balance constraint is written as a weak inequality.

Consider the net supply vector $y\in y(p)$. Let $\rho(y)$ be the cone of support prices for y. If Y is 'ridged' or 'kinked' at y there will be at least two linearly independent support prices.

Suppose $x(q)$ is a production efficient allocation, i.e. $x(q)=y$ for $y\in y(p)$. Let $\nabla x(q)$ be the matrix of aggregate demand partial derivatives. With $\tilde{p}\in\rho(y)$, $\tilde{p}^{\mathrm{T}}\nabla x(q)\gamma$ represents the cost in terms of these support prices of the demand changes induced by a differential change in consumer prices γ.[8] Let

$$\psi(q)=\{\psi|\psi=\tilde{p}^{\mathrm{T}}\nabla x(q), \tilde{p}\in\rho(y), y=x(q), y\in y(p) \quad \text{for some} \quad p\}. \tag{15}$$

To a first-order approximation

$$Q(q)=\{\gamma|\psi^{\mathrm{T}}\gamma\leqq 0 \quad \text{for all} \quad \psi\in\psi(q), \gamma\in T(q)\} \tag{16}$$

is the set of all directions of consumer price changes which lead to a feasible change in demands. In other words, the value of the demands decreases or remains constant regardless of which support prices are used in the evaluation.

Assuming $\Lambda(q)$ is pointed, from theorem 1 it is known which directions of consumer price changes are strictly Pareto-improving. Now (16) provides the

[8] It is easy to show that $w^{\mathrm{T}}\nabla x(q)\in T(q)$ for any weights w.

directions of consumer price changes which lead to feasible changes in demands. A necessary condition for $\hat{x}(q)$ (with $x^h(q)\neq 0$ for all h) to be Pareto optimal is that these sets have an empty intersection.

Theorem 3. Suppose $\Lambda(q)$ is pointed, $x^h(q)\neq 0$ for all h, $y=x(q)$ where $y\in y(p)$ for some p, and $\rho(y)$ is a polyhedral cone. A necessary condition for $\hat{x}(q)$ to be Pareto optimal is: $\tilde{p}^{\mathrm{T}}\nabla x(q)\in -\Lambda(q)\backslash\{0\}$ for some $\tilde{p}\in\rho(y)$.

Proof. Suppose $Q(q)\cap \operatorname{int} P(q)=\emptyset$. Since $\rho(y)$ is a polyhedral cone, $\rho(y)$ has a finite number of generators $p^g, g=1,\ldots, G$. In this case,

$$Q(q)=\{\gamma|p^{g\mathrm{T}}\nabla x(q)\gamma\leqq 0, \quad \text{for all} \quad p^g\}. \tag{17}$$

By theorem 1,

$$\operatorname{int} P(q)=\{\gamma|-x^h(q)^{\mathrm{T}}\gamma>0, \quad \text{for all} \quad h\}. \tag{18}$$

By supposition, no γ satisfies (17) and (18) simultaneously. Hence, by Motzkin's theorem,

$$\exists w\geqq 0 \quad \text{and} \quad \exists \tilde{w}>0 \quad \text{s.t.} \quad -\sum_h \tilde{w}_h x^h(q)^{\mathrm{T}}=\sum_g w_g p^{g\mathrm{T}}\nabla x(q). \tag{19}$$

By (12) neither side of (19) is zero. Letting $\tilde{p}^{\mathrm{T}}=\Sigma_g w_g p^{g\mathrm{T}}$, this implies $\tilde{p}^{\mathrm{T}}\nabla x(q)\in -\Lambda(q)\backslash\{0\}$ for some $\tilde{p}\in\rho(y)$.[9]

Theorem 3 is illustrated in fig. 1. The construction of $-\Lambda(q)$ and $P(q)$ were considered in the description of fig. 2. The derivation of $Q(q)$ from $\psi(q)$ is analogous to the derivation of $P(q)$ from $\Lambda(q)$. If $\hat{x}(q)$ is Pareto optimal, then $Q(q)\cap \operatorname{int} P(q)=\emptyset$, as shown in fig. 3.

2.5. Optimality with unique support prices

Now make the *local* assumption that $y(p)$ is a differentiable function at p.[10] Let $\nabla y(p)$ be the symmetric matrix of supply partial derivatives evaluated at p. From the first-order conditions for profit maximization,

$$p^{\mathrm{T}}\nabla y(p)=0. \tag{20}$$

From (20) the rank of $\nabla y(p)$ is at most $n-1$. Guesnerie (1977) assumes

[9]This method of proof follows a suggestion made by A. Dixit. I conjecture that the assumption that $\rho(y)$ is polyhedral could be relaxed.

[10]Using $y(p)$ to denote a function involves an abuse of the notation introduced earlier. If Y is not smooth at $y(p)$, a sufficient condition for this differentiability assumption would be to suppose p is in the relative interior of $\rho(y(p))$.

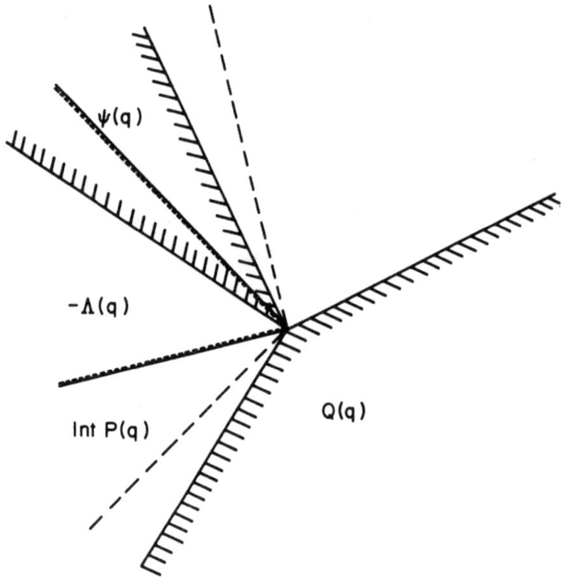

Fig. 3. Necessary conditions for second-best optimality.

that $\nabla y(p)$ is precisely of rank $n-1$. He demonstrates that this assumption implies that the government has local control of the production sector in the sense that it is possible to induce a differential change in supplies in any direction along the frontier of Y by a suitable *differential* change in producer prices.

Another important implication of this rank assumption is that p is the unique (to a positive scaling factor) support price to $y(p)$. This will be established as a corollary to a theorem which generalizes (20).

Theorem 4. If $\tilde{p} \in \rho(y(p))$, *then* $\tilde{p}\nabla y(p)=0$.

Proof. Since p and $\tilde{p}$ support $y(p)$, so does $p(\mu)=p+\mu(\tilde{p}-p)$ for $0 \leqq \mu \leqq 1$. Differentiating $y(p(\mu))$ with respect to μ and evaluating at $\mu=0$, $(\tilde{p}-p)^{\mathrm{T}}\nabla y(p)=0$. From (20), $p^{\mathrm{T}}\nabla y(p)=0$ so $\tilde{p}^{\mathrm{T}}\nabla y(p)=0$ as well.

Corollary 1. If the rank of $\nabla y(p)$ *is* $n-1$, *then* $y(p)$ *has a unique* (*to a positive scaling factor*) *support price.*[11]

Proof. Suppose p and $\tilde{p}$ are linearly independent and both support $y(p)$. By

[11] A. Dixit suggested this result. I have used his proof to establish the more general theorem 4.

theorem 4 both $p^{\mathrm{T}}\nabla y(p)=0$ and $\tilde{p}^{\mathrm{T}}\nabla y(p)=0$ which contradicts the rank assumption.

Corollary 2. If the rank of $\nabla y(p)$ is $n-1$, $\tilde{p}^{\mathrm{T}}\nabla y(p)=0$ if and only if $\tilde{p}=\lambda p$.

Proof. The result is a trivial implication of (20) and the rank assumption.

Combining these results with theorem 3 establishes the necessary conditions for optimality corresponding to Guesnerie's (1977) assumptions.

Theorem 5. Suppose $\Lambda(q)$ is pointed, $x^h(q)\neq 0$ for all h, $x(q)=y(p)$ for some p, and $\nabla y(p)$ is of rank $n-1$. A necessary condition for $\hat{x}(q)$ to be Pareto optimal is $p^{\mathrm{T}}\nabla x(q)\in -\Lambda(q)\backslash\{0\}$.

3. Optimality conditions using supply functions

3.1. *Optimality conditions*

If a change in demands is evaluated using producer prices and the value of the change is nonpositive for all support prices of the initial production decision, then the change is feasible. In this section linear approximations of the supply functions at the initial producer prices are used to determine the feasibility of a change.

Market balance requires

$$x(q)\leqq y(p). \tag{21}$$

Eqs. (9) and (21) are the equilibrium conditions for the model. Supposing that (9) and (21) hold with equality initially, assuming $y(p)$ is differentiable at p, for differential changes

$$\begin{pmatrix} -M, & -X, & 0 \\ 0, & -\nabla x(q), & \nabla y(p) \end{pmatrix} \begin{pmatrix} \mathrm{d}u \\ \mathrm{d}q \\ \mathrm{d}p \end{pmatrix} \geqq 0. \tag{22}$$

A necessary condition for second-best optimality is that there be no solution to (22) which also satisfies (10). By Motzkin's theorem, this obtains if and only if

$$\exists \begin{pmatrix} w^1 \\ w^2 \end{pmatrix} \geqq 0 \quad \text{and} \quad \exists \tilde{w}>0 \quad \text{s.t.} \quad \begin{pmatrix} w^1 \\ w^2 \end{pmatrix}^{\mathrm{T}} \begin{pmatrix} M, & X, & 0 \\ 0, & \nabla x(q), & -\nabla y(p) \end{pmatrix} = \tilde{w}^{\mathrm{T}}(I,0,0). \tag{23}$$

Theorem 6. Suppose $x^h(q) \neq 0$ for all h and $x(q) = y(p)$ for some p. A necessary condition for $\hat{x}(q)$ to be Pareto optimal is: $\exists w^1 > 0$ and $\exists w^2 \geqq 0$ such that

$$w^{1\mathrm{T}} X = -w^{2\mathrm{T}} \nabla x(q) \tag{24}$$

and

$$w^{2\mathrm{T}} \nabla y(p) = 0. \tag{25}$$

Proof. With $\partial m^h / \partial u^h > 0$, (24) and (25) follow immediately from (23).

Corollary 1. Suppose $\Lambda(q)$ is pointed, $x^h(q) \neq 0$ for all h, and $x(q) = y(p)$ for some p. A necessary condition for $\hat{x}(q)$ to be Pareto optimal is: $\exists w^2 > 0$ such that (25) holds and $w^{2\mathrm{T}} \nabla x(q) \in -\Lambda(q) \backslash \{0\}$.

Proof. Since $\Lambda(q)$ is pointed, (12) implies $w^{1\mathrm{T}} X \neq 0$ for $w^1 > 0$ so $w^{2\mathrm{T}} \nabla x(q) \neq 0$ and $w^2 \neq 0$. The result follows from the definition of $\Lambda(q)$.

Corollary 2. Suppose $\Lambda(q)$ is pointed, $x^h(q) \neq 0$ for all h, $x(q) = y(p)$ for some p, and $\nabla y(p)$ is of rank $n-1$. A necessary condition for $\hat{x}(q)$ to be Pareto optimal is $p^{\mathrm{T}} \nabla x(q) \in -\Lambda(q) \backslash \{0\}$.[12]

Proof. By corollary 1, $w^2 \neq 0$. By corollary 2 to theorem 4 and (25), $w^2 = \lambda p$ for $\lambda > 0$.

3.2. A reconciliation

Theorem 6 together with its corollaries are the major results from the use of supply functions. But corollary 2 is identical to theorem 5. In other words, by adding to the assumptions of theorem 6 the requirement that strictly Pareto-improving price changes exist and by assuming $\nabla y(p)$ is precisely of rank $n-1$ reconciles the results of Guesnerie (1977) and Diewert (1978). The key to this reconciliation was noting that in these circumstances the only solutions to (25) must be proportional to p.

[12]Diewert (1978) requires (9) and (21) to hold with equality; this necessitates the use of a slightly different form of Motzkin's theorem. In (8) he has $Eb = 0$ which means that w in (6) obeys no sign restrictions. With the assumptions of corollary 2, it is only possible to conclude that $w^2 = \lambda p$ for $\lambda \neq 0$ rather than for $\lambda > 0$. In effect, by working only with the frontier of Y these techniques cannot determine the sign of the support prices. Dixit (1979) avoids this problem by working with weak inequalities.

Diewert also develops his conditions using compensated demand functions rather than ordinary demand functions. His theorems can be reduced to those of this paper using the Slutsky equation.

Further insight can be gained by comparing theorem 3 with these new results. The relevant comparison is to corollary 1 as strictly Pareto-improving price changes were assumed to exist in theorem 3.

Knowledge of the semipositive solutions to (25) is needed for corollary 1, i.e. one must solve for the kernel to (25) and consider semipositive vectors in this kernel. From theorem 4 is it known that all support prices in $\rho(y(p))$ are solutions. However, only when the dimension of the kernel to (25) is one will the support prices coincide with the set of all semipositive solutions to (25). In other words, the converse to theorem 4 is false when the rank of $\nabla y(p)$ is less than $n-1$. So, while theorem 5 and corollary 2 are identical, theorem 3 and corollary 1 differ.

In section 2 two features of the assumption that $\nabla y(p)$ is of rank $n-1$ were noted: (a) there are unique (to a scaling factor) support prices and (b) it is possible to induce a differential change in supplies in any direction along the frontier of Y by a suitable differential change in producer prices. When the rank of $\nabla y(p)$ is less than $n-1$ there are some directions of supply changes which cannot be achieved by differenetial changes in producer prices, although all directions can be attained by suitable finite changes. When considering the feasibility of a change in demands, in section 2 the change was not required to be achieved by a differential change in producer prices. However, to use the techniques developed in this section only differential changes in producer prices could be considered. In tax reform problems only differential changes are allowed, so it is possible that reforms could terminate although a small change in demands would lead to a feasible Pareto improvement.

An example is instructive. Suppose $n=2$ and the initial supply vector is at a kink on the frontier of Y with p in the interior of $\rho(y(p))$. This is illustrated in fig. 4(a). With differential price changes it is not possible to achieve any change in supplies. The matrix $\nabla y(p)=0$, so the semipositive solutions to (25) are all of $R^2_+\backslash\{0\}$. This set is all the support prices to the technology depicted in fig. 4(b). For differential changes these technologies are indistinguishable.

The only changes in demands considered in this paper were changes achieved by differential changes in consumer prices. If $\nabla x^h(q)$ has rank $n-1$ for all h, where $\nabla x^h(q)$ is defined analogously to $\nabla x(q)$, each consumer will have q as the unique prices supporting $\hat{x}(q)$. In this situation theorems 3 and 5 and corollary 2 to theorem 6 provide necessary and sufficient conditions for $\hat{x}(q)$ to be a local optimum, where an allocation is considered to be Pareto optimal if and only if it is impossible to make *all* consumers better off.

4. Variable profit taxation

In Diewert (1978) and Dixit (1979) profits are returns to factors which are

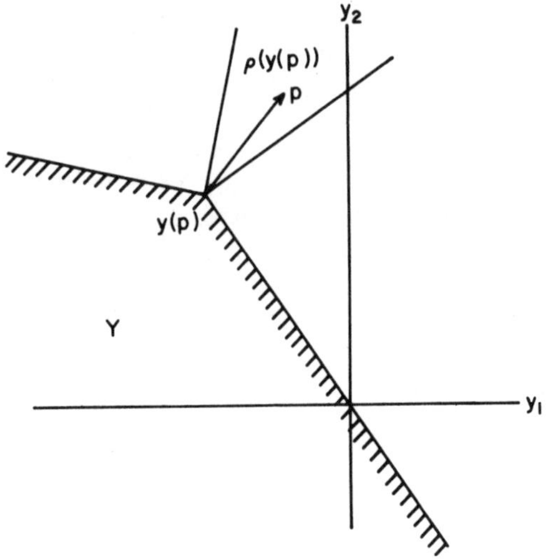

(a)

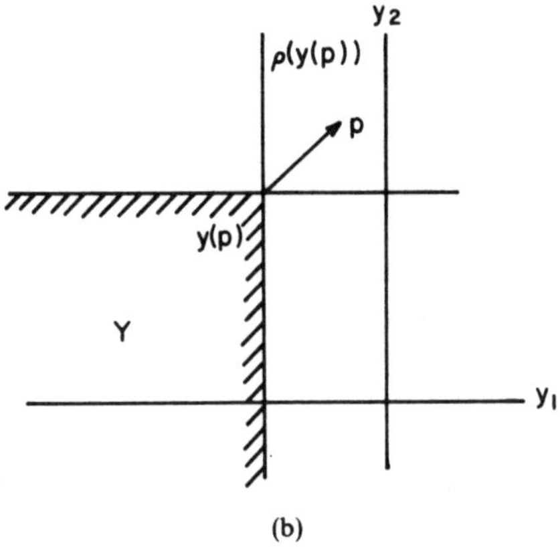

(b)

Fig. 4. Technologies with $\nabla y(p)=0$.

in inelastic supply. Each household is endowed with a vector of these fixed factors v^h for which they receive an after-profit-taxation return of s. Given $v=\Sigma_h v^h$, the aggregate technology for variable inputs and outputs is Y, as before. As v is supplied inelastically, there is no need explicitly to consider the prices firms pay for these factors.[13]

[13]Diewert (1978) and Dixit (1979) provide further details of the model. In the presence of fixed factors the assumption that Y is irreversible should be relaxed to the requirement that $Y\cap R^n_-$ be bounded.

The two equilibrium conditions are now

$$m^h(u,q) \leqq sv^h, \qquad h=1,\dots,H \tag{26}$$

and

$$x(q,\hat{m}) \leqq y(p), \tag{27}$$

where $\hat{m}=(m^1,\dots,m^H)$. For differential changes and supposing (26) and (27) hold with equality initially,

$$\begin{pmatrix} -M, & -X, & 0, & V \\ 0, & \nabla_q x(q,\hat{m}), & \nabla y(p), & -N \end{pmatrix} \begin{pmatrix} \mathrm{d}u \\ \mathrm{d}q \\ \mathrm{d}p \\ \mathrm{d}s \end{pmatrix} \geqq 0, \tag{28}$$

where V has rows v^{hT}, N has entries $\Sigma_h(\partial x_i^h/\partial m^h)v_i^h$, and $\nabla_q x(q,\hat{m})$ is the matrix of derivatives of $x(q,\hat{m})$ with respect to q.

Ignoring feasibility, it is a simple matter to apply Motzkin's theorem to establish that strict Pareto improvements are possible if and only if

$$\nexists w>0 \quad \text{s.t.} \quad w^{\mathrm{T}}X=w^{\mathrm{T}}V=0. \tag{29}$$

If $v^h>0$ for all h, strict Pareto improvements can be achieved by increasing s proportionally.

Now taking account of feasibility, attention is restricted to the case where strict Pareto improvements exist and where $\nabla y(p)$ is of rank $n-1$. It is clear from (28) that (25) must hold for Pareto optimality.

Theorem 6. Suppose $x^h(q)\neq 0$ for all h, (29), $x(q,\hat{m})=y(p)$ for some p, and $\nabla y(p)$ is of rank $n-1$. A necessary condition for $\hat{x}(q,\hat{m})$ to be Pareto optimal is: $\exists w^1>0$ and $\exists \lambda>0$ such that

$$\lambda p^{\mathrm{T}}\nabla_q x(q,\hat{m}) = -w^{1\mathrm{T}}X \neq 0 \tag{30}$$

and

$$\lambda p^{\mathrm{T}}N = w^{1\mathrm{T}}V \neq 0. \tag{31}$$

The proof of this theorem is essentially the same as theorem 5 together with its corollary 2, so it is omitted. Eq. (30) simply requires $p^{\mathrm{T}}\nabla_q x(q,\hat{m}) \in -\Lambda(q,\hat{m})\backslash\{0\}$. Dropping the requirement that a strict Pareto improvement exists, (29), λ could be zero. With this modification (30) and (31) are eqs. (21) and (22) in Dixit (1979).

Diewert (1978) suggests that the presence of supply derivatives in his conditions and their absence in Guesnerie's (1977) conditions is related to the fact that there is 100% profit taxation in Guesnerie's model. From (30) and (31) it is clear that optimality conditions can be written without reference to supply derivatives even in the case of variable profit taxation. With only differential changes in instruments allowed, this would not be possible if the rank of $\nabla y(p)$ is less than $n-1$.

5. Conclusions

The key feature of the model thus appears to be the local controllability of the production sector. When it is possible to induce an arbitrary feasible direction of supply changes by a differential change in producer prices, the results of sections 2 and 3 coincide. Since both Guesnerie (1977) and Diewert (1978) explicitly restricted themselves to differential changes, the relative simplicity of Guesnerie's propositions can now be understood to depend largely on his local controllability assumption.

In tax reform problems, where the optimality conditions are derived for small changes in the instruments, the optimality conditions can always be written with explicit reference to the supply derivatives. It is only in the case where local controllability is assumed is it possible to express the optimality conditions with no explicit reference to the supply derivatives for, in this case, there are unique support prices. However, in characterizing second-best optima, the use of supply derivatives is inappropriate except when local controllability is present, and even then their use complicates the statement of the results.

This resolves the apparent conflict between Guesnerie and Diewert. The possibility of variable profit taxation (or the existence of fixed factors) is not at issue; rather, it is the extent to which the private production sector may be controlled in a decentralized fashion.

Appendix

This appendix summarizes various results on cones which are used in the text. Theorems stated here without proofs may be found in either Berman (1973) or Gale (1960). The universal set is assumed to be a real vector space. To avoid ambiguity, λ will be a vector while μ will be a scalar.

A set K is a *cone* iff $k \in K$ implies $\mu k \in K$ for all $\mu \geqq 0$.

A convex cone K is *pointed* iff $K \cap (-K) = \{0\}$.

A convex cone K is *solid* iff $\operatorname{int} K \neq \emptyset$.

The *negative polar cone* of a convex cone K is

$$K^- \equiv \{k' \mid k^T k' \leqq 0 \quad \text{for all} \quad k \in K\}.$$

The *positive polar cone* of a convex cone K is $K^+ \equiv -(K^-)$.

A cone K is *finite* or *polyhedral* iff there exists a matrix M such that

$$K = \{k \mid k = M\lambda \quad \text{for some} \quad \lambda \geqq 0\}.$$

In this definition the columns of M may be chosen to be nonzero, in which case the columns of M are called *generators* of K. As a notational convention denote a column of M by M^i and the cone generated by M by $K(M)$.

It is straightforward to establish that a polyhedral cone is convex and that K^- is closed.

Theorem A.1. *If K is a polyhedral cone, then K is pointed iff K^- is solid.*

Theorem A.2. *If K is a pointed polyhedral cone, then*

$$\operatorname{int}(K^-) = \{k' \mid k' \in K^- \quad \text{and} \quad k^{\mathrm{T}}k' < 0 \quad \text{if} \quad k \in K \backslash \{0\}\}.$$

Corollary. *For a matrix M with nonzero columns, if $K(M)$ is pointed, then $k \in \operatorname{int}(K(M)^-)$ iff $M^{i\mathrm{T}}k < 0$ for all i.*

Proof. (a) Suppose $M^{i\mathrm{T}}k < 0$ for all i, then $(\Sigma_i \lambda_i M^i)^{\mathrm{T}} k < 0$ for all $\lambda > 0$. Applying the definitions of $K(M)$ and $K(M)^-$ to theorem A.2, $k \in \operatorname{int}(K(M)^-)$.

(b) Trivial.

Theorem A.3. *For a matrix M with nonzero columns, $K(M)$ is pointed iff $\nexists \lambda > 0$ such that $\Sigma_i \lambda_i M^i = 0$.*

Proof. (a) Suppose $K(M)$ is not pointed. Then, $\exists a, b \in K(M)$ with $a = -b \neq 0$. That is, $a = \Sigma_i \lambda_i^1 M^i$ for $\lambda^1 > 0$ and $b = \Sigma_i \lambda_i^2 M^i$ for $\lambda^2 > 0$ with $\Sigma_i \lambda_i^1 M^i = -\Sigma_i \lambda_i^2 M^i$. Letting $\lambda_i = \lambda_i^1 + \lambda_i^2$, this implies $\Sigma_i \lambda_i M^i = 0$ with $\lambda > 0$.

(b) Suppose $\exists \lambda > 0$ such that $\Sigma_i \lambda_i M^i = 0$. Consider any $\lambda^1 > 0$ and $\lambda^2 > 0$ such that $\lambda^1 + \lambda^2 = \lambda$. Then, $a = -b$ with $a, b \in K(M)$ where $a = \Sigma_i \lambda_i^1 M^i$ and $b = \Sigma_i \lambda_i^2 M^i$. So $K(M)$ is not pointed.

References

Berman, A., 1973, Cones, matrices and mathematical programming (Springer-Verlag, Berlin).

Diamond, P.A. and J.A. Mirrlees, 1971, Optimal taxation and public production I–II, American Economic Review 61, 8–27, 261–278.

Diewert, W.E., 1978, Optimal tax perturbations, Journal of Public Economics 10, 139–177.

Dixit, A.K., 1979, Price changes and optimum taxation in a many-person economy, Journal of Public Economics 11, 143–157.

Gale, D., 1960, The theory of linear economic models (McGraw-Hill, New York).

Guesnerie, R., 1977, On the direction of tax reform, Journal of Public Economics 7, 179–202.

Mangasarian, O.L., 1969, Nonlinear programming (McGraw-Hill, New York).

Matthews, S., 1978, Directional cores in simple dynamic games, California Institute of Technology, July.

Weymark, J.A., 1978a, On Pareto-improving price changes, Journal of Economic Theory 19, 338–346.

Weymark, J.A., 1978b, Undominated directions of tax reform, University of British Columbia Discussion Paper 78–26, August.

[31]

Productivity- and Pareto-Improving Changes in Taxes and Tariffs

W. E. DIEWERT
University of British Columbia

A. H. TURUNEN-RED
University of Texas at Austin

and

A. D. WOODLAND
University of Sydney

The paper investigates the problem of tariff reform in a small open multi-household economy that only has tariffs and domestic commodity taxes as policy instruments. The concept of a productivity improvement in tariffs and taxes is introduced and conditions for its existence are established. We prove that a Pareto-improving change in tariffs and domestic taxes exists if a productivity-improving change in tariffs exists and if the Weymark condition on the matrix of household demands holds. Conditions are established for particular tariff reforms, such as proportional reductions and reductions of extreme rates, to yield Pareto improvements in welfare.

1. INTRODUCTION

Until recently, proofs establishing the existence of gains from trade have used the assumption that the government can alter the distribution of income by a set of lump-sum transfers; i.e. the government has at its disposal a set of household-specific transfer instruments. However, recent work has been devoted to situations where these transfer instruments are inadmissible. Dixit and Norman (1980, pp. 79–80) demonstrate that a government that can alter all domestic commodity taxes can ensure that no individual is made worse off by moving from autarky to free trade. More recently, the question of whether the availability of commodity tax instruments alone (without the use of lump sum transfers) is sufficient to ensure that a strict Pareto improvement will occur in moving from autarky to free trade has been debated by Kemp and Wan (1986) and Dixit and Norman (1986).

The literature on tariff reform, on the other hand, has typically dealt with a single household economy and has assumed the availability of a lump sum transfer between the government and the household. Such studies by Foster and Sonnenschein (1970), Bertrand and Vanek (1971), Bruno (1972), Lloyd (1974), Hatta (1977) and Fukushima (1979) do not, therefore, concern themselves with the problems of the distribution of benefits of a tariff reform among households. Nor do they consider whether such tariff reforms will be beneficial if the government does not have lump sum transfer instruments available, but has to rely solely upon domestic commodity taxes as the redistributive instrument.

The purpose of this paper is to investigate the problem of tariff reform in a small open, multi-household economy for the case where the government only has tariffs and domestic commodity taxes as policy instruments. By assuming a small open economy, the world prices for tradeable commodities are fixed and our results may be readily compared with the substantial literature based upon the same assumption. The case of a large trading nation with variable world prices for tradeables is considered within the context of the gains from trade by Dixit and Norman (1986). Our paper also restricts the government's policy instruments to tariffs and domestic commodity taxes, thus ruling out other tax instruments such as lump sum transfers and poll taxes. A primary reason for this choice is that transfers and poll taxes are seldom used by governments, and so it is of considerable interest to examine the possibilities of obtaining welfare gains using a subset of politically feasible tax instruments, namely commodity taxes.

The plan in the paper is as follows: the general equilibrium model of the economy is developed in Section 2. In Section 3, we introduce the concept of a productivity-improving change in tariffs. This concept is of interest not only in its own right, but also in providing sufficient conditions for the existence of a Pareto-improving change in tariffs and commodity taxes. It is shown that various tariff reform policies that have been suggested in the literature, such as proportional reductions and the reduction of the highest ad valorem rate, are capable of creating a productivity improvement.

In Section 4 we show that if a productivity improving change in tariffs exists and if the Weymark (1979) condition on the matrix of household demand vectors holds, then there exists a differential change in tariffs that yields a strict Pareto improvement in welfare. We note that an autarky equilibrium may be replicated in an open economy if the government chooses a set of tariffs and export taxes that will just induce zero net exports for each internationally traded good. Thus, the existence of gains from trade for a small open economy may be regarded as a special case of the existence of a Pareto-improving change in tariffs.

In Section 4 we also establish conditions under which particular tariff reforms, such as proportional reductions and the reduction of the highest ad valorem rate, can yield a strict Pareto improvement in welfare. These results extend the validity of such reforms, which were previously only shown to be beneficial in a single-household economy with lump sum transfers. Section 5 provides some concluding comments.

2. MODEL FORMULATION

In this section we set out the model that is used for the discussion in subsequent sections. The model is a perfectly competitive general equilibrium model of a small open economy, which includes a government that buys and sells goods in fixed amounts (possibly to produce a public good), imposes commodity and trade taxes (called tariffs), and makes transfer payments to households.

The economy is assumed to consist of H households, a production sector, and a government. There are $M+N$ commodities, M of which are internationally tradeable at fixed world price vector, w, the remaining N commodities being non-tradeable.[1] The government imposes a vector of trade taxes ("tariffs"), τ, on net imports of tradeable commodities and a vector of domestic commodity taxes, (s, t), on both tradeable (s) and non-tradeable (t) commodities.[2] The producer price vector is thus $(r, p)=(w+\tau, p)$,

1. The term commodity refers to all outputs and inputs and therefore includes factors of production. The production, consumption and trade vectors may therefore have both positive and negative elements.

2. The "tariff" vector τ includes any export taxes or subsidies and any import subsidies. If $\tau_m>0$ (<0) and the m-th internationally traded good is being imported into the country, then τ_m is a tariff (subsidy); if $\tau_m>0$ (<0) and the m-th good is being exported, then τ_m is a subsidy (export tax).

TABLE 1

Notation

	Non-tradeable goods	Tradeable goods
world prices		w
trade taxes (tariffs)		τ
producer prices	p	$r = w + \tau$
commodity taxes	t	s
consumer prices	$q = p + t$	$v = w + \tau + s$
net outputs (private)	y	f
net outputs (government)	y_0	f_0
consumption (household h)	x_h	e_h
consumption (total)	x	e
number of goods	N	M

while the consumer price vector is $(v, q) = (w + \tau + s, p + t)$. The government has a fixed net output vector, (f_0, y_0), for commodities and chooses a vector, m, of net lump sum transfers to households. A summary of the notation is provided in Table 1.[3]

The production sector chooses net output vector, (f, y), in its feasible production set, Y, so as to maximize profit given the vector of producer prices, (r, p). It is assumed that the production set, Y, is a non-empty, closed and convex cone; that is, there are constant returns to scale in production.

It will be convenient to carry out the profit maximization sequentially, thus defining the revenue function

$$G(r, y) = \max_f \{r'f: (f, y) \in Y\} \qquad y \in \bar{Y}, \tag{2.1}$$

as the maximum value of traded goods produced given the net output vector for non-traded goods, y, where $\bar{Y}$ is the set of y for which (f, y) is feasible for some f. The remainder of the profit maximization problem is

$$\pi(r, p) = \max_y \{G(r, y) + p'y: y \in \bar{Y}\}. \tag{2.2}$$

If $G(r, y)$ is differentiable then the optimal choice of f from (2.1) and the optimal choice of y from (2.2) will satisfy

$$f = G_w(r, y) \equiv \partial G(w + \tau, y)/\partial w; \qquad -p = G_y(r, y) \equiv \partial G(r, y)/\partial y. \tag{2.3}$$

Moreover, the revenue function $G(r, y)$ is linearly homogeneous and convex in r and hence w (since $r = w + \tau$).[4] If $G(r, y)$ is twice continuously differentiable in r (and hence w) then these properties imply that

$$\begin{aligned} G_{ww}(r, y) &\equiv \partial^2 G(w + \tau, y)/\partial w \partial w' \\ &\equiv \partial^2 G(r, y)/\partial r \partial r' \text{ is a positive semi-definite matrix such that} \\ &(w + \tau)' G_{ww}(w + \tau, y) \equiv 0. \end{aligned} \tag{2.4}$$

Each household $h = 1, \ldots, H$ maximizes a utility function subject to its budget constraint characterized by the vector of consumer prices (v, q) and net lump sum transfers

3. Other notational conventions used throughout this paper are as follows. Subscripts will be used to denote partial differentiation. All vectors are column vectors, with ′ denoting transposition. Also, if vector $x \geqq 0$ every element is non-negative, if $x \gg 0$ every element is positive, and $x > 0$ denotes a semi-positive vector, i.e. $x \geqq 0$ and $x \neq 0$.

4. For further details on the revenue or gross national product function see Samuelson (1953), Diewert and Woodland (1977), Dixit and Norman (1980, pp. 30-36) or Woodland (1982, pp. 52-60).

m_h. As is well known, this problem may be divided into two parts. The first defines the expenditure function $E^h(u_h, v, q)$ as the minimum expenditure needed to obtain the level of utility u_h. If satiation is ruled out then the level of utility is obtained by solving

$$E^h(u_h, v, q) = m_h, \qquad h = 1, \ldots, H, \tag{2.5}$$

where m_h is the (possibly negative) lump sum transfer from the government to household h. This set of equations may be expressed in vector form as

$$M(u, v, q) = m, \tag{2.6}$$

where $M = (E^1, \ldots, E^H)'$ and $m = (m_1, \ldots, m_H)'$ are H-dimensional vectors.

It is also convenient to define the aggregate expenditure function[5]

$$E(u, v, q) = \sum_{h=1}^{H} E^h(u_h, q, v), \tag{2.7}$$

as the minimum expenditure needed to attain utility vector $u = (u_1, \ldots, u_H)'$. If the expenditure functions are differentiable with respect to prices then the aggregate demand vectors x and e are given by

$$x = E_q(u, v, q) \equiv \partial E(u, v, q)/\partial q; \qquad e = E_v(u, v, q) \equiv \partial E(u, v, q)/\partial v. \tag{2.8}$$

Moreover, the household expenditure functions, and hence the aggregate expenditure function $E(u, v, q)$, are linearly homogeneous and concave in the consumer price vector $\rho \equiv (v, q)$.[6] Thus, if $E(u, \rho)$ is twice continuously differentiable in ρ then

$$E_{\rho\rho}(\mu, \rho) \equiv \partial^2 E(u, \rho)/\partial\rho\partial\rho' \text{ is a negative semi-definite matrix such that } \rho' E_{\rho\rho}(u, \rho) \equiv 0. \tag{2.9}$$

Since we assume that the household expenditure functions are increasing in utility, we may normalize these functions such that

$$M_u(u, \rho) = I; \qquad \text{i.e. } \partial E^h(u_h, \rho)/\partial u_h = 1, \qquad h = 1, \ldots, H. \tag{2.10}$$

If the revenue function, G, and the vector of expenditure functions, M, are differentiable and all prices are positive then the model for a small open economy may be compactly written as follows:

$$M(u, w + \tau + s, p + t) = m, \tag{2.11}$$

$$G_y(w + \tau, y) + p = 0, \tag{2.12}$$

$$y + y_0 - E_p(u, w + \tau + s, p + t) = 0, \tag{2.13}$$

$$b = w'[f_0 + G_w(w + \tau, y) - E_w(u, w + \tau + s, p + t)]. \tag{2.14}$$

Equation (2.11) states that the levels of household utility are those for which household expenditure equals household income. Equation (2.12) indicates that the market price for non-tradeables, p, equals the shadow price for non-tradeables in production. Condition (2.13) is the market equilibrium condition for non-traded goods, recognizing that $E_p(u, w + \tau + s, p + t)$ is the consumption sector's demand vector for non-traded goods and y_0 is the government demand vector. Finally, (2.14) defines the net balance

5. The function $E(u, v, q)$ may be interpreted as the minimum expenditure function corresponding to a Scitovsky indifference map. See Woodland (1982, pp. 162-164).

6. For further details on expenditure functions see Diewert (1982).

may also be interpreted as a net transfer of income from the home nation to the rest of the world, an interpretation that is used subsequently in Section 4.

Given the world price vector, w, the vector of lump sum transfers, m, the government net output vectors, f_0 and y_0, and tax vectors, τ, s, and t, the model (2.11)-(2.14) determines endogenously the vector of utilities, u, the price and net production vectors of non-traded goods, p and y, and the balance of trade, b. Alternatively, the balance of trade may be exogenously given (perhaps at zero), in which case the government's choices of m, r, s, and t are constrained by (2.14).

It is assumed that there exists a unique solution to (2.11)-(2.14), which is referred to as the initial (tax-distorted) equilibrium. It is further assumed that all functions in (2.11)-(2.14) are continuously differentiable at the initial equilibrium. Finally, it is assumed that the economy is small implying that the world price vector is fixed, that the government net output vectors are fixed, and that the government does not have household lump sum transfers as available policy instruments implying that m is fixed. Accordingly, the differential comparative static system corresponding to (2.11)-(2.14) is

$$\begin{bmatrix} M_u \\ 0 \\ -E_{pu} \\ -w'E_{wu} \end{bmatrix} du + \begin{bmatrix} 0 \\ 0 \\ 0 \\ -1 \end{bmatrix} db + \begin{bmatrix} M_w \\ G_{yw} \\ -E_{pw} \\ w'(G_{ww} - E_{ww}) \end{bmatrix} d\tau + \begin{bmatrix} M_w \\ 0 \\ -E_{pw} \\ -wE_{ww} \end{bmatrix} ds$$

$$+ \begin{bmatrix} M_p \\ 0 \\ -E_{pp} \\ -w'E_{wp} \end{bmatrix} dt + \begin{bmatrix} M_p \\ I \\ -E_{pp} \\ -w'E_{wp} \end{bmatrix} dp + \begin{bmatrix} 0 \\ G_{yy} \\ I \\ w'G_{wy} \end{bmatrix} dy = \begin{bmatrix} 0 \\ 0 \\ 0 \\ 0 \end{bmatrix} \tag{2.15}$$

which may be compactly written as

$$C_u du + C_b db + C_\tau d\tau + C_s ds + C_t dt + C_p dp + C_y dy = 0, \tag{2.16}$$

where the matrices C_i have obvious definition and are evaluated at the initial equilibrium, and matrices E_{pp} and E_{wp} are sub-matrices of $E_{\rho\rho}$ defined by (2.9).

The differential approach to tariff reform is to find conditions under which differential changes in the policy variables (τ, s and t) with consequent changes in the endogenous variables (p, y, u) will result in $du \gg 0$, that is, a *strict Pareto improvement* in welfare.[7] It is to this problem that attention is now turned.

3. PRODUCTIVITY-IMPROVING CHANGES IN TARIFFS

It is well known that one of the important sources of gains from trade arises from the restructuring of the production sector. In the context of tariff reform we are interested in whether a small change in tariffs will lead to a restructuring of the production sector such that the benefits can be passed on to consumers. As a step towards that aim we define a particular concept of productivity improvement that relates only to the production sector.

7. In Diewert, Turunen and Woodland (1984) the net balance of trade, b, was also assumed to be available as a policy instrument. However, most of the results presented in the current paper are independent of whether db is restricted to be zero (as here) or positive (as in the 1984 paper).

We say that there exists a *productivity-improving change in tariffs* if there exists a tariff reform such that the value of traded goods at world prices is increased while maintaining the initial net output vector for non-traded goods. If we define

$$\beta(\tau) = w'G_{w}(w+\tau, y), \tag{3.1}$$

as the value of the production of traded goods at world prices, then a productivity-improving change in the tariff vector, τ, increases the value of β. If attention is restricted to differential changes in τ, then a *productivity-improving differential change in tariffs, $d\tau$,* exists when $d\beta(\tau) = (\partial\beta(\tau)/\partial\tau)'d\tau > 0$ for some $d\tau$.

We make the following assumption.

Assumption 1. At the initial equilibrium the tariff vector satisfies

$$\tau'G_{ww}(w+\tau, y) \neq 0. \tag{3.2}$$

Theorem 1. *Let the revenue function $G(w+\tau, y)$ be twice continuously differentiable in $(w+\tau)$ at the initial equilibrium. Then a necessary and sufficient condition for there to exist a productivity-improving differential change in tariffs is that Assumption 1 holds.*

Proof. The total differential of $\beta(\tau)$ is

$$d\beta(\tau) = w'G_{ww}(w+\tau, y)d\tau = -\tau'G_{ww}(w+\tau, y)d\tau, \tag{3.3}$$

since $(w+\tau)'G_{ww}(w+\tau, y) \equiv 0$ by (2.4). If Assumption 1 does not hold, then $\tau'G_{ww}(w+\tau, y) = 0$ and so $d\beta(\tau) = 0$ for all $d\tau$. If Assumption 1 holds, then $d\tau \neq 0$ can always be found to make $d\beta(\tau) > 0$. ‖

When will Assumption 1 *not* hold, thus preventing productivity improvements arising from differential tariff changes? One obvious case occurs if $G_{ww} = 0$. This corresponds to the production possibilities surface among traded goods having a sharp point at the initial production vector, so that small changes in price do not have any effect upon production. The "Ricardian point" in a model with a Leontief technology is an example where G_{ww} vanishes.

Even if G_{ww} does not vanish there are two other cases where Assumption 1 may fail to hold. The first case occurs if $\tau = 0$ (free trade), or if $\tau = \alpha w$ for some $\alpha > 0$ (tariffs are imposed at a uniform rate, α, with no distortionary effect upon production). A second, more subtle, possibility exists. If Assumption 1 does not hold then

$$w'G_{ww}(w+\tau, y) = 0 \quad \text{and} \quad \tau'G_{ww}(w+\tau, y) = 0, \tag{3.4}$$

which implies that w and τ are distinct (if $\tau \neq \alpha w$ for some scalar α) eigenvectors of matrix G_{ww} corresponding to zero eigenvalues. This situation corresponds to a ridge on the efficiency frontier orthogonal to w. For some changes in τ the production vector will change ($G_{ww} \neq 0$) but all such changes are orthogonal to w so that the world price evaluation of production does not increase. Production is not "controllable" by prices.

In general, therefore, there are cases where Assumption 1 will not hold even though the initial tariffs are non-zero. On the other hand, if the production substitution matrix G_{ww}, has maximal rank $(M-1)$, and if the tariff vector does not yield uniform ad valorem rates on all traded commodities, Assumption 1 will hold. Accordingly, there will exist productivity-improving differential changes in tariffs.

If (3.4) has a solution then productivity improvements resulting from differential changes in tariffs are not possible. This does not, however, rule out the possibility that productivity improvements are possible for discrete, but possibly small, changes in τ.

That is a difficulty in dealing with differential changes. Another difficulty is that, in general, the function $G(w+\tau, y)$ may not be differentiable with respect to prices at the initial equilibrium. This occurs if the optimal production is a point in a linear subspace forming part of the efficiency frontier. In that case, a small change in τ may shift production to the boundary of that subspace resulting in an increase in β. G is pointed at the initial producer price vector and has no derivative. However, it does have well-defined left- and right-hand derivatives. Thus, at such a point the (first and second) derivatives depend upon the direction of movement in τ and hence producer prices. The same comments apply to $\beta(\tau)$, which is a correspondence at the initial τ. The problem posed in (3.3) remains valid: we seek some $d\tau$ for which $d\beta(\tau)>0$ holds, where G_{ww} is the derivative matrix that applies in the direction $d\tau$. However, further consideration of these issues is beyond the scope of the present paper.[8]

The preceding theorem indicates the condition for the existence of a productivity-improving differential change in tariffs, but it does not provide us with specific policy prescriptions. Some are provided, by the following theorem.

Theorem 2. *Let the revenue function $G(w+\tau, y)$ be twice continuously differentiable in $(w+\tau)$ at the initial equilibrium. Then a productivity-improving differential change in tariffs of the form $d\tau = a d\alpha$ with $d\alpha > 0$ exists if*

$$\tau' G_{ww}(w+\tau, y) a < 0, \tag{3.5}$$

where a is an M-dimensional vector.

Proof. The proof is similar to that for Theorem 1. ||

A consideration of various special configurations of vector a yields the following corollary to Theorem 2.

Corollary 2.1. *The conclusion of Theorem 2 applies if Assumption 1 holds and*

(i) *The vector a in (3.5) is chosen as*

$$a = (\gamma w - \varepsilon \tau), \qquad \gamma + \varepsilon > 0, \tag{3.6}$$

where γ and ε are scalars defining a particular direction of tariff change; or

(ii) *Only τ_k is reduced, other tariffs remaining unchanged, and*

$$G_{ik} \leqq 0 \quad \text{and} \quad \sigma_k \equiv \tau_k / w_k \geqq \tau_i / w_i \equiv \sigma_i \quad \text{for all } i \neq k,$$

$$G_{jk} < 0 \quad \text{and} \quad \sigma_k > \sigma_j \quad \text{for some } j \neq k. \tag{3.7}$$

The proofs of Corollary 2.1 and subsequent theorems are provided in the Appendix.

The first case in Corollary 2.1 moves the producer price vector for tradeable goods, $w+\tau$, towards the world prive vector, w, along a linear path. If $\varepsilon = 1$, then $d\alpha$ is an

8. The case dealt with in this paragraph may arise if the number of tradeable commodities exceeds the number of non-tradeable commodities in the traditional international trade model with no joint production. An alternative production sector specification is to assume that the national production set is strictly convex, thus implying the existence of well-defined derivatives of the revenue function $G(w+\tau, y)$. This case may be cast into the present specification by defining an artificial commodity in fixed supply and whose earnings are profits, which are taxed at a rate given by the appropriate component of the domestic tax vector.

equi-proportional reduction in the distortion between τ and the uniform tariff structure γw. If $\gamma = 0$, then $\varepsilon d\alpha$ is an equi-proportional reduction in τ. Finally $\varepsilon = 0$ implies that $d\tau = \gamma w d\alpha$ so all tariffs are increased proportionately with w.

The second case indicates that a reduction of the highest ad valorem rate on good (k) will be productivity-improving if no commodity is complementary in production with k and at least one product with a lower ad valorem rate is a substitute for k in production.

The above policy recommendations are similar to those developed by Foster and Sonnenschein (1970), Bruno (1972), Lloyd (1974), Hatta (1977) and Fukushima (1979); here they apply to the production sector alone, whereas Lloyd and Hatta were concerned with welfare improvements.

While the second case of Corollary 2 provides for a reduction in a single tariff, it relies heavily upon the assumption of substitutability. Independently of such an assumption, we can demonstrate that there always exists a commodity for which a reduction in its tariff will be productivity-improving.

Theorem 3. *Let the revenue function $G(w+\tau, y)$ be twice continuously differentiable in $(w+\tau)$ at the initial equilibrium and let Assumption 1 hold. Then there exists a commodity k such that a differential reduction in its tariff is productivity-improving, and a commodity l such that a differential increase in its tariff is productivity-improving.*

While Theorem 3 indicates existence, it does not specify how to identify commodities k and l. However, to do this we need only check the signs of the elements of the vector $\tau' G_{ww}(w+\tau, y)$. According to the proof of Theorem 3, this vector has at least one positive, and at least one negative, element. If element k is positive then $d\tau_k < 0$ will be productivity-improving, whereas if element l is negative $d\tau_l > 0$ will be productivity-improving.[9]

In this section we have shown that a productivity improvement in tariffs exists under very mild conditions on the revenue function describing the production technology. The question arises as to whether the government is able to construct a domestic taxation policy to convert the productivity gain arising from a change in tariffs into a Pareto improvement in welfare for households. In the following section we consider this question for the case where commodity taxes are the available policy instruments, but lump sum transfers are not.

4. PARETO-IMPROVING CHANGES IN COMMODITY TAXES AND TARIFFS

4.1. *Preliminaries*

In this section we provide conditions under which Pareto-improving changes in commodity and trade taxes (τ, s, t) exist, and develop various specific policy proposals.

A change in (τ, s, t) that creates an increase in utility for every household is called a *strict Pareto-improving change in commodity taxes and tariffs*. If attention is restricted

9. This can be seen by reference to (3.3).

to differential changes in (τ, s, t), a ***strict Pareto-improving differential change in commodity taxes and tariffs*** is defined to be a vector $(d\tau, ds, dt)$ such that there exists a solution to (2.16) with $db = 0$ and $du \gg 0$.[10]

We now introduce an assumption that is necessary if commodity tax adjustments are to be able to yield a strict Pareto improvement in welfare.

Assumption 2. At the initial equilibrium there does *not* exist a solution $\lambda = (\lambda_1, \ldots, \lambda_H)'$ to

$$\lambda' M_\rho(u, \rho) = 0, \quad \lambda < 0, \tag{4.1}$$

where $\rho' = (v', q')$.

The importance of Assumption 2 is made clear by considering the question of whether there exists *any* differential change in the consumer price vector, ρ, that will raise the level of utility for every household when transfer payments remain fixed.[11] The question posed is whether there exists a solution $(du, d\rho)$ to

$$du = M_\rho(u, \rho) d\rho, \qquad du \gg 0. \tag{4.2}$$

Motzkin's Theorem of the Alternative (Lemma 1 in the Appendix) states that either (4.2) has a solution $(du, d\rho)$, or (4.1) has a solution λ, but not both. Thus, there exists a strict Pareto-improving differential change in commodity prices if, and only if, Assumption 2 holds. Thus, Assumption 2 is necessary for the success of any policy that aims for a strict Pareto improvement in welfare by adjusting consumer prices.

When will (4.1) fail to have a solution? One case is if M_ρ has full row rank. For this case to occur it is necessary, but not sufficient, that $H \leqq M + N$, i.e. the number of households must be less than the number of goods. This condition is related to the early literature on economic policy: it says that the number of policy instruments (commodity prices) must be at least as great as the number of targets (household utility levels). The plausibility of this rank condition being satisfied in the real world is clearly debatable. It is, of course, more likely to be satisfied if H is redefined as the number of homogeneous types of households and the analysis conducted in terms of homogeneous types rather than individual households. A second case where (4.1) has no solution is where at least one column of the $H \times (M + N)$ matrix of households' net demand vectors, M_ρ, has all positive, or all negative, elements. In this case, there is at least one commodity that is either demanded by all households or supplied by all households. All households are on the same side of the market for at least one good.

These conditions are individually sufficient for (4.1) to have no solution, but they are not necessary. What is necessary and sufficient is that all households' (net) demand vectors lie in the same half-space and form a pointed cone. If they do, it is possible to find a vector $d\rho$ that is at an acute angle to every demand vector. This is equivalent to saying that the inner product between every demand vector and $d\rho$ is positive. By (4.2), these inner products are precisely the elements of the vector du, so $du \gg 0$ is achieved.

10. The reader may well wonder why we don't look for a weak Pareto improvement that merely raises the utility of at least one household without reducing the utility of any household; i.e. why do we not replace $du \gg 0$ by $du > 0$? The problem is that if a variable such as u_h has a zero directional derivative (i.e. $du_h = 0$), then the actual change in u_h can be positive or negative for arbitrarily small finite changes in the exogenous tax variables. The difficulty is discussed further in Diewert (1978, p. 155).

11. Assumption 2 is sometimes referred to as the Weymark (1979) condition, and goods satisfying it may be called Diamond-Mirrlees (1971) goods. For further details see Weymark (1979).

4.2. *Existence results*

We now consider the question of whether a strict Pareto improvement is possible as a result of differential changes in tariffs accompanied by changes in domestic taxes that preserve all of the equilibrium conditions.

Our main result is contained in the following theorem.

Theorem 4. *Let the revenue function G and the total expenditure function E be twice continuously differentiable at the initial equilibrium. If, in addition, Assumptions* 1 *and* 2 *hold at the initial equilibrium then there exists a solution to* (2.16) *with* $du \gg 0$ *and* $db = 0$; *that is, there exists a strict Pareto-improving differential change in tariffs and commodity taxes.*

Conditional upon the differentiability assumption, Theorem 4 gives sufficient conditions for the existence of a differential change in tariffs and commodity taxes that will raise the utility of every household and therefore provide a strict Pareto improvement in welfare. The first of these, Assumption 1, is the necessary and sufficient condition for the existence of a productivity improvement in tariffs. As noted above, this is one of the traditional sources of gains from trade or, in the present context, a source of gain from freer trade. By itself, a productivity improvement is not sufficient for the existence of a Pareto improvement in welfare.

The second condition, Assumption 2, has previously arisen as the necessary and sufficient condition for the existence of strict Pareto-improving differential change in consumer prices. In that context, the prices changes considered were arbitrary. Here, they are no longer arbitrary, but are constrained by all of the equilibrium conditions. Assumption 1 permits the creation of a productivity improvement, and Assumption 2 ensures that this productivity improvement can be converted into a strict Pareto welfare gain by a suitable choice of tariff and commodity tax changes.

Theorem 4 tells us that a productivity-improving change in tariffs can be converted into a Pareto-improving change in tariffs and commodity taxes even if household-specific transfer instruments are not available, provided only that the mild regularity condition (Assumption 2) on household preferences and endowments is satisfied.

An interesting special case of Theorem 4 occurs if τ is a vector of prohibitive tariffs, so that the initial equilibrium is interpreted as an autarky equilibrium. Then Theorem 4 may be interpreted as a Dixit–Norman (1980, 1986) existence of the gains from trade theorem when no lump sum transfer instruments are available. Dixit and Norman deal with a trading world of large economies and with the movement from autarky to free trade. Our result, as a special case, gives conditions for the existence of gains from a differential movement away from autarky for a small open economy.

The possibility of strict Pareto improvements is enhanced if the initial commodity taxes are not Pareto optimal given the initial tariff vector, τ, since a strict Pareto improvement may then be possible by changing commodity taxes alone and leaving tariffs unchanged. In order to prevent the wrongful assignment of such welfare gains to tariff reform, we now consider the case where commodity taxes are initially Pareto optimal given the initial tariff vector.

The initial commodity taxes vector (s, t) is Pareto optimal given τ if there does not exist a solution to (2.16) with $du > 0$, $db = 0$ and $d\tau = 0$. Given that the initial commodity tax vector is Pareto optimal for the initial tariff vector, τ, the problem is to characterize conditions under which τ can be altered so as to achieve a strict Pareto improvement in welfare. Theorem 5 (below) shows that the existence of a productivity-improving differential change is necessary for this outcome.

Theorem 5. *Let* (i) *G and E be twice continuously differentiable at the initial equilibrium and* (ii) *the initial commodity tax vector* (s, t) *be Pareto optimal given* τ. *Then, a necessary condition for there to exist a solution to* (2.16) *with* $du \gg 0$ and $db = 0$ *is that Assumption* 1 *holds.*

If commodity taxes are Pareto optimal, given τ, the only source of potential gain in welfare is via a change in tariffs. Theorem 5 indicates that the existence of a productivity improvement in tariffs is essential for the existence of a Pareto improvement in welfare, because the commodity tax rates have already been chosen to minimize any distortion created by tariffs in the consumption sector. If productivity gains do not exist then a differential change in tariffs is of no benefit.

Theorem 5 shows that Assumption 1 is necessary for the existence of a strict Pareto-improving differential change in tariffs and taxes. Assumption 1 will also be sufficient for this outcome if Assumption 2 also holds (irrespective of whether initial commodity taxes are optimal), as indicated by Theorem 4. Assumption 2 provides the appropriate initial conditions for the construction of a suitable redistributive commodity tax policy.

Assumption 2 may be given an interpretation in terms of providing the appropriate initial conditions for a gift of income to or from abroad to be distributed by changes in commodity taxes so as to yield a strict Pareto improvement in welfare. This is the content of the following theorem.

Theorem 6. *Let G and E be twice continuously differentiable at the initial equilibrium. Then, there exists a differential change in transfer income from abroad, with accompanying changes in p, y, s and t, that yields a strict Pareto improvement in welfare if and only if Assumption* 2 *holds.* (*That is, there exists a solution to* (2.16) *with* $du \gg 0$ *and* $d\tau = 0$ *if and only if Assumption* 2 *holds.*)

This theorem relates our results on tariff reform to the literature on international transfers of income, and provides an interesting interpretation of Assumption 2. It states that Assumption 2 (the Weymark condition) is a necessary and sufficient condition for the existence of some exogenous change in the balance of trade (international transfer of income) that will, after all adjustments to re-establish equilibrium have been made, yield a strict Pareto improvement in welfare. The redistributive mechanism is via commodity tax policy, not lump sum household transfers. An implication of Theorem 6 is that Assumption 2 in Theorem 4 may be replaced by the equivalent assumption: that there exists a solution to (2.16) with $du \gg 0$ and $d\tau = 0$.

4.3. *Specific policy recommendations*

The results presented above establish the existence of strict Pareto-improving differential changes in tariffs and commodity taxes, but they do not give any specific guidance for policy makers. We now develop some specific recommendations that are guaranteed to yield strict Pareto improvements.

The following theorem provides a general family of tariff reforms that are guaranteed to be welfare improving.

Theorem 7. *Let* (i) *G and E be twice continuously differentiable at the initial equilibrium and* (ii) *suppose that there exists a solution to* (2.16) *with* $du \gg 0$, $db < 0$ *and* $d\tau = 0$. *Then there exists a solution to* (2.16) *with* $du \gg 0$, $db = 0$, $d\tau = a d\alpha$ *and* $d\alpha > 0$ *if*

$$\tau' G_{ww}(w + \tau, y) a < 0, \tag{4.3}$$

at the initial equilibrium, where a is an M-dimensional vector.

This theorem differs from Theorem 4 above in several respects. First, there is a requirement for a particular direction of tariff reform defined by the vector a and the specification that $d\alpha > 0$. Because of this requirement, the sufficiency conditions have to be strengthened. Thus a second difference is that Assumption 1 is replaced by the stronger condition that (4.3) holds. It is easily demonstrated that (4.3) is equivalent to the statement that the directional derivative of the function $\beta(\tau)$ is positive in the direction of the tariff reform; that is, there is a productivity improvement in this direction. The third difference between Theorems 4 and 7 is that Assumption 2 is replaced by the stronger assumption (ii), which may be interpreted as a type of normality condition on preferences. Assumption (ii) states that a gift of income from abroad (an exogenous decrease in the balance of trade) may be accompanied by suitable changes in commodity taxes to ensure a strict Pareto improvement in welfare; that is, a gift is beneficial. While stronger than Assumption 2 (recall Theorem 6), this assumption seems rather mild.[12]

This theorem can be used to demonstrate the welfare gains from several different types of tariff changes. Just as we were able to derive various specific tariff policies that yield an improvement in productivity as in Corollary 2.1 of Theorem 2, we can similarly demonstrate that the same tariff policies will yield a strict Pareto improvement in welfare. For completeness, these results are presented in the following corollaries to Theorem 7.

Corollary 7.1. *The conclusion of Theorem 7 applies if either*

(i) *The vector a in* (4.3) *is chosen as*

$$a = (\gamma w - \varepsilon \tau), \qquad \gamma + \varepsilon > 0, \tag{4.4}$$

where γ *and* ε *are scalars defining a particular direction of tariff change; or*

(*ii*) *Only* τ_k *is reduced, other tariffs remaining unchanged, and*

$$G_{ik} \leqq 0 \quad \text{and} \quad \sigma_k \equiv \tau_k / w_k \geqq \tau_i / w_i \equiv \sigma_i \quad \text{for all } i \neq k,$$

$$G_{jk} < 0 \quad \text{and} \quad \sigma_k > \sigma_j \quad \text{for some } j \neq k. \tag{4.5}$$

Corollary 7.2. *Let assumptions* (i) *and* (ii) *of Theorem 7 hold. Then there exists a commodity k such that a differential reduction in its tariff, with appropriate adjustments in domestic commodity taxes, is strictly Pareto-improving, and a commodity l such that a differential increase in its tariff, with appropriate adjustments in domestic commodity taxes, is strictly Pareto-improving.*

The first corollary shows that there is a class of tariff changes that move the domestic producer price towards the world price vector and are guaranteed to yield a strict Pareto

12. It is worth noting that assumption (ii) may be replaced by the weaker Assumption 2 if the outcome specified in Theorem 7 is amended to be the existence of a solution to (2.16) with $du \gg 0$, $db > 0$, $d\tau = a d\alpha$ and $d\alpha > 0$; that is, if we replace $db = 0$ by $db > 0$. In this case the nation has an additional policy instrument, which may be used to ensure a welfare improvement when preferences are not normal (in the sense of (ii)).

improvement in welfare so long as domestic commodity taxes are appropriately adjusted. It also shows that the policy of reducing the highest ad valorem tariff rate, or of increasing the lowest ad valorem tariff rate, will also work if traded commodities are substitutes in production.

Corollary 7.1 extends to a multi-household economy with commodity taxes as the only redistributive instrument, the validity of piecemeal policies demonstrated by previous authors to work in a single-household economy with lump sum taxes as a redistributive instrument. Radial reductions in tariff distortions were shown to be welfare-improving in a single household economy with a lump sum transfer mechanism by Foster and Sonnenschein (1970, p. 290), who assumed normality and constant producer prices, Bruno (1972, p. 379), Lloyd (1974, p. 381) and Fukushima (1979). Part (i) of Corollary 7.1 deals with tariff changes that are linear functions of w and τ, containing radial reductions as a special case, and indicates that such tariff reforms are strictly welfare-improving for all households in a multi-household economy with only domestic commodity taxes as available redistributive instruments. Part (ii) of Corollary 7.1 shows that the removal of extreme tariff distortion will also be strictly Pareto-improving for a multi-household economy with commodity tax rates as the only other tax instrument if all goods are net substitutes in production. Previously, Lloyd (1974), Hatta (1977) and Fukushima (1979) proved that such tariff reforms are welfare-improving in single household economies with lump sum transfers available. Theorem 7 and Corollary 7.1 thus generalize and extend the relevance of previous tariff reform policies to multi-household economies with domestic commodity taxes rather than lump sum transfers as the only redistributive taxation instruments.

Corollary 7.2 shows that, even without special assumptions regarding substitution, the policy of changing a single tariff will yield a strict Pareto improvement in welfare. Unfortunately, the corollary does not give guidance as to which tariff to change. However, that can be established by examining the sign structure of vector $\tau' G_{ww}$.

5. CONCLUSION

In this paper we have investigated the existence of strictly Pareto-improving changes in tariffs and domestic commodity taxes in a small open, multi-household economy. We introduced the concept of a productivity improvement in tariffs, which proved to be very useful. In particular, we showed that if a productivity improvement in tariffs is feasible and if the Weymark condition on household consumption vectors is satisfied, then there exists a tariff reform that increases the welfare of every household.

In addition to this general existence theorem we have obtained various piecemeal tariff policy results. Piecemeal tariff policies, such as the reduction of an extreme tariff distortion or a radial reduction of all tariff distortions, have previously been shown to be welfare-improving in single household economies with lump sum transfers available. Elsewhere we show these piecemeal policies are strictly Pareto-improving in a multi-household economy with lump sum transfers available.[13] In the present paper the successful application of these policies in economies with many households and domestic commodity taxes as the only available redistributive instrument is demonstrated. Further results dealing with various restrictions on the subset of commodity taxes that can be varied are available in Turunen (1985).

13. See Diewert, Turunen and Woodland (1984).

APPENDIX

This appendix contains a statement of a Lemma based upon Motzkin's Theorem of the Alternative and the proofs of the theorems presented in the text.

Lemma 1 (Motzkin) *Let D_1 and D_2 be given matrices and let x_1, x_2 and y be conformable vectors. Then either*

$$D_1x_1 + D_2x_2 = 0, \qquad x_1 \gg 0, \tag{A.1}$$

has a solution (x_1, x_2), or

$$y'D_1 < 0, \qquad y'D_2 = 0, \tag{A.2}$$

has a solution y, but never both.

Proof. Apply Motzkin's Theorem of the Alternative as given in Mangasarian (1969, p. 34) with $A = [I, 0]$, $C = 0$, *and* $D = [D_1, D_2]$. *Motzkin's alternative to* (A.1) is

$$z'A + y'D = 0, \qquad z > 0,$$

which is equivalent to

$$y'D_1 = -z' < 0, \qquad y'D_2 = 0,$$

which is (A.2). ||

Lemma 2. *Let A be a symmetric positive semi-definite matrix $(n \times n)$ such that $Ax = 0$ for some $x \neq 0$. Let τ be a vector such that $A\tau \neq 0$. Then $\tau' A \tau > 0$.*

Proof. The proof is available from the authors upon request. ||

Proof of Corollary 2.1. (i) If $a = (\gamma w - \varepsilon\tau)$, and $\gamma + \varepsilon > 0$, then

$$\begin{aligned} \tau' G_{w'w'}(w+\tau, y)a &= \gamma\tau' G_{w'w'}(w+\tau, y)w - \varepsilon\tau' G_{w'w'}(w+\tau, y)\tau \\ &= -(\gamma+\varepsilon)\tau' G_{w'w'}(w+\tau, y)\tau \quad \text{using (2.4)} \\ &< 0, \end{aligned} \tag{A.3}$$

since $\gamma + \varepsilon > 0$ and $\tau' G_{w'w'}(w+\tau, y)\tau > 0$ by Lemma 2.

(ii) If only τ_k is reduced than $a = -e_k$, where e_k is the kth unit vector. Then

$$\begin{aligned} \tau' G_{w'w'}(w+\tau, y)a &= -\tau' G_{wk} \quad (G_{wk} \text{ is column } k \text{ of } G_{w'w'}) \\ &= -\textstyle\sum_{i \neq k} \tau_i G_{ik} - \tau_k G_{kk} \\ &= \textstyle\sum_{i \neq k} w_i G_{ik}(\sigma_k - \sigma_i)/(1+\sigma_k) \quad \text{using (2.4) and } \sigma_i \equiv \tau_i / w_i \\ &< 0, \end{aligned} \tag{A.4}$$

if $G_{ik} \leqq 0$ and $\sigma_k \geqq \sigma_i$ for all $i \neq k$ and $G_{ik} < 0$ and $\sigma_k > \sigma_i$ for at least one $i \neq k$.

Thus in each case (i) and (ii) the inequality in (3.5) was shown to hold, proving the corollary. ||

Proof of Theorem 3. It is assumed that $w \gg 0$ and $r = w + \tau \gg 0$. Because of (2.4) it follows that

$$\tau' G_{w'w'}(w+\tau, y)(w+\tau) = 0. \tag{A.5}$$

Since $(w+\tau) \gg 0$, it follows that either (i) $\tau' G_{w'w'} = 0$, or (ii) $\tau' G_{w'w'}$ has both positive and negative elements. Since (i) is ruled out by Assumption 1, (ii) must hold. If element k is positive, then $d\beta(\tau)$ given by (3.3) will be positive if $d\tau_k < 0$ and $d\tau_i = 0$ for all $i \neq k$. If element j is negative then $d\beta(\tau)$ will be positive if $d\tau_j > 0$ and $d\tau_i = 0$ for all $i \neq j$. ||

Proof of Theorem 4. We are required to prove that there is a solution to (2.16) with $du \gg 0$ and $db = 0$. By Lemma 1 such a solution exists if and only if there is no solution λ to

$$\lambda' C_u < 0, \quad \lambda'[C_p, C_y, C_t, C_s, C_\tau] = 0, \tag{A.6}$$

which is the "Motzkin alternative".

Suppose (A.6) has a solution λ. Then, partitioning λ conformably with (2.16) as $\lambda' = (\lambda_1', \lambda_2', \lambda_3', \lambda_4)$, we can establish the following relations:

$$\begin{aligned} &\text{(i)} \quad \lambda'(C_p - C_t) = \lambda_2' = 0, \\ &\text{(ii)} \quad \lambda' C_y = \lambda_4 w' G_{wy} + \lambda_3' = 0 \qquad \text{due to (i)}, \\ &\text{(iii)} \quad \lambda'(C_\tau - C_s) = \lambda_4 w' G_{ww} = 0 \qquad \text{due to (i)}, \\ &\text{(iv)} \quad \lambda' C_u = \lambda_1' - \lambda_3' E_{pu} - \lambda_4 w' E_{wu} < 0 \qquad (\text{recalling } M_u = I). \end{aligned} \tag{A.7}$$

Assumption 1 implies that $w'G_{ww} \neq 0$ so (iii) implies that $\lambda_4 = 0$. Thus (ii) implies that $\lambda_3 = 0$ and (iv) implies that $\lambda_1 < 0$. It follows that

$$\text{(v)} \quad \lambda'[C_\tau, C_p] = \lambda_1'[M_w, M_p] = \lambda_1' M_p = 0.$$

However, this contradicts Assumption 2 which states that (v) has no solution $\lambda_1 < 0$. Accordingly, the supposition that (A.6) has a solution is incorrect. Thus, (A.6) has no solution and, by Lemma 1, there exists a solution to (2.16) with $du \gg 0$ and $db = 0$. ‖

Proof of Theorem 5. Since (s, t) is Pareto optimal given τ, there is no solution to (2.16) with $du > 0$, $db = 0$ and $d\tau = 0$. Thus, there is a solution λ to

$$\lambda' C_u \ll 0, \quad \lambda'[C_p, C_y, C_t, C_s] = 0, \tag{A.8}$$

using Tucker's Theorem of the Alternative.[14]

On the other hand, by Lemma 1, a solution to (2.16) with $du \gg 0$ and $db = 0$ exists if and only if there is no solution λ to (A.6).

If (A.6) has no solution then the λ that solves (A.8) cannot also solve (A.6). But this λ satisfies every condition of (A.6) except the condition $\lambda' C_\tau = 0$. Now if λ solves (A.8) then it can be shown, as in the proof of Theorem 4, that $\lambda_2 = 0$. Hence, if (A.6) has no solution,

$$\lambda'(C_\tau - C_s) = \lambda_4 w' G_{ww} \neq 0, \tag{A.9}$$

which implies that $w'G_{ww} = -\tau' G_{ww} \neq 0$. ‖

Proof of Theorem 6. By Lemma 1, there exists a solution to (2.16) with $du \gg 0$ and $d\tau = 0$ if and only if there is no solution λ to

$$\lambda' C_u < 0, \quad \lambda'[C_p, C_y, C_t, C_s, C_b] = 0. \tag{A.10}$$

By definition, Assumption 2 is satisfied if and only if there is no solution λ_1 to

$$\lambda_1'[M_w, M_p] = 0, \quad \lambda_1 < 0. \tag{A.11}$$

The theorem is proved by showing that the existence of a solution to (A.11) (violation of Assumption 2) implies the existence of a solution to (A.10) (non-existence of a solution to (2.16) with $du \gg 0$ and $d\tau = 0$), and vice versa.

First, suppose that Assumption 2 does *not* hold, implying that there exists a solution λ_1 to (A.11). If we now choose $\lambda_2 = 0$, $\lambda_3 = 0$, $\lambda_4 = 0$ and λ_1 as the solution to (A.11), it is easily shown that $\lambda' = (\lambda_1', \lambda_2', \lambda_3', \lambda_4')$ is a solution to (A.10). Thus, it has been shown that if Assumption 2 does not hold, then (A.10) has a solution and hence there is no solution to (2.16) with $du \gg 0$ and $d\tau = 0$.

Second, suppose that there is no solution to (2.16) with $du \gg 0$ and $d\tau = 0$, implying that there is a solution λ to (A.10). Then, as in the proof of Theorem 4 it can be shown that (A.7.i), (A.7.ii) and (A.7.iv) hold. In addition, it is easily shown that $\lambda' C_b = -\lambda_4 = 0$ and, hence, from (A.7.i) and (A.7.ii) that $\lambda_2 = 0$ and $\lambda_3 = 0$, and so from (A.7.iv) that $\lambda_1 < 0$. It follows that

$$\lambda[C_s, C_t] = \lambda_1'[M_w, M_p] = \lambda_1' M_p = 0. \tag{A.12}$$

However, this implies that (A.11) has a solution, which means that Assumption 2 is violated. It has been shown, therefore, that no solution to (2.16) with $du \gg 0$ and $d\tau = 0$ implies that Assumption 2 is violated. ‖

14. See Mangasarian (1969, p. 34). Tucker's theorem of the alternative is used here rather than Motzkin's, since the required inequality condition on du is now $du > 0$ (no household loses and at least one gains) rather than $du \gg 0$ (all households gain).

Proof of Theorem 7. Condition (ii) of Theorem 7 implies, by Lemma 1, that there does not exist a solution λ to

$$\lambda'[C_u, -C_b] < 0, \qquad \lambda'[C_p, C_y, C_t, C_s] = 0. \tag{A.13}$$

We wish to show that if (4.3) holds then (2.16) has a solution with $du \gg 0$, $db = 0$, $d\tau = ad\alpha$ and $d\alpha > 0$ and so, by Lemma 1, there does not exist a solution λ to

$$\lambda'[C_u, C_\alpha] < 0, \qquad \lambda'[C_p, C_y, C_t, C_s] = 0, \tag{A.14}$$

where $C_\alpha = C_\tau a$.

Suppose, to the contrary, that (A.14) has a solution λ. Then it is easily shown that

$$\lambda' C_\alpha = \lambda'(C_\alpha - C_s a) = -\lambda_4 \tau' G_{ww} a \leqq 0, \tag{A.15}$$

which, together with (4.3), implies that $\lambda_4 \leqq 0$. Since $\lambda' C_b = -\lambda_4$ we see that $\lambda' C_\alpha$ and $-\lambda' C_b$ have the same sign depending upon the sign of λ_4. Comparing (A.13) with (A.14) we conclude that the solution to (A.14) is also a solution to (A.13). This contradicts the assumption that (A.13) has no solution. Our supposition that (A.14) has a solution is therefore incorrect. Accordingly, (A.14) has no solution and the conclusion of the theorem follows. ||

Acknowledgement. The authors are indebted to the Social Science and Humanities Research Council of Canada and the Yrjo Jahnsson Foundation for financial support, and to R. Harris, M. Kemp, P. Lloyd, E. Sieper and the referees for their helpful comments on earlier drafts. This paper is a substantial revision and extension of Sections 1-4 of Diewert, Turunen and Woodland (1984).

REFERENCES

BERTRAND, T. J. and VANEK, J. (1971), "The theory of tariffs, taxes and subsidies: some aspects of the second best", *American Economic Review*, **61**, 925-931.

BRUNO, M. (1972), "Market distortions and gradual reform", *Review of Economic Studies*, **39**, 373-383.

DIAMOND, P. A. and MIRRLEES, J. A. (1971), "Optimal taxation and public production I-II", *American Economic Review*, **61**, 8-27 and 261-278.

DIEWERT, W. E. (1978), "Optimal tax perturbations", *Journal of Public Economics*, **10**, 139-177.

DIEWERT, W. E. (1982), "Duality approaches to microeconomic theory", Chapter 12 in Arrow, K. J. and Intriligator M. D. (eds) *Handbook of Mathematical Economics* (Amsterdam: North-Holland Publishing Company), 535-599.

DIEWERT, W. E., TURUNEN, A. H. and WOODLAND, A. D. (1984), "Productivity and Pareto improving changes in taxes and tariffs" (Discussion paper #84-06, University of British Columbia).

DIEWERT, W. E. and WOODLAND, A. D. (1977), "Frank Knight's theorem in linear programming revisited", *Econometrica*, **45**, 375-398.

DIXIT, A. and NORMAN, V. (1980) *Theory of International Trade* (Welwyn, U.K.: James Nisbet).

DIXIT, A. and NORMAN, V. (1986), "Gains from trade without lump-sum compensation", *Journal of International Economics*, **16**, 111-112.

FOSTER, E. and SONNENSCHEIN, H. (1970), "Price distortion and economic welfare", *Econometrica*, **38**, 281-296.

FUKUSHIMA, T. (1979), "Tariff structure, nontraded goods and the theory of piecemeal policy recommendations", *International Economic Review*, **20**, 427-435.

HATTA, T. (1977), "A recommendation for a better tariff structure", *Econometrica*, **45**, 1859-1869.

KEMP, M. C. and WAN, H. Y. (1986), "Gains from trade with and without lump-sum compensation", *Journal of International Economics*, **16**, 99-110.

LLOYD, P. J. (1974), "A more general theory of price distortions in open economies", *Journal of International Economics*, **4**, 365-386.

MANGASARIAN, O. L. (1969) *Nonlinear Programming* (New York: McGraw-Hill).

SAMUELSON, P. A. (1953), "Prices of factors and goods in general equilibrium", *Review of Economic Studies*, **21**, 1-20.

TURUNEN, A. H. (1985), Optimal public policies in small open economies" (Ph.D. thesis, University of British Columbia).

WEYMARK, J. A. (1979), "A reconciliation of recent results in optimal taxation theory", *Journal of Public Economics*, **12**, 171-189.

WOODLAND, A. D. (1982) *International trade and resource allocation* (Amsterdam: North-Holland Publishing Company).

[32]

Econometrica, Vol. 59, No. 4 (July, 1991), 1127–1152

STRICT PARETO-IMPROVING MULTILATERAL REFORMS OF TARIFFS

BY ARJA H. TURUNEN-RED AND ALAN D. WOODLAND[1]

We consider a model of a trading world consisting of an arbitrary number of nations engaged in international trade in an arbitrary number of commodities. Starting from an arbitrary tariff-distorted initial equilibrium, we examine the possibilities of undertaking a gradual multilateral reform of tariffs (and other trade taxes and subsidies) so as to attain a strict Pareto improvement in welfare. Necessary and sufficient conditions for the existence of strict Pareto-improving multilateral (differential) tariff reforms, accompanied by international transfers of income, are obtained. These results are then applied to various concrete tariff reform proposals such as proportional reductions in tariffs and the reduction of the highest ad valorem tariff rates. Some of our theorems extend the generality of previously obtained results, and some new tariff reform proposals are also made.

KEYWORDS: Tariff reform, Pareto improvements, multilateral.

1. INTRODUCTION

DESPITE THE LONG-HELD and predominant view among economists that free international trade is desirable, there exist significant barriers to international trade in the form of tariffs and quantitative restrictions. Moreover, attempts to undertake gradual reform of international trade barriers under the auspices of GATT (General Agreement on Tariffs and Trade), which undertakes regular multilateral tariff reduction negotiations, have never been easy. Such negotiations are difficult because they involve many traded commodities, tariff reductions in all participating nations, and nations will only agree to the proposed reforms if they will be better off as a consequence.

In view of the importance of multilateral tariff reform, it is surprising that economic theorists have given it relatively little attention. Indeed, most of the literature on tariff reform has focused upon unilateral tariff reform in small open economies.

The essence of the tariff reform problem is that it is a special case of the general theory of second best, pioneered by Meade (1955) and Lipsey and Lancaster (1956). The implication of the theory of second best is that the reduction or elimination of a subset of distortions in a competitive equilibrium may not be welfare improving. In the context of international trade, while free trade may be Pareto optimal, the partial reduction of import tariffs (or other trade taxes) or even the complete elimination of some of them may not be welfare improving. For example, it is now well known that free trade is optimal (first best) for a small open economy, but that the reduction of the rate of import duty on one commodity may actually reduce welfare. Indeed, there may

[1] The first author acknowledges the University of Sydney for its hospitality and the University of Texas at Austin for a Summer Research Grant.

exist commodities such that an increase in their tariff rates will increase welfare. In this example, a full reduction of all tariffs to zero is a welfare improvement but this shift may be practically and politically infeasible. Hence, the problem of tariff reform arises: the problem is to design small feasible changes in the country's existing tariff structure that will improve welfare when the first best (free trade) is not immediately available.

In a many-country competitive world a similar situation arises: free trade is the first best choice but, starting from an equilibrium distorted by arbitrary country-specific tariffs, a shift to entirely free trade is not usually considered attainable. Again, attention focusses upon the search for directions of tariff reform (small feasible changes in tariffs) that will improve the welfare of all nations, rather than upon first best, but unattainable, solutions.

The purpose of the present paper is to specify a many-nation, many-commodity model of international trade containing distortions arising from trade taxes (tariffs) and to examine the possibilities for the gradual multilateral reform of tariffs. Attention is focussed upon the attainment of strict Pareto improvements in welfare, whereby every nation gains from the tariff reform, since only these reforms are guaranteed to get unanimous approval. Apart from obtaining general existence theorems, we consider concrete tariff reform proposals. Some of the results extend previously obtained results concerning tariff reform proposals, but new tariff reform formulae are also proposed.

The tariff reform problem closely resembles the closed economy tax reform problem, where the goal is to design changes of the country's existing commodity tax structure so that a welfare improvement (a strict Pareto improvement in the many-household case) results. Our analysis of the tariff reform problem applies some of the methods developed by Guesnerie (1977), Diewert (1978), and Weymark (1979) in the tax reform context.[2]

The literature on tariff reform consists of two distinct parts. The first and by far the largest part of this literature deals with unilateral tariff reform by a small open economy under the assumption that world prices for tradeable commodities and trade policies of the rest of the world are given. Two broad policy conclusions emerge from this literature: proportional reductions in all tariffs and a reduction of extreme ad valorem tariff rates can be welfare improving. Demonstrations that a proportional reduction in all tariffs is welfare improving in a small open, single-household economy have been provided by Foster and Sonnenschein (1970), Bruno (1972), Lloyd (1974), Hatta (1977b), and Fukushima (1979). Various results concerning welfare improvements arising from the reduction of extreme ad valorem tariff rates, which typically rely upon substitutability assumptions, have been derived by Bertrand and Vanek (1971), Hatta (1977b), and Fukushima (1979). These results have been extended to a many-household context by Diewert, Turunen-Red, and Woodland (1991) and, further, to the case where only domestic taxes, not household transfers, are

[2] The methodology of our paper is also closely related to Diewert (1983). Keen (1987) addresses an analogous problem of domestic tax reform (harmonization) in a multilateral context.

available as a distributive device by Diewert, Turunen-Red, and Woodland (1989).[3]

The second and much smaller part of the tariff reform literature deals with multilateral tariff reforms, whereby many nations simultaneously alter their tariffs. Vanek (1964) and Hatta and Fukushima (1979) consider tariff reform in a many nation world that trades in just two commodities and show that a reduction of the world's highest ad valorem tariff rate will yield a potential increase in welfare for all nations.[4] Hatta and Fukushima also prove that a proportional reduction in all tariff rates is potentially welfare improving. More recently, Fukushima and Kim (1989) extend the Hatta-Fukushima result on proportional reductions in tariffs to a many-commodity setting.

While these extensions of the welfare-improving properties of proportional and extreme ad valorem rate tariff reforms to the multilateral context are very important, they suffer from several weaknesses. The first is that these results have been obtained under fairly stringent assumptions. Vanek (1964) and Hatta and Fukushima (1979) assume that there are just two tradeable commodities, an assumption that implicitly ensures that these commodities are net substitutes in every nation. They also assume that all commodities are normal in every nation. While Fukushima and Kim (1989) allow for many tradeable commodities, they maintain this rather extreme normality assumption and, moreover, assume that no pair of commodities can be net complements in either production or consumption in any nation. The question naturally arises as to whether it is possible to prove that proportional and extreme tariff reductions yield Pareto improvements in welfare under somewhat weaker assumptions.

The first purpose of our paper is to answer this question in the affirmative by deriving more general results than have been obtained thus far. The second purpose is to provide general theorems on the existence of Pareto-improving tariff reforms in a multilateral context. The resulting necessary and sufficient conditions may be checked for any tariff reform proposal to determine its welfare effects. The third purpose is to provide new multilateral tariff reform proposals that are strict Pareto improving in welfare.

In Section 2 we specify a model of a trading world consisting of an arbitrary number of nations engaged in international trade in an arbitrary number of commodities. In Section 3 a general existence theorem is obtained and interpreted from an economic viewpoint. Specifically, we provide the necessary and sufficient conditions for the existence of a strict Pareto-improving (every nation attains a strict welfare improvement) multilateral tariff perturbation. Using this result, we note that a strict Pareto-improving multilateral tariff reform exists, for example, if the domestic price vectors for traded goods differ across the nations and the net substitution matrices of at least two nations are of maximal rank.

[3] The case of unilateral tariff reform in a nation large enough to affect world prices has been considered by Dixit (1987).

[4] To convert a potential increase in welfare into an actual Pareto improvement, the tariff reform has to be accompanied by a set of international transfers of income. Our analysis deals with actual welfare improvements.

Our primary focus is upon the welfare implications of specific multilateral reforms of tariffs, dealt with in Section 4. In order to provide specific tariff reform recommendations, we consider the existence of a multilateral strict Pareto-improving tariff reform when the change in the world tariffs is restricted to a particular *direction*. Our existence theorems for this type of tariff reform allow us to derive several interesting special cases: we consider proportional changes and reductions of all tariffs, shifts of domestic prices toward world market prices, shifts of domestic prices toward a specifically defined shadow price vector for traded products, unilateral tariff reforms including unilateral reductions of extreme tariffs, and changes of single tariffs. Our results extend old and provide new recommendations for unilateral and multilateral tariff reform in a very general model of world trade. Concluding comments and suggestions for further research are provided in Section 5.

Methodologically, our paper does not adopt the standard comparative static procedure to derive existence and specific policy recommendation results. Instead, we follow recent practice and make extensive use of Motzkin's Theorem of the Alternative.[5] This theorem plays a pivotal role throughout our analytical sections, and allows us to establish definite policy statements in a very general model of a trading world without the need to obtain an explicit solution to the differential comparative system for our model.

2. THE MODEL

In this section we set out the formal model that is used in subsequent sections for the analysis of tariff reforms. We consider a perfectly competitive general equilibrium model of the world, consisting of K ($\geqslant 2$) nations trading in N ($\geqslant 2$) internationally tradeable commodities. Each nation consists of many producers, a single consumer, and a government. The national governments impose taxes and/or subsidies (to be referred to as "tariffs") on international trade, undertake lump-sum transfers to or from the consumer (domestic transfers), and many undertake lump-sum transfers to or from foreign governments (international transfers).[6] Given the policies of the national governments, a competitive equilibrium for the world is established. The tariff reform problem is to perturb this equilibrium by altering the national tariff vectors so as to achiéve a Pareto improvement in welfare.

The K nations are assumed to engage in international trade in the N tradeable commodities at the world price vector $p^T = (1, q^T)$, which is normalized so that the first commodity serves as the numeraire, where ^{T} denotes the transpose of a vector. The prices facing the domestic consumer and producers in nation k are given by the domestic price vector p^k, $k = 1, \ldots, K$. This domestic price vector differs from the world price vector by a vector of (specific)

[5] See Mangasarian (1969, p. 34) for a statement of this theorem. It has been used extensively in the tax and tariff reform literature following early uses by Diewert (1978) and Weymark (1979).

[6] The governments may also have fixed demand vectors for tradeable and nontradeable commodities, possibly to produce a fixed amount of a public good. However, since these demands play no role in the analysis of tariff reform, they are ignored in the model specification.

trade taxes, τ^k, levied on the net imports of the tradeable commodities. Thus, $p^k = p + \tau^k$. It should be noted that, since the trade tax vector and the net import vector may have both positive and negative elements, the trade tax vector may include export taxes and subsidies as well as import taxes (tariffs) and subsidies. Thus, if $\tau_i^k > 0$ (< 0) and commodity i is being imported by nation k, then τ_i^k is an import tariff (import subsidy); and if $\tau_i^k > 0$ (< 0) and commodity i is being exported by nation k, then τ_i^k is an export subsidy (export tax). Accordingly, the model is very general in allowing for all types of trade taxes and subsidies. While, strictly speaking, tariffs are a special case, we shall adopt the convenient convention of referring to τ^k as the tariff vector and to the policy of changing it as tariff reform.

The production sector of each nation is modelled in terms of the net revenue or gross national product (GNP) function. Commodities are divided into two groups: internationally tradeable and internationally nontradeable commodities. As in the traditional international trade model, the nontradeable commodities may be regarded as domestic factors of production but our model formulation does not require this and some nontradeable commodities may be outputs. However, it is assumed that the net outputs of nontradeable commodities are fixed in order to keep the model as simple as possible. Given the fixed net supply of nontradeable commodities and the exogenous prices of tradeable commodities, it is well known that the perfectly competitive production sector in nation k may be characterized by the net revenue or GNP function $G^k(p^k)$, which indicates the maximum value of net production of tradeable commodities that can be achieved.[7] It also represents the net revenue earned by the consumer from the sale of the fixed vector of nontradeable commodities (factors) to the production sector.

The GNP function $G^k(p^k)$ is a convex, linearly homogeneous function of prices, and it is assumed to be twice continuously differentiable. Hotelling's lemma implies that the gradient with respect to prices, denoted $G_p^k(p^k)$, is the vector of net supply functions for tradeable commodities.[8,9]

The consumption sector in nation k is characterized by the expenditure function $E^k(p^k, u^k)$ for tradeable commodities, where u^k is the level of utility or welfare for the single consumer.[10] The expenditure functions are concave and linearly homogeneous in prices, increasing in utility, and assumed to be twice continuously differentiable. Shephard's lemma implies that the gradient

[7] Debreu (1959, p. 45) indicates that net revenue of the production sector is maximized if and only if each firm maximizes net revenue.

[8] Properties of the net revenue or GNP function are provided in Diewert (1974, pp. 133–141), who calls it a variable profit function. Applications of the GNP function in international trade theory may be found in Woodland (1982, p. 58) and Dixit and Norman (1980, p. 30), who call it the revenue function. If the nontradeable commodities consist only of all the primary factors of production, then G^k is indeed gross national product.

[9] Throughout the paper we use subscripts to denote derivatives. For example, $G_p^k(p^k)$ is the vector of partial derivatives of $G^k(p^k)$ with respect to p^k while $G_{pp}^k(p^k)$ is the matrix of second derivatives with respect to p^k.

[10] The assumption of a single consumer is for simplicity, though it may be justified if the government undertakes household lump-sum transfers to maximize a social welfare function, as proved by Samuelson (1956).

with respect to prices, denoted $E_p^k(p^k, u^k)$, is the vector of Hicksian or compensated demand functions for tradeable commodities.[11]

It will be convenient to define the country-specific maximal *compensated net revenue functions*:

$$(2.1) \qquad S^k(p^k, u^k) \equiv G^k(p^k) - E^k(p^k, u^k) \qquad (k = 1, \ldots, K),$$

as the difference between the revenue earned by the production sectors and the expenditures by the consumers on tradeable commodities. Thus, $S^k(p^k, u^k)$ represents the excess of income over expenditure on tradeable commodities for the private sector of nation k. The properties of the GNP and expenditure functions ensure that the maximal compensated net revenue functions are convex and linearly homogeneous in prices, decreasing in utility, and twice continuously differentiable. The lemmas of Hotelling and Shephard may be used to show that the gradient of the net revenue function, denoted as $S_p^k(p^k, u^k) \equiv G_p^k(p^k) - E_p^k(p^k, u^k)$, is the vector of compensated net export functions for nation k. It is because of this property that the net revenue function may be used to conveniently specify the equilibrium conditions for the model.[12]

Because of the interpretation of the gradient of the net revenue functions with respect to prices, $S_p^k(p^k, u^k)$, as the vector of compensated net export functions, the matrix of second-order derivatives with respect to prices, denoted by $S_{pp}^k(p^k, u^k)$, may be regarded as the matrix of responses of net exports of tradeable commodities to changes in their domestic prices. Since the compensated net revenue functions are convex, the matrices S_{pp}^k are positive semidefinite, and since the compensated net revenue functions are linearly homogeneous, the second-derivative matrices satisfy the identity

$$(2.2) \qquad p^{kT} S_{pp}^k(p^k, u^k) = 0 \qquad (k = 1, \ldots, K).$$

The consumer in nation k has a budget constraint given by

$$(2.3) \qquad E^k(p^k, u^k) = m^k + G^k(p^k), \qquad (k = 1, \ldots, K).$$

This states that expenditure equals income, which consists of net transfers (possibly negative or zero) from the government, m^k, and income derived from the sale of the fixed endowment of nontradeable commodities to the production sector, $G^k(p^k)$.

The national governments are assumed to impose a vector of taxes (tariffs) on net imports of tradeable commodities, τ^k, and undertake lump-sum transfers of income to the domestic consumer, m^k, or to foreign governments, b^k. It is the change in these policy instruments that is the focus of this paper. The initial values of these policy instruments are assumed to be arbitrarily given, but they

[11] See, for example, Diewert (1982, pp. 537–553) for properties of the expenditure function.

[12] See, for example, Woodland (1982, pp. 169–172) for further information on the net revenue function. If $Y^k(v^k)$ is the production possibility set for tradeable commodities, v^k is the fixed net input vector of nontradeable commodities, and $Z^k(u^k)$ is the set of consumption vectors yielding at least utility level u^k, then we may define the net revenue function as

$$S^k(p^k, u^k) = \max_x \{ p^{kT} x : x \in Y^k(v^k) - Z^k(u^k) \}.$$

must satisfy the government budget constraint. The government budget constraints may be written as

$$(2.4)\qquad m^k + b^k = -\tau^{kT} S_p^k(p^k, u^k) \qquad (k = 1, \dots, K).$$

This states that the net transfers from nation k's government to the consumer, m^k, plus the net transfers to foreign governments, b^k, must equal the net revenue received from the trade taxes, $-\tau^{kT} S_p^k(p^k, u^k)$. Evidently, the value of one of these policy variables is determined once the values of the remaining policy variables are determined. In the subsequent model specification and analysis the net transfers from the government to the consumer, m^k, is taken to be the instrument so determined and so no specific reference to it will be made.

Under the assumptions that the net revenue functions are differentiable and that the world price vector p is positive, the equilibrium conditions for the world economy may be compactly written as follows:

$$(2.5)\qquad \sum_{k=1}^{K} S_p^k(p + \tau^k, u^k) = 0,$$

$$(2.6)\qquad p^T S_p^k(p + \tau^k, u^k) = b^k \qquad (k = 1, \dots, K),$$

$$(2.7)\qquad \sum_{k=1}^{K} b^k = 0.$$

The first N equations (2.5) are the world market equilibrium conditions for tradeable commodities, stating that the world excess supplies for these are zero. The K equations in (2.6) are the national budget constraints, which state that the value at world prices of nation k's net exports (its balance of trade) equals its net transfer to foreign governments, b^k. This national budget constraint may be derived from the consumer budget constraint (2.3) and the government budget constraint (2.4) by eliminating m^k and making use of (2.2). Conversely, if the national budget constraint (2.6) is satisfied, then the consumer and government budget constraints will also be satisfied by an appropriate choice of m^k. Finally, condition (2.7) requires the international transfers to be consistent with a zero world balance of payments.

Given the tariff vectors τ^k, $k = 1, \dots, K$, and a vector $b = (b^1, \dots, b^K)^T$ of international transfers satisfying (2.7), the market equilibrium conditions (2.5) and the national budget constraints (2.6) may be solved for the competitive equilibrium world price vector for tradeable commodities, p, and the vector of national utilities $u = (u^1, \dots, u^K)^T$. The transfers m^k, $k = 1, \dots, K$, to consumers consistent with the government budget constraint may then be obtained from (2.3) or (2.4).

The existence of a competitive equilibrium solution with $p \gg 0$ is assumed.[13] As is well known, Walras' Law ensures that one of the market equilibrium conditions in (2.5) is redundant and may be safely ignored. In the subsequent

[13] Notation: If $x = (x_1, \dots, x_N)^T$ then $x \gg 0$ means $x_n > 0$ for all $n = 1, \dots, N$; $x > 0$ means $x_n \geqslant 0$ for all $n = 1, \dots, N$, and $x \neq 0$; and $x \geqslant 0$ means $x_n \geqslant 0$ for all $n = 1, \dots, N$. Also, I_K denotes a K-dimensional identity matrix, while l_K denotes a K-dimensional vector of ones.

analysis the market for the first tradeable commodity is ignored. Moreover, the equilibrium world price vector is only determined up to a factor of proportionality and so, as previously indicated, it has been normalized by setting the price of the first commodity to unity.

In this paper attention is focussed upon differential tariff reform. A differential tariff reform given by the vectors $d\tau^k$, $k=1,\dots,K$, accompanied by a differential change in international transfers, db, will cause adjustments in the world price vector and the utility levels of all of the consumers to re-establish a competitive equilibrium. The changes in these policy instruments and endogenous variables consistent with the re-establishment of a competitive equilibrium are obtained by computing the differential comparative static system for the model. Given our differentiability assumptions concerning the maximal net revenue function S^k, the system (2.5)–(2.7) can be differentiated at the initial equilibrium to yield

$$A\,du + B\,dq + C\,db + D\,d\tau = 0, \tag{2.8}$$

where the matrices $A,\dots,D$ are defined by

$$A = \begin{bmatrix} S^1_{qu} & \cdots & S^K_{qu} \\ p^T S^1_{pu} & \cdots & 0 \\ \vdots & \cdots & \vdots \\ 0 & \cdots & p^T S^K_{pu} \\ 0 & \cdots & 0 \end{bmatrix}, \quad B = \begin{bmatrix} S_{qq} \\ S^{1T}_q + p^T S^1_{pq} \\ \vdots \\ S^{KT}_q + p^T S^K_{pq} \\ 0 \end{bmatrix}, \tag{2.9}$$

$$C = \begin{bmatrix} 0 \\ -I_k \\ l^T_K \end{bmatrix}, \quad D = \begin{bmatrix} S^1_{qp} & \cdots & S^K_{qp} \\ p^T S^1_{pp} & \cdots & 0 \\ \vdots & \cdots & \vdots \\ 0 & \cdots & p^T S^K_{pp} \\ 0 & \cdots & 0 \end{bmatrix},$$

and

$$S = \begin{bmatrix} S_{11} & S_{1q} \\ S_{q1} & S_{qq} \end{bmatrix} = [S_{p1}, S_{pq}] \equiv \sum_{k=1}^{K} \begin{bmatrix} S^k_{11} & S^k_{1q} \\ S^k_{q1} & S^k_{qq} \end{bmatrix}. \tag{2.10}$$

The matrix S defined in (2.10) gives the aggregate (world) net substitution effects upon world excess supplies of traded commodities of changes in the international prices p, keeping utility levels fixed in every nation.

Before proceeding to examine the solutions to (2.8) it will be useful to introduce a harmless simplifying normalization of the compensated net revenue functions at the initial equilibrium. Since we assume that the country specific expenditure functions are increasing in utility and, hence, the net revenue functions are decreasing in utility, we may normalize these functions so that

$$(2.11) \quad S_u^k(p^k, u^k) = -1 \qquad (k = 1, \ldots, K),$$

at the initial equilibrium. This money metric scaling of utilities implies that the vectors $-S_{pu}^k = E_{pu}^k$, $k = 1, \ldots, K$, can be regarded as the income derivatives of the nations' ordinary (Marshallian) demand functions at the initial equilibrium.[14] Further, (2.11) and linear homogeneity of the functions $S_u^k(p^k, u^k)$ in prices p^k yield the identity

$$(2.12) \quad p^{kT} S_{pu}^k(p^k, u^k) = -1,$$

which will be used in the subsequent analysis.

3. EXISTENCE OF STRICT PARETO-IMPROVING TARIFF REFORMS

3.1. *Existence Results*

In this section, we develop necessary and sufficient conditions for the existence of strict Pareto-improving multilateral reforms of tariffs under the assumption that tariff reforms are accompanied by a system of international transfers of income. The existence conditions are interpreted from an economic viewpoint and are expressed in terms of income derivatives of the consumer demand functions and the national substitution matrices. Central to the analysis is a vector of shadow prices that plays a crucial role in the specific tariff reform recommendations to be considered in Section 4.

Multilateral tariff reform is defined in the present context to be a differential change or perturbation in the vector of all nations' tariffs, $d\tau$. Assuming that the national governments can agree on a perturbation of the initial international transfers, db, as a part of a multilateral tariff and transfer reform, we wish to determine the necessary and sufficient conditions under which there exists a (differential) change $(d\tau, db)$ such that the welfare level of each country is improved. That is, we wish to specify conditions for the existence of a strict Pareto-improving (differential) multilateral tariff and transfer reform, assuming that international prices adjust to maintain a competitive equilibrium. Formally, the problem is to establish the circumstances where there exists a $(du, dq, db, d\tau)$ such that (2.8) holds and $du \gg 0$.[15]

We first state the general necessary and sufficient conditions for the existence of a strict Pareto-improving tariff and transfer reform as a lemma. This lemma forms the basis for the proofs of the theorems contained in this paper and is proved using Motzkin's Theorem of the Alternative.[16] Unfortunately, the lemma

[14] Diewert (1978, p. 146).

[15] Attention is restricted to a *strict* Pareto improvement in welfare, $du \gg 0$, rather than a weak Pareto improvement, $du > 0$, following Diewert (1978, p. 155). Diewert argues that the latter requirement does not guarantee that a small *finite* tariff reform will make no nation worse off, whereas the former does.

[16] Motzkin's Theorem of the Alternative is stated and proved in Mangasarian (1969, pp. 28–29, 34).

does not lend itself easily to a simple economic interpretation but it is used to prove subsequent theorems that do have useful economic interpretations.

LEMMA 1: *A strict Pareto-improving (differential) multilateral tariff and transfer reform exists if and only if there is no vector $\lambda \in R^{N-1}$ and no scalar $\mu \in R$ such that the net export substitution matrices S^k_{pp} and the export income derivatives S^k_{pu}, $k = 1, \ldots, K$, satisfy the conditions*

$$(3.1) \quad \lambda^T S_{qq} + \mu p^T S_{pq} = 0,$$

$$(3.2) \quad \lambda^T S^k_{qp} + \mu p^T S^k_{pp} = 0 \qquad (k = 1, \ldots, K),$$

$$(3.3) \quad [\lambda^T, \mu p^T] \begin{bmatrix} S^1_{qu} & \cdots & S^K_{qu} \\ S^1_{pu} & \cdots & S^K_{pu} \end{bmatrix} < 0.$$

We now make an additional assumption that enables us to provide a new and simpler characterization of the existence conditions (3.1)–(3.3). Let us assume that the $(N-1) \times (N-1)$ dimensional submatrix, S_{qq}, of the world net substitution matrix S_{pp} has full rank $(N-1)$. Then, we can define scalars

$$(3.4) \quad \beta^k \equiv \hat{p}^T S^k_{pu} = p^T S^k_{pu} - p^T S_{pq} S^{-1}_{qq} S^k_{qu} \qquad (k = 1, \ldots, K),$$

where

$$(3.5) \quad \hat{p}^T = p^T - (0, p^T S_{pq} S^{-1}_{qq})$$

is the world shadow price vector introduced by Turunen-Red and Woodland (1988, p. 256) and discussed further in subsection 3.2 below. Our new characterization of the existence conditions is provided in the following theorem.

THEOREM 1: *Let the world substitution matrix S_{qq} have full rank $N-1$ and let p_1 be fixed. Then, a strict Pareto-improving multilateral (differential) tariff and transfer reform exists if and only if there is no scalar $\mu \in R$ such that*

$$(3.6) \quad \mu \hat{p}^T S^k_{pp} = 0 \qquad (k = 1, \ldots, K),$$

$$(3.7) \quad \mu[\beta^1, \ldots, \beta^K] < 0.$$

Whether the system of equations and inequalities (3.6)–(3.7) has a solution depends in a fairly complicated way upon the nature of the substitution possibilities in both production and consumption (S^k_{pp}), the response of consumer demand to income changes in each nation ($-S^k_{pu}$), the shadow price vector $\hat{p}$, and, implicitly, upon the tariff structures.

If the equations and inequalities in (3.6) and (3.7) have a solution, then Theorem 1 indicates that a strict Pareto-improving tariff and transfer reform does not exist. Conversely, if (3.6) and (3.7) do not have a solution, then there does exist a tariff reform $d\tau$, accompanied by a change of international transfers db, such that the utility levels of all consumers increase, that is, $du \gg 0$. Thus, the tariff reform problem reduces to the question of whether (3.6) and (3.7) have a solution.

3.2. *Normality and Shadow Prices*

Before proceeding to discuss the implications of Theorem 1, we provide an interpretation of the scalars β^k and the vector $\hat{p}$. In the analysis of tariff reform in a small open economy the term $p^T E^k_{pu} \equiv -p^T S^k_{pu}$ often appears, and the requirement that $p^T S^k_{pu} < 0$ may be referred to as the *Hatta normality condition* for nation k. In the context of a closed economy, Hatta (1977a) refers to this expression, with p interpreted as the producer price vector, as the aggregate of income terms weighted by marginal costs (AIM). Dixit (1975) notes, further, that this term will be positive in a closed economy if and only if an increase in the consumer's endowment increases consumer welfare. In the context of a small open economy, Lloyd (1974) refers to $p^T E^k_{pu}$ as the aggregate marginal propensity to consume evaluated at world prices and assumes that it is positive. This expression also appears in Hatta (1977b), Dixit (1985, p. 344), and Fukushima (1981), who calls it the aggregate income term evaluated by world prices (AIW) and interprets the condition that $p^T E^k_{pu}$ be positive as a stability condition for a small open economy. Moreover, the condition $p^T E^k_{pu} > 0$ is easily shown to be the necessary and sufficient condition for a transfer of income to nation k to increase welfare in that nation if it is a small open economy, that is, if world prices do not change.

The prices used to weight the income effects in the Hatta normality condition are the world prices for tradeable commodities. This is appropriate for small open economies, but not for large ones that have an influence upon world prices. It turns out that the appropriate price vector to use for this purpose is the price vector $\hat{p}$ defined by (3.5). Accordingly, by analogy with the Hatta normality condition for a small open economy, we follow Turunen-Red and Woodland (1988) and define for a large open economy the requirement that $\beta^k = \hat{p}^T S^k_{pu} < 0$ as the *generalized Hatta normality condition* for nation k.

In Turunen-Red and Woodland (1988) the vector $\hat{p}$ defined by (3.5) is given an interpretation as the shadow price vector that should be used to evaluate public projects. If a public project that affects world prices is evaluated at the shadow price vector $\hat{p}$ and the generalized Hatta normality condition holds for nation k, then it can be shown that nation k experiences an increase in welfare (other utility levels constant) if and only if the project yields a positive (shadow) profit.

The world shadow price vector $\hat{p}$ may be further interpreted as follows. If there is a unit increase in world excess supplies of each traded commodity (due to some public project, say) there will be an adjustment of prices required to re-establish equilibrium in the commodity markets. If utility levels are held constant, the effect upon market prices q is given by the matrix $-S^{-1}_{qq}$. This change in market prices then affects the world tariff revenue by an amount given by $p^T S_{pq}$.[17] The total effect upon world tariff revenue is then given by $-p^T S_{pq} S_{qq}^{-1}$, which is the adjustment to the unnormalized part of the world price vector, p, to obtain the shadow price vector, $\hat{p}$. Thus, $\hat{p}$ takes into account the facts that world prices will be affected by any project that alters world excess supplies and that the world tariff revenue will be affected in turn.

It may also be shown that $\hat{p}$ differs from p by a weighted average of tariff rates. To facilitate this demonstration let it be assumed, without loss of generality, that tariffs on commodity 1 are zero in every nation and partition the tariff vectors as $\tau^{kT} = (0, \sigma^{kT})$. Then it can be shown that (3.5) reduces to

$$\hat{p}^T = p^T + \left(0, \sum_{k=1}^{K} \sigma^{kT} S_{qq}^k S_{qq}^{-1}\right). \tag{3.8}$$

This shows that $\hat{q}$ differs from q by a matrix weighted average of the national tariff vectors σ^k, since the matrix weights $S_{qq}^k S_{qq}^{-1} = S_{qq}^k (\Sigma_{j=1}^K S_{qq}^j)^{-1}$ sum to the identity matrix. In the special case where there are just $N = 2$ traded commodities the weights are scalars that are nonnegative and sum to unity. Thus, in general, $\hat{p}$ differs from p by a weighted average of tariff rates with the weights reflecting the relative importance of each nation in the world substitution matrix, S_{pp}.

3.3. *Economic Interpretation of Existence Theorem*

With the interpretation of $\beta^k < 0$ as a generalized Hatta normality condition and $\hat{p}$ as a world shadow price vector, we now return to the interpretation of Theorem 1.

Elsewhere, Turunen-Red and Woodland (1988) showed that a multilateral set of international transfers by themselves could yield a strict Pareto-improvement in welfare if the scalars β^k, $k = 1, \ldots, K$, are not all of the same sign. Thus, for example, if all nations except one satisfies the generalized Hatta normality condition, then a strict Pareto improvement in welfare is possible without changing any tariffs. Because of this result it is necessary to assume that all nations satisfy the generalized Hatta normality condition in order to focus unambiguously upon welfare gains arising directly out of tariff reforms. Under this normality assumption it is clear from Theorem 1 that inequalities (3.7) always have a solution and so the question of whether a Pareto-improving tariff and transfer reform exists reduces to whether equation (3.6) has a solution.

This reasoning yields the following corollary to Theorem 1.

COROLLARY 1.1: *Let all nations k, $k = 1, \ldots, K$, satisfy the generalized Hatta normality condition. Then a strict Pareto-improving multilateral reform of tariffs and transfers exists if and only if there is at least one nation k such that*

$$\hat{p}^T S_{pp}^k \neq 0. \tag{3.9}$$

[17] See Turunen-Red and Woodland (1988, p. 253).

This corollary indicates that condition (3.9) is necessary and sufficient for the existence of a Pareto-improving multilateral tariff and transfer reform when all nations satisfy the generalized Hatta normality condition.[18] If there are no tariff distortions, then it is readily shown that the shadow price vector $\hat{p}$ and all the domestic price vectors p^k reduce to the equilibrium world price vector p and so, by (2.2), equation (3.9) will be violated. Conversely, if tariff distortions do exist it is to be expected that condition (3.9) will hold, and hence the opportunity for welfare improving tariff and transfer reforms will be present. That this is indeed the case is made explicit by the following Assumption A and Lemma 2.

ASSUMPTION A: *There are at least two nations* (k, j) *such that the domestic prices* p^k *and* p^j *in the two nations are not proportional, and the net substitution matrices* S^k_{pp} *and* S^j_{pp} *are of maximal rank* $(N-1)$.

LEMMA 2: *If Assumption A holds, there exists a nation k such that* $\hat{p}^T S^k_{pp} \neq 0$, *i.e.* (3.9) *holds.*

In conjunction, Lemma 2 and Corollary 1.1 show that some tariff distortions, accompanied by a curvature (rank) condition, are sufficient to ensure that $\hat{p}$ does not coincide with every domestic price vector and hence that (3.9) holds. In other words, Assumption A is sufficient for the existence of strict Pareto-improving tariff and transfer reforms.

The following corollary gives an interpretation for (3.9) in terms of *sources* of strict Pareto improvements in a many-country world.

COROLLARY 1.2: *If there is a nation* k, $k = 1, \dots, K$, *such that* (3.9) *holds, then there exists a unilateral tariff reform* $d\tau^k$ *for which* $du = 0$ *and*

$$(3.10) \quad d\sum_{j=1}^{K} b^j = \hat{p}^T S^k_{pp}\, d\tau^k > 0.$$

Corollary 1.2 points out that when condition (3.9) is satisfied a unilateral tariff reform $d\tau^k$ can be chosen so as to improve the constant utility net trade balance of the world. This increase in world wealth generated by the tariff reform can then be redistributed among the nations in a strict Pareto-improving fashion using international transfers of income according to Corollary 1.1.

That strict Pareto-improving multilateral tariff and transfer reforms exist under very weak conditions should not be particularly surprising. These results are important in providing the precise conditions for such reforms, however. Moreover, they form the springboard for the analysis of particular tariff reform proposals to be considered in the following section.

[18] Actually, it can be shown that (3.9) is sufficient for this outcome without any normality condition.

4. TARIFF REFORM RECOMMENDATIONS

4.1. *General Results*

In this section we consider several particular recommendations for multilateral tariff reform and establish the conditions under which they will yield a strict Pareto improvement in welfare under the assumption that the tariff reforms are accompanied by suitable multilateral transfers of income.[19] Some of our results are generalizations of those previously obtained by Vanek (1964), Hatta and Fukushima (1979), and Fukushima and Kim (1989). Others involve new policy recommendations and are related closely to the world shadow price vector, $\hat{p}$, introduced in the previous section.

The particular tariff reform proposals that are investigated in this section may be shown to be special cases of a more general specification of tariff reform. Accordingly, it will facilitate the exposition and the proofs of results for particular tariff reforms if the more general case is dealt with first. This general case emphasizes the role played by the world shadow price vector, $\hat{p}$, and the national substitution matrices, S^k_{pp}.

Two general types of tariff reform are considered. A *change of tariffs along vector a* is defined to be reform of the world tariff vector such that $d\tau = a\,d\alpha$, where a is a vector indicating the hyperplane of feasible changes in τ and $d\alpha \neq 0$ is the distance of movement along a. Because the scalar $d\alpha$ is unrestricted in sign, the change in the tariff vector is restricted to a hyperplane passing through a and the origin. Our second general tariff reform is obtained by restricting $d\tau$ to be on this hyperplane, but in the direction a from the origin. Thus, we define a *change of tariffs in direction a* to be a $d\tau$ such that $d\tau = a\,d\alpha$, where $d\alpha > 0$. Whether tariff changes involve increases or decreases depends upon the precise specification of the vector a, which defines the unique direction of tariff reform.

Our general results concerning tariff reforms along a and in direction a are contained in the following theorem and its corollary. In particular, Theorem 2 provides the general necessary and sufficient conditions under which a tariff reform in a particular direction is strict Pareto improving.

THEOREM 2: *Let the world net substitution matrix S_{qq} be of full rank $(N-1)$. Then*:

(i) *a change of tariffs along a (i.e., a change of tariffs of the form $d\tau = a\,d\alpha$, $d\alpha \neq 0$) is strict Pareto improving if and only if there is no scalar $\mu \in R$ such that*

$$(4.1) \qquad \mu[\beta^1,\dots,\beta^K] < 0, \qquad \mu\gamma = 0; \qquad \gamma \equiv \sum_{k=1}^{K} \hat{p}^T S^k_{pp} a^k,$$

where a^k is the subvector of a corresponding to nation k;

[19] For convenience, specific reference to this assumption will not be made in the formal statements of the theorems, but the assumption is implicitly made.

(ii) *a change of taxes in direction a* (*i.e., a change of the form* $d\tau = a\,d\alpha$, $d\alpha > 0$) *is strict Pareto improving if and only if there is no scalar* $\mu \in R$ *such that*

$$\mu[\beta^1, \ldots, \beta^K; \gamma] < 0. \tag{4.2}$$

Theorem 2 yields the following corollary.

COROLLARY 2.1: (i) *If* $\gamma \neq 0$, *then a strict Pareto-improving change of tariffs along a exists.*

(ii) *If* $\gamma > 0$ *and there is at least one country,* k, $k = 1, \ldots, K$, *satisfying the generalized Hatta normality condition, then a change of tariffs in direction a is a strict Pareto improvement.*

Theorem 2 and Corollary 2.1 show that the ability of a tariff reform, accompanied by suitable international transfers of income, to yield a strict Pareto improvement in welfare depends upon both income and substitution effects as well as the extent of the initial tariff distortion. The income effects are captured by the terms β^k while the substitution effects are captured directly by the national substitution matrices, S^k_{pp}. The world shadow price vector, $\hat{p}$, is affected by the tariff distortions and the degree of substitutability.

Theorem 2 and its corollary focus attention upon the term γ. Corollary 2.1 shows that the condition $\gamma \neq 0$ is sufficient for a strict Pareto-improving tariff reform along a to exist. If attention is restricted to tariff reforms in direction a (i.e. $d\alpha > 0$), then the condition on γ is that it be positive. In this case, however, a very weak normality condition is used to ensure that the increase in disposable income generated by the improved efficiency of allocation of world resources can be converted into an improvement in welfare for all consumers.

In the following, particular tariff reform proposals are considered. Each such proposal defines a particular specification of the direction vector a and a particular sign for $d\alpha$. The research strategy is to show that in each case either $\gamma \neq 0$ or $\gamma > 0$ and $\beta^k < 0$ for some k, $k = 1, \ldots, K$. Then Corollary 2.1 may be used directly to demonstrate the existence of strict Pareto improvements in welfare.

4.2. *Tariff Changes Linear in World Prices and/or Tariffs*

The first important class of tariff changes that we consider may be expressed in terms of the direction vector

$$a^k = (\delta p - \varepsilon \tau^k), \qquad (\delta + \varepsilon) > 0 \qquad (k = 1, \ldots, K), \tag{4.3}$$

where δ and ε are scalars. In the special case where $\delta = 0$ we have that $d\tau^k = a^k d\alpha = -\varepsilon \tau^k d\alpha$ so that the changes in individual tariff rates (in specific form) are proportional to the initial tariff rates. If $d\alpha > 0$, then all nations reduce all tariffs equi-proportionately. Another special case of (4.3) occurs where $\varepsilon = 0$ in which case $d\tau^k = \delta p\, d\alpha$. In this case all tariff changes are proportional to the world price vector. If $d\alpha > 0$, then all tariffs are *increased* proportionately with world prices. Superficially, this appears to be a movement away from free trade but it is not. In particular, it is easy to demonstrate that the general specification (4.3) together with $d\alpha > 0$ causes the national price vectors, $p^k = p + \tau^k$, to move closer to the world price vector in the sense that the price ratios p_j^k / p_j become closer to unity.

The following theorem provides conditions under which linear tariff reforms are strict Pareto improving in welfare.

THEOREM 3: *Let Assumption A hold. Then:*
(i) *a change in tariffs along a, defined by* (4.3), *is strict Pareto improving;*
(ii) *a change in tariffs in direction a, defined by* (4.3), *is strict Pareto improving if there is at least one nation in which the generalized Hatta normality condition is satisfied.*

Assumption A requires that there exist a tariff distortion and that there exist sufficient substitutability in production or consumption for the tariff change to have an effect on net exports. Part (i) of Theorem 3 then indicates that a change in tariffs that is linear in p and/or τ^k will be welfare improving. If attention is restricted to a reform in the direction a, then a weak normality condition is required to ensure a welfare improvement.

This theorem provides a generalization of the results of Hatta and Fukushima (1979) and Fukushima and Kim (1989). Hatta and Fukushima consider a model of international trade in just two commodities, assume that both commodities are normal in every nation, and show that a proportional reduction in all tariffs in all nations is potentially welfare improving. Our result is for an arbitrary number of commodities, thus allowing for complementarities in production and consumption, our normality assumption is much weaker, our class of feasible tariff reforms is more general ($\delta \neq 0$ is permitted), and we are explicit about the attainment of a strict Pareto improvement (as opposed to a potential welfare improvement).[20] Recently, Fukushima and Kim (1989) have considered a many-product model of trade and, assuming that all commodities are normal and that there is no complementarity in either production or consumption in any nation, proved that a linear change in tariffs towards δp is potentially welfare improving. Our result is more general in that it requires weaker assumptions. We do not require normality for each commodity in each nation, merely that the generalized Hatta normality condition holds in at least one nation. Also, we do not require any assumption to be made concerning the sign structure of the national substitution matrices. Finally, our class of tariff reforms (4.3) is more general and reduces to theirs as the special case where $\varepsilon = 1$.

[20] Hatta and Fukushima (1979) and Fukushima and Kim (1989) demonstrate potential welfare improvements by keeping all utility levels fixed except one and show that this utility level increases. Our results allow for international income transfers and we show that each nation actually experiences an increase in welfare.

Theorem 3 is also closely related to Proposition 1 of Keen (1989, p. 199), who proves that a multilateral uniform proportional reduction in all domestic taxes and trade tariffs is potentially Pareto improving in welfare.[21] Keen's model is more general than ours in that he explicitly incorporates nontraded commodities and allows for domestic commodity taxes. His proof proceeds by showing that the utility of one nation (the first) increases while holding the utility levels of all other nations fixed, and relies upon a particular normality assumption. If nontraded commodities and domestic taxes are ignored, it is readily demonstrated that Keen's normality assumption is equivalent to the assumption that nation 1 exhibits generalized Hatta normality (i.e., our β^1 is negative). Thus, for the case of equi-proportional reforms, Keen's result is a generalization of our Theorem 3 to cover nontraded goods and domestic commodity taxes and relies upon a similar normality assumption. On the other hand, we deal with a wider class of reforms than does Keen.

4.3. *Unilateral Tariff Reform*

Theorem 3 provides conditions under which *multilateral* tariff reforms along a and in direction a, defined by (4.3), are strict Pareto improving in welfare. It is interesting to consider the question of whether a *unilateral* tariff reform of this type by one nation k can be welfare improving. The general conditions for a unilateral tariff reform to be strict Pareto improving are fairly complex, but a special case is of particular interest.

Consider then the unilateral tariff reform defined by

$$(4.4) \qquad a^k = (\delta p - \varepsilon \tau^k), \qquad (\delta + \varepsilon) > 0, \qquad \text{and} \qquad a^j = 0 \qquad \text{for all} \quad j \neq k.$$

Then the following result may be established.

THEOREM 4: (i) *A unilateral change of tariffs of nation k along a^k, defined by* (4.4), *is strict Pareto improving if*

$$(4.5) \qquad \hat{p}^T S^k_{pp} \tau^k \neq 0;$$

(ii) *a unilateral change of tariffs of nation k in direction a^k, defined by* (4.4), *is strict Pareto improving if the generalized Hatta normality condition is satisfied in at least one nation and*

$$(4.6) \qquad \hat{p}^T S^k_{pp} \tau^k < 0.$$

This theorem, which is easily proved by making use of the homogeneity condition (2.2) in the expression for γ in Theorem 2, provides general conditions that determine whether a unilateral tariff reform (4.4) is welfare improving. For example, condition (4.6) implicitly defines a subspace of tariff vectors

[21] We are indebted to a referee for bringing Keen's paper to our attention.

τ^k. If τ^k is in this subspace, the unilateral tariff reform by nation k is guaranteed to yield a strict Pareto improvement in welfare.

While conditions (4.5) and (4.6) may be checked to determine whether a strict Pareto-improving unilateral tariff reform is feasible, the conditions do not easily lend themselves to simple economic interpretations. However, there is a special case that is of some interest, as illustrated by the following corollary to Theorem 4.

COROLLARY 4.1: *Let nation k have a representative substitution matrix in the sense that* $S^k_{pp} = \sigma S_{pp}$ *for some* $\sigma > 0$. *Then:*

(i) *a change of tariffs of nation k along* a^k, *defined by* (4.4), *is strict Pareto improving;*

(ii) *a change of tariffs of nation k in direction* a^k, *defined by* (4.4), *is strict Pareto improving if the generalized Hatta normality condition is satisfied in at least one nation.*

The assumption in Corollary 4.1 is that nation k has a substitution matrix that is proportional to the world substitution matrix, meaning that nation k is "representative" or "average." This is a very strict requirement. However, it may be argued, in view of Corollary 4.1, that if a nation has a substitution matrix sufficiently close to σS_{pp}, then a unilateral change in tariffs by that nation would be strict Pareto improving.

4.4. *Tariff Reforms Proportional to the World Shadow Prices*

The world shadow price vector, $\hat{p}$, plays a prominent role in the crucial term, γ. It turns out that the following tariff reform specification is welfare improving:

$$(4.7) \qquad a^k = \hat{p}, \quad \text{and} \quad a^j = 0 \quad \text{for all} \quad j \neq k \qquad (j = 1, \ldots, K).$$

In this case the tariff vector for nation k is unilaterally increased proportionately with the world shadow price vector $\hat{p}$.

It follows immediately from the definition of γ and (4.7) that

$$(4.8) \qquad \gamma = \hat{p}^T S^k_{pp} \hat{p},$$

which will be positive in view of the positive semidefiniteness of S^k_{pp} and the requirement that there be some distortion (i.e., that (3.9) be satisfied). This reasoning leads to the following result.

THEOREM 5: *Let there be a nation k satisfying* (3.9) *and the generalized Hatta normality condition. Then a unilateral tariff reform* $d\tau^k = \hat{p}\, d\alpha$, $d\alpha > 0$, *is strict Pareto improving in welfare.*

The unilateral tariff reform by nation k may involve tariff increases and/or decreases depending upon the sign structure of $\hat{p}$. Elsewhere, Turunen-Red and Woodland (1988, pp. 259, 266) show that $\hat{p} > 0$ if the world substitution matrix exhibits net substitutability. Under these circumstances the tariff reform requires the changes in tariffs to be semipositive (i.e. all are nonnegative and at least one is positive). Yet this tariff reform moves the domestic prices towards world prices, creates greater efficiency, and hence allows a strict Pareto improvement in welfare.

This tariff reform recommendation is new. Like the tariff reforms linear in world market prices and tariff vectors, this tariff reform is shown to be welfare improving because γ becomes a positive definite quadratic form. Unlike these other reforms, however, this tariff reform formula can only be calculated once the world shadow price is known. This, in turn, depends upon knowledge of the world substitution matrix. Given this knowledge, the reform proposed may be easily implemented and is guaranteed to be welfare improving.

4.5. *Reduction of Extreme Tariff Rates*

Vanek (1964) demonstrated that the reduction of extreme tariff rates in a two-product model of international trade can be welfare improving. This result was formalized and proved by Hatta and Fukushima (1979, Theorem 1) in a many-nation model, retaining the assumption of two traded commodities. In this section a similar but quite different result is obtained.

THEOREM 6: *Let all goods be normal in consumption in the nation k, and let both the world net substitution matrix S_{pp} and the nation k net substitution matrix S^k_{pp} exhibit nonpositive off-diagonal elements (all traded goods are net substitutes in nation k and the world as a whole). Then a unilateral reduction by nation k of the tariff on commodity j is strict Pareto improving if the shadow ad valorem tariff rate on the jth commodity in country k, defined by*

$$\hat{t}^k_j \equiv \frac{p^k_j - \hat{p}_j}{\hat{p}_j} \qquad (j = 1, \ldots, N;\ k = 1, \ldots, K), \tag{4.9}$$

satisfies $\hat{t}^k_j \geqslant \hat{t}^k_i$, $i \neq j$.

Theorem 6 shows that a reduction of a nation's highest shadow ad valorem tariff, calculated with respect to the world prices $\hat{p}$, is strict Pareto improving, given normality in consumption in that country and net substitutability of all traded goods in that particular country and in the world. It provides a means for obtaining welfare improvements through unilateral tariff reductions by individual nations. It implies that every nation k has one commodity j whose tariff can be reduced and a Pareto improvement in welfare obtained. Accordingly, the welfare improvements will be higher if all nations join the reform, each reducing their highest shadow ad valorem tariff rate.

This theorem differs from the Vanek-Hatta-Fukushima result in several important ways. First, our result is obtained in a model containing an arbitrary number of traded commodities, whereas their results are for a two-commodity model. Second, the proposed tariff reform is on the *commodity* with the highest shadow ad valorem tariff rate within nation k. For any nation k that satisfies the regularity assumptions, one chooses that commodity with the highest shadow ad valorem tariff rate and reduces that tariff. By contrast, the Vanek-Hatta-Fukushima result is for the reduction of the ad valorem tariff for the *nation* with the highest tariff rate on the one good subject to tariffs. Third, our ad valorem tariff rates, which are the basis for the choice of the most extreme rate, are not the normal ad valorem tariff rates defined with respect to world prices. Rather, they are shadow ad valorem rates defined with respect to the world shadow price vector.

The assumptions required to establish our result are somewhat weaker than those used by Hatta and Fukushima to establish their result. Our result is based upon a model consisting of an arbitrary number of traded commodities, whereas their result is for a two-commodity model. In a two-commodity model the commodities are necessarily net substitutes. Our theorem requires explicit statement of the substitutability conditions needed to establish a strict Pareto improvement in welfare as a result of a reduction of an extreme tariff. Hatta and Fukushima also assume that all commodities are normal in all nations, whereas we merely require that all commodities be normal in the nation in which the tariff reduction takes place.[22]

The question arises as to whether the Vanek-Hatta-Fukushima theorem can be generalized to the case where there are an arbitrary number of traded commodities. While their result may be readily obtained from an examination of γ when the number of traded commodities is $N=2$, it is unclear how to proceed in the case where $N>2$. It therefore remains an open question as to whether their result generalizes.[23]

[22] However, as pointed out by a referee, the normality assumption in the statement of Theorem 1 of Hatta and Fukushima (1979) is stronger than the normality assumption actually used in their proof. The assumption actually used is that all goods are normal in one (not every) nation—the nation for which the increase in utility is demonstrated. The same comment applies to the extension of the Hatta-Fukushima result by Fukushima and Kim (1989, p. 386). In other words, these authors' results actually rely upon a normality assumption similar to, and no stronger than, ours.

[23] Indeed, it is possible that our Theorem 6 is the natural generalization of the Vanek-Hatta-Fukushima theorem. In the case of $N=2$ commodities with the simplification of no tariffs on commodity 1 in any nation, it may be shown that

$$\hat{\tau}_2^k \equiv p_2^k - \hat{p}_2 = p_2 \sum_{j \neq k} (t_2^k - t_2^j)(S_{22}^j S_{22}^{-1})$$

where $t_i^k \equiv \tau_i^k / p_i$ is the ad valorem tariff rate of commodity i in nation k. If $t_2^k \geqslant t_2^j$ for all $j \neq k$, the Vanek-Hatta-Fukushima theorem implies a Pareto improvement if t_2^k is reduced. But if t_2^k is the highest rate (over j), then the above relationship shows that $\hat{\tau}_2^k \geqslant \hat{\tau}_1^k \equiv 0$.

That is, if nation k has the highest ad valorem tariff rate on commodity 2, it also follows that the shadow ad valorem tariff rate on commodity 2 is nonnegative ($\hat{t}_2^k = \hat{\tau}_2^k / \hat{p}_2 \geqslant 0$) and so is the highest shadow ad valorem rate in nation k. Thus, Theorem 6 and the Vanek-Hatta-Fukushima theorem both show that a reduction in the tariff on commodity 2 in nation k is welfare improving.

The reverse is not true, since $\hat{\tau}_2^k \geqslant 0$ does not necessarily imply that $t_2^k \geqslant t_2^j$ for all $j \neq k$. Moreover, Theorem 6 implies that every nation has one commodity whose tariff can be reduced. The implication may well be that Theorem 6 is the natural generalization of the Vanek-Hatta-Fukushima theorem on extreme tariff reductions.

4.6. *Remarks*

Let us now complete this section with some remarks on our results obtained thus far. Firstly, we note the importance that our general existence result (Theorem 1) places upon both the generalized Hatta normality condition and the existence of initial tariff distortions. The importance of these two initial conditions is also reflected in the results of the present section, which deals with specific directions of tariff reform. Secondly, in this section we have distinguished between movements in the world tariff vector along a given vector in any direction, and movements in only one direction. The condition for a strict Pareto improvement are, of course, weaker in the former case (see Theorem 2).

Thirdly, we have considered a variety of specific tariff reforms based upon particular specifications of vector a. Theorem 3 provides for strict Pareto-improving tariff and transfer reforms that move domestic prices towards world prices under fairly weak conditions. Theorem 4 establishes a similar result for a unilateral tariff reform accompanied by a multilateral transfer. A new tariff reform recommendation is given by Theorem 5, namely the change of a single nation's tariff vector proportionally to the world shadow prices $\hat{p}$. Naturally, additional welfare gains accrue if all nations follow this policy. Theorem 6 provides for a unilateral reduction in a single tariff rate when normality and net substitutability at the world level prevail in the initial equilibrium. This is an example of the reduction of an extreme tariff distortion in which the tariff rates are expressed in ad valorem form, not relative to world prices but to the world shadow prices $\hat{p}$.

Finally, we note that the tariff reforms considered vary in the informational requirements for their implementation. The central requirement is for the calculation of the world shadow price vector $\hat{p}$. These prices depend on the world substitution matrix and initial world prices. The world substitution matrix, and hence $\hat{p}$, can be estimated in principle by econometric methods. Alternatively, one may be willing to make sufficient a priori assumptions (such as normality and net substitutability) to avoid data and computational obstacles. In either case, our results specify the precise conditions for tariff and transfer reforms to be strictly Pareto improving.

5. CONCLUSIONS

This paper has been concerned with the problem of obtaining conditions under which cooperative multilateral reforms of tariffs and transfers that increase the welfare of every nation exist. Our results provide necessary and sufficient conditions for the existence of such reforms, and demonstrate that various particular tariff reform proposals satisfy these conditions.

We have strengthened the existing literature by adding several new policy prescriptions to the list of tariff and transfer reforms that result in a strict welfare improvement for all nations. We have also weakened the previously determined conditions under which proportional reductions of tariffs and reductions of extreme tariffs are welfare improving for every nation.

We have not considered tariff reforms from a strategic point of view, i.e. as a noncooperative game, as have Johnson (1953), Riezman (1982), McMillan (1986), and Mayer (1981). Johnson and Riezman point out that free trade cannot be an outcome of strategic tariff reductions if some of the participants are gaining from imposing tariffs ("winning a tariff war"). Mayer investigated the end results of tariff reforms constrained to strict Pareto-improvements and showed that the outcomes of negotiated tariff reforms are Pareto superior to the tariff war (Nash) equilibrium, even if they may not be free trade situations. However, none of the above authors provides results concerning the exact directions of strict Pareto-improving tariff and transfer reforms. This question has been one focus of our paper.

Finally, it is noted that the present paper and the previous literature assumes that the tariff reforms are explicitly or implicitly accompanied by a set of accommodating international transfers of income. While this assumption makes the analysis more straightforward, it is clearly desirable to develop tariff reform results in models without allowance for international transfers of income. This is a challenging task, towards which our current research is directed.

Dept. of Economics, University of Texas at Austin, Austin, TX 78712, U.S.A.
and
Dept. of Econometrics, University of Sydney, Sydney, NSW 2006, Australia.

Manuscript received November 1987; final revision received March 12, 1990.

APPENDIX

PROOF OF LEMMA 1: A strict Pareto-improving $(d\tau, db)$ exists if and only if there is a $(du, dq, db, d\tau)$ such that (2.8) holds and $du \gg 0$. Applying Motzkin's Theorem of the Alternative (Mangasarian (1969, p. 34)), an equivalent condition is: there is no vector $\gamma \in R^{(N-1)+K+1}$ such that

$$\text{(A.1)} \qquad \gamma^T[B,C,D] = 0, \qquad \gamma^T A < 0.$$

Let γ be partitioned as $\gamma = [\gamma_q^T, \gamma_2^T, \gamma_3]$, where $\gamma_q \in R^{N-1}$, $\gamma_2 \in R^K$, and $\gamma_3 \in R$. The equations $\gamma^T C = 0$ imply $\gamma_2 = \gamma_3 l_K$, where l_K is a K-dimensional column vector with every element equal to unity. Thus, (A.1) can be written in the form

$$\text{(A.2)} \qquad \gamma_q^T S_{qq} + \gamma_3 p^T S_{pq} = 0,$$

$$\text{(A.3)} \qquad \gamma_q^T S_{qp}^k + \gamma_3 p^T S_{pp}^k = 0 \qquad (k = 1, \dots, K),$$

$$\text{(A.4)} \qquad \gamma_q^T S_{qu}^k + \gamma_3 p^T S_{pu}^k \leqslant 0 \qquad (k = 1, \dots, K, \text{ with strict inequality for at least one } k).$$

Redefining $\gamma_q \equiv \lambda$ and $\gamma_3 \equiv \mu$, we see that (A.2)–(A.4) are identical to (3.1)–(3.3), thus completing the proof of Lemma 1.

PROOF OF THEOREM 1: If the matrix S_{qq} is of full rank $(N-1)$, the inverse matrix S_{qq}^{-1} exists. Hence, the equations (A.2) can be solved for γ_q as

$$\text{(A.5)} \qquad \gamma_q^T = -\gamma_3 p^T S_{pq} S_{qq}^{-1}.$$

Substituting (A.5) into (A.3)–(A.4) yields (3.6)–(3.7).

PROOF OF COROLLARY 1.1: If (3.9) holds, then (3.6) implies that $\mu = 0$. However, (3.7) cannot have a solution $\mu = 0$. Thus Theorem 1 implies that a strict Pareto-improving tariff and transfer reform exists.

Conversely, if (3.6) and (3.7) have a solution, then $\mu \neq 0$ and (3.8) cannot be true for any $k = 1, \ldots, K$.

PROOF OF LEMMA 2: The rank condition in Assumption A and the homogeneity condition (2.2) imply that the equation system $z^T S^i_{pp} = 0$ has a unique solution p^i up to a factor of proportionality, where $i = j, k$. Since p^j and p^k are not proportional to each other by assumption, it follows that $\hat{p}$ cannot be equal to both p^j and p^k up to a factor of proportionality and therefore cannot solve the equations $z^T S^i_{pp} = 0$, $i = j, k$ simultaneously. Therefore, (3.9) must hold for at least one of these nations, say k.

PROOF OF COROLLARY 1.2: Since $du^k = 0$ for all k, differentation of (2.6) yields

$$\text{(A.6)} \qquad db^k = S^{kT}_q dq + p^T S^k_{pq} dq + p^T S^k_{pp} d\tau^k.$$

Summing (A.6) over k, $k = 1, \ldots, K$, and using $dq = -S^{-1}_{qq} S^k_{qp} d\tau^k$ (derived from (2.5) assuming that $du^k = 0$ for all k), we obtain

$$\text{(A.7)} \qquad \sum_{j=1}^{K} db^j = \left(p^T S^k_{pp} - p^T S_{pq} S^{-1}_{qq} S^k_{qp} \right) d\tau^k = \hat{p}^T S^k_{pp} d\tau^k.$$

Condition (3.9) implies that the right side of (A.7) can be made positive by an appropriate choice of $d\tau^k$.

PROOF OF THEOREM 2: (i) Using (2.8) and the constraint $d\tau = a\,d\alpha$, $d\alpha \neq 0$, Motzkin's Theorem of the Alternative indicates that the necessary and sufficient condition for the existence of a strict Pareto-improving tariff change in the direction a is: there is no vector $\gamma \in R^{(N-1)+K+1}$ such that

$$\text{(A.8)} \qquad \gamma^T A < 0, \qquad \lambda^T [B, C] = 0, \qquad \lambda^T Da = 0.$$

The equations $\gamma^T C = 0$ yield $\gamma_2 = \gamma_3 1_K$, where the vector γ has been partitioned as in the proof of Lemma 1. The equations $\gamma^T B = 0$ can be solved for the first component of the vector γ as in (A.5). Then, the inequalities $\gamma^T A < 0$ give (3.7), i.e. the inequality in (4.1). The equations $\gamma^T Da = 0$ yield

$$\text{(A.9)} \qquad \gamma^T_q \sum_{k=1}^{K} S^k_{qp} a^k + \gamma_3 \sum_{k=1}^{K} p^T S^k_{pp} a^k = 0.$$

Using the definition of the shadow prices $\hat{p}$ in (3.5) and the solution λ_q in (A.5), (A.9) can be rewritten as

$$\text{(A.10)} \qquad \gamma_3 \sum_{k=1}^{K} \hat{p}^T S^k_{pp} a^k = 0,$$

which coincides with the equality in (4.1).

(ii) The equations and inequalities (A.8) are now transformed to

$$\text{(A.11)} \qquad \gamma^T [B, C] = 0, \qquad \gamma^T [A, Da] < 0.$$

Proceeding as above, (4.2) is obtained.

PROOF OF COROLLARY 2.1: (i) If $\gamma \neq 0$, the equality $\mu\gamma = 0$ in (4.1) must be violated. Note that also $\mu \neq 0$ if the inequalities in (4.1) are to hold.

(ii) If $\gamma > 0$, the scalar μ in (4.2) must be negative for (4.2) to be satisfied. However, if the generalized Hatta normality condition holds for country k, then $\beta^k < 0$ and hence the condition (4.2) cannot hold.

The following lemma is used in the proof of Theorem 2. It is essentially the same as Lemma 3 of Fukushima and Kim (1989), but we do not require that all national substitution matrices be of maximal rank $(N-1)$.

LEMMA 3: *The scalar* $\hat{S}_{11} \equiv S_{11} - S_{1q}S_{qq}^{-1}S_{q1} \geqslant 0$. *If Assumption A holds, then* $\hat{S}_{11} > 0$ *and the world substitution matrix* S_{pp} *is positive definite* (*i.e. has full rank* N).

PROOF OF LEMMA 3: Since S_{pp} is positive semidefinite and its submatrix S_{qq} is of full rank with $|S_{qq}| > 0$, it follows that $|S_{pp}| = (S_{11} - S_{1q}S_{qq}^{-1}S_{q1})|S_{qq}| \geqslant 0$ and, hence, that $\hat{S}_{11} \equiv S_{11} - S_{1q}S_{qq}^{-1}S_{q1} \geqslant 0$.

Since S_{pp} is positive semidefinite, $z^T S_{pp} z \geqslant 0$ for all $z \neq 0$. To prove that $z^T S_{pp} z > 0$ for all $z \neq 0$, i.e. that S_{pp} is positive definite and hence that its determinant is positive, suppose to the contrary that $z^T S_{pp} z = 0$ for some $z \neq 0$. Then $z^T S_{pp} z = \Sigma_{k=1}^{K} z^T S_{pp}^k z = 0$ implies that $z^T S_{pp}^k z = 0$ for all $k = 1, \ldots, K$. By Lemma 1 of Turunen-Red and Woodland (1988) this implies that $z^T S_{pp}^k = 0$ for all $k = 1, \ldots, K$. But this contradicts Assumption A, as shown in the proof of Lemma 2. Thus the supposition that $z^T S_{pp} z = 0$ for some $z \neq 0$ is incorrect and so $z^T S_{pp} z > 0$ for all $z \neq 0$. Therefore, S_{pp} is positive definite and its determinant, and hence $\hat{S}_{11}$, are positive.

PROOF OF THEOREM 3: (i) Using Corollary 2.1(i), it is sufficient to show that (4.1) is violated when the tariff reform is of the form (4.3). Using $a^k = (\delta p - \varepsilon \tau^k)$, $(\delta + \varepsilon) > 0$, $k = 1, \ldots, K$, and (2.2), the expression γ defined in (4.1) can be rewritten as

$$\sum_{k=1}^{K} \hat{p}^T S_{pp}^k (\delta p - \varepsilon \tau^k) = (\delta + \varepsilon) \hat{p}^T S_{pp} p. \tag{A.12}$$

Now we observe that

$$\hat{p}^T = p^T - \left[0, p^T S_{pq} S_{qq}^{-1}\right] = \left[1, q^T\right] - \left[0, S_{1q} S_{qq}^{-1} + q^T\right] = \left[1, -S_{1q} S_{qq}^{-1}\right]. \tag{A.13}$$

It follows that (A.12) can be rewritten as

$$\sum_{k=1}^{K} \hat{p}^T S_{pp}^k (\delta p - \varepsilon \tau^k) = (\delta + \varepsilon)\left[S_{11} - S_{1q} S_{qq}^{-1} S_{q1}\right]. \tag{A.14}$$

By assumption, $(\delta + \varepsilon) > 0$. The second term on the right-hand side of (A.14) is also positive in view of Assumption A and Lemma 3. Hence, the expression γ defined in (4.1) is positive and equation (4.1) cannot hold.

(ii) Consider (4.2). Using the above argument, the scalar μ in (4.2) must be negative for (4.2) to have a solution. However, since there is a country k for which $\beta^k < 0$, (4.2) cannot have a solution.

PROOF OF THEOREM 4: Using $a^k = (\delta p - \varepsilon \tau^k)$, $(\delta + \varepsilon) > 0$, and (2.2), the expression γ defined in (4.1) can be written as

$$\gamma = (\delta + \varepsilon) \hat{p}^T S_{pp}^k p = -(\delta + \varepsilon) \hat{p}^T S_{pp}^k \tau^k. \tag{A.15}$$

Since $(\delta + \varepsilon) > 0$ it follows that $\gamma \neq 0$ and $\gamma > 0$ respectively imply (4.5) and (4.6). Application of Corollary 2.1 yields Theorem 4.

PROOF OF COROLLARY 4.1: If $S_{pp}^k = \sigma S_{pp}$ for some $\sigma > 0$ the expression (A.15) for γ becomes $\gamma = (\gamma + \varepsilon)\sigma \hat{p}^T S_{pp} p$. The remainder of the proof follows that of Theorem 3.

PROOF OF THEOREM 5: Since (3.9) holds for the kth country, $\hat{p}^T S_{pp}^k \hat{p} > 0$. Hence, since also $\beta^k < 0$, there is no solution $\mu \in R$ for (4.2).

PROOF OF THEOREM 6: Here $\hat{p}^T S_{pp}^k a^k = -\hat{p}^T S_{pp}^k e_j$, where e_j is the jth unit vector. It follows that

$$(A.16) \qquad -\hat{p}^T S_{pp}^k e_j = -\sum_{i=1}^{N} \hat{p}_i S_{ij}^k = -\sum_{i \neq j} \hat{p}_i S_{ij}^k + \frac{\hat{p}_j}{p_j^k} \sum_{i \neq j} p_i^k S_{ij}^k,$$

and further simplification of expression (A.16) gives

$$(A.17) \qquad -\hat{p}^T S_{pp}^k e_j = -\sum_{i \neq j} S_{ij}^k \left[\frac{p_j^k}{\hat{p}_j} - \frac{p_i^k}{\hat{p}_i} \right] \frac{\hat{p}_i \hat{p}_j}{p_j^k} = \sum_{i \neq j} S_{ij}^k (\hat{t}_i^k - \hat{t}_j^k) \frac{\hat{p}_i}{(1+\hat{t}_j^k)},$$

where the shadow ad valorem tax rates $\hat{t}_i^k$ are defined in (4.9). Now, net substitutability of all traded goods in the world implies that all $\hat{p}_i > 0$ (Turunen-Red and Woodland (1988, p. 266)), net substitutability of all traded goods in the country k implies $S_{ij}^k < 0$, $i \neq j$, and, since the shadow ad valorem tax rate on the jth good is the highest in country k, we must therefore have $\hat{p}^T S_{pp}^k a^k > 0$. On the other hand, normality of all goods in country k and positivity of the shadow prices $\hat{p}$ gives $\beta^k < 0$. Hence, there cannot be a solution $\mu \in R$ for (4.2).

REFERENCES

BERTRAND, T. J., AND J. VANEK (1971): "The Theory of Tariffs, Taxes and Subsidies: Some Aspects of Second Best," *American Economic Review*, 61, 925–931.

BRUNO, M. (1972): "Market Distortions and Gradual Reform," *Review of Economic Studies*, 39, 373–383.

DEBREU, G. (1959): *Theory of Value*. New York: John Wiley and Sons.

DIEWERT, W. E. (1982): "Duality Approaches to Microeconomic Theory," Chapter 12 in *Handbook of Mathematical Economics*, ed. by K. J. Arrow and M. D. Intriligator. Amsterdam: North-Holland Publishing Company, 535–599.

——— (1978): "Optimal Tax Perturbations," *Journal of Public Economics*, 10, 139–177.

——— (1974): "Applications of Duality Theory," in *Frontiers of Quantitative Economics*, Vol. II, ed. by M. D. Intriligator and D. A. Kendrick. Amsterdam: North-Holland Publishing Company, 106–171.

——— (1983): "Cost-Benefit Analysis and Project Evaluation," *Journal of Public Economics*, 22, 265–302.

DIEWERT, W. E., A. H. TURUNEN-RED, AND A. D. WOODLAND (1989): "Productivity- and Pareto-Improving Changes in Taxes and Tariffs," *Review of Economic Studies*, forthcoming.

——— (1991): "Tariff Reform in a Small Open Multihousehold Economy with Domestic Distortions and Nontraded Goods," *International Economic Review*, forthcoming.

DIXIT, A. (1975): "Welfare Effects of Tax and Price Changes," *Journal of Public Economics*, 4, 103–123.

——— (1985): "Tax Policies in Open Economies," in *Handbook of Public Economics*, ed. by A. Auerbach and M. Feldstein. Amsterdam: North-Holland, 313–374.

——— (1987): "On Pareto Improving Redistribution of Aggregate Economic Gains," *Journal of Economic Theory*, 41, 133–153.

DIXIT, A., AND V. NORMAN (1980): *Theory of International Trade*. Welwyn, U.K.: James Nisbet.

FOSTER, E., AND H. SONNENSCHEIN (1970): "Price Distortion and Economic Welfare," *Econometrica*, 38, 281–296.

FUKUSHIMA, T. (1979): "Tariff Structure, Nontraded Goods and the Theory of Piecemeal Policy Recommendations," *International Economic Review*, 20, 427–435.

——— (1981): "A Dynamic Quantity Adjustment Process in a Small Open Economy, and Welfare Effects of Tariff Changes," *Journal of International Economics*, 11, 513–529.

FUKUSHIMA, T., AND N. KIM (1989): "Welfare Improving Tariff Changes: A Case of Many-Goods and Countries," *Journal of International Economics*, 26, 383–388.

GUESNERIE, R. (1977): "On the Direction of Tax Reform," *Journal of Public Economics*, 7, 179–202.

HATTA, T. (1977a): "A Theory of Piecemeal Policy Recommendations," *Review of Economic Studies*, 44, 1–12.

——— (1977b): "A Recommendation for a Better Tariff Structure," *Econometrica*, 45, 179–202.

HATTA, T., AND T. FUKUSHIMA (1979): "The Welfare Effect of Tariff Rate Reductions in a Many Country World," *Journal of International Economics*, 9, 503–511.
JOHNSON, H. G. (1953): "Optimum Tariffs and Retaliation," *Review of Economic Studies*, 21, 142–153.
KEEN, M. (1987): "Welfare Effects of Commodity Tax Harmonization," *Journal of Public Economics*, 33, 107–113.
——— (1989): "Multilateral Tax and Tariff Reform," *Economic Studies Quarterly*, 40, 195–202.
LIPSEY, R. G., AND K. LANCASTER (1956): "The General Theory of Second Best," *Review of Economic Studies*, 24, 11–32.
LLOYD, P. J. (1974): "A More General Theory of Price Distortions in Open Economies," *Journal of International Economics*, 4, 365–386.
MANGASARIAN, O. (1969): *Nonlinear Programming*. New York: McGraw-Hill.
MAYER, W. (1981): "Theoretical Considerations on Negotiated Tariff Adjustments," *Oxford Economic Papers*, 33, 135–153.
McMILLAN, J. (1986): *Game Theory in International Economics*. Chur: Harwood Academic Publishers.
MEADE, J. E. (1955): *Trade and Welfare*. Oxford: Oxford University Press.
RIEZMAN, R. (1982): "Tariff Retaliation from a Strategic Viewpoint," *Southern Economic Journal*, 48, 583–593.
SAMUELSON, P. A. (1956): "Social Indifference Curves," *Quarterly Journal of Economics*, 70, 1–22.
TURUNEN-RED, A. H., AND A. D. WOODLAND (1988): "On the Multilateral Transfer Problem: Existence of Pareto Improving International Transfers," *Journal of International Economics*, 25, 249–269.
VANEK, J. (1964): "Unilateral Trade Liberalization and Global World Income," *Quarterly Journal of Economics*, 78, 139–147.
WEYMARK, J. A. (1979): "A Reconciliation of Recent Results in Optimal Taxation Theory," *Journal of Public Economics*, 12, 171–189.
WOODLAND, A. D. (1982): *International Trade and Resource Allocation*. Amsterdam: North-Holland Publishing Company.

Name Index

The International Library of Critical Writings in Economics

1. Multinational Corporations
   Mark Casson
2. The Economics of Innovation
   Christopher Freeman
3. Entrepreneurship
   Mark Casson
4. International Investment
   Peter J. Buckley
5. Game Theory in Economics
   Ariel Rubinstein
6. The History of Economic Thought
   Mark Blaug
7. Monetary Theory
   Thomas Mayer
8. Joint Production of Commodities
   Neri Salvadori and Ian Steedman
9. Industrial Organization
   Oliver E. Williamson
10. Growth Theory (Volumes I, II and III)
    R.Becker and E. Burmeister
11. Microeconomics: Theoretical and Applied (Volumes I, II and III)
    Robert E. Kuenne
12. The Economics of Health (Volumes I and II)
    A.J. Culyer
13. Recent Developments in Macroeconomics (Volumes I, II and III)
    Edmund S. Phelps
14. Urban and Regional Economics
    Paul C. Cheshire and Alan W. Evans
15. Modern Public Finance (Volumes I and II)
    A.B. Atkinson
16. Exchange Rate Economics (Volumes I and II)
    Ronald MacDonald and Mark P. Taylor

17. The Economic Value of Education: Studies in the Economics of Education
Mark Blaug

18. Development Economics (Volumes I, II, III and IV)
Deepak Lal

19. The New Classical Macroeconomics (Volumes I, II and Ill)
Kevin D. Hoover

20. The Economics of the Environment
Wallace E. Oates

21. Post Keynesian Theory of Growth and Distribution
Carlo Panico and Neri Salvadori

22. Dynamic Labor Demand and Adjustment Costs
Giorgio Galeazzi and Daniel S. Hamermesh

23. The Philosophy and Methodology of Economics (Volumes I, II and III)
Bruce J. Caldwell

24. Public Choice Theory (Volumes I, II and III)
Charles K. Rowley

25. Evolutionary Economics
Ulrich Witt

26. Economics and Psychology
Shlomo Maital and Sharone L. Maital

27. Social Choice Theory (Volumes I, II and Ill)
Charles K. Rowley

28. Non-Linear Dynamics in Economic Theory
Marc Jarsulic

29. Recent Developments in Experimental Economics (Volumes I and II)
John D. Hey and Graham Loomes

30. Monopoly and Competition Policy (Volumes I and II)
F.M. Scherer

31. The Economics of Technical Change
Edwin Mansfield and Elizabeth Mansfield

32. The Economics of Exhaustible Resources
Geoffrey Heal

33. The Economics of Institutions
Geoffrey M. Hodgson

34. The Economics of Transport (Volumes I and II)
Herbert Mohring

35. Implicit Contract Theory
Sherwin Rosen

36. Foundations of Analytical Marxism (Volumes I and II)
John E. Roemer

37. The Economics of Product Differentiation (Volumes I and II)
Jacques-François Thisse and George Norman

38. Economic Growth in Theory and Practice: A Kaldorian Perspective
John E. King

39. Markets and Socialism
Alec Nove and Ian D. Thatcher

40. Recent Developments in the Economics of Education
Elchanan Cohn and Geraint Johnes

41. The Theory of Inflation
Michael Parkin

42. The Economics of Location (Volumes I, II and III)
Melvin L. Greenhut and George Norman

43. Financial Intermediaries
Mervyn K. Lewis

44. The Political Economy of Privatization and Deregulation
Elizabeth E. Bailey and Janet Rothenberg Pack

45. Gender and Economics
Jane Humphries

46. Macroeconomics and Imperfect Competition
Jean-Pascal Bénassy

47. Labor Economics (Volumes I, II, III and IV)
Orley C. Ashenfelter and Kevin F. Hallock

48. The Economics of Altruism
Stefano Zamagni

49. The Economic Analysis of Rent Seeking
Robert D. Tollison and Roger D. Congleton

50. Economics and Biology
Geoffrey M. Hodgson

51. The Economics of Ageing
John Creedy

52. Fiscal and Monetary Policy (Volumes I and II)
Thomas Mayer and Steven M. Sheffrin

53. The Economics of Information (Volumes I and II)
David K. Levine and Steven A. Lippman

54. Transaction Cost Economics (Volumes I and II)
Oliver E. Williamson and Scott E. Masten

55. Agricultural Economics
George H. Peters

56. International Debt (Volumes I and II)
Graham Bird and P. Nicholas Snowden

57. Economics and Discrimination (Volumes I and II)
William A. Darity, Jr

58. Business Cycle Theory
Finn E. Kydland

59. International Trade (Volumes I and II)
J. Peter Neary

60. The Money Supply in the Economic Process
Marco Musella and Carlo Panico

61. Small Firms and Economic Growth (Volumes I and II)
Zoltan J. Acs

62. Producer Cooperatives and Labor-Managed Systems (Volumes I and II)
David L. Prychitko and Jaroslav Vanek

63. Ethics and Economics (Volumes I and II)
Alan P. Hamlin

64. The Economics of the Family
Nancy Folbre

65. The Economics of Training (Volumes I and II)
Orley C. Ashenfelter and Robert J. LaLonde

66. Chaos Theory in Economics: Methods, Models and Evidence
W. Davis Dechert

67. General Equilibrium Theory (Volumes I, II and III)
Gérard Debreu

68. Economic Growth: Theory and Evidence (Volumes I and II)
Gene M. Grossman

69. Long Wave Theory
Christopher Freeman

70. The Economics of Communication and Information
Donald M. Lamberton

71. The Foundations of Public Finance (Volumes I and II)
Peter Jackson

72. The Theory of the Firm
Mark Casson

73. The Economics of Uncertainty (Volumes I and II)
John D. Hey

74. The Economics of Global Warming
Tom Tietenberg

75. The Development of Ecological Economics
Robert Costanza, Charles Perrings and Cutler Cleveland

76. Economic Growth in the Long Run: A History of Empirical Evidence (Volumes I, II and III)
Bart van Ark

77. The Economics of Productivity (Volumes I and II)
Edward N. Wolff

78. The Economics of Population: Key Modern Writings (Volumes I and II)
Julian L. Simon

79. Political Business Cycles
Bruno S. Frey

80. Cultural Economics: The Arts, the Heritage and the Media Industries (Volumes I and II)
Ruth Towse

81. Law and Economics (Volumes I, II and III)
Richard A. Posner and Francesco Parisi

82. Independent Central Banks and Economic Performance
Sylvester Eijffinger

83. Culture, Social Norms and Economics (Volumes I and II)
Mark Casson

84. Industrial Policy and Competitive Advantage (Volumes I, II and III)
David B. Audretsch

85. The Economics of Housing (Volumes I and II)
John M. Quigley

86. Economic Demography (Volumes I and II)
T. Paul Schultz

87. Trade and the Environment: Economic, Legal and Policy Perspectives
Alan M. Rugman and John J. Kirton with Julie A. Soloway

88. The Economics of Fiscal Federalism and Local Finance
Wallace E. Oates

89. Price Theory and its Applications
Bernard Saffran and F.M. Scherer

90. Women in the Labor Market (Volumes I and II)
Marianne A. Ferber

91. Market Process Theories (Volumes I and II)
Peter Boettke and David Prychitko

92. Input–Output Analysis (Volumes I, II and III)
Heinz Kurz, Erik Dietzenbacher and Christian Lager

93. Mathematical Economics (Volumes I, II and III)
Graciela Chichilnisky

94. The Foundations of Regulatory Economics (Volumes I, II and III)
Robert B. Ekelund, Jr.

95. The Economics of Marketing
Martin Carter, Mark Casson and Vivek Suneja

96. Service Industries in the Global Economy (Volumes I and II)
J.R. Bryson and P.W. Daniels

97. Economic Justice (Volumes I and II)
Giorgio Brosio and Harold M. Hochman

98. Foreign Exchange Intervention: Objectives and Effectiveness
Sylvester C.W. Eijffinger

99. Economic Anthropology
Stephen Gudeman

100. Consumer Theory
Kelvin Lancaster

101. The Economics of Famine
Jean Drèze

102. Microeconomic Theories of Imperfect Competition
Jean J. Gabszewicz and Jacques-François Thisse

103. The Economics of Executive Compensation (Volumes I and II)
Kevin F. Hallock and Kevin J. Murphy

104. The Foundations of Long Wave Theory (Volumes I and II)
Francisco Louçã and Jan Reijnders

105. The Economics of Commodity Markets
David Greenaway and C.W. Morgan

106. Corporate Governance (Volumes I, II, III and IV)
Kevin Keasey, Steve Thompson and Mike Wright

107. Economic Welfare: Concepts and Measurement (Volumes I and II)
John Creedy

108. Economic Forecasting
Terence C. Mills

109. Recent Developments in Game Theory
Eric S. Maskin

110. The Economics of Increasing Returns
Geoffrey Heal

111. The Economics of Corruption and Illegal Markets (Volumes I, II and III)
Gianluca Fiorentini and Stefano Zamagni

112. The Economics of Price Discrimination
George Norman

113. The Economic Theory of Auctions (Volumes I and II)
Paul Klemperer

114. The Economics of Regional Policy
Harvey W. Armstrong and Jim Taylor

115. Economic Integration and International Trade
Carsten Kowalczyk

116. The Political Economy of Science, Technology and Innovation
Ben Martin and Paul Nightingale

117. The Economics of Science and Innovation (Volumes I and II)
Paula E. Stephan and David B. Audretsch

118. Innovation, Evolution of Industry and Economic Growth (Volumes I, II and III)
David B. Audretsch and Steven Klepper

119. The Economics of Energy (Volumes I and II)
Paul Stevens

120. Privatisation in Developing Countries (Volumes I and II)
Paul Cook and Colin Kirkpatrick

121. The Economics of Tourism (Volumes I and II)
Clem Tisdell

122. The Economics of Unemployment (Volumes I, II, III and IV)
P.N. Junankar

123. Privatisation and Corporate Performance
David Parker

124. Income Distribution (Volumes I, II and III)
Michael Sattinger

125. International Finance (Volumes I and II)
Robert Z. Aliber

126. Welfare Economics (Volumes I, II and III)
William J. Baumol and Charles A. Wilson

127. The Theory of Trade Policy Reform
Carsten Kowalczyk

Future titles will include:

The Economics of Defence
Keith Hartley and Todd Sandler

Economic Theory and the Welfare State
Nicholas Barr

The Economics of Property Rights
Svetozar Pejovich

The Economics of Politics
Dennis C. Mueller

The Economics of Sport
Andrew Zimbalist

The Political Economy of Development
Amitava Krishna Dutt

The Regulation and Supervision of Banks
Maximilian J.B. Hall

Public Procurement
Sue Arrowsmith and Keith Hartley

The Economics of Advertising
Kyle Bagwell

Forms of Capitalism: Comparative Institutional Analyses
Ugo Pagano and Ernesto Screpanti

The Economics of Business Strategy
John Kay

The Economics of Crime
Isaac Ehrlich

The Economics of Organisation and Bureaucracy
Peter Jackson

Realism and Economics: Studies in Ontology
Tony Lawson

The International Economic Institutions of the Twentieth Century
David Greenaway and Robert C. Hine

The Economics of Structural Change
Harald Hagemann, Michael Landesmann and Roberto Scazzieri

The Economics of the Mass Media
Glenn Withers

Alternative Theories of the Firm
Richard Langlois, Paul Robertson and Tony F. Yu

International Financial Integration
Sylvester C.W. Eijffinger

The Economics of Budget Deficits
Charles Rowley

The Economics of Intellectual Property
Ruth Towse and R.W. Holzhauer

Path Dependence
Paul David

The Economics of Contracts
Lars A. Stole

New Developments in Exchange Rate Economics
Lucio Sarno and Mark P. Taylor

The Political Economy of Monetary Union
Paul De Grauwe

New Institutional Economics
Claude Ménard

The Economics of Barter and Countertrade
Bernard Yeung and Rolf Mirus

Comparative Law and Economics
Gerrit de Geest and Roger Van Den Bergh

Cost-Benefit Analysis
Arnold C. Harberger and Glenn P. Jenkins

The Economics of Migration
Klaus F. Zimmermann and Thomas Bauer

The Economics of Networks
Michael Katz and Carl Shapiro

The Economics of Technology Transfer
Sanjaya Lall

Regulation, Economics and the Law
Anthony I. Ogus

The Economics of Labor Unions
Alison Booth

The Economics of Poverty and Inequality
Frank A. Cowell

The Economics of Business Strategy
John Kay

The Economics of Free Trade
Robert W. Staiger

Forecasting Financial Markets
Terence C. Mills